THE PAPERS OF ULYSSES S. GRANT

OVERLEAF:
President Ulysses S. Grant.
Courtesy James A. Bultema.

THE PAPERS OF

ULYSSES S. GRANT

Volume 21:
November 1, 1870–May 31, 1871

Edited by John Y. Simon

ASSISTANT EDITORS
William M. Ferraro
Aaron M. Lisec

TEXTUAL EDITOR
Sue E. Dotson

SOUTHERN ILLINOIS UNIVERSITY PRESS
CARBONDALE AND EDWARDSVILLE

Library of Congress Cataloging in Publication Data (Revised)

Grant, Ulysses Simpson, Pres. U.S., 1822–1885.
The papers of Ulysses S. Grant.

Prepared under the auspices of the Ulysses S. Grant Association.
Bibliographical footnotes.
CONTENTS: v. 1. 1837–1861—v. 2. April–September 1861.—v. 3. October 1, 1861–January 7, 1862.—v. 4. January 8–March 31, 1862.—v. 5. April 1–August 31, 1862.—v. 6. September 1–December 8, 1862.—v. 7. December 9, 1862–March 31, 1863.—v. 8. April 1–July 6, 1863.—v. 9. July 7–December 31, 1863.—v. 10. January 1–May 31, 1864.—v. 11. June 1–August 15, 1864.—v. 12. August 16–November 15, 1864.—v. 13. November 16, 1864–February 20, 1865.—v. 14. February 21–April 30, 1865.—v. 15. May 1–December 31, 1865.—v. 16. 1866.—v. 17. January 1–September 30, 1867.—v. 18. October 1, 1867–June 30, 1868.—v. 19. July 1, 1868–October 31, 1869.—v. 20. November 1, 1869–October 31, 1870.—v. 21. November 1, 1870–May 31, 1871.
1. Grant, Ulysses Simpson, Pres. U.S., 1822–1885. 2. United States—History—Civil War, 1861–1865—Campaigns and battles—Sources. 3. United States—Politics and government—1869–1877—Sources. 4. Presidents—United States—Biography. 5. Generals—United States—Biography. I. Simon, John Y., ed. II. Ulysses S. Grant Association.
E660.G756 1967 973.8′2′0924 67–10725
ISBN 0-8093-2197-1 (v. 21)

Printed in the United States of America

Ulysses S. Grant Association

Contents

Introduction

MIDWAY THROUGH HIS FIRST TERM, Ulysses S. Grant was so beset by policy issues and partisan skirmishes that he looked forward to his last day in office as "the happiest of my life, except possibly the day I left West Point, a place that I felt I had been at always and that my stay at had no end." His views might have differed if major initiatives had achieved greater success.

Foreign policy during this period consisted primarily of two initiatives: one aimed at annexing Santo Domingo to the United States, the other at settling with Great Britain the vexing issue of the Alabama Claims. Senate rejection of an earlier Santo Domingo annexation treaty prompted Grant to take charge of a renewed effort: "So convinced am I of the advantages to flow from the acquisition of San Domingo, and of the great disadvantages, I might almost say calamity, to flow from non acquisition, that I believe the subject has only to be investigated to be approved." Carefully marshaling support from both houses of Congress, newspaper editors, and philanthropic leaders, he sidestepped the scornful opposition of U.S. Senator Charles Sumner of Massachusetts and other annexation foes to win congressional approval for a commission to explore the political, economic, and social situation in Santo Domingo. Grant's adroit selection of commissioners temporarily disarmed enemies, and the ensuing report advocated annexation. After laboring over his April 5, 1871, message submitting this report to Congress, Grant endured more verbal abuse and the bitter disappointment of watching Congress once again reject annexation.

Negotiations involving the Alabama Claims achieved far better results. Under the leadership of Grant's most trusted and indispensable cabinet officer, Secretary of State Hamilton Fish, the United States and Great Britain agreed on May 8 to arbitrate the disputed claims. While congratulations followed Senate ratification, Grant, Fish, and others knew that ultimate resolution of this extraordinarily sensitive issue awaited the legal, intellectual, and diplomatic maneuvers of subsequent arbitration hearings set for Geneva. In other foreign policy areas, Grant welcomed the end of the Franco-Prussian War, enthusiastically acknowledged the unification of Germany, and sought stronger ties with Japan.

Domestically, "a deplorable state of affairs existing in some portions of the South" and the specter of the Ku Klux Klan riding roughshod over freedmen and Unionists moved Grant to ask Congress for special powers to check violence and intimidation. Congressional adversaries responded to his formal request on March 23 with a torrent of condemnation of Grant as a tyrant trampling state prerogatives. Firmly believing in the moral as well as constitutional correctness of his course, Grant persisted. The "Ku Klux Klan" Act passed on April 20 gave the president authority to protect public safety and the ballot box by suspending the writ of *habeas corpus* and imposing martial law where appropriate. Calls for federal assistance came from elected officials and citizens throughout the South, taxing the limited numbers of troops available and forcing Grant to make hard decisions. Attorney General Amos T. Akerman, a former Confederate officer, worked energetically to assist Grant in executing these new presidential powers.

From the West, frequent reports of clashes between Indians and whites reached the White House, ranging from legal battles over treaty rights to battles in recently settled remote areas. Grant placed considerable hope in the gathering of tribal leaders at Okmulgee in December, 1870, that framed a constitution for a self-governing Indian Territory. Congress, however, refused to relinquish control over this domain. Senators and representatives withheld support unless the principal offices in the proposed territory went to whites, and Grant bowed to this pressure. Grant never hid his dislike of patronage: "There is no duty which so much embarrasses the Executive and heads of departments as that of appointments; nor is there any such arduous and thankless labor imposed on Senators and representatives as that of finding places for constituents."

Rifts among Republicans in New York, Nebraska, Arkansas, and Louisiana caused additional problems. The central role of brother-in-law James F. Casey complicated factional issues in Louisiana. Unable to appease all sides in these internecine struggles, Grant typically emphasized the need to display good sense and to preserve order. Grant did have favorites, but in extending assistance he shrewdly refrained from making "absolute promises."

Apart from his presidential duties, Grant directed operations on his farm near St. Louis through its manager, William Elrod, a rather inept distant relative; worried about finances and snarled property interests; encouraged his oldest son, Frederick Dent, through a trying final year at West Point; reassured his second son, Ulysses, Jr., nicknamed Buck, then at Harvard; and endeavored to stay in touch with relatives and friends. He declined invitations to many celebrations, unveilings, and testimonials. Overwhelming public and private demands compelled Grant to postpone an anticipated trip to California.

Grant's prominence as president and war hero brought appeals from people in virtually every circumstance of life and various parts of the globe. Vacant offices provoked floods of letters of application and endorsement. Our volumes present selected items from such correspondents while sustaining a previous commitment to include all letters addressed to Grant concerning major issues of the administration. The overall goal of the series remains a comprehensive edition of Grant's substantive writings and effective coverage of incoming correspondence bearing upon significant personal and historical subjects.

We are indebted to Timothy Connelly for assistance in searching the National Archives; to Harriet F. Simon for proofreading; and to Joni Eberhart, Vera Horvath, and Laurel Petrich, graduate students at Southern Illinois University, for research assistance.

Financial support for the period during which this volume was prepared came from Southern Illinois University, the National Endowment for the Humanities, and the National Historical Publications and Records Commission.

JOHN Y. SIMON

February 1996

Editorial Procedure

1. Editorial Insertions

A. Words or letters in roman type within brackets represent editorial reconstruction of parts of manuscripts torn, mutilated, or illegible.

B. [. . .] or [— — —] within brackets represent lost material which cannot be reconstructed. The number of dots represents the approximate number of lost letters; dashes represent lost words.

C. Words in *italic* type within brackets represent material such as dates which were not part of the original manuscript.

D. Other material crossed out is indicated by ~~cancelled type~~.

E. Material raised in manuscript, as "4th," has been brought in line, as "4th."

2. Symbols Used to Describe Manuscripts

AD	Autograph Document
ADS	Autograph Document Signed
ADf	Autograph Draft
ADfS	Autograph Draft Signed
AES	Autograph Endorsement Signed
AL	Autograph Letter
ALS	Autograph Letter Signed

ANS	Autograph Note Signed
D	Document
DS	Document Signed
Df	Draft
DfS	Draft Signed
ES	Endorsement Signed
LS	Letter Signed

3. Military Terms and Abbreviations

Act.	Acting
Adjt.	Adjutant
AG	Adjutant General
AGO	Adjutant General's Office
Art.	Artillery
Asst.	Assistant
Bvt.	Brevet
Brig.	Brigadier
Capt.	Captain
Cav.	Cavalry
Col.	Colonel
Co.	Company
C.S.A.	Confederate States of America
Dept.	Department
Div.	Division
Gen.	General
Hd. Qrs.	Headquarters
Inf.	Infantry
Lt.	Lieutenant
Maj.	Major
Q. M.	Quartermaster
Regt.	Regiment or regimental
Sgt.	Sergeant
USMA	United States Military Academy, West Point, N.Y.
Vols.	Volunteers

4. Short Titles and Abbreviations

ABPC	*American Book Prices Current* (New York, 1895–)
Badeau	Adam Badeau, *Grant in Peace. From Appomattox to Mount McGregor* (Hartford, Conn., 1887)
CG	*Congressional Globe.* Numbers following represent the Congress, session, and page.
J. G. Cramer	Jesse Grant Cramer, ed., *Letters of Ulysses S. Grant to his Father and his Youngest Sister, 1857–78* (New York and London, 1912)
DAB	*Dictionary of American Biography* (New York, 1928–36)
Foreign Relations	*Papers Relating to the Foreign Relations of the United States* (Washington, 1869–)
Garland	Hamlin Garland, *Ulysses S. Grant: His Life and Character* (New York, 1898)
Julia Grant	John Y. Simon, ed., *The Personal Memoirs of Julia Dent Grant* (New York, 1975)
HED	*House Executive Documents*
HMD	*House Miscellaneous Documents*
HRC	*House Reports of Committees.* Numbers following *HED, HMD,* or *HRC* represent the number of the Congress, the session, and the document.
Ill. AG Report	J. N. Reece, ed., *Report of the Adjutant General of the State of Illinois* (Springfield, 1900)
Johnson, Papers	LeRoy P. Graf and Ralph W. Haskins, eds., *The Papers of Andrew Johnson* (Knoxville, 1967–)
Lewis	Lloyd Lewis, *Captain Sam Grant* (Boston, 1950)
Lincoln, Works	Roy P. Basler, Marion Dolores Pratt, and Lloyd A. Dunlap, eds., *The Collected Works of Abraham Lincoln* (New Brunswick, 1953–55)
Memoirs	*Personal Memoirs of U. S. Grant* (New York, 1885–86)
Nevins, Fish	Allan Nevins, *Hamilton Fish: The Inner History of the Grant Administration* (New York, 1936)
O.R.	*The War of the Rebellion: A Compilation of the Official Records of the Union and Confederate Armies* (Washington, 1880–1901)

O.R. (Navy)	*Official Records of the Union and Confederate Navies in the War of the Rebellion* (Washington, 1894–1927). Roman numerals following *O.R.* or *O.R.* (Navy) represent the series and the volume.
PUSG	John Y. Simon, ed., *The Papers of Ulysses S. Grant* (Carbondale and Edwardsville, 1967–)
Richardson	Albert D. Richardson, *A Personal History of Ulysses S. Grant* (Hartford, Conn., 1868)
SED	*Senate Executive Documents*
SMD	*Senate Miscellaneous Documents*
SRC	*Senate Reports of Committees.* Numbers following *SED, SMD,* or *SRC* represent the number of the Congress, the session, and the document.
USGA Newsletter	*Ulysses S. Grant Association Newsletter*
Young	John Russell Young, *Around the World with General Grant* (New York, 1879)

5. Location Symbols

CLU	University of California at Los Angeles, Los Angeles, Calif.
CoHi	Colorado State Historical Society, Denver, Colo.
CSmH	Henry E. Huntington Library, San Marino, Calif.
CSt	Stanford University, Stanford, Calif.
CtY	Yale University, New Haven, Conn.
CU-B	Bancroft Library, University of California, Berkeley, Calif.
DLC	Library of Congress, Washington, D.C. Numbers following DLC-USG represent the series and volume of military records in the USG papers.
DNA	National Archives, Washington, D.C. Additional numbers identify record groups.
IaHA	Iowa State Department of History and Archives, Des Moines, Iowa.

I-ar	Illinois State Archives, Springfield, Ill.
IC	Chicago Public Library, Chicago, Ill.
ICarbS	Southern Illinois University, Carbondale, Ill.
ICHi	Chicago Historical Society, Chicago, Ill.
ICN	Newberry Library, Chicago, Ill.
ICU	University of Chicago, Chicago, Ill.
IHi	Illinois State Historical Library, Springfield, Ill.
In	Indiana State Library, Indianapolis, Ind.
InFtwL	Lincoln National Life Foundation, Fort Wayne, Ind.
InHi	Indiana Historical Society, Indianapolis, Ind.
InNd	University of Notre Dame, Notre Dame, Ind.
InU	Indiana University, Bloomington, Ind.
KHi	Kansas State Historical Society, Topeka, Kan.
MdAN	United States Naval Academy Museum, Annapolis, Md.
MeB	Bowdoin College, Brunswick, Me.
MH	Harvard University, Cambridge, Mass.
MHi	Massachusetts Historical Society, Boston, Mass.
MiD	Detroit Public Library, Detroit, Mich.
MiU-C	William L. Clements Library, University of Michigan, Ann Arbor, Mich.
MoSHi	Missouri Historical Society, St. Louis, Mo.
NHi	New-York Historical Society, New York, N.Y.
NIC	Cornell University, Ithaca, N.Y.
NjP	Princeton University, Princeton, N.J.
NjR	Rutgers University, New Brunswick, N.J.
NN	New York Public Library, New York, N.Y.
NNP	Pierpont Morgan Library, New York, N.Y.
NRU	University of Rochester, Rochester, N.Y.
OClWHi	Western Reserve Historical Society, Cleveland, Ohio.
OFH	Rutherford B. Hayes Library, Fremont, Ohio.
OHi	Ohio Historical Society, Columbus, Ohio.
OrHi	Oregon Historical Society, Portland, Ore.
PCarlA	U.S. Army Military History Institute, Carlisle Barracks, Pa.

PHi	Historical Society of Pennsylvania, Philadelphia, Pa.
PPRF	Rosenbach Foundation, Philadelphia, Pa.
RPB	Brown University, Providence, R.I.
TxHR	Rice University, Houston, Tex.
USG 3	Maj. Gen. Ulysses S. Grant 3rd, Clinton, N.Y.
USMA	United States Military Academy Library, West Point, N.Y.
ViHi	Virginia Historical Society, Richmond, Va.
ViU	University of Virginia, Charlottesville, Va.
WHi	State Historical Society of Wisconsin, Madison, Wis.
Wy-Ar	Wyoming State Archives and Historical Department, Cheyenne, Wyo.
WyU	University of Wyoming, Laramie, Wyo.

Chronology

November 1, 1870–May 31, 1871

Nov. 11–13. USG and Horace Porter visited Philadelphia for the weekend.

Nov. 24. USG and family attended Thanksgiving services.

Dec. 5. USG submitted his annual message to Congress.

Dec. 9. Secretary of State Hamilton Fish informed the cabinet of an overture from Great Britain to settle the Alabama Claims and other issues.

Dec. 10. USG invited Horace Greeley to dinner. On Jan. 3, USG and Greeley met at length.

Dec. 12. On USG's behalf, U.S. Senator Oliver P. Morton of Ind. and U.S. Representative Nathaniel P. Banks of Mass. introduced a joint resolution to send a commission to investigate Santo Domingo.

Dec. 21. USG nominated Robert C. Schenck as minister to Great Britain.

Dec. 21. In an evening speech, USG opposed moving the national capital to the midwest.

Dec. 28. USG's father Jesse Root Grant visited the White House.

Jan. 1. USG attended the funeral of Carita Belknap, wife of Secretary of War William W. Belknap.

Jan. 5. A delegation from Ore. urged USG to appoint George H. Williams to the cabinet.

Jan. 9. Fish and British envoy Sir John Rose began to negotiate a framework for settling the Alabama Claims.

Jan. 13. USG appointed members of the Santo Domingo Commission. On Jan. 24, the commission arrived at Santo Domingo.

JAN. 19. James Longstreet, surveyor of customs, New Orleans, discussed La. political affairs with USG.

JAN. 25. USG attended the unveiling of Vinnie Ream's statue of Abraham Lincoln at the Capitol rotunda.

JAN. 28. Frederick Dent Grant testified before a House subcommittee investigating cadet misconduct at USMA.

JAN. 30. USG asked Congress to consider a proposed constitution adopted in Dec., 1870, for a self-governing Indian Territory.

FEB. 2. USG held a state dinner for the diplomatic corps.

FEB. 7. Adolph E. Borie and his wife arrived for a week as USG's guests.

FEB. 9. USG submitted nominations to the Senate for a joint U.S.-British commission to meet at Washington, D.C., to settle the Alabama Claims.

FEB. 15. USG protested but did not veto a bill easing restrictions on office-holding for former Confederates.

FEB. 21. USG signed legislation creating a D.C. territorial government. On Feb. 27, USG nominated Henry D. Cooke as D.C. governor.

FEB. 22. A delegation of Irish exiles met USG.

FEB. 27. The Joint High Commission on the Alabama Claims held its first meeting.

MAR. 2. USG welcomed the first Japanese legation to the U.S.

MAR. 3. Congress passed legislation for a centennial celebration at Philadelphia in 1876.

MAR. 9. USG held a state dinner for the Joint High Commission.

MAR. 10. USG congratulated Prussian minister Baron Gerolt on the unification of Germany. On March 16, USG wrote to Emperor William I.

MAR. 17. While the weekend guest of Anthony J. Drexel at Philadelphia, USG attended a Hibernian Society dinner.

MAR. 23. After outbreaks of violence in many southern states, USG asked Congress to strengthen executive power.

MAR. 24. USG issued a proclamation ordering armed bands in S.C. to disperse within 20 days.

MAR. 30. Members of the Santo Domingo Commission dined at the White House. USG's failure to invite Frederick Douglass provoked controversy. On April 5, USG submitted the commission's report to Congress.

APRIL 5. USG sent to the Senate a report recommending the annexation of Hawaii.

APRIL 20. USG called a special session of Congress for May 10 to consider a possible treaty with Great Britain, still under negotiation. In the evening, USG left for the midwest.

APRIL 22. USG spoke to an evening rally at Indianapolis.

APRIL 23–25. In St. Louis to inspect his property, USG visited friends.

APRIL 26. USG and Vice President Schuyler Colfax attended an Odd Fellows meeting at Lafayette, Ind.

APRIL 28. USG returned to Washington, D.C.

APRIL 29. USG hosted a state dinner for foreign ministers.

MAY 3. USG proclaimed the "Ku Klux" act, passed on April 20 by Congress to enforce the Fourteenth Amendment against violent resistance.

MAY 6–7. USG joined Julia Dent Grant and their son Jesse as weekend guests of Jay Cooke, near Philadelphia.

MAY 8. U.S. and British commissioners signed the Treaty of Washington, establishing a tribunal at Geneva to arbitrate disputes. On May 10, USG submitted the treaty to the Senate.

MAY 13. USG ordered troops to assist federal officials in arresting suspected Ku Klux Klan members in S.C.

MAY 22. Colfax collapsed in the Senate and remained at the Capitol, where USG visited him on May 24 and 27. On May 31, Colfax left for South Bend, Ind.

MAY 24. The Senate ratified the Treaty of Washington, which USG signed the following day.

MAY 26. A Washington, D.C., newspaper reported that USG had bought a former parsonage for $7,500.

MAY 27. USG, Julia Grant, and Ellen (Nellie) Grant visited the Naval Academy at Annapolis.

MAY 30. USG attended Decoration Day ceremonies at Arlington National Cemetery.

The Papers of Ulysses S. Grant

November 1, 1870–May 31, 1871

To Charles W. Ford

Washington, D, C,
Nov. 3d 1870

Dear Ford:

On reflection I do not deem it necessary to have my Carondelet land surveyed. The deeds are all on record in St. Louis. From them, and the plats in the Recorders Office, any competant surveyer can make a plat. John F. Long will do this for me. Of course I expect to pay him for his services. In paying taxes my share amounts to only 4/5 of that assessed to the property got from Burns. Jesse Holliday holds the other interest.

All of that land that will rent for garden purpose~~d~~s I would like to have rented out. There is a mistake I understand about anything being due for holding possession of the Carlin tract. Elrod can explain that to you.—I was glad to learn that my horses had arrived safely. All of that batch I value highly.

Yours Truly
U. S. Grant

ALS, DLC-USG.

To Charles W. Ford

Washington D, C,
Nov. 6th 1870.

Dear Ford;

If my offer to compromise ten arpents, more or less, with a Mr. [1] whos name I have forgotten,—has not been accepted, I withdraw the proposition. I will continue to pay $100 00 pr. arpent in settlement but will sell none except where I have a full title.

Yours Truly
U. S. GRANT

ALS, DLC-USG.

1. George T. Hulse. See letter to Charles W. Ford, March 15, 1871.

To Alexander Shaler

~~City~~ Washington, D. C.
November 7, 1870.

MAJOR GENERAL ALEXANDER SHALER;[1]
COMMANDING 1ST DIVISION
NATIONAL GUARD, STATE OF NEW YORK
NEW YORK CITY, N. Y.
SIR,

By virtue of authority conferred upon the President of the United States to use the land, naval, and militia forces of the United States in maintaining the laws, you are hereby notified that the Division under your command is called into the service of the United States, and you are directed to hold it, or so much of it as you may deem necessary, [in rea]diness to cooperate with the United States Marshal, ~~and~~ the Brigadier General commanding the Military Department of the East, "to enforce the faithful execution of the laws of the United States," during the election[2] to be held in the City of New York to-morrow the 8th instant.

You will please acknowledge the receipt of this, and report your action

U. S. GRANT

Copies, NjP; DNA, RG 107, Telegrams Collected (Bound). At the foot of this letter, Secretary of War William W. Belknap wrote: "Above Telegraphed to Marshal Sharpe. Agreement having been made with City Authorities, order withdrawn—" AN, NjP. On Nov. 7, 1870, a correspondent reported: "The Secretary of War was closeted with the President for a long time to-day, issuing the final orders to the commander of the troops in and around New-York, preparatory to any service they may be called upon to perform to-morrow. All the news from New-York, the President says, indicates a quiet election, which he hopes may be true." *New York Tribune*, Nov. 8, 1870. On the same day, Belknap wrote to Brig. Gen. Irvin McDowell, New York City. "An order from the President Calling out Genl. Shaler's Division or so much of it as may be necessary goes to Marshal Sharpe for delivery to Genl. Shaler to-day by telegraph and Mail. Gen Sharpe may consult with District Attorney as to propriety of calling out Militia and if not recommended by them inform me by telegraph for further instructions. See Sharpe at once" ADfS (the second sentence in USG's hand), DNA, RG 94, Letters Received, 799W 1870. Also on Nov. 7, Secretary of State Hamilton Fish, New York City, wrote to USG. "The day of my arrival here I called on Genl Sharpe, & requested him to advise me of any movements of importance—I have not heard from him since—I have seen Gen Cushing several times—last Evening he informed me of the probability of an understanding between the Marshal & the ~~May~~ Governor, looking to the non employment of any State Troops, & an agreement as to the mode of exercising their authority by the United States Marshals, & Supervisors—Genl McDowell has been very anxious to have the State Militia called out under your orders—The Marshal, I understand has been disinclined to have them so called—He and the Governor are to meet this afternoon, for a further conference—Hoffman, I am satisfied, desires to avoid any military conflict—it is his interest that the Election pass quietly, and he will work to that end. whether he can control his men, is questionable—Genl McDowell shewed me last night, what he said was a secret order (in copy) issued by Fisk to part of his Regiment, to meet at their Armory, tomorrow morning at Eight oclk—in fatigue dress—& Genl Sharpe insists on having the U. S. troops in the City, and distributed in small detachments—this I think is unfortunate—There is a great deal of deep earnest feeling, but thus far I see nothing that may not be consistent with a peaceful day tomorrow—" ALS (press), DLC-Hamilton Fish.

On Feb. 13, 1871, USG wrote to the House of Representatives. "I transmit herewith in answer to the resolution of the House of Representatives of the 6th instant, copies of the correspondence between the Governor of the State of California and the President of the United States, in the month of October 1868 relative to the use of the military forces of the national government in preserving the peace at the approaching state election." Copy, DNA, RG 130, Messages to Congress. On Feb. 11, Belknap had written to USG transmitting these papers. Copy, *ibid.*, RG 107, Letters Sent, Military Affairs. Representatives from Calif., Pa., and N. Y. sought this information because in 1870 USG had ordered troops to supervise state elections without obtaining the consent of the governors. See *HED*, 41-3-126; *CG*, 41–3, 790, 999–1000, 1192.

1. See *PUSG*, 10, 405–6.

2. On Nov. 2, Fish telegraphed to USG. "The Circuit Court has declared the Election law to be constitutional—One man has been convicted for false registering. Another trial pending—" ALS (press), DLC-Hamilton Fish. On Nov. 3, Fish wrote to USG. "I saw Senator Conkling last Evening—He hesitates as to the propriety of vacating his seat in the Senate, on the same grounds that Govr Morton placed his declension, but seems to entertain the proposal with favor & wishes time to consider—I mentioned the desirableness of speedily filling the place, but stated that an answer by the next week will be in time—He speaks more hopefully of our prospect of carrying the State, than any others whom I have seen—Should the Republicans Carry a majority in the Assembly large enough to overcome the Democratic majority in the Senate, my impression is that he will take the Mission—Genl Sharpe tells me that there is some reason to apprehend that several of the State Regiments will be ordered un-

der arms on the day of Election—He named the 22d—69th & Fisks'—He expects further & more certain information Mr Murphy complains of great apathy among prominent Republicans, & I hear the same complaint from many others—The judgment rendered yesterday in the Circuit Court will have the most beneficial effects—it encourages our friends greatly A prominent Democrat told me yesterday, however, that they would have in this city, the largest majority they have ever had—I doubt it—" ALS (press), *ibid.*

To Marcus P. Norton

Washington D. C. Nov. 10. 70.

DEAR SIR:

Your favor of the 8th inst. is at hand and has been read with interest. I do not write to express any views upon the subjects which you write upon, but to express my appreciation of your motives, and to say that I am, at all times, glad to get the candid views of sensible thinking men who mingle with the people as my duties preclude the possibility of my doing. I shall be glad to hear from you at all times though I cannot promise to answer.

Yours truly
U. S. GRANT

MARCUS P. NORTON,
KANKAKEE, ILLS.

Copy, DLC-USG, II, 1. Marcus P. Norton, born in 1829, graduate of Union College (1855), was a patent attorney in Troy, N. Y. On Dec. 27, 1871, Norton, Kankakee, Ill., wrote to USG. "Enclosed you will please find a letter upon matters concerning the 'Civil Service' as it is called by certain Ones who have opposed your Administration only to oppose your renomination as well as to oppose you in every movement you make in Office or in the great Republican Party who nominated and elected you to your present honorable position. I hope you will find time to read it. The next letter on same subject will be more full &c. Permit me to say, that in my opinion, were Congress to pass any Law covering the ground 'set out' by Senator Schurz, Trumbull, and the *Democratic* Senators concerning the so called 'Civil Service' that the same would be the 'Death Knell' of the Republican Party as I will try to show in a few words. In my judgment the whole thing is intended as a *fraud* against your re-nomination, as well as against the *Republican* Party. It is a *trick* on the part of the Democracy, aided by a few *dis*appointed and '*sore headed*' Politicians in our Party, to overthrow the Republican Party, and to prevent if possible your *re*nomination—Now let us see. It takes *labor* and *money* to successfully work any Political Party. If there is to be no reward, or hope of reward for *services* rendered and *money* expended—by appointment to some official position, do you, or can any one suppose, that this *necessary labor* and *money* will come to the Party freely or in any other manner? No, Sir, not *any honest* labor—nor *a dollar* in money could be had with such a 'Civil Service' Law as by them proposed. What would then be the result? Why, of course that class would either go over to the Democratic Party or form a new Party whereby *to repeal* the 'Civil Service' Law created by Republicans. *This* is the only thing that will ever help the Democratic Party into power. The men that the proposed 'Civil Service' Law would certainly drive from the Republican Party as I have stated, are *the very* men, who by *their labour* and *money* make *successful* the great Republican Party. It will never do for those *in office* to attempt to hold their places by any such work No change of the manner of appointment can be successfully made. It is right, *when,* and as *it now is,* only, let *all* who prove themselves unqualified or unworthy *to hold* their appointment, be removed by those who made *the* appointment. I am glad to say to you, that *the plan* of *re*-nominating you *in 1872 is rapidly* spreading *into all parts* of the country The several letters that I have written on that subject with Speaker BLAINE for *Vice President,* have been extensively copied and referred to, throughout the West, Northwest, and quite favorably in *the East*—the same have been received. There are *Six* of those letters exclusive of the one now enclosed. The plan here is to make me a delegate to the next National Convention, and nothing will prevent *it,* unless *it be* that of *citizenship,* as Troy N. Y. has been my home. until about one year ago, when expecting to have gone to one of the Territories I closed up my *Law Business* there, and came here, in order *to finally* settle up my business in the East, and make the West my *permanent* home; and yet, we may get along *with that point*" ALS, Ford Collection, NN.

On Dec. 14, 1876, Norton, Troy, wrote to USG. "It having been a long time since you have had a letter from me, perhaps you will not object to receiving one from me at this time—a time when the liberties of a great People seem to be in imminent peril and danger under the leadership of a Man and a Political Party, whose 'no still hunt' cry not long ago—'reform and better times'—was sounded from one end of the land to the other—not as an *honest* sentiment right from the heart, but for *false* and *fraudulent* purposes, whereby to deceive the American People—and to let in the great '*Reformer*' to those places now and for the past eight-years, occupied by yourself to the satisfaction of of all *true—honest,* and *Patriotic* citizens everywhere. Yes, sir, when Revolution and Civil War is again suggested by the Democratic Party, and the great Republic saved by you in the war of, say, 16 years ago—by your *genius, skill, Patriotism,* and bold *Courage*—is again threatened by an armed Democratic Mob—bordering upon another Civil War—I have thought best to write you. The enclosed '*cutting*' from 'The Troy Times' Daily Newspaper will explain the object of my writing. I beg of you to most carefully examine all and every of the matters suggested in the enclosed printed slip. The Troy Times Newspaper is not onlly thoroughly Republican, but it is strongly tinctured with '*Grantism*' as it ought to be. You will remember me as one who wrote and published in January 1871, in the New York Tribune—*the first*—letter ever written and published urging upon the People, for reasons then stated, your *re nomination* and *re-election* to the Presidency, and thereafter following it up in the newspaper Press until at last you were *re-nominated* When that was done, I took the field in that campaign and fought as good a fight as was in my Power to do—until you were *re-elected.* I hope you have not forgotten these things—nor forgotten that, from the time when you won the Battle at Ft Donaldson, all through the War—down to this very writing, I have been your fast friend, and devoted admirer. I have only to regret that I could not have the privilege of voting for you for the '*Third Term*'. So you see that I am not only troubled with '*Grantism*', but also with '*Caesarism*'. When it became apparant that you were not to have the 'third Term'—then I did all I could for my personal friend—the Honorable Roscoe Conkling, whom I would very much desire to be your successor at the 'White House'. But Sir—the Republican Party nominated Mr Hayes, and *the People* of this Country have *fairly* and *honestly* elected him to the Presidential Chair. Now, the question, is, shall he be inaugurated in March next *in an honest* and *peaceful* manner, or shall *Tilden* be sworn in by a system of braggbluster, 'Bulldozing', and threats of civil War. It is for you to determine at the proper time. Mr President, as a citizen of this Republic—I much prefer—*Peace*—but if *War* with all it horrors must come—then I say, by all means let it—be War. But let not the blow come first from those who support Hays, no, but let it *first* come from those who now so meanly threaten it, and then, by the Eternal—'let slip the dogs of War'—The great North and West would in a short time give you a greater Army than you had under your command when you met Gen'l Lee at Appomattox. Mr President—I am *with* you until the end of your present Term, and shall be *for* you ever thereafter. I am but one among your friends, but no one did more than I for you in the Campaign of 1872" ALS, USG 3. The enclosed newspaper clipping is *ibid.*

To John Russell Young

Washington, D. C. Nov. 15 *18~~6~~70*

DEAR SIR:

Though I am a general reader of the Standard,[1] as well as of the other~~s~~ leading New York City papers, I have not seen your issue of the 11th of Nov. until to-day. I am much pleased with it. Mr. Greeley[2] is an honest, firm, untiring supporter of the republican party. He means its welfare at all times. But he is a free thinker: jumps at conclusions; does not get the views of others who are just as sincere as himself in the interest of the party that saved the country, and now wants to pay its honest debts, protect its industries and progress to a prosperous future, as well as himself. I have long desired a free, full talk with Mr. Greeley because I have confidence in his intentions. I have thought, at times, of inviting him to Washington for that purpose; but I have been afraid that the object might be misinterpreted. If he ever does come to Washington, and I can find he is here before the hour of his leaving, I certainly try to see him.

But the key note of your Article is just right! Fentonism in New York means simply a yealding of the Executive to Mr. Fenton for the punishment of all who do not agree that the republican party has no higher mission than to place him in controll of it.[3]

Yours Truly
U. S. GRANT

J. RUSELL YOUNG,
ED. N. Y. STANDARD,

ALS, DLC-John Russell Young. Born in 1840, John Russell Young, a reporter for the *Philadelphia Press* during the Civil War, served as managing editor, *New York Tribune* (1866–69), then, with the support of U.S. Representative Benjamin F. Butler of Mass., established the *New York Standard* in May, 1870. On Nov. 26, Young, New York City, wrote to USG. "I had a long conference with Mr Greeley on Thanksgiving Day, reading him ~~a lett~~ an extract from your letter. We had a full conversation. He said he was anxious for your fullest success in the administration, and a good deal more in the way of friendly criticism. Was pleased with Mr Akerman in the Cabinet,—and felt it would do much towards holding Georgia. He thought Mr Boutwell had had the greatest opportunity ever given to a Secretary,—such a one as would never occur again,—but he had missed it,—and his sixty millions in the Treasury was a blunder. Was sorry we had no Secretary from Missouri, which might be saved, and liked Cresswell immensely. Of Mr Fish he spoke with great respect and esteem, believing there was no better and truer man in the country. He requested me to write you and recommend Mr Edwards Pierrepoint for England, as a clean, square man,—and was very angry with the Free Traders, and thoroughly pleased with your course on that subject. Furthermore he said he would go to Washington in a few days, and see you. The invitation evidently pleased him I had a conversation with Mr L. P. Morton yesterday. He will do what our friends would like. . . . I had a long talk with Mr E D. Webster yesterday He complains of Jourdan's appointment, and is very sore and will 'retire from politics'—" ALS, USG 3. On Dec. 6, USG nominated James Jourdan as assessor of Internal Revenue, 3rd District, N. Y. See letter to Roscoe Conkling, Nov. 18, 1870.

On Nov. 7, Edwards Pierrepont, New York City, wrote to Julia Dent Grant. "The speech I sent you was full of printers blunders, *this* is correct—Mrs Pierrepont from taking a severe cold by getting wet in Boston has not been well & seeing me writing to you she desires me to say that she is now pretty well again and wishes to know whether you are not coming to Newyork before the autumn is over & if so she wishes you to come to our house (of course you know I do) Read the speech some day, and *doubt* no more that Gen. Grant will be the next Pres'dnt" ALS, IHi. On Nov. 3, Pierrepont had addressed a Republican meeting at Cooper Institute. *New York Times*, Nov. 4, 1870. A printed fragment of this speech is in USG 3.

On Jan. 28 and 29, 1871, Pierrepont wrote to USG. "CONFIDENTIAL:. . . Judge Hilton, at a party last evening, in a quiet corner of the room, had a conversation with me of some interest to us—He commenced, 'Well Judge, you had better come back as I have done, they were glad enough to have me and I am now *inside*; you ca'nt make any thing out of Grant.' I became a good listner and learned much—He says their candidate is agreed upon; Did not name him, but made it clear that he was of the West. He spoke with the most absolute confidence of success. Said Fenton and Conkling would keep this State divided and that the South was sure in *every* state—that the organization for 1872 had begun and that they did not rely upon *'spontaneous combustion'* for success. As we had been old Democrats and friends he wanted me to come into a movement which was of sure success. He spoke with much ridicule of the idea that the Republicn Party could prolong their power. He seemed to suppose that as I held no office, ~~that~~ I was free to act and to go into a movement which promised a long lease of power—that the Democrats would know how to *keep* power. When I couple this with what I learned in Washington, I see clearly that they have begun in *earnest*; they expect by *force*, in the South and by money and fraud in the North, to win in '72. They are playing for an Empire, and they will take any risk, run any hazzard, do any desperate act:—they are animated by the same spirit which caused the war and they now mean to rule the whole, instead of a part of the Country:—and if our side cannot smother their petty jealousies and work in harmony for a great end, we shall get what we deserve and be trampled down because we do not believe the desperate things which the enemy will do—We have the game in our hands, and we are *cowards* if we lose it. I was vastly encouraged by my visit to you—I found you awake and advanced and all that I could wish. I have precisely the same faith as last Fall, when in a public speech I said; We must organise and *unite*—I saw Fenton again; He has no hope but in Republican success. He assures me that he is *earnestly* for you; that all his interests are that way; that he wants political influence, of course, but with no end but the success of the party and that the party success is your success—He protests most earnestly that he will be your zealous supporter if you give him a chance—*Let him have the chance*—I saw our friend Senator Conkling; He is a little morbid, and in his mind exagerates the acts of Greeley and of Fenton towards him—you have not to do with individual quarrels. As the head of the Nation, if Greeley and Fenton will work honestly for you, give them the fair opportunity. I want to call your attention to one thing which I deem very important—There is danger that individuals from personal jealousy and spite may try to keep men from serving you who would gladly be your friends—If this suggestion takes root in your mind it can do no harm and may do you great service—It is one of the schemes of men when they wish to sever you from other influences to play upon each, & thus from *mis-representation* misunderstandings arise which do great mischief. I know that you will believe this some day, and that to day you will feel that the suggestion comes from your true friend . . . I do not doubt the wisdom of new things with the new Congress—" "I saw Mr Greeley last night. He is strongly in favor of the repeal of the income tax—of the San Domingo treaty and of Gen. Grant for next Presidnt He says he wants you to put your hand on the quarrel of the Newyork Senators and extinguish it—he is very earnest about that. I find that certain leading Democrats fear that you will keep the fishery the St Lawrence and the Alabama questions OPEN, and that next year it may look so warlike that the country will think it safer to keep a successful General in power. This is a fear which the wisest of the Democrats have—consider it—I saw Mr Roberts to-day—he says that the statements of his opposition, or that he knew of a single article in the Sun are lies, and that you will find him a better friend than his slanderers are—He will come out all right for you—" ALS, *ibid.*

1. On Nov. 5, Young had written to USG. "I have been trying to write you the substance of General Butlers conversation, when here the other day, and the nature of which I promised to acquaint you. The elections however, have kept me very busy. The General would have gone at once to Washington, in obedience to your suggestion, but he had an engagement with a committee of Congress at the soldier's home in

Augusta. He assumed the subscription of Mr Garrison himself and opened negotiations with Mr Paran Stevens on the subject which will mature on some day next week. After the election he will go on to see you, and give you his views, based upon a close and analytical examination of our business. As you honored me with so much attention when I spoke of *The Standard* the other day, I am sure you will permit me to make one or two suggestions and explanations. The *Standard* was started to compete directly with *The Sun* by those friends of your administration who resented its brutality and cowardice towards yourself—It was made the same size, and was the chief journal of a new Press Association, which I founded as a rival of the old news monopoly, and which is now a great success—numbering over a hundred journals. *The* Sun began with nearly $400000 (I think) and bought the franchise of a newspaper 35 years old and in its day a most successful newspaper. I began with $50000 promised, and had to start from the very foundation. We could purchase no machinery, and everything, press-service &c, had to be hired. This was not the best economy, but as *The Standard* was an experiment, it was deemed best, to lay out no useless capital. Of this amount $50000,—only $25.000 was paid in. One subscriber,—Mitchell made me a personal loan of $2500, wishing to aid me but not caring as a Democrat to hold stock in a Republican journal. Personally I have advanced nearly $10.000, although my business interests elsewhere ~~although~~ while prosperous are not available and scarcely will be for a year or two. Practically I have had little or no support from the business of the government The success of *The Standard* has surpassed my expectations. My aim has been to make a decorous,—able,—moderate Republican journal, giving direct and affirmative support to ~~the masses~~ your administration—and so cheap as to reach the masses and gain a large circulation—*I cannot print a larger circulation* with my present press,—and the ceaseless complaint is *that people cannot obtain the paper.* A circulation of 16.000 is unusually large in six months,—but it should be made 50.000 and could be in a city like NewYork,—the centre of 2.000.000 of people. So we are at a stand-still. *As a business,* I could readily turn the paper over to Tammany Hall who would be glad to buy it. Tammany give *The World* and *Star* a subsidy of $100.000 a year,—and neither of them suit them. I would, turn it over ~~it~~ to a free-trade alliance,—as a conservative Republican. So as a business, I can see no peril. but either of these transformations would involve my retirement for I would not be connected with any journal in either interest. I want to do the work set down for me in my own way,—to give your administration what no other newspaper here does,—a generous, hearty, fighting support. If I cannot do that I will give it up. I state these things, generally Mr President, that you may know where ~~I~~ *The Standard* is. Some of these points may arise in conversation with Gen. Butler. My brother will hand you this,—and receive any communication you may care to make. I commend him to your confidence, as a man of discretion and honor who represents *The Tribune* in your city,—but is thoroughly informed on my affairs." ALS, *ibid.* See John Russell Young, *Men and Memories: Personal Reminiscences,* ed. May D. Russell Young (New York, 1901), pp. 164–65; Hans L. Trefousse, *Ben Butler: The South Called Him BEAST!* (New York, 1957), pp. 211, 311.

2. On Oct. [27], Horace Porter had written to William Orton, president, Western Union Telegraph Co., New York City. "The President requests me to write you and say that, the appointment of Mr Costar as Collr of the 6th Dist. was made out and signed by him upon your recommendation, but it has occurred to him that Mr. Greeley being a candidate for Congress in that District, and the Administration wishing to further his election in every way possible, it might be well to consult him before an appointment is made. Will you therefore please be kind enough to

consult with Mr. Greeley and advise the President as to his views—whether it would be better for his interest to retain the present incumbent for the present." Copy, DLC-USG, II, 1. On Oct. 29, Orton wrote to Porter. "Your note of 27th instant was received yesterday as I was concluding the dictation of a second message to be conveyed to the President through General Babcock. I have just forwarded to you the following: 'Mr Greeley does not wish to express any opinion in the matter of the Collectorship of the Sixth District, and prefers that the President shall be governed by the wishes of those recognized as his (Greeley's) friends. I take the liberty to add on my own responsibility that the change which I have requested will meet his approval, although for obvious reasons he would not care to have the removal understood to be procured by him.' Fearing that I might not be able to get access to Mr Greeley on account of his illness, I requested his brother-in-law, J. F. Cleveland, late Assessor of the Thirty-second District, and formerly assessor, and still a resident of the Sixth District, to convey to him the Presidents wishes as communicated by you to me, and to report Mr Greeleys response thereto; and the message of which the above is a copy is the result of Mr Clevelands communication to me. I knew what Mr Greeley's opinions of Collector White were before the removal was solicited, but the reasons which would restrain him from the expression of any opinion at the present time will readily occur to the President on a moments reflection. I confidently expect that Thomas E. Steward, who has been nominated by the faction led by Collector White, in opposition to Mr Greeley, will withdraw in a day or two—not because of his desire to produce harmony in the District, or even to promote Mr Greeleys election, but because he is unwilling by remaining in the field, to permit the fact to be demonstrated that his backers consist only of the little handful of office holders for whom he has hitherto been able to provide places. It would not be politic for Mr Greeley, by expressing any wish in the premises to place it in the power of Collector White to charge the latters removal to the former. It is proper, however, that the President should know for his own satisfaction, and as a personal confidence, that Mr Greeley's views and wishes are precisely in accordance with my own. Please convey to the President assurances of my earnest desire to do and to have done only that which will promote the best interests of the Republican party, and reflect the highest credit upon his administration. I can not resist availing of this opportunity to make a single remark. I earnestly hope that the rumor in circulation here concerning the probable appointment of a successor to Mr Delano from this city is without foundation. The appointment to which I refer would be, in my judgment, a graver error than any with which the Presidents' enemies have heretofore charged him." LS, CSmH. On Dec. 6, USG nominated Charles R. Coster as collector of Internal Revenue, 6th District, N. Y., then nominated him for the 8th District on Feb. 9, 1871.

On Oct. 26, 1870, Orton had written to USG. "I beg leave very respectfully to recommend the appointment of Marshall B. Blake Esq to the office of Appraiser at the Port of New York. I have known Mr Blake commercially, politically and personally during the past ten years, and knowing also something of the qualifications requisite to a proper discharge of the duties of Appraiser, I am confident that he would fill the office so satisfactorily as to reflect especial credit upon your administration. As a merchant Mr Blake has had opportunities for acquiring knowledge of the wants of that portion of the public directly interested in the business department of the office. As a Collector of Internal Revenue during a period of eight years he has become familiar with the routine of official business with Executive Departments. . . ." LS, DNA, RG 56, Appraiser of Customs Applications. On Jan. 26, 1871, USG nominated Marshall B. Blake as collector of Internal Revenue, 32nd District, N. Y.

On Feb. 16, George H. Sharpe, U.S. marshal, Southern District, N. Y., wrote to USG. "I learn that it is proposed to make a change in the General Appraiser-Ship at the city of New York—an office now held by Mr John T. Hogeboom. I have nothing to say in regard to the present incumbent, who is a highly respectable gentleman, as I have had no means of knowing any thing concerning his administration of the duties of his office. But I also learn that in case there is a change made, Col George G. Hastings, now an Assistant Appraiser at this port, is a candidate for the place. . . ." ALS, *ibid.* Related papers are *ibid.*, including one dated Oct. 15, 1870, from Governor Joshua L. Chamberlain of Maine to USG. "It gives me much pleasure to commend Col. George G. Hastings for appointment as United States Judge for the Eastern District of Texas. I had ample acquaintance with his ability and skill as a Judge Advocate during the recent war to enable me express a confident opinion as to his ability and fitness for the position he now desires. I know of no one whom I would more cordially recommend for the place for which I recently commended my friend General Appleton of this state now deceased. I hope Colonel Hastings will receive the appointment." ALS, *ibid.* No appointment followed.

On April 3, 1871, Porter wrote to Secretary of the Treasury George S. Boutwell. "The President directs me to request that you have prepared, and sent to this office by one o'clock today, a nomination for A. H. Laflin to be Naval Officer vice Grinnell, and a nomination for Wm. A. Darling to be Appraiser of Mdse vice Palmer, both at New York City." LS, *ibid.*, Letters Received. On March 20, Porter had written to Addison H. Laflin. "In reply to your letter of this date the President directs me to say that the contract you desire is now held by the Messrs. Willcox of Philadelphia and will not expire till the first of next July. He wishes me to assure you that he fully appreciates your business qualifications and your earnest labors in behalf of the Republican party and that at the proper time he will be pleased to aid you in any manner consisting with his duties" Copy, DLC-USG, II, 1.

On Jan. 4, 1872, Horace Greeley, New York City, testified before the Committee on Investigation and Retrenchment. "Q. . . . How many employés of the custom-house have you known to be removed because they were Fenton men and their places supplied by Conkling men?—A. I should think about a hundred in all had been, though I could not name so many. . . . Mr. Murphy was the first change; General Merritt, naval officer, was the next. . . . General Palmer, the appraiser of the port, a Fenton man, was also removed, and Mr. Darling, a Conkling man, put in his place. . . . General Merritt was naval officer first. He was removed to make a place for Mr. Grinnell when he was taken out of the collectorship. Then after awhile Mr. Grinnell was removed and Mr. Addison H. Laflin, a Conkling member of Congress, appointed in his place. Mr. Cornell, the surveyor, was also a Conkling man. He holds the same place he has always held since General Grant made his first disposition of offices. . . . Q. These leading appointments, those of collector, appraiser, and naval officer, I suppose, were made by the President and confirmed by the Senate?—A. Yes, sir; originally with the intent to equalize, to keep things about balanced between the two factions. . . ." *SRC*, 42-2-227, I, 13. See *PUSG*, 20, 140–41; letter to Thomas Murphy, Nov. 20, 1871.

On Jan. 10, 1872, George W. Palmer, New York City, testified before the committee. "Well, sir, I got a letter from a gentleman in the Treasury Department, or information through that source, that it was being stated to President Grant that I was a Tammany Hall republican, or it went even so far as to say that I was a democrat, and that I worked at the polls for the democratic ticket and voted it, and all that kind of thing; and then further it was said to him that I was opposed to him personally and to his administration, which was not true; and finally I got a note from there asking me to come to Washington. I went and saw the President myself, after much difficulty in getting to see him.... I stated to him what I heard had been told him, the same as I have stated it here. He said such statements had been made to him, and he was glad to see me, because he wanted to know what I had to say about it.... I said I understood the reason for these reports, and the only reason, was that people thought that I was a personal friend of Governor Fenton, and it was understood that Governor Fenton's friends were to be put out of office in case they had any office. I said that my being a friend to Governor Fenton did not make any difference so far as he was concerned; and that whatever statements were made to him that I had done or said unkind things of his administration were not true, and I would be glad to meet the persons who made the charge face to face, and if he was not satisfied when we got through that I was correct I would consent to be sent away cheerfully. He said that was very fair; that he had never heard any charge as to my official conduct. I said, 'Mr. President, if you want my place for any one else, without either official or political charges being made against me, I will give you my resignation at any moment; but if you are going to discharge me on political charges, then I claim, as your appointee, the right to be heard, and I will leave the result with you.' He said that was fair, and it should be done, and he told me a good many things about his former life; I really had a very pleasant conversation with him. He said to me that I need not have any fear of removal; that if there was anything further in the matter he would give me a chance to be heard. I said that was all I asked, and bid him goodbye. I think it was not to exceed three weeks after that, that the first knowledge I had of being removed was that I saw the announcement in the Evening Post." *SRC*, 42-2-227, I, 275–76.

3. On Jan. 13, 1871, Isaac F. Quinby, U.S. marshal, Rochester, N. Y., wrote to USG. "My own conscience would condemn me as a false friend to you who have proved one so true and generous to me did I conceal from you facts which have come to my knowledge in reference to the conduct of at least two persons in this State holding among the best and most lucrative positions in your gift. The one is the appraiser of customs in New York who in the presence of his clerks and other subordinates has repeatedly denounced you as a 'failure' a 'dead-beat' &c and who exerted himself to the utmost throughout the State to secure what was known as a 'Fenton delegation' at the late Saratoga Convention; the avowed purpose being to reprove you for the removals and appointments which, at that time, had been recently made in this State. Another person who made himself particularly active at and before the Convention in this attempt was General Curtis Supervisor of Customs for the Northern frontier of this State. The denunciations and conduct of Mr Palmer have become almost common talk and I myself am cognizant of the fact that General Curtis voted with Fenton's friends at the Saratoga Convention. No one can desire more earnestly than I to see the dissentions allayed which exist in the republican party in this State, but I for one cannot consent to such a consummation if it is to be brought about by keeping men in office who openly speak in disparaging and contemptuous terms of you, and take sides with those who attempt to destroy your influence with the republican party in this State. With kindest regards to Mrs Grant ... P. S. I have no advice to give in reference to the above mentioned persons, my only desire being to acquaint you with facts. Your own good judgement will determine what action to take if any" ALS, USG 3. In 1870, U.S. Senator Reuben E. Fenton of N. Y. had written to USG about dissension in the Republican party, exonerating himself and defending his policy. William Evarts Benjamin, Catalogue No. 42, March, 1892, p. 10.

On April 12, 1869, Fenton had written to USG. "The President will permit me with the utmost respect & kindness, to make my earnest protest in writing against the appointment of Genl Barlow to the office of Marshall of the Southern district of N. Y. Genl Barlow is a pronounced opponant to me; he is well known as the active & devoted friend of Gov Morgan, who has, in the appointments already made received as much consideration, it seems to me, as his political position entitles him to. The names I have presented for appointment, have not been without fitness & merit; the name of Genl Jones for the place in question is all that can be desired in respect of integrity & capacity, & I am unable to conceive why Genl Barlow should be preferred upon any ground. But not to argue the matter,—as I gave expression to my regret last evening at the interview you kindly accorded to me,—I most respectfully submit the fairness of my case,—and in this I am persuaded that I faithfully represent the sentiment of the party in our great city & state. Also, permit me the further suggestion, that in my judgement it would be wise to recognise the loyal Irish sentiment of my state as represented in the person of Genl Jones; a true man & a brave & devoted soldier of the Republic" ALS, Joseph W. P. Frost, Eliot, Maine. See *PUSG*, 19, 232–33.

To John Coon

Washington, D. C. Nov. 17. 1870

DEAR SIR:

It would afford me great pleasure to be with you on the occasion of the meeting of the Society of the Army of the Cumberland, on the 24th and 25th. inst., if it were possible. The time however is so near the beginning of the next session of Congress, for which I have to prepare, that it will be impossible.

I very much appreciate these Army Society reunions and hope they may long be kept up. The dead who lost their lives in their Country's cause and those who have died since exposing their lives in the same cause should be ever held in grateful remembrance. No more conspicuous or beloved soldier has gone to his final rest than your late commander.[1] His memory will be kept green in history and in every meeting of your society in the future.

With great respect
your obt. svt.
U. S. GRANT

JOHN COON, ESQ
CH: SOCIETY ARMY OF THE CUMBERLAND.
CLEVELAND. O.

Copy, DLC-USG, II, 1. See *New York Times*, Nov. 26, 27, 1870. John Coon was a former maj. and paymaster.

1. George H. Thomas. See *PUSG*, 20, 128–29.

To Roscoe Conkling

Washington, D, C,
Nov. 18th 1870

DEAR SENATOR:

Your favor of the 15th inst. is rec'd. I have no doubt but benefits have accrued to the republican party, in New York, from the change of officials there. There were not quite enough of them made is my opinion after the fight.[1]

Yours Truly
U. S. GRANT

HON. ROSCOE CONKLING U. S. S.

ALS, DLC-Roscoe Conkling. On Nov. 22, 1870, U.S. Senator Roscoe Conkling of N. Y., Utica, wrote to USG. "I have the honor to state that with a full acquaintance with Saml. T. Maddox of Brooklyn, I think him a very fit man for appointment as Collector or assessor of Internal Revenue. If Mr Scanlan's place is to be filled, I think no better man than Mr Maddox could be chosen" ALS, OFH. On Nov. 25, Orville E. Babcock wrote to Conkling. "The President directs me to inform you that your letter of the 22d reached him on the 24th. and that he had appointed Gen. Jourdan on the 23d. He directs me to say that he thinks as you do, very highly of Mr Maddox." Copy, DLC-USG, II, 1.

1. On Nov. 19, Horace Porter telegraphed to Thomas Murphy, collector of customs, New York City. "Hope you will come over to-night. President wishes to see you. Stop at Arlington." Copy, *ibid.*, II, 5. On Nov. 20 and 23, a correspondent reported from Washington, D. C. "There has been some excitement in political circles, to-day, caused by the presence here of a large number of New-York politicians. Among the number are Collector Murphy, William Orton, E. D. Webster, H. A. Bowen, Major Haggerty, Col. Lansing, Chauncey M. Depew, and Mr. Darling. Mr. Murphy came here at the direct solicitation of the President, and with Mr. Orton, spent the whole afternoon with His Excellency. The President assured Mr. Murphy that he has no intention of removing him, and expressed himself as fully satisfied, not only with the manner in which he has collected the revenues, but also with his efforts to secure the success of the Republican ticket in the late campaign in New-York." "Supervisor Dutcher, Gen. Barlow, and Mr. Tracy have been here for a day or two, and had an interview with the President to-day. There have been rumors of changes among the Revenue officers in New-York and Brooklyn, but there is good authority for repeating

the assertion that none are immediately contemplated." *New York Tribune*, Nov. 21, 24, 1870. See letter to John Russell Young, Nov. 15, 1870, especially note 2.

To William T. Davis

MR. WM T. DAVIS
PLYMOUTH, MASS.
DEAR SIR:

I am in receipt of your letter of the 12th. inst., inviting me to attend the celebration of the 250th anniversary of the landing of the Pilgrims.

It would afford me great pleasure to be present upon an occasion of so much interest, but it will be impossible to leave the Capital at that time, and I am compelled to decline your very cordial invitation.[1]

Respectfully yours
U. S. GRANT

EXECUTIVE MANSION.
NOV. 19TH. 1870.

LS, Pilgrim Society, Plymouth, Mass. William T. Davis, born in 1822, graduated from Harvard (1842), practiced law in Boston, then settled in Plymouth, becoming president, Plymouth National Bank (1859) and beginning a long association with the Pilgrim Society. On Nov. 19, 1870, USG had written to Mayor Nathaniel B. Shurtleff of Boston. "Your favor of the 10th inst. inviting me to be present at the 250th anniversary of the landing of our Pilgrim forefathers, at Plymouth, Mass. on the 21st of Dec. is received. As much pleasure as it would afford me, to be present on that interesting occasion I am compelled to send my regrets. Public duties will require my presence here. Please express my regrets to the good people of Plymouth, and my appreciation of their kind invitation." Copy, *ibid.* See *Boston Transcript*, Dec. 21, 1870.

1. On Nov. 19, Horace Porter wrote to J. C. Bancroft Davis, asst. secretary of state. "I received your note and showed it to the President. He has received several invitations, to attend the anniversary of the landing of the Pilgrims, from different people, but is compelled to decline them." LS, DLC-J. C. Bancroft Davis. In a letter dated Dec. 19 (possibly written earlier), Porter wrote to U.S. Representative James Buffinton of Mass. "The enclosed is a sentiment which the President directs me to forward to you for the meeting, celebrating the landing of the Pilgrims. . . . Our Pilgrim Fathers—May their children ever be as pure in motive, as patient in toil, and as brave in danger." Copy, DLC-USG, II, 1.

To Charles W. Buckley

Washington D. C. Nov. 21st *1870*.

DEAR SIR:

It is not my desire as a usual thing to indicate a preference among republicans for office, when the chose is not with myself; but seeing how close the Legislature of the State of Ala. is, and how the defection of two or three republican members might defeat the party altogether in the Senatorial Contest,[1] I drop a line to express my appreciation of the services of Senator Warner.[2] He has been a true representative of his party and of his adopted state. I know that it would please his many friends, in Congress and out of it, if he could be returned again. Disclaiming any desire to dictate, ~~between Candidates of~~ or to express a preference for one Candidate of the party over another, but believing Senator Warner to be the choice of the great majority of the republicans in the Legislature, I write this

With great respect,
your obt. svt.

HON. C. W. BUCKLEY M. C.

P. S. I desire that this letter should not be published.

U. S. G.

AL (initialed), Warner Papers, Tennessee State Library and Archives, Nashville, Tenn. Born in N. Y. in 1835, Charles W. Buckley graduated from Beloit College (1860) and Union Theological Seminary (1863), served as chaplain with the 8th La. Colored Inf., and became superintendent of education in Ala. for the Freedmen's Bureau (1866–67). Delegate to the Ala. constitutional convention (1867), he was elected U.S. representative in 1868. On Nov. 25, 1870, U.S. Senator Willard Warner of Ala., Montgomery, wrote to USG. "Your very kind and flattering letter of 21st inst to Mr. Buckley enclosed to me was duly received. Please accept my most earnest thanks and allow me to express the hope that many opportunities may offer for me to return your unusual and prompt kindness. I shall be nominated in Caucus by a vote of 60 out of 70 members and I now feel sanguine of getting every Republican vote at the election, and of being elected, unless the Democrats shall obtain a majority by turning out our members." ALS, OFH.

On Nov. 17, Warner had written to USG. "Hon. Lewis E. Parsons visits Washington to procure an injunction from one of the U. S. Supreme Judges to restrain the President of our Senate from declaring the count of votes as returned of our late election, until an investigation shall be had into the frauds practiced at the polls and by the returning of supevising offices. These have been of the most stupendous and infamous character and much more than sufficient to change the result. Gov. Parsons will explain them fully and in detail, and I commend him to your full confidence and ask for him all the support which you can lawfully give him. The crisis is a vital one. The Democrats of this state have shown in this contest and since the election a desperation and a malignity which you can scarcely imagine. The old Union men say that their spirit and tone now is more bitter, intolerant and defiant than in 1860, and that they are resorting to the same means to accomplish their ends which they used then; viz: fraud intimidation and open violence. At bottom it is a contest between the enemies and the friends of the United States Government. If the conduct of the former in the late election is to be submitted to, then no limit can be placed on their aggressions. At a low estimate we have been defrauded of 10.000 votes. We were so strong, that but for folly and treachery in our ranks, we should have beaten them despite all their violence and fraud. Senator Spencer was the leading traitor. To gratify his personal malice against Gov. Smith, he labored for the defeat of the Republican Party. Gov. Parsons labored earnestly for our success, and now in his mission to Washington represents the will and wish of the entire Republican Party of the state. The strong arm of the General Gov't should be reached out to show these defeated leaders of Secession and Rebellion, who yet nurse their wrath against the power that baffled them, that their violence ~~must cease~~ will be fruitless and must cease. If the injunction is granted then the U. S. Marshal should have ample military force at his command in this city in order to prevent any outbreak or violence, for the excitement and rage will be intense when our opponents find themselves brought to a halt in their violent course. I most earnestly recommend this, and that the command of the troops in this state be restored to Gen. Crawford or that Gen. Terry come to Montgomery It is but necessary that the same preparation and will be shown here, which you so wisely displayed in New York, to insure quiet obedience to the mandate of the court. The official returns from all but twelve counties, and reliable reports from eight of those twelve counties, show that a count and return of the votes actually put in the ballot boxes would elect Governor Smith by more than a thousand majority. We have a just majority of eight in the Legislature in joint ballott but I fear the Democrats intend to turn out, in one pretext or another, enough Republicans to get a majority. But for Senator Spencer I should have no Republican opposition to my re-election. Of the 38 Republican members of the House elect all are for me but one, and only two or three Senators out of 32 are known to be against me. My only danger is that Spencer can carry over enough votes four—to the Democrats to elect a Democrat. He has avowed his purpose to do this. Trusting that you will give Gov. Parsons a patient hearing and that your sense of duty will incline you to support the loyal people of this state in the position which we take . . ." ALS, DNA, RG 107, Letters Received from Bureaus. On Nov. 18, Governor William H. Smith of Ala. wrote to USG. "The election in this state has been carried by the Democrats by intimidation and fraud, I propose to make a case under the law to infor[c]e the 15th amendment, & for this purpose I have employed Gov Parsons as my attorney, & he will visit Washington for the purpose obtaining legal process to determine the right to the Executive Office of this State. Things ~~here~~ look here very much as they did in 1860. The difference ~~we hope is that~~ is t[hat] we now feel confident of the support of the Government of the U. S. in all proper efforts ~~for the~~ to sustain the laws of the country. There is nothing but the positive support of the Government of the U S. can save the entire south from the control of the old secession [l]eaders, If Alabama can be carried by intimidation & fraud so can every other state South, & the whole south will be lost to the Republican party. Many of our most prudent men believe that violence is intended. & that every precaution should be used; that the [troops] now in this state should remain & that either General Crawford or some other efficient Commander should have the immediate Command ~~of the Forces in the state~~ of them." ALS, *ibid.* See Endorsement, Nov. 30, 1870.

1. On March 16, 1871, Warner, Washington, D. C., wrote to USG. "Please permit me to call your attention to your intention expressed to me and Mr. Buckley to send back to the Senate the name of Colonel Buck as appraiser at Mobile Ala, vice Myers sent in a few days ago. I feel *very deeply* in regard to this matter and more on *your own account* than any other, because to put Myers in office is to *reward* him for his *treason* in aiding to elect a Democratic *Governor* and a Democratic *Senator.* You could strike the Republican Party of Alabama and myself, no harder blow than this would be." ALS, DNA, RG 56, Collector of Customs Applications. On the same day, Orville E. Babcock wrote to Secretary of the Treasury George S. Boutwell. "The President directs me to forward the enclosed letter of Senator Warners and say that Mr. Myers was removed from a position as Postal Agent and that he thinks his name should be withdrawn, and the name of Mr. Buck send in again as Appraiser of Merchantdise at Mobile" Copy, DLC-USG, II, 1. On March 9, USG had nominated Alfred E. Buck as appraiser of merchandise, Mobile; on March 13, he withdrew this nomination; on March 20, he again nominated Buck; on April 19, the Senate tabled this nomination.

On May 24, U.S. Senator George E. Spencer of Ala. wrote to USG. "Immediate and Important . . . The office of Appraiser at Mobile being a newly created position, a careful examination of the Tenure-of-office act decides it cannot be filled during the recess. It therefore must be filled now, or not until December. In view of the fact that we are at this moment entering upon an exciting canvass for County officers, sheriffs *etc, etc,* and upon these elections depend the machinery of the election for the Presidency, the new Legislature and Governor, these officers of the counties now to be elected, being for the term of the latter elections, *you cannot do me a greater or more important personal and political favor than to immediately appoint Col. H. Ray Myers, Appraiser at Mobile. . . .*" ALS, DNA, RG 56, Appraiser of Customs Applications. On the same day, USG endorsed this letter. "I have no objection to the nomination of Mr. Myers." AES, *ibid.* On March 13, Spencer and U.S. Representatives Charles Hays and Benjamin S. Turner of Ala. had written to USG recommending H. Ray Myers. LS, *ibid.* On March 14, USG nominated Myers as appraiser of merchandise, Mobile; on March 20, he withdrew this nomination; on May 24, he again nominated Myers. Resolutions dated Oct. 24 and Nov. 27 from Republicans in Mobile to USG requesting the removal of Myers and George L. Putnam, postmaster, Mobile, for promoting party dissension are *ibid.*

On May 13, 1873, Spencer, St. Louis, wrote to USG. "Mr. Jones having declined the Consulate at Hesse Darmstadt, I have recommended the appointment of Col. H Ray Myers in lieu and the Secretary of State has consented, very kindly, to submit his name to you. But I learn that some objection has been urged because Col. Myers was born in Germany. I hope this objection will not be pressed in his case; for he left Germany when a child, and has no kith or kin there, nor any associations with the German Nation. He served through the Mexican War, and was severely wounded; and also through the War for the Suppression of the Rebellion. Without his own admission, no one would suppose he had a drop of foreign blood in his veins. He is as essentially an American as I am, and understands fully the proprieties of representing America abroad, and would not interfere in any political matters. If this objection cannot be overcome, I hope he will receive an equal appointment on the Continent, at some temperate climate, where he is obliged to go because of the illness of his wife, now suffering from prostration incident to residence in the South. Col. Myers' appointment will give universal Satisfaction to all of our party in Alabama, without exception. For this I make myself personally responsible, and your kind consideration in these premises will be highly appreciated . . ." ALS, *ibid.*, RG 59, Letters of Application and Recommendation. Related papers are *ibid.* On Dec. 2, USG nominated Myers as consul, Hamilton, Canada.

2. Warner, born in Ohio in 1826, graduated from Marietta College (1845), served as col., 180th Ohio, then moved to Prattville, Ala., in 1867 to become a cotton planter. In 1868, he was elected U.S. senator. See *PUSG*, 15, 520. On April 23, 1871, Warner wrote to USG. "Ten years hard work in public life leaves me now penniless, and for the time stranded. I would feel deeply grateful to you personally for remunerative work, I prefer to remain in Ala, and think I can do you and the cause more good there than elsewhere, but would be glad to go to Brazil as Minister, and can support my application with the hearty endorsement of many of the best men of the country, South and North." ALS, DNA, RG 59, Letters of Application and Recommendation. On May 1, Buckley, New York City, wrote to USG. "I intended to hand you the enclosed before I left Washington, but was called here before your return from St Louis. Neither the interests of the government nor those of party can allow Genl Warner to go abroad so long as his services are so valuable and indispensable to the State of Alabama. The only position within the state important enough to induce him to remain is the Custom House at Mobile. His appointment to that position will give general satisfaction and strength to the party of the State" ALS, *ibid.* On March 14, 1869, Warner, Spencer, and four others had written to USG. "We, the undersigned Senators and Representatives from Alabama, respectfully recommend to you for appointment to the office of Collector of the Port of Mobile Alabama, Judge William Miller of Eutaw, Alabama. Judge Miller is an old resident of our state, has always been a steadfast Union man and an active earnest supporter of the Reconstruction policy of Congress and is a man whose honesty and fitness for the place no one can question for a moment. His appointment will give satisfaction to all classes of Republicans, and will command the respect of all men of all parties in Alabama." DS, *ibid.*, RG 56, Collector of Customs Applications. On May 4, 1871, William Miller, collector of customs, Mobile, wrote to USG. "PERSONAL. . . . I hope you will pardon my intrusion. I am informed in various ways that a combined effort of the 'Outs' is soon to be made for my removal. When in Washington in May last I mentioned that something of the kind was being urged in some quarters. I am fully aware of the fact that you have a very arduous duty to perform, and, also, that many reports have gone to Washington well calculated to lower me in your estimation, none of which have, so far, changed your feelings towards me, and I trust they may not. I am using my feeble efforts for the interest of the Government with at least an honest intention of deserving the confidence of the Government. Now, I have one favor to ask, and that is, if any effort is made for my removal I hope you will have me advised at once, so that I may be able before a decision is had to present my side of the case. Thanking you for past favors, and hopeing to merit and receive more . . ." LS, *ibid.* On May 18, USG nominated Warner as governor, New Mexico Territory. See Endorsement, Feb. 6, 1871, note 1; telegram to John W. Forney, March 22, 1871, note 1.

On May 30, Jacob D. Cox, Cincinnati, wrote to Warner. "Your letter came this morning & I hasten to reply. It is very hard to give any satisfactory answer to your question as to my opinion on N. Mexico. First I need to vent my wrath & disgust that there should be a moments hesitation in giving you what would be really satisfactory to you. The offer of the Governorship of N. Mexico is so far below what your station or your merit demanded, that I strongly incline to say you cannot at all afford to take it. Santa Fé I have understood to be a dirty village of one story adobe houses, with a rough frontier population of greasers, frontiers men & indians, a little indian trading & whiskey drinking being the only business, & the whole country in as utter a stagnation as is possible.... On the whole, Warner, I am inclined to say, Dont go—You can make a better living on your plantation, or in working your way into trade in Alabama, & surely there never was an emptier honor than the Governorship of N. Mexico—..." ALS, Warner Papers, Tennessee State Library and Archives. On May 31, a correspondent reported from Washington, D. C.: "Ex-Senator Willard Warner, who was nominated for Governor of New Mexico by the President, and subsequently confirmed by the Senate, does not regard with favor the disposition which has been made of him. He desired to be appointed collector at Mobile, and has no fancy for being sent away off on the frontier, outside of the arena of national politics. He waited upon the President to-day to ascertain if his wishes as to the appointment at Mobile could not be complied with, but the former did not give him any satisfaction. Pending a further appointment Warner will hold himself in readiness to proceed to New Mexico, provided his fortunes cannot be otherwise bettered." *Missouri Democrat*, June 1, 1871. On June 5, Babcock telegraphed to USG, West Point, relaying a dispatch from U.S. Senator Alexander Caldwell of Kan., Leavenworth, to USG. "I understand Warren declines Governorship of New Mexico. Can you not give it to Legate. Do so for me" Copy, DLC-USG, II, 5. On June 7, Warner, Washington, D. C., wrote to USG. "Having now received my commission as Governor of New Mexico I beg leave to renew to you the expression of my sincere thanks for this very kindly and flattering indication of your personal regard and confidence, and to beg leave ~~to~~ again to express my respectful declination. I think I can do more good in Alabama than in New Mexico. With the assurance of my sincere friendship, personally and politically, ..." ALS, OFH. On June 9, Cox wrote to Warner. "... You ought to let Grant know in some polite but unmistakeable form, that you do not think you were complimented in the attempt to send you into exile. He ought not to suppose that you regard him as having shown special honour & friendship to you in the nomination made...." ALS, Warner Papers, Tennessee State Library and Archives.

On March 28, Buckley had written to USG. "I beg leave to recommend to your favorable consideration Judge Timothy Pearson of Alabama...." ALS, DNA, RG 56, Collector of Customs Applications. On March 30 and April 3, U.S. Representative Benjamin S. Turner of Ala. wrote to USG. "I have the honor to reccommend Col. Timothy Pearson of Wilcox County, Alabama, for the position of Collector of Customs, at Mobile Alabama—Col. Pearson stands high as a citizen and a lawyer, and he commands the respect and confidence of all who know him,—He served in the U. S. Army with much distinction, and has been living in Alabama since the War;—owns property there and has at heart the welfare of the Country and the interest of the Republican party—He is a warm and zealous supporter of the Administration—and is always ready to forward and advance its interest.—Col. Pearson labored faithfully for my election, and I will therefore deem it a personal as well as political favor to have a favorable consideration of this application—He is eminently qualified to fill the office to the satisfaction of all parties—and to the best interest of the Government.—" "I have the honor to address you for the purpose of requesting the removal of William Miller Esq. Collector of Customs at the Port of Mobile, Alabama, and in his stead the appointment of Timothy Pearson Esq. The reasons for this request of removal are manifest. Mr Miller has mis-used the patronage of his office to the great detriment of the Republican Party; he was active in the bolting movement in Mobile in the State election in November last. Mr. Miller and all of his appointees in the CustomHouse fraternize with the Democrats, and with but two exceptions, openly voted the Democratic Ticket at the election for County School superintendent which took place on the 4th of March 1871. As I have heretofore had the honor, to represent to your Excellency in the matter of the removal of Mr. Bromberg, this bolting movement lost to the Republican party five members of the State Legislature, and the election of five Democrats, the result of which was the defeat of a Republican U. S. Senator. . . ." ALS, *ibid.* Another petition supporting Timothy Pearson is *ibid.* On May 25, Babcock wrote to Spencer. "The President directs me to submit the accompanying affidavit, and four protests against Mr Putnam's appointment to the Mobile Post Office, and to request that they be read by yourself and Mr Turner, and returned to him with any remarks the subject may suggest. . . . Abstract of papers accompanying letter. 1. Copy of Affidavit of Chas. Chambers stating that he received money from G. L. Putnam, candidate for Supt of Education, for stuffing ballot boxes in Putnam's favor. 2. Telegram. Protesting against the apptm't of Putnam as P. M. at Mobile, Ala. 3. Protest against removal from P. O. at Mobile, Ala, of F. G. Bomberg, by German citizens. 4. Same as No 3. 5. Protest irrespective of party against Putnam's apt to P. O." Copy, DLC-USG, II, 1. On June 15, James H. Burdick, probate judge, Camden, Ala., wrote to Warner. "I received a few days ago a 'Chronicle' of the 1st inst over the frank of Hon E Spencer which contained a marked article stating that Gen Spencer had had an interview with President Grant and pressed the claims of 'Col T Pearson' to be appointed Collector of the Port of Mobile. Permit me in behalf of the *entire* Republican party of this County through you to protest to the~~e~~ President against such appointment. Mr Pearson has been a resident of this county since the close of the war, and I speak but the simple plain truth when I say that he has never at any time during *any* canvass acted with the party, true he may have voted the republican ticket when he *did* vote, but during the presidential campaign to my own personal knowledge as well as that of every other citizen of the county he during the entire canvass advocated the election of Seymour & Blair, but on election day did come to Camden and vote an open ticket for the Republican candidates, saying at the time that he was *now* sure that was the winning ticket and he wanted the bystanders to see that he voted it. Col Buck informs me that Gen. Spencer represented to the President that Mr Pearson canvassed this Dist during the last canvass in company with Mr Turner, and that he was the *only* one who did do so. This is not true in a single particular. Mr Turner attempted to make the canvass of the District and got as low as Monroe Co and then returned to Selma saying he dared not go farther that it would cost him his life and he would not risk it further. Col Buck and Mr Reynolds *did* canvass the *entire* District and are the *only* ones who did do it. In conclusion permit me to say further that Mr Pearson is regarded by every white republican in this county as a notoriously dishonest and corrupt man, and if after the very grave mistake (the respect we feel for the president forbids our using a stronger term) of the appointment of Putnam to the Post office Mr Pearson is to succeed to the Collectorship, we *must* feel that true worth and faithful service are no longer to be rewarded by the republican party. You My dear Gen *know* that I have no selfish motive in view in writing as I do, *I* want nothing, save that *good* and *true* men represent the party in the federal appointments, there are many such to select from. If the president should however be forced to conclude that we are all 'a bad lot' together, beg him for Gods sake appoint an honest respectable man to the position from the democratic ranks rather than Mr Pearson Is it not possible that the appointment of Putnam can be revoked Should you deem it best you have my permission to remind the president of my relation to him as a member of his Staff (Ordnance officer) during the operations against Vicksburg, and he may thereby perhaps recollect what weight my statements are entitled to. Thanking you in behalf of the entire party of this county for your past kindnesses, and for your declining the honor recently conferred upon you, electing thereby to remain and give us the benefit of your consel and voice in the future which seems so dark to us, . . ." ALS, DNA, RG 56, Collector of Customs Applications. On June 24, Warner wrote to USG enclosing this letter. ALS, *ibid.*

On June 30 and July 6, Spencer wrote to USG. "Upon my return from Alabama last evening, whither I had gone for the especial purpose of organizing and preparing for the coming campaign, I was at once surprised and mortified to learn that Willard Warner had been appointed Collector of the Port of Mobile. Relying upon the understanding previously had that, under no circumstances would Mr Warner receive this appointment, and that no change would be made in the Collectorship until after August, I had accommodated and arranged all the important complications and misunderstandings in our party, and I flattered myself that the pathway to future Republican success in Alabama had been cleared of the many obstacles which had previously brought defeat upon us. Upon arriving here to consummate all that had been understood and agreed upon, I find that my labor had been utterly lost and thrown away, . . . I telegraphed, while *en route* to Washington to Secretary Boutwell to delay action in this matter until my arrival, and was more than chagrined to find that I was not accorded the delay of a single hour. As a Republican Senator in the Congress of the United States, I find myself compelled, most respectfully, but no less emphatically, to interpose my protest against the unnecessary haste with which this appointment was made, particularly when it is considered that I have been furthering the wishes of the Hon. B. S. Turner, the Republican Representative in Congress from the Mobile District, who is in accord with me in vehement opposition to Mr Warner's appointment as Collector. The blow struck at him is a serious one, considering that his nomination and election to Congress were opposed by Warner and his special friends, but who, notwithstanding, carried the Mobile district by an increased majority of three thousand. Acting upon your suggestion, I had procured from Collector Miller the appointment of ten or twelve prominent Republicans in the Mobile Custom House, and had succeeded in displacing a number of Democratic office-holders, who held positions there, while actively supporting the Democratic party. As these new appointees are upright, honest, active-working Republicans, whose fealty to their party rises superior to personal considerations, they must, of course, in view of Warner's appointment, be displaced for the benefit of those marplots and disorganizers who bolted the Republican nominees, and by carrying 210 votes out of 4500 in Mobile county, succeeded in electing the entire Democratic Legislative ticket in Mobile county. There can be no mistaking the issues and facts presented. This clique, consisting of self-constituted Committees, office-holders and bolters, have all testified their approbation of Warner's course, which gave the State to the Democracy. The masses of honest Republicans, not office-holders, but simple soldiers in the ranks, have openly and vigorously denounced and repudiated Warner and his co-conspirators. This appointment, therefore, endorses the bolters and conspirators, spurns the protestations of the masses, and places power in the hands of my enemies to further persecute me and my friends I have hitherto used mild words and terms in connection with Willard Warner, not because I was justified in so doing, but in deference to his late position as a Senator. As he is no longer a Senator, I feel myself at liberty to charge that his career, while such Senator, has been fraught with lying, fraud, deceit and treachery, deftly and aptly concealed under the hypocritical garb of sanctimony, and his demeanor toward my friends and myself has been, as you must admit, vindictive, dishonest, disreputable and vicious. He has not hesitated to be accessory to forgery and subornation of perjury, and this is attested by the record of public papers and of courts. To accomplish his selfish ends, personal and political, no act has been too base, no scruple either of honesty or of conscience has interposed, and no practices of petty, mean, low device and deceit have been allowed to interrupt his actions. Last winter, he saw fit to circulate in the Departments what purported to be a remonstrance against the appointment of any of my friends to office, and demanding that I should be ignored by yourself and your cabinet advisers. This petition, so called, contained the names of persons, who have under their own hands certified to me that they did not sign such a paper, while others stated that their signatures were obtained by fraud and deceit. Bogus telegrams were resorted to for the purpose of giving weight to Warner's asservations, and but recently he was convicted of interpolating a forged and fraudulent statement purporting to have emanated from the Republican Council of Mobile, which was promptly nailed as an audacious forgery by Judge McKinstry of Mobile, the President of the Council. I had the honor to urge the appointment of the Hon. G. L. Putnam as Postmaster of Mobile. I did so, because, in common with other leading Republicans, I believed him to be the ablest and most reliable Republican politician in that section of the State, and I earnestly desired to place him in position to aid our party success in the coming effort to redeem the State from the Democracy. Mr Putnam had, in the face of the most violent opposition, succeeded in establishing a system of free schools, white and colored, in a community utterly hostile to these ideas of progress. The Democracy, by the expenditure of large sums of money, had determined to drive Mr Putnam and his schools away. The usual persecutions followed, but Mr Putnam bravely met them in the Courts, and conquered in this unequal fight. As Mr Putnam's influence could not be secured to aid the bolters and the Democracy in disguise, the influence of Warner and his clique was brought to bear to crush him. When presented for the office of Postmaster, they revamped all the disproved charges and persecutions of the Democracy, but were repulsed by the force of simple truth. By subornation of perjury, accomplished by the money of Ex-Congressman Buck, Warner succeeded in procuring an indictment for bribery against Mr Putnam, and upon trial therefor, a few days since, before a politically hostile court, the honorable Judge charged the Jury that there was not a particle of evidence against Mr Putnam, and that the prosecution was absolutely infamous. The Jury acquitted Mr Putnam without leaving their seats; and so, in spite of the machinations and subornations of Warner, truth and justice have been again vindicated—at least, until some new phase of outrage is again launched against this gentleman, whose only crime is that he is a true Republican, and one of my many friends. . . ." "Herewith, I have the honor to transmit brief of the documents on file in the Treasury Department, favoring and opposing the appointment of Willard Warner as Collector at Mobile. Mr Vanderbilt will forward you today the originals, which I sincerely hope and most earnestly beg you will personally examine. You will please observe and especially note that this appointment of Mr Warner is earnestly opposed by Messrs. Hays and Turner, who, with myself, constitute the entire Republican delegation, with the single exception of Mr Buckley of the Montgomery District. It certainly does appear marvellous that a single Congressman, who monopolizes the entire patronage of his own District, should outweigh the influence and overcome the protests of the only Republican Senator, and the other Republican Representatives, including the Representative from the Mobile District, Mr Turner. You will also be kind enough to note the vast preponderance of opposition to this appointment, which I urgently submit as proof positive that, so far from uniting the Republican party of Alabama, the preferment of Mr Warner will only serve to widen the breach already existing, and utterly defeat our prospects of carrying the State in 1872. Please remember that in a few weeks, we enter upon a campaign for county officers, who are to govern and manage the next Presidential election; and it will be beyond my power to stem the tide, when I am, at the same time, forced to battle with recalcitrant Republicans as well as with the KuKlux Democracy. I cannot, therefore, become responsible for the defeat which must inevitably follow, unless you will put a stop to the unnatural warfare which has been, for the past two years, mercilessly waged against my friends and myself, under the auspices of Mr Warner. . . . You have, as you remarked to me some weeks since, done more for Mr Warner than almost any other man. I do not desire to pay Mr Warner back in his own coin of persecution, nor to dilate upon his abilities as a 'past-master in the high art' of treachery, deceit and fraud. I am willing that he shall be more than adequately provided for, so that it be not at the expense of the harmony of the Republican party of Alabama. Let him be tendered the Mission to Venezuela, or the Governorship of New Mexico! Either place should suffice a moderate ambition. There is no reason why he should be permitted to eclipse the brightness, or blight the hopes of our political success in Alabama, where, if he remains in the position of Collector, defeat is inevitable. In order to accommodate and reconcile all conflicts, permit me to recommend the appointment of the Hon R. S. Heflin, late Republican Congressman from the 3d Ala. District. . . . I certainly have more claim upon your personal and political consideration than Lewis E. Parsons, Andrew Johnson's Provisional Governor of Alabama, against whom I carried the State in 1868, for 'Grant and Colfax'—who villified and abused you and your platform in that memorable campaign—who, by a sweeping order, while Provisional Governor, continued all the rebel authorities in office—who has done more than any other man to ostracise and imperil Alabama Republicans—who has heretofore bitterly opposed and still is inimical to colored suffrage.—whose plausibility and duplicity stamp him as a perfect political Judas, and whose Syren song has been so successfully sung in praise of Mr Warner's questionable virtues. Pardon this long letter, and again begging that you will personally inspect the documents sent by Mr Vanderbilt, . . ." ALS, *ibid.* On Sept. 9, Hays, Haysville, wrote to USG. "I have the honor to transmit a letter, from Chancellor A. W. Dillard, recommending the removal of Ex. Senator Warner as Collector of the Port of Mobile. I have taken no part in the war between Senator Spencer, & Ex. Senator Warner, but claim them both as friends, I do not believe that the Existence of the Republican party, rests upon the shoulders of Either of them. As I expressed my views briefl[y] to you while in Washington upon this Subject, I have only to say, I reiterate those views and fully endorse the letter of Chancellor Dillard." ALS, *ibid.* See letter to Roscoe Conkling, Jan. 17, 1872.

To William Elrod

Washington D. C. Nov. 24th *1870*

DEAR ELROD:

Richard[1] has returned and reports horses all safely delivered on the farm. You will have to keep one hand who is a good horseman, after this Winter, to look after the colt. As I do not want him to go to a single mare, except my own, before he is four years old the same hand can do a good deal of work in addition the first year. After that he will have enough to do in looking after the stallion, young colts, and mares.

I was sorry to hear you had rented out any portion of the farm! It will make no difference however for one year. I think the place will feed 300 head of cows the ~~The~~ horses and sheep, and pork enough for yourself and hands. To do that you may have to buy some grain each year but the pasturage and hay, and a portion of the grain, can be raised on the place. It will be several years however before you can have any such amount of stock. I want you to raise all the heiffer calves here after until you get the maximum amount of cattle that you can feed. I think too you should keep two or three sows and raise your own hogs.—If I can borrow the money I will send you $3.000 00/100 in a week or two. Out of that I want you to buy 25 young cows and plank enough to straiten the road up the creek with a plank fence on each side of the ~~creek~~ lane. As fast as you have the means I want you then to buy plank, and make a plank fence from the turnpike out to Mr. Pipkins[2] place; along the turnpike from where the plank fence now ends along the front of the land bought from Mrs. Orr, and the whole length of my land on the Garrison road. With the rails you can then get you can make cross fences so as to throw the farm into convenient fields. As fast as the land gets fit for timothy you should set a good deal in timothy. The money I now send you is the last I want to send to the farm. In fact I shall hope soon to get a dividend from it. Before that however I want a Lime kiln built, another barn and a large addition to your house to accomodate the increased number of hands you will have to keep.

Yours U. S. GRANT

ALS, Illinois Historical Survey, University of Illinois, Urbana, Ill.

1. See memorandum to Richard Curtin, April 9, 1873.
2. William L. Pipkins.

To Ulysses S. Grant, Jr.

Washington D. C. Nov. 24th *1870*

DEAR BUCK,

We have just returned from hearing a most capital Thanks Giving sermon from Dr. Newman. Your Ma, Nellie and I went but Jesse did not. He has taken to riding Jeff of late and ~~while~~ did not get back this morning in time. Jessie seems quite delicate this Fall. He suffers particularly from headach, and often from bleading of the nose. I hope he will grow stronger as he grows older for he is a very bright, as well as good, boy. I think he and Nellie are learning now better than ever before. Fred has done quite well in his studies this half year, but is on tinderhooks about his demerit. On the 1st of Dec. a new half year, his last, begins. If he is all right then he need have no further trouble.[1] All send much love to you. We expect to see you now in about three weeks.

Yours Affectionately
U. S. GRANT

U. S. GRANT, JR.
HARVARD UNIVERSITY.

ALS, Robert S. Ruwitch, Northbrook, Ill. On Oct. 9, probably in 1870, USG had written to Ulysses S. Grant, Jr. ". . . to have the respect of all with whom you come in contact . . . To gain this never deceive nor act an artificial part. Be simply yourself . . . never resort to any means to make believe you know more than you really do . . . you should thoroughly understand what you go over. Call on Mr. Richardson and present to him, and to his family, my very kindest regards. Mr. R. beside being a very able and worthy man, I regard as one of the very best friends I have in Mass." ALS (incomplete facsimile and transcription), *Scriptorium* (1973).

1. On Aug. 25, 1874, James W. Smith, Columbia, S. C., wrote "*To the Editor of the New National Era:* . . . In July, 1870, the President was in Hartford, Ct., and in a conversation with my friend the Hon. David Clark, in reference to my treatment at West Point, he said: 'Don't take him away now; the battle might just as well be fought now as at any other time,' and gave him to understand that he would see me protected in my rights; while his son Fred, who was then a cadet, said to the same gentleman, and *in the presence of his father*, that 'the time had not come to send colored boys to West Point.' Mr. Clark said if the time had come for them to be in the United States Senate, it had surely come for them to be at West Point, and that he would do all in his power to have me protected. Fred Grant then said: 'Well, no d——d nigger will ever graduate from West Point.' This same young gentleman, with other members of his class, entered the rooms of three cadets, members of the fourth class, on the night of January 3, 1871, took those cadets out, and drove them away from the 'Point,' with nothing on but the light summer suits that they wore when they reported there the previous summer. Here was a most outrageous example of Lynch law, disgraceful alike to the first class, who were the executors of it, the corps of cadets, who were the abettors of it, and the authorities of the Academy, who were afraid to punish the perpetrators because the President's son was implicated, or, at least, one of the prime movers of the affair. Congress took the matter in hand, and instructed the Secretary of War to dismiss all the members of the class who were implicated, but the latter gentleman 'was extremely liberal in his interpretation of the regulations,' and declined to be influenced by the action of Congress, and let the matter drop. . . ." Henry Ossian Flipper, *The Colored Cadet at West Point* (New York, 1878), pp. 305–6. See letter to Frederick Dent Grant, Jan. 15, 1871.

On July 30, 1874, Smith wrote "*To the Editor of the New National Era:* As I told you in my last communication, I shall now proceed to give you an account of my four years' stay at West Point. I reported there on the 31st of May, 1870, and had not been there an hour before I had been reminded by several thoughtful cadets that I was 'nothing but a d——d nigger.' Another colored boy, Howard, of Mississippi, reported on the same day, and we were put in the same room, where we stayed until the preliminary examination was over, and Howard was sent away, as he failed to pass. While we were there we could not meet a cadet anywhere without having the most opprobrious epithets applied to us; but after complaining two or three times, we concluded to pay no attention to such things, for, as we did not know these cadets, we could get no satisfaction. . . . Finding there was no redress to be had there, I wrote my friend Mr. David Clark, of Hartford, Ct., to do something for me. He had my letter published, and that drew the attention of Congress to the matter, and a board was sent to West Point to inquire into the matter and report thereon. That board found out that several cadets were guilty of conduct unbecoming a cadet and a gentleman and recommended that they be court-martialled, but the Secretary of War thought a reprimand would be sufficient. Among those reprimanded were Q. O'M. Gillmore, son of General Gillmore; Alex. B. Dyer, son of General Dyer; and James H. Reid, nephew of the Secretary of War (it is said). I was also reprimanded for writing letters for publication. Instead of doing good, these reprimands seemed only to increase the enmity of the cadets, and they redoubled their energies to get me into difficulty, and they went on from bad to worse, until from words they came to blows, and then occurred that 'little onpleasantness' known as the 'dipper fight.' . . ." Flipper, *Colored Cadet*, pp. 290–92. On July 8, 1870, P. Clark [*David Clark*?], New York City, wrote to USG. "I trust I shall be pardoned for sending the Enclosed, and begging in the name of justice & humanity, that an inquiry be made into the case of young Smith, Such treatment of this noble Boy, is disgraceful to the country, and its correction would not be beneath the dignity of your Exalted Station" ALS, DNA, RG 94, Correspondence, USMA. David Clark, born in 1805 in Chaplin, Conn., had prospered as a businessman in Hartford and donated large sums for the education of freedmen and other charitable purposes. *Hartford Courant*, Oct. 8–9, 1889. See *CG*, 41–2, 5471, 5513; *New York Times*, July 15, 1870; William P. Vaughn, "West Point and the First Negro Cadet," *Military Affairs*, 35, 3 (Oct., 1971), 100–2; Walter Scott Dillard, "The United States Military Academy, 1865–1900: The Uncertain Years," Ph.D. Dissertation, University of Washington, 1972, pp. 190–202.

On Aug. 7, 1874, Smith wrote "*To the Editor of the New National Era:* SIR: In my last communication I related the circumstances of the 'dipper fight,' and now we come to the court-martial which resulted therefrom. . . . The court to try me sat in September, with General O. O. Howard as President. I plead 'not guilty' to the charge of assault on Cadet Wilson, and also to the charge of making false statements. The court found both Cadet Wilson and myself 'guilty' of assault, and sentenced us to be confined for two or three weeks, with some other light punishment in the form of 'extra duty.' The finding of the court was approved by President Grant in the case of Cadet Wilson, but disapproved in my case, on the ground that the punishment was not severe enough. Therefore, Cadet W. served his punishment and I did not serve mine, as there was no authority vested in the President to increase it. . . . I was released in November, after the proceedings and findings of the court had been returned from Washington, where they had been sent for the approval of the President, having been in arrest for three months. But I was not destined to enjoy my liberty for any length of time, for on the 13th of December, same year, I was in the ranks of the guard, and was stepped on two or three times by Cadet Anderson, one of my classmates, who was marching beside me. As I had had some trouble with the same cadet some time before, on account of the same thing, I believed that he was doing it intentionally, and as it was very annoying, I spoke to him about it, saying: 'I wish you would not tread on my toes.' He answered: 'Keep your d——d toes out of the way.' Cadet Birney, who was standing near by, then made some invidious remarks about me, to which I did not condescend to reply. One of the Cadet Corporals, Bailey, reported me for 'inattention in ranks,' and in my written explanation of the offence, I detailed the circumstances, but both Birney and Anderson denied them, and the Commandant of Cadets took their statement in preference to mine, and preferred charges against me for falsehood. I was court martialled in January, 1871, Captain Piper, Third Artillery, being President of the court. By this court I was found 'guilty,' as I had no witnesses, and had nothing to expect from the testimony of the witnesses for the prosecution. Cadet Corporal Bailey, who made the report, Cadets Birney and Anderson were the witnesses who convicted me; in fact they were the *only* witnesses summoned to testify in the case. The sentence of the court was that I should be dismissed, but it was changed to one year's suspension, or, since the year was almost gone before the finding of the court was returned from Washington, where it was sent for the approval of President Grant, I was put back one year. . . ." Flipper, *Colored Cadet*, pp. 293–95.

On Jan. 14, David Clark, Hartford, had written to U.S. Representative Charles H. Porter of Va. ". . . I notice your proposal in the House of Representatives to investigate the treatment of Cadet Smith, for which I thank you with all my heart. I desire to give you a few facts about Cadet Smith. Soon after the close of the war,

I sent a teacher to Columbia, S. C. In January, 1867, I visited her school. My attention was called to the boy Smith, then 15 years old. My teacher said that he was a remarkable scholar, and possessed an excellent character. The boy was most anxious for an education, and wished me to take him North and educate him. The appeal was so earnest that I decided to do so. . . . On the 1st of May I sent him to the Howard University, intending to educate him there. During the month Judge Hoge, Representative of the Third Congressional District of South Carolina, gave him an appointment to West Point. He desired to get General Howard's approval of the plan. I differed, but yielded. He went, and God only knows how much he has suffered from the day he trod that ground until this last court-martial. I have been there three times to look after him. He would have left in July had it not been for me. I had an interview with President Grant when here, on the 2d and 3d of July last. He said, 'Don't take him away; the battle might as well be fought now as any time.' So he was permitted to stay. Scarcely a day has passed when he has not been assaulted by words, or blows inflicted, to force him to do something for which they might expel him. I beg you to continue your efforts in behalf of this persecuted young man." *New National Era*, Jan. 26, 1871. On Feb. 17, Secretary of State Hamilton Fish recorded in his diary. "Cabinet. All present. . . . West Point Matters discussed Cadet Smith (Colored) has been convicted by Court Martial of lying & sentenced to be dismissed—Judge Advocate General recommends, a remittal of the sentence—(WHY?)" DLC-Hamilton Fish. On June 13, Secretary of War William W. Belknap ordered: ". . . In conformity with the 65th of the Rules and Articles of War, the proceedings of the General Court Martial in the foregoing case have been forwarded to the Secretary of War for the action of the President of the United States. The proceedings, findings and sentence are approved, but in view of all the circumstances surrounding this case and believing that the ends of public justice will be better subserved and the policy of the Government—of which the presence of this cadet in the Military Academy is a signal illustration—better maintained by a commutation of the sentence than by its rigid enforcement, the President is pleased to mitigate it by substituting, for dismissal from the service of the United States, reduction in his academic standing one year. Cadet Smith will join the succeeding fourth class at the commencement of the next academic year. The sentence as commuted will be duly executed." Copy, DNA, RG 107, Letters Sent, Military Affairs. See *New York Times*, Oct. 21–22, 1870, Jan. 5, June 9, 15, 20, 1871; "The West Point Troubles," *The Nation*, 293 (Feb. 9, 1871), 84–85; *CG*, 41–2, 5471, 5513, 41–3, 494, 583, 997; Tom D. Phillips, "The Black Regulars: Negro Soldiers in the United States Army, 1866–1891," Ph.D. Dissertation, University of Wisconsin, 1970, pp. 1064–1125.

On July 22, 1872, Clark, Hartford, wrote to Sayles J. Bowen, Washington, D. C. ". . . On June 30 [*1870*] I received from Cadet Smith the following letter: DEAR FRIEND AND PATRON: Your kind letter should have been answered long ere this, but really I have been so harrassed with examination and the insults and ill treatment of these cadets that I could not write or do anything else scarcely. I passed the examination all right and got in, but my companion Howard failed and was rejected. Since he went away I have been lonely indeed. And now these fellows appear to be trying their utmost to run me off, and I fear they will succeed if they continue as they have begun. . . . I have borne insult upon insult, till I am completely worn out. I have written a plenty of bad news, and I wish I had some good news for you; but, alas! it seems to be getting worse and worse. I forgot to tell you that out of 86 appointees only 39 passed the examination. They had prepared it to fix the colored candidates, but it proved most disastrous to the whites. I hope my brightest hopes will be realized, but I doubt if they ever will be here. Give my kind regards to all, and write soon to your much benefited and thankful servant. J. W. SMITH. Knowing that President Grant was to spend a few days with a friend of his in this city in the early part of July, I caused the foregoing letter to be published in *The Morning Courant* of the 2d of that month, so that it might come to the observation of the President. Through a mutual friend it was agreed that I should have an interview with the President on the subject of this letter. Accordingly, I met him. After giving him a history of my interest in Cadet Smith, including his having been a member of my household while attending school in Hartford, and then referring to the contents of the above letter, I said to the President that my opinion was that Smith could never remain at West Point in peace, and that he had better resign his position at once and return to Howard University. President Grant replied, 'I think differently; let him remain there, and I will do all that I can to protect him in his rights, and so shall the officers of the Academy, for I understand he passed the best examination of any of the appointments this year.' He then added that 'the officer who had used the abusive language on parade,' as quoted in the letter, 'should be expelled.' With this assurance from the President, I reluctantly assented that he should remain. The President informed me at this interview that his son Frederick, who was a member of the Academy, was with him, and he would introduce him and I could talk with him about the matter. I then met Master Frederick, and he said he had never spoken to Cadet Smith, nor had he any knowledge of any indignities heaped upon him, though he had heard about them. He said he should take neither one side nor the other in the quarrel, if one existed. He thought that it was premature to admit colored cadets at this time. That was about substantially all he said. I replied that if the white cadets would let the boy 'severely alone,' it would be all any of his friends asked. Our interview then closed.... Gen. Howard visited me during the month of December following, and in conversation with regard to the court-martial, said there was great disappointment at Washington that sufficient cause was not found by the court to expel Cadet Smith. I inquired of him, 'Who were disappointed?' and he replied, 'Both the President and Secretary of War.' I then inquired, 'Why are they disappointed?' Gen. Howard replied, 'In conversation with the Secretary of War, he informed me that President Grant had called upon him prior to the appointments of the courts-martial and said: "I suppose, Mr. Secretary, that you are about to appoint a court-martial for the trial of the colored Cadet Smith, at West Point. I have received two or three letters from my son Fred, who informs me that the cadet is very objectionable there; that there are strong prejudices existing against him, &c. Now, as this trial is to come off, Mr. Secretary, I trust that you will so make up the court as to cause his removal." There can be no doubt that the Secretary of War, acting upon the suggestion of President Grant, did constitute the Court, including the Judge-Advocate, of whom I have spoken, with a special view to secure the dismissal of Cadet Smith; and Gen. Howard was placed at the head, so that in case a majority of the Court should meet the expectations of the President, his name might add weight to the verdict before the people of the country. But the record of the cadet was so good, the testimony of his accusers so flimsy, that the Court could not find even an excuse for ordering his expulsion; and because of this fact the verdict as found was disapproved by the Secretary of War, as it answered in no way to serve the plot to disgrace the persecuted colored boy. I was astonished at this announcement, remembering what President Grant had promised me, when in Hartford, in the July preceding, that he would do all in his power to protect Cadet Smith in his rights, and also see that the officers at West Point did the same; for he had broken faith with me, by ignoring all the expressions of his own and carrying out the views of his son Fred., whose conversation at my interview with him in Hartford, it will be observed, exactly tallies with President Grant's remarks to the Secretary of War. This son Fred, has all along assumed to be a sort of Governor of West Point, and has made himself obnoxious to the professors by advising them of what 'his father' desired or did not desire. Upon Gen. Howard's return to Washington I wrote him a letter expressive of my disappointment and astonishment at the course pursued by President Grant and the Secretary of War, claiming that if it was right under the guarantees of the Fourteenth and Fifteenth Amendments to the Constitution that colored men should be elected as Senators and representatives in Congress, then it was equally right that the representatives of the colored race should be educated at the public expense at West Point—that there should be no discrimination under the general system of equality of citizenship; and, after enlarging upon these points, I requested him to show the letter to both the President and the Secretary of War, or supply them with copies. Gen. Howard subsequently advised me that he had done as I requested. From that moment up to the present time I have never believed that Gen. Grant has been in sympathy with the colored people. But I am convinced that all his professions of friendship for them have been for the sake of his own personal or political advancement. Following the result of the last court-martial alluded to, in which President Grant and his War Secretary took such an active interest, Cadet Smith was constantly harassed by persecutions, the extent of which may be imagined when it is stated that, during his first year at West Point, he was, during ten months of the time, kept under arrest. Evidently it was well understood at West Point what the views and wishes of President Grant and the Secretary of War were. The most frivolous charges were preferred against Smith for special reasons; just before the ball season opened he was placed under arrest, for no other reason but to keep him out of the ball-room, and was subsequently released without trial. In contrast to all this abuse of the colored cadet, there is something striking in the position and treatment of Fred. Grant at West Point. He was graduated 37 in a class of 41, and at once granted, by request of his father, the President, a furlough of six months, to visit the Pacific coast, and upon his return that furlough was extended to allow him to visit the courts of Europe, and be presented as the great American Prince. Contrasting again the treatment of the poor colored cadet at the close of his first year, President Grant condescended to absolve for all past offenses, only inflicting upon him the punishment that he should be set back one year, and commence anew his career at West Point. It is proper that I should add that during the past year he has been unmolested and left to the enjoyment of all his rights and privileges as a cadet. He now stands in his class the first among his equals. The foregoing is an unembellished narrative, plainly stating my knowledge of the whole case. I am very glad that your letter has enabled me to present it, as I have long felt that there were facts in the history of Cadet Smith at West Point which the people, and especially the colored people of the country, should know." *New York Tribune*, July 31, 1872. See *New York Times*, Aug. 2, 1872; *Washington Chronicle*, Aug. 2, 1872.

On Aug. 1, Belknap telegraphed to Brig. Gen. Oliver O. Howard, Sante Fé, New Mexico Territory. "In a letter from David Clark to Sayles J. Bowen, dated July 22d 1872, published in yesterday's New York Tribune, he states that in December following Cadet Smith's trial you said to him as follows:. . . Did you make that statement? Answer by telegraph." LS (telegram sent), DNA, RG 107, Telegrams Collected (Bound). On Aug. 3, Belknap telegraphed to Howard. "I have received no answer to my telegram of August 1st about colored cadet. The President and I desire a reply at once." LS (telegram sent), *ibid.* Howard telegraphed to Belknap. "CAMP AT CAVE SPRINGS, A. T. August 8, VIA SANTA FE August 14. . . . Your telegrams of August 1 and 3, this moment received. Mr. Clark is certainly mistaken, for I never had such a conversation with the Secretary of War, and could not have made so untrue a report." *Baltimore Gazette,* Aug. 16, 1872. On Aug. 16, Clark wrote. "General Howard in a telegraph despatch to the Secretary of War denies the conversation had with me relative to the appointment of the court martial to try colored cadet Smith. I solemnly affirm that my report of that conversation is substantially true. Could I meet General Howard and remind him of the intimations he gave me at West Point, at the time of the trial, which he fully explained at my house in Hartford, in the December following, then stating to me the position of the President and Secretary of War on this matter, I am sure he would withdraw his denial and acknowledge his forgetfulness. . . ." *Philadelphia Public Ledger,* Aug. 17, 1872. On Aug. 17, Belknap telegraphed to Horace Porter, Long Branch. "In papers to-day David Clark speaks of letter to Howard of which, he says, copies were given to me and to President. I have no recollection of such letter and can find no copy. Was one given President: If so please mail copy to me at once? Answer—" ALS (telegram sent), DNA, RG 107, Telegrams Collected (Bound). On the same day, Porter telegraphed to Belknap. "President has no recollection of any such letter from Clark." Telegram received (at 5:15 P.M.), *ibid.* In an undated letter, R. R. Fish wrote to Belknap charging Howard with duplicity toward USG. ALS, PHi. For Smith's final dismissal from USMA, see Flipper, *Colored Cadet,* pp. 289–90; Peter S. Michie, "Caste at West Point," *North American Review,* CIII, CCLXXXIII (June, 1880), 609–11; George L. Andrews, "West Point and the Colored Cadets," *International Review,* IX (Nov., 1880), 479–84.

To William W. Smith

Washington D. C. Nov. 26th *1870*

DEAR SMITH:

Can you and Emma, (if Emma is able to travel) not come and spend ChristMass week with us? If Emma cannot come then you come alone.

Please present my kindest regards to Judge and Mrs. McKennan, Emma & the children

yours Truly
U. S. GRANT

ALS, Washington County Historical Society, Washington, Pa. See letter to Ulysses S. Grant, Jr., Dec. 8, 1870.

Endorsement

Respectfully refered to the Sec. of War. No reply has been sent to Mr. Lindsay.[1] I think probably it will be well to inform the comd.g officer[2] at Montgomery the substance of his dispatch and ask for information as to his orders and the present status.

No reply is necessary to Lindsay further than an acknowledgement of the receipt of his dispatch and a statement that U. S. troops will not be used to obstruct any legal decision of the questions existing between the two canditates for Governor of Ala.

U. S. GRANT

NOV. 30TH /70

AES, DNA, RG 94, Letters Received, 720P 1870. Written on a telegram of Nov. 29, 1870, from Governor Robert B. Lindsay of Ala. to USG. "Having on saturday twenty sixth 26th inst duly qualified as Governor of the state of alabama in accordance with the Constitution and laws thereof—In an official Communication made to captain Drum commanding united states forces at this post I requested him to withdraw soldiers which on the requisition of my predecessor Governor Smith he had placed on guard in the building of the state capitol capt Drum has not complied with my request I therefore respectfully ask your interposition in this behalf I am satisfied capt Drum believes that he is acting in strict perfor[m]ance of his duty" Telegram received (at 5:15 P.M.), *ibid.* On Nov. 27, Governor William H. Smith of Ala. had telegraphed to USG. "I omitted to say in my dispatch of yesterday that because of the excitement and threats of violence I deemed it prudent and necessary to ask the Officer Commanding here to place troops at the Capitol. I urgently recommend that more be sent here" Telegram received (at 10:25 A.M.), *ibid.* Related papers are *ibid.*

1. Born in Scotland in 1824, Lindsay immigrated to N. C. in 1844, settled at Tuscumbia, Ala., in 1849, where he practiced law and was elected to the legislature. Lindsay served in the C.S. Army, returned to the legislature after the war, and was the Democratic candidate for governor in 1870.

2. Capt. William F. Drum, 2nd Inf.

Endorsement

[*Nov. 1870*]

I concur with the Sec. of War so far as he indicates your worth to the Army; but I believe the course you have pursued a wise one and that you will prove quite as valuable to the country, out of the service, as you always have in it. Should the country ever require your services as a soldier, which I trust it may not, I know that your patriotism would lead you to make any sacrifice in its cause.

Wishing you prosperity and happiness in the new field you have marked out for yourself, I subscribe myself,

Your friend
U. S. GRANT

AES (facsimile), Joseph M. Maddalena [Spring, 1993], no. 54. Written on a letter of Nov. 26, 1870, from Secretary of War William W. Belknap to Lt. Col. James H. Wilson. "... You are the first and only Field Officer who has, since the passage of the Army bill, voluntarily retired, and I can sincerely say, that I would accept the resignation of none, with so much hesitation. You bear with you to your new field my earnest wishes for your continued success, and I know that in saying this, I express the feelings of the President as well as my own." *Ibid.*, p. 38.

On Aug. 29, Belknap, Keokuk, had written to AG Edward D. Townsend. "Genl. J. H. Wilson (Lieut. Col. unassigned) now stationed here, proposes to resign under the Act of Congress—to take effect Jany. 1. 70.—Genl. Wilson is so valuable an officer that I have endeavored to change his purpose, but without effect. I had a conversation with the President as to his case, and the latter desired Wilson to remain in the service, but also desired his discharge under the law if W. insisted upon. When his application comes you will please grant it to take effect Dec. 31. 70 (I believe that is the date fixed by him). He also, I think, asks for transportation &c which it appears to me is not allowable, but of this, you are better informed than I am—" ALS, DNA, RG 94, ACP, 1871 130. On Sept. 2, Wilson, Keokuk, wrote to Townsend. "Under the provisions of the late Act of Congress providing for the reduction of the Army I have the honor to tender herewith the resignation of my commission as Lieutenant Colonel, United States Army, unassigned (late 35th Regiment of Infantry), and to request that I may be honorably discharged from the service, with one year's pay and allowances, milage for myself, and transportation for my horses and servants to my home at Wilmington, Delaware...." ALS, *ibid.*

On the same day, Horace Porter, Long Branch, wrote to Wilson. "I received, upon my return from Newport and West Point, your three letters, which I read with great interest, particularly the one referring to your resignation, You are right, If I had the same prospects I should not hesitate a day about my course. I got a letter from Belknap yesterday, He speaks of the matter, and says he does not want you to resign, because you are a good officer, and as head of the Army he is anxious to keep all good officers in service. This is very complimentary but not very strong argument. Your letter to Humphreys has the right ring, When you come East we shall talk over matters at length. The President says you need have no apprehension about your success in civil life, that you are bound to win, which is more than he generally says about any body, you know...." AL (initialed), DLC-James H. Wilson. On Sept. 10, Wilson wrote to Hiram Barney, New York City. "... Grant directed Belknap to offer me any transfer that the law would allow, said he would have made me Brigr General had not the vacancies been abolished, & added that I could go to West Pt. next year as Supt if I would stay in the Army—closing with the opinion that I would not and ought not to accept. Belknap seconded all this and added that anything he could do to advance my wishes should be done. It all made no difference with me—particularly as the talk about promotion is a little late...." ALS, CSmH. For papers relating to Wilson's resignation, see DNA, RG 94, Letters Received, 885W 1870 and 886W 1870. See also *PUSG*, 6, 295–96; *ibid.*, 19, 256–58, 261; letter to Ministers and Consuls, Feb. 14, 1871; James Harrison Wilson, *Under the Old Flag* (New York, 1912), II, 380–95.

Draft Annual Message

[*Dec. 5, 1870*]

TO THE SENATE
AND HOUSE OF REPRESENTATIVES
GENTLEMEN:

Since my last Annual ~~last~~ Message a year of peace, and general prosperity to this Nation, has transpired. We have, through a kind providence, been blessed with abundent crops, and have been spared from complications, and war, with foreign nations. ~~and have~~ In our own midst comparitive harmony has been restored. The states states of Virginia, Mississippi and Texas have been restored to representation in our National Council. ~~and t~~The state of Georgia, the only state now without representation, may confidently be expected to take her place there also at the beginning of the new year, and then, let us hope, will be completed the work of reconstruction. ~~A~~ It is to be regreted however that a free exercise of the franchise has been denied to citizens in exceptional cases ~~throughout the South, however and, in some instances, have, no doubt, changed~~ the ~~true verdict of the people has, no doubt, been reversed~~ in several of the recently re-admitted states, and in some instances no doubt to the extent of changing the verdict of the people. ~~As each House of Congress however is the judge of the "qualification, and election, of its own members" this subject will receive your consideration in such way as you may deem most proper.~~

With an acquiescence on the part of the whole people in the National obligation to pay the public debt, created as the price of our Union, and the pensions to our disabled soldiers, ~~their and~~

soldiers widows and orphans, and in the changes to the constitution made necessary by a great revolution, there is no reason why we should not ~~go on to~~ advance in material prospirty and happiness as no other nation ever did after so protracted and devatating a war.

In the year just passed[1]

Millions of our public debt has been paid. The tax collected from the people has been reduced more than Eighty Millions of dollars per Annum. By steadiness in our present course there is no reason why, in a few short years, the national tax gatherer may not disappear from the doors of of the Citizen almost entirely. With the revenue stamp, dispensed by postmasters in every community, a tax upon liquors of all sorts, tobacco in ~~every shape~~ all its forms, and a wise adjustment of the tarriff which will put a duty only upon those articles which we could dispense with, known as luxuries, and on those which we use more of than we produce, revenue enough may be raised after a few years of peace and consequent reduction of obligations to fulfill all our obligations ~~after a few more years of peace and consequent reduction of obligation~~. A further reduction of expenses, in addition to a reduction of interest account, may be relied on to make this practicable. Revenue reform, if it means this has my hearty support. If it implies a collection of all the revenue for the support of government, for the payment of principle and interst of the public debt, pensions &c. by directly taxing the people, then I am against revenue reform and confidently believe the people are with me. If it means failure to provide the necessary means to defray all the expenses of government, and thereby repudiation of the public debt, and bounties, then I am against revenue reform all the more. Revenue reform has not been defined by any of its advocates, to my knowledge, but seems to be accepted as something which is to fill every mans purse and stomache without any effort or exertion on his part.

A true revenue reform can not be made in a day but must be the work of numerous acts of Congress, and of time. As soon as the revenue can be dispensed with all duty should be taken off of ~~sug~~ Coffee, tea, and other articles of universal use, not produced by ourselves. The necessities of the country compell us to collect revenue from our imports. An army of Assessors and Collectors is not a pleasant sight to the citizen, but they, or a tarriff for revenu, ~~are~~ is necessary.

During the last session of Congress a treaty for the Annexation of the Rebublic of San Domingo to the United States ~~was rejected by~~ failed to receive the requisite two third vote of ~~the~~ the Senate: I was thoroughly convinced then that the best interest of this country, commercially and materially, demanded its ratification. Time has only ~~convinced me more strongly to~~ confirmed me more strongly in this view~~s~~. ~~I then entertained~~. I now firmly believe that the moment it is known that the United ~~s~~States ~~give up~~ has entirely abandoned the project of accepting as a part of its territory the island of San Domingo a Free Port will be negociated for, by European nations in the Bay of Samina. ~~It will~~ A large commercial city will spring up which we will be tributary to without corresponding benefits, and then will be seen the folly of our rejecting so great a prize. [~~Some of the advantages which I believed would~~ My views on this subject were imperfectly set forth in a special Message to the senate which are here recapitulated] In view of the importance of this ~~matter~~ question I earnestly urge upon Congress early action expressive of their views upon it and providing the way to acquire San Domingo. My suggestion is that by ~~J~~joint resolution of the two houses of Congress the Executive be authorized to appoint a commission to negociate a treaty with the Authorities of San Doming for the acquisition of that island.[2] The treaty then may be subject either to the action of the Senate or to the joint action of the two houses of Congress as in the case of the acquisition of Texas. So convinced am I of the advantages to flow from the acquisition of San Domingo, and of the great disadvantages, I might almost say calamity, to flow from non acquisition, that I believe the subject has only to be investigated to be approved.

~~to the maximum standard for the future~~. The War Department buildin is an~~d~~ old structure, not fireproof, and entirely inadequate in dimen~~t~~[s]ions to our present wants. Many thousands of dollars are now paid annually for rent of [private] buildings, ~~outside~~, to accomodate the various bureaus of the Department. I recommend an appropriation for ~~the building of~~ a new War Department building, suited to the present and growing wants of the nation. The report of the Sec. of War shews a very satisfactory reduction in the expenses of the Army for the last fiscal year. For details you are refered to his ~~report herewith~~ accompanying [report].

The [accompanying] report of the Post Master General, ~~herewith accompanying~~, shows a most satisfactory working of that Dept. With the adoption ~~of some~~ of the recommendations contained ~~in this report~~ therein, particulary those relating to a reform in the franking privelege, and adopting the '~~card~~ "Correspondence Cards," a self sustaining postal system may speedily be looked for, and at no distant day a further reduction ~~reduction~~ of the rate of postage ~~attainable~~ [be attained].

~~Commissions eminate in the Departments under which appointees rep serve and receive instructions except in the Postmaster Generals Department. Post Masters are commissioned by the Sec. of State. I would recommend that the duty of issueing these commissions be transfered to the Post Master Genl.~~

I recommend authorization by Congress to the Post Master General, and Attorney General, to issue all ~~the~~ commissions to officials appointed through their respective departments. ~~Here to fore~~ [At present] these commissions, where ~~the~~ appointments are Presidential, ~~have been~~ [are] issued by the State Department. The custom in all the departments of Government except those of the Post Office and Attorney General, ~~has been~~ [is] for each ~~department~~ to is[sue] its own commissions.

Always favoring practical reforms I ~~will~~ respectfully call your attention to one abuse, of long standing, which I would like to see remedied by this Congress. It is a reform in the civil service of the country. ~~and~~ I would have ~~that reform~~ [it] go beyond the mere fixing of the tenure of office of clerks and employees who do not require "the advice and consent of the Senate" to make their appointment complete, ~~and~~ I would have it govern, not the tenure but the manner of making all appointment[s?]. There is no duty which so much embarrasses ~~an~~[the] Executive, and heads of departments as that of appointments; nor is there ~~other so~~ [any such] arduous and thankless ~~a~~ labor imposed on Senators and representatives as that of finding places for constituents. The present system does not secure the best men, and often not even fit men, for ~~place~~ for public place. The elevation and purification of the civil service of the government will be hailed with approval by the whole people of the United States

my views.

Reform in the management of Indian Affairs has received the special attention of the Administration from its inauguration to the present day. The experiment of making it a missionary work was tried with a few agencies, given to the denomination of Friends And has been found to work most ~~ad~~ advantageously. All agencies and Superintendencies not so disposed of were given to Officers of the Army. The Act of Congress reducing the Army ~~rendering these latter~~ renders Army Officers ~~of the Army~~ ineligible for civil positions. ~~and deeming~~ Indian Agencies ~~as~~ being civil Offices, I determined to give all the Agencies to such religious denominations as had heretofore established Missionaries among the Indians, and perhaps to some other~~s~~ denominations who would undertake the work on the same terms; i. e. as a Missionary work.[3] The societies selected are allowed to name their own agents and are expected to watch over them, and aid them, as missionaries, to Christianize and Civilize the Indian, and to train him in the arts of peace. The government watches over the~~ir~~ official acts of these agents and require of them as strict an accountability as if they were appointed in any other manner.—I entertain the confident hope that the policy now pursued will, in a few years, bring all the Indians on to reservations, where they will live in houses, have school houses and churches, and will be pursuing peaceful and self sustaining avocations, and where they may be visited by the law abiding white man with the same impunity that he now visits the civilized White settlements. I call your special attention to the report of the Commissioner of Indian Affairs for full information on this subject.

Our depressed commerce is a subject which I called your special attention to, at the last session, and suggested that we will, in the future, have to look more to the states south of us, and to China and Japan for a revival of it. Our representatives to all these Countries have exerted their influence to encourage trade between the United States and them. But the fact exists that the carrying is all done in foreign bottoms, and while this state of affairs exists we can not controll our due share of the commerce of the world. That between the Pacific states and China & Japan is about all the carrying trade no[w] conducted in American vessels. I would recommend a liberal policy towards that line, ~~which~~ one that will insure its success, and even extension.

The cost of building iron vessels, the only vessels that can compete with foreign vessels in the carrying trade, is so much greater in the United States than in foreign countries that without some assistence from the government they cannot be successfully built ~~with us~~. here. There will be several propositions laid before Congress, in the course of the present session looking to remedying this evil. Even if it should be at some cost to the National Treasury I hope such encouragement will be given as will secure American shipping on the ~~h~~High Seas, and American ship building at home.

[During the last fiscal year 8,095,413 acres of public land were disposed of, being 429,261.03 acres in excess of the amount disposed of during the year which preceded it. Of this quantity, 3,698,910.05 acres were taken under the Homestead law, and 2,159,515.81 sold for cash. The remainder was located with military warrants,[4] college or Indian scrip, or applied in satisfaction of grants to railroads or for other public uses. The entries under the Homestead law during the last, covered 961,545 acres more than those during the preceding, year.

Surveys have been vigorously prosecuted to the full extent of the means applicable to the purpose. The quantity of land in market will amply supply the present demand. The claim of the settler under the homestead or the preëmption laws is not, however, limited to lands subject to sale at private entry. Any unappropriated surveyed public land may, to a limited amount, be acquired under the former laws, if the party entitled to enter under them will comply with the requirements they prescribe in regard to residence and cultivation. The actual settler's preference right of purchase is even broader, and extends to lands which were unsurveyed at the time of his settlement. His right was formerly confined within much narrower limits, and at one period of our history was conferred only by special statutes. They were enacted from time to time to legalize what was then regarded as an unauthorized intrusion upon the national domain. The opinion that the public lands should be regarded chiefly as a source of revenue is no longer maintained. The rapid settlement and successful cultivation of them are now justly considered of more importance to our well-being than is the fund which the sale of them would produce. The remarkable growth and prosperity of our new States and Territories attest the wisdom of the legislation which invites the tiller of the soil to secure a permanent home on terms within the reach of all. The pioneer who incurs the dangers and privations of a frontier life and thus aids in laying the foundation of new commonwealths, renders a signal service to his country and is entitled to its special favor and protection. These laws secure that object and largely promote the general welfare. They should, therefore, be cherished as a permanent feature of our land system. Indeed it is worthy of serious consideration whether the residue of our public lands should not be disposed of solely to actual settlers.

The work of the Census Bureau has been energetically prosecuted. The preliminary report, containing much information of special value and interest, will be ready for delivery during the present session. The remaining volumes will be completed with all the dispatch consistent with perfect accuracy in arranging and classifying the returns. We shall thus, at no distant day, be furnished with an authentic record of our condition and resources. It will, I doubt not, attest the growing prosperity of the country, although during the decade ~~now drawing to a close~~ which has just closed it was so severely tried by the great war waged to maintain its integrity, and to secure and perpetuate our free institutions.]

The subjects of Education and Agriculture are of great interest to the success of our ~~r~~Republican institutions, happiness and grandure as a Nation. In the interest of one a bureau has been established, in the Interior Department, the Bureau of Education, and in the interest of the other the Bureau of Agriculture. I believe great general good is to flow from the operations of both these bureaus, if properly fostered. I cannot commend to your careful consideration to highly the ~~the~~ reports of the Commissioners of Education and of Agriculture, nor urge to strongly such liberal legislation as to secure their efficiency.

In conclusion I would sum up ~~our~~ ~~true~~ the policy ~~to~~ ~~be~~ of the Administration to be; a thorough enforcement of every law; a faithful collection of every tax provided for; economy in the disbursment of the same; a prompt payment of every debt of the nation; a reduction of taxes as rapidly as the requirements of the country will admit of; reductions of taxation to be so ~~made~~ arranged as to afford the greatest relief to the greatest number; honest and fair dealings with all other peoples to the end that war with all its blighting consequences may be avoided, but without surrendering any right or obligation due to us; a reform in the treatment of indians and in the whole civil service of the country; and finally in securing a pure, untrammeld ballot, where every man entitled to cast a vote may do so, just once at each election, without fear of molestation an proscription on account of his politics.

ADf (bracketed material not in USG's hand), DLC-USG, III. On Nov. 21, 25, 30, 1870, Secretary of State Hamilton Fish had written in his diary. "read to the President the portions proposed for his Annual Message, relating to matters ~~from~~ in charge of the State Dept—Reading the part relating to San Domingo & the Bay of Samana, he said that he had written something about San Domingo, which he thought he would substitute for what I had read, but would consider it—so too with respect to a passage renewing the recommendation for allowing the purchase of foreign built vessels—he says he has prepared something submitting alternative courses—that there is objection to the purchase of British vessels while the parties objecting would be willing to allow the purchase of German or French vessels—I urge him to recommend one policy—that if he submit alternative propositions his friends in Congress will be divided, & nothing may result—& as to the objection to purchasing British vessels many of the German & French Steamers are British built & call attention to the condition of our Commerce on the Lakes, where the British tonnage, in our own Ports is fifty percent larger than the American tonnage—" "President read draft of his message—He has altered the passage, in the draft which I submitted to him, respecting the Bay of Samana—making a recommendation to Congress to authorise a Commission who may negotiate for annexation either by Joint Resolution, or by Treaty, 'to be submitted to Congress' After conclusion of the reading, I express doubt whether I had correctly understood that passage & state that if by Treaty, the treaty can only be submitted to the *Senate*, & the action of the House is necessary only for appropriating what money may be needed, or for Legislation to carry out the objects of the Treaty—It wd be a Constitutional blundre, to propose submitting a Treaty to both Houses of Congress—I further suggest, in reply to the Presidents remark that his object was to submit to Congress, the question, ~~whether~~ in order to obtain an expression of their opinion upon the question of annexation, that he has the Constitutional right to appoint Commissioners, & that the object he suggests will be attained by asking an appropriation for the Expenses &c of the Commission—on which the merits of the proposed Annexation, can be discussed—this view appearing to be acquiesced in, he says he will re-write that part—He has also changed the part of the draft submitted from the Department, respecting the purchase of foreign built vessels—" "In reply to my enquiry he says that he has altered that portion of his message relating to San Domingo, where he had suggested the submission of a Treaty, (in case one should be negotiated) to the two Houses of Congress, & that he made no mention of any particular European Govt as having an intention or desire to obtain the harbor of Samana—he had named Prussia as the nation desiring the purchase—" DLC-Hamilton Fish.

On Dec. 8, Henry Adams, Harvard College, wrote to Jacob D. Cox. ". . . The Message is a queer document. It is curious to watch Fish's position? How is it possible for him to stand the joint-resolution part of it? I never have been able to comprehend Mr Fish's theory of management. He certainly cannot approve such a step. As to Revenue Reform it is peculiarly droll, but rather in the style of a very ignorant collegian. It is to be regretted that the President does not know what Revenue Reform means, but I think we shall teach him as much as he will be able to learn, before long. It is at all events something to have got to the mark on Civil Service, and for this you are responsible. But I still see a long fight before us here, and I look on your article as our first step forward. . . ." ALS, Cox Papers, Oberlin College, Oberlin, Ohio.

On Dec. 12, Governor Lucius Fairchild of Wis., Washington, D. C., wrote to USG. "I desire to testify to the great satisfaction your message gave me—On all hands it is commended highly by your party friends—and proves a shot below the water line to—the opposition—Not the least of its merits is the fact that it has taken the breath out of the 'new party' faction—I would have been glad to have said this much to you personally had opportunity offered—but the constant calls on your time prevented—" ALS, ICarbS. On Dec. 22, Adam Badeau, London, wrote to USG. "Confidential . . . Although I have pestered you with letters of late, I cannot refrain from writing one line to say that the text of the Message has arrived and been printed every where here. I am delighted with it, and consider it an admirable state paper, both in style and matter. The part about San Domingo seems to me admirable and eloquent and unanswerable; I hope it may be effective. Every syllable on the Fishery and Alabama questions appears to me just, well considered, firm and yet calm. The summary of the policy of the administration at the close, warmed up all my old enthusiasm for my chief; I felt that he deserved and must command the same success in civil as in military life. I enclose a letter for Mrs Grant, which I beg you will hand her and accept my best wishes for your health and happiness, and entire success during the new year. I learned a day or two ago that Mr. Motley submitted his concluding and long despatch, to Mr. Hughes, so as to be sure of the correctness of his legal points. As Mrs. Hughes told me this, I know you will pardon me for asking you to regard it as confidential; but it lessens my esteem for Mr. Motley, that in a dispute with his own government, he, while a subordinate of that government, should go with his grievances and defence, for counsel to a foreigner . . . Mr. Froude has again expressed his anxiety that you may permit me to write the article I spoke of. I still make no suggestion." ALS, USG 3.

1. A lengthy discussion of foreign policy occurs at this point in the final version. See following Annual Message.

2. On Dec. 8, Stephen Preston, Haitian minister, Washington, D. C., had written to Fish. "I have the honor to call your serious attention to the following passage in the message of His Excellency the President of the United States, addressed to Congress on the 5th instant: 'My suggestion is that by a joint resolution of the two Houses of Congress, the Executive be authorized to appoint a commission to negotiate a treaty with the authorities of San Domingo for the acquisition of that island, etc.' This passage in the message of the President of the United States, asking Congress for authority to make a treaty to annex the *Island of San Domingo* (the name formerly given to Hayti by Europeans, and still commonly used in the United States) has caused me deep and painful surprise, which it will be very easy for you to appreciate. My quality as Minister of Hayti, accredited near your Government, imposes upon me the obligation to address you, in order to receive explanations touching the meaning of this phrase, which seems to me to be a formal menace to the independence of Hayti, with regard to which the Haytians are susceptible in a very high degree. The idea of destroying the autonomy of my country can only be based upon a serious error, and this is the more to be regretted, as it comes from the Great Republic of the United States of the North, which we considered as our ally, and as one that would, in case of necessity, protect us against the aggressions of European Powers. I shall be very happy to be able to transmit to my Government, with the message of the President of the United States, such communications as you may be pleased to address me on this subject, which, I hope, will be sufficiently satisfactory to calm its legitimate anxieties, and will aid in preventing unfortunate complications for my country in future, . . ." LS (in French), DNA, RG 59, Notes from Foreign Legations, Haiti; translation, *ibid.* On Dec. 12, Fish wrote to Preston. ". . . A message of the President is a communication between two distinct branches of this government and as such is strictly and exclusively a domestic document, to which it is conceived no foreign power can take just exception. If recommendations, contained in such a message should be adopted by Congress and should become a law a foreign power which may suppose that its rights or interests would be affected thereby may then properly object through its representative here to the measure proposed. No such contingency having yet occurred, your interference in the matter must be regarded as at least premature." Copy, *ibid.*, Notes to Foreign Legations, Haiti; *SED*, 41-3-17, 113. See message to Senate, Jan. 16, 1871.

On Dec. 8, 1870, James Watson Webb, New York City, had written to USG. "*In Bed.* . . . You are only *begining*, while I am closing a long *Political* career; and I ask your perusal of, and careful pondering over, the enclosed article. They are neither the views of a Partizan nor of an interested manufacturer or Politician; but they are the honest results of my nearly fifty years of reflection. I was a soldier before I was an Editor; and consequently, I always proclaimed, that I would only be guided by *party*, when the action of *party*, involved great principles. That is, to say, I would support a fool, if to defeat him would remotely endanger the principles involved in our cause; but would & did oppose nominations of Fools & Knaves for Governor or Mayor, when to defeat *them*, endangered no principles of our party:—and immediately before going to Brazil, I made oath before a Committee of Congress as follows,—'During the thirty odd years I have edited the Cour. & Enq. I have annually made trips to Washington and Albany in the interest of our merchans; but never in a single instance, have I ever received any reward for so doing, nor have I ever had my expenses paid. And further, neither congress nor our Legislature, ever passed a Law in which I have had a present or prospective interest of one Dollar.' This may not have been a good record to live by; but it is a good one to close life with. A thousand thanks for your frank & manly language in relation to our foreign affairs. I am, & ever have been, thoroughly with you in the matter of St. Domingo; and if my life is spared, as now seems probable, I shall yet aid that wise measure. Give ship-builders, what wd be equal to duties, when they use American Iron.—Never forget that the Tariff is for the protection of *farmers*" ALS, NjP. See *PUSG*, 15, 507–15.

3. On Oct. 31, a correspondent had reported from Washington, D. C. "The President had a conference to-day with Simon Wolf, of this district, in regard to recognizing Israelites in his division of the Indian agencies, among the various religious denominations. The President said that they had not been neglected, but the agencies had only been given to such denominations as had missionary organization. He would, however, be glad to recognize the Israelites of this country by appointing such a one as might be properly indorsed by one of the superintendencies." *Cincinnati Gazette*, Nov. 1, 1870.

4. On Dec. 14, William McCoy, Gentryville, Ind., wrote to USG. "I see in your adress to congress that their is sutch thing as Bounty land warrants for soldiers I desire to know what class of soldiers is entitled to warrants and how they may be procured I desire to go west and if their is a land warrant for me all right . . ." ALS, DNA, RG 48, Lands and Railroads Div., Miscellaneous Letters Received. On Dec. 17, John B. Buchanan, Kansas City, Mo., wrote a similar letter to USG. ALS, *ibid.*

Annual Message

[*Dec. 5, 1870*]

TO THE SENATE AND HOUSE OF REPRESENTATIVES: . . .

Soon after the existing war broke out in Europe, the protection of the United States Minister in Paris was invoked in favor of North Germans domiciled in French territory. Instructions were issued to grant the protection. This has been followed by an extension of American protection to citizens of Saxony, Hesse and Saxe-Coburg, Gotha, Columbia, Portugal, Uruguay, the Dominican Republic, Ecuador, Chili, Paraguay and Venezuela, in Paris. The charge was an onerous one, requiring constant and severe labor, as well as the exercise of patience, prudence and good judgment. It has been performed to the entire satisfaction of this Government, and, as I am officially informed, equally so to the satisfaction of the government of North Germany.

As soon as I learned that a Republic had been proclaimed at Paris, and that the people of France had acquiesced in the change, the Minister of the United States was directed, by telegraph, to recognize it, and to tender my congratulations and those of the people of the United States. The re-establishment, in France, of a system of government disconnected with the dynastic traditions of Europe appeared to be a proper subject for the felicitations of Americans. Should the present struggle result in attaching the hearts of the French to our simpler forms of representative government, it will be a subject of still further satisfaction to our people. While we make no effort to impose our institutions upon the inhabitants of other countries, and while we adhere to our traditional neutrality in civil contests elsewhere, we cannot be indifferent to the spread of American political ideas in a great and highly civilized country, like France.

We were asked by the new government to use our good offices, jointly with those of European Powers, in the interests of peace. Answer was made that the established policy, and the true interests of the United States forbade them to interfere in European questions jointly with European Powers. I ascertained, informally and unofficially, that the government of North Germany was not then disposed to listen to such representations from any powers, and though earnestly wishing to see the blessings of peace restored to the belligerents, with all of whom the United States are on terms of friendship, I declined, on the part of this government, to take a step which could only result in injury to our true interests, without advancing the object for which our intervention was invoked.

Should the time come when the action of the United States can hasten the return of peace, by a single hour, that action will be heartily taken.

I deemed it prudent, in view of the number of persons of German and French birth living in the United States, to issue, soon after official notice of a state of war had been received from both belligerents, a proclamation defining the duties of the United States as a neutral, and the obligations of persons residing within their territory, to observe their laws and the laws of nations.

This proclamation was followed by others, as circumstances seemed to call for them. The people, thus acquainted, in advance, of their duties and obligations, have assisted in preventing violations of the neutrality of the United States.

It is not understood that the condition of the insurrection in Cuba has materially changed since the close of the last Session of Congress.

In an early stage of the contest, the authorities of Spain inaugurated a system of arbitrary arrests, of close confinement and of military trial, and execution of persons suspected of complicity with the insurgents, and of summary embargo of their properties, and sequestration of their revenues by Executive warrant.

Such proceedings, so far as they affected the persons or property of citizens of the United States, were in violation of the provisions of the Treaty of 1795., between the United States and Spain. Representations of injuries resulting to several persons claiming to be citizens of the United States, by reason of such violations, were made to the Spanish government.

From April 1869 to June last, the Spanish Minister at Washington had been clothed with a limited power to aid in redressing such wrongs. That power was found to be withdrawn "in view", as it was said, "of the favorable situation in which the Island of Cuba" then "was"; which however did not lead to a revocation or suspension of the extraordinary and arbitrary functions exercised by the Executive Power in Cuba; and we were obliged to make our complaints at Madrid.

In the negotiations thus opened, and still pending there, the United States only claimed that, for the future, the rights secured to their citizens, by Treaty, should be respected in Cuba, and that, as to the past, a joint tribunal should be established in the United States, with full jurisdiction over all such claims.

Before such an impartial tribunal, each claimant would be required to prove his case. On the other hand, Spain would be at liberty to traverse every material fact, and thus complete equity would be done. A case, which, at one time, threatened seriously to affect the relations between the United States and Spain, has already been disposed of in this way. The claim of the owners of the "Col. Lloyd Aspinwall," for the illegal seizure and detention of that vessel, was referred to arbitration, by mutual consent, and has resulted in an award to the United States, for the owners, of the sum of nineteen thousand, seven hundred and two dollars and fifty cents, in gold. Another, and long pending claim of like nature, that of the whale ship "Canada", has been disposed of by friendly arbitrament, during the present year. It was referred, by the joint consent of Brazil and the United States, to the decision of Sir Edward Thornton, Her Britannic Majesty's Minister at Washington, who kindly undertook the laborious task of examining the voluminous mass of correspondence and testimony submitted by the two governments, and awarded to the United States the sum of one hundred thousand, and seven hundred and forty dollars, and nine cents, in gold, which has since been paid by the Imperial government.

These recent examples show that the mode which the United States have proposed to Spain, for adjusting the pending claims, is just and feasable, and that it may be agreed to by either nation without dishonor. It is to be hoped that this moderate demand may be acceded to by Spain, without further delay. Should the pending negotiations, unfortunately and unexpectedly, be without result, it will then become my duty to communicate that fact to Congress, and invite its action on the subject.

The long deferred peace conference between Spain and the allied South American Republics has been inaugurated in Washington, under the auspices of the United States. Pursuant to the recommendation contained in the Resolution of the House of Representatives, of the 17th. of December 1866, the Executive department of the government offered its friendly offices for the promotion of peace and harmony between Spain and the Allied Republics. Hesitations and obstacles occurred to the acceptance of the offer. Ultimately, however, a conference was arranged, and was opened in this City, on the 29th. of October last, at which I authorized the Secretary of State to preside. It was attended by the Ministers of Spain, Peru, Chili and Ecuador. In consequence of the absence of a representative from Bolivia, the conference was adjourned until the attendance of a Plenipotentiary from that Republic could be secured, or other measures could be adopted towards compassing its objects.

The Allied and other Republics of Spanish origin on this continent, may see in this fact a new proof of our sincere interest in their welfare; of our desire to see them blessed with good governments, capable of maintaining order, and of preserving their respective territorial integrity; and of our sincere wish to extend our own commercial and social relations with them. The time is not probably far distant, when in the natural course of events, the European political connection with this continent will cease. Our policy should be shaped, in view of this probability, so as to ally the commercial interests of the Spanish American States more closely to our own, and thus give the United States all the pre-eminence, and all the advantage which Mr Monroe, Mr Adams and Mr. Clay contemplated, when they proposed to join in the Congress of Panama.

. . . The government of San Domingo has voluntarily sought this annexation. It is a weak power, numbering probably less than one hundred and twenty thousand souls, and yet possessing one of the richest territories under the sun, capable of supporting a population of ten millions of people, in luxury. The people of San Domingo are not capable of maintaining themselves, in their present condition, and must look for outside support. They yearn for the protection of our free institutions and laws; our progress and civilization. Shall we refuse them?

The acquisition of San Domingo is desirable because of its geographical position. It commands the entrance to the Caribbean Sea, and the Isthmus transit of commerce. It possesses the richest soil, best and most capacious harbors, most salubrious climate, and the most valuable products of the forest, mine and soil, of any of the West India islands.

Its possession by us will in a few years build up a coast-wise commerce of immense magnitude, which will go far towards restoring to us our lost Merchant Marine. It will give to us those articles which we consume so largely, and do not produce, thus equalizing our exports and imports. In case of foreign war, it will give us command of all the islands referred to, and thus prevent an enemy from ever again possessing himself of rendezvous upon our very coast. At present, our coast trade between the states bordering on the Atlantic and those bordering on the Gulf of Mexico, is cut in two by the Bahamas and the Antilles. Twice we must, as it were, pass through foreign countries to get, by sea, from Georgia to the west coast of Florida.

San Domingo, with a stable government, under which her immense resources can be developed, will give remunerative wages to tens of thousands of laborers, not now upon the island. This labor will take advantage of every available means of transportation to abandon the adjacent islands, and seek the blessings of freedom and its sequence—each inhabitant receiving the reward of his own labor. Porto Rico and Cuba will have to abolish slavery, as a measure of self-preservation, to retain their laborers.

San Domingo will become a large consumer of the products of northern farms and manufactories. The cheap rate at which her citizens can be furnished with food, tools and machinery will make it necessary that contiguous islands should have the same advantages, in order to compete in the production of sugar, coffee, tobacco, tropical fruits, &c.,

This will open to us a still wider market for our products. The production of our own supply of these articles will cut off more than one hundred millions of our annual imports, besides largely increasing our exports. With such a picture, it is easy to see how our large debt abroad is ultimately to be extinguished. With a balance of trade against us (including interest on bonds held by foreigners, and money spent by our citizens traveling in foreign lands,) equal to the entire yield of the precious metals in this country, it is not so easy to see how this result is to be otherwise accomplished. The acquisition of San Domingo is an adherence to the "Monroe doctrine"; it is a measure of national protection; it is asserting our just claim to a controlling influence over the great commercial traffic soon to flow from west to east, by way of the Isthmus of Darien; it is to build up our Merchant Marine; it is to furnish new markets for the products of our farms, shops and manufactories; it is to make slavery insupportable in Cuba and Porto Rico, at once, and ultimately so in Brazil; it is to settle the unhappy condition of Cuba, and end an exterminating conflict; it is to provide honest means of paying our honest debts, without overtaxing the people. It is to furnish our citizens with the necessaries of every day life at cheaper rates than ever before; and it is, in fine, a rapid stride towards that greatness which the intelligence, industry and enterprise of the citizens of the United States entitle this country to assume among nations. . . .

It is to be regretted that our representations in regard to the injurious effects, especially upon the revenue of the United States, of the policy of the Mexican government, in exempting from impost duties a large tract of its territory on our borders, have not only been fruitless, but that it is even proposed, in that country, to extend the limits within which the privilege adverted to has hitherto been enjoyed. The expediency of taking into your serious consideration proper measures for countervailing the policy referred to, will, it is presumed, engage your earnest attention.

It is the obvious interest, especially of neighboring nations, to provide against impunity to those who may have committed high crimes within their borders, and who may have sought refuge abroad. For this purpose extradition treaties have been concluded with several of the Central American Republics, and others are in progress.

The sense of Congress is desired, as early as may be convenient, upon the proceedings of the commission on claims against Venezuela, as communicated in my messages of March 16. 1869, March 1. 1870 and March 31. 1870. It has not been deemed advisable to distribute any of the money which has been received from that government, until Congress shall have acted upon the subject.

The massacres of French and Russian residents at Tien Tsin, under circumstances of great barbarity, were supposed by some to have been premeditated, and to indicate a purpose, among the populace, to exterminate foreigners in the Chinese Empire.[1]

The evidence fails to establish such a supposition, but shows a complicity between the local authorities and the mob. The government at Pekin, however, seems to have been disposed to fulfill its Treaty obligati[o]ns, so far as it was able to do so.

Unfortunately, the news of the war between the German States and France reached China soon after the massacre.

It would appear that the popular mind became possessed with the idea that this contest, extending to Chinese waters, would neutralize the Christian influence and power, and that the time was coming when the superstitious masses might expel all foreigners, and restore Mandarin influence.

Anticipating trouble from this cause, I invited France and North Germany to make an authorized suspension of hostilities in the East, (where they were temporarily suspended by act of the commanders,) and to act together for the future protection, in China, of the lives and properties of Americans and Europeans.

Since the adjournment of Congress, the ratifications of the treaty with Great Britain, for abolishing the mixed courts for the suppression of the Slave trade, have been exchanged. It is believed that the Slave trade is now confined to the eastern coast of Africa, whence the slaves are taken to Arabian markets.

The ratifications of the naturalization convention between Great Britain and the United States have also been exchanged during the recess; and thus, a long standing dispute between the two governments has been settled, in accordance with the principles always contended for by the United States.

In April last, while engaged in locating a military reservation near Pembina, a corps of Engineers discovered that the commonly received boundary line between the United States and the British possessions, at that place, is about forty-seven hundred feet south of the true position of the 49th parallel, and that the line, when run on what is now supposed to be the true position of that parallel, would leave the Fort of the Hudson's Bay Company, at Pembina, within the territory of the United States. This information being communicated to the British government, I was requested to consent, and did consent that the British occupation of the Fort of the Hudson's Bay Company should continue for the present. I deem it important, however, that this part of the boundary line should be definitely fixed by a joint commission of the two governments, and I submit herewith estimates of the expense of such a commission on the part of the United States, and recommend that an appropriation be made for that purpose.[2] The land boundary has already been fixed and marked from the summit of the Rocky Mountains to the Georgian Bay. It should now be, in like manner, marked from the Lake of the Woods to the summit of the Rocky Mountains.

I regret to say that no conclusion has been reached for the adjustment of the claims against Great Britain, growing out of the course adopted by that government during the rebellion.

The Cabinet of London, so far as its views have been expressed, does not appear to be willing to concede that Her Majesty's government was guilty of any negligence, or did, or permitted any act, during the war, by which the United States has just cause of complaint. Our firm and unalterable convictions are directly the reverse. I therefore recommend to Congress to authorize the appointment of a commission to take proof of the amounts, and the ownership of these several claims, on notice to the representative of Her Majesty, at Washington, and that authority be given for the settlement of these claims by the United States, so that the government shall have the ownership of the private claims, as well as the responsible control of all the demands against Great Britain.

It cannot be necessary to add that, whenever Her Majesty's government shall entertain a desire for a full and friendly adjustment of these claims, the United States will enter upon their consideration, with an earnest desire for a conclusion consistent with the honor and dignity of both nations.[3]

The course pursued by the Canadian authorities towards the fishermen of the United States, during the past season, has not been marked by a friendly feeling. By the first Article of the Convention of 1818, between Great Britain and the United States, it was agreed that the inhabitants of the United States should have forever, in common with British subjects, the right of taking fish in certain waters therein defined. In the waters not included in the limits named in the Convention, (within three miles of parts of the British coast,) it has been the custom, for many years, to give to intruding fishermen of the United States a reasonable warning of their violation of the technical rights of Great Britain.

The Imperial government is understood to have delegated the whole, or a share of its jurisdiction or control of these in-shore fishing-grounds, to the Colonial authority, known as the Dominion of Canada, and this semi-independent, but irresponsible agent has exercised its delegated powers in an unfriendly way. Vessels have been seized without notice or warning, in violation of the custom previously prevailing, and have been taken into the Colonial ports, their voyages broken up, and the vessels condemned. There is reason to believe that this unfriendly and vexatious treatment was designed to bear harshly upon the hardy fishermen of the United States, with a view to political effect upon this gov[er]nment. The Statutes of the Dominion of Canada assume a still broader and more untenable jurisdiction over the vessels of the United States.

They authorize officers or persons to bring vessels, hovering within three marine miles of any of the coasts, bays, creeks, or harbors of Canada, into port, to search the cargo, to examine the Master, on oath, touching the cargo and voyage, and to inflict upon him a heavy pecuniary penalty if true answers are not given; and if such a vessel is found "preparing to fish," within three marine miles of any of such coasts, bays, creeks or harbors, without a license, or after the expiration of the period named in the last license granted to it, they provide that the vessel, with her tackle, &c, &c, shall be forfeited. It is not known that any condemnations have been made under this statute. Should the authorities of Canada attempt to enforce it, it will become my duty to take such steps as may be necessary to protect the rights of the citizens of the United States.

It has been claimed by Her Majesty's Officers, that the fishing vessels of the United States have no right to enter the open ports of the British Possessions in North America, except for the purposes of shelter and repairing damages, of purchasing wood, and obtaining water; that they have no right to enter at the British Custom houses, or to trade there except in the purchase of wood and water; and that they must depart within twenty-four hours after notice to leave.

It is not known that any seizure of a fishing vessel, carrying the flag of the United States, has been made under this claim. So far as the claim is founded on an alleged construction of the Convention of 1818, it cannot be acquiesced in by the United States. It is hoped that it will not be insisted on by Her Majesty's government.

During the conferences which preceded the negotiation of the Convention of 1818, the British commissioners proposed to expressly exclude the fishermen of the United States from "the privilege of carrying on trade with any of His Britannic Majesty's subjects, residing within the limits assigned for their use"; and also that it should not be "lawful for the vessels of the United States, engaged in said fishery, to have on board any goods, wares or merchandize whatever, except such as may be necessary for the prosecution of their voyages to and from said fishing grounds. And any vessel of the United States which shall contravene this regulation may be seized, condemned and confiscated, with her cargo."

This proposition, which is identical with the construction now put upon the language of the Convention, was emphatically rejected by the American Commissioners, and there upon was abandoned by the British Plenipotentiaries, and Article I, as it stands in the Convention, was substituted.

If, however, it be said that this claim is founded on Provincial or Colonial statutes, and not upon the Convention, this government cannot but regard them as unfriendly, and in contravention of the spirit, if not of the letter of the Treaty, for the faithful execution of which the Imperial government is alone responsible.[4]

Anticipating that an attempt may possibly be made by the Canadian authorities, in the coming season, to repeat their unneighborly acts towards our fishermen, I recommend you to confer upon the Executive the power to suspend, by proclamation, the operation of the laws authorizing the transit of goods, wares and merchandize, in bond, across the territory of the United States to

Canada, and further, should such an extreme measure become necessary, to suspend the operation of any laws whereby the vessels of the Dominion of Canada are permitted to enter the waters of the United States.

A like unfriendly disposition has been manifested on the part of Canada, in the maintenance of a claim of right to exclude the citizens of the United States from the navigation of the St. Lawrence. This river constitutes a natural outlet to the ocean for eight states, with an aggregate population of about 17.600.000. inhabitants, and with an aggregate tonnage of 661.367 tons upon the waters which discharge into it. The foreign commerce of our ports on these waters is open to British competition, and the major part of it is done in British bottoms. If the American Seamen be excluded from this natural avenue to the ocean, the monopoly of the direct commerce of the Lake Ports with the Atlantic would be in foreign hands; their vessels on trans-atlantic voyages having an access to our Lake Ports, which would be denied to American vessels on similar voyages. To state such a proposition is to refute its justice.

During the administration of Mr John Quincy Adams, Mr Clay unanswerably demonstrated the natural right of the citizens of the United States to the navigation of this river, claiming that the act of the Congress of Vienna, in opening the Rhine and other rivers to all nations, showed the judgement of European jurists and statesmen, that the inhabitants of a country, through which a navigable river passes, have a natural right to enjoy the navigation of that river to and into the Sea, even though passing through the territories of another Power. This right does not exclude the cöequal right of the Sovereign possessing the territory through which the river debouches into the sea, to make such regulations relative to the police of the navigation as may be reasonably necessary; but those regulations should be framed in a liberal spirit of comity, and should not impose needless burdens upon the commerce which has the right of transit. It has been found, in practice, more advantageous to arrange these regulations by mutual agreement.

The United States are ready to make any reasonable arrangement as to the police of the St. Lawrence which may be suggested by Great Britain.

If the claim made by Mr Clay was just when the population of states bordering on the shores of the Lakes was only 3.400.000., it now derives greater force and equity from the increased population, wealth, production and tonnage of the states on the Canadian frontier. Since Mr Clay advanced his argument in behalf of our right, the principle for which he contended has been frequently, and by various nations, recognized by law or by treaty, and has been extended to several other great rivers.

By the Treaty concluded at Mayence, in 1831, the Rhine was declared free from the point where it is first navigable into the sea. By the convention between Spain and Portugal, concluded in 1835, the navigation of the Douro, throughout its whole extent, was made free for the subjects of both crowns.—In 1853, the Argentine Confederation, by Treaty, threw open the free navigation of the Parana and Uruguay to the merchant vessels of all nations. In 1856, the Crimean War was closed by a treaty which provided for the free navigation of the Danube. In 1858, Bolivia, by treaty, declared that it regarded the rivers Amazon and La Plata, in accordance with fixed principles of national law, as highways or channels, opened by Nature, for the commerce of all nations. In 1859, the Paraguay was made free by treaty, and in December 1866, the Emperor of Brazil, by Imperial decree, declared the Amazon to be open, to the frontier of Brazil, to the merchant ships of all nations. The greatest living British authority[5] on this subject, while asserting the abstract right of the British claim, says—"It seems difficult to deny that Great Britain may ground her refusal upon strict *law*; but it is equally difficult to deny, first, that in so doing she exercises harshly an extreme and hard law; secondly, that her conduct with respect to the navigation of the St. Lawrence is in glaring and discreditable inconsistency with her conduct with respect to the navigation of the Mississippi. On the ground that she possessed a small domain, in which the Mississippi took its rise, she insisted on the right to navigate the entire volume of its waters. On the ground that she possesses both banks of the St Lawrence, where it disembogues itself into the sea, she denies to the United States the right of navigation, though about one half of the waters of Lakes Ontario, Erie, Huron and Superior, and the whole of Lake Michigan, through which the river flows, are the property of the United States."

The whole nation is interested in securing cheap transportation from the Agricultural states of the West to the Atlantic sea-board. To the citizens of those states, it secures a greater return for their labor; to the inhabitants of the sea-board, it affords cheaper food; to the nation, an increase in the annual surplus of wealth.

It is hoped that the government of Great Britain will see the justice of abandoning the narrow and inconsistent claim, to which her Canadian Provinces have urged her adherence. . . .

The condition of the archives at the Department of State calls for the early action of Congress. The building now rented by that Department is a frail structure, at an inconvenient distance from the Executive Mansion, and from the other Departments; is ill adapted to the purpose for which it is used; has not capacity to accommodate the archives; and is not fire-proof. Its remote situation, its slender construction, and the absence of a supply of water in the neighborhood, leave but little hope of safety for either the building or its contents in case of the accident of a fire. Its destruction would involve the loss of the rolls containing the original acts and resolutions of Congress, of the historic records of the Revolution and of the Confederation; of the whole series of diplomatic and consular archives, since the adoption of the Constitution, and of the many other valuable records and papers left with that Department when it was the principal depository of the governmental archives. I recommend an appropriation for the construction of a building for the Department of State.

I recommend to your consideration the propriety of transferring to the Department of the Interior, to which they seem more appropriately to belong, all powers and duties in relation to the territories with which the Department of State is now charged by law or usage; and from the Interior Department to the War Department, the Pension Bureau, so far as it regulates the payment of soldiers' pensions. I would further recommend that the payment of naval pensions be transferred to one of the bureaux of the Navy Department.

The estimates for the expenses of the government for the next fiscal year are $18.244.346.01. less than for the current one, but exceed the appropriations for the present year, for the same items, $8.972.127.56. In this estimate, however, is included $22.338.278.37. for Public works heretofore begun under Congressional provision and of which only so much is asked as Congress may choose to give. The appropriation for the same works, for the present fiscal year, was $11.984.518.08.

The average value of gold, as compared with National currency, for the whole of the year 1869 was about 134, and for eleven months of 1870, the same relative value has been about 115. The approach to a specie basis is very gratifying, but the fact cannot be denied that the instability of the value of our currency is prejudicial to our prosperity, and tends to keep up prices to the detriment of trade. The evils of a depreciated and fluctuating currency are so great, that now, when the premium on gold has fallen so much, it would seem that the time has arrived when by wise and prudent legislation Congress should look to a policy which would place our currency at par with gold at no distant day. . . .

Such a tariff, so far as it acts as an encouragement to home production, affords employment to labor, at living wages, in contrast to the pauper labor of the old world, and also in the development of home resources.

Under the act of Congress of the 15th day of July 1870, the army has gradually been reduced, so that, on the 1st day of Jany. 1871, the number of commissioned officers and men will not exceed the number contemplated by that law. . . .

The expenses of the Navy for the whole of the last year, i, e, from December 1. 1869, the date of the last report, are less than $19.000.000, or about $1.000.000 less than they were the previous year. The expenses since the commencement of this fiscal year, i, e, since July 1st, show, for the five months, a decrease of over $2.400.000. from those of the corresponding months of last year.

The estimates for the current year were $28.205.671.37. Those for next year are $20.683.317., with $955.100. additional for necessary permanent improvements. These estimates are made closely for the mere maintenance of the naval establishment as it now is, without much in the nature of permanent improvement.

The appropriations made for the last and current years were evidently intended by Congress, and are sufficient, only to keep the Navy on its present footing, by the repairing and refitting of our old ships. This policy must, of course, gradually but surely destroy the Navy, and it is in itself far from economical, as each year that it is pursued, the necessity for mere repairs in ships and Navy Yards becomes more imperative and more costly; and our current expenses are annually increased for the mere repair of ships, many of which must soon become unsafe and useless. I hope, during the present Session of Congress, to be able to submit to it, a plan by which Naval vessels can be built and repairs made with great saving upon the present cost.

It can hardly be wise statesmanship in a government which represents a country with over 5.000. miles of coast line, on both oceans, exclusive of Alaska, and containing 40.000.000. of progressive people, with relations of every nature with almost every foreign country, to rest with such inadequate means of enforcing any foreign policy, either of protection or redress. Separated by the ocean from the nations of the Eastern continent, our Navy is our only means of direct protection to our citizens abroad, or for the enforcement of any foreign policy. . . .

Good faith requires us to give full effect to existing grants. The time honored and beneficent policy of setting apart certain sections of public land for educational purposes in the new states should be continued. When ample provision shall have been made for these objects, I submit as a question worthy of serious consideration, whether the residue of our national domain should not be wholly disposed of under the provisions of the homestead and preëmption laws.

In addition to the swamp and overflowed lands granted to the states, in which they are situated, the lands taken under the Agricultural College acts, and for internal improvement purposes, under the act of September 1841., and the acts supplemental thereto, there had been conveyed, up to the close of the last fiscal year, by patent or other equivalent evidence of title, to states and corporations, twenty-seven million, eight hundred and thirty-six thousand, two hundred and fifty-seven and sixty-three hundredths acres, for railways, canals and wagon roads. It is estimated that an additional quantity of one hundred and seventy-four millions, seven hundred and thirty-five thousand, five hundred and twenty-three acres, is still due, under grants for like uses. The policy of thus aiding the states in building works of internal improvement was inaugurated more than forty years since, in the grants to Indiana and Illinois, to aid those states in opening canals to connect the waters of the Wabash with those of Lake Erie, and the waters of the Illinois with those of Lake Michigan. It was followed, with some modifications, in the grant to Illinois of alternate sections of public land, within certain limits, of the Illinois Central railway. Fourteen states and sundry corporations have received similar subsidies in connection with railways, completed or in process of construction. As the reserved sections are rated at the double minimum, the sale of them, at the enhanced price, has thus, in many instances, indemnified the Treasury for the granted lands. The construction of some of these thoroughfares has undoubtedly given a vigorous impulse to the development of our resources, and the settlement of the more distant portions of the country. It may, however, be well insisted that much of our legislation in this regard has been characterized by indiscriminate and profuse liberality. The United States should not loan their credit in aid of any enterprise, undertaken by states or corporations, nor grant lands in any instance, unless the projected work is of acknowledged national importance. I am strongly inclined to the opinion that it is inexpedient and unnecessary to bestow subsidies of either description; but should Congress determine otherwise, I earnestly recommend that the rights of settlers and of the public be more effectually secured and protected by appropriate legislation.

During the year ending September 30. 1870. there were filed in the Patent Office, 19.411 applications for patents, 3.374 caveats, and 160 applications for the extension of patents. 13,622 patents, including re-issues and designs, were issued, 110 extended, and 1,089 allowed, but not issued by reason of the non-payment of the final fees. The receipts of the office during the fiscal year were $136.304.29. in excess of its expenditures. . . .

During the last fiscal year, the sum paid to pensioners, including the cost of disbursement, was $27.780.811.11., and 1,758 bounty land warrants were issued. At its close, 198.686 names were on the pension rolls.

The labors of the Pension Office have been directed to the severe scrutiny of the evidence submitted in favor of new claims, and to the discovery of fictituous claims which have been heretofore allowed. The appropriation for the employment of special agents, for the investigation of frauds, has been judiciously used, and the results obtained have been of unquestionable benefit to the service. . . .

U. S. GRANT

DS, DNA, RG 46, Annual Messages. Ellipses represent material covered by preceding draft. On Dec. 16, 1870, USG acknowledged as oversights in his annual message the failure to comment on amnesty for disenfranchised Southerners and "the propriety of removing the disqualifications from holding office imposed by the Fourteenth Amendment." *New York Tribune*, Dec. 20, 1870.

1. On Nov. 11, William H. Fogg & Co., New York City, had written to USG. "In forwarding the enclosed *Petition* signed by the *Firms* engaged in trade with *China*, and some, (the same as ourselves) having business houses there:—We feel deeply interested in the matter and pray you will give it your [e]arly Consideration—" ALS, DNA, RG 45, Miscellaneous Letters Received. The undated petition requested that USG increase "the number of United States vessels of war in Chinese waters. The recent lamentable massacre of foreign residents at the port Tientsin, occurring during the absence of every vessel of war from the port, and the indications that massacre was only a part of a preconcerted plan, having larger objects and originating in a strong anti-foreign feeling prompted by Mandarins high in office and power, gives rise to serious apprehensions that similar attacks will be attempted at other ports, with the object of expelling citizens of the United States and other foreign residents from that country altogether. . . ." DS (18 signatures), *ibid.*

2. On Nov. 7, Sir Edward Thornton, British minister, Washington, D. C., had written to Lord Granville about preliminary negotiations concerning the U.S.-Canadian boundary: ". . . Mr: Davis promised to consult the President on the subject and did so on the 4th Inst., subsequently intimating to me that if I would address him a note in the sense of the Report of the Privy Council, he would give me an answer in

accordance with my wish. I therefore addressed to him on the 5th Instant the Note of which I have the honour to enclose a copy. Mr: B. Davis at the same time communicated to me verbally the desire of the President that no time should be ~~appointe~~ lost in appointing a commission for definitively marking the Boundary, and that he had applied to the War Department to make an estimate of the expenses which would be probably incurred by such a Commission. On the meeting of Congress in December, the President would send a message to it, recommending that he should be authorised to agree to the appointment of such a Commission on the part of the U. S., and asking an appropriation for the expenses which the salaries and operations of the Commission would involve.—I replied to Mr: Bancroft Davis that I had reason to believe that H. M.'s Govt: would be prepared to meet the views of that of the U. S. upon this matter.—Mr: Davis remarked that when the Commission should begin its operations, it might be expedient that it should first lay down the point where the 49th Parallel touches the Red River, so that the Jurisdiction over the Hudson's Bay Company's post might be decided and that it should then proceed to the Lake of the Woods and work Westward.—I have now the honour to enclose Mr: B. Davis answer to my note in which he informs me that the President consents that for the present the post erected by General Pope in 1850 shall be considered as indicating the Boundary. . . ." Copy, Thornton Letterbook, ICarbS. See *HRC*, 41-3-19, 42-2-1; *HED*, 42-1-12.

On Jan. 21, 1871, Philip S. Beebe, Lakeville, Conn., wrote to USG. "In your Message to Congress at the commencement of the present session—you refer to a portion of the boundary on the northern frontier, as not well defind and marked—and reccommend a joint commission to run the line and fix the boundary so that there may be no mistake about it—hereafter—If I can satisfy you that I am a suitable man for the position, and you can, consistently do it—I will respectfully, ask you to give me a place on the commission I suppose it is the usual custom for a man who wants a favor from the President, to make his request through a Member of Congress or some other Official or hanger on at Washington—I prefer to make the request myself, and then if I can have some intimation that I may have the appointment, if you are satisfied with regard to my fitness for it, I will endeavour to satisfy you on that point—It is sometimes said, by ardent and *patriotic* gentlemen that, if they, or their particular friends dont get this or that office, the Republican party will go to smash right away—Now so far as I am concerned, I dont think it will make one hair white or black whethe I get it or not—I shant fly the track I dont think any body else will on my account—but I say frankly if you can, consistently, give me the appointment I shall be gratified" ALS, DNA, RG 59, Letters of Application and Recommendation. No appointment followed.

In 1871, U.S. Senator Henry W. Corbett of Ore. wrote to USG suggesting Archibald Campbell as commissioner to establish the U.S.-Canadian boundary. Conway Barker Catalogue, Jan. 12, 1963. Campbell was appointed. See *SED*, 44-2-41.

3. See *PUSG*, 20, 29–31. On Nov. 20 and 28, 1870, Fish had written in his diary. "Sir Edward Thornton—In the course of a long friendly conversation, the subject of the Alabama claims being referred to, he expresses a wish that they may be settled, & would like to know, what we wish—I reply full payment for all losses actually sustained, & some satisfaction for the general wrong—he says that involves the admission of wrong on their part, which no Governmt cd make & sustain itself—which I controvert—but insist that we will not submit the question of *liability* of Gt Britain to Arbitration—we will submit the question of amount of damages—we regard these claims as *National* & not to be mixed up with, or be liable to be offset by any ordinary Commercial Claims, which continually arise between Nations—We

must have some recognition of a wrong *done, some expression of regret—some kind word*—That the recent amendment of the Foreign Enlistment Act, is an acknowledgment that their laws were insufficient for the observance of their International duties—it will not be any humiliation, to say that under the previous laws, by accident, or carelessness a wrong had befallen us for which they are ready to make ~~payment~~ satisfaction &c &c . . . Although he did not say so, but on the contrary, professed to entirely discredit the telegraphic rumor, of Instructions being given to Moran, to press a settlement of the claims, I think a principal object of his visit, to day was to be assured that the report was unfounded—He enquired, as he continually does when we meet, if any appointment of a Minister to England has yet been made" "Sr Edward Thornton, enquires about the names & address of some of the principal Woolen & Worsted manufactures in the State of NY—for a list of which I write to Mr Murphy Collector &c He refers to 'exaggerated newspaper rumors' with respect to the relations of Gt Britain & Russia, which gives me the opportunity to refer to a newspaper rumor that Ld Granville had expressed to some private parties representing some claim for loss sustained by the Alabama a willingness on the part of the British Govt to settle the amt of losses with the individual claimants & to say that this Govt would not recognize any settlement—with individual claimants, as a satisfaction or in diminution of the demands of the Govt, that the Govt claimed the entire control of the claims, & that . . . no settlement can be made with any party other than itself—He tells me that he wrote to Ld Granville a full statement of the Conversation we had on Sunday 20th inst—. . . & is reminded that that was not an official interview, & the conversation on that subject was accidental, & private. He says it was so much of a summary of former conversations that he had deemed it of sufficient importance to relate it, at length—Some Conversation ensues respecting the Fisheries &c" DLC-Hamilton Fish. See Nevins, *Fish*, pp. 430–35.

4. On Nov. 10 and 11, 1870, Fish had written in his diary. "Sir Edward Thornton opens the question of the Fisheries & asks if it cannot be settled on something like the principle of the Reciprocity Treaty—I think not—He reminds me that last winter I suggested a concession of free entry of four articles (Coal—lumber—Salt—& Fish) for the Free navigation of the Canadian Canals & St Lawrence River, & the Fisheries . . . I reply that whatever might then have been done, the unfriendly, action of both Imperial & Canadian Authorities during the past season, changed our feelings, & I did not think they could now get what might then have been conceded—He again intimated a willingness to refer the construction of the Treaty of 1818, as to the 'Fisheries' to Arbitration, & was told very decidedly that we would not submit it to arbitration—we mean to settle it ourselves—He says that without yielding the question of right, the Imperial Govt decided to forego the exercise of the right claimed, to exclude American fishing vessels from Ports of Entry, & the privilege of shipping their fish in Bond—& in reply is told that 'it is very well,' at the end of the season, when the fishing vessels have returned hence, & all the injury that could be inflicted has been done, to say that they forego the question—that we feel an injury has been done to the extent of the ability of both Imperial & Dominion Govt upon our Fishing Interests—He produces a Memorandum, giving the present rates of duties (as he says) on the Articles which were admitted free under the Reciprocity Treaty—& names Breadstuffs, Animals Fish, Hides, Furs & Skins, Butter & Cheese, Horns, Ores, Timber, & Firewood, as articles to be admitted free, & Coal at a reduced rate in consideration of which they may grant freedom of the Fisheries & the free Navigation of the Canals & St Lawrence—He receives no encouragement, but asks to leave the memorandum with me—" "Thorntons conversation of yesterday, with

regard to the Fisheries, & a Trade treaty was mentioned—Delano says the western interests will object strongly to the Free introduction of Grain, Animals, & Butter/Cheese—No objection was anticipated with regard to Fish, Hides Furs, Skins, Horns, Ores, or Timber—but the general policy of a Trade Convention, was not regarded with favor—The President inclines to the opinion that the question had better be left open for settlement with the Alabama Claims—" DLC-Hamilton Fish. See *PUSG*, 20, 268.

5. Robert Phillimore, *Commentaries on International Law* (1854; reprinted, Littleton, Colo., 1985), I, 163–64.

To Senate

TO THE SENATE OF THE UNITED STATES.

I nominate, *Vice Admiral David D. Porter*,[1] to be Admiral in the Navy, from the 15th of August 1870, *vice* Admiral David G. Farragut, deceased;

Rear Admiral Stephen C. Rowan,[2] to be Vice Admiral in the Navy, from the 15th of August 1870, *vice* Vice Admiral David D. Porter, nominated for promotion;

Commodore Thornton A. Jenkins,[3] to be a Rear Admiral in the Navy, from the 15th of August 1870, *vice* Rear Admiral Stephen C. Rowan, nominated for promotion.

Captain James R. M. Mullany,[4] to be a Commodore in the Navy, from the 15th of August 1870, *vice* Commodore Thornton A. Jenkins, nominated for promotion.

U. S. GRANT

WASHINGTON CITY,
5TH DECEMBER 1870.

DS, DNA, RG 46, Nominations. On Dec. 5, 1870, Secretary of the Navy George M. Robeson had written to USG. "I have the honor to transmit, herewith, Nominations of Officers of the Navy and Marine Corps, appointed and promoted during the interim of Congress, all of which are to fill vacancies in their respective grades." Copy, *ibid.*, RG 45, Letters Sent to the President. On the same day, USG wrote five additional letters to the Senate nominating Navy and Marine Corps officers for promotion. DS, *ibid.*, RG 46, Nominations.

1. On Dec. 3, Vice Admiral David D. Porter wrote to USG. "My first impulse on reading the letter published in *The New-York World* was to go to you at once and pronounce it a fabrication, for as such I considered it; but, as it purported to have been written six years ago, and published by a person who once held a prominent position

under the Government, I determined to ascertain fully if I had ever indited such a letter before addressing you on the subject. Neither myself nor my secretary, who has served with me eight years, could recall to our recollection any circumstance of the kind. I could not conceive that I had uttered sentiments I know I never felt, and which are so at variance with those that I have uniformly expressed toward you. The letter, it appears, was a private one; and vindictive must have been the heart of the man that could be guilty of so grave a breach of confidence; and depraved indeed must be the character who, to gratify his mischievous instincts, could make public a confidential letter, written, perhaps, under great excitement, and at this distant day not even remembered. It seems like a poor return for your uniform confidence and kindness to me; and I am too glad that I remember nothing connected with the letter. At about the date of the letter I had passed through a long and fatiguing contest with Fort Fisher, and my numerous fleet was almost overpowered by the elements. I saw the coveted prize within my grasp and then slip from me. For another month I had to battle with the storms of Winter, anchored on an open coast, with the responsibility of that large fleet on my hands, and my mind and body harassed by extraordinary fatigues. The whole nation was looking on excited, dreading a defeat that might prolong a contest that was already sapping its vitals. You and others know what I had to undergo bodily and mentally. I presume it was while under this excitement that I wrote the letter which, you say, has made you lose your faith in human nature. I have no recollection of it any more than I would have of other passing circumstances of six years ago. When several persons have at different times informed me that a letter would be published in which I had abused Gen. Grant, I treated the matter with indifference, thinking it impossible that such a letter could exist. I do not write for the purpose of exonerating myself, for I would rather be the writer of the letter than its publisher. The peace of political parties and of society would be placed in great jeopardy if all the private letters written the last six years were published. Nothing that I have said will affect your fair fame, and your many friends would be sadly wanting in judgment if they were at all influenced by the silly exultations of a few unscrupulous persons who, after all, are only rejoicing over the most contemptible breach of confidence I ever heard of. I regret exceedingly the loss of your friendship, and do not hesitate to disapprove the sentiments of which, I suppose, I must bear the odium. They appear in a letter of which I have no recollection. They are so different from the sentiments I always express toward yourself and the gallant officers of our army, and are so inconsistent with all my antecedents, that I scarcely consider them entitled to a moment's thought." *New York Tribune*, Dec. 6, 1870.

On Jan. 24, 1865, Porter, Cape Fear River, had written to Secretary of the Navy Gideon Welles. "I received your kind letter of the 17th inst., and thank you warmly for the confidence you reposed in my opinion that this place could be taken. To the Navy Department alone is the country indebted for the capture of this rebel stronghold, for had it not been for your perseverance in keeping this fleet here, and your constant propositions made to the army, nothing would have been done. As it was, after the proposition had been received and Gen. Grant promised that troops should be sent, it was not done until Gen. Butler consented to let the matter go on, and when he hoped to reap some little credit from the explosion of the powder boat. Now the country gives Gen. Grant the credit of inaugurating the expedition, when on both occasions he permitted it to go improperly provided. In the first place, it had neither head nor tail, as far as the army was concerned. In the second place, he (Grant) sent too few men, when he ought to have calculated that the rebels would have more strongly defended the works after seeing what a narrow escape they had. Nothing but the most desperate fighting and determination to win on the part of the army gave us the victory. The gallant band of sailors who fearlessly went into the works, amid a shower of cannister and bullets, drew the enemy's attention away from the assault on the land side, and enabled the troops to obtain a secure footing. I don't say this to detract from the gallantry of the soldiers, for never did men fight harder or more handsomely than did our troops on that day. Now that the most important fort on the coast has been gained, as usual you will hear but little of what the navy did, and no doubt efforts will be made again to show that the work was 'not substantially injured as a defensive work.' To Gen. Grant, who is always willing to take the credit when anything is done, and equally ready to lay the blame of the failure on the navy, when a failure takes place, I feel under no obligations for receiving and allowing a report to be spread from his headquarters that there were three days when the navy might have operated and did not. He knows as much about it as he did when he wrote to me, saying that the 'only way in which the place could be taken was by running the ships past the batteries,' showing evidently that he had not studied the hydrography of Cape Fear river, and did not know the virtue there was in our wooden walls when they went in for a fair stand-up fight. Any fort in rebeldom can be taken, if we can only get within reach of it. I have served with the Lieutenant-General before, where I never worked so hard in my life to make a man succeed as I did for him. You will scarcely notice in his reports that the navy did him any service, when, without the help it has given him all the way through, he would never have been Lieutenant-General. He wants magnanimity, like most officers of the army, and is so avaricious as regards fame that he will never, if he can help it, do justice to our department. When the rebels write the history of this war, then, and only then, will the country be made to feel what the navy has done. I do not feel at all kindly toward Gen. Grant for the indifference he displayed in this matter, until he found his reputation at stake; then he was glad to throw the elephant overboard that had weighed him down so heavily. He could not help but know that Gen. Butler was going in command of this expedition. The matter was constantly discussed with him. He knew that he had placed himself and all his numerous staff on board the flagship Ben De Ford, and everybody spoke of him as commander of the troops. In a conversation with Gen. Grant, I expressly told him that I wanted nothing to do with Gen. Butler, and he promised me faithfully that he should not have any connection with the expedition. Two months I waited, the fleet ready to sail at an hour's notice, and I acquiesced in the Lieutenant-General's decision that he could not spare troops for fear of endangering the defences in his front. I said, 'Then the expedition will never go until Butler has a finger in the pie;' and sure enough, when Butler said go, we went. The fear of weakening the defences disappeared on Butler's presenting his plan of blowing the forts down, and an army was shipped so quick (unprepared) on the transports, that they almost sailed in the middle of a heavy gale. Gen. Grant knew that I did not care a fig for the powder-boat, though I was very willing to try it as an experiment, but not disposed to trust to it altogether. I think it was most unhandsome in him to listen for a moment to the idle talk of Butler's staff, and his timid, calculating engineer Comstock, who wanted some excuse for not doing their duty. The Lieutenant-General and I were together eighteen months before Vicksburg; he never had to wait for me, nor did any of his Generals (but I have had to wait for them); and he should have supposed from the past and my anxiety to go to work that I had not become any slower in my movements than I was on the Mississippi. His course proves to me that he would sacrifice his best friend rather than let any odium fall upon Lieut.-Gen. Grant. He will take to himself all the credit of this move now that it is successful, when he deserves all the blame for the first failure to take the place. All this now is saddled on Gen. Butler, and history will tell nothing of Gen. Grant's share in it. I tell it to you for your own personal satisfaction, that you may know and feel that you are entitled to the entire credit for getting this expedition off and for its success. I am merely the agent, and only use to advantage the ample means placed at my disposal, which any one else could have done as well as I. I expect you sometimes think I am a little too impolitic in what I say, but that is my nature. I am always ready to fight right away, if any one reflects upon the navy. I know that no country under the sun ever raised a navy as you have done in the same space of time, and that no navy ever did more. Could the navy operate in James river, Richmond would now be ours. Vicksburg, a stronger place, fell when the navy was brought to bear upon it. Every place has [f]allen where naval cannon have been brought into play. Our success here has been beyond my most sanguine expectations. I knew we would have Caswell in less than a month; but I had no idea that the rebels would blow that and other works up so soon and leave us sole possession. I am uneasy now for fear the enemy may turn all their force this way, and throw 40,000 men into this peninsula. They would retake Fort Fisher, even with the gunboats we have here, and turn the guns of the fort on us. The object is a great one, and if I was general of their forces, I would do it at all hazards. Yet this is not a pet place with the Lieutenant-General, and he leaves it with about 7,000 men, and I don't think knows much of the situation. An army man thinks if he has a gunboat at his back he is all safe; but this is one case where, at times, the gunboats are driven off by bad weather, and those inside cannot coöperate effectively. I have given you a long letter, but find an apology for myself in the fact that I know your whole heart is in the navy, and that everything concerning it interests you. Again permit me to thank you kindly for the confidence you have always placed in me and the opportunities you have given me for distinction; and assuring you that it has been my warmest wish to merit only your approbation, . . ." *New York Sun*, Dec. 2, 1870. A slightly variant and abbreviated version of this letter, dated Jan. 21, 1865, appeared in the *New York World*, Dec. 2, 1870.

The letter provoked controversy that hindered Porter's immediate confirmation. In [Dec.], Edwin D. Morgan wrote to USG. "I have no ill feeling against Porter, and before this had no prejudice. But he is not the right man for so great a distinction, and he is already filling a higher grade in the Navy than his merits entitle him to." William Evarts Benjamin, Catalogue No. 27, Nov., 1889, p. 8.

On Dec. 8, 1870, Gen. William T. Sherman wrote to Maj. Cyrus B. Comstock. "I want to fix as near as possible the date when General Grant accompanied by Gn Schofield visited the fleet inside Cape Fear River *after* the Capture of Fort Fisher—Fort Fisher was taken Jan 15, 1865—General Grant wrote me from Washington Jan 2[1], about it, & about his proposed dispositions of Schofields troops then Coming from the West. Afterwards in a letter dated City Point Jan 31, he says 'after visiting Admiral Porter and Gen Terry in Cape Fear accompanied by Genl Schofield' he had ordered so & so. Porters awful letter is dated ~~D~~*Jan 24.* Could Genl Grant have been there at that time, before? or after? You can imagine what feeling this letter has begotten. It cannot injure General Grant—Nor must you notice publicly his allusion to you, but it may ruin Porter for I fear that the Senate will confirm Rowan, & leave Porter out by NonConfirmation, or even by abolishing the office. I dont intend to meddle one way or the other, but would like to see the thing dropped as far as possible. The President has sent to the Senate Porters name for Admiral—since the publication of the letter & does not intend as I understand to take an interest one way or the other, but in fixing some motive for the writing of that letter I want to fix the exact time when Genl Grant was *there.* If as I suppose you kept a Journal, that will doubtless note the event of his arrival & departure. I know that I in January did not want Fort Fisher to be attacked at all, and after the Butler failure, Porter sent to me at Savannah for troops which I denied because I preferred that Hoke's Division should be there than in my front in the Interior. I dont think Genl Grant attached as much importance to it as Porter did, & the latter on the supposition that he had achieved some thing of infinite importance, may have thought that Gnl Grant was disposed to belittle it, and his consequent unhappy letter resulted. Present me kindly to your wife . . ." ALS, DLC-Cyrus B. Comstock. On Dec. 11, Comstock, Detroit, wrote to Sherman. "I have your letter asking about the date of Gen. Grants visit to the Cape Fear River in Jany 1865, and find that Porter sent us up word on Jany 28 that Genl Grant was with him, whereon Gen. Terry & I went down to the 'Malvern', Porters flag ship whe[re] Genl Grant was. The latter left that night for the North and I dont think was there more than twenty four or thirty six hours. He was certainly not there on the date of Porters letter, Jany 24, for that day Terry & I went down to urge Porter to attack a little battery—Ft. Anderson—across the Cape Fear from Ft. Fisher, & which closed the river to us. I suspect the actual irritation at that time, must have been that the Northern papers which would have by that time reached him with the accounts of the capture of Fort Fisher, justly gave the main credit of the capture to the Army which did the hard fighting, instead of attributing all to Porter. As to his reference to the 'timid engineer,' I'll leave that to Terry's official report of the capture—Terry was probably as competent and certainly as honest a judge as Porter. Porter probably disliked me at that time for criticising his attempt to blow up & take Ft. Fisher all by himself, while the Land forces under Butler were 60 miles away—& for urging upon him & upon Grant that Porter should run a vessel into Cape Fear river to silence a rebel gun boat known to be there, & which at one time annoyed Terry's troops. The original letter did not surprise me, but the recent one did. Between the two it would be difficult for any one to place themselves in a more unpleasant position. If I can give you any further recollections I shall be glad to do so . . ." ALS, DLC-William T. Sherman. See *PUSG*, 13, 308–9, 324, 331, 349; Richard S. West, Jr., *The Second Admiral: A Life of David Dixon Porter, 1813–1891* (New York, 1937), pp. 327–34; *Julia Grant*, pp. 178–79.

2. Stephen C. Rowan, born in Ireland (1808), entered the navy in 1826, served in the Mexican and Civil wars, and was promoted rear admiral in 1866. On Dec. 5, 1870, a correspondent reported from Washington, D. C. "The President gave a dinner at the White House this evening in honor of Admiral Rowan. Many of the most prominent officers of the Navy were present with their wives and daughters. Admiral Porter did not attend." *New York Tribune*, Dec. 6, 1870. On Jan. 21, 1871, Robeson wrote to USG transmitting commissions for Rowan *et al.* Copy, DNA, RG 45, Letters Sent to the President.

3. Thornton A. Jenkins, born in Va. (1811), joined the navy in 1828, served on lighthouse boards and participated in coastal surveys, then, during the Civil War, became chief of staff to Rear Admiral David G. Farragut. On Feb. 5, 1872, Jenkins, Washington, D. C., wrote to USG. "Being under preparatory orders to proceed to China and Japan to relieve Rear Admiral Rodgers in command of the naval forces in Asiatic waters, I would, before leaving for my command, most respectfully solicit at your hands, either now or at such time hereafter as may be convenient, the appointment of Cadet at West Point for my son Presley Thornton Jenkins, who is about seventeen years of age, and a student at Williston Seminary, East Hampton, Mass., for entry with the class of 1873, and the appointment to be sent to my son-in-law, Col. P. C. Hains, US. Corps of Engineers on lighthouse duty at Baltimore, Md. In making this application, I beg leave to say that there is not a single member of my family name but

myself now in the military or naval service; that my son's great-grandfather, the late Col. Presley Thornton of Virginia, served with honor and distinction during the entire war of the Revolution, at the close of which he found himself greatly reduced in his pecuniary circumstances; that his grandfather, the late Francis A Thornton, served in the Navy with honor and credit from 1812 to the time of his death in 1857. For my own services in the Navy, since my entry in 1828, having been actively employed in the Mexican war, in the settlement of our difficulties with Paraguay (1858–9), and in the late war of the rebellion, I would respectfully refer to the records of the Navy Department." LS, *ibid.*, RG 94, Correspondence, USMA. Related papers are *ibid.* Presley T. Jenkins did not attend USMA.

4. James R. M. Mullany, born in N. Y. (1818), appointed a midshipman in 1832, served in the Mediterranean and Brazil squadrons before the Civil War, then commanded the *Bienville* (1862–65) on the Gulf Coast.

Speech

[*Dec. 6, 1870*]

VISCOUNT: You are welcome as the Envoy Extraordinary and Minister Plenipotentiary of France. Your former acceptable abode here in another diplomatic character gives occasion to congratulate you upon your promotion. It is believed that full confidence may be entertained in your friendly disposition. You may be assured that in our intercourse with you we shall always bear in mind the origin of our kind relations with your country, and shall endeavor to preserve and strengthen them.

Washington Chronicle, Dec. 7, 1870. USG spoke after Jules Treilhard had presented his credentials as French minister. *Ibid.* Treilhard served as chargé d'affaires *ad interim* (1859–60, 1864) while in Washington, D. C., as secretary, French legation. On Dec. 6, 1870, Secretary of State Hamilton Fish recorded in his diary. "Presented Viscount Treillard, newly appointed Minister from France—to the President After the presentation Treillard in conversation with me refers to the Presidents Message, & especially to the sentence where he states that 'if the U S. can shorten the continuance of the War, by a single hour, by any act of theirs it will gladly be done' & enquires its meaning—He is informed that this Govt early desired to tender its good offices to both belligerents in the interests of Peace, but learnt that Germany was not then inclined to listen to any intervention—That the same disposition which had formerly been expressed, continued, & whenever it could be made to appear to the President, that both Governments are inclined to listen to friendly Counsels in the direction of Peace, this Govt will be ready to act—" DLC-Hamilton Fish.

On March 12, 1871, Fish wrote. "Genl Cushing calls to say that Mr Treillard the French Minister, has become insane, & been taken to the Insane Hospital—that his mind has been greatly disturbed by the events occuring in France, but more especially by the conduct of the French Consul in NY, who he says has been largely defrauding his Govt in overcharges &c for the immense quantity of arms purchased by France in the U. S." *Ibid.*

To Ulysses S. Grant, Jr.

Washington D. C. Dec. 8th *1870*

DEAR BUCK,

Enclosed I send you check for $100 00 which should have been sent ten days ago but forgot it. I hope you have had money to pay your mess bills and other expense accounts!—We are all looking anxiously for your return. Will Smith will be here to spend Christ-Mass week, and, what may interest you more, Sussie Felt[1] will also be here.

All send much love to you. Fred is on his last half year since the 1st of Dec. As I have not heard of him being in any difficulty I presume he got off enough of his demerit to save him. He had an even 100 the first three months of the half year, and had three more for the fourth month. I will be glad when he gets through as I know he will be. I do not want Fred to stay in the Army longer than to report for duty and serve a week or two.

Good buy
U. S. GRANT

ALS, ICarbS. See letter to Frederick Dent Grant, Jan. 15, 1871. On Dec. 16, 1870, Jesse Root Grant, Covington, Ky., wrote to Isaac N. Morris. "Yours of the 14th inst is this moment recd, and as you request I avail myself of the earliest moment to reply Your letter was recd mingled pleasure & regret I am glad to hear from you, & that you have some confidence in my kind feelings in the welfare of the *needy*. But as I am going to start to Washington in the morning, & made *large* calculation on meeting you there, & find I shall be disappointed in that I am thrown back—wont you be there before NewYears day. I dont expec[t] to leave here before that time—I will take your letter with me, and if I can get a situation for your friend I will certainly do so . . . Cant you be there before Cristment? Well I will be in Washington two or three weeks & would be glad to meet you there If I can find any situation for your friend I will do so do so & allow you by mail In the mean time would like to hear from you as often as possibe" ALS, Morris Family Papers, IHi.

1. Susan M. Felt, seventeen-year-old daughter of Galena merchant Lucius S. Felt, attended Miss Porter's School, Farmington, Conn. See *PUSG*, 2, 53–54, 247, 290; *ibid.*, 20, 278–79.

For Benjamin F. Peixotto

Executive Mansion
Washington Dec 8. 1870

The bearer of this letter Hon Benj F. Peixotto, who has accepted the important though unremunerative position of U. S. Consul-General to Roumania[1] is commended to the good offices of all representatives of this government abroad.

Mr Peixotto has undertaken the duties of his present office more as a missionary work for the benefit of the people who are laboring under severe oppression than for any benefits to accrue to himself, a work which all good citizens will wish him the greatest success in.

The United States knowing no distinction of her own citizens on account of religion or nativity naturally believe in a civilization the world over which will secure the same universal liberal views.

U S. GRANT

LS, American Jewish Historical Society, Waltham, Mass. Born in 1834 in New York City, Benjamin F. Peixotto had been an editor of the *Cleveland Plain Dealer* and grand master of B'nai B'rith, and was a lawyer in San Francisco when nominated by USG on June 16, 1870, as consul at Bucharest. On June 2, Abraham Hart, president, Board of Delegates of American Israelites, Philadelphia, telegraphed to USG. "In behalf of my Coreligionists in Maldava & Wallachia who are being persued for Slaughter by the Christians I ask your own influence and that of our Government to Stop this horrible massacre by an [i]mmediate telegraph dispatch being sent from Washington to Roumana the effect of which may yet Spare the lives of those unfortunate beings whose [o]nly crime is that of being non Christians who are yet being hunted down as the telegraph dispatch published from Constantinople dated June first it is vented the fury of the continuous unabated finding fresh Victims to glut its insatiable fury" Telegram received, DNA, RG 59, Miscellaneous Letters. On the same day, Israel Joseph, New York City, telegraphed to USG. "Report from Turkey speaks of thousands of Israelites murdered by the butchering hand of biggotted fanaticism. For God sake do something to stay further blood shed." Telegram received, *ibid.* Related papers are *ibid.* On June 6, USG transmitted to the Senate a report of Secretary of State Hamilton Fish stating that he had no official information "concerning a reported persecution and massacre of Israelites in Roumania." DS, *ibid.*, RG 46, Presidential Messages. See *SED*, 41-2-97; *New York Times*, June 9, 1870.

On April 19, 1869, Rabbi H. Z. Sneersohn of Jerusalem had called on USG to discuss the plight of Jews in Palestine. *National Intelligencer*, April 20, 1869; Sneersohn, *Palestine and Roumania* . . . (New York, 1872; reprinted, New York, 1977), pp. 85–86. On Jan. 19, 1870, Sneersohn, Chicago, wrote to USG at length. "To the chosen Chieftain of the United States of America, warrior, hero and prince of peace, Ulysses S.

Grant. 'May the splendor of the Lord cover him all his days.' May his name be a blessing over the confines of the earth. Amen! Several months ago, I was honored by the good fortune of beholding thy countenance. The kind reception which thou didst then award me, was a blessing to my spirit as though I had viewed the face of an Angel of Mercy. I then represented to thee the distress of my brethren in faith at Jerusalem. In the appointment of a new U. S. Consul for Jerusalem I see the fulfillment of the promise thou gavest me that the Government of the United States would do all in its power toward ameliorating the lot of my wretched brethren residing there. Thanks and praises to thee, O! noble one, for thy kindness which thou hast shown to the children of Abraham, of Isaac, and of Jacob. Also accept my thanks, springing from the innermost recesses of my heart, for favorable mediation which thou hast tendered for my unfortunate brethren in Russia. . . . Therefore, I feel myself encouraged in again praying to the great American people and their chosen chieftain. Five hundred thousand souls in Roumania are being trodden upon, and like the beasts of the field and the birds of the air, subjected to the malicious will of all. Their crime is their belief in one God; their sin, that they are scions of the stock of Abraham and faithful adherents of the words of Moses, which have even also been the fountainhead of the Christian religion. . . . The influence of the United States can be exerted in two different ways for the benefit of these unfortunates. First, in the appointment of Consuls friendly toward our race in that country; but more especially would such an appointment prove efficacious, namely, if a Jewish citizen were sent there as Consul. Such an example of so great and mighty a nation in its appreciation of men and its honor of their rights without regard to religious belief, could not fail of making an impression. Secondly, by friendly mediation and intercession with the Roumanian government made in the ordinary diplomatic manner. Pardon me, mighty ruler, beneficent chieftain, beloved of God and of men—pardon a stranger of a strange land—pardon a son of Jerusalem, which is dear to all civilized people—pardon him if in his grief over the woes of his brethren in faith he annoys thee with his prayers, and if his cries disturb thee in thy labors and rob thee of the precious time which belongs to the government of thy good people, 'for out of the abundance of my complaint and grief have I spoken hitherto.'" *Ibid.*, pp. 86–89. See Lloyd P. Gartner, "Roumania, America, and World Jewry: Consul Peixotto in Bucharest, 1870–1876," *American Jewish Historical Quarterly*, LVIII, 1 (Sept., 1968), 25–117.

On Nov. 30, 1869, Simon Wolf *et al.*, Washington, D. C., had written to USG. "We your humble petitioners, beg to represent to your Excellency, that the melancholy news by cable, has reached us, that recently, by the enforcement of a harsh, inhuman and sectarian law, some two thousand Jewish families have been expatriated from their homes into the interior of primitive Russia. They have been banished for no crime or fault, either, of omission or commission, but simply because they adhere steadfastly and heroicaly to the faith in which they were born, and with the historical firmness of the Hebrew, remain faithful to the traditions and truths of their people, to live and die for the freedom of conscience. It can scarcely be credited that in this enlightened Age, for no other Sin than worshipping God, according to the dictates of conscience, such cruel persecution can be practiced. we have for years admired the growing tendency on the part of the Czar to liberal and enlightened views, and are impressed that this Edict has not his sanction, but that it has been, if at all, wrung from him to appease, an ignorant and cruel peasentry. We appear before your Excellency to plead the cause of these unfortunates, and although we live in, and are citizens of this free and tolerant land, where every man can pursue his religious convictions without let or hindrance, still we cannot help but feel the woes of our coreligionists, and sympathize with them in their affliction. May it please your Excellency, although we well know, that it is against the policy of this Government to interfere with the internal affairs of any other people, yet there are crimes committed in the name of municipal jurisdiction, that by their nature and magnitude become offences against humanity, and thus are violations and infractions of the law of nations. We are confident that the instance we bring to your honored notice, although it may not call for the active interposition of the United States, still we deem it a proper subject of friendly interposition from this government to a friendly and faithful ally, and we most respectfully request that instructions may be sent to our honored representative at St Petersburgh, asking him to represent to the Russian Government that this subject has been brought to the notice of the President of the United States, with the suggestion that [he] use whatever influence he can within the limits of diplomatic duty, to have the ukase revoked or modified, and as the matter is of the most pressing character, in the middle of a Russian winter, helpless families are being dragged from their firesides, we respectfully urge a cable telegram to be forwarded, for time in this case is the essence of our appeal. Your Excellency needs no suggestion of ours to reflect that while all nations are striving to facilitate the means of intercommunication by liberal and friendly commercial treaties—by subjecting all the appliances of modern science to break down the estrangements that have by narrow policies divided peoples created in the image of that Deity, who is father of all, it will be a hopeless task to endeavor to permanently unite the nations of the Earth, in bonds of amity, unless one universal law of humanity is recognized, it is exacted in time of war of an Enemy, is it foreign to the genius of our enlightened institutions to urge it on a friendly power in time of peace? The equality of all men before the law, the divine rights, expressed in our matchless Declaration, are the Watchwords of our polity, ~~that~~ these principles are the birth rights of the human family, is it too much to ask ~~her~~ the U. S. to proclaim that henceforth it shall be an integral part of her intercourse with the nations, that international law recognizes *only*, as members of the family of nations those people who are guided by the unchangeable laws of a common humanity. Therefore we most humbly and respectfully ask that a copy of this appeal be forwarded to the representative of the United States near the Russian government, with such other instructions as may be thought proper by your Excellency in order to afford relief to the people so harshly dealt with" DS (5 signatures), DNA, RG 59, Miscellaneous Letters. An expanded version is in *Washington Chronicle*, Dec. 1, 1869. "The President replied that the paper should receive his careful consideration; he had seen a telegraphic report of the circumstance, and was grieved at it. He was free to say that in this age of enlightenment it is too late in the day to persecute any one on account of condition, birth, creed, or color, and no one ought to be molested or punished except after conviction by due process through the courts. The address, he added, should be presented to the Cabinet at the meeting about to convene." *Ibid.* See Evelyn Levow Greenberg, "An 1869 Petition on Behalf of Russian Jews," *American Jewish Historical Quarterly*, LIV, 3 (March, 1965), 278–95; Ronald J. Jensen, "The Politics of Discrimination: America, Russia and the Jewish Question, 1869–1872," *American Jewish History*, LXXV, 3 (March, 1986), 280–95.

1. In [*July*] 1869, T. N. Kornbach wrote to USG. "In the name and for the sake of humanity, justice and the integrity of the American Nation I begg and entreat you most submissively, having my reclamations before your worthy notice, to do justice to one who has been deeply wronged as an American cityzen from the part of one Mr. Czapkay in the quality of Consulate here, who instead of raising the American Nation in the eyes of the people where he has had the honour of beeing sent to represente such, has on the contrary through his public as well as private life contribuated to bring dishonour and discredit upon our beloved republic May God enlighten and

keep you Sire, in safety and wellfare many, many years to come, that the splendid hopes America is looking forward to may be realized through you as is the prayer and heartfelt wish of one deeply insulte[d] and who awaits satisfaction to be don[e] him," ALS (docketed as received on July 23), DNA, RG 59, Miscellaneous Letters. An additional letter from Kornbach, Bucharest, to USG complaining about Louis J. Czapkay, consul, Bucharest, is *ibid.* Papers related to Czapkay are *ibid.*, Letters of Application and Recommendation. On June 3, 1870, USG nominated Adolphe Buchner as consul, Bucharest, withdrew the nomination on June 16, and named Peixotto instead.

On Dec. 1 and 21, Fish wrote in his diary. "B F Peixotto—Consul to Bucharest calls in company with Simon Wolf—Peixotto says he goes to the Consulate not with the ordinary objects of a Commercial agency but with a special view to the interests of a large class of religionists, resident there &c—& for their advancement, & social & political improvement—He is told very distinctly, that he mistakes the object of his appointment—that as Consul he has no political functions or responsibilities, but on the contrary is expressly enjoined from interference ~~ther~~ with any questions of the kind . . . he is advised to remember the prejudices of race & of religion that exist, & overcome them by kindness & charity rather than by force or by extreme claims" "Met Simon Wolf at the Presidents—& express to him strong disatisfaction with the conduct of Peixotto (appointed Consul at Bucharest) in obtaining & publishing a letter from the President—& intimate a desire to revoke his appointment—that his Conduct in this matter implied an intention to transcend his proper duties, & was an indignity to me after my refusal to give him a special letter, & my explanation to him of the limited sphere of his duties—Wolf expresses concurrence in my answer—but hopes he may not be recalled—In the Evening he sends me a letter, enclosing copy of one from him to Peixotto" DLC-Hamilton Fish. See Esther L. Panitz, *Simon Wolf: Private Conscience and Public Image* (Rutherford, N. J., 1987), pp. 41–47.

To Charles H. Rogers

TO MR. CHAS. H. ROGERS
CONTINENTAL HOTEL PHILA. PA.
MY DEAR SIR:

I have just received your letter of the 6th. inst.

We shall be glad to see you and Miss. Post[1] at any time, either this week or next.

Please let me know, by telegraph, what train you are coming on, that the carriage may meet you at the depot.

Yours truly
U. S. GRANT

EXECUTIVE MANSION.
DEC. 8. 1870.

LS, DLC-USG. For Charles H. Rogers, a former Galena banker, see *PUSG*, 10, 215; *ibid.*, 12, 284–85; *ibid.*, 18, 273, 357–58; *ibid.*, 19, 198–99, 478; *Julia Grant*, p. 128; letter to Charles H. Rogers, June 22, 1872.

On July 28, 1870, USG, Long Branch, had written to Rogers. "Your letter in regard to the retention of two employees in the Custom House was rec'd, and forwarded to the collector with my endorsement of yours Also your second letter announcing the shipment of a box of grapes. The grapes have arrived for which accept my thanks. Mrs. Grant and my self will be pleased if we can have a visit from you and Mrs. Rogers the latter part of next week, or at any time after that that best suits you. We have company now, and more coming, who will stay until about the last of next week. I hope you will find it convenient to come. Mrs. Grant joins me in kindest regards to Mrs. Rogers, John & yourself." ALS, *ibid.*

On Aug. 27, 1868, Bvt. Maj. Gen. John A. Rawlins, Washington, D. C., had written to Rogers. "Mrs Rawlins has been dangerously ill and is now slowly recovering though still very low—Your fine grapes seem to be first on her mind when she speaks of what her apetite would relish. I have tried to get the same kind here and have I think quite nearly succeeded but they dont taste to her like those that grow on your grapery. Will you therefore please send her a few bunches—the purple ones she most craves, and increase by one more the many, many kindness you have shown me and mine. My own health is not so good I fear as I have been led to suppose it was. The loss of rest and anxiety I had when Mrs Rawlins was so ill. produced a return of Hemorhage which I had not had for near three years—I am now quite well & feel if anything better than before it occurred, but still I feel considerable fears as to the real condition of my lungs. As soon as Mrs Rawlins is well enough to go to Danbury I shall try the West again My love to Mrs Rogers & John" ALS, *ibid.* On Dec. 31, 1869, Orville E. Babcock wrote to Rogers thanking him for a $500 contribution to the Rawlins memorial fund. ALS, *ibid.*

1. Lily Post became a correspondent of Julia Dent Grant.

To Oliver P. Morton

Washington, D. C. Dec 9th *18~~6~~70.*

DEAR SIR:

When your note of last evening was received I was in company with Senators Howard and Carpenter, and at the moment of receiving it was saying that I thought the resolution in regard to San Domingo should start in the Senate.

Both Senators agreed with me, and, as the chairman of the Committee on Foreign Relations cannot be got to introduce the subject,[1] it should be introduced by some other member of that Committee. The result would have been, had I not received your note, that I should have written this morning requesting you to do what you have kindly offered to do.

I do not suppose that the Sec. of State can have a resolution drawn to day, in the shape it should go before the Senate, but if you do not think it improper I wish you would give notice to day that you will introduce such a resolution on Monday.[2] How would it do to recommend also that the resolution be referred to a special committee instead of to your comt?

Yours truly
U. S. GRANT

HON. O. P. MORTON. U. S. S.[3]

Copy, USG 3. On Dec. 8, 1870, U.S. Senator Oliver P. Morton of Ind. wrote to USG. "If no body else in the Senate has the matter in charge I will introduce the resolutions in regard to St Domingo in accordance with the suggestions in the message. I should be glad to have Mr Fish prepare them as he is doubtless considering them as to form and substance. ~~The~~ They should be started without delay. If any body else has the matter in hand it is all right . . . If convenient please answer by bearer." ALS, DLC-Hamilton Fish. On Dec. 9, USG endorsed this letter. "Will the Sec. of State please read the enclosed and prepare such resolution as is contemplated." Copy, USG 3.

J. C. Bancroft Davis, asst. secretary of state, prepared a draft of the contemplated resolutions. "Resolved by the Senate and House of Representatives of the United States of America in Congress assembled. 1 That the sum of   thousand dollars be and hereby is appropriated to defray the expenses of a Commission to be appointed to negotiate and agree with the Government of the Dominican Republic upon the terms of the cession of the Territories of the said Dominican Republic to the United States, either by Treaty to be submitted to the Senate, or by Articles to be submitted to the two Houses of Congress, as the President may elect. 2. And be it further Resolved: That Congress doth consent that the Territory properly included in and rightfully belonging to the said Dominican Republic may be annexed to the United States as one of the Territories thereof, upon the following conditions. *First*: That all the Custom Houses, Fortifications, Barracks, Ports, Harbors, Navy and Naval Docks, Magazines, Arms, Armaments and Accoutrements, Archives and ~~p~~Public Documents of the said Dominican Republic shall become the absolute property of the United States. *Second*: That the United States shall pay therefor to the Dominican Republic in the gold coin of the United States a sum not exceeding one million three hundred and fifty thousand dollars. *Third*: That the sum so paid shall be applied by a Commission to be appointed by the United States after the cession to the payment of the existing debt of the Dominican Republic. *Fourth*: That the United States shall, in no event, be responsible for any part of said debt." Copy, DLC-Hamilton Fish. Secretary of State Hamilton Fish wrote on this document. "This Copy of Mr Davis draft, was submitted to the President Sunday Eveng Decr 11 /70, & subsequently, on the same Evening, to Senator Morton—Both requested me to prepare another draft & I noted in pencil, on the back of this Copy, the points of enquiry suggested in the interviews with Morton, & returnig home prepared another draft, which I submitted on Monday Morng, to the President, Morton, Chandler, Howard Robeson, Cresswell—" AN, *ibid.*

E. Peshine Smith, solicitor, dept. of state, prepared a draft of the contemplated resolutions. "Resolved by the Senate and House of Representatives of the United States of America in Congress assembled. 1. That the sum of   dollars be and the same hereby is appropriated to defray the expenses of missions and negotiations to agree upon the terms of the admission and cession of the Republic of Dominica either by Treaty to be submitted to the Senate, or by Articles to be submitted to the two Houses of Congress as the President may determine. 2. And be it further Resolved. That the President be requested to appoint, by and with the advice and consent of the Senate, one or more special Commissioners, or Envoys Extraordinary, to negotiate with the authorities of the Republic of Dominica, a Treaty, or to agree upon Articles to be submitted to Congress for the reception of that Republic into the United States, as one of the Territories thereof, to be hereafter erected into one or more States, when and as Congress in its discretion shall determine; upon these conditions, to wit: ~~1~~I. That the United States shall pay a sum not exceeding   dollars for the forts, arsenals, and other public buildings or establishments of the Republic of Dominica, not including its public domain not already specifically devoted to and employed in the civil, military, or naval service of the Republic. II That the above mentioned sum of   dollars may be paid by using the same, or so much thereof as may be necessary, in the redemption and cancellation of the public debt of the Republic of Dominica existing at the date of the Treaty, whether the same be liquidated and acknowledged or having been claimed, remains under discussion. III That so much of the public domain of the Republic of Dominica as shall under the Treaty be transferred absolutely to the United States, shall stand charged with the residue of the public debt of the Republic of Dominica after its annexation to the United States, and the revenue or the proceeds of the sale thereof shall in the discretion of Congress be devoted to the extinguishment of such debt, if any there be found to remain, as a primary charge before such revenue or proceeds be appropriated to the expenses of the Territory of Dominica, or the State or States that may be formed therefrom." Copy, *ibid.* Fish wrote on this document. "This copy of Mr Peshine Smiths draft was submitted to the President, Sunday Evng Decr 11 /70 subsequently to Senator Morton same Evenig—Both requested me to prepare another draft" AN, *ibid.*

On Dec. 11, Fish wrote in his diary. "A letter from the President requests me to call in the afternoon or Evening & bring the draft resolution in regard to San Domingo—I call in the Evening—President still at Dinner table with, V. P. Colfax—Genl Hamilton, Ben Wade, & Collector Murphy—He reads the Resolutions, & desires some alteration—preferring the draft made by Peshine Smith—requests me to see Morton, & consult him—Genl Banks comes in & Prsdt mentions the subject to him—Banks advises that they be introduced simultaneously in both Houses, & states that the subject in his Committee has been referred to Mr Orth, & recommends that he be requested to introduce them—Go to see Senator Morton—in the office of the National Hotel, . . . Read to Morton the two Resolutions (Davis & Smiths) & mention Presidents desire, as to the form, & my own views, in ~~which~~ the theory of which he concurs—I request him to indicate the *points* & subjects to which enquiry should be directed—(the theory of my idea of what the resolutions should be) will appear in the draft which I prepare on my return home—I then request him to suggest the subjects of inquiry & note them, in pencil, as stated by him, on the back of one of the Sets of Resolutions, which I had read to him—going over these carefully two or three times, they seem at length to embrace all that he thinks necessary—Mentioning Banks suggestion that the resolutions be introduced simultaneously in both Houses—he objects—does not wish to seem to be introducing Resolutions that have been prepared by some one else—says that he has requested some three or four Senators to meet him tomorrow morning at 9½ at the Presidents, wishes me to be there, & to have the Resolution, which I may prepare, embodying the points we have considered, & hand it to him—He desires me not to say that the resolution has been prepared by me—but let him have it without drawing attention thereto—Returning home I prepare the Resolution before going to bed—" *Ibid.*

On Dec. 12, Morton introduced a joint resolution. "*Resolved, &c.*, That the President of the United States be authorized to appoint three commissioners, and also a secretary, (the latter to be versed in the English and Spanish languages,) to proceed to the island of San Domingo, and to inquire into, ascertain, and report—1. The political state and condition of the republic of Dominica. 2. The desire and disposition of the people of the said republic to become annexed to and to form part of the people of the United States. . . . 8. The terms and conditions on which the Dominican Government may desire to be annexed to and become part of the United States as one of the Territories thereof. 9. Such other information with respect to the said Government or its territories as to the said commissioners shall seem desirable or important with reference to the future incorporation of the said Dominican republic into the United States as one of its Territories. SEC. 2. *And be it further resolved*, That the said commissioners shall, as soon as conveniently may be, report to the President of the United States, who shall lay their report before Congress. SEC. 3. *And be it further resolved*, That the said commissioners shall serve without compensation, (except the payment of expenses,) and the compensation of the secretary shall be determined by the Secretary of State, with the approval of the President." *CG*, 41-3, 53.

On Dec. 21, U.S. Senator Charles Sumner of Mass. delivered a speech later entitled "Naboth's Vineyard." ". . . This whole measure of annexation, and the spirit with which it is pressed, find a parallel in the Kansas and Nebraska bill, and in the Lecompton constitution, by which it was sought to subjugate a distant Territory to slavery. The Senator from Indiana was not here during those days, although he was acting well his part at home; but he will remember the pressure to which we were then exposed; and now we witness the same things—violence in a distant island, as there was violence in Kansas; also the same presidential appliances; and, shall I add, the same menace of personal assault? In other days, to carry a project, a President has tried to change a committee. It was James Buchanan. And now we have been called this session to witness a similar endeavor by our President. He was not satisfied with the Committee on Foreign Relations as constituted for years. He wished a change. He asked first for the removal of the chairman. Somebody told him that this would not be convenient. He then asked for the removal of the Senator from Missouri, [Mr. SCHURZ,] and he was told that this could not be done without affecting the German vote. He then called for the removal of my friend the Senator from New Hampshire, [Mr. PATTERSON,] who unhappily was not a German. It was finally settled that this could not be done. I allude to these things reluctantly and only as part of the case. They illustrate the spirit we are called to encounter. They illustrate the extent to which the President has fallen into the line of bad examples. Sir, I appeal to you, as Vice President. By official position and by well known relations of friendship you enjoy opportunities which I entreat you to use for the good of your country, and, may I add, for the benefit of that party which has so justly honored you. Go to the President, I ask you, and address him frankly with the voice of a friend to whom he must hearken. Counsel him not to follow the example of Franklin Pierce, James Buchanan, and Andrew Johnson; tell him not to allow the oppression of a weak and humble people; ask him not to exercise War Powers without authority of Congress, and remind him kindly that there is a grandeur in Justice and Peace beyond anything in material aggrandizement, beyond anything in war.... There is one other consideration, vast in importance and conclusive in character, to which I allude only, and that is all. The island of San Domingo, situated in tropical waters and occupied by another race, never can become a permanent possession of the United States. You may seize it by force of arms or by diplomacy, where a naval squadron does more than the minister; but the enforced jurisdiction cannot endure. Already by a higher statute is that island set apart to the colored race...." *Ibid.* (brackets in original), pp. 227, 230–31; variant, *The Works of Charles Sumner* (Boston, 1870–83), XIV, 89–124.

On the same day, Morton spoke. "Mr. President, the Senator from Massachusetts, [Mr. SUMNER,] this afternoon, in the course of his speech, thought proper to refer to my personal relations to the President of the United States, and he presented me as the confidential adviser of the President, a frequent visitor at the White House, and as conferring with the President alone in the Blue Room. I have seen the President in the Blue Room on several occasions, for I am somewhat lame and unable to go up stairs, and the President is kind enough when I visit the White House on business to come down stairs and see me, and I presume he would do the same for any Senator or Representative, or any other person who was not able to climb the stairs without difficulty.... I have been his friend and admirer ever since the battle of Fort Donelson; and although I sometimes disagree with him, perhaps in regard to appointments, or perhaps in regard to measures, I always try to differ with him in such a way as not to assail his personal character or to demoralize the party of which he is the head. A series of assaults have been made on the President, from time to time, ever since his inauguration; scarce has one subsided before another is begun. And I think he has been treated with a bitterness of persecution and a torrent of calumny that have not been lavished upon any Executive of the United States perhaps since the days of Thomas Jefferson.... Now, sir, allow me to say that nearly all the Senator's points are immaterial—immaterial to the purpose of this resolution. He has spent his force upon matters that, so far as the merits of this resolution are concerned, may be designated as frivolous, wholly unimportant. We are not now proposing to examine whether the treaty was correctly and properly negotiated. We have passed by the treaty; we are beginning *de novo;* we are proposing to examine this question as if a treaty had never been made, and we propose to go to the vital and material points in the matter, and to do that we propose to send a commission to the island, where this information is most accessible and can be most accurately obtained...." *CG*, 41–3 (brackets in original), p. 236.

On Dec. 22, 6:37 A.M., the Senate passed the joint resolution, 32–9. *Ibid.*, p. 271. On the same day, USG received congratulatory calls from "numerous Senators and Members." *New York Times*, Dec. 23, 1870. On Dec. 23, Fish wrote in his diary. "After leaving the President, he (Boutwell) speaks of Sumner, & his speech in the Senate day before yesterday on San Domingo—refering to Sumners appeal 'to the Secretary of State, & Secretary of the Treasury' he says that within a week Sumner mentioned to him charges against the President of a nature so outrageous & violent, that he is unwilling to repeat them—that he has not repeated & will not unless under some compulsion that at present he cannot conceive can be brought to bear upon him—He adds that 'Sumner forgets what he says'—I express the opinion that Sumner is 'crazy—a monomaniac upon all matters relating to his own importance—& his relations toward the President'—& state that S. more than once in speaking of the Presidents interviews with him last Winter at Sumner's house, about San Domingo had said that Grant was drunk—'he called me Chairman of the *Judiciary* Committee'. Boutwell, who was present at the interview says 'he was no more drunk, or excited than he was when we left him upstairs five minutes since—no more so than Sumner himself'" DLC-Hamilton Fish. See *CG*, 41–3, 183–84, 190–98, 222–23, 238–71; *PUSG*, 19, 209–10; *ibid.*, 20, 123–24, 311–12; letter to Nathaniel P. Banks, Dec. 12, 1870; message to Senate, Jan. 11, 1871; letter to Buenaventura Báez, Jan. 15, 1871; message to Senate, Jan. 16, 1871; William D. Foulke, *Life of Oliver P. Morton* (1899; reprinted, New York, 1974), II, 150–68; Edward L. Pierce, *Memoir and Letters of Charles Sumner: Period 1860 to Death* (London, 1893), IV, 456–62; David Donald, *Charles Sumner and the Rights of Man* (New York, 1970), pp. 468–75.

1. On Dec. 8 and 20, 1870, a correspondent reported: "The San Domingo question is the most prominent one before the Committee on Foreign Relations, though perhaps not the most important. The Committee is supposed to have a majority of one against acquisition on any terms. But this is not so certain. Some Senators who voted against the treaty last session, express a willingness to support the action asked for by the President, and it may turn out that an additional member of the Committee may entertain the same view. It is not thought however, that the Committee will reverse its expression of last session." "Pertinent to the San Domingo matter, it may be said that during the past two weeks several gentlemen have been earnestly endeavoring to bring about a pacification between the President and Mr. SUMNER, but without success. Prominent in these efforts have been Senator WILSON, Senator ANTHONY, and Gov. JEWELL. Mr. SUMNER remains as bitter as ever, and the President maintains a firm attitude, inconsistent with anything like an approach toward conciliation. . . ." *New York Times*, Dec. 9 and 21, 1870. On Dec. 25, U.S. Representative Cadwallader C. Washburn of Wis. wrote to Elihu B. Washburne. ". . . We have had a good deal of excitement of late over St Domingo. The President as you saw in the Message, crowded annexation very hard, & I think very unwisely—Well a proposition came up this last week to send Commissioners to SanDomingo to make inquiry. Sumner who has been nursing his wrath to keep it warm ever since the recall of Motley, attacked the President with great bitterness, & the result was a general cat fight, lasting all night. Sumner was utterly floored, & badly kickd & cuffed around. The President in my opinion is sending the party to the devil at lightening speed—With Ben Butler for adviser what more could be expected—Without any decent reason he has quarrelled with Fenton & taken Roscoe Conkling to his bosom. The Schurz quarrel might be healed if the President was less obstinate or self willed. Shurz was all wrong, but we cannot afford to drive him from the party. He has now great power with the Germans. They are very proud that one of their Countrymen holds so high a position & they will make his quarrel theirs—With the loss of the German vote the party is surely doomed, & with it we can hardly save ourselves—. . ." ALS, DLC-Elihu B. Washburne.

2. Dec. 12.

3. On Jan. 11, Orville E. Babcock wrote to Fish. "I return herewith the several papers on Sto Domingo matters, forwarded to me by Senator Morton and others." Copy, DLC-USG, II, 1.

To Horace Greeley

Washington D. C. Dec. 10th *1870*

DEAR SIR:

May I have the pleasure of your company at dinner[1] this afternoon, at 5 O'clock, and to spend the evening with me, and night if it is your intention to remain in the city over Sunday? There will be no one else but yourself and my family present.

I shall be at the funeral of your tried friend, Gen. Walbridge, this afternoon and will receive your answer there if not convenient to send it before.

Yours Truly
U. S. GRANT

HON. H. GREELEY
ARLINGTON HOUSE

ALS, Ford Collection, NN. On Dec. 10, 1870, Horace Greeley served as a pallbearer in Washington, D. C., for Hiram S. Walbridge, who died on Dec. 6. *New York Tribune*, Dec. 12, 1870. Walbridge, born in N. Y. in 1821, attended Ohio University, practiced law in Toledo, was appointed brig. gen., Ohio militia (1843), moved to New York City (1847), and was elected Democratic U.S. representative (1853–55). On April 26, 1869, Horace Porter wrote to Secretary of the Interior Jacob D. Cox. "The President directs me to inform you that Mr Greely has declined his appointment as an Inspector of the Union Pacific Rail Road, and requests that the Hon Hiram Wallbridge of New-York be appointed in his place." Copies, DLC-USG, II, 1, 4. On April 28, Walbridge, New York City, telegraphed to USG. "Please accept my grateful thanks for my unexpected designation as one of the Pacific Rail Commissioners which I first learned this morning. I shall endeavor to conscientiously discharge its duties to your entire satisfaction and the credit of your administration which for the interest of the country must be continued the next eight 8 years" Telegram received (at 1:00 P.M.), DNA, RG 107, Telegrams Collected (Bound). On Sept. 4, Walbridge, San Francisco, wrote to USG. "Since arriving in this city, on the duty you assigned me, as a Commissioner to examine the Union and Central Pacific Railroads I observe that the Mission to China is vacant On account of my health and the advice of my physicians, I fear I will be compelled to seek its restoration in a milder climate. For this reason, if I should be deemed worthy and competent, by you, it would at this time, be most agreeable and acceptable to me, to receive the nomination for that place—My long association with trade and commerce in New York city, would I venture to suggest, give me some fitness to extend our commercial relations, with this numerous and interesting people I am sure, I need not speak of my entire accord with and my earnest desires for the success of the views and policy of your Administration, and my warm admiration for you personally. Should the appointment be conferred upon me, my best efforts will be to advance the interests and honor of our country, and to do no discredit to your preference." ALS, *ibid.*, RG 59, Letters of Application and Recommendation. A related letter is *ibid.* On Sept. 7, Walbridge telegraphed to USG. "I have written to you about chinese mission Please suspend appointment if you can till my letter arrives" Telegram received (at 3:00 P.M.), *ibid.*, RG 107, Telegrams Collected (Bound). No appointment followed.

1. Julia Dent Grant remembered that Greeley accepted the invitation. *Julia Grant*, p. 180. An invitation to dinner on Jan. 19, 1870, from USG to Greeley is in the Ford Collection, NN.

To Hamilton Fish

Washington D. C. Dec. 12th *1870*

HON. H. FISH;
SEC. OF STATE.
DEAR SIR;

Will it be convenient for you to furnish Gen. Banks[1] a copy of the San Domingo resolution so that it may be presented in the two houses simultaneously?

Gen. Banks expressed the opinion that he thought it advisable to have the resolution so presented, and said that if he could be furnished a copy by 12 m. to-day, he would give it to Judge Orth[2] for that purpose.

I do not rember whether the resolution provides for a specific number of Commissioners or not? If it does not it seems to me it should, and that the number should be five.

Yours Truly
U. S. GRANT

ALS, DLC-Hamilton Fish.

1. On Dec. 10, [1870], Horace Porter wrote to U.S. Representative Nathaniel P. Banks of Mass. "The President will be obliged to you if you will be kind enough to call at the Executive Mansion this evening, between 7 & 10 O'Clock to converse on the subject which I mentioned to you on Friday last." ALS, DLC-Nathaniel P. Banks.

2. Born in 1817 near Lebanon, Pa., Godlove S. Orth attended Gettysburg College and moved in 1839 to Lafayette, Ind., where he practiced law and served as Whig state senator (1843–48). Orth helped to organize the Republicans in Ind., and, in July, 1862, raised troops following a call for vols. Entering the U.S. House of Representatives (1863), he focused on foreign policy.

On July 11, 1870, U.S. Senator Oliver P. Morton of Ind. had written to USG. "The Hon G. S. Orth is well qualified to fill the mission to Berlin. He is a gentleman of fine education, a good lawyer, of decided ability, and an earnest republican, and I recommend him for the appointment . . . P. S. He speaks and writes the German language as I am informed" ALS, DNA, RG 59, Letters of Application and Recommendation. U.S. Senator Daniel D. Pratt of Ind. favorably endorsed this letter. AES, *ibid.* On July 12, William E. Chandler, Washington, D. C., wrote to USG. "In case of a change in the incumbency of the mission to Prussia I trust that *Hon G. S. Orth* of Indiana may receive the appointment. Judge Orth's natural talents, legal attainments, long service in Congress, experience on the Committee of Foreign Relations and his thorough knowledge of public affairs would abundantly vindicate the wisdom of the selection. His appointment would also be an appropriate recognition of the Republicans of Indiana who are entitled to all honor from the Republican party and from the present administration. In the political contests of the past, Indiana has received the heaviest shock of the battle. In October 1868 our triumph by small majorities in Indiana and Pennsylvania saved the Presidential election, and no political battle-ground was ever more closely contested. In that campaign in Indiana as well as in all other critical fights Judge Orth acted a conspicuous part, and without disparagement of others, he is deserving of high credit for our important success. It is my knowledge of the character and importance of the conflicts in Indiana and of Judge Orth's participation there in that impels me to give my testimony in his behalf. As a member and officer of the Republican National Committee I respectfully urge his appointment. If made I shall consider it a personal favor to myself because conferred upon one whom I earnestly esteem as a most valued friend." ALS, *ibid.* On the same day, Simon Wolf, Washington, D. C., wrote to USG. "I learn with great pleasure that the friends of Hon Godlove S Orth, are advocating his claims for the Berlin Mission, I trust that his well known services, his eminent fitness, his untiring zeal and energy, his devotion to Liberty and the Defenders of the Union, will be remembered and recognized, but more than all, his superior *Representative* Capacity, for not alone as an American, but as a German is he everywhere recognized and esteemed. I am within the bounds of facts, when I state, that no appointment will give greater satisfaction to the Germans and Israelites of the whole Country, the taint of Prejudice has never tarnished the Shield of his fame, I hope for his appointment" ALS, *ibid.* On July 13, Governor Conrad Baker of Ind. telegraphed to USG. "If there is to be a change in the Minister to Berlin the appointment of Mr Orth would be gratifying to me personally and would be entirely acceptable to the people of this state," Telegram received (at 10:20 A.M.), *ibid.* On the same day, U.S. Representative John A. Logan of Ill. wrote to USG. "Genl Coburn & Myself came to see you this moring in ref'ence to Judge Orth of Indiana for Minister to Berlin. This would be an xcellent appt would give great satisfaction to the Ho of Reps, and, would be a good thing to do for the West. I hope that you may do this, the present Minister &c is of no advantage to you or the party, This appt. would, be. We send you reccomendations. I hope you will look them over at once, and if you do anything in the matter, do it before Congress adjourns." ALS, *ibid.* Also on the same day, Speaker of the House James G. Blaine wrote to USG. "I have heard that the name of Godlove S. Orth of Inda is before you for appointment as Minister to Prussia—I entered Congress with Mr Orth and have known him intimately for eight years—He is a gentleman of the most honorable type—a lawyer of conceded ability—a statesman of discretion, ability, probity and purity—There is no man within my knowledge better fitted to represent our country at a foreign Court—especially of German nationality—for from this great stock Mr. Orth is descended—He speaks the language, is familiar with the history traditions, manners and customs of Germany—while he has six generations of the best American blood in his veins—" ALS, *ibid.* On Oct. 1, Col. Joseph J. Reynolds, Austin, wrote to USG.

"I desire to invite your special attention to *Hon Godlove S. Orth* in connection with the mission to Prussia—I have been personally & intimately acquainted with Mr Orth for many years—He sustains the highest character as an able Jurist—Mr Orth is of German lineage and familiar with that language—With his public history as a representative in Congress for the last eight consecutive years, from the state of Indiana you are familiar—Mr Orth is fully imbued with the progressive, enlightened, Republican ideas of the times and has had a full share in their development thus far—He is particularly well fitted to represent us in Prussia, at this time, and his appointment will be highly appreciated by the whole country and especially the state of Indiana—" ALS, *ibid.* Additional recommendations are *ibid.* No appointment followed. See following letter.

To Nathaniel P. Banks

Washington D. C. Dec. 12th *1870*

HON. N. P. BANKS, M. C.[1]
DEAR SIR:

Govr Fish think that it probably is better that the same resolution, in relation to San Domingo, should not be introduced simultaneously in the two houses of Congress. I think too it might be better if the house should present its own resolution and the Senate do the same.

I shall be glad to learn this evening that resolutions have been introduced in both branches of the Nation legislature looking to the carrying out of my recommendation in regard to Santa Domingo.[2]

Respectfully Yours
U. S. GRANT

ALS, Mrs. Arthur Loeb, Philadelphia, Pa.

On Dec. 12, 1870, U.S. Representative Nathaniel P. Banks of Mass. introduced a joint resolution providing: "That the President be, and hereby is, authorized to appoint a commission, consisting of five members, to negotiate a treaty with the authorities of San Domingo for the acquisition of the territory of that Government, and to ascertain and report such information as a full and complete examination of the subject may enable them to present; and that the report of the said commission shall be considered a privileged report and in order whenever it shall be presented by the said commission." *CG*, 41–3, 66. On the same day, the measure was referred to the Foreign Affairs Committee under a motion "that the committee shall be authorized to report after five days' notice to the House, in order that the subject may not be sprung suddenly upon the House." *Ibid.*, p. 67.

On Dec. 19, Secretary of State Hamilton Fish wrote in his diary. "Govr Swann, member of Comm. on For. Affr H. R—calls on subjects referred to his Committee. . . .

he remarked that the San Domingo proposition wd probably be reported against by the Committee of the House—that Ambler (of Ohio) had said to him that if he (Swann), Wood (the Democrats on the Committee) would join them they wd defeat it—He named only Ambler & Willard (of Vermont) of the Republican Members, as opposed to the proposed Commission of Inquiry—there must be others, ~~or he wd not thi~~ to justify his opinion that the measure will fail—" DLC-Hamilton Fish.

On Jan. 6 and 7, correspondents reported: "Notwithstanding the apparent adverse vote in the Committee on Foreign Affairs yesterday, on Gen. Banks' San Domingo resolution, this gentleman is confident that it, or one similar to that of the Senate, will pass the House. It would appear from the representations of prominent friends of annexation, that at least two Democrats of the House will vote for the appointment of a commission." *Philadelphia Public Ledger*, Jan. 7, 1871. "The President was informed today that a majority of the Foreign Affairs Committee were favorable to Morton's resolution, and that it would be reported on Monday, but that it would be some days before the vote could be reached, as a number of gentlemen wished to discuss it." *Boston Transcript*, Jan. 7, 1871.

On Jan. 9, U.S. Representative Godlove S. Orth of Ind. substituted the Senate joint resolution regarding a commission of inquiry to Santo Domingo for the measure proposed by Banks. *CG*, 41–3, 382. See letter to Oliver P. Morton, Dec. 9, 1870. On the same day, U.S. Representative Jacob A. Ambler of Ohio proposed an amendment. "*Provided*, That nothing in this resolution contained shall be held, understood, or construed as committing Congress to the policy of annexing the territory of said republic of Dominica." *CG*, 41–3, 383.

On Jan. 10, U.S. Representative Samuel S. Cox of N. Y. spoke. "This measure authorizes the President to appoint three commissioners and a scribe, to proceed to and rove about San Domingo. They are to feel the pulse of its colored community of two hundred thousand, and report its physical, mental, and moral condition. The commission is especially to ascertain how that enlightened community is disposed toward us. . . . Although this is done with reference to the incorporation of the Dominican republic into the United States as one of its 'territories,' there was not enough of sugar-coating over the dose to make it go down here, until the proviso of my friend from Ohio [Mr. AMBLER] was introduced. His proposition has this absurdity. It pretends not to commit us to annexation by the passage of the resolution; yet we all know that unless the annexation is accomplished there is no necessity of such a commission. If the thing is foregone, the commission is a senseless waste of time and money. No one is deceived by this proviso. It is well meant, but whether it will be voted down or not, the annexation will be practically a fact. . . . I do not know how things can be done under this present Administration. God only knows how this Administration is conducted in its arcana, its secret recesses. It is run by aid-de-camps and military people, who even come to the floor of this House for the purpose of assisting us in our legislation. . . . Is the 'Tennessee' fired up, and the favorable report already drawn to befool the people with a sham observation, under the guidance of a lot of interested speculators or ductile flunkeys? Why, we do not treat the Indians half so cavalierly as this bill proposes to treat both contracting parties. Is there to be no frank, fair consent of both peoples to this measure? When have they spoken?. . ." *Ibid.* (brackets in original), pp. 407–8.

On the same day, Orth spoke about USG. ". . . He has been charged with favoring those who, it is alleged, have acted corruptly, and, with the knowledge of this charge, there is a most strenuous opposition to the creation of this commission, which will have the power to give to us all the facts embraced in this question. No one worthy of the least consideration has charged, and no one will for a moment believe that the President's action in this matter is otherwise than conscientious, pure, and honorable.... If there be any foundation for suspecting the existence of a 'job' or a 'ring' in this question of annexation, that is an additional reason why this resolution should pass, and an opportunity given for the most searching investigation by a commission of gentlemen whose characters shall be a sufficient guarantee for the correctness of the results at which they may arrive...." *Ibid.*, pp. 415–16.

Also on the same day, the House approved the amendment, 108–76, and then passed the joint resolution, 123–63. *Ibid.*, p. 416. On Jan. 11, after additional debate on annexation and the defeat of amendments proposed by U.S. Senators Charles Sumner of Mass. and Willard Saulsbury of Del., the Senate passed the joint resolution as received from the House, 57–0. *Ibid.*, pp. 403–6, 426–31. USG signed the joint resolution on Jan. 12. See letter to William G. Temple, Jan. 14, 1871; letter to Buenaventura Báez, Jan. 15, 1871; Fred H. Harrington, *Fighting Politician: Major General N. P. Banks* (Philadelphia, 1948), pp. 188–91.

1. On Dec. 8, 1870, a correspondent reported: "The House Committee on Foreign Affairs met today and briefly considered the work before them. That portion of the President's Message referring to our relations with Great Britain was referred to Mr. BANKS, and that portion referring to San Domingo to Judge ORTH." *New York Times*, Dec. 9, 1870.

On April 5, 1869, Edward Prince, Jr., Washington, D. C., had written to Banks. "Learning upon my arrival in this City, that the annexation of the Republic of Santo Domingo to the U. S. was under consideration in your Comtee, and having spent a month in that country during a recent tour through the West India Islands, I presume some statement, based on personal observation, may be of service. My intimate personal relations with President Baez, as well as with Messrs Gautier, Hungria & Delmonte all members of his Cabinet, including many other prominent Citizens of the State, fully justify me in stating that the one prevailing sentiment of the peop[le] from the highest to the lowest is in favor of immediat[e] annexation to the United States From personal observation I can assure your honorable Comtee that in point of mineral wealth agricultural and commercial resources, this country justly merits its exalted reputation—The advantage to our own Government, of possessing in those waters a central naval dépôt, is admitted by all and there can be no doubt that th[e] Bay of Samana possesses a harbor unexcelled throughout the world—" ALS, DNA, RG 59, Consular Despatches, Santo Domingo.

2. On Dec. 28, 1870, Orville E. Babcock wrote to Winslow Pierce, Indianapolis. "The President directs me to acknowledge the receipt of your letter enclosing your very able article on the acquisition of San Domingo, and to thank you for sending it to him." Copy, DLC-USG, II, 1.

On Dec. 31, Babcock wrote to Fish. "The President will be pleased to have you send him an official copy of a letter written by Col. Picket, when Consul at Turks Island some 25 years ago—on the subject of San Domingo. He will be pleased to receive it at as early a date as convenient." LS, DLC-Hamilton Fish. Fish endorsed this letter. "handed copy to President Jany 2" AE, *ibid.* On Sept. 22, 1846, John T. Pickett, consul, Turks Island, had written to Secretary of State James Buchanan promoting U.S. commercial relations with Santo Domingo and praising the political and social conditions of the Dominican Republic. ALS, DNA, RG 59, Consular Despatches, Turks and Caicos Islands.

On Jan. 3, 1871, a correspondent reported: "Hon. HORACE GREELEY arrived here this morning, and, after a long interview with the Postmaster General, accompanied that gentleman to the White House, where an interview was had with the President. Mr. GREELEY has latterly been here at the invitation of the President, and his mission now is understood to be to aid in the San Domingo movement." *New York Times*, Jan. 4, 1871. On Jan. 9, Horace Greeley published a card. "All I ever saw or heard of Gen. Grant assures me that he has too much sense to think of sending me to San Domingo. Thus far he has honored and gratified me by never suggesting to me that I could be more useful to the country, or to his Administration, in any other position than in that which I have filled for almost thirty years. At all events, I assure you that I never thought of going to San Domingo, and am not, I trust, wanted to go to San Domingo, and at all events I wont go to San Domingo." *Boston Transcript*, Jan. 9, 1871.

On Jan. 4, Speaker of the House James G. Blaine wrote. "I have been round to the White House since dinner to call on the President. He sent for me, and we had a frank chat on San Domingo. I will support the resolution of inquiry, but am against the final acquisition." Gail Hamilton, *Biography of James G. Blaine* (Norwich, Conn., 1895), p. 248.

To Edwin D. Morgan

HON. E. D. MORGAN,
NEW YORK.
DEAR SIR:

Mrs. Grant and I shall be happy to have you and Mrs. Morgan visit us on the thirtieth of January next and spend a week with us at the Executive Mansion. Washington will be very pleasant at that time and we shall endeavor by every means to contribute to your enjoyment.

Very truly yours
U. S. GRANT

EXECUTIVE MANSION
DEC 14 1870

LS, New York State Library, Albany, N. Y. See *New York Times*, Feb. 2, 1871.

On Nov. 11, 1870, Edwin D. Morgan, New York City, wrote to USG. "The Hon E. A. Rollins fought well for us against all the schemes and corruptions of Andy Johnson. You are aware that he offered to resign if Columbus Delano could be appointed. *This* Johnson declined. Now what I have to suggest is, that Rollins is a true man, and will be with us through evil report and through good [r]eport, and if some thing could be offered to him, It would shew that a Republican Administration is not ungrateful to its real friends: I do not name any particular office But I know Rollins to be an honest man," ALS, DLC-USG, IB.

On Sept. 25, 1868, William E. Chandler, New York City, wrote to "My dear General." "Your letter received. All looks well today Hamilton Fish has given us $5000—& several smaller subscriptions of 1000 & 2000 have come in all of which we are pouring rapidly into Indiana & Penn. Isn't Gen Dix' letter a good one. It states the case against against Seymour with terrible severity & truthfulness. The enclosed slip shows the character of the testimony fabricated by Johnson & Binkley against Rollins. It is perjured & infamous. And yet the are people who will believe it" ALS, USG 3. On Sept. 29, Adam Badeau, Galena, endorsed this letter. "Respy referred to J. R Jones Esq by A B" AE, *ibid.*

On March 6, 1869, Edward A. Rollins, commissioner of Internal Revenue, wrote to USG. "John M. Binckley was appointed solicitor in August last On the second day of the following month I requested his removal upon the ground that he was a wilful perjurer, or so weak and credulous as to make him the convenient tool of corrupt and malicious men. Not having changed my opinion of him since that time, I have assigned him no duty whatever, and for the last five months I do not know that he has even ostensibly done a single hour's labor for the Government. Meanwhile I have repeatedly urged his removal, and he has repeatedly drawn his monthly salary, at the rate of $4,000 per annum. Mr Binckley is notoriously unqualified for his place. I do not know that he even claims to be a lawyer; certain it is that he never undertook the practice of law, and the farce of his employment as Solicitor of Internal Revenue I do not believe should be continued under the present administration. The Acting Secretary of the Treasury, unadvised by you, may hesitate, perhaps, to change the officers of the department, in anticipation of the early appointment and qualification of its permanent Secretary, and I respectfully recommend, therefore, that you request him to dismiss Mr. Binckley immediately." *National Intelligencer*, March 9, 1869. For John M. Binckley's controversial investigation of fraud in collecting taxes on whiskey, see *HRC*, 40-3-3; *Biographical Encyclopedia of Illinois of the Nineteenth Century* (Philadelphia, 1875), pp. 304–5.

On April 1, Chandler, Washington, D. C., wrote to USG. "*Personal* . . . I have been endeavoring to see you for several days but am reluctant to intrude upon you when you are so pressed. My object is to suggest that it would be gratifying to Hon E. A. Rollins, to his friends and to the country if you should tender him the *Naval Office at Boston.* Mr. Rollins has had a hard time of it, has served the country and the Republican party faithfully; he goes out of office where he has controlled millions worth in all less than *ten thousand* dollars. Mr Rollins is undecided what disposition in life to make of himself. He ought to rest this summer; he will hardly himself, apply for government office. But I feel confident that you could not do a more gracious or appropriate act than to assure him that he can if he desires it now or at any time during the next few months be appointed to the Naval Office." ALS, DNA, RG 56, Naval Officer Appointments. On the same day, Badeau, Washington, D. C., wrote to Chandler. "I presented your letter to the President when he was alone, so that he had the chance to read it immediately." ALS, DLC-William E. Chandler. On Jan. 30, 1872, Secretary of the Interior Columbus Delano wrote to USG. "I omitted to speak to you this morning of the fact that Hon. E. A. Rollins, ex-Commissioner of Internal Revenue would be very much gratified to receive the appointment of one of the Com'r's from New Hampshire to the Centennial Anniversary of 1876." LS, Wayde Chrismer, Bel Air, Md. No appointments followed. See *PUSG*, 17, 553; Proclamation, April 29, 1871.

To John M. Langston

December 15, 1870

The bearer John M. Langston, Professor of Law in the Howard Institute, is a gentleman of liberal education and of high standing. He has much influence with the people of his own race, is a thorough republican and in full accord with the Administration. He is commended to all good people with whom he may come in contact while executing his inspection in the south.

U. S. GRANT

FOR PROF. JNO. M. LANGSTON.
HOWARD UNIVERSITY.

Copy, DLC-USG, II, 1. John M. Langston, born a slave in Va. (1829), grew up in Ohio, graduated from Oberlin College (1849), received a theology degree (1853), and practiced law. During the Civil War, he raised black troops, later served as inspector gen., Freedmen's Bureau (1868), and became dean of the law dept., Howard University (1869). On Dec. 13, 1870, Orville E. Babcock had written to Brig. Gen. Oliver O. Howard. "*Personal.* . . . The President directs me to write you and say that, he will be pleased to have you send Prof. Longston to Tenn, and Ark. to examine into and report upon the condition of the colored schools in those states, and any other information concerning the condition of the colored people, that may be of interest to the government." LS, DNA, RG 105, Letters Received. For USG's nomination of Langston to the D. C. Board of Health, see letter to Hannibal Hamlin, Feb. 21, 1871.

On Feb. 3, 1874, Secretary of War William W. Belknap wrote to USG. "I have the honor to report in answer to the communication referred to me, from Professor J. M. Langston and others endorsed by Senator Morton asking that a change be made in the Surgeonship of the Freedmen's Hospital, that I have learned from the Surgeon General that the appropriations for the support of the Freedmen's Hospital and Asylum were not made in the interest of the Howard University, nor is its right to selection and control of the officers of the Hospital at all recognized. The discontinuance of the Freedmens Bureau left the inmates of the Hospital the wards of the Government, and that the appropriations for its continuance under the charge of the War Department are considered temporary is clear by the prohibition of admission of additional cases at the expense of the appropriation. Clinical instruction at regular hours is as open as ever to the students of Howard University, but unauthorized and irregular visits by students to the wards, proving destructive to all discipline, and most annoying and injurious to the sick, was forbidden by order of the Surgeon General much to the relief and gratification of the inmates. This is not a question of preference or of race, or as between the interests of the Howard University and the Surgeon in charge, but one of the efficient and economical administration of a government trust, involving large appropriations, and the very best means to this end have been taken, as is proved by the large reduction in expenditure under its present admirable administration. The sale of a portion of the grounds now included in the Hospital, by the Howard University may make a change in its control desirable; but neither justice to the Government or to the Hospital and its inmates sanctions a change that would inure to the benefits of the University, at the expense of far greater interests. In connection with this subject I have also the honor to append the following extract from the report of the Surgeon General of November 29th last:—'Upon the discontinuance of the Freedmen's Bureau, certain aged and infirm people of color in a hospital controlled by the Freedmen's Bureau and Howard University had to be provided for, and to do this and at the same time disconnect the hospital from the Freedmen['s] Bureau and the Howard University, an Act was carefully framed looking to the ultimate discontinuance of this hospita[l] by requiring that no part of the Government appropriation should be expended for other than the inmates. The appointments regulations and orders now in force, as well as the system of accounts and expenditures all originated with the Surgeon General, and were approved by the Secretary of War to whom alone is he responsible for the proper execution of his duty. As has been stated in previous communications upon this subject, while Dr. Reyburn possesses peculiar qualifications for this position and has proven that by his able and economical administration, Dr. Purvis has no claim for any higher position than the one he now holds, and is without the necessary qualifications or experience for the position of Surgeon in charge.'" Copy, DNA, RG 107, Letters Sent.

On July 29, Langston, act. president, Howard University, *et al.* wrote to USG. "The undersigned Trustees of Howard University and friends of universal education, respectfully represent, that the interests of colored medical students and of the Medical Department of this University, absolutely require that they should have an opportunity for Clinical Instruction; that there is no Sanitary Institution in the city where colored students can be admitted for that instruction equally with white students, except the Freedman's Hospital; that the surgeon in charge of this Hospital (appointed by the War Department, and formerly a Professor in the Medical Department of this University), has left the University and joined a Medical school whose Faculty are *notoriously opposed* to granting *equal rights* to *colored Medical men*, and he has thus *transferred privileges, which naturally belong* to colored students, to those unfriendly; that the continuance of this will utterly destroy the usefulness of the Medical Department of this University, and break up the education of colored medical students in the City of Washington. We therefore respectfully ask that the President will if consistent with the interests of the country, secure through the Hon. Sec. of the Interior the assignment of officers to the Freedmans Hospital, who are in sympathy with the education of colored people, and friendly to this Institution; and that such assignment be made as soon as practicable." DS (10 signatures—including Frederick Douglass), *ibid.*, RG 48, Appointment Div., Letters Received.

To Schuyler Colfax

Washington D. C. Dec. 16th *1870*

DEAR SIR:

Mrs. Grant and myself accept with pleasure your invitation to dinner to-morrow at *5* p. m.

There is not one word of truth, so far as I know, in the rumors in regard to Mr. Boutwell. There is no man in or out of the Cabinet who has more fully my confidence than he has, and if he is not thoroughly satisfied he has consealed his feeling from me very successfully.

yours Truly
U. S. GRANT

HON. S. COLFAX VICE PRESIDENT

ALS, University of Rochester, Rochester, N. Y. For the rumor that Secretary of the Treasury George S. Boutwell would resign because of a disagreement with USG, see *New York Tribune*, Dec. 16, 1870.

To William Elrod

Washington D. C. Dec. 17th *1870*

DEAR ELROD:

You may strip the piece of land you spoke of next to Mr. Longs. Make in to rails all that is fit for it and the balance into cord wood; but do not sell any wood. I think in the Spring I will have a lime kiln[1] built and if so we will want all the wood we can get from the place. If I do not go to California in the Spring I will spend at least a week on the place and give definite directions as to improvements. Sixty bushels of lime to the acre would bring up the land more than all the stable manure that can be pu[t] on it.—I would not hawl grain to the mill to be ground for feed. The toll will amount to more than the a[d]vantage of feeding ground feed, besid[e]s the time consumed in hawling. If you had a few sows to follow your cows grain will go as far without grinding as with. The work of cleaning up undergrouth should go on as your hands have the spare time. How is the colt doing? He should be handled enough to keep him gintle. He is finely disposed and if there is any thing in pedigree or form he should be very fast. I do not want him tried however in the least until I have him put in the hands of a regular trainer.

Yours Truly
U. S. GRANT

ALS, Dorothy Elrod, Marissa, Ill. On Dec. 31, 1870, USG telegraphed to Charles W. Ford. "I withdraw my dispatch of yesterday. Please have Elrod stop change of road until I go to St Louis or write him definitely. . . . Please despatch immediately" Copy, DLC-USG, II, 5. On Jan. 21, 1871, William Elrod petitioned the St. Louis County Court for USG. "The undersigned begs leave to change the location of the 'Grant Road' slightly upon his own land and at his own expense, that is to say, begin at the Bridge at the Gravois Road, thence nearly on a strait line to the north bend of the Gravois Creek near my old Barn, intersecting a bend in the said Road thence from this point in nearly a strait line to the S. E. corner of H. L. Long's Meadow field, intersecting again said Road. The proposed route is shorter and on better ground than the present location." ADS, Highway Engineer, St. Louis County, Clayton, Mo. On May 28, 1874, USG signed an authorization. "I hereby accept the change of a portion of the 'Grant Road' over a portion of my Gravois Farm, as reported to the Saint Louis County Court, by Road Supt. A. Elbring, on the 18th day of May 1874, and now on file in office of Clerk of Saint Louis County Court." DS, *ibid.*

1. See letter to William Elrod, July 8, 1871.

Speech

[*Dec. 21, 1870*]

I cannot thank you appropriately for the honor you have done me in calling upon me this cold and blustering night, nor would I detain those out of doors to hear a speech. Knowing that you are to make calls at other places, upon gentlemen who no doubt will thank you in appropriate terms, I will only say that it has been my desire to see this great national capital built up in a manner worthy of a great and growing republic like ours. As to the removal of the capital, I think that is improbable in the extreme. Nor do I believe that the removal should be subject to a mere majority of the representatives of the people elected for a single term. I think the question of removal, if ever presented, should go through the same process at least as amendments to the Constitution, even if there be the Constitutional power to remove it, which is not settled. This language may seem rather unpopular for a person coming from the part of the country I do, but it is expressed with earnestness, nevertheless, and without reserve. Gentlemen, I thank you for your attention and kindness.

Washington Evening Star, Dec. 22, 1870. USG responded to a demonstration by Washington, D. C., firemen, Boys in Blue *et al.* O. D. Barrett also spoke, thanking USG "for his efforts to preserve the Union, and for his expressions of kindness toward the District, especially for having declared that the capital can be removed by no less a power than that required to erase an article from the Constitution." *Ibid.*

On Jan. 22, twelve leading citizens of D. C., including William W. Corcoran and John W. Forney, had called on USG expressing concern about efforts to relocate the nation's capital to the Mississippi Valley and requesting that significant improvements be made to public buildings and streets. "The President said he wished to see the now a great nation, and he thought our capital should be improved in a manner worthy of our national position. We have now some of the grandest public buildings in the world, and the business of the Government required several new Department structures. The country was now paying more rent for the use of private property in Washington for Government purposes than would pay the interest on the amount required to construct permanent and substantial buildings. Many of the structures now rented and occupied by the Government were unsuitable for the purposes used, and afford no protection against destruction by fire of the invaluable archives of the Government, which they contain. He thought the capital should be made attractive, and merit the just pride of the American people, while at the same time it would command the respect of the people of the old world visiting it. He did not think it proper that an appropriation for all of these improvements should be made at one time, but that substantial improvements should be made from year to year. . . . At the conclusion of the interview the President stated that he appreciated the disadvantages under which the citizens of the District labored, and that he would help them out to the full extent of his power." *Washington National Republican*, Jan. 24, 1870. On Jan. 24, the Washington Board of Aldermen and Board of Common Council resolved unanimously "That the thanks of these Boards are hereby tendered to his Excellency President Grant for the interest manifested by him during a recent interview with a number of our citizens concerning the perpetuity, prosperity, improvement, and adornment of this, the national capital; and that his Honor the Mayor be respectfully requested to forward a copy of the above resolutions to his Excellency." *Washington Chronicle*, Jan. 25, 1870. On Jan. 27, Mayor Sayles J. Bowen and Simon Wolf, recorder of deeds, met with USG to discuss D. C. problems. "The President replied that he did not know how it came, but the gentlemen who had seen him seemed to suppose that he would recommend to Congress that appropriations ought to be made for this city. Such had not been, nor was it his intention now. A recommendation of this character at present would be disregarded. Western members were specially tenacious in regard to this subject. Time and more information would soften the asperities of the moment. It had been his desire for years, and was his wish now, to see, before the close of his term of office, the capital take rank with the first in the world; to beauty, adorn, and improve it, so as to be a source of pride to the nation, worthy of our great achievements, and admiration to the foreigners visiting us. The year closing March 3 would show a great reduction of the public debt, and less taxation, and by that time Congress might see the necessity of improving our avenues, public buildings and other important public works; and he had no doubt the time would come when Cabinet Ministers would be furnished with houses free of rent by the Government. To suppose that men representing the nation could, on the pittance of eight thousand dollars a year, give grand dinners and receptions was simply ridiculous. . . . The President replied that he would take great pleasure in being the medium of transmitting such a letter to Congress, with such endorsement as he might deem proper and expedient; that he could not see why the Government, which owned half of the taxable property of the city, should be exempt from its due share of liability to adorn and embellish the capital, &c." *Washington National Republican*, Jan. 28, 1870.

On Jan. 1, 1871, Logan U. Reavis, St. Louis, wrote to USG. "... But it is not my object, Mr. President, to address you with analysis and criticism, but to vindicate against your opposition the cause of Capital-removal by systematic and irrefutable argument, ... Mr. President, having passed over the field of dis[sen]sion and presented to your mind an array of facts and arguments that are positively incontestable by any man and can only be ignored by a stolid stupidity at varia[nce] with the genius of our national progress and contine[ntal] greatness, I now insist that the immediate removal of the National Capital is demanded; the facts, as well as the enlightened judgment of the American people, decide that Washington is unfit to be the nation[al] metropolis of our Government, and the universal [con]viction that the removal of the Capital is only a ques[tion] of time, coupled with the fact that its present removal would not, in any possible way, adversely affect the general interest of the Government, but rather give it [new] life, argues incontrovertibly the wisdom of taking immediate steps for the removal to the grand Valley of the Mississippi. Every day of delay, Mr. President, in taking positive initiatory steps for the removal, so much the more st[alls] the Republic, retards the great mission of our people in their peaceful conquest of the Continent, and the complete organization of the Government into an imperial Republic of States. The mission of our people is sublime, why stand ye in the way? Why not move with our progress? Let us celebrate our hundredth anniversary with a new Capital, and the inauguration of the new Republic, whose all-embracing rule shall be the new liberty which this nation has given to mankind. ..." *New York Tribune*, Jan. 28, 1871. See L. U. Reavis, *A Change of National Empire; or Arguments in Favor of the Removal of the National Capital from Washington City to the Mississippi Valley* (St. Louis, 1869).

To Senate

TO THE SENATE OF THE UNITED STATES.

I nominate Robert C. Schenck,[1] of Ohio, to be Envoy Extraordinary and Minister Plenipotentiary of the United States, to Great Britain.

U. S. GRANT

WASHINGTON, 21 DECEMBER, 1870.

DS, DNA, RG 46, Nominations. On Dec. 2, 4, and 20, 1870, Secretary of State Hamilton Fish wrote in his diary. "Genl Schenck called this morning—as appeared when we parted, he called expecting me to 'pump him' on the subject of the British Mission—He says the President requested him to call—The President says he asked him if I had talked with him about it" "Genl Schenck dined with me—He is anxious to go to England hesitates on account of private & business considerations—is offereed the confidential Counsel-ship of the North Pacific RR (Jay Cookes) at a Salary of $20.000. & has some other employment in view, which will yield him an additional compensation: thinks these may be kept open for him, for a short time:—enquires whether the Alabama negotiations would be entrusted to him—is told that they will be committed to Any Minister enjoying the Confidence of the President—the present condition of this question is explained to him also Motleys course & the reason why they were taken out of Motleys charge—He evidently is very ambitious of the position—but (prudently) is considering the cost—He has been told by the President, & I repeat to him, that the place will not be offered to any one without knowing that it will be accepted—" "Dined at P. M. G—Cresswell—afterward drove the President to Judge Swayne, returning home, I enquired to what extent he was inclined to let Schenck take up the Alabama Claims—He replied that he was willing to give him the same instructions that had been originally given to Motley—I reminded him that Motley was instructed to say that the circumstances of the time seemed unfavorable to continue negotiations just then, but that he (the President) hoped the necessity for suspending them wd be of short duration—that now the British Govt had a right to expect that this Govt having rejected the Treaty, would indicate the time when the discussion should be resumed, & that it seemed to me adviseable to have the question settled—He assented, & said that he wished Schenck to take the question up & endeavor to effect a settlement—This is the first he has expressed such desire" DLC-Hamilton Fish. See *Washington Star*, Dec. 21, 28, 1870. On Dec. 9, a correspondent had reported from Washington, D. C. "The subject of the English mission is no longer in doubt. There is the highest authority for stating that the mission was formally tendered to Gen. Schenck, and that he has accepted it. . . . The President several weeks ago, during Gen. Schenck's visit to this city, asked him if he would accept the appointment, and it was only within a fortnight that he decided to accept, and he has so informed the President." *New York Tribune*, Dec. 10, 1870. On Jan. 5, 1871, USG wrote to Queen Victoria presenting Robert C. Schenck as minister to Great Britain. Copy, DNA, RG 84, Great Britain, Instructions.

On March 10, Schenck, Washington, D. C., wrote to USG. "I have the honor to recommend & request the appointment of Colonel William H. Chesebrough of New York to the place of Second Secretary of Legation at London. Col. Chesebrough was, for nearly three years during the war, on my staff, & with me, first as Aide de Camp & afterwards as Assistant Adjutant General, & I know him to be well qualified & adapted to the position. I would ask that his appointment may be made to take effect on the 1st of May 1871 vice Nadal, the present incumbent. He will not be prepared to accept the office before that date" ALS, *ibid.*, RG 59, Letters of Application and Recommendation. On April 20, William H. Chesebrough, New York City, wrote to USG. "It is with extreme regret, that I am compelled, on account of my business affairs, to decline the position of Assistant Secretary of the Legation of the United States at London to which I have been appointed by you and Confirmed by the Senate under date March 17 /71—" ALS, *ibid.*, Letters of Resignation and Declination.

On May 2, Schenck wrote to USG. "Colonel William H. Chesebrough having, to my regret, declined the position of Assistant Secretary of Legation at London, to which he was appointed & confirmed, I consider myself fortunate in being able to recommend & request the appointment of another gentleman whom I had thought of at first, & who is now willing to accept the office at once, & to accompany me to England as soon as I can proceed to my post. I refer to General Maxwell Woodhull of this city. I have known him all his life. He is a gentleman of fine qualities & attainments—Was on my staff during my service in the Army, & afterwards, & until the close of the War, successively Assistant Adjutant General of the Fifteenth Army Corps, & of the Army of the Tennessee—& has my entire confidence. I shall be gratified if Genl Woodhull can be appointed immediately, & his name sent to the ~~confirm~~Senate for confirmation as soon as that body convenes. In the mean time I can employ him officially & usefully here. Begging your immediate decision upon this recommendation & request, . . ." ALS, *ibid.*, Letters of Application and Recommendation.

On May 10, USG nominated Maxwell Woodhull as asst. secretary of legation, London.

On June 1, Secretary of War William W. Belknap wrote to Schenck, London. "You will remember that just prior to your departure for England, the Adjutant General spoke to you in my office concerning some papers belonging to the Department which it is supposed may be found among the Archives of the U. S. Legation in London. At the President's desire they were loaned to General Badeau, to aid in preparing his history of the War and he is believed to have had them in London while attached to the U. S. Legation, in 1869. As these papers are of great value and cannot be replaced, I request you will do me the favor to have a thorough search made for them, and if found, to have them shipped to my care. General Badeau has asked for the use of them again, being under the impression that he has returned them; but I prefer they should, if found, be sent to me when I can furnish him copies. A list of the missing papers is herewith enclosed." Copy, *ibid.*, RG 107, Letters Sent.

1. Schenck, born in Ohio in 1809, graduated from Miami University (1827), began to practice law in Dayton (1833), served as a Whig in the Ohio legislature (1839–43) and as U.S. representative (1843–51), then became minister to Brazil (1851–53). During the Civil War, he was a brig. gen. and maj. gen. of vols. before returning to Congress (1863–71) where he chaired the Committee on Ways and Means. See *PUSG*, 7, 396; *ibid.*, 10, 555; *ibid.*, 16, 12, 311–12; *ibid.*, 17, 11–12. On Jan. 9, 1871, Orville E. Babcock wrote to U.S. Representative Samuel Hooper of Mass. "The President desires me to acknowledge the receipt of the polite invitation to attend the complimentary dinner to Gen. Robt. C. Schenck, on the evening of the 11th. instant. He wishes me to say that he had already accepted an invitation to dine with Senator Edmunds upon that evening and therefore has to decline the pleasure it would afford him to be present at the dinner given to Gen. Schenck." Copy, DLC-USG, II, 1. On April 28, a note from the White House stated that "Mrs Grant requests the pleasure of Miss. Schenck's company this afternoon, to receive with her from three to five o'clock." AN, OFH.

To Hamilton Fish

Washington D. C. Dec. 21st *1870*

HON. H. FISH;
SEC. OF STATE:
DEAR SIR:

Will you be kind enough to call at the Executive office about 12 m to-day? Please also bring nomination of Mr. Patridge[1] for Peru and Mr. Antonio M. Soteldo for Venezuela with you, and we will then agree as to the propriety or impropriety of sending them in.

Yours Truly
U. S. GRANT

ALS, DLC-Hamilton Fish. On Dec. 5 and 21, 1870, Secretary of State Hamilton Fish recorded in his diary. "President says Davis Hatch has been naturalized as a Spanish-subject—that Babcock has a copy of his naturalization papers—wherein he renounces allegiance to the US. He also mentions that a person in the Employ of the NY Sun, has a memorandum shewing the various sums paid to C. A Dana, for his assaults upon him & me, & other parties—the levying of black Mail—&c—that on one occasion Articles were printed in the Sun, attacking Jim Fiske Jr & a copy was sent to Fisk, in the Evening before it was to have appeared, with a message that unless an arrangement was made the Edition of the following day wd contain~~ing~~ the Article—~~Fiske~~ Fiske replied telling them to 'go to H___L'—a large Edition was printed—but before its issue, at 3 or 4 o'clk in the morning Fiske drove to the Office of the Paper & paid five thousand dollars to suppress the Article—The Edition printed was destroyed—except one or two copies which this party has—Genl Ingalls & Mr Lamont have the matter in hand, & are, as I understand, the Presidents informants—The man is willing to disclose his evidence, but represents that it will implicate a number of persons, & that his life will not be safe in NY—Wants some temporary employment, to enable him to get away, for a time—He is a Venezuelan by birth—a naturalized Citizen" "Rcd a note from Prsdt—requesting me to call & bring nominations of Jas R Partridge as Envoy Ex'or to Peru, & Antonio M. Soteldo, for Venezuela—The latter name I had never heard—& did not know, or what, or whence, he is—Carried the nominations to the Prsdt—find that Soteldo is the person who has been engaged as an Assistant Editor of the N. Y. Sun, & is now making public certain disclosures relating to that Paper & its Editor—that he was one of its reporters in Washington last Winter—President in his note had ~~requested~~ expressed a desire to *consult* with regard to the nomination—Seeing him, he stated as a reason that Soteldo imagined himself in danger of violence, from some of the 'roughs' who may be instigated by the Parties who maybe exposed by his statements—hands me the recommendations in his favor—utterly insignificant—J. W. Husted (member of Assembly from Westchester) & Mr Munos y Castro—late Minister from Venezuela, (& not a *strong* endorser) & two or three others whose names I had never heard—I remonstrate against the appointment—that it will bring the whole Diplomatic appointments of the Govt—into disrepute & contempt—will be severely & justly criticised in the Senate—will be taxing his friends in the Senate too heavily to sustain it, under the opposition it must meet—that to appoint a man thus unknown, will be considered as the price paid for the disclosures which the man proposes to make (the Tribune of a day or two since contained a chapter of his forthcoming Pamphlet) & will be regarded as making the President responsible for, or at least as having paid for, the disclosures by this appointment—He admits the force of these objections—especially of the last—I further urge the fact of his being a Venezuelan as an objection to his being sent to Venezuela—President says Mr Lamont ('Greeleys friend') had urged his appointment—I think that Pleasanton, Ingalls, Babcock & Porter have also urged it—He expresses a wish to provide for him in some way—I suggest that some employment in the secret service of the Treasury will be the most adviseable, as not attracting attention—It is suggested that possibly he may be made Bearer of Dispatches—& I mention that the Naturalization Treaty with Austria will soon have to be sent to Vienna for Exchange—The appointment as Minister to Venezuela, at all events, seems abandoned—" *Ibid.* See *New York Tribune*, Dec. 19, 1870; *New York Times*, Feb. 10–12, 15, 1882. See also *The Biter Bit; or The Robert Macaire of Journalism. Being a Narrative of Some of the Black-Mailing Operations of Charles A. Dana's "Sun"* (Washington, D. C., 1870). On Dec. 17, 1870, James W.

Husted, N. Y. Assembly, had written to USG. "A. M. Soteldo Jr in whose behalf I write has done probably as good service with his Pen for the cause of good government and for the success of Republican Principles as any foreign man connected with the Press in this Country. Last winter at Albany he was outspoken in his denunciation of corruption—He is a man of marked ability of high social standing and of widely acknowledged influence—I sincerely trust his application to your Excellency may receive the most favorable consideration" ALS, DNA, RG 59, Letters of Application and Recommendation. Related papers, including a letter from Manuel Munos y Castro, former Venezuelan minister, to Fish, are *ibid.* See letter to John A. J. Creswell, June 20, 1871.

1. On March 18, 1869, John P. Kennedy, Baltimore, wrote to Fish. "I take great pleasure in introducing to your acquaintance and regard, my friend Mr James R. Partridge of this City, who must be already known to you as the Resident Minister of Our Government for some four or five years during Mr Lincoln's administration, in Salvador and Honduras in which posts he served the government with the full approbation of the Country. He had been before that distinguished in this State, as The Secretary of State under Governor Hicks. I need say nothing more to assure you of his entire fitness for a renewed appointment of the same character in the diplomatic service of South America, towards which he now looks with the hope of a favorable consideration by yourself and General Grant. He is anxious to obtain the post of Minister to The Argentine Republic—where his acquaintance with their public affairs, ~~and~~ his knowledge of the language of the country and his familiarity with the temper and character of their society, I am convinced would render him a most efficient and acceptable representative of our Country." ALS, DNA, RG 59, Letters of Application and Recommendation. Related papers are *ibid.* On March 25, Thomas N. Stillwell, Anderson, Ind., telegraphed to USG. "Would be Complimented by my name sent in as U S Minister Venzula as the Committee on foreign Relations unanimously Recommended my Confirmation to the position I held will if nominated & Confirmed Resign, Refer to senators Morton & Pratt." Telegram received, *ibid.* On Dec. 18, 1868, President Andrew Johnson had nominated Stillwell as minister to Venezuela; the Senate tabled his nomination on March 3, 1869. On April 12, USG nominated James R. Partridge as minister to Nicaragua, then withdrew the nomination; the next day, USG nominated Partridge as minister to Venezuela. On May 18, 1871, USG nominated Partridge as minister to Brazil. See telegram to John W. Forney, March 22, 1871, note 1.

To George W. Dent

Washington D. C. Dec. 21st *1870*

DEAR DENT:

In paying taxes on the Carondelet property, or that portion of it which I compromised for, I paid for the portion belonging to Mr. Holliday. The whole amount was $183 69 of which his proportion would probably be about $35 00 though I cannot figure out the exact amount. I wish he would either buy from me or sell his, or give me a power of Atty. to dispose of his interest in case the suit before the Supreme Court goes in his favor.

Yours Truly
U. S. GRANT

ALS (facsimile), USGA. See *PUSG*, 19, 228–29; letter to Charles W. Ford, Feb. 2, 1871.

To John M. Thayer

Washington, D. C. Dec 22d *18~~6~~*70

DEAR SENATOR:

I regret to hear that in the Senatorial contest about to take place in Neb. the argument is used against you that, in consequence of differences between yourself and your colleague, your standing and influence with the administration is impaired.

Such is not the case. Our acquaintance commenced in the field and has continued through the whole of your senatorial term, so far, with always the best of feeling towards you personally and politically. I have always had your support in my present trying place as I had your support on the battle field.

I must disclaim any desire to suggest to a republican legislature what republican shall be elected to the United States Senate. Whoever may be the choice of a republican legislature I shall hope to be supported by him.[1] But it is due to you, who have been a personal and political friend, to say that, to have proper weight with the Executive, it is not necessary that you ~~must~~ be in harmony with your colleague, who has been very consistent in opposing an administration elected by the same constituency as himself.

I do not write this for publication, and shall regret seeing it published, but do write it as a contradiction to grounds I have heard are being urged against your reelection, and so that you can authoritatively deny such statements.

Very Truly Yours
U. S. GRANT

HON. J. M. THAYER U. S. S.

ALS (incomplete facsimile), Gerard A. J. Stodolski, Inc., Catalogue 2, Dec., 1992, no. 147; copy, USG 3. A former brig. gen., U.S. Senator John M. Thayer of Neb. had been elected in 1867. See *PUSG*, 2, 21; *ibid.*, 5, 185; *ibid.*, 9, 123–25; *ibid.*, 16, 475; Earl G. Curtis, "John Milton Thayer," *Nebraska History*, XXIX, 1 (March, 1948), 64–65.

On Oct. 17, 1870, Thayer had written to USG concerning the election in Neb. and the activities of Mr. Lipton [U.S. Senator Thomas W. Tipton of Neb.?]. The Scholar Gypsy, Ltd., Catalogue 6 [1979], no. 362. On Dec. 29, Thayer, Omaha, telegraphed to USG. "I want ten days leave from Jany fifth for Gov Burbank of Dakota to go to Lincoln to assist me Please telegraph leave to me I must have him there" Telegram received (on Dec. 30, 2:00 A.M.), DNA, RG 59, Dakota Territorial Papers. On Dec. 30, Orville E. Babcock wrote to Secretary of State Hamilton Fish. "The President directs me to say that he has no objection to the granting of the 'leave.'" LS, *ibid.*

1. On Jan. 18, 1871, Phineas W. Hitchcock was elected to replace Thayer. See *New York Times*, Jan. 24, 1871. On March 25, 1869, Thayer had written to USG. "I most earnestly ask for the following appointments: Gen Robert R. Livingston of Nebraska, to be Surveyor General of Nebraska and Iowa, in place of P. W. Hitchcock, who has been a *thorough Johnson man.* Further more, Hitchcock has been absent from his office more than two thirds of his time since he was appointed by Johnson, two years ago. This I know to be literally true, of my own knowledge. Gen Livingston was Captain in the First Nebraska at Fort Donelson, and Pittsburg Landing, and became its Colonel when I became Brigadier General, and served throughout the war. He is thoroughly competent, and honest. His application is on file with the Secretary of the Interior. *John B. Furay* to be U. S. Marshal for *Nebraska*, in place of C. E. Yost. Yost has been a Johnson man. Furay served gallantly in the Union army in the late war. Yost did not. He is entirely comptent and honest. His application is filed with the Attorney General. Col. *Robert W. Furnas*, to be Superintendent of Indian offairs for the Northern Superintendency located at Omaha, Nebraska, in place of H. B. Denman, a democrat, who made speeches in our state last fall in support of Seymour and Blair, The Superintendency embraces only the state of Nebraska. Col Furnas is wellfitted for the position, strictly upright. He served creditably in the late war. His application is on file with the Secretary of the Interior. These appointments are of the most *vital importance to me politically.*" ALS, OFH. On April 7, USG nominated Robert R. Livingston as surveyor gen., District of Neb. and Iowa.

On March 20, Tipton wrote to USG. "I hereby recommend the appointment of J. T. Hoile of Neb. to the office of Marshal for that state. Mr Hoile is a man of good ability, fidelity, and moral standing. Often Elected to the Legislature he is known and trusted by the people; and his appointment would give very general satisfaction." ALS, DNA, RG 60, Records Relating to Appointments. On April 30, Thayer wrote to USG. "Mr Tipton has recommended Joseph T. Hoile for Marshall of Nebraska. I have recommended said Hoile for Collector of Internal Revenue, as there ought to be a change in that office. He (Hoile) can thus be provided for. The Governor of the state, Mr Taffe, (my colleague in the House,) and myself earnestly ask for the appointment of John B. Furay as Marshall. He was a soldier in the late war. The present incumbent was not. He Secured his present appointment by being a Johnson man." ALS, *ibid.* Related papers are *ibid.* On Dec. 6, USG nominated Joseph T. Hoile as marshal, Neb. On April 4, 1871, Hitchcock and U.S. Representative John Taffe of Neb. wrote to USG. "We beg respectfully to recommend George P. Tucker Esq. for appointment as United States Marshal of Nebraska—Mr. T—was one of the first settlers of the State—was one of the earliest and has always been one of the most active of our Republicans—We believe he would make a competent and popular officer—" LS, *ibid.* On May 15, Judge Elmer S. Dundy, U.S. District Court, Omaha, telegraphed to USG. "Cannot mr Hoile be retained as U. S. Marshall for Nebraska Hoile is a sound Republican and a first rate marshal I should deeply regret his removal." Telegram received (at 4:42 P.M.), *ibid.* On Feb. 19, 1872, USG nominated George P. Tucker as receiver, Lincoln, Neb., and, on April 15, nominated William Daily as marshal, Neb.

To John M. Thayer

Washington D. C. Dec. 22d *1870*

DEAR SENATOR:

It would have afforded me much pleasure to have nominated Gen. Strickland for Govr of Idaho[1] had you mentioned his name in connection with that office before the nomination of another had been made.

Yours Truly
U. S. GRANT

HON. J. M. THAYER U. S. S.

ALS, Abraham Lincoln Book Shop, Chicago, Ill. On Nov. 28, 1870, U.S. Senator John M. Thayer of Neb., Omaha, had written to USG. "I find that I cannot reach Washington till the 10th inst. I respectfully request that you will not send in the nomination of Governor of *Utah* till I can see you." ALS, OFH. On Dec. 21, Thayer, Washington, D. C., wrote to USG. "I have known Gen. S. A. Strickland for fifteen years. I know him to be a man of *strict integrity*. He is a bold, positive man. He is admirably adapted for the Govership of Utah. He will carry out your policy and execute the laws. He served through the whole war, was Brigade Was with me at Donaldson and Pittsburg Landing, was all through the Atlanta campaign, and then with Scofield at Franklin and Nashville. He was chairman of the Nebraska delegation at the Chicago convention. I would not ask his appointment if I did not know ~~he~~ it would be a good one." ALS, DNA, RG 59, Letters of Application and Recommendation. Related papers are *ibid.* On Jan. 12, 1871, USG nominated Silas A. Strickland, former col., 50th Ohio, as governor, Utah Territory. On Jan. 23, USG withdrew Strickland's name and nominated George L. Woods.

On May 18, 1869, Governor Charles Durkee of Utah Territory and fourteen others telegraphed to USG. "C. C. Clements is trustworthy and efficient. The people wish him retained as Register of Land Office for Utah." Telegram received (at 7:45 P.M.), *ibid.*, RG 107, Telegrams Collected (Bound). On Dec. 6, USG nominated Courtland C. Clements as surveyor gen. and George R. Maxwell as register, Land Office, Utah Territory. On July 21, Durkee wrote to USG. "In reply to your letter of the 15th inst in relation to the sentence passed upon Branigan for murder, I have to state that the Supreme Court have this day reversed the decision of the Court below, and sent the case back for a new trial. Should future events in his further examination make it necessary to act agreeably to your suggestion, rest assured I shall be pleased to do so." ALS, *ibid.*, RG 60, Letters from the President. On July 15, USG had granted a reprieve until Oct. 1 for Thomas Branigan, convicted of murder. Copy, *ibid.*, RG 59, General Records. See *Deseret Evening News*, May 4, June 7, July 23, Oct. 8, 15, 1869; *Pacific Reporter*, 24 (July 3-Dec. 4, 1890), 767–71.

On March 16, J. Wilson Shaffer, Washington, D. C., had written to USG. "In view of the fact that both my own and Mrs Shaffers health is so very poor I most earnestly ask that you appoint me minister to Switzerland. I mention this position because it has been strongly recomended on account of the climate and then too the salery is sufficient to support me and educate my children there This is the first time in my life that I have asked for an appointment and would not do it now had I the means to do what I feel is of such vitel importence to both myself & Wife. Should this position have passed beyond your control some one eaquelly accepteble may suggest itsef to your mind and while I desire above all things the position I ask for I leave the matter to your own good judgemnt to do what seems best" ALS, DNA, RG 59, Letters of Application and Recommendation. On Dec. 16, USG nominated Shaffer as governor, Utah Territory. On April 10, Thomas L. Kane, Washington, D. C., had written to USG. "The Senators of Pennsylvania will recommend you to appoint me Governor of Utah Territory. My reasons for desiring this place I ask permission to impart to you personally. They are of sufficient importance, I think, to justify me in soliciting you to place me in communication with an Officer of your Staff or a confidential friend, instructed by you to report if you are called upon to notice my request farther." ALS, *ibid.* On April 15, Morton McMichael, publisher, *North American and United States Gazette*, Philadelphia, wrote to USG. "Gen: T. K. Kane has been presented to you in connection with the Governorship of Utah. I respectfully recommend his appointment. Though belonging to a family which, both before & during the war, was intensely democratic, his own convictions always on the side of freedom, led him to join the Republican organization of which he became an active & conspicuous member. He fought gallantly in the field until disabled by a [severe] wound, & has since contributed both by his voice & pen to the success of the great principles which triumphed in your election. Gen: Kane is highly cultivated, has ample attainments & is a thorough gentleman." ALS, *ibid.* Related papers are *ibid.*

On March 17, William Bross, publisher, *Chicago Tribune*, wrote to Orville E. Babcock. "I have a letter from Gen P. E. Conner stating that he will be a candidate for Gov. of Utah. I send the inclosed to you, begging the favor that at the proper time you will bring the matter personally to the attention of the President. Gen Conner is in my judgement specially adapted to solve the mormon question. If his papers (application &c) have not arrived, please if possible keep the matter in abeyance till they do. With kind regards to your excellent wife, & to Col Campbell & wife & *much love* to *Miss Jessie* . . ." ALS, *ibid.* On the same day, Bross wrote to USG. "I beg leave earnestly to recommend Gen. P. E. Conner, of Stockton Utah for the office of Governor of that Territory. When Vice. Prest. Colfax & his party crossed the continent in '65 we saw much of Gen. Conner & learned more of his efficient, wise, and able management of the Mormons while in command at Salt Lake City. I fully believe he will peaceably & surely solve the knotty Mormon question, if appointed, during his administration. Of all men I believe him best fitted for this particular duty." ALS, *ibid.* On Aug. 18, Vice President Schuyler Colfax, San Francisco, wrote to USG. "I hope, ere this, you have seen some of our public men who visited Salt Lake, on the way out here, & have returned East, such as Trumbull, Kelly & others. They all concur in the belief that the golden moment has arrived for the appointment of Gen. P. E. Conner as Governor of Utah. I learn that the U. S. officers there concur in this, as the Gentiles there do. A schism, led by the young Smith's who are for obedience to the law, ags't Polygamy, & for loyalty to the U. S., is widening beneficently, & will be more potential for the Right if they have a firm Governor to sustain & protect them. I understand further that Gov. Durkee offered to resign in Conner's favor last winter, but Gen. C. did not wish to accept it from Mr. Johnson." ALS, *ibid.* Related papers are *ibid.* See *PUSG*, 15, 457; *ibid.*, 16, 174–77.

On Feb. 12, 1870, Shaffer wrote to USG. "In the event of the rejection by the Senate of Joseph M Orr as marshel of Utah I would esteem it a great personel favor to myself to have Col M T Paterick of Nebraska appointed marshel of that Teritory I ask this knowing Col Paterick intimately and feeling the necessity of having men about me that I can rely upon which of course you can fully appreciate" ALS, DNA, RG 60, Records Relating to Appointments. Related papers are *ibid.* On Sept. 4, 1869, Cyrus M. Hawley, associate justice, Utah Territory, had written to USG. "J. M Orr Esqr of this City is an applicant for the office of U. S. Marshall for this Territory. From my acquantance with him for three months past I regard him in all respects fitted for the position. He is a Republican, and a '*gentile*', & will make an efficient officer. The public *interests* require a new marshall in this Territory: & his appointment would give Satisfaction to the *loyal* people here—" ALS, *ibid.* On Dec. 6, USG nominated Joseph M. Orr as marshal, Utah Territory, withdrew his name on April 1, 1870, and nominated Mathewson T. Patrick.

On May 24, USG nominated Charles C. Crowe as secretary, Utah Territory, to replace Samuel A. Mann. On March 13, 1869, U.S. Senator George E. Spencer of Ala. had written to USG. "Yesterday in conversation with me you stated that you could not give my friend Col Crowe of Alabama the Governorship of Wyoming but would be glad to give him one of the other Territories, I filed with the Hon E B Washburn, Secretary of State several days ago an application for Col, Crowe recommended strongly by all the Senators and most of the Representatives of the reconstructed States and others, Col, Crowe is one of the most accomplished gentlemen, and gifted Orators of the South, and possesses admirable executive qualities, He was in the Confederate Army, but as soon as the surrender took place, accepted the situation, and has been, and is as thorough a Republican as there is in the whole country, To his exertions more than any other man is due the result of the election in November in Alabama in favor of the Republican party, he having canvassed the entire State, as Elector at large on the Republican ticket. I would suggest that his application be changed to *Arizona* or any one of the other Territories where a vacancy exists. I most sincerely hope that Col, Crowe's claims will not be forgotten." LS, *ibid.*, RG 59, Letters of Application and Recommendation. On March 30, Crowe, Washington, D. C., wrote to Secretary of War John A. Rawlins. "Should the President honor me with an appointment to a Territorial Governorship, I would be glad and grateful if New Mexico were assigned me. I wish the appointment not for political purposes; not to make the Territory a mere way-station on the road to Congress;—but to make it a permanent home for myself & my family; so that, thoroughly identified with all its interests, I may devote my time and energies to developing it's resources, to building it up,—making it a pleasant & prosperous country, & inviting to American emigration. Arizona offers no social or educational advantages, New Mexico does. And to speak frankly, as all men should, I am not able pecuniarily to carry my family to Arizona. A distinguished physician of the City advises me that New Mexico has the only climate on the Continent that will restore my shattered lungs. Under these circumstances, Gen'l, you will add to the weight of lasting obligation which your kindly interest in my promotion has already imposed upon me, if you will press my appointment to New Mexico in preference to any other Territory" ALS, *ibid.* Related papers are *ibid.* On April 3, USG nominated Crowe as governor, New Mexico Territory. On Feb. 8, 1870, USG nominated Crowe as register, Land Office, Wyoming Territory. On June 20, U.S. Senators William M. Stewart and James W. Nye of Nev. wrote to USG. "Mr C C Crowe recently appointed and confirmed Secty of the Territory of Utah having suddenly deceased, we request and reccomend that no other appointment be made in his place but that Hon S A Mann the present incumbent, appointed by you from Nevada in April last, be left undisturbed" LS, *ibid.*

On July 7, Shaffer wrote to USG. "I most respectfully request that you again appoint a successor to Hon S. A. Mann, our Secy. of State. Our best lawyers here are of the opinion that the office is vacant, and all official acts performed by Mr. Mann are void. Whether this be true or not, I, of course, am not a judge, but as matters now stand, it will be obvious to you that a change in the office is essential to our perfect harmony of action here. Since my return to Utah I have began to do what I intended doing previous to my being summoned home. A few ~~days~~ days ago I appointed new Commissioners for the Penitentiary, and will this week appoint a Warden, and will continue to fill all the Territorial offices, that the organic act provides shall be appointed by the Governor as fast as I can find good and well qualified men for the places. I presume the present incumbents (although illegally elected) will refuse to surrender their positions to my appointees; hence the necessity of Justice McKanes' being here as soon as possible, as he will preside over this (Salt Lake) Judicial District. If the present officers will not give up; writs of quo-warranto will have to be issued by Judge McKane. I am determined, as far as the law will support me, to clean this 'Augean Stable'. During my first few weeks here, keeping quiet, and doing substantially nothing that would interfere in any way with Mormons or Mormon officers, (to the end that I might fully understand the situation of affairs and study the law before I acted) I received nothing but opposition, neglect and abuse from them, but since I have began to act, and give them fully to understand, that what few laws we have got, shall be executed, they have treated me with *extreme* consideration and politeness. Brigham Young clearly is beginning to feel that we have a President and a Government. I earnestly hope that Congress, if it can do no more for us this session, will at least, give loyal citizens of this Territory a chance to select our jurors. As the law now stands the Mormons have entire control, and a verdict in favor of the Government or a Gentile cannot be had. Thanking you most kindly for the manner in which you have sustained me here, . . ." LS, *ibid.* A petition of May 7 from Orr *et al.*, Salt Lake City, to USG requesting the removal of Mann and Charles C. Wilson, chief justice, Utah Territory, is *ibid.* See letter to Amos T. Akerman, June 2, 1871.

On July 11, 1870, USG nominated Vernon H. Vaughn as secretary, Utah Territory. On Oct. 31, Vaughn telegraphed to USG announcing Shaffer's death. Telegram received, DNA, RG 59, Utah Territorial Papers. On the same day, James B. McKean, chief justice, Obed F. Strickland, associate justice, Utah Territory, and Hawley, Salt Lake City, telegraphed to USG. "Governor Shaffer is dead we send important facts by mail" Telegram received (at 9:27 P.M.), ICarbS. On Dec. 1, Toussaint Mesplié, "Roman Cath Priest," Salt Lake City, wrote to USG. "You will, I hope, pardon the liberty that I now take: I am almost irresistably constrained to write you this letter.

You may have forgotten me, and probably the exciting, and may I not say, the terrible events through which you have passed since we met, have been sufficient to blot me from your memory. I well remember our pleasant and to me agreable meeting at Fort Vancouver, W. Terr. in 1849 or 1849; and also at Fort Astoria, the same year. I am also well acquainted with General Sheridan, and well known to your brother in Law, General Dent whom I last met at Walla Walla W. Terr. Having been in the Territories since 1846, may I not say that I am a territorial man. I am at least deeply interested in all that partains to any of them; Especially am I now interested in Utah, with many others, For utah is in state of transition, and constitutes one of the difficulties of your administration. Therefore it is that I now write, and for the sake of justice and truth. For myself and many others, I now thank you for having appointed Gov. Vaughan. You all about the Morman people and the difficulties here. You could not have appointed a better man than Gov. Vaughan to solve the difficulties. This afternoon, I met gentlemen, (men of wealth and influence, but silent; men that will not speak) that told me that effords were being made to enduce your Excellency to remove Gov. Vaughan They are deeply interested in the welfare of the Territory and ~~not~~ do not want him removed. Nothing that is said about him of a damaging character is true. A Morman band serenaded him and made a great many men made; G. Vaughan could not help it; he told the Morman band that they had taken the wrong time to serenade him. Being an ardent friend of yours, he, when Secretary, had a warm dispute with one of the officials that wants Gen. Logan for the next President; and that official is opposed to Gov. Vaughan I have thoroughly investigated every charge againts Gov. Vaughan, and they are only pretences growing out of selfish motives. Gov. Vaughan is the firts Governor that the Territory ever had that not controle by others; he discretly keeps his plans to himself, and rebukes any intruder. an intuitive discoverer of character; with agreable and fascinating manners; energetic, determined, courageous, and possessing powerfull executive ability; capable of graspling with anything, or fighting againts any odds; he is proven preeminently the man to governe the people of Utah Territory and a better selection never can be made. I plead my deep interest in the welfare of the Territory for my enthusiasm in behalf of Gov. Vaughan, and earnestly ask you and the Senate to retain him in his present position until the Morman difficulties are fully settled. In the hope that my petitions will be taken into consideration, . . ." ALS, DNA, RG 59, Letters of Application and Recommendation. On Dec. 2, William S. Godbe, publisher, *Salt Lake Tribune, et al.*, wrote to USG. "Hearing that efforts are being made to prevent the confirmation of Mr Vernon H. Vaughan as Governor of this Territory, we desire to state that in our opinion his rejection would be very undesirable from the fact that he is already practically engaged in grappling with the difficulties of the situation, and the confirmation of a new appointee could but add to the intricacies attending the solution of matters here. From all we have learned of Mr Vaughan's spirit and course, we conceive that he will maintain the supremacy of the Government with firmness and moderation, and be found equal to the situation." DS (3 signatures), *ibid.* On Dec. 5, Mason Brayman, editor, *Illinois State Journal*, Washington, D. C., wrote to USG. "I have the honor to request appointment to the office of *Governor* of the Territory of *Utah*, recently made vacant by the decease of Hon. Wilson Shaeffer." ALS, *ibid.* A letter recommending William M. Fliess for governor of Utah Territory is *ibid.* On Dec. 9, a correspondent reported from Washington, D. C. "Several members of Congress called upon the President today to protest against the appointment of Vaughn as Governor of Utah. They have information direct from the Territory that he is working in the interest of Brigham Young, and that he is a man of dissipated habits. The appointment of a man like Representative

Cullom of Illinois, whose sentiments concerning polygamy are well known, is absolutely necessary to carry out the reforms already inaugurated. . . ." *Boston Transcript*, Dec. 9, 1870. On Jan. 16, 1871, USG nominated George A. Black to replace Vaughn as secretary.

On Jan. 10, McKean wrote to USG. "Major C. H. Hempstead, U. S. Attorney for this Territory, is now absent from this city and is in attendance upon a term of the First District Court at Provo, where Justice Strickland is presiding. But I have been shown a letter addressed to Mr. Hempstead by the acting Attorney General, conveying to him your Exclleny's appreciation of his services, and your earnest request that he withdraw his tendered resignation and continue in the office which he now holds. Mr. President, you have done Major Hempstead no more than justice by the high compliment which you have paid him; and I trust that for a time, at least, he will accede to your request. He is a studious and learned counselor, an eloquent advocate, and an honorable man;—one who knows how to do his duty in a gentlemanly manner without unnecessary asperity. Such qualities are of great importance, nay, they are indispensable, *just now*, in the office of U. S. Attorney of Utah. May I explain why *I* feel a deep interest in this matter? As a member of the Supreme Court I preside over the whole Territory, but as Judge of the Third District Court I preside, without my associates, but with a Grand and a Petit Jury, in the District in which forty nine fiftieths of all the litigation in the Territory originates. Mr. President, I cannot, I absolutely cannot enforce the laws without a prosecuting attorney of a high order of ability, industry, and integrity. And yet, Sir, this great government pays a U. S. Attorney for Utah a salary of *two hundred and fifty dollars*! In causes in which the United States are a party he is allowed fees in addition; but as there are almost no causes of that kind, *practically* his salary is $250. per annum. I have found it to be my duty to render a decision turning the Mormon 'Attorney General' out of court, and throwing all the crimical prosecutions into the hands of the U. S. Attorney. This adds ten-fold to the duties and labors of the latter officer, but nothing to his compensation. Should your Excellency see fit to call the attention of congress, or of the proper committees to this matter, and should congress, during its present session, provide for paying the U. S. Attorney of Utah a salary of $3.000. or at least $2.500. per annum, I shall allow myself to hope that Maj. Hempstead will yield to your request, and withdraw his resignation. But if something of this kind is not done, I greatly fear that no *capable* and *trustworthy* man can be induced to hold the office;—and without such a man in that office, I should despair of satisfactorily discharging the duties of mine." ALS, OFH. On Sept. 1, Attorney Gen. Amos T. Akerman wrote to Secretary of State Hamilton Fish. "I am directed by the President to request you to issue a Commission appointing J. H. Wickizer to the office of Attorney of the United States for Utah Territory, in place of C. H. Hempstead, resigned." Copy, DNA, RG 60, Letters Sent to Executive Officers. On Oct. 9, John H. Wickizer, Salt Lake City, wrote to Akerman declining the appointment: ". . . I respectfully ask permission to add the following, in explanation. I persistently objected to the appointment of the Atty-ship. But by the *importunity* of the Governor and Judges of the Territory I finally consented upon the express condition, that the P O Dept. should be perfectly willing I should hold the Attyship concurrently with the spl. Agency of P O Dept. That Department—very properly I think, is unwilling. I feel *unable* to resign the spl. Agency, and accept the salary of the Attyship. But there is a much graver reason than *this*, why I *should* refuse to accept it. The responsibility of the U. S. Atty for Utah, just at *this* time, is much greater than that of any other Territory or State in the Republic. The sympathy of the great mass of the people here, is *with* the parties to be prosecuted. Ninety thousand ignorant and fanatical people have been moulded into a Theocracy inimical *to*, and in direct conflict *with*, the Government and Laws of the U. S. and of Christian civilization. They *honestly* believe their leader to be the vice regent of God on earth, Hence the trial of Brigham Young, is not simply the trial of one man, but the trial of a Theocracy, numbering ninety thousand, ignorant, but *honest* Religious fanatics, Hence, the Pros. Atty, should know *all* things, human and divine as it were. He should know all Law, Religion and Politics All History, Mythology, Logic, Rhetoric and the human heart—And should have a grace of style and suavity of manner, as to charm and convince Hence it requires the best talent of the Nation, to prevent possible or even probable bloodshed, The Prosecutor who fills the bill perfectly, will be immortal, for, the civilized world will read the legal proceedings Therefore, were I at perfect liberty to accept the position, I should feel inability to perform the duties, as I am *impressed* they should be [performed.] Pardon this *long* dissertation, but, thus much I deemed it proper to say in relation to the situation here, and of the necessary accomplishments of the U. S. Atty for Utah" ALS, *ibid.*, Letters Received, Utah. On the same day, McKean wrote to USG. "Pardon me for writing you again so soon. I cannot well avoid it. When Mr. Hempstead persisted in his determination to resign the office of U. S. Attorney for this Territory, we saw the necessity of his being succeeded by some one now here and familiar with the situation. *Col. John H. Wickizer*, a man of superior talents, formerly a successful lawyer in Illinois, and now the Special Agent of the Post Office Department, was therefore recommended. He consented to serve for a time if it did not involve the resignation of his Postal Agency. Your Excellency appointed him. An assistant was necessary, and I appointed *George R. Maxwell*, the Register of the Land Office. Both these gentlemen were willing to serve the public in these positions for some months, without any regard to compensation. You are informed, Sir, of the great progress that we have lately made. But now comes an order from the Post Office Department forbidding Wickizer, and another from the Land Office forbidding Maxwell, to act as a public prosecutor unless he resigns his other position,—and this, Sir, right on the eve of the trial of important indictments. I am sure I shall be pardoned if the conviction is slowly but surely forcing itself upon me, that the obstacles constantly rising up before me, are too great for me to surmount. The most discouraging of all obstacles is the fact, that so many government officials, outside of Utah, utterly fail to appreciate the situation here. I cannot now see any way but to adjourn my court. But I shall try to act with as much deliberation as the circumstances will permit." ALS, *ibid.* See letter to John P. Newman, Nov. 6, 1871.

1. See Endorsement, Feb. 6, 1871.

Endorsement

[*Dec. 31, 1870*]

I would make no change now. If meritorious officers are left out they may get back to fill vacancies occuring, in their grade, during the year for which they receive pay.

U. S. G.

AE (initialed), DNA, RG 94, ACP, K93 CB 1863. Written below an undated note from Gen. William T. Sherman to USG. "Please look over the enclosed, and write your decision—Edie is to me a stranger, and this is the *last* day." ANS, *ibid.* On Dec. 31, 1870, Sherman had written to Secretary of War William W. Belknap. "Excuse my intruding on you at this momt—Lt Col Edie is here—He is the only Lt Col left out, unprovided for He has served continuously since 1861—and was with us at Atlanta & Jonesboro—By accepting Stevensons resignation, & promoting a Lt Col we can retain Edie. Are you willing—" ALS, *ibid.* In an undated note, Belknap wrote to Sherman. "I have accepted Stevesons resignation this morning & have arranged as to the promotions thereby occurring. Col. Mack has the list & left here a few moments ago. As to Edie I have heard so much against him that I do not like to retain him. Carlin spoke to me about his conduct at Jonesboro, which was very *un*favorable—However I leave the matter to you & the President. If any change is made see Mack & correct his list. But I cannot conceal my unfavorable opinion as to Edie" AN (initialed), *ibid.* Related papers are *ibid.* Born in Pa., John R. Edie entered USMA in 1828, did not graduate, but served in the Civil War as capt. and maj., 15th Inf., and lt. col., 8th Inf., receiving bvt. promotions for service at Missionary Ridge and Jonesboro, Ga. See *PUSG*, 6, 207.

On Feb. 11, Attorney Gen. Amos T. Akerman wrote to Belknap interpreting Edie's case under the Army Bill enacted July 15, 1870: ". . . On the 31st day of December 1870, Colonel John D. Stevenson of the 25th Infantry, was, at his own request, by the direction of the President, honorably discharged from the service of the United States, said discharge to take effect January 1st 1871. This discharge was in pursuance of section 3 of said act. Lieutenant Colonel Edie insists that he was entitled to the vacancy thus created by the resignation of Colonel Stevenson. He was not so promoted to Colonel Stevenson's place, but on the 2nd of January 1871. was honorably mustered out of the service under the provisions of said section 12. There can be no question that on the 1st day of January Lieutenant Colonel Edie was a supernumerary officer, and that if he then possessed the proper rank, seniority, and fitness, he would have had a valid claim to promotion to a vacancy which had occurred prior to that day. I do not think that he had any just claim to a vacancy which did not begin to exist until that day. Colonel Stevenson's resignation took effect on that day. . . . I am, therefore, of opinion that Lieutenant Colonel Edie was not lawfully entitled to the place made vacant by the resignation of Colonel Stevenson, and that he was lawfully mustered out of service by the order of January 2. 1871." LS, DNA, RG 94, ACP, K93 CB 1863.

On Dec. 14, 1870, Akerman had written to USG. "The eleventh section of the act of July 15, 1870, entitled 'An Act making Appropriations for the Support of the Army for the Year ending June 30, 1871, and for other Purposes' (16 U. S. Stat., p. 318), provides for the constitution of a board of officers, who shall consider the cases of officers reported by the general of the army and commanding officers of the several military departments as unfit for the proper discharge of their duties, and further provides that, 'on recommendation of such board, the President shall muster out of the service any of the said officers so reported with one year's pay, but such muster-out shall not be ordered without allowing such officer a hearing before such board to show cause against it.' The question which you submit to me is, whether the President has a discretion in acting upon the recommendation of the board, or whether such recommendation compels him to muster out the officer in question. The language of the statute being mandatory and positive, I think that no discretion is reserved to the President, and that when the reported officer has been allowed a hearing before the board, and the board recommends that he be mustered out, the President must carry the recommendation into effect." LS, *ibid.*, A503 CB 1870.

On March 11, John A. Dix, New York City, wrote to John A. Darling. "I heard with great regret that, under the recent reduction of the Army, you had been disbanded. Your faithful and efficient services on my staff during our unhappy civil war, and your gentlemanly bearing, as well as your professional merit, led me to hope that the Army would continue to number you among its members and to have the benefit of your experience and companionship. I shall always retain a grateful remembrance of your association with me, and it will afford me great pleasure to be of service to you, should any opportunity present itself." *SRC*, 44-2-615, 5. On May 11, USG endorsed letters related to Darling. "Respectfully referred to the Secretary of War for his consideration. Major Darling's recommendations are of the highest character." *Ibid.* On May 13, Darling, Washington, D. C., wrote to USG. "I have been informed by the Sec. of War., that he told you today, that the action of the Dept. in my case, was fully justified by a report of Lt. Col. George Crook, 23d. Infty. As you have read the testimonial letters in support of my character and ability as an officer, I beg respectfully to call your attention to the fact that the testimony of four distinguished officers of high rank, covering a period of seven (7) of the ten (10) years of my service, is, in the judgement of the War Dept., offset by the adverse report of one. That this report was uncalled for, and the result of personal prejudice I can fully establis[h] when the opportunity is afforded me. The official report of Genl. Canby, my Dept. Commander, made in compliance with the law, was favorable to me. My object in addressing your Excellen[cy] is simply to ask the suspension of you[r] judgement in my case, until I can obtain the hearing that justice deman[ds.]" ALS, DNA, RG 94, ACP, 1608 1871. On April 24, 1878, Darling was reappointed capt., art.

On March 27, 1871, Maj. Gen. George G. Meade, Philadelphia, wrote to U.S. Senator Simon Cameron of Pa. "I am advised by I. R. Dunkelberger late Bvt Lt-Col US Army that you have interested yourself in his behalf to repair what seems to been a mistake in his case.—Lt. Col. Dunkelberger has been under the act of Congress July 15—/70 honorably discharged the service with one years pay—Col Dunkelbergers services of over ten years, and his good record during the war, would seem to justify his expectation of being better provided for, ~~than~~ and there is reason to believe if all the facts of the case had been before the Department Lt—Col—D would have been retired from wounds received in battle—but unfortunately for him, he was not examined till December 1870, and the proceedings of the Board, did not reach Washington till some months after the final action of the Department.—The only practicable way that now remains to correct the mistake—would be to have Col D—reappointed for the purpose of his being subsequently retired—. . ." ALS, *ibid.*, R506 CB 1870. On April 12, USG endorsed this letter. "Refered to the Sec. of War. If this officer can be sent before a retiring board, legally, I think he should be so sent." AES, *ibid.* On July 19, 1876, Isaac R. Dunkelberger, Washington, D. C., wrote to Secretary of War James D. Cameron. "I have the honor to respectfully request that I be appointed a 2nd Lt in the Cavalry service of the U. S. Army to date from Jany 1st 1871 in order to make my service continuous; rank & pay to commence from date of appointment." ALS, *ibid.* Related papers are *ibid.* On July 26, 1st Lt. Francis V. Greene endorsed these papers to AG Edward D. Townsend. "Papers in case of Dunkelberger returned herewith. The President directs that his name be placed on the list of candidates for 2nd Lt. to be appointed next after Eldridge—mentioned in Mem. of 24 July" AES, *ibid.* On Aug. 11, USG nominated

Dunkelberger, 2nd lt., 10th Cav. In Oct., Dunkelberger, Sunbury, Pa., after being refused retirement, wrote to Townsend declining his commission because of physical incapacity. ALS, *ibid.* On Feb. 2, 1877, USG nominated Dunkelberger as postmaster, Los Angeles. See *CR*, 56–2, 3464–65; *SRC*, 56-1-558; *HRC*, 56-1-1186.

On April 12, 1871, Charles Robinett, New York City, wrote to USG. "... I had every reason to flatter myself that I was second to no line officer of my late regiment in tactical knowlege general efficiency and scholastic attainment—having been educated partly at a New York University and partly at a second rate College at Oxford England. My honesty and moral character generally are unimpeachable and yet shortly after my arrival, I learned from New York papers that I was transferred to the list of supernumeraries and mustered out. I have not yet learned specifically what allegations have been made against me although I have made repeated efforts to know and to refute them. I am convinced that the law has not been properly applied in my case...." ALS, DNA, RG 94, ACP, H400 CB 1870. On Dec. 10, 1870, Capt. Henry G. Thomas, 20th Inf., Fort Ransom, Dakota Territory, had written to Maj. Oliver D. Greene, asst. AG. "Under the letter from the War Dept of October 13th & the endorsement of the Dept Commander of Oct 19th I feel it my duty to report that 1 Lt Chs Robinett can be advantageously transferred to the list of Supernumeraries. He is neither efficient or discreet. He is incapable of controlling men or inspiring them with respect. Any responsibility whatever puts him in a state of mental fermentation...." ALS, *ibid.* Related papers are *ibid.*

On April 20, 1871, U.S. Delegate Selucius Garfielde of Washington Territory wrote to USG. "I desire once more, respectfully but urgently, to ask that Col. Samuel Ross, whose case has been favorably reported upon by the Retiring Board which sat at San Francisco, Cal., be placed upon the retired list in accordance with the recommendations of said ~~b~~Board.... The Secretary of War recently read to me statements made by one Col. Shepard in which he charges Col. Ross with grave offences committed in the year 1848. I expressed great astonishment, and then declared to the Secretary, that if these charges were true, I should decline to press the claims of Col. Ross, whatever his legal rights might be. Since that time I have had abundant reason for believing that the charges referred to were without foundation at the time and have slept through many years until called up by some malicious influence to defeat the just claims of a wounded soldier...." ALS, *ibid.*, 1867 1871. On Feb. 2, 1872, L. D. Ingersoll, Washington, D. C., wrote to USG. "I would feel under special obligations to You if You would appoint Col. Sam Ross a Second Lieutenant, with the object of having him retired. He is in every way worthy. This is all the favor I have to ask of You, and as You turned me out of office—who was your only genuine hearty friend of the press of Chicago except Mr. Medill—at the request of a Member of Congress who has admitted that therein he did a grievous wrong, I wish You may at once comply with my desire." ALS, *ibid.* On Feb. 5, USG nominated Samuel Ross as 2nd lt., 7th Inf. On March 13, Belknap wrote to Attorney Gen. George H. Williams ordering the retirement of Ross. AN (initialed), *ibid.* Ross had served as private, non-commissioned officer, and bvt. 2nd lt. (1837–49) and returned as capt., 14th Inf. (1861), being breveted maj. as of May 3, 1863, lt. col. as of Dec. 13, 1864, and col. as of March 13, 1865. In 1869, he was assigned as superintendent of Indian Affairs, Washington Territory.

On May 22, 1871, Maj. Henry R. Rathbone wrote to USG. "Adverting to your conversation had on the 18th inst with Judge Harris, I now venture to transmit to your Excellency the enclosed letter of resignation, and to respectfully request that you will cause it to be accepted." ALS, *ibid.*, 2340 1871. The enclosed letter to

Belknap is also dated May 22. "I have the honor to request that so much of General Order No 1, current Series, as musters me out of the Army may be revoked, and that the enclosed resignation may be accepted, and made to take effect as of the date thereof; viz: (Decr 31st/70)" ALS, *ibid.* On the same day, USG favorably endorsed this letter. AES, *ibid.* In Dec., 1878, bills were introduced in the Senate and House on Rathbone's behalf. *CR*, 45–3, 3, 43. On Jan. 18, 1879, Charles Ewing, Rathbone's attorney, argued before the House Committee on Military Affairs that Rathbone had been illegally mustered out and asked "that his request to be placed on the Retired List of the Army, that was approved by General Sherman and disapproved by Secretary of War Belknap, be granted." Charles Ewing, *Argument for Major Henry R. Rathbone, of the 5th U. S. Infantry* (n.p., [1879]), p. 11.

On June 5, 1871, Lorenzo W. Cooke, Washington, D. C., wrote to USG, Long Branch. "As I did not have an opportunity to submit my case to you in person, I beg briefly to state that when mustered out of the service, I was awaiting trial by a court martial at Fort Harker, Kansas, before which I had been ordered on charges involving alleged embezzlement, &c. Confident of acquittal, I was anxious to submit my case to the court, and then and there vindicate my reputation as an officer and a gentleman. It was no fault of mine that I was so unexpectedly deprived of the opportunity. If guilty I should have rejoiced at an act which at once enabled me to escape the severe sentence which attaches to such criminality. But the fact that, pending trial, I was *honorably* mustered out of service may I think, fairly be claimed as evidence that there was no case against me. At the same time there can be no doubt that the order was designed as a punishment for the alleged offence, and that for this reason I was summarily deprived of my commission, and of an honorable career in a profession which I had chosen from patriotic motives and as a means of support. But this action against me, severe though it was, is not the only punishment to which I have been subjected. The order of the War Department stopping my pay, issued in September 1869, and renewed in October 1870, still continues in force, and while preventing me from receiving the amount which has accumalated from the date first named, prevents from drawing a year's pay and allowances under the Act of Congress approved July 15th 1870. . . . My record as an officer is one of which I am not ashamed & is alone marred by my muster out under charges. Only eighteen months since, thinking I had a bright career before me I married, now my prospects have been blighted and the future filled with gloom. Without hesitation, I appeal to you, who, as General of the Army and now as President of our great Republic, has ever held the scales of justice evenly balanced with a firm and steady hand. Enlisting as a private at the early age of fifteen when the great rebellion began, I was in 1866, appointed a second Lieutenant, and having made arms my profession beg that you will consider my case and by a favorable decision enable me again to serve my country as a military officer." ALS, DNA, RG 94, Letters Received, 639C 1870. Related papers are *ibid.* On April 3 and May 31, Cooke had written to USG requesting appointment as 2nd lt., 3rd Inf. ALS, *ibid.*, ACP, 4401 1871. U.S. Senators Samuel C. Pomeroy and Alexander Caldwell of Kan. favorably endorsed the letter of April 3. ES (undated), *ibid.* On May 17, Lt. Gen. Philip H. Sheridan also favorably endorsed Cooke's letter. AES, *ibid.* On Oct. 13, Belknap wrote to Townsend. "The President directs the appointment as 2d Lieutenant 3d Infantry (if there is a vacancy—if not in some other Infantry regiment) of L. W. Cooke late 1st Lt. 3d Infantry—~~The~~ Appointment to be made at once—" AN (initialed), *ibid.*

On March 30, 1872, Samuel B. Lauffer, Washington, D. C., wrote to USG. "I again respectfully place myself before you appealing to you for aid.—*I am totally disabled with Chronic Muscular and Inflamatory Rheumatism, unfitted for any business or occupation, by which to obtain a livelihood, with no hope of ever getting any better and this brought about by disease contracted by exposure in the line of duty while in the Service of the United States* . . . I ask that my order discharging me may be *revoked* and that *I be restored similar as in the case of Asst. Surg. B. F. Pope* who was discharged Dec 31st 1870 (under Section 3 of Act Approved July 15th 1870) *same as myself,* and was restored June 17th 1871; *that I may be retired* . . ." ALS, *ibid.,* ACP, L115 CB 1863. On Feb. 6 and March 6, Lauffer had written to USG on the same subject. ALS, *ibid.* On Jan. 25, USG had endorsed papers concerning Lauffer. "Respectfully refered to the sec. of War." AES, *ibid.* On Feb. 5, Belknap wrote to USG. "In the matter of the application of late Captain Samuel B. Lauffer, for permission to withdraw his request for discharge under Sec. 3 of the Act approved July 15, 1870, with a view of going before a Retiring Board, for retirement because of disability, herewith returned, I have the honor to send you an extract from a report of the Adjutant General upon this case, in whose views I fully concur." Copies, *ibid.*; *ibid.,* RG 107, Letters Sent, Military Affairs. Facing retirement on grounds of unfitness for duty, Lauffer had been granted an honorable discharge as of Jan. 1, 1871.

In an undated letter, John C. Graham wrote to USG. ". . . In October, 1870, I resigned my Commission in the U. S. Army. . . . Before receiving any notice of action upon it, I saw a notice in the 'Army and Navy Journal' that my resignation had been accepted, but not mentioning the Section of the Act under which it was made. Writing to the Adjutant General, in regard to it, I received an answer, stating, in effect, that Second Lieutenants were not entitled to the benefit of said Act. . . . My resignation was expressly 'under Section 3d of the Act of July 15 1870. which is as follows, . . ." ALS, *ibid.,* RG 94, ACP, G143 CB 1870. Section 3 granted one year's pay to officers who resigned before Jan. 1, 1871. Related papers, *ibid.,* indicate that Graham eventually received the pay.

Endorsement

[*Dec. 1870*]

Refered to the Sec. of War. If it is legal to reconsider the "muster out" of Col. Hatch, and to date his "muster out" three months later, and to give him the difference of pay between that of Capt. & Lt. Col. for the time he was allowed only the former, I have no objection to making such an order knowing that Col. Hatches

AE (incomplete), DNA, RG 94, ACP, 241 1872. Written on a letter of Dec. 9, 1870, from Reuben B. Hatch, Washington, D. C., to Secretary of War William W. Belknap. "I would respectfully represent that on the 3rd of June, 1865, I was relieved from duty at Vicksburg, by orders of the Commanding General, Department of Mississippi, with a view to my being mustered out of service; that by Special Orders of the War Dept., dated July 28th 1865—I was mustered out of the service of the United States, as Assistant Quartermaster; that previously to the date of the order last mentioned, and while *en route* to St Louis, Mo. on the Steamer 'Atlantic,' with an amount of Government funds to turn over to Genl Wm Myers, the Quartermaster from whom I received the same, the steamer's safe, in which I had placed the said funds, together with my own, for safe Keeping, was robbed; that the United States instituted suit, in its own behalf, against the corporation owning said Steamer, and recovered judgment; that during this period, namely, from the date of my muster out of service to the date of the rendition of said judgment, to wit, the 7th of June 1866., I was almost constantly employed, *at my own expense*, in trying to recover the said Government funds; in obtaining testimony, and in attending the trial. That since that time I spent three months in this city for the purpose of settling my accounts with the Government, but returned to my home without effecting a settlement, for want of proper facilities and competent assistance; that on the 22nd of October, ultimo, I came here again with competent help, and have been constantly and unremittingly engaged to this date in settling my accounts with the Government, and *at my own expense*; that my accounts are now settled and closed, and that *I am not indebted to the Government for any amount.* In view, therefore, of my early entry into service, August 1861, and continuance in it during the war; the onerous duties imposed upon me at Cairo in 1861–2; the many hardships to which I have been subjected; the utter neglect and ruin of my private business; the service I have legitimately rendered for more than a year after my muster out, for the Government, and the pecuniary expenditure necessary in pursuance of said extra official service, in simple justice I respectfully request that the Special Order of the War Department, dated July 28th, 1865, mustering me out of service, be so amended as to date from the 28th day of October, 1865—I would further state, that by Special Order No. 126 War Dept. March 24th. 1864, I was assigned to duty as *Lieutenant Colonel* by the President; that I was never relieved from that assignment, though afterward, in an order emanating from the War Department, changing my station, I was addressed as Captain, which order, by misconstruction on the part of Paymasters, deprived me of a large portion of my pay from the date of said last order forward; that in view of General Order No 40. Adjutant Generals Office, April 15, 1862, setting forth the fact that no one but the President can discharge an officer or reduce his rank, I further respectfully request, that in the order of muster out, asked to be amended to date from Oct 28th 1865, I be addressed and designated as Lieutenant Colonel, both as a matter of pride and to facilitate the payment of my accounts for arrearage pay." LS, *ibid.* On July 2, 1865, Maj. Gen. Stephen A. Hurlbut had written to Maj. Gen. Grenville M. Dodge. "I wish you to give Col R B Hatch the fullest opportunity to clear his skirts for the money robbed from him on this Steamer—I have known Hatch long & well. He has been robbed beyond doubt & thinks by some one acquainted with the boat & without *his fault.* Attend to this promptly and oblige your friend & old Commanding officer" ALS, *ibid.*, Staff Papers. Related papers are *ibid.* Hatch died on Feb. 28, 1871. See *CG*, 42–2, 2012–13, 2285.

On March 22, 1869, Hatch had written to USG. "I apply to you for appointment as Commercial Agent at Acapulco, Mexico. I trust that I am in some degree qualified for the duties of the position. I would not be an applicant if pressing pecuniary necessities did not compel me. If you find yourself able and disposed to confer upon me this, or any other position which, from your knowledge of my qualifications, you may believe me a suitable person to have, I will promise you to faithfully perform the duties of the same, to the best of my ability" ALS, DNA, RG 59, Letters of Application and Recommendation. U.S. Senator Richard Yates of Ill. endorsed this letter. "I most earnestly desire that Col. Hatch may receive the appointment of Commercial agent at

Acapulco Mexico—You know him well and therefore I need not say that he rendered the Government most faithful and effective service during the war and that he is a man of the highest honor and integrity and in every respect worthy and competent to the position for which he applies and I most earnestly request that ~~the~~ he may receive the appointment." AES (undated), *ibid.* U.S. Senator Lyman Trumbull and U.S. Representatives John A. Logan and Shelby M. Cullom of Ill. added favorable endorsements. AES (undated), *ibid.* Related papers are *ibid.* See *PUSG*, 2, 230; *ibid.*, 4, 44, 79–84; *ibid.*, 19, 414–15.

Veto

TO THE HOUSE OF REPRESENTATIVES:

I herewith return without my approval, House Bill No 1395, entitled, "An Act for the relief of Charles Cooper, Goshorn A. Jones, Jerome Rowley, William Hannegan and John Hannegan," for the following reasons:—

The act directs the discontinuance of an action at law said to be now pending in the United States District Court for the Northern District of Ohio, for the enforcement of the bond executed by said parties to the United States; whereas in fact no such suit is pending in the District Court, but such a suit is now pending in the Circuit Court of the United States for the Sixth Circuit and Northern District of Ohio.

Neither the body of said act nor the proviso requires the obligors in said bond, who are released from all liability to the United States on account thereof, to abandon or release their pretended claim against the Government.

Since these parties have gone to Congress to ask relief from liability for a large sum of money on account of the failure of the principals in the bond to execute their contract, it is but just and proper that they at the same time should abandon the claim heretofore asserted by them against the Government growing out of the same transaction.

U. S. GRANT

EXECUTIVE MANSION
JANUARY 4TH 1871

Copy, DNA, RG 130, Messages to Congress. The contract in question involved the Des Moines rapids of the Mississippi River. See *CG*, 41–2, 856, 2549–50, 4385; *HRC*, 41-2-30. On Dec. 20, 1870, Horace Porter wrote to Benjamin H. Bristow, solicitor gen. "I am directed by the President to submit H. R. 1395 entitled 'An Act for the relief of Charles Cooper, Goshorn A. Jones, Jerome Rowley, Wm Hannegan and John Hannegan' and to ask whether any reasons exist against its receiving his approval" Copy, DLC-USG, II, 1. On Jan. 17, 1871, Orville E. Babcock wrote to Bristow. "Will you please send to this office, for temporary use, the letter of Gen. J. H. Wilson, which accompanied your reasons why House Bill No 1395 should not receive the approval of the President." Copy, *ibid.*

On Feb. 4, U.S. Representative Michael C. Kerr of Ind. reported a bill "intended to obviate the objections of the President in his veto message dated January 4, 1871, to House bill No. 1395, bearing the same title as this bill, which passed the Senate and House at the last session. The subject-matter of the bill was at that session very fully and carefully examined by the Judiciary Committee, and they considered the relief proposed by that bill to be distinctly and eminently just and proper to be granted. The first objection made by the President is that the court in which the action is pending is not correctly indicated, and the objection is good, and the bill I now offer removes it. The other objection is that the bill No. 1395 gives to the persons named therein not only relief against the demand of the Government, which is the basis of the action referred to, but also authorizes them to prosecute an action in the Court of Claims against the Government for any claim they may have under or on account of their contract. The Judiciary Committee accept this objection, and in the bill I offer it is removed by entirely omitting the proviso in the original bill which gave to the contractors the right to maintain that action in the Court of Claims. I think that now there can be no question made either as to the propriety and justice or the form of this bill." *CG*, 41–3, 962. See *ibid.*, pp. 974–75, 1720–21, 1942.

To John M. Palmer

Washington D. C.
Jan.y 6th 1871

Govr. J. M. Palmer
Springfield Mass? (Ills)

Govt. officials are not in Springfield by any official direction. They are acting upon their own judgment exercising the privileges of citizens, and if they neglect no official duty I do not see how they can be interfered with by Executive orders.

U. S. Grant.

Copy, DLC-USG, II, 5. On Jan. 5, 1871, Governor John M. Palmer of Ill. telegraphed to USG. "Capt Church Revenue Officer from Montana, Capt Whamm Indian agent from Wyoming and Mr Bangs Postal Agent and many collectors and assessors of Internal Revenue are here openly interfering in the election, which produces much bad feeling amongst republicans. I call your attention to this not as a partisan of any candidate Your friends in Illinois cannot understand how it is that you are neutral in the Senatorial contest when Capt Proutt [*Routt*] U. S. Marshall and Bangs Postal Agent and nearly all your office holders are permitted to be here doing duty under Genl Logan. We do not want you to interfere and ask you to order these men to their duties." Telegram received, DLC-John A. Logan. On the same day, USG replied to Palmer. "I knew nothing of the assembling of government officials at Springfield and know nothing now beyond your dispatch received late last night." Copy, DLC-USG, II, 5. Palmer, U.S. Representative John A. Logan, Gustavus Koerner, and Richard J. Oglesby sought the Republican legislative caucus endorsement for U.S. senator. Logan won the endorsement and subsequent election. See *Illinois State Journal*, Jan. 2–19, 1871; Mrs. John A. Logan, *Reminiscences of a Soldier's Wife* (New York, 1913), pp. 283–89; James P. Jones, *John A. Logan: Stalwart Republican from Illinois* (Tallahassee, 1982), pp. 45–54.

On Feb. 21, 1869, Bvt. Maj. Gen. James H. Wilson, Wilmington, Del., wrote to Edward Kitchell, Olney, Ill. "I received your nice letter a few days ago—& since then, at the request of Genl Grant for the name of an honest man for Marshal of the Southern District of Ills. I took the liberty of suggesting you. He wants a man whom *he can trust*, and *who would rather die than compromise with rascality*, & as he wrote your name on a card & put it in his pocket, I am sure you can have & *will have* the office if acceptable to you. It is honestly worth 6000 dollars a year and no more. I understand that Col. Biggs is Collector of your district & hope you'll do nothing to get him out. Please write me at Keokuk, Iowa, what you think of being Marshal. Wishing you success in all good things, . . . P. S. Please consider this *confidential*." ALS, DNA, RG 60, Records Relating to Appointments. On Feb. 26, Kitchell wrote to Wilson. "(Confidential) . . . On yesterday I wrote you in answer to your very kind letter of the 21st inst—Since then I have been thinking very seriously over the contents of your letter—and must confess that I have a strong desire to be Marshal of Southern Illinois—And as you were kind enough to suggest my name to Gen Grant, and assure me that I could get the appointment, I desire to be guided alone by your advice—The Office of Collector of this District, for which I had intended applying is not worth over $1500 per year clear of expenses—And it is not a desirable office, if any thing better is tangible—The present Collector is a very good man (Capt R. D. Noleman of Centralia) and although he has held the office for more than six years, it may not be deemed advisable to remove him, for the sake of giving place to some other person. . . ." ALS, *ibid.* On Feb. 28, Wilson, Keokuk, wrote to USG. "This note will be handed to you by Genl Edward Kitchell of Olney Ills, of whom I spoke to you as the best man of my acquaintence for Marshal of the Southern District of Illinois. The General would like the office, and I am entirely sure if any change is to be made you need not look further for a man to fill the vacancy. You can rely not only upon the fidelity and zeal of Genl Kitchell but also upon his scrupulous honesty." ALS, *ibid.* On March 15, U.S. Senator Lyman Trumbull of Ill. wrote to USG. "I respectfully recommend Gen. Edward Kitchell for Marshall for the Southern Dist. of Ill. Gen. Kitchell performed gallant service during the war, is a Lawyer by profession, a Gentleman of the strictest integrity & would make an able honest & efficient officer." ALS, *ibid.* On the same day, U.S. Senator Richard Yates of Ill. wrote to USG. "I beg to introduce Genl E Kitchell late Republican

Presidential Elector for the 11th District of Illinois. He was a brave soldier an intelligent officer and is a prominent and influential citizen of Southern Illinois—He desires a moment's speech with you—" ALS, *ibid.*

On March 17, S. A. Buckmaster, Chicago, wrote to USG. "Permit me to add my recomendation to the already very strong Petitions & Letters in favor of the appointment of Mr Thos. J. Larrison of Logan Co Illinois for the position of Marshall for the Southern District of this State. His Experience in the performance of the duties of Sheriff of his own County, & his general buisness qualities, would seem to point to him as the right man for the position, My own opinion is that a better appointment could not be made, nor one, that would give more general Satisfaction" ALS, *ibid.* On March 22, David Davis, U.S. Supreme Court, wrote to Attorney Gen. Ebenezer R. Hoar recommending Thomas J. Larison. ALS, *ibid.* A related petition is *ibid.* See *PUSG*, 3, 294; *ibid.*, 20, 344–45. On April 4, 1870, USG nominated John L. Routt as marshal, Southern District, Ill.

On April 3, 1871, George S. Roper, Alton, Ill., wrote to USG. "The following is an application to be appointed Marshal for the Southern Dist of Illinois and is based upon your former kindness to me, and my reputation as an officer & man. I was appointed Capt Com of Sub by President Lincoln and I think that my Army record will justify me in saying that I did not disappoint your selection. I have always been a Republican from principle and a Grant man from preference, I have never before sought office, but I now feel the need of the help it would give me and that I can discharge its duties satisfactorily. I do not know of anything Mr President that can be brought against me as a man except that I once honestly tried to make an *honest, living making whiskey* and I succeeded in demonstratining that that could not be done 'In that have I offended'. This will be handed you by Hon John B Hay who is our member from this District and who can more fully urge my claims" ALS, DNA, RG 60, Records Relating to Appointments. On the same day, Roper wrote to U.S. Representative John B. Hay of Ill. "I enclose with this a Letter which I desire you to hand in person to President Grant. . . . Capt Routt the present marshal says he has contemplated resigning for some time so that I judge from that, that he is not at all anxious to hold the position—I have not said this in my letter to the President nor do I say it for his ears I prefer to risk my claims indipendent of that fact, . . ." ALS, *ibid.* See *PUSG*, 2, 101.

On Oct. 13, Mrs. John Cook, Springfield, Ill., wrote to USG. "It is with no little hesitation & diffidence I address you this morning—but under the peculiar circumstances & having always regarded you as a personal friend of Mr Cooks I have laid aside or rather sacrificed my own feelings most cheerfully for my husbands sake & I assure you entirely without his knowledge make this appeal in his behalf—for the position of U. S. Marshall of the southern district of Illinois—From the morning papers I learn that it is vacant—Mr Cook has been a great sufferer with many others in the terrible calamity that has befallen our state & I know the office would be an acceptable one—His qualifications for the office are of course known to you & every one will testify to his enering & faithfulness in filling every place of trust ever entrusted to him Do if possible consider favorably my request—& with very kind remembrances to Mrs Grant & your family . . ." ALS, DNA, RG 60, Records Relating to Appointments. On May 22, Logan had written to Secretary of State Hamilton Fish withdrawing "all the papers relating to the application of General John Cook, Springfield, Ill; for the appointment as Consul Genl at Paris." LS, *ibid.*, RG 59, Letters of Application and Recommendation. See *PUSG*, 2, 171–72; *ibid.*, 4, 275, 376; *ibid.*, 10, 239–40.

On Oct. 13, Charles E. Lippincott, Ill. auditor, wrote to USG. "I see by the papers this morning that Capt Jno. L. Routt has been appointed Second Asst P. M. General *vice* Gen Giles A. Smith resigned. This appointment (which gives universal satisfaction here) leaves the Marshallship of the Southern District of this State vacant. I hear that Hon Edwd R. Roe, now a member of the State legislature would be gratified if he were appointed. To me it is a matter of pleasure, as it is of justice, to say that I know Col Roe well, and in many relations of life. I served with him in the Army; I knew him before and since the war in civil life, and can bear willing testimony to his excellence every where and in every place. As a gentleman, soldier, citizen and man he deserves the highest testimony from all who know him. His appointment to the vacant Marshallship will give great pleasure to your friends in this State." ALS, DNA, RG 60, Records Relating to Appointments. On Dec. 6, USG nominated Edward R. Roe as marshal, Southern District, Ill. On Nov. 15, 1875, Roe, Springfield, wrote to Bluford Wilson, solicitor of the treasury. "I forward herewith letters to the President, in my behalf, from eminent Republicans here. The public sentiment is *unanimous* for my re-appointment, so far as I can see. Judge Treat said to Judge David Davis that no such efficient marshal as I, ever filled the office in this district. Senator Logan will lay my letter to the President, with his own endorsement, before his Execellency. Senator Oglesby, owing to his relationship which he bears to certain parties, will take no part in the re-appointment, *pro* or *con.* No local news of importance." ALS, *ibid.* On Nov. 20, Wilson favorably endorsed this letter. ES, *ibid.* On Nov. 16, Roe wrote to USG. "My commission as Marshal of the United States for the southern district of Illinois will expire by its own limitation on the 12th day of December, *proximo.* You will appreciate my gratification in being able to report that after four years' personal devotion to the duties of my office, I have recieved the approval of the court, the bar and the people, and especially of the Department of Justice. I desire to return you my sincere thanks for your past confidence; and I very respectfully solicit a re-appointment to my present position" ALS, *ibid.* Logan endorsed this letter. "I can see no reason why Col Roe should not be reappointed. I hope he may" AES (undated), *ibid.* On Nov. 24, Asa C. Matthews, supervisor of Internal Revenue, Springfield, wrote to USG. "To the numerous petitions forwarded to your Excellency, by the friends of Col. Roe the presant Marshal of the Southern District of Illinois, for his re-appointment, I desire to add mine & In his behalf I beg to say that he is a gentleman of unblemished reputation and tried integrity. He served as the Lieut. Col. of the 33d Illinois Inf'try Vol's under your command until badly wounded through the body on the 22d day of May 1863. during the assault upon the rebel fortifications in the rear of Vicksburg Miss. He is a gentleman of learning and large experience, and of much influence in the central portion of Illinois. As Marshal of this District he has performed his work thoroughly and well, and has rendered promptly and efficiently, aid in the discovery of frauds against the Internal Revenue. That he can fill acceptably the position has been demonstrated by an experience of years and in the presant condition of revenue matters in Illinois I think the best interests of the Government demand his re-appointment" ALS, *ibid.* On Dec. 17, USG renominated Roe.

On May 8, George W. Lynn, Mattoon, Ill., had written to USG. "In view of a possible vacancy by reason of the resignation of Col Roe U S Marshal for the Southeren Dist. of Ills; If it meet your approval I would be glad to accept the appointment to fill said vacancy" ALS, *ibid.* On Nov. 18, 1873, USG had suspended Lynn as postmaster, Mattoon. On Dec. 6, 1875, U.S. Representative Charles B. Farwell of Ill. wrote to USG. "I hear that a change is contemplated in the office of Marshall in the

Southern Dist of Ill—Without consulting him—I suggest (our old friend) Jesse K Dubois—" ALS, *ibid.*

To House of Representatives

TO THE HOUSE OF REPRESENTATIVES:

I transmit to the House of Representatives, in answer to their resolution of the 5th instant, a report from the Secretary of State with accompanying documents.

U. S. GRANT

WASHINGTON, JANUARY 9TH 1871.

Copies, DNA, RG 59, General Records; *ibid.*, RG 130, Messages to Congress. On Jan. 5, 1871, on motion of U.S. Representative Benjamin F. Butler of Mass., the House of Representatives "Resolved, That the President be, and hereby is, requested, if not incompatible with the public service, to furnish for the information of the House the Reports of John Hogan United States Commissioner upon the resources and condition of the Dominican Republic, made to the State Department in the administration of President Polk, also the Report of Captain Geo. B. McClellan upon the same subject made during the administration of President Pierce." D, *ibid.*, RG 59, Miscellaneous Letters. On Jan. 9, Secretary of State Hamilton Fish wrote to USG. "The Secretary of State, to whom was referred the Resolution of the House of Representatives of the 5th instant, . . . has the honor to submit a copy of the Report of John Hogan, requested by the Resolution, and to state that no report of Captain George B. McClellan is now, or, so far as the records show, ever has been on file in this Department" Copy, *ibid.*, General Records. On Jan. 10, Secretary of War William W. Belknap wrote to USG transmitting a copy of the report of Capt. George B. McClellan. Copy, *ibid.*, RG 107, Letters Sent. On Jan. 11, USG wrote to the House of Representatives. "I transmit herewith in reply to the resolution of the House of Representatives of the 5th instant, copies of the reports of Captain George B. McClellan upon the Dominican Republic, made in the year 1854." Copy, *ibid.*, RG 130, Messages to Congress. See *HED*, 41-3-42, 41-3-43.

To Franz Sigel

Washington D. C. Jany 10. 1871

DEAR SIR:

The resolution authorizing me to send commissioners to Santo Domingo having passed the House of Representatives, it would not seem premature for me now to get the consent of those whom I would like to undertake the service. My choice is for yourself as Secretary of the Commission. If you accept will you be kind enough to notify me by telegraph. The aim will be to get this commission off at as early a day as practicable. A naval vessel will be in readiness at Norfolk, Va. as soon as the party is ready to start, and will be fully provided for the comfort of all.

Yours truly
U. S. GRANT

GEN FRANZ SIGEL
NEW YORK

Copy, DLC-USG, II, 1. On Jan. 14, 1871, USG wrote to Franz Sigel. "I regretted receiving your despatch declining to accompany the Santo Domingo Commission, but perfectly understood your reasons, i. e. that is that you did not regard yourself as sufficiently conversant with the Spanish language to fulfill the requirements of the law. I am yet anxious that you should accompany the Commission, though the place legally provided for are filled. If you consent to go however, you may regard this letter as an invitation to do so, and as directions to Capt. Temple Commander of the Steamer Tennessee, which conveys the expedition, to receive you, and provide for you, in the same manner as he provides for the appointed Commissioners." Copy, *ibid.* See *PUSG*, 3, 251; *ibid.*, 10, 222–23, 286–87; *ibid.*, 11, 185; *ibid.*, 15, 169–70; letter to William G. Temple, Jan. 14, 1871; letter to Buenaventura Báez, Jan. 15, 1871.

On March 18, 1869, Sigel, Morrisania, N. Y., had written to USG. "The Undersigned respectfully presents, that he is an Applicant for the position of Minister to Switzerland and bases his application on the following grounds: 1, That he has propagated and defended the principles of Republican Government in theory and practice for more than twenty years in Europe and America, sometimes even under the greatest difficulties and dangers. 2, That he defended to the best of his abilities the Unity of the United-States before and during the late war and faithfully helped to enlist the German-American element of the Country in this struggle for the maintenance of the Republic. 3, That before his arrival in this Country he has been living in Switzerland for three years, from 1848 to 1851, in German, French and Italian Cantons, speaks and writes the three languages declared national by the Swiss Constitution and is well acquainted with the leading men, the people and the institutions of the Swiss-Confederation. 4, That being a Republican in principle, he would prefer to be sent to a Government,—Republican in form—, and where the greater part of the people is intimately affiliated to the German nationality. 5, That, having been educated a professional man and a soldier, and being a graduate of a scientific High-School and of a Military-Academy he would prefer a position not chiefly commercial or financial in its character; he would therefore refrain from applying for or expecting to receive a position in any other Department of the United-States. 6, That, though not a professional politician, he ever was prepared to give his support, when needed, to the party of progress, with moderation, impartiality and unselfishness. In making this application I stand on the principle of a fair competition and leave the decision of the merits of this case to your Excellency." LS, DNA, RG 59, Letters of Application and Recommendation. On March 22, Sigel wrote to Orville E. Babcock. "You will undoubtedly remember the time when I saw you at Cumberland, Md, and when I received certain instructions and orders from then General Grant, now President of the United States. Whatever may have been the result of my subsequent actions, you will concede to me, that I was very anxious to have things done according to the best interest of the service and my instructions received; I therefore beg leave to address you. I have sent an Application through the Secretary of State to the President for the Mission to Switzerland. To be judged fairly, I would say, that I have done it solely on my own responsibility, privately and without any ostentation or political pressure, leaving the President free to decide on the inherent merits of the case. In my letter to the Secretary of State I have refered to a few Gentlemen now in Washington and have addressed some of them in my behalf. In addition, however I think it proper to say, that having never found an opportunity to explain certain circumstances connected with the Battle of NewMarket and my position as commander of the Department of West-Virginia, I should be glad, if you would read the enclosed letter of Surveyor General Campbell of Pa, who commanded the 54th Pa Regiment at the said Battle and was at that time its Colonel. The letter is a verbal and certified copy of the original and was written as a private document on my request, to have a frank and impartial statement from the Colonel's own hand. Since I left the service I was so much taken up by private business (as an editor of a paper in Baltimore) that I could never find time and leisure enough to write a detailed report of the operations in West-Virginia, but at this moment, when I claim the confidence of my former Superior, now the President of the United States, even to a position which is not military, I can not refrain from adducing the opinion of a brave soldier and very honest man and should feel greatly obliged to you, if you would bring it to the knowledge of the President." ALS, *ibid.* The enclosure and related papers are *ibid.* On Jan. 25, 1870, USG nominated Sigel as assessor of Internal Revenue, 6th District, N. Y.

On June 3, Rudolph Wieczorek, New York City, wrote to USG. "Allow me to say, that General Franz Seigel would be the most proper person for the Custom-House—Collectors Office at New York. By this appointment You would please all the german population of the U. S." ALS, *ibid.*, RG 56, Collector of Customs Applications. On May 18, 1871, USG nominated Sigel as collector of Internal Revenue, 9th District, N. Y. On May 22, Horace Porter wrote to Sigel, New York City. "The President has learned with great regret that you contemplate declining the office of the Ninth District of New York, and he directs me to say that he hopes you may reconsider this determination. He wishes me to assure you that you will enter upon the duties of your office with the full confidence and support of himself and the officers of the Treasury Department, and that your acceptance will in no manner prejudice your claims to any other position under the government to which it might at any time be advisable to appoint you. By entering this office you can rest assured that you are displacing no one, and that you will receive your appointment in such a manner as to leave no grounds for cavil on the part of any one." Copy, DLC-USG, II, 1. On June 7, USG wrote to Sigel on an unknown subject. "Presidents and Near-Presidents," *University of Kentucky Library Bulletin*, Number XX [1960], p. 10. Sigel served as collector of Internal Revenue.

To Senate

TO THE SENATE OF THE UNITED STATES

In view of a proclamation having been published in newspapers of the United States, purporting to eminate from ~~Gen~~. Cabral, a chieftain who now opposes the constitutional authorities of the Republic of Santo Domingo,[1] I deem it but just to communicate to the Senate of the United States, ~~as a part of the treaty making power of this Government~~, the views of that Chieftain, and his followers, as voluntarily communicated by him, through the U. S. Minister to the Republic of Hayti, in June last. It will be observed by the letter of Minister Bassett that ~~Gen~~. Cabral did not wish his views to be made public before the question of Annexation was disposed of, in a way to work prejudice to his interest. But, as the object which ~~Gen~~. Cabral had clearly in view was to declare to the treaty making ~~treaty making~~ power of the United States, his views, and those of his followers, upon the subject of Annexation of the Republic of Santo Domingo, and as the Senate is ~~as much~~ a branch of that power, I deem it no breach of confidence to communicate this letter to the Senate. I ask however that it may be read in Executive session, and that the request of ~~Gen~~. Cabral be observed "so ~~as to prevent~~ that in no case they shall be made public or used against him, until the question of Annexation is disposed of."

EXECUTIVE MANSION
JANUARY 11TH 1871

ADf, Mr. and Mrs. Philip D. Sang, River Forest, Ill. On June 14, 1870, Ebenezer D. Bassett, U.S. minister, Port-au-Prince, wrote to Secretary of State Hamilton Fish. "PRIVATE No 5. . . . General Valverde, formerly Governor of Santo Domingo under the Spanish rule, and afterwards Minister of War when General Cabral was President, recently, through Mr Galvan the Spanish Consul here, requested a private interview with me. As I could see no good reason for declining to listen to anything General Valverde might have to say, I acceded to the request. The Spanish Consul Mr Galvan is himself a citizen of St. Domingo, and assured me that full faith might be given to General Valverde's statements. General Valverde said he had been sent from General Cabral's headquarters to lay before me certain strictly confidential statements, and solicit my view of them. He went on to say that, the feeling of national pride being dropped, it was a fact acknowledged by all the leading men of St. Domingo that the people there are really incapable of Self Government. 'There is not,' said he, 'a single enlightened or patriotic Dominican who would not wish to see his country under the control of some civilized and powerful Government like the United States. All the intelligence of whatever party in St. Domingo is in favor of annexation to the United States. General Cabral is strongly in favor of it. He was the first to propose this scheme. General Baez by appealing to the ignorant masses and telling them that Cabral wished to sell them to the Americans, succeeded in overthrowing Cabral. And in turn Cabral and his partizans have used the same means against Baez, whilst at heart Cabral and his party are thorough annexationists. Cabral is fighting, not against the proposed annexation of St. Domingo to the United States, but against Baez and his usurpations, and he makes use of this as one of the means of carrying on his warfare. The war is simply a party feud. All that General Cabral asks is that in case the annexation is consummated, neither he nor Baez shall be placed in power in St. Domingo by the United States Government. If Baez is placed in power there under your Government, he will find means of persecuting and oppressing those who are now opposed to him, and Cabral will feel obliged to continue his war. He knows that he could not defeat the power of the United States. But he knows also that he can continue his guerilla warfare in the interior indefinitely. General Cabral has commissioned me to lay before you his true position, because he is desirous of having it understood by the United States, and thought that perhaps you might be able to tell him how far this single wish of his might be acceded to' 'Well, General,' said I, 'I must decline to give any guarantee as to the position which my Government would be disposed to assume. But I can assure you of this, that if the annexation is consummated, Baez and Cabral will be simply citizens of the United States, and no political persecutions will be tolerated. Every man will find perfect safety in an adherence to the laws which will be put in force.' 'Can you then,' said General Valverde, 'convey Cabral's views as I have expressed them to your Government in a strictly confidential manner, so that in no case they shall be made public or used against him, until the question of annexation is disposed of?' 'I think I can promise to do that, General,' said I, 'but you must remember that the annexation has been consummated already, as far as the action of St. Domingo is concerned, in spite of Cabral's ostensible opposition, and that Cabral has really no claims upon us. Perhaps however my Government may think it well to quietly accede to Cabral's simple request, if by so doing it can avoid the expense of blood and treasure which may be required at its hands if Cabral should be so unwise as to continue his warfare after annexation. But I am sure that it will not be disposed to give any open pledges now.' 'Let the assurance in any way be given,' said General Valverde, 'that Baez shall not be appointed Governor of St. Domingo or placed in any other position there which will afford him more or less means of wreaking vengeance on Cabral and his followers, and I assure you that the United States will meet with no trouble or opposition from any party in St. Domingo. Let your Government appoint any disinterested person from the States as Governor, and peace and tranquillity will be guaranteed throughout St. Domingo.' 'You will observe,' continued he, 'that no movement has been made by Cabral lately, although he has frequent calls to do so from different parts of the country. He does not intend to make any further demonstration until he can get some idea of the disposition of your Government as to the single point which I have stated, for he is not opposed to the annexation of St. Domingo to the United States, but sees clearly the great advantages which would result from it to his country.' General Valverde impressed me as a man of candor and ability. I did not understand his statement of Cabral's wishes and purposes to be in the character of a menace, but as one made in simple candor and frankness. It is not for me to discuss the bearings of the point suggested. But I think the foregoing is a faithful epitome of my long interview with General Valverde, and I shall be glad if you can give it such consideration as you may think it merits. Perhaps you may judge it worth while to write me privately or otherwise in reference to the subject." LS, DNA, RG 59, Diplomatic Despatches, Haiti. Fish endorsed this letter to Robert S. Chilton, clerk, dept. of state. "acknowledge—may say confidentially to Genl V. that in case of annexation the policy of the U S. would unquestionably suggest the appointment of a Citizen from United [*States*] as Govr & that an impartial measure of justice will be observed toward the sever[al] parties who have heretofore been estranged & have distracted the Island" AE, *ibid.* Fish's endorsement was incorporated in a letter of July 6 from Fish to Bassett. Copies, *ibid.*, Diplomatic Instructions, Haiti and Santo Domingo; *ibid.*, RG 46, Presidential Messages, Foreign Relations, Santo Domingo. On Dec. 28, Babcock wrote to Fish. "I am directed by the President to request you to send to him a copy of Minister Bassetts letter addressed to you, relative to the annexation of Sto. Domingo, and the request of Mr Cabral, through his late Secretary of War, and a copy of your reply." LS, DLC-Hamilton Fish. On Jan. 15, 1871, Babcock wrote to J. C. Bancroft Davis, asst. secretary of state. "The President will be pleased to have you send him to day a copy of Minister Bassetts letter on Cabral & the Sectys Answer. I send this to you, not to go over the head of the Secty, as you know—but to facilitate matters and not annoy him." ALS, DNA, RG 59, Miscellaneous Letters. See *PUSG*, 20, 8–15; letter to Oliver P. Morton, Dec. 9, 1870.

1. Ousting Gen. Pedro Antonio Pimentel as president of the Dominican Republic (1865), José María Cabral expressed friendship toward the U.S., lost his office to Buenaventura Báez, and returned as president in 1866 until again unseated by Báez in 1868. On Dec. 23, 1870, Cabral issued an address condemning Báez as "faithless to us. In exchange for gold he wants to sacrifice our independence; and our independence we must maintain, as the only thing we have and as the most precious jewel we can bequeath to future generations." *New York Tribune*, Jan. 9, 1871. For another statement of Cabral's opposition to U.S. annexation of Santo Domingo, see message to Congress, April 5, 1871 (2), note 1.

To George S. Boutwell

Washington D. C. Jan.y 12th *1871*

HON. G. S. BOUTWELL
SEC. OF THE TREAS.
DEAR SIR:

This will introduce to you Capt. Phelps, formerly of our Navy, and who rendered distinguished service during the rebellion. Capt. Phelps is now the representative of the Pacific Steamship line between San Francisco and China, and desires to see you in relation to the interests of the company which he represents.

Yours Truly
U. S. GRANT

ALS, Ford Collection, Minnesota Historical Society, St. Paul, Minn. On Dec. 8, 1873, USG wrote to "U. S. Ministers and Consuls in Europe." "It affords me great pleasure to introduce to you Capt. S. L. Phelps, late of our Navy and now a resident of this City, who proposes spending some time in Europe. Capt. Phelps is a gentleman greatly esteemed by his friends and neighbors and I beg to commend him to your good offices while he may remain in your vicinity." Copy, DLC-USG, II, 2. See *PUSG*, 2, 188–89; *ibid.*, 4, 313–14; *New York Times*, June 25, 1885.

Endorsement

[*Jan. 13, 1871*]

The President is thus lenient in view of the youth and inexperience of the offenders, and must not be regarded as a precedent for the future.

AE, DNA, RG 94, Correspondence, USMA. On Dec. 10, 1870, Edwin P. Andrus, Myron W. Howe, George R. Smith, and Robert P. P. Wainwright were expelled from USMA for "[u]nauthorized and highly improper interference with the cadet sentinels duly posted on the night of November 16, 1870," and Alpheus E. Frank was expelled for "[w]illful violation of his pledge of honor not to interfere with new cadets." *HRC*, 41-3-28, 51. On Jan. 13, 1871, Secretary of War William W. Belknap wrote to Col. Edmund Schriver. "The President directs that the order dismissing Cadets Wainwright, Smith, Howe, Frank and Andrus ~~who~~ be revoked and that the sentences be changed to suspension until June 20, 1871—He desires it stated in the order of revocation that he '*is thus lenient in view of the youth & inexperience of the offenders, and that this change of sentence must not be regarded as a precedent for the future, as he intends to use all the means at his command to put a stop to the disgraceful practice of hazing*' &c" AD (initialed), DNA, RG 94, Correspondence, USMA. Andrus, Howe, Smith, and Wainwright graduated from USMA in 1875.

On Dec. 13, 1870, George R. Frank, Boscobel, Wis., had written to USG. "I have just learned with much regret, from my son, Alpheus E Frank, a Cadet at West Point, being information which he obtained from your son, also a Cadet there, that you had dismissed him (Alpheus) from the Academy for holding the door of his room against a Cadet sentinel on duty I am very anxious to have my son obtain a Military education, but my pecuniary circumstances are such as to render it impossible for me to give such an education as I would like to, or as he desires, should he be compelled to leave the academy at West Point. He assures me that he held the door but for a moment and regrets very much the unfortunate occurrence He also states that he thought the new Cadets were no longer regarded as such, the Officers over them having been relieved from such duty and they admitted to the Battallion &c and did not think he was violating his word of honor If you can by any means consistent with your duty as the Chief Magistrate of this great nation, retain him in the Academy, you will receive the blessings of his many friends here who ever delight to honor General Grant As to myself I can only say that on the 14th day of Aug, 1862 I enlisted a company of men and soon after took the field, went immediately to the front and remained there till the close of the war, performing my duty to the best of my ability in many a hard fought battle; and I do hope you will not let my son be disgraced by dismissing him from the Academy at West Point. He has ever borne the reputation at home of a steady industrious upright boy and I am confident will make amends for any errors he may have committed and be a true and faithful soldier. I have relied implicitly on you amid the storm of battle. I do the same now and with you I leave the fate of my dear boy, hoping and trusting, And may the blessing of God rest upon you." ALS, *ibid.* A related letter is *ibid.* Frank, who entered USMA in 1869, did not graduate and was appointed 2nd lt., 10th Cav., in 1873.

To William G. Temple

Washington D. C. Jan.y 14th *1871*

CAPT. TEMPLE,
COMD.G STR. TENNESSEE:

If you can provide accomodations for Col. McMichael,[1] representative of the Phila ~~Leg~~dger, I will be obliged.

Yours Truly
U. S. GRANT

ALS, NNP. Born in 1824 in Rutland, Vt., William G. Temple was appointed midshipman (1840), served in the Mexican War, and spent much of the next decade conducting coast surveys. During the Civil War, he was on blockade and ordnance duty and participated in the attacks on Fort Fisher. Promoted to commander (1865) and capt. (1870), he was reassigned in Dec., 1870, from his post as asst. judge advocate, Navy Dept., to special service as commander of the *Tennessee.* See *SED*, 42-1-9, 57–58; *Cincinnati Gazette*, Dec. 24, 1870.

On Jan. 12, 1871, Orville E. Babcock wrote to Horace Porter. "You will proceed to New York City without delay and comply with the verbal instructions communicated to you by the President in relation to the sailing of the U. S. Steamer 'Tennessee'. After completing this duty you will rejoin your station in this City. By order of the Prest." Copy, DLC-USG, II, 1.

On the same day, Secretary of State Hamilton Fish wrote to USG. "Mr Ramsdell has called upon me, & mentions that you had requested me to write to Mr Greeley & other proprietors of papers, to designate some persons to accompany the Commission to San Domingo—I had not understood you to desire me to make the request but will do so immediately if you direct, & will indicate the Papers to which you wish the offer to be made. I think that it will be adviseable to require the Papers to which the permission shall be given, to indicate in writing by letter Either to Genl Porter or Babcock, or to this Department, the name of the Correspondent whom they wish to send—" ALS (press), DLC-Hamilton Fish. Also on Jan. 12, Babcock wrote to Fish. "The President is in receipt of your note and directs me to say in reply that, he did not intimate to Mr Ramsdell any wish to have you write to Mr. Greeley or the proprietor of any newspaper. That he simply remarked that accommodation might be made for about five correspondents. It is not his desire to have you write any such letters." LS, *ibid.*

On Jan. 13, Fish wrote in his diary. "Robeson submits draft of Instructions to the Commander of the Tennessee. Question of Newspaper Reporters being allowed to accompany the expedition is considered—Concluded that Mr Fulton of the Balt American—H V Boynton correspondent of the Cincinnati Gazette, & a correspondent to be designated by each of the papers, NY Tribune—Times—Herald & World—& Phil Ledger, & Washington Republican be allowed—Genl Porter to go to NY this Evening to arrange with these Papers—" *Ibid.* On Feb. 14, Allan A. Burton, Santo Domingo City, wrote to Fish. "By desire of the commission of inquiry to Santo Domingo, I have the honor to state, for the information of the Department, the circumstances under which Mr. Rebello was admitted aboard the United States steamer Tennessee on the departure of the commission from New York. Mr. Rebello was employed by me as clerk and copyist, and to assist me in such duties as might be proper for him to perform for me as the secretary of the commission, and with the understanding that his relations to the commission and to me were to be strictly confidential. Soon after setting out on the voyage, Mr. Rebello refused to render me any assistance, and applied to the commissioners for employment. The commissioners declined to employ him except in some capacity in which he could be useful to me in the discharge of my duties as its secretary, and to which I would recommend him. Finding that I could not conscientiously do this, I was forced to discharge him. He had already received $200 payment of his wages, which I understood to be at the rate of $200 a month. I beg leave to add that, after the commission declined to employ Mr. Rebello, except upon the terms above stated, he avowed himself to be the assistant editor of the New York Sun." *SED*, 42-1-9, 48–49. See also *ibid.*, pp. 39–40.

On Jan. 9, U.S. Representative Nathaniel P. Banks of Mass. had written to Fish. "Mr. James F. Farrell, attached to the 'Free Press' office, in New York, who was with Admiral Poor at San Domingo, desires that he may be allowed to have passage on board the vessel which is to take the San Domingo commissioners out to that Island. So far as I know, he is a reliable and worthy man, and will justify the liberality of the Government if it shall accord to him his request." LS, DNA, RG 59, Letters of Application and Recommendation. On Jan. 14, E. F. Waters, "Publisher Boston Advertiser," telegraphed to Secretary of the Navy George M. Robeson. "Secy. Fish has referred the Boston Advertiser to you for permission to send correspondent with San Domingo commission. We have had correspondence tendered us but we desire to send Mr Herbert Tuttle of our own staff whom we know to be friendly to the Administration" Copy, DLC-USG, II, 5.

On Jan. 16, a newspaper reported that "Ex-Senator Wade and President White, of Cornell University, left here last night for New York, and will be joined in that city by Dr. Howe, of Boston, the third commissioner, and Judge Burton, the secretary. The commissioners were accompanied from this city last night by Secretary Robeson, Gen. Porter, of the President's staff, and Commodore Alden, of the bureau of equipment, Navy Department, who went on to perfect the arrangements for the departure of the Tennessee. They were also accompanied by Professor Blake, of the State Department, as geologist of the expedition; Dr. Parry, botanist of the Agricultural Department, and an assistant; Frederick Douglass, who has been appointed one of the secretaries to the commission; J. P. Foley, Esq., phonographer to the commission and correspondent of the New York *Times*; R. R. Hilt, Esq., assistant phonographer; Gen. H. V. N. Boynton, correspondent of the Cincinnati *Gazette*; Arthur Shepherd, of the Washington *Republican*; H. J. Ramsdell, of the Cincinnati *Commercial* and Charles Douglass, (colored,) of the *New Era*. In New York they were joined by Dr. Phillips, who goes out for the *Herald*, C. C. Fulton, of the Baltimore *American*, and others." *Washington Star*, Jan. 16, 1871. For a final list of those authorized to accompany the Santo Domingo Commission, see *SED*, 42-1-9, 36.

On Jan. 18, Babcock wrote to "L. Prang & Co.," Boston. "The President directs me to inform you that your letter came too late to send any answer before the sailing of the Steamer Tennessee. He does not know that any artist accompanied the expedition. He would be pleased to have such views as you mention published." Copy, DLC-USG, II, 1.

On Feb. 17, a correspondent reported from Washington, D. C. "The Navy Department is still without any news concerning the Tennessee. The President informed Gov. Morton yesterday that he did not expect to hear from the Tennessee until the arrival of the Tybee steamer at Key West or New York. He added that if he did not hear from her by next Wednesday, he would begin to be uneasy." *Boston Transcript*, Feb. 17, 1871. On Feb. 20, Horace Porter telegraphed to Morton McMichael, Philadelphia. "Steamer North America from Brazil at New York, reports Tennessee at San Domingo all right." Copy, DLC-USG, II, 5. The Santo Domingo Commissioners had reached their destination on Jan. 24. *SED*, 42-1-9, 4.

1. Son of publisher and politician Morton McMichael, William McMichael was born in 1841, graduated from the University of Pennsylvania (1859), and became a lawyer. He served during the Civil War as staff officer and was mustered out as maj. and bvt. col. See *PUSG*, 3, 217–22; *ibid.*, 5, 34; *ibid.*, 20, 129; *New York Times*, April 21, 1893. On March 14, 1871, USG nominated McMichael as solicitor of Internal Revenue; on Dec. 6, as asst. attorney gen.; on March 13, 1873, as U.S. attorney, Eastern District, Pa. On Nov. 3, 1875, McMichael, Philadelphia, wrote to USG resigning his post "to engage in a general law practice." ALS, DNA, RG 60, Letters from the President.

To Hamilton Fish

Washington D. C. Jan.y 15th *18*71

HON. H. FISH:
SEC. OF STATE,
DEAR SIR:

Mr. Wade informs me that the "form of an oath" alluded to in his instructions is not found among the papers furnished to him. I presume there has been an oversight in not putting this in.

Can you furnish the required blanks to-day so that the Commission need not be delayed.

Yours Truly
U. S. GRANT

ALS, DLC-Hamilton Fish. See following letter. On Jan. 16, 1871, Horace Porter, New York City, telegraphed to Orville E. Babcock. "Shall stay over tomorrow They sail at half past ten AM, *Ship* and *frigate supplies* sound the vessel employs Foley. Everything works satisfactorily" Telegram received, DLC-Hamilton Fish.

On the same day, Secretary of State Hamilton Fish wrote to USG. "A telegram from Messrs Spofford & Tileston, in answer to one from me enquiring when the Tybee will sail on her next trip says 'probably one week from Saturday next'." Copy (press), *ibid.* On Jan. 25, Babcock wrote to "Spofford Bros & Co.," New York City. "Will you greatly oblige Mr Burton the Sect'y. of the Commission to San Domingo, by sending him the enclosed package of letters. If the Commission has left the Island, or it will be impracticable to send these letters to him, may I ask you to have Capt. Delanoy bring the package back, and return it to Washington under cover to the President, . . ." Copy, DLC-USG, II, 1. On Feb. 28, William J. Reid, New York City, wrote to Babcock. "I propose sailing in the next trip of the 'Tybee' for Santo Domingo, & if you can have me made bearer of despatches for the State Department I shall be happy to take charge of its despatches as well as any you or any of your friends may have. The 'Tybee' will sail next wednesday week March 8 /71. Mrs. Reid, who goes with me, sends her regards to you & Mrs. Babcock, . . . P. S. Anything you may have for me, please send to the care of Spofford Bros & Co." ALS, DNA, RG 59, Letters of Application and Recommendation.

To Buenaventura Báez

Washington, D. C., Jany. 15. 1871.

His Excellency, B. Baez,
Pres. Republic of San Domingo
Sir:

In accordance with a joint resolution of the two houses of the Congress of the United States, I have appointed three distinguished Citizens of the United States, towit: Hon. B. Wade,[1] many years a Senator, President A. D. White,[2] Cornell University, and Dr S. G. Howe,[3] distinguished for his philanthropy, learning and services in relieving the blind and mute of much of the monotony of life, natural to their infirmities, by opening to them the world of letters, as Commissioners to visit the Republic of Santo Domingo, and to obtain the information called for by the resolution. Associated with the Commission is also Judge A. A. Burton,[4] Secretary[5] to the same, a gentleman who has honored his Country by serving it in a diplomatic Capacity. I beg to introduce these gentlemen and to ask for them your kind offices.

With Great respect,
Your Obedient Servant,
U. S. GRANT.

Copies, DLC-Frederick Douglass; DLC-USG, II, 1. On Feb. 2, 1871, after receiving USG's letter from Benjamin F. Wade, president of the Santo Domingo Commission, Buenaventura Báez spoke. "GENTLEMEN: I have received with pleasure the autograph letter which his excellency President Grant has sent through a medium so highly appreciated by me. I understand that your mission, ordered by the Congress of the United States, is one of absolute peace. This is the aspiration and object of this republic. One of the principal causes that have brought about the present negotiation is the strong desire of our people for the pacification of their country, the development of its resources, and a guarantee for the existence of the liberty and property of the citizens. You may count on the most ample and absolute liberty in pursuing the objects of your mission. The government offers whatever data you may consider necessary for your purposes, and will take especial pleasure in affording everything desired. In making your investigation as to the spontaneity of the resolution of the Dominican people, we ardently desire that you will consult not only the immense majority in favor of annexation to the United States, but also those who oppose it." *SED*, 42-1-9, 40. See letter to Oliver P. Morton, Dec. 9, 1870; message to Congress, April 5, 1871.

On Jan. 10, 1871, Secretary of State Hamilton Fish recorded in his diary that USG "had determined upon the Commissioners to be sent to San Domingo in case of the adoption of the pending resolution on that question—they are Benjamin F. Wade—Andrew G. White, and the Rt Revd Bishop Simpson—& Genl Sigel for Secretary" DLC-Hamilton Fish. On Jan. 13, Fish wrote. "Cabinet—All present—The San Domingo Commission occupies the most of the time Ben. Wade, & President White accept the appointment—Bishop Simpson cannot go. Dr S. G. Howe of Boston has been recommended by Mr Burt Post Master at Boston, & by Senator Wilson—Robeson advocates the appointment—'if he concurs in a favorable report it will disarm Sumner, & his immediate advocates—if he disagrees it will be accepted as Sumner's view—Howe is a man of integrity & intelligence—well known & universally respected—his selection will be received favorably, & be an earnest of a desire to appoint a fair, & an intelligent Commission—' these views being generally agreed to President telegraphs to Howe, tendring him the appointment—Sigel declines the appointment of Secretary on the ground that he is not sufficiently familiar with the Spanish language—Allan A Burton of Ky formerly Minister to Colombia is appointed—& Fred Douglass appointed as Assistant to the Secretary—Ben. Wade attends the Meeting of the Cabinet I submit the form of Commission to be given to the Comrs & to the Secretary—which is approved . . . Call upon the President, to submit draft instructions to the Commissioners and Secretary, on the San Domingo Commission—and to determine the amount of compensation to the Secretary—He proposes five thousand dollars—which I think too large—as the time occupied will probably not exceed two or three months, & suggest a compensation at a certain rate per annum—which he approves—I suggest the rate of five thousand a year—

he proposes six thousand a year, which is agreed upon—" *Ibid.* On the same day, USG issued appointments for Benjamin F. Wade of Ohio, Andrew D. White of N. Y., and Samuel G. Howe of Mass. as commissioners, and Allan A. Burton as secretary. Copy, DNA, RG 59, General Records. On Jan. 14, a correspondent reported: "THE SAN DOMINGO COMMISSION, As now constituted, gives unqualified satisfaction. Even Mr. Sumner's most intimate friends and supporters express their pleasure at the appointment of Dr. Howe. It is understood Mr. Wade is the President's first and own choice for the head of the Commission. Mr. Wade is known by every one to be incorruptible. The choice of President White, of the Cornell University, is partly due to Secretary Fish and Senator Conkling, though the President has before desired to honor him. He was at one time selected for the English Legation, and but for the wish to have Morton go, he would have received the commission. Dr. Howe the President has never met personally. His name was suggested in a telegram from Boston, sent by a friend of the President." *Philadelphia Public Ledger*, Jan. 16, 1871. On Feb. 17, Governor Rutherford B. Hayes of Ohio wrote in his diary. "I saw the President; called with Mr. Delano at a Cabinet meeting. All informal.... Then turned and talked about San Domingo. Said he chose the commissioners on account of their high character. Two of them he had never seen, Messrs. White and Howe; didn't know the opinions of any of them. Didn't want them to find facts to sustain anybody's opinions. That if they reported unfavorably, that would end the matter; if favorably, then he hoped annexation would take place." Charles Richard Williams, ed., *Diary and Letters of Rutherford Birchard Hayes* (Columbus, 1922–26), III, 131. On April 25, U.S. Senator Charles Sumner of Mass. wrote to Francis W. Bird. "*private* ... Prof. Agassiz when here mentioned a curious fact. He was waited upon last Jan. by *Postmaster Jones* of N. Y, in the name of the Prest, & invited to be a St Domingo Commr. The Professor saw at once that the object was to enlist a personal friend of Mr Sumner, & he *was determined not to get caught in this way....*" ALS, MH.

On Jan. 10, USG had telegraphed to Matthew Simpson. "Commission will probably leave about Monday 17th. I am anxious for favorable answer from you." Copy, DLC-USG, II, 5. About this date, Simpson wrote to USG declining the appointment as commissioner. William Evarts Benjamin, Catalogue No. 42, March, 1892, p. 20.

On Oct. 20, 1870, Ebenezer D. Bassett, minister to Haiti, "New York Bay," wrote to Frederick T. Dent. "Allow me to introduce to you the bearer my distinguished friend Frederick Douglass. The President expressed to me his desire to see and converse with Mr. Douglass, and I promised His Excellency that I would call at the Executive Mansion with him. But when I was last in Washington, I had, as you may remember, no opportunity to do so. I am now on ship board in NewYork Bay on my way to Hayti, and I therefore beg you to do me the favor to present Mr. Douglass to His Excellency the President." ALS, Harry S. Truman Library, Independence, Mo. On Jan. 11, 1871, Horace Porter wrote to Frederick Douglass, Washington, D. C. "The President directs me to say that he will be obliged to you, if you will call at the Executive Mansion about twelve o'clock today, and if not convenient to come today then at about that hour tomorrow." Copy, DLC-USG, II, 1. On Jan. 12, U.S. Senator Willard Warner of Ala. wrote to USG. "I know that you will appreciate rightly my motives in stating to you my conviction that it will be fitting and wise for you to appoint Frederick Douglas as one of the San Domingo Commissioners. I understand him not to be committed on the question of annexation. His race are deeply interested, and a strong effort is being made to prejudice them against annexation. Has Mr. Chase's name occurred to you?" ALS (misdated 1870), OFH. On the same day, Brig. Gen. Oliver O. Howard wrote in his diary. "I began to urge upon him (General Grant, at an interview at the White House) the thought that he might have kept Senator Sumner from opposition [to himself] if he had exercised his accustomed wisdom and knowledge of human character. He smiled, and finished my idea before the sentence was complete, and then told us simply how Mr. Sumner had disappointed him. Mr. Douglass, who was present, presented some thoughts about the unfulfilled mission of the Republican party, and how necessary it still is to continue it. General Grant said, earnestly, 'Yes, it is so, whoever may lead.' I plead, as usual, for *education*, presenting the idea of a full-fledged *department*, with a seat in the Cabinet." Brackets in original; Laura C. Holloway, *Howard: The Christian Hero* (New York, 1885), p. 225. In 1871, Douglass wrote to USG "that his son will go in his stead as Secretary of the San Domingo Commission." William Evarts Benjamin, Catalogue No. 27, Nov., 1889, p. 6. See *Life and Times of Frederick Douglass: Written By Himself* (1892; reprinted, New York, 1962), pp. 407–11; Philip S. Foner, *The Life and Writings of Frederick Douglass* (New York, 1950–55), IV, 64–72.

On Jan. 6, Douglass had written to Sumner. ". . . The article to which you take exception was written in the interest of peace between you and the President—and not in furtherance of the scheme of *annexion* of San Domingo. I reserve my sentiments for the moment on that subject. The point at which I thought you bitterly severe upon the President was where you exposed his ignorance in regard to the names of Senate Committees: and more especially where you associate his name with the infamous names of Pierce, Buchanan and Johnson. These names in the minds of all loyal and liberty loving men stand under the heaviest reproach—and I candidly think you did wrong to place Grant in that infamous category even by implication. I may be wrong—but I do not at present see any good reason for degrading Grant in the eyes of the American people. Personally, he is nothing to me, but as the president, the Republican President—of the country—I am anxious if it can be done to hold him in all honor. But I am free, I am slave to no man—and if the future shall show that General Grant is unworthy—I will join with the '*World*' the '*Sun*'—and the whole Democratic party in denouncing him. . . ." ALS, MH.

On Dec. 16, 1870, J. Watson Webb, New York City, had written to USG. "The Commissioners to be appointed under Senator Morton's resolution, are not to receive any remuneration: and therefore, I beg leave to be considered an applicant for the appointment. I am, as you know, thoroughly in favour of the annexation of St. Domingo; but at the same time, I could act impartially in reporting the *facts* in the case,—a duty for which I think, my whole public life peculiarly qualifies me. I believe too, that the information sure to be elicited by Senator Morton's resolution, will insure favorable action my Congress. Permit me to add, that I am not directly or indirectly, interested in the annexation of St. Domingo, to the amount of one Dollar; and probably, my appointment might induce friends, now opposed to the purchase, to examine more critically any report favorable to the acquisition of the Island,—which would virtually, be securing to the U. S. the control of the West Indies Group." ALS, DNA, RG 59, Letters of Application and Recommendation.

On Dec. 26, Secretary of War William W. Belknap endorsed to USG a letter of Dec. 23 addressed to him by Winthrop DeWolf, Providence, R. I. "As I see it is proposed to send a Commission to San Domingo to obtain further information respecting the values and capabilities of that island, and presuming, that if the measure passes, the appointment of one or more of the Commissioners will be within your control, directly or indirectly, I beg leave to suggest for that position the name of Col John Winthrop, my uncle, and your former client in Keokuk matters, when, as you will remember, he was a heavy loser. Shortly before the time when his affairs were placed in your hands, he had retired from a successful law practice of many years in New Orleans. During the war with Mexico, he held for some time a position on Gen. Taylor's staff in that country. Col Winthrop is a man of quick observation and clear judgment—speaks Spanish and Italian fairly—French and German fluently, and seems peculiarly qualified for the mission, not only from having no private interests to serve, but from having spent much time in the West Indies, particularly in Cuba, when he had the management, as Executor, of a large sugar estate, for a considerable period. Should you think proper to give him the appointment, he will call upon you whenever it is desired." ALS, *ibid.*

On the same day, Charles V. Dyer, Chicago, wrote to U.S. Senator Lyman Trumbull of Ill. "If it would not be doing too much for Illinois—I would accept very gladly the San Domingo commissionership—having all along felt a lively interest in the matter." ALS, *ibid.* On Dec. 31, Trumbull endorsed this letter to USG. "I presume you know Dr. Dyer. He was formerly one of the judges under the Treaty with Great Britian for the suppression of the slave trade—He is an enterprising & intelligent Gentleman—" AES, *ibid.*

On Dec. 27, L. C. Norvell, New Orleans, had written to USG. "having always advocated the annexation of the Island of St Domingo to the U. S: as a political as well as a national necesity, I now write to make application for the appointment of one of the Commissioners soon to be sent there, to look into the expediency of such an arrangement as will be of mutual benefit to both countries. should the appointments be made before this letter reaches you, you will please make such mention of me to the commissioners as will give me a friendly reception by them, as I propose to go with ~~them~~ or meet them in St Domingo" ALS, *ibid.*

On Dec. 31, U.S. Senator Richard Yates of Ill. wrote to USG. "The writer of the within letter Hon. Edwd A. Turpin is an old friend of mine, and I feel compelled, though reluctantly, to trouble you with his application. He was long a Minister resident at Carracas, and is complete master of the Spanish language. He is quell qualified for such a place and is in every respect worthy. Supposing the Commission has probably been determined on, I think it useless to say more. I have been debarred by sickness from calling to pay my respects to the President this session which it would have afforded me pleasure to do" ALS, *ibid.* The enclosure is *ibid.*

On Jan. 10, 1871, U.S. Senator John Sherman of Ohio wrote to USG. "I have known Thos. Webster Esq of Philadelphia—the writer of the enclosed letter—as an ardent active Republican of character and abilities—I believe he would be if selected a good Commissioner to San Domingo and that he would with energy & thoroughness perform the duties enjoined by the pending Resolution" ALS, OFH.

On Jan. 12, Orville E. Babcock wrote to Wade. "The President will be pleased to have you see the bearer Mr J. P. Foley, a short hand writer. Mr. Foley is highly recommended to the President for the place of clerk to the commission. From the personal knowledge we have of the gentleman we believe he will be the best man for the position." Copy, DLC-USG, II, 1. On the same day (3:20 P.M.), Babcock telegraphed to U.S. Senator Oliver P. Morton of Ind. "If you have not committed yourself to appointment of Mr Hitt, the President will be pleased to have Mr Foley appointed." Copy, *ibid.*, II, 5. John P. Foley and Robert R. Hitt went with the Santo Domingo Commission as stenographers. *SED*, 42-1-9, 35.

1. On Jan. 9, 1871, Wade, Washington, D. C., wrote to Caroline Wade. ". . . I have just returned from a visit to the President, he is extremely cordial seems to think that I am about the best man in the nation, but he will be undeceived before it is over.

Bishop Simpson will be one of the Commissioners if he will serve, the other one is not yet fixed on—. . . The House will take up the Resolutions to day, and the President is fuller in the faith that they will pass at once than I am, He tells me that he mentioned my name to all the members of the Cabinet, and many of the leading members of the House, and they all agreed that it would be the best appointmt that could be made, he enjoined secrecy on them and wonderful to relate it has not yet got out. I should not be disappointed if it was a week yet before we get off. . . ." ALS, DLC-Benjamin F. Wade.

2. Born in 1832 in Homer, N. Y., White was raised in Syracuse, graduated from Yale College (1853), and studied and traveled in Europe before becoming a history professor at the University of Michigan. Returning to N. Y. during the Civil War, he became a state senator (1864) and helped found Cornell University, which opened with him as president in 1868. On Jan. 2, 1871, Archibald C. Powell, Syracuse, wrote to Fish. "I write to suggest to the Prest. through you the name of Hon. Andrew D. White Prest of Cornell University as one of the Commissioners to St. Domingo Mr White is a ripe Scholar, of unsullied reputation as a man & a Politician; a fine Linguist speaking very fluently the French language and is withal an uncompromising friend of the Administration. He is favorably known throughout this country and to a great extent abroad. In fact he is so well known to you that he needs no commendation at my hands. I think the appointment would be very gratifying to him and to the entire Republican Party in this State. . . ." ALS, DNA, RG 59, Letters of Application and Recommendation. On Jan. 10, USG wrote to White. "May I ask of you the favor to accept the position of Commissioner to visit Santo Domingo, in accordance with the resolution which has just passed the House of Representatives? Should you accept, and should each of the other gentlemen whom I have asked to go accept also, the commission will be composed of yourself, B. F. Wade of Ohio, and Bishop Simpson of Pa. Gen. F. Sigel has been invited to go as Secretary to the Commission. Please notify me by telegraph your determination in this matter." Copy, DLC-USG, II, 1. On Jan. 11, White, Ithaca, N. Y., wrote to USG. "I have the honor to receive your letter informing me of the choice of Commissioners to visit Santo Domingo and, among them, of myself. In renewing my acceptance—already telegraphed—of the position, permit me to return my thanks for this mark of confidence and to present assurances that it shall be my constant endeavor to discharge with fidelity the highly honorable duties thus imposed" ALS, OFH. Possibly on the same day, White telegraphed to Porter. "I telegraphed acceptance this morning, I leave for Washington immediately," Telegram received (on Jan. 12), DNA, RG 107, Telegrams Collected (Bound). On Jan. 15, a correspondent reported: "The Hon. Andrew J. White, member of the San Domingo Commission, arrived to-day, and had a pleasant interview with the President, who said to Mr. White that he was earnestly anxious to have everything probed to the bottom. He remarked further, with a broad smile, that he wanted all the villany exposed if they could find any, and especial search made for those lots on Samana Bay, said to be marked 'Grant,' 'Babcock,' &c. He further said that he trusted he was as open to conviction against the policy of annexation as he was desirous that others should be converted to such policy." *Philadelphia Public Ledger*, Jan. 16, 1871. On Nov. 30, 1870, Joseph W. Fabens, New York City, had written to Fish. "I observed in the New-York Herald of 22d instant, a report of an interview with Secretary Sumner at Chicago, at which he states that a friend of his who had been in Santo Domingo told him that the coast of Samana Bay was staked off into lots marked. Baez. Cazneau and Babcock and that some large ones were marked Grant. I have been looking daily for a disclaimer by Mr Sumner

of this statement attributed to him. but have seen none up to this date. I hardly need to assure you that there is not the slightest foundation for the assertion made by Mr Sumner's friend—. . ." ALS, DNA, RG 59, Notes from Foreign Legations, Dominican Republic. See *Autobiography of Andrew Dickson White* (New York, 1905), I, 483–507; Glenn C. Altschuler, *Andrew D. White—Educator, Historian, Diplomat* (Ithaca, 1979), pp. 108–11.

3. Born in 1801 in Boston, Howe graduated from Brown University (1821), received an M.D. from Harvard (1824), and spent the next six years assisting the Greek struggle for independence. Returning to Mass., he directed the Perkins School for the Blind, married Julia Ward (1843), and became associated with educational and humanitarian reforms. On Dec. 30, 1870, Sumner wrote to Howe. ". . . I am in the midst of a struggle as in the olden time for the down-trodden. This St Domingo business is of heartless cruelty, & the Haytien govt. appeal to me for protection. The minister is full of distress & emotion. The same pressure now as against Kansas!" ALS, MH. On Jan. 13, 1871, USG telegraphed to Howe. "I will be pleased if you will go as one of the Commissioners to Santo Domingo. If you accept please notify me, by telegraph and meet the other Commissioners in New York City, to sail in Steamer Tennessee, on Monday next." Copy, DLC-USG, II, 5. On Jan. 14, Babcock wrote to Fish. "The President directs me to inform you, in reply to your note just received, that, Dr Howe has accepted the position of Commissioner; that, the name is J. P. Foley, and that we do not know here what Mr. Hitt's full name is." LS, DLC-Hamilton Fish. See Harold Schwartz, *Samuel Gridley Howe: Social Reformer, 1801–1876* (Cambridge, Mass., 1956), pp. 296–320.

On March 30, 1869, Governor William Claflin of Mass. had written to USG. "The friends of Dr Saml G Howe are very desirous that he should receive the appointment of Minister to Greece—Such a nomination will be most gratifying to the people of this State, where his life long service and devotion, to the cause of freedom and humanity are so well know.—His labors in behalf of the blind, the poor and the oppressed demand high recognition, from the Government, but, added to these, is the consideration that he is peculiarly fitted for the duties of the position, by a thorough knowledge of the language, the habits and institutions of the people ~~to which~~ of the country to which he would be sent.—An opportunity is rarely afforded the nation of being represented abroad, by a man, whose reputation as a benefactor of his race is worldwide, whose ability and culture are of the highest order and whose name is a synonym of all, that is noble and magnanimous in human nature. I never ask of the Executive any thing on *personal* grounds, but I will say, that no appointment would afford me so much gratification—" ALS, DNA, RG 59, Letters of Application and Recommendation. On April 1, Gerrit Smith, Peterboro, N. Y., wrote to Fish. "I take no part in the matter of appointments. But hearing this hour (as I do for the first time) that Dr S. G. Howe is spoken of for Minister to Greece, I can hardly refrain from saying to you that, in my judgment, this would be an eminently fit appointment. Dr Howe is a highly intellectual gentleman—& in point of patriotism & benevolence, I know not by whom he is surpassed. No other American is so well acquainted, as he is, with Greece, her people & her interests; and no other American has made such generous, brave & sublime sacrifices for her, as he has made. But I need not, in writing to you dwell upon the merits of Dr Howe. You are familiar with them." ALS, *ibid.*

4. Born in 1820, raised in Lancaster, Ky., and self-educated, Burton practiced law, being designated as associate justice, Dakota Territory, in 1861. President Abraham Lincoln instead appointed him minister to New Granada, and he became minis-

ter to Colombia (1863–67). See Lincoln, *Works*, IV, 294, 408; *ibid.*, VII, 37; *New York Times*, July 21, 1878.

On Nov. 17, 1870, Speed S. Fry, Cincinnati, wrote to USG. "The Hon. Allen A. Burton. of Lancaster Garrard Co. Ky. by whom this note will be handed you, visits the Federal Capital for the purpose of Laying before you, the unsettled condition of affairs in Ky, and especially in that portion of the state, from which he hails. You are doubtless well acquainted with the character and standing of Mr Burton, and it is therefore only necessary for me to say that he will give a you a history of recent events in his portion of the state, which I hope may convince you of the necssity of affording such relief as they demand. Allow me however to say Sir that Mr Burton is a refugee from the threats and persecutions of those who are not only his enemies, but the enemies of the General Govt. These men, composed mainly of original rebels and Ku Klux, seem to be determined to override all Law and to disregard the rights of those who uphold and sustain the Govt in its efforts to restore the Country to peace and good order. Mr Burton is incapable of misrepresenting the matter and I hope Sir you may find it in your power to furnish the relief he comes to seek at your hands. Some thing must be done for the protection not only of the Colored voters of the state, but for many white voters who favor the enfranchisement of the blacks" ALS, DNA, RG 107, Letters Received from Bureaus. A similar letter of Nov. 16 from John T. Croxton, Paris, Ky., to USG is *ibid.* On Aug. 5, 1871, Burton, Lancaster, wrote to Fish. "If the President should be pleased to nominate me Minister Resident to Constantinople, a post understood to be vacant, I would discharge the duties of the office to the best of my poor abilities." ALS, *ibid.*, RG 59, Letters of Application and Recommendation. No appointment followed.

5. See letter to Franz Sigel, Jan. 10, 1871. On Dec. 26, 1870, H. S. Washburn, Washington, D. C., had written to USG. "Permit a a very humble citizen to express his high estimation of, and thanks for your efforts to secure the annexation of San Domingo. It is barely possible a fair knowledge of the Spanish languge acquired by a three years residence in Mexico and considerable study would enable me to be of some service as Secretary of the Commission about to be sent out there. I have been a Surveyor and Miner which experience would be of service in judging of the Mineral & Agricultural advantages of a new country. Wishing the annexation Scheme every success . . ." ALS, *ibid.* No appointment followed.

To Frederick Dent Grant

Washington D. C. Jan.y 15th *1871*

DEAR FRED:

Your letter written after examination is rec'd. You may direct your bills to me to an amount not exceeding $500 00 and I will pay them on presentation. Let me advise you however to get but little uniform clothing. It may be that you will never join a regiment. I advise you to get one suit however, but no sword, sash, epauletsts or other paraphernalia which you will not wear on furlough.—I do not think it necessary for you to come home before graduation. Not now certainly. I would try from this to June to make up all possible.

We are all well. Your Aunts Jennie & Mary will spend this week with us. Kittie Felt[1] will also be here this week and will spend the balance of the Winter with us.—I believe Buck is in fForm "A," in a class of 189; but he is too diffident to say anything about it. It is but a little over four months now until you will go into your final examination. The time will soon pass, so be of good cheer.

Yours Affectionately
U. S. GRANT

ALS, USG 3. See letter to Ulysses S. Grant, Jr., Nov. 24, 1870, note 1.

On Jan. 28, 1871, Frederick Dent Grant, West Point, testified to the Committee on Military Affairs subcommittee investigating the expulsion of Cadets Enoch H. Flickinger, William Baird, and McDowel E. Barnes. ". . . On the 2d of January, while we had release from quarters, Mr. Baird, of the fourth class, went to Buttermilk, where he got drunk. He returned in the afternoon, and in the evening he told one of his classmates, Mr. Dallon, that he was going down again. Mr. Dallon told him not to go, that he would be 'hived' if he was caught during the inspection. He replied something to the effect that he was all right; that he had arranged with Flickinger; that he had him under his control, so that he would do what he told him to. At the sentinel's inspection at the first relief, Flickinger answered 'all right;' the sentinel, however, suspected that all was not right, and so reported to the corporal. Q. You need not go through with the details. Your class were satisfied that these cadets were guilty of falsehood, and held a meeting for the purpose of taking measures to expel them from the Point?—A. Yes, sir. There had been a great many court-martials before that, and out of 29 that had been dismissed within the last ten years, only one has remained away. Q. You divided your class into three squads who were to take care of these boys?—A. Yes. Q. The principal part of the class were engaged in the affair?—A. The whole of it. Q. Are you a member of that class?—A. Yes, sir. Q. You took part in the affair the same as the rest?—A. Yes, sir. By Mr. SLOCUM: Q. Speaking about the number of cases in which sentences have been remitted, in how many of these cases have you applied for a remission of the sentences?—A. Only three, sir. Q. What were they?—A. One was the case of Mr. Clark, class of 1868. He was dismissed for going down to Buttermilk. I wrote a letter to father, but he took no action upon it; Mr. Johnson remitted it; and the other two were the cases of Mr. Groom and Mr. Davenport. I wrote to have their sentences remitted, as they were not guilty of any offense. Their sentence was remitted to suspension for one year. Q. What were they charged with?—A. Conduct unbecoming an officer and a gentleman; the specification was for erasing a report. They did not erase it—at least I understood they did not; and out of the five men who were court-martialed at that time, three of them for lying, the two who were not guilty were sentenced to be dismissed, and only one that was dismissed finally was afterward proven to be innocent, and that was Barnes. Q. Do you recollect the case of Shortelle?—A. That was another case about which I wrote. I forgot that. Q. You wrote on about that?—A. Yes, sir. Q. He was reinstated?—A. Yes, sir. Q. These four cases are the only ones you can call to mind?—A. Yes, sir. By Mr. ASPER: Q. Were you present in the room calling up these boys, and what part did you take personally in sending them off?—A. I was merely in the room. I was appointed treasurer of the committee. I think there were six or eight men in the committee to which I belonged. Q. Did you have a meeting on the day of the 3d, in which you heard testimony in reference to these boys?—A. We had a meeting of the class, I think, on the 3d. We had enough testimony to convince me. Q. The boys were not present at any of these meetings?—A. No, sir. Q. They did not know what was going on?—A. No, sir; we didn't intend to do anything until we were satisfied that they were guilty. Q. Who were the movers?—A. There were no movers. Q. Who were the leaders?—A. No one; all acted together. Q. Did you see anything about violence?—A. There was none that I saw. I only remember seeing three men touch them, and that was only to wake them, which was not roughly at all; just enough to wake them up. They were informed that they had been lying, and that they knew it, and that we were going to send them off. We took them up the road toward Fort Putman and sent them off. I didn't see them touched going up. Q. The talk going up was rather menacing than otherwise toward the boys?—A. I did not pay any attention to it. I believe something was said, if they came back in the morning they would be tarred and feathered. . . . Q. Were there any other threats?—A. Not that I heard. Q. Were they not told to run?—A. Perhaps so; they ran about fifty yards. Q. Were any missiles thrown?—A. None whatever. Q. Did not some of the boys have rocks in their hands?—A. I did not see any. By Mr. SLOCUM: Q. Your class base their action in this matter wholly on the ground that it was found impossible to punish such offenses here?—A. That was one of the reasons; another was, the sentences being remitted as often as they are. We did not consider this the place for liars. Q. Was there not a difficulty between your class and these boys before?—A. None whatever that I know of. I know that Mr. Baird, particularly, had friends in our class. Mr. Barnes had been arrested two or three times for lying, twice I think altogether, and was known to be a liar." *HRC*, 41-3-28, 42–44.

On Feb. 14, 1870, USG had written to Secretary of War William W. Belknap. "Please revoke order approving sentence in the case of Cadet Jas. E. Shortelle and commute his sentence to restriction of limits for the balance of the present Academic year, and loss of rank as a cadet non-commissioned officer for the same period, with the addition of a reprimand for his insubordination. This leniency is shown not because the course of cadet Shortelle is approved, but upon the ground of previous good conduct, the belief that his objectionable conduct will not be repeated, and the provocation which he seemed to have in the excitable manner of a superior officer who appeared intent upon making him convict companions, who were no more guilty than he himself was, morally, of a violation of regulations." Copy, DLC-USG, II, 1. James E. Shortelle, who did not graduate from USMA, was appointed 2nd lt., 11th Inf., as of June 12, 1871, and died on Aug. 5.

The subcommittee recommended that the Secretary of War "restore Cadets Baird, Flickinger, and Barnes to the Military Academy at West Point, to take effect with the beginning of the next academic year; and then permit them to proceed with the fourth class without further punishment for the offenses heretofore committed by them. . . . That the House of Representatives recommend that the Secretary of War convene a court of inquiry for the purpose of ascertaining what members of the first class were instigators and leaders in the affair of January 3 at the United States Military Academy, and that such leaders and instigators be at once dismissed from the Military Academy, and the remaining members of the class engaged in the affair be punished at the discretion of a general court-martial to be convened for their trial."

HRC, 41-3-28, 9–10. See *CG*, 41–3, 465, 701, 1035–37, 1150, 1230–40, 1313–21; Peter S. Michie, *The Life and Letters of Emory Upton* . . . (New York, 1885), pp. 257–72; Stephen E. Ambrose, *Upton and the Army* (Baton Rouge, 1964), pp. 72–74; Walter Scott Dillard, "The United States Military Academy, 1865–1900: The Uncertain Years," Ph.D. Dissertation, University of Washington, 1972, pp. 83–87, 199–200.

On Feb. 11, 1871, an editorial stated: ". . . On the 3d of January three cadets of the Fourth or lowest Class were placed in arrest, by order of the commandant, for the following reasons: BAIRD, for being absent from his quarters during part of the previous night; FLECKINGER, for reporting 'all right,' knowing that his roommate BAIRD was absent without authority; and BARNES, for making a false statement to a sentinel, and under cover of it paying visits, without authority. The offense of the latter was quite distinct from that of the other two. Drunkenness had nothing to do with the matter, for none of the cadets were accused of it, although BAIRD tried to escape punishment by declaring that he was drunk. The proper penalty for drunkenness is dismissal, though it has been customary to remit this punishment when the entire class of which the offender is a member agree to take the pledge of total abstinence. . . . The First Class having learned all the facts regarding these three members of the Fourth Class, and having other additional proofs of their want of veracity, held a meeting, and with but two dissenting voices resolved to administer a lesson to the offenders which would impress upon the entire corps the necessity and importance of truthfulness. . . . The three culprits were quietly visited at midnight on Tuesday, and directed to clothe themselves in citizens' dress, and ordered to leave the Academy. They were led to the Highland Falls road, behind the barrack, and were bid good-bye with a caution never to return, as their trunks would be sent after them. No violence was used, no disturbance raised, none of the party wore masks, and there was no disguise. This is a simple statement of the facts of the case. The action of the cadets was a mistaken effort in behalf of a good cause, and was no mere boyish freak. The punishment for this offense was the severest it was in the power of the Superintendent to inflict. The right of dismissal is vested only in the authorities at Washington, but Col. PITCHER ordered that the cadets of the First Class should be deprived of all privileges, and be confined to even narrower limits than is the case under ordinary circumstances. . . . the class submit to these restrictions without a murmur, being now convinced of their error and of the justice of their sentence. . . ." *New York Times*, Feb. 11, 1871.

On Feb. 14, U.S. Representative Henry W. Slocum of N. Y. (former maj. gen.) spoke in Congress. ". . . It has been asserted that this riotous proceeding on the part of the senior class was prompted solely by a desire of elevating the moral tone of the corps. I believe nothing of the kind; on the contrary, I believe these young men were actuated by a desire to exhibit their own power and independence; and that they were prompted to do it by a conviction on their part that one or more of their number possessed the ability to screen them from punishment, no matter what crime they might commit. . . . When I was a member of the Board of Visitors last spring one of the oldest and most highly respected professors of the Academy stated to me that the discipline of the institution was being lowered by the influence of a cadet who seemed to possess the power of overruling those placed in authority. As an instance, he referred to the case of an instructor who had been grossly insulted by a cadet, and had preferred charges against the cadet which resulted in his conviction by a court. The cadet, however, was reinstated, as it was supposed at the instance of one of his classmates. This professor stated to me that a single instance of this kind tended to intimidate and demoralize all those in immediate authority over the corps. . . . Every officer, without a single exception, summoned before the committee testified to the injurious effect upon the discipline of the Academy which has resulted from the constant interference on the part of the authorities at Washington, the frequent remission of sentences, and sending back to the institution boys who had been justly dismissed. In view of this evidence who can believe that one of these cadets doubted for a moment but that he would be protected in the crime that it was proposed to commit? Who can believe that but for this supposed protection these boys who had been nearly four years under military training would have ventured upon this palpable and willful violation of the law, upon this heartless and cruel treatment of boys who had for only six months enjoyed the advantages of the Academy, and who during that time had maintained good reputations? No one can doubt it. . . . It will teach to the youth of the Academy, to those who may hereafter enter it, and to the country at large that in the United States there is at least one place where mob law is discountenanced, one place where the laws can be executed. It will teach these young men and the young throughout the country that in this land no one, whatever may have been his birth, whatever may be his family connections, can with impunity violate the laws. . . ." *CG*, 41–3, 1234–35.

U.S. Representative Benjamin F. Butler of Mass. then spoke. ". . . There ever has been, and doubtless there still is, an idea there that men of high influence, whose sons are there, will interfere for their protection against breaches of discipline. From the beginning of the history of the Academy this has been the fact, well known of all men. And there is there too much also of the idea that members of Congress will each protect the young man he sent there, and that we will go to the Executive, and go to the Secretary of War, and sustain as against the consequences of their wrongful acts those we have appointed. And we too frequently so do. Let us look to our own action a moment and see whether we do not too frequently do that; whether we are not too frequently impelled so to do by the influence of our constituents, before we attach too much blame to the Executive for listening to our appeals, and before we blame the young cadet, his son, who has perhaps not all that discretion he will have when the frosts of winter will have silvered his hair, as it has done ours. Before we too much blame the action of the son, whose good conduct no doubt caused his father to pardon the offenses of fellow classmates, I trust we shall be entirely sure that members of Congress have not been to the President and asked him, in like manner with the boy, to interfere with the discipline of West Point. . . ." *Ibid.*, pp. 1235–37.

On Feb. 16, U.S. Representative William L. Stoughton of Mich. also spoke. ". . . It is true, sir, that a son of the President of the United States is a member of the first class of the Military Academy and implicated in this transaction. And it is equally true that the committee have endeavored to mete out equal and exact justice to all the cadets. No effort has been made by the committee or by any officer of the Government, civil or military, to shield this young man or palliate his offense. Why, then, the covert attack upon the President by the gentleman from New York? Is it quite fair and chivalric or worthy the high character of that gentleman to attack the father by an assault upon the son? But, aside from this, I propose to show that the assumptions of the gentleman are not supported by a single particle of evidence or a single fact proved or fairly inferable. . . ." *Ibid.*, pp. 1318–19.

Also on the same day, Orville E. Babcock wrote to Lt. Col. Emory Upton, West Point. "Personal. . . . The President will be pleased to know just how long that Committee remained at West Point, and the manner they pursued to procure evidence, and any other points you may be able to give touching the matter. I suppose he would like to have the information come in a shape that could be used officially." Copy, DLC-USG, II, 1.

On June 17, Edward Flickinger, Toledo, wrote to USG. "Could I ask what chance or hopes there is to have my Brother reinstated He feels and we all feel it a duty to try and get back to the academy. we also feel like its a duty you owe to us to reinstate him to the academy The vacancy is still held for him in this District would like much to hear from you in behalf of my Brother If this Brother had any dislike for the academy I would not ask for him to return Hoping to hear from you soon as he is waiting to return . . ." ALS, DNA, RG 94, Correspondence, USMA. Flickinger and Barnes did not graduate.

On Jan. 18, 1869, Nealie Baird, St. Paul, had written to USG. "My husband has just made a formal application to the Sec: of War for an appt. as a Cadet at West Point for our son William, and, altho' I know there are a thousand & one cares, public, & private, that must necessarily press upon you at this time, I *hope* you will not consider me intrusive in calling your attention to this matter, so momentous to us—& in begging from you as favorable a consideration of the case of our boy as you can give—I know General you will deliberate on the case, but I am most anxious you should decide *favorably*—Of Gen. Baird's unwearying services in the field, as well as ever since his entrance into the army nearly 20 years ago, I will say nothing, since the record is familiar to you—His Great GrandFather was killed in battle at Fort Duquesne,—his GrandFather was an officer during the Revolutionary War. & we are naturally anxious that Willie should embrace the same honorable career as his ancestors—He will be 18 next August, & is well advanced in his studies, having recited for two years to Gen. B. who was *seven* years Instructor at West Point—And laying aside my Mother feeling, I believe him to be one of the *best* boys I ever knew, & one who I trust will be an *Honor* to his Country. I have watched the career of your cadet son with great interest, & trust he may fulfil *your* highest expectations—and those of the country—by following in your footsteps—With kindest regards to Mrs. Grant & yourself in which Gen. Baird joins me . . ." ALS, *ibid.* On Feb. 7, 1870, USG endorsed this letter. "Let special attention be called to this application when appointments come to be made." AES, *ibid.* On June 25, 1869, Nealie Baird, Boston, had telegraphed to Horace Porter. "What chance for getting Willie as sep at WestPoint? Could I accomplish anything by immediate interview with the President" Telegram received (on June 26, [1869], 9:00 A.M.), *ibid.*, RG 107, Telegrams Collected (Bound). On June 26, Porter telegraphed an answer to Charlestown, Mass. "President promises Willie shall be the next one appointed No necessity of coming on" Telegram received, *ibid.*, RG 94, Correspondence, USMA.

On March 9, 1871, Lt. Col. Absalom Baird, Washington, D. C., wrote to USG. "While thanking you for the promise you kindly made my [w]ife some weeks ago in relation to the reinstating of our son as a Cadet at the Military Academy, I desire to submit for your consideration a few notes in relation to the same matter intended to meet objections made by the Inspector of the Academy to the Action which you proposed to take It is claimed by the Inspector that the resignation of an individual having been accepted—he is therby out of service, and that the President has no legal authority to reconsider previous action, and by revoking the order of acceptance to put him back in service. In reply to this I desire to state first—that I can discover no statute imposing this prohibition, and no recorded judicial decision or interpretation of law on the subject—Second—that there is no regulation of Army to that effect—and third—that it has been the Custom of the War Department to reconsider the action by which Officers have been separated from the Army, and to restore them—. . . I would further state that the resignation of my son was extorted from him, under an amount of pressure that may fairly be regarded as compulsion—that he is a minor and not legally comptent to act in a matter of the kind, without my consent; while a regulation of the Academy expressly forbids the acceptance of a cadets resignation without the consent of his parent—Had the Superintendant of the Academy sent a telegram to the Hd. Quarters where I am known to be stationed, as soon as the trouble occurred, my refusal to consent would have reached him before he acted—as it [w]as although I only learned of the occurrences through the intervention of a friend who saw them noticed in the public prints—a telegram from me did reach him immediately afterwards—Under all of the circumstances I do not think that the resignation of my son can be regarded as a legal act—" ALS, *ibid.* William Baird graduated USMA in 1875.

1. On Dec. 11, 1870, Julia Dent Grant invited Katherine Felt to visit. "Do not delay for any preparation—I would be very glad to assist you with my advice & taste which I flatter myself is as good at least as your N. York dress maker . . . Dont see company but once a week except in the Evening when of course we are at home. . . . Papa is well & sends regards . . ." *The Collector*, No. 842 (1975), I-693; Charles Hamilton Auction No. 111, March 23, 1978, no. 124.

To Senate

TO THE SENATE OF THE UNITED STATES.

I transmit to the Senate, in answer to their resolution of the 4th instant, a report from the Secretary of State,[1] with accompanying documents, relating to the proposed annexation of the Dominican portion of the island of St. Domingo.

Washington, Jan. 16. 1871.

U. S. GRANT

DS, DNA, RG 46, Presidential Messages. On Dec. 9, 1870, U.S. Senator Charles Sumner of Mass. introduced a resolution passed on Jan. 4, 1871. "That the President of the United States be requested to communicate to the Senate, if, in his opinion, not incompatible with the public interests, copies of all papers and correspondence relating to the proposed annexation of the Dominican portion of the Island of San Domingo, or the purchase of any part thereof, including the first and all subsequent instructions to any agent or consul, of the United States, with the correspondence of such agent or consul; also, any protocol or convention signed by such agent or consul; also, an account of the debt and liabilities of the Dominican government, especially its obligations to the neighboring republic of Hayti; also, the provisions of the existing constitution of Dominica, so far as the same relate to the sale or transfer of the national domain; also, any treaty with Hayti or France, by which Dominica is bound or affected; (also any communication from the neighboring republic of Hayti, or from our minister there, relating to the proposed annexation;) also, instructions to the commander of our naval squadron in the waters of the island since the commencement of the late negotiations, with the reports and correspondence of such commander; also, any information tending to show what European power, if any proposes to acquire jurisdiction of any part of the island, and if so, of what part; also, any information with regard to the position of President Baez, under whom the treaty of annexation was negotiated, and the extent to which he has been maintained in power by the presence of United States vessels of War; also, any information with regard to the sentiments of the people in Dominica and the reported pendency there of Civil War; also any information with regard to any claim of jurisdiction by the republic of Hayti over the territory of Dominica" D, *ibid.*, RG 59, Miscellaneous Letters; *CG*, 41-3, 51. See *ibid.*, pp. 53, 183–85, 190–91, 291; *SED*, 41-3-17.

On Jan. 31 and Feb. 3, Orville E. Babcock wrote to J. C. Bancroft Davis, asst. secretary of state. "Can you have the part within the blue pencil mark translated and returned to me? It does not look like concealing the matter from the Dominicans," ALS, DLC-J. C. Bancroft Davis. "Have you yet had made the translation of the newspaper article? If you have will you please have it sent down. Also the copies of the report in answer to Sumner's resolution on San Domingo, of which we were speaking." LS, DNA, RG 59, Miscellaneous Letters. Davis sent ten copies. AE (undated), *ibid.*

On Nov. 16, 1870, Secretary of State Hamilton Fish had written to Ebenezer D. Bassett, U.S. minister, Port-au-Prince. "Representations have been made to this government by that of the Dominican Republic, that the government of Haiti is constantly putting in jeopardy the tranquillity of that Republic by conniving at the organization of factions in Haiti and by furnishing war material to Dominican insurgents. It is also represented that this is done despite professions of strict neutrality on the part of the Haytien government. It is presumed that that government must be aware that, at this juncture especially the government of the United States is peculiarly interested in the exemption of the Dominican Republic both from internal commotions and from invasions from abroad. If, therefore, there should be any just foundation for the complaint of the Dominican government adverted to, this government expects that at least so long as the relations of the United States with that Republic shall continue to be as intimate and as delicate as they now are the Haytien government will as a proof of its good will towards us do every thing which may be in its power towards avoiding any cause for such complaint. You will address a note to this effect to the Haytien Minister for Foreign Affairs" Copy, *ibid.*, Diplomatic Instructions, Haiti and Santo Domingo. On Jan. 25, 1871, Bassett wrote to Fish reporting his discussion with Haitian officials. LS, *ibid.*, Diplomatic Despatches, Haiti. On the same day, Bassett wrote twice more to Fish. "Private No 8. . . . There is much excitement here just now in reference to the annexation of St. Domingo to the United States, though the reports which appear in the New York papers are ridiculously absurd. The public meetings therein reported to have taken place, have been and are practically prohibited. It is true however that the Haïtien newspapers teem with accounts of the 'terrible question of annexation.' And it is true that the ruling sentiment here is opposed to any and every thing looking to a possibility of giving up the nationality of Haïti. But it is also true that the intelligent people of the cities begin to open their eyes to the advantages of a stable Government. Some of the men who fume most unreasonably in the public prints against annexation, have privately assured me of their warm sympathy with the annexation scheme. The very man who heads the movement for a testimonial to Senator Sumner for his opposition to the annexation of St. Domingo, has over and over again assured me that he is in favor of that annexation. . . ." "Private No 9. . . . The Mr. Delmonte who was sent with Mr. A. Folsom as a Commissioner to Washington for this Government on the downfall of Salnave, and who is, I believe, a nephew of one of President Baëz's ministers, has often called to express to me the views of Genl Cabral, both himself and General Cabral being warmly in favor of the annexation of St. Domingo to the United States, but ostensibly opposed to it. Recently he has inquired of me whether you would receive a special and private messenger from General Cabral. I told him 'Yes,' if he went to you in a purely personal and private character. I asked him the nature of General Cabral's message to you. He replied that General Cabral wished to see if arrangements could not be made by which he could withdraw his (pretended) opposition to Annexation and leave St. Domingo. Having received the promise that neither himself (General Cabral) nor Baëz should be appointed Governor in case of annexation, he wished to know if some arrangement could not be made whereby his debts of a public character could be paid. He hinted that a few thousand dollars in addition would be desirable to satisfy his chief followers. The whole amount would probably not exceed, he estimated, a hundred and fifty thousand dollars. He wished also to ascertain what would be the fate of those who are in prison and in exile under Baëz. I told him that I could not give him one word of assurance about money, but that the United States would not tolerate for a single hour after annexation the idea of holding persons in prison or in exile for political offenses said to have been committed against either General Cabral or President Baëz. It is my impression that the peaceful annexation of St. Domingo to the United States depends entirely upon the action of Congress. There is not the slightest ground for fear of hostile opposition after it is consummated, from either Haïti or any faction in St. Domingo itself." LS, *ibid.* On Feb. 7, Fish wrote in his diary. "*Cabinet*—All present—Read Bassetts No 66 Jany 25 (Port au Prince) & No 64 same date also his '*Private*' despatches No 8 & 9 of same date—the latter stating that Delmonte (Cabrals friend) had applied in Cabrals name to know if a special messenger would be received from him—& that Cabral was in favor of annexation, & would like to receive a sum of money—&c—President desires these two to be shown to Morton, Harlan Cameron—" DLC-Hamilton Fish. On Feb. 9, Fish wrote to Bassett. "Your despatch No. 64, of the 25th ultimo, has been received. The assurances offered to you by the Haytien government as to its disposition to keep wholly neutral in the contest between the Dominican parties severally headed by Baez and Cabral, do not seem to be expressed in a way to inspire perfect confidence in their sincerity. . . . It may easily be understood that the Haytiens, being mostly descended from those of African extraction, who once held in slavery won their freedom and independence by expelling their former masters, should be reluctant to allow any nation tolerating slavery to acquire dominion in St. Domingo. This feeling should not now, however, include the United States, especially in view of the fact, that the equality of races here before the law, is signally exemplified in the person of our diplomatic representative accredited to them." Copy, DNA, RG 59, Diplomatic Instructions, Haiti and Santo Domingo. See letter to Oliver P. Morton, Dec. 9, 1870; message to Senate, Feb. 7, 1871; message to Congress, April 5, 1871 (2), note 1.

On Dec. 30, 1871, Pedro Melas, "Officer in the domn Army," New York City, wrote to USG. "*Private* . . . The underhand circulation of certain pamphlets in the shape of a protest, maliciously represented as emanating from citizens of 'Santo Domingo', against annexation to the United States, having at length come to light, I cannot, as a true born dominican & sincere patriot, allow, without doing great injustice to all my countrymen, such unwarrantable acts of infamy to pass over in silence without denouncing them as those of an impostor & calculated to deceive the credulous public, nor can I leave you in ignorance of the fact that the 'prime mover' of all the mischief is the 'Haytian Minister,' Mr Preston who, to serve his own purpose & private interests, has resorted to the like stratagem by having the said pamphlets prepared & elaborated in this city by his paid agents & associates, to throw, if possible, every impediment in the way of an understanding between Santo Domingo and the United States govt. in relation to the annexation question. It is well, Mr President, that you should know that Mr Preston, who resides in this city, aided by his *paid agents,* has been constantly engaged in all such fabrications, as the documents referred to, and the vilest machinations, unworthy of a Minister, to deceive public opinion while prejudicing the good disposition & views of the U S. Government towards the dominican people, who are all eagerly waiting for a favorable solution of the question at issue—The Haytian Minister, Mr Preston's sole object, while manoeuvring as depicted above, is to speculate upon his own govt. & the people of Hayt[i] by making them believe that he has, through the channel of some influential political men at Washington, who lent him their assistance for certain pecuniary considerations, succeeded in counteracting the designs of the U. S government & defeating annexation. Therefore to attain his ends, he has on several occasions drawn for large sums of money on his govt. under the false pretext of having to compensate those influential men at Washington for their services—&c in the matter. These few lines, I trust, Mr President, will suffice to convince you that the pamphlets alluded to never came from dominican citizens, who are all unanimously longing for 'annexation,' but are the work of Mr Preston as every body knows—" ALS, DNA, RG 59, Miscellaneous Letters. On Jan. 20, 1872, Fish wrote to Melas. "I understand that you have addressed a letter to the President of the United States marked 'Private,' in which you charge that certain pamphlets are covertly circulated containing slanders on him and that Mr Preston, the Minister from Hayti, is the instigator of the proceeding. Before any notice can be taken of such an accusation, it would be desirable to know what are the titles and the subjects of the pamphlets to which you refer and what proof you have of the participation of Mr Preston in circulating them—" LS, *ibid.* John H. Haswell, clerk, State Dept., endorsed Fish's letter as "returned by the Postmaster at New York." AE (initialed), *ibid.*

1. On Jan. 10, 1871, Fish wrote in his diary. "I then read to the Cabinet a draft reply to the Senates Call (Sumners Resolution) for information as to San Domingo—before the meeting, I had mentioned to the President that I had such a paper, & he replied that he was not inclined to make any answer to it—but on the suggestion that the refusal to answer was unusual & might be misapprehended into a supposed inability to answer, he at once said, that he merely felt 'a little disposed' not to answer—The paper was read and approved—" DLC-Hamilton Fish.

On Feb. 9, Ebenezer R. Hoar, Boston, wrote to Jacob D. Cox. ". . . I am more and more astonished at what you say of the President's statements, and of those which he allowed to be made—I came to the very decided opinion before I left, and your experience gave the strongest evidence to confirm it, that the President had the most crude and imperfect notions of the true relations between himself and the head of a department; and that his personal interference with the duties which the law imposes upon a Cabinet officer, in the details of administration, and which often arose from impressions made on his mind from untrustworthy sources, was the cause of a great deal of evil. It has done more than any thing else to shake the public confidence in him—A driver, who, instead of holding the reins steadily, does nothing but give one of them an occasional twitch, will not find his team very serviceable. But he is the best we have—and the prospect of any thing better at present is not as good as I wish it were—which silences public criticism—Gov. Fish has chafed under his treatment almost ever since he joined the administration—and for a considerable time was only induced to hold on by strong persuasions, and from a sense of public duty—Whether he has since become more reconciled to the situation, I have no personal knowledge. But in spite of all evidence, I find myself unable to believe in such double-dealing, and mean attempts to escape responsibility, as this McGarrahan business seems to impute to Grant—There *must* be some explanation to it—for with all that simple frankness that we have so long known & valued, it is impossible that he could all at once become a trickster & knave. My experience of him was this; that all that I saw of him, or had to do with him, was perfectly true and upright; simple, direct, and manly—But as soon as I had communication with him through other people, I hardly knew what to believe, or what he would do. . . . The St. Domingo business, which has caused more mischief than any thing else for the last two years, is understood, as I am informed, to be pretty much disposed of—The commission was intended merely to let the administration down 'easy'; it cannot report in season to do any thing in this Congress—and the next will be strong against it. I hope it will disappear with McGarrahan—. . ." ALS, Cox Papers, Oberlin College, Oberlin, Ohio. See *PUSG*, 20, 292–302.

On March 13, Charles F. Cox, New York City, wrote to Jacob Cox. ". . . Now that Grant's financial policy,—I suppose we may call it his,—is likely to come to naught he seems to be doing his best to ruin his chances for popularity in other directions also. His personal quarrel with Sumner is calculated to hurt Grant very considerably even if it does not absolutely settle the question of his renomination & reelection. I had a conversation with Mr. Curtis on Friday and asked him what he thought of Mr. Sumner's removal from the Foreign Relations Committee. He said very decidedly 'It is fatal, it is *fatal*.' From what he subsequently said I judged that he meant to say it was fatal to the Republican Party and I am inclined to think he is about right. Not, as Mr. Curtis said, because Mr. Sumner is altogether innocent in this quarrel, for in that he and Grant are about equal, but because a quarrel on *any* grounds between men in their positions must necessarily result unfortunately to the party with which they are connected. . . . I have been hoping that what you said about the San Domingo Commission when you were here would prove true, vz, that it would make a half & half kind of report and that under cover of it, the President would back down; but the commissioners seem to have become intoxicated with the San Domingo air, if not with something else, and I imagine they are preparing to make a favorable report, and hence Grant's anxious preparation of Senate Committees &c. for its reception & favorable consideration. I am afraid this miserable job will yet go through. And here the country stands an apparently uninterested observer of this scheme, indifferent to the manner of its manipulation and the probable consequences of it,—indifferent simply because Gen Grant is the father & manager of it! When will the country recover its senses sufficiently to demand that the Government shall give its attention to something more useful?. . . Perhaps Sumner's removal from the Foreign Relations Committee—('*Personal* Relations Com.' Mr. Plimpton proposes to call it.)—has something to do with this Alabama business, as the Post—(which Doug sent you on Saturday) suggests. Do you think so, or do you think that it is only an excuse to cover the packing of the Committee for the Annexation report?. . ." ALS, Cox Papers, Oberlin College.

Endorsement

Refered to the Sec. of the Treas. I think it likely it will be well, in rearranging the Supervisor of Int. Rev. and in reducing the number, to apt. Col. Hughes,[1] and to transfer Dr. Presbury[2] to one of the other districts.

U. S. GRANT

JAN.Y 16TH /71

AES, MeB.

1. Robert W. Hughes, born in 1821, practiced law in Richmond, wrote for the *Richmond Examiner*, and edited the *Washington Union* (1857–61), which supported James Buchanan's administration. Returning to the *Richmond Examiner*, he favored the C.S.A., opposed Jefferson Davis, and later edited the Republican *Richmond Republic* (1865–66) and *State Journal* (1869–70). On Feb. 3, 1871, USG nominated Hughes as U.S. attorney, Western District, Va. See *New York Times*, Aug. 3, 1873.

2. Otis F. Presbrey, born in 1820, graduated from Berkshire Medical College and, in 1862, was named assessor of Internal Revenue, Buffalo, where he had promoted commercial development. He served as special agent, U.S. Treasury Dept. (1866–70); in March, 1869, USG appointed Presbrey supervisor of Internal Revenue, Washington, D. C., Va., and West Va. See *Eminent and Representative Men of Virginia and The District of Columbia of the Nineteenth Century* (Madison, Wis., 1893), pp. 254–58.

To Senate

TO THE SENATE OF THE UNITED STATES:

In answer to their resolution of the 16th of December 1870,[1] I herewith transmit copies of certain reports received at the War Department, relative to disloyal organizations in the State of North Carolina intended to resist the laws, or to deprive the citizens of the United States of the protection of law, or the enjoyment of their rights under the Constitution of the United States. These reports are in addition to the abstracts of those sent to the Senate on the 13th instant.[2]

U. S. GRANT

EXECUTIVE MANSION,
JANUARY 17TH 1871.

DS, DNA, RG 46, Presidential Messages. Related papers are *ibid.* See *CG*, 41–3, 479, 548; *SED*, 41-3-16, part 2; *SRC*, 42-1-1.

On Jan. 1, 1871, William W. Holden, Raleigh, wrote to USG. "In addition to the former evidence of the existence of a dangerous conspiracy, in this State, which I have laid before you, I desire to transmit the accompanying papers, as an appendix to my former official letter. The pamphlet, containing the evidence against the Lenoir County prisoners, is of sufficient notoriety and authenticity to warrant its acceptance; and indeed Judge C. R. Thomas, before whom the examination was had, and who has since been chosen a member of the 42nd Congress, stands ready to corroborate it. This was the first exposition of the conspiracy. You will further find numerous confessions of members of the Ku-klux Klan, obtained through the means of the militia movement of last Summer; and also a copy of the oath required of members of one of its degrees, 'the White Brotherhood.' The other two degrees are known as 'the Constitutional Union Guard,' and 'the Invisible Empire.' The accompanying lists of outrages committed in Alamance and Lincoln Counties are full up to date. It will be observed that fear of injury on the part of informants has induced them to ask that their names be withheld. The government can obtain them at any moment however. Extracts from letters from citizens are also transmitted, and one or two 'specimen' statements made by parties, who have been outraged in this State. If all such statements were compiled, it would be a tale of terror and woe that the people of this country have never heard before. This organized conspiracy is in existence in every County of the State. And its aim is to obtain the control of the government. It is believed that its leaders now direct the movements of the present Legislature. It is proven, (page 210 of my Message & ACC. Doc.,) that the Speaker of the present House, T. J. Jarvis, is a member, and one other prominent leader in the Legislature, Fred. Strudwick, was seen on his way at Gilbreath's bridge to murder a State Senator, (page 226,); and (page 218), that the leading Democratic paper of this State is in direct sympathy with this organization of conspirators and assassins. In conclusion, I enclose you a printed list of outrages, which is not one-twentieth of the number committed in the State. But they are the most prominent, and serve as examples to show what has been already done, and to warn the government that unless active measures are taken that the lives of its loyal citizens are no longer safe and their libertyies a thing of the past." ALS, DNA, RG 94, Letters Received, 60 1871. Enclosures are *ibid.* See *PUSG*, 20, 210–13; note to William W. Belknap, Jan. 30, 1872, note 2.

1. On Dec. 16, 1870, U.S. Senator Oliver P. Morton of Ind. introduced this resolution, and U.S. Senator Samuel C. Pomeroy of Kan. spoke. "I have no objection to that, and I am glad that the Senator has introduced it, because one hour in the day we are for general amnesty or universal amnesty, and the next hour of the day we are after the rebels who are murdering our people. I shall not vote for any more amnesties as long as we have to inquire what the rebels are doing in murdering Union men." *CG*, 41–3, 146.

2. On Jan. 13, 1871, USG wrote to the Senate. "In reply to the resolution of the Senate of the 16th of December 1870, requesting to be furnished with information relative to the organization of disloyal persons in North Carolina, having in view resistance of the United States laws; denial of protection, and the enjoyment of the rights and liberties secured under the United States, &c. I transmit herewith abstracts of reports and other papers on file in the War Department relative to outrages in North Carolina, and also, for the information of the Senate, those relative to outrages in the other Southern States. The original reports and papers are too voluminous to be cop-

ied in season to be used by the present Congress, but are easily accessible for reference and copies of such papers can be furnished, as the Senate may deem necessary." DS, DNA, RG 46, Presidential Messages. Related papers are *ibid.* On Jan. 16, Secretary of War William W. Belknap submitted to USG additional reports regarding N. C. Copy, *ibid.*, RG 94, Letters Received, 510R 1870.

To Congress

To the Senate and House of Representatives
~~I have the honor to~~ I transmit herewith ~~the Resolutions and Constitution adopted by the united indian tribes~~ an official copy of the proceedings of the Council [of Indian tribes] held at Okmulgee, in December last,[1] which resulted in the adoption of a declaration of rights, and a constitution for their Government;[2] together with a copy of the report of the Com. of Indian Affairs; and the views of the Sec. of the Interior thereon.

It ~~looks me~~ [would seem] highly desirable that the civilized indians of the country should be encouraged in establishing for themselves forms of ~~civil~~ territorial government, compatible with the Constitution of the United States, and with the previous custom towards other communities laying outside of State limits.

I concur in the views expressed by the Sec. of the Interior. I do not believe [that] it would [not] be advisable to receive the new terriory with the constitution precisely as ~~th~~ it is now framed. So long as a territorial form of government is preserved Congress should hold the power of approving or disapproving of all legislative action of the territory; and the Executive should, with "the advice and concent of the Senate" have the power to appoint the Governer and Judicial officers, (and possibly some others) of the territory. This ~~however being~~ [is] the first indication of the aborigines ~~to~~ desiring to ~~come into~~ [adopt] our form of government, ~~and~~ it ~~being~~ [is] highly desirable that ~~that~~ they become self sustaining, self relying, Christianized and Civilized, ~~and~~. ~~i~~[I]f successful in this their first attempt at territorial government, ~~hoping to~~ [we may hope for a] gradual~~ly~~ concentrate[ion of] other indians in the new territory. I would [therefore] recommend as close an adherence to their wishes as is consistent with safety. It might be well to limit the appointment of all territorial officials, appointed by the Executive, to native citizens of the territory. If any exception is made to this rule I would recommend that it should be limited to the Judiciary.

It is confidently hoped that the policy now being pursued towards the indian will fit him for self government, and make him desire to settle among people of his own race where he can enjoy the full privileges of Civil, and enlightened government.

[E. M JANY 30. 1871.]

ADf (bracketed material not in USG's hand), DLC-George B. Cortelyou. On Jan. 25, 1871, Secretary of the Interior Columbus Delano wrote to USG. "I have the honor to transmit, herewith, the following papers: Copy of a letter from the Commissioner of Indian Affairs, Honorable E. S. Parker, of this date, transmitting an official copy of the proceedings of the Council held at Okmulgee, in December last, which resulted in the adoption of a declaration of rights, and a Constitution of Government, by which certain tribes and bands of Indians have confederated for the purpose of civilization and education. I also enclose a copy of a letter from the Commissioner of Indian Affairs, dated the 4th instant, containing his report of the proceedings of the Council while in session and during his presence and attendance thereupon. This assemblage was held under acts of Congress, authorizing the establishment of a 'General Council' in the Indian Country; and before it was convened, I regarded its probable proceedings of such importance as to require the Commissioner of Indian Affairs to be present, in order to give such aid and advice as the Department might afford, in properly directing its deliberations. The report of General Parker, is highly interesting in its account of the agricultural and educational condition of the tribes, in the Indian Country. The Constitution, declaration of rights, and entire proceedings of the Council, evince great wisdom and judgment, and I trust they will lead to the organization of a Government, originated by the Indians themselves, and in which they feel a deep interest, which in its results will greatly aid in the work of civilization and education. If Congress shall conclude to take the proceedings of this Council as the basis for Civil government among the Indians, reserving the right of disapproving of all acts of legislation, and placing the appointments to Office under the Constitution, in the hands of the President, and Senate of the United States, I shall hope for the happiest consequences from this experiment. In the event that this course is adopted, the Indians will feel that their government is, to some extent, a work of their own creation and they will, I have no doubt, acquiesce in all needful and proper alterations of their Constitution; but I am compelled to express the hope that no change in that instrument will be made, which will require or permit any nonresident to fill any office in the Government, unless it be one of high judicial character. I am also convinced that, for the present, there should be no change in existing laws, regulating the settlement and occupancy of said Territory, hoping and believing that this course will lead rapidly to the establishment of most if not all, the Indian tribes within this Territory. I have the honor, respectfully, to suggest that the proceedings of this Council be transmitted to Congress as early as practicable, with such recommendations and suggestions as in your judgment may seem necessary.... P. S.—Since writing the foregoing, I have received through Vincent Colyer, Esq, Secretary of the Honb Board of Indian Commissioners, the following report, which with his permission I forward with this communication. The views of the Commission are so much in accord with my own on the subject, that I deem it proper to submit them for your consideration." LS, DNA, RG 46, Presidential Messages. On Jan. 4, Ely S. Parker, commissioner of Indian Affairs, had written to Delano. "In obedience to your instructions, dated the 2nd December, 1870, I proceeded to the capital of the Creek Nation, in the Indian Territory, to attend the session of the General Council of Indian Nations and tribes resident in said Territory, convened in pursuance of treaties made in 1866 between the United States and the Cherokee, Creek, Seminole, Choctaw and Chickasaw Nations of Indians, and the Act of Congress approved July 15, 1870. I reached Okmulgee, the place where the council was held, on the 12th December. On the 13th I met the council. There were present Messrs. Robert Campbell, J. V. Farwell and J. D. Lang, of the Board of Indian Commissioners; Superintendent Hoag, presiding Officer of the council, and fifty six Indian Delegates, representing the Cherokee, Creek, Seminole, Choctaw, Chickasaw, Great and little Osage, Ottawa, Eastern Shawnee, Quapaw, Seneca, Wyandotte, Confederated Peoria, Sac and Fox and the Absentee Shawnee Nations or tribes of Indians, all residing in said Territory and numbering all together about sixty thousand souls. The only tribes of said Territory not represented,—and this was said to be owing to their not having had sufficient notice, and the great distance they are from the council ground,—were the Wichitas and other affiliated bands, the Kiowas and Comanches, and the Cheyennes and Arapahoes. Being duly introduced to the Council by the Presiding Officer, I was invited to address them, which I did briefly, stating to them that their assemblage was the most important council ever held among the Indian tribes of the country.... Several delegates responded, expressing gratitude for the suggestions made to them; they appreciated highly the interest manifested in their behalf by the Government; they felt gratified for the presence of the Special Indian Commission among them, for the words of encouragement they had given them—evidencing the kindly sympathy the good people of the Country entertained for them. They said that up to that Morning their minds had been depressed, as they had been left in the dark as to how far they could go in the organization of an Indian government, but the remarks of the Commissioner of Indian affairs had made evry thing clear, and they felt now that they could safely proceed in their work. They thanked the President and secretary of the Interior for not forgetting the Indians in the multiplicity of the duties devolving on them ..." DS, *ibid.* Related papers are *ibid.* On the same day, a correspondent reported: "Commissioner Parker is engaged in the preparation of a report to the Secretary of the Interior and the President relative to his visit to Okmulgee, Creek Nation, and attendance on the grand Indian Council that has been in session there. General Parker says the Council is one of the most important bodies ever assembled. There was a great deal of talent exhibited, and a general harmony of effort, which augured well for the success of the movement. The constitution framed by the Council organizes a full-fledged State, and provides for the election of all the officers. The Commissioner, in advising with the leading Indians, suggested that Congress might not be willing to allow such large powers to the proposed confederation. The Indians themselves are convinced that it is the only way by which they and their race can be protected from the rapacity of the railroad and other land operations. They ask that their government shall be allowed to grow from within and not be imposed upon from without, as is the case in a House bill now pending, providing for a territorial government. This is made in the interests of the Kansas and Missouri Gulf Railroad schemers. The council, before adjourning, represented a civilized population of about 55,000 Indians and about 3000 negroes, who are entitled to the rights of citizens. The tribes in the western part of the Territory, about 7000 in all, have not yet given in their adhesion, though it is probable they will." *Philadelphia Public Ledger*, Jan. 5, 1871. See *SED*, 41-3-26; *HRC*, 42-2-61, 42-2-89; *CG*, 41–3, 600–5, 699–701, 42–2, 2954–55, 42–3, 1522; "Journal of the General Council of the Indian Territory," *Chronicles of Oklahoma*, III, 1 (April, 1925), 33–44; "Journal of the Adjourned Session of First General Council of the Indian Territory," *ibid.*, 2 (June, 1925), 120–36; "Okmulgee Constitution," *ibid.*, 3 (Sept., 1925), 216–28; Curtis L. Nolen, "The Okmulgee Constitution: A Step Towards Indian Self-Determination," *ibid.*, LVIII, 3 (Fall, 1980), 264–81; William H. Armstrong, *Warrior in Two Camps: Ely S. Parker Union General and Seneca Chief* (Syracuse, 1978), p. 151.

On March 14, Samuel Checote, chief, Creek Nation, and others wrote to USG. "We the citizens of the Creek or Muskokee Nation of Indians, in National council assembled would most earnestly present to You—and through You to the Intel[l]igent and Honurable United States Senate and House of representatives—our Solemn protest—against the action of the Congress of the United States. in the introduction of Bills for the establishment of a Teritorial Goverment for the the Indians. Inhabiting the Indian Teritory—other than the one framed by the Delegates in Grand Council assembled at Okmulgee Creek Nation Indian Teritory and which has been forwarded to Your Excellency We deny the right of the Congress of the United States to frame a Constitution, or enact Laws for us or to interfere with our internal relations in any way whatever—The only right conceded is that of regulating Trade and Intercourse between citizens of the United States and ourselves We have been induced to believe. that the policy of Your administration and the desire of the whole people of the United States—was to Civilize—Christianise—and to establish relations of the most lasting and perfect Peace—not only with Indians of this Teritory but with the Tribes of the West known by us as the Prairie Indians—Who we were induced by the peace commissioners our Superintendant and others to believe you were attempting to have follow in the course of Industry. and peacefulness as have the Tribes who inhabit this Teritory to wit, the Cherokees Chocktaws Chickasaws Seminoles ourselves and other Tribes and bands . . . They cannot understand why Congress should attempt to establish for them a Teritorial government—and cause the official positions created by them to be filled by persons who are Citizens of the United States—persons whose sympathies and interests are not with them—and not by citizens of their own country—Is there any Independance to us in this—Is there any freedom in it—~~is not the right~~ Is there any Justice in it Is not the right granted by Treaty to the Authorities of the United States to suspend any Laws which may conflict with the constitution of the U. S—restrictions and check enough upon us?—~~They~~ We were invited to frame a constitution and establish a government of ~~their~~ our own and for ~~them~~ ourselves—This ~~they~~ we done in Grand Council assembled at Okmulgee Creek Nation—During the framing of that Constitution—Our relation to each other and the government of the United States was fully and freely discussed and understood—The constitution was adopted by nearly a unanimous vote and the Indians were satisfied. The Good results and expectations of that Council—are already being realized—The Cheyennes Arapahoes—and others, have sent word to our chief that they desire to be with us in our Councils—to Act with us and to follow our examples—We feel that we are not mistaken when we say, that if left alone to adopt our own constitution, that was framed at Okmulgee as it was without any change in it—except what may be made by the citizens of the Indian Teritory—It will do more to insure lasting and permanent peace—than can all the

Teritorial Bill introduced—having the Executive—and Judiciary departments filled by citizens of the United States—we want our Laws administered by Officers of our own choice—we desire our own Judiciary to decide our disputes and Lawsuits—we earnestly feel and believe that if we would become civilized—and Christianized to the full extent—that we must be permitted to make our own Laws—control our own people—and to decide as to our own wants—All of this has been Guarantied to us by Treaty, and we, well knowing the stability and Integrity of the Government of the United States expect all of the above—We also feel that our perfect security in, and control of our country—lies in the strength of the Government and Wisdom of the administration—We earnestly hope that Your Excellency will use the Great influence You possess, to this end, that our constitution as adopted by ourselves, may remain unchanged—and that the Teritorial forms of Government may be of our own creation—and not one created by parties who are entirely unacquainted with our manners, Customs—or wants—" DS, DNA, RG 75, Letters Received, Creek Agency. See O. A. Lambert, "Historical Sketch of Col. Samuel Checote, Once Chief of the Creek Nation," *Chronicles of Oklahoma*, IV, 3 (Sept., 1926), 275–80; John Bartlett Meserve, "Chief Samuel Checote, with Sketches of Chiefs Locher Harjo and Ward Coachman," *ibid.*, XVI, 4 (Dec., 1938), 401–9.

1. This council convened Dec. 6–20, 1870.

2. On Jan. 12, 1871, a correspondent reported from Washington, D. C.: "THE CHEROKEE DELEGATES Arrived here last night, namely, Principal Chief Downing, Colonel Adair, Colonel Vaux [*Vann*], Captains Smith and Scraper. Their business is to secure the ratification of the treaty sent to the Senate by the President during the latter part of the former session of Congress, providing for the payment of $32,000,000 agreed upon under the treaty of 1868 for twenty odd million of acres land lying in the southern part of Kansas, and west of the 96th deg. of longitude in their country. This treaty was favorably reported upon by the Commissioner of Indian Affairs prior to the expiration of the last session, and is now pending. These delegates also represent in part the new State Territorial Govenment of Oklohama, being a confederation of the various nations of the Indian Territory, namely—the Cherokees, Creeks, Choctaws, Chickasaws, Seminoles and others. It is understood that Commissioner Parker has brought with him the official copy of the new constitution adopted at Ocmulgee, by the delegates of these nations, in accordance with the provisions of the treaty of 1866, and that the President in his interview with the delegation of Friends yesterday expressed himself favorable to this new Territorial Government, and opposed to the projects of railroad and land speculators, whose interests are sought to be secured through other measures now pending before Congress." *Philadelphia Public Ledger*, Jan. 13, 1871. See *SMD*, 41-2-148.

On Jan. 20, 1872, USG met with a delegation of Cherokees, Creeks and Choctaws. "They informed him that they did not want a Territorial Government, but were satisfied with such institutions as they had, which were adapted not only to the civilized Indians, but to those not yet brought under educating influences. They desired to be allowed to work out their own destiny, and prepare for their inevitable absorption in the white population crowding upon them, with as few attendant evils as possible. The President expressed gratification at their social progress, and assured them that, as far as he was concerned, the Territorial Government should not be extended over the Cherokee Country unless they wanted it." *Philadelphia Public Ledger*, Jan. 22, 1872. See also *Washington Evening Star*, Jan. 20, 1872.

To Amos T. Akerman

Will the Atty Gn. please see Mr. Lathers and recommend what action should be taken in the case which he will present.

U. S. GRANT

FEB. 2D /71

ANS, DNA, RG 60, Letters from the President. Born about 1820 in S. C., Richard Lathers entered business, moved to New York City in 1847, and prospered as a merchant and insurance executive. Maintaining S. C. ties, Lathers lobbied USG on behalf of Alfred Huger, former Charleston postmaster (1834–67), prosecuted for surrendering U.S. funds to C.S.A. officials. "... I called upon President Grant, who expressed great sympathy for the Union Ex-Postmaster as soon as he heard his story, and promised me that he would relieve Huger of a disgraceful prosecution.... He offered to give me a letter to the Attorney-general expressing his sympathy for Mr. Huger. I told the President that I feared the prejudice of his official, who, being an old Secessionist transformed into a carpet-bag Union man, would resent everything friendly to a genuine Union man's cause. The letter was received by the Attorney-general exactly as I had feared it would be. With great pomposity, he informed me that he was too busy to listen to these rebel appeals." Alvan F. Sanborn, ed., *Reminiscences of Richard Lathers: Sixty Years of a Busy Life in South Carolina, Massachusetts and New York* (New York, 1907), pp. 293–94.

On July 7, 1870, John J. Martin, 6th auditor, Treasury Dept., had written to William E. Dodge, New York City. "Your appeal in behalf of Mr. Alfred Huger, so long & through so many consecutive administrations, Deputy Postmaster at Charleston, South Carolina, referred by order of the President to the Post Master General, has been submitted to this office in correspondence with the United States District Attorney for S. C. since the suit was commenced. Mr Huger's own statement, in 1865, was a clear & explicit one, and he rests the merits of his case on pleas of duress, by which certain moneys & other funds belonging to the Post Office Department passed from him, as the custodian, into the possession of the so called Confederate States. The pleas filed were learnedly drawn & so ably argued before the United States District Court, that the Defendants had verdict & judgment, for which there was an appeal to the Supreme Court of the United States. The remission of the whole judgment, in the face of the recent decision of that tribunal, overruling the Court below, would be inadmissable, as the Huger case was, in fact, a test one...." Copy, DNA, RG 60, Letters Received. A letter from Huger's attorneys is *ibid.*

To Charles W. Ford

Washington D. C. Feb.y 2d *18*71

DEAR FORD;

Enclosed I send you a letter from Jesse Holliday. It explains itself. Will you make enquiries for me as to how much interest Holliday has in the Sigerson tract; how much, if any, outside of that which I bought from Burns, and about what it would be worth with a clear title.

I wrote to Long what I wanted in the way of straitening the road through my farm. He has probably attended to it.

Yours Truly
U. S. GRANT

ALS, DLC-USG. On Jan. 27, 1871, USG had telegraphed to Charles W. Ford, collector of Internal Revenue, St. Louis. "You have authority as requested to absent yourself" Telegram sent, DNA, RG 107, Telegrams Collected (Bound).

Endorsement

If the Govornorship of Idaho is declined by Gen. Connor[1] the apt. may be given to Gen. Dumont.

U. S. GRANT

FEB.Y 6TH /71

AES, DNA, RG 59, Letters of Application and Recommendation. Written on an undated petition from U.S. Senator Oliver P. Morton of Ind. *et al.* to USG. "The undersigned Members of Congress from Indiana, unite in presenting the name of General Ebenezer Dumont of our state for a federal Appointment. We would mention as pointing to the grade of appointment it might be proper to say that Gen Dumont is a Lawyer of many Years practice and of acknowledged ability, that he was a Brig Genl of Volunteers in the late war, proved himself a good soldier and won distinction, that he was an able Member of the 38 & 39 Congress, and has held many places of honor and trust in his own State, in all of which he has proved himself competent and acquitted himself honorably." DS (9 signatures), *ibid.* Ebenezer Dumont, born in 1814, served as lt. col. in the Mexican War and as col., 7th Ind., then brig. gen., during the Civil War. On March 15, 1871, Horace Porter wrote to Secretary of State Hamilton Fish. "The President requests that a nomination be prepared and send to him to day for Ebenezer Dumont of Indiana, to be Governor of Idaho Territory, vice Alexander H. Conner resigned" Copy, DLC-USG, II, 1. Dumont died on April 16.

On April 18, U.S. Delegate Samuel A. Merritt of Idaho Territory wrote to USG. "I take the liberty of addressing you on the subject of the Governorship of Idaho Territory, which Territory I have the honor to represent in the 42nd Congress—The office of Governor is vacant by the recent demise of Genl Dumont, lately appointed by your Excellency—The office has not been filled by an actual incumbent since May 1st 1870 at which time the term of David W Ballard expired. Samuel Bard of Georgia was appointed the successor of Governor Ballard, but never came to the Territory—Genl Marston of New Hampshire was then appointed with a like result—He was succeeded by Mr H H Connor of Indianna, and he by Ebenezer Dumont of the same state who died very recently—Thus it will be seen that Idaho Territory has been practically without a Governor for nearly a year—The office is not a lucrative one, the salary being only $2500. per annum, barely sufficient, in view of the high price of being in that Territory, to give a decent support Not being a member of the Republican party I have no suggestions to make in regard to the person to be appointed to the Governorship of Idaho Territory, but I hope your Excellency will pardon the suggestion from me, that some person who will discharge the duties of the office, shall be appointed, and if consistent with your Excellency's views and policy that a resident of the Territory be appointed. There are many gentlemen, members of the Republican party, residents of Idaho Territory, fully competent to fill the office of Governor, among whom I would name Hon Thos J Butler the Republican candidate, at the last two elections, for Congress—Also Col Isaac Jennings a Pioneer of the Territory. Also E J Curtis Esq the present efficient Secretary of the Territory. Also Judge W. C. Whitson associate Justice of Idaho Territory. Hoping your Excellency will pardon the liberty I take in addressing you on this subject . . ." ALS, DNA, RG 59, Letters of Application and Recommendation. See *PUSG*, 20, 285–86, 289–91.

On May 24, 1870, USG had nominated Gilman Marston as governor, Idaho Territory. On Dec. 3, Marston, Exeter, N. H., wrote to USG. "I desired very much to accept the office of Govenor of Idaho which you were kind enough to offer me, and I have delayed a long while—much too long—in the hope that I should be able to do so, but I am obliged to decline it." ALS, DNA, RG 59, Letters of Resignation and Declination.

On Nov. 25, Samuel Shellabarger, Springfield, Ohio, had written to USG. "The friends of James Stout, late of Illinois Ills., now receiver and disburser of public money at Boice city Idaho Territory, inform me that he applies to be appointed governor of that territory. . . . I very cordially recommend him to the president for the place he applies for." ALS, *ibid.*, Letters of Application and Recommendation. On April 17, 1869, USG had nominated James Stout as receiver, Land Office, Boise.

On April 18, 1871, D. W. Lafollette, New Albany, Ind., wrote to USG. "In consequence of the death of our late friend Gen Dumont, I presume you will have another appointment to make of Gov of Idahoe Sir, please consider me as an applicant, and if you desire it I will forward recommendations of my friend Judge Gresham and other leading republicans. I am now as was ever your warmest Supporter from the time your name was first named in connection with the office of President." ALS, *ibid.*

On March 31, U.S. Senator Powell Clayton of Ark. had telegraphed to USG. "In consideration with Secretary Fish I learn the Brazillian Mission is the only one vacant I urgently request Judge Bowen's appointment thereto. You will find few who will bring as much ability and represent our government with more credit. You will be entirely satisfied with him." Telegram received, *ibid.* A related letter is *ibid.* On April 17, Orville E. Babcock wrote to Fish. "The President desires me to say that he understands that the Governor of Idaho is dead and he will be pleased to have you send down, to go to the Senate to day, a nomination for Mr. Bowen of Arks: as Governor of Idaho. We do not know the initials of Mr. Bowen but the nomination may be left blank as regards the initials and we will notify you of the full name, after we ascertain it." Copy, DLC-USG, II, 1. On Sept. 15, Governor Thomas M. Bowen wrote to USG. "I have the honor to tender this my resignation as Governor of the Territory of Idaho to take effect Sept 30th 1871 For ten years I have been an active participant in the great events which have transpired and am impeled to this step because my position here cuts me off from efficient participation in the great strugle of 1872 which I look upon as equal in importance to any during the years of the Rebellion or those of reconstruction thereafte[r] following—In going out of office instead of asking for one it is not in bad taste for me to say that I regard your reelection as absolutely necessa[ry] to the preservation of what was gained by the war and to the future security of the lives and property of the loyal men of the south. Entertaining these views and feeling that my duty calls upon me to take part in the coming campaign I return you the high office with which you were pleased to honor me—Thanking you again for your expression of confidence . . ." ALS, DNA, RG 59, Idaho Territorial Papers.

On Sept. 23, Ohio Representative Wilson W. Griffith, Toledo, wrote to USG. "I notice that Mr Bowen Governor of Idaho has resigned—and remembering that there have been a number of changes of this kind in a comparatively ~~a~~ short space of time—and believeing I that I know somewhat of the difficultes that environ Republican Governors in that Democratic stronghold I made up my mind to write you a short letter on the subject—If you have in mind the gentleman to be Mr Bowens successor I have nothing to offer. But if not I am not sure but I would like the appointment. I could probably come to you as strongly supported by the Press and influential parties as moste men for the position but will not ask for such till I know it is needed. nor will any know that I might accept such a position if tendered till I recive an answer to this letter Will briefly state on my own behalf without mock modesty—That I am a retired successful business man. Forty Eight years old. In prime of life. Now a member of the Ohio Legislature. and One of the two Commissioners of this state (by nomination of Gov Hayes and your appointment) for the centennial Exposition of 1876. I have had much to do with the world and the world of mankind—having traveled in the four quarters of the Globe and have had more or less Experience with a majority of the peoples thereof. and too spent about a year on the Pacific coast.—moste of which time in the Territory of Idaho—settling up the affairs of a large mining business at Atlanta City. This brought me in contact with about every shade of Character of that *speckled* population—. . ." ALS, *ibid.*, Letters of Application and Recommendation. No appointment followed.

Also on Sept. 23, Morton, Indianapolis, wrote to USG. "I learn that Gov Bowen of Idaho Territory has resigned and I desire earnestly to recommend for the place Gen T. W. Bennet of Richmond Indiana. Gen Bennet was a gallant soldier, and served throughout the war entering the service as a captain. He is a lawyer by profession a fine speaker and is well qualified for the position. He is about 37 years of age. The appointment would be a good one, and would strengthen the hands of your friends in eastern Indiana. Judge Wilson who will present this can give you a full account of Gen Bennet. . . . Gen Bennet is a thorough Republican who has never wavered." ALS, *ibid.* USG endorsed this letter. "Respectfully refered to the Sec. of State. I have no objection to this apt. if the vacancy exists." AES, *ibid.* Related papers are *ibid.* On Dec. 6, USG nominated Thomas W. Bennett as governor, Idaho Territory. See Ronald H. Limbaugh, *Rocky Mountain Carpetbaggers: Idaho's Territorial Governors, 1863–1890* (Moscow, Idaho, 1982), pp. 90–99.

On Sept. 18, 1872, Bennett wrote to USG. "I have been urgently requested by the Republicans of Oregon to canvas that State for our cause, and having nothing of importance to attend to here just now, I have consented to do so, but having no, leave of absence, and not having time to wait for one, I have forwarded my application to the State Department, and will go at once to Oregon. I write you because I know that there are some disaffected men here, who would report me to you. And while on that subject allow me to say that Mr James S Reynolds who was an applicant for the place I now hold, is a violent and abusive opponent of your Administratio[n] and a supporter of Greeley, and he holds the position of clerk in Assa[y] office. I do not mention this as reason for his removal *now*, but that he and a little 'ring' of his here may not prejudice the interests of better men, and your friends. Asking pardon for troubling you with such small matters. . . ." ALS, DNA, RG 59, Idaho Territorial Papers.

1. On Feb. 23, 1869, David W. Voyles, New Albany, Ind., wrote to USG. "Hon. A. H. Conner of Indiana, will at the proper time, be an applicant for the position of *Commissioner of Indian Affairs* Mr. Conner has been fully identified with the Republican party of this state, as one of its most efficient and untireing workers since its first organization. In 1860 he discharged the arduous and responsible duties of Chairman of the State Central Committee, and in that capacity, contributed largely towards achieving the first great victory of Republicanism over Democracy and Treason. Again in 1868 he occupied the same honorable position, and through his efficiency, his untireing zeal and indefatigable labors, conducted us safely through the storms of the most determined political conflict that has ever occurred in any state, within the history of the government . . ." ALS, *ibid.*, RG 48, Appointment Div., Letters Received. Related papers are *ibid.*

On Nov. 4, 1870, Morton wrote to USG. "I intended to speak to you in behalf of A. H. Connor Esq. of Indianapolis. He is the chairman of our state central Committee, and acted in that capacity in 1860. 62. 64 & 68. He is a lawyer by profession, is an able politician, and has rendered very valuable service to the Republican party. His fortunes ~~are~~ is somewhat impaired and he is anxious to procure an appointment and would prefer to go to one of the territories. . . ." ALS, *ibid.*, RG 59, Letters of Application and Recommendation. On Dec. 16, USG nominated Alexander H. Conner as governor, Idaho Territory. On June 20, 1871, U.S. Senator Daniel D. Pratt of Ind., Logansport, wrote to USG. "You may remember that I once asked for the appointment of Judge John S. Watts for Governor of N. Mexico. You then indicated your purpose to nominate my friend Genl. Warner & recognizing its entire fitness, I did not further urge the claims of Judge Watts—In the mean time, one of the citizens of my own State, would like the place—A. H Conner, whom you once nominated for Governor of Idaho—Mr Conner is an able man, and I have no doubt in point of qualifications and fitness generally, quite up to the standard of that grade of appointments. I was sorry he did not accept the Governorship of Idaho, as I felt confident the appointment would reflect credit upon your administration. I believe his appointment to the Governorship of N. Mexico would be equally creditable." ALS, *ibid.* No appointment followed.

Veto

[*Feb. 7, 1871*]

To the Senate of the United States:

I herewith return, without my approval, Senate resolution No 92 entitled "A resolution for the relief of certain contractors for the construction of vessels of war and steam machinery," for the following reasons:—

The Act of March 2, 1867, (14th United States Statutes at Large page 424) directs the Secretary of the Navy "to investigate the claims of all contractors for building vessels-of-war and steam machinery for the same under contracts made after the first day of May 1861, and prior to the first day of January 1864, and said investigation to be made upon the following basis: He shall ascertain the additional cost which was necessarily incurred by each contractor in the completion of his work by reason of any changes or alterations in the plans and specifications required, and delays in the prosecution of the work occasioned by the government, which were not provided for in the original contract; but no allowance for any advance in the price of labor or material shall be considered, unless such advance occurred during the prolonged time for completing the work rendered necessary by the delay resulting from the action of the government aforesaid, and then only when such advance could not have been avoided by the exercise of ordinary prudence and diligence on the part of the contractor" etc.

The present joint resolution transfers the investigation to the Court of claims, and repeals "so much of said act as provides against considering any allowance in favor of any such parties for any advance in the price of labor or material, unless such advance could have been avoided by the exercise of ordinary diligence and prudence on the part of the contractor."

It seems to me that the provision thus repealed is a very reasonable one. It prevents the contractor from receiving any allowance for an advance in the price of labor and material when he could have avoided that advance by the exercise of ordinary prudence and diligence. The effect of the repeal will be to relieve contractors from the consequences of their own imprudence and negligence. I see no good reason for thus relieving contractors who have not exercised ordinary prudence and diligence in their business transactions.

U. S. GRANT

DS, DNA, RG 46, Presidential Messages. On Feb. 16, 1871, the Senate, 57-2, sustained USG's veto. *CG*, 41–3, 1291. See *SRC*, 41-2-163; *CG*, 41–2, 323, 696–97, 5368, 5411, 5657–58, 41–3, 840, 1023; *SED*, 41-3-33.

To Congress

TO THE SENATE AND HOUSE OF REPRESENTATIVES

The union of the States of Germany into a form of government similar in many respects to that of the American Union, is an event that cannot fail to touch deeply the sympathies of the people of the United States.

This Union has been brought about by the long continued, persistent efforts of the People with the deliberate approval of the Governments and people of twenty four of the German States, through their regularly constituted representatives[1]

In it, the American people see an attempt to reproduce in Europe some of the best features of our own Constitution, with such modifications as the history and condition of Germany seem to require. The local governments of the several Members of the Union are preserved, while the powers conferred upon the chief impart strength for the purposes of self defence, without authority to enter upon wars of conquest and ambition[2]

The cherished aspiration for National Unity, which for ages has inspired the many millions of people, speaking the same language, inhabiting a contiguous and compact territory, but unnaturally separated and divided by dynastic jealousies, and the ambition of short sighted rulers, has been attained; and Germany now contains a population of about thirty four millions, united, like our own, under one Government, for its relations with other powers, but retaining in its several members, the right and power of control, of their local interests, habits and institutions.

The bringing of great masses of thoughtful and free people under a single government must tend to make governments, what alone they should be, the representatives of the will, and the organization of the power of the people.

The adoption, in Europe, of the American system of Union, under the control and direction of a free people, educated to self restraint, cannot fail to extend popular institutions, and to enlarge the peaceful influence of American ideas.

The relations of the United States with Germany are intimate and cordial—The commercial intercourse between the two countries is extensive, and is increasing from year to year, and the large number of citizens and residents in the United States, of German extraction, and the continued flow of emigration thence to this country, have produced an intimacy of personal and political intercourse, approaching if not equal to that with the country from which the founders of our Government derived their origin.

The extent of these interests, and the greatness of the German Union seem to require that in the classification of the Representatives of this Government to Foreign Powers, there should no longer be an apparent undervaluation of the importance of the German Mission such as is made in the difference between the compensation allowed by Law to the Minister to Germany, and those to Great Britain and France. There would seem to be a great propriety in placing the Representative of this Government at Berlin on the same footing with that of its Representatives at London and Paris. The union of the several States of Germany under one Government, and the increasing commercial and personal intercourse between the two countries will also add to the labors and the responsibilities of the Legation.

I therefore recommend that the salaries of the Minister and of the Secretary of Legation at Berlin be respectively increased to the same amounts as are allowed to those at London and at Paris.

U. S. GRANT

WASHINGTON, 7TH FEBRUARY 1871.

DS, DNA, RG 46, Presidential Messages. See *SED*, 41-3-99; *HED*, 42-2-1, part 1, pp. 358–59, 378–81, 410; Theodore Stanton, *General Grant and the French: extracted from*

"The Cornell Magazine," October, 1889 (n.p., n.d.). On Feb. 5, 6, and 7, 1871, Secretary of State Hamilton Fish wrote in his diary. "Gerolt—has instructions from Bismarck to express the desire of the German Govt that Bancroft may not be recalled—Wishes to communicate it to the Prsdt asks if he may—is told that he has the right to see the President, who will doubtless listen to any communication his Govt instructs him to make" "President—I take to him draft of proposed message relating to Germany, & recommending an increase of the Compensation of the Minister & Secretary—which he approve He consents to say nothing about the like increase at St Petersburgh which he had directed to embody in the same message—Mention Orth's declension of the Brazilian Mission—He says he has no intention at present of making any change at Berlin—" "Baron Gerolt again potters about Bancrofts retention at Berlin—has been to see the President about it—got no reply—wishes I would give him some assurance—which I decline—saying it is not our habit to do so—we make no promises to retain ~~People~~ any one in Office—especially not to Foreign Powers" DLC-Hamilton Fish.

On Feb. 28, Elihu B. Washburne, Paris, wrote to Fish. "The Message of the President of the United States to Congress in relation to the new German Empire and the United States Mission to Berlin has been very much misunderstood here and has been commented upon very generally and very unfavorably by the Paris journals. It is looked upon as being complimentary to the monarchical institutions of Germany and a 'slap in the face' to the new Republic of France. I have the honor to enclose you herewith various extracts on this subject" Copy, DLC-Elihu B. Washburne.

On the same day, Count Otto von Bismarck, Versailles, wrote to Baron Gerolt, Prussian minister. "Mr. Bancroft has had the kindness to communicate to Mr. von Thile an extract from a dispatch of Mr. Fish, Secretary of State, whereby he is directed to present the congratulations of His Excellency the President on the union of the German states under a common constitution and on the renewal of the Empire in Germany. I have brought this communication to the notice of His Majesty the Emperor and King, who has received it with lively satisfaction. He directs you to thank His Excellency the President and to assure him that he also feels confident that the German Empire, reëstablished upon a federative basis, will afford a guaranty for the peace of the world. His Majesty sees an indication of the fulfillment of this hope in the friendly relations which have always uninterruptedly existed between Germany and America, and in the congratulations which have just been offered by His Excellency the President. You will, in accordance with this most high order, express yourself to Mr. Fish in the sense of this dispatch, and hand him a copy of the same, if he desires it." Copy (translation), DNA, RG 59, Notes from Foreign Legations, Germany.

On March 22, George Bancroft, U.S. minister, Berlin, wrote to Fish. "Before leaving Versailles the Emperor of Germany addressed a letter to the President of the United States, informing him of the new title which he had assumed on the occasion of the union of the Southern German states with the northern. The German minister at Washington was also instructed to communicate to the President the cordial response of the German government to the words of sympathy in which the President announced to Congress the Union of Germany. To this I can add that the state paper has attracted attention from one end of Europe to the other, and that I am constantly receiving evidences of the satisfaction which it has excited in every class of Germany, from extreme liberals to extreme conservatives. The new Empire contains a little more than forty millions of people who are almost exclusively of one nationality; even in the new province of Alsace and Lorraine 1,350,000 are Germans & only about 300,000 are of French descent. In Posen, in the eastern part of the Empire, a majority of the people are Polish; and about half a million of Jews are scattered through the country, but these all speak the German language, and have for centuries been resident in Germany. This unity of nationality already gives evidence that it will control the policy of the empire. It is held in memory that in centuries long gone by the German Emperor professed to be the successor of the Roman, and as such was constantly involved in foreign, especially Italian, wars to the ruin of the country. No plans of future conquest are now cherished, but instead of it the culture and development of the homogeneous population are the great ends which are proposed. The unity of nationality shows itself already as a guarantee of a policy of peace. I have met no one who wants territory occupied by men of another race and language. Another guarantee of peace is the character of the army, composed as it is of the people, and as with us disinclined to any war, except for self defence. Still another guarantee is found in the federal constitution of the Empire, the several governments having reserved to themselves the right of being consulted before war can be declared. The President in his message to congress expressed his confidence that the body which represents the people would be marked by a love of liberty, and it has proved so. The Grand-Duchy of Baden is entitled to twelve representatives in the German Diet and, though the majority of the people of Baden are catholics, the national party has elected ten of the representatives, the ultramontanes only two The victory of the liberal national party in Württemberg is still more remarkable. Three years ago it did not elect to the German eCustoms-parliament one single national member, while in the present election out of seventeen to which Württemberg is entitled, all are national and liberal, except two. Bavaria was looked upon by the ultramontanes as their strong hold, and in Bavaria, where the catholics compared with the Protestants are as five to two, the ultra-montanes and the separatists combined are left in a decided minority. Thus south Germany comes into the German Parliament with all its States on the side of Union, and with a great majority for the developement of the country on the principle of Freedom. Yesterday the Parliament of Germany had its first sitting. The day began with divine service in the Royal chapel, after which the speech of the Emperor was delivered in a large hall in the palace to the members of the two houses of parliament, of whom nearly every one seemed to be present. It was addressed to them as the representatives of the German people, who have at last attained to consciousness of life and unity; and the object of the constitution was declared to be the protection of Justice in Germany and the fostering of the welfare of the German people. Next to the recognition of the Union of Germany as the result of the efforts of the nation, the most remarkable point in the speech is the pledge which it gives for the maintenance of peace, for respect for the rights of all other powers whether strong or weak and for emulation in the victories of Peace. Before the day closed the Emperor, as King of Prussia, not as Emperor of Germany, raised Count Bismarck to the rank of Prince." LS, *ibid.*, Diplomatic Despatches, Germany. See Speech, March 10, 1871.

1. On Nov. 29, 1870, Bancroft had written to Fish. "The day which the President selected for the National Thanksgiving was also the day on which the Diet of North Germany convened for the last time. With the opening of the New Year the North German Union will be merged in the United States of Germany. I am able to inclose to you to-day a copy of the substance of the treaties effecting this Union with Bavaria and Würtemberg. The grand result is brought about by the liberal and orderly tendencies of the German people, by the patriotic wisdom of a part of its rulers and the

apprehensions of the rest. The new organization bears the marks of its origin. The aristocratic party who desired an upper house of Princes and nobles has found no hearing; and as yet the chief of the United States of Germany retains the name of President. Should the South German dynasties desire that he should be called Emperor the North would probably yield its assent; but thus far the change of name has not been made; the title of Kaiser is not specially in favor. Regenerated Germany renounces all affinities with the Roman empire of the middle ages. When the deliberations on the new constitution are at an end, I will endeavor to report to you the final result of the complicated negotiations. At present I call your attention to the restrictions imposed on the President of Germany as to the declaration of war which hereafter will require the previous consent of the German Council. In my former reports I have led you to expect for United Germany the establishment of the most liberal government on the continent of Europe, and all that I may have led you to expect seems likely to be realized. In one sense the new government is the child of America; but for our success in our civil war it would not have been established. Our victory in that strife sowed the seeds of the regeneration of Europe. . . ." LS, DNA, RG 59, Diplomatic Despatches, Germany.

2. On Jan. 18, 1871, Bancroft wrote to Fish. "I have been informed by Count Bismarck that a proclamation will very soon be issued, perhaps before this despatch reaches you, announcing to the world the union of the States of Germany under the King of Prussia as President with the title of Emperor of Germany. I beg leave to suggest that as the United States' President wrote a congratulatory letter to the King of Prussia on occasion of the formation of North Germany so now there is much greater cause for it from the more auspicious event of the union of all Germany. This union cannot but especially touch the sympathies of the people of the United States, partly because it is in so many respects a copy of our union, and because it has been brought about not only without the effusion of a single drop of blood or the compulsory acclimations of a mob, but on the contrary by the deliberate approval of the government and people of every one of the German United States through their regularly constituted representatives; just as in our country the constitution did not go into effect until it had been ratified by the authority of the separate States. United America may see in United Germany a reproduction of its own constitution with such modifications as the history and condition of Germany seemed to require. I give it as my opinion that it is the greatest step in favor of political order and freedom that has been made in Europe in the last century or in this Nor will it escape your attention that Germany thus united becomes the leading power on the continent of Europe. Its constitution in another respect resembles our own; it imparts exceeding strength for the purposes of self defence & takes from its chief the power of entering upon wars of conquest & ambition." LS, *ibid.*

To Senate

TO THE SENATE OF THE UNITED STATES:

In answer to that part of your Resolution of the 4th of January last,[1] requesting copies of "Instructions to the commander of our Naval Squadron in the waters of the island (of San Domingo) since the commencement of the late negotiations, with the reports and correspondence of such commander"—I herewith transmit a report with accompanying papers, received from the Secretary of the Navy.

U. S. GRANT

EXECUTIVE MANSION
FEBRUARY 7TH 1871.

DS, DNA, RG 46, Presidential Messages, Foreign Relations, Santo Domingo. On Feb. 6, 1871, Secretary of the Navy George M. Robeson wrote to USG. "The Secretary of the Navy, to whom was referred, on the 11th day of January, the hereinafter quoted portion of the Resolutions of the Senate of the 4th of that month . . . has the honor to report to the President that he herewith transmits all the orders, instructions, reports and correspondence asked by the portion of the Resolution of the Senate above quoted. A technical answer to the call of the Senate on this subject would have confined the report to the particular orders and reports given to and received from the officer commanding the North Atlantic Fleet, but as the Secretary of the Navy understands the spirit of the inquiry to extend to all the orders of the Department and reports of its officers, during the period and on the subject referred to, he has caused to be transmitted in response thereto every thing on the subject found on the files of the Department from the commencement of this administration to the present time, with only such explanations as are necessary to their proper understanding. In the copies of some of the orders and reports those portions relating to mere details of the naval service are omitted, but everything is copied which bears any relation to the subject matter of the Senate's inquiry. The long distances from which the various orders and reports are transmitted render an exact chronological sequence impossible, but the order of time has been preserved as far as is consistent with a proper understanding of the subjects referred to in each." LS, *ibid.* The enclosures are *ibid.* See *SED*, 41-3-34.

1. See message to Senate, Jan. 16, 1871.

Endorsement

Refered to the Sec. of the Treas. I have no objection to the change asked.

U. S. GRANT

FEB.Y 8TH 1871

AES, DNA, RG 56, General Appraisership Applications. Written on a petition of Feb. 2, 1871, from James F. Casey, collector of customs, Stephen B. Packard, U.S. marshal, Lt. Governor Oscar J. Dunn of La. *et al.*, New Orleans, to USG. "We, the undersigned, in view of the resignation by Dr L. D. Kellogg, of the U. S. General Appraisership for the South, would respectfully commend to your consideration Jno. R. G. Pitkin, Esq of New Orleans, as one who would prove a thoroughly capable trustworthy incumbent of that post. Mr Pitkin is a native of New Orleans, a member of its bar, a tried and resolute Union man and both in this and many Northern states has contributed invaluable service as a Republican orator. In the hope that his name may be favorably considered with reference to the Appraisership in question, . . ." DS (7 signatures), *ibid.* On Feb. 7, U.S. Representative Benjamin F. Butler of Mass. wrote to USG. "John G. R Pitkin Esq of NewOrleans has been long well and intimately known to me . . . Any place he may be given he will be competent to fill as well by ability as integrity" ALS, *ibid.* On Feb. 9, USG nominated John R. G. Pitkin as general appraiser of merchandise for the South. Descended from a Conn. family, Pitkin was born in 1841 in New Orleans. After traveling through the Mediterranean for health reasons, he graduated from the University of La. (1861) and was admitted to the bar. He enlisted in the 176th N. Y., returned to La., attended the Southern Loyalist Convention at Philadelphia (1866), and subsequently served as a Republican campaign speaker. Appointed register in bankruptcy for La. (1867), Pitkin later wrote for the "anti-Warmoth" *National Republican and Citizens' Guard.* See telegram to James F. Casey, March 27, 1871; *HMD*, 42-2-211, 334, 401.

On March 7, 1869, Col. Joseph A. Mower, New Orleans, wrote to USG. "The bearer of this, Mr. J. R. G. Pitkin who is already somewhat known to you is about to visit Washington. . . . He is strongly endorsed for the mission to Florence and his appointment to that position would gratify all the *good* union people of this State:—both the old residents and the new comers." ALS, DNA, RG 59, Letters of Application and Recommendation. On March 17, Maj. Edward G. Beckwith, Washington, D. C., wrote to USG. "The Hon: J. R. G. Pitkin of La. an accomplished scholar and Attorney at Law is he informs me an applicant for the Office of U. S. Marshal of La. His unswerving devotion to the Union throughout the late rebellion was marked and conspicuous. For those convictions he was driven from his State to which he returned in the ranks as a private soldier of the Union cause, and was soon afterwards employed in my office showing very superior ability and a zeal worthy of all commendation. . . ." ALS, *ibid.* On March 25, Thomas J. Durant, Washington, D. C., wrote to U.S. Senator Charles Sumner of Mass. recommending Pitkin. ALS, *ibid.* Related papers are *ibid.* On April 26, Pitkin, New Orleans, wrote to Sumner. "I have taken the liberty to urge our Common friend, Hon. Thos J. Durant, to confer with you as to the Brazilian mission. I went to Wash. some weeks ago, wanting a mission, but was there bidden not to abandon La. now,—plea, I was needed at home to assist the Republican re-organization. I asked, therefore, for the Marshalship here,—was heavily Endorsed therefor—and I am less chagrined at not securing it than at being distanced by a vicious trickster like Packard, who has long been the incumbent of a State office, (yet unrelinquished) worth $30.000 a year. I have striven persistently for the Union and must confess that the zest afforded by my discomfiture to factious leaders here, (whom Mr Durant can fully describe to you) pricks me to secure, if possible, the mission indicated. . . ." ALS, MH.

On Dec. 18, 1872, Casey wrote to USG. "Mr. Pitkin was prominent several years ago as a powerful Republican speaker and writer and since my first knowledge of him, has been unwearied in his efforts for the Union. Eighteen months ago he was made General Appraiser of the South at the request of Senators Kellogg and Buckingham, General Butler and others,—this position he now holds. He is in bad health, owing in considerable measure to his strenuous exertions on the stump in September and October last and if you can assign him a foreign mission I am certain that Louisiana, to which he is native, will appreciate it. Of his talents there is no question whatever." LS, DNA, RG 59, Letters of Application and Recommendation. On Dec. 19, Charles W. Lowell, postmaster, New Orleans, wrote to USG recommending Pitkin for a foreign mission. LS, *ibid.* On Dec. 20, Packard, chairman, La. Republican Executive Committee, wrote to USG. "J R G Pitkin of Louisiana aspires to a mission abroad and I respectfully ask that he receive a hearty recognition, Not only was he zealous as a speaker in the recent national canvass but he has, ever since my first entering Louisiana as a soldier in 1862 been a prominent champion of the Union. At that period few here and yet fewer native Louisianians like Mr Pitkin cared to challenge the local Public opinion by standing by Genl Butler—who I may add as also Mr Durant of Washington knows him thoroughly. In the spring of 68 he refused as a Republican to espouse Mr Warmoth's candidature although most active in the National Canvass in the fall of that year—and down to the present hour has held no relations whatever with that official. He has rendered signal service in the campaigns of other states as well as Louisiana, and his attainments, personal worth and careful avoidance of all disreputable Combinations command the general respect of this people No Man in Louisiana can have fuller and heartier endorsement. I earnestly trust he may be allotted a mission" LS, *ibid.* On the same day and on Feb. 27, 1873, William P. Kellogg, New Orleans, wrote to USG. "John R. G. Pitkin, General Appraiser of the South since March. 1871, a native of Louisiana and admitted to her bar in '61, desires a foreign mission. A resolute supporter of the Union, anterior to and during Gen. Butler's rule here, and an eloquent orator and writer he has labored assiduously and with great effect for Republican interests, until now after a recent exhaustive canvass, his health is seriously impaired, as Dr Roudanez can tell you. He is a gentleman of marked culture, legal and general, and I feel that you can confer such an appointment in no better Southern instance. I ask earnestly in his behalf." "Numerous responsible recommendations of John. R G. Pitkin, of Louisiana for a foreign mission were not long since placed in your hands, by Messrs Durant and Roudanez. No Louisianian could be more handsomely accredited to your notice than he has been. He apprehends however that Senator West may in consequence of an old personal misunderstanding prove inimical to him. I have to supplement my letter already on file in his matter with the expression of a conviction that Mr. Pitkin's assignment would be a thoroughly acceptable tribute to this, his native State. All the Lower House members from La. endorse him." LS, *ibid.* On Jan. 3 and April 14, Louis C. Roudanez, New Orleans, wrote to USG. "I beg leave to place in your hands an application, supported by numerous recommendations, from my friend J. R. G. Pitkin of New-Orleans, Louisiana, who solicits from your favor an appointment abroad of a diplomatic character, in a region where the climate may be more favorable to his health which is now suffering and failing. . . ." "I was privileged at the beginning of the year to present in company with Thos J. Durant Esq, a large number of papers to you subscribed by the most responsible names of Louisiana, Republican and otherwise. These papers embodied an extraordinarily strong resquet for a forein mission for John R G. Pitkin, a native Louisianian, who has done more than almost any other man in our State to uphold the cause of Republican liberty during our Successive trials. I desire as a colored man, native also to this State and thoroughly familiar with the views of my race to be understood as earnestly urging Mr Pitkin's appointment as a recognition, especially deserved now that his health is as I personnally know, failing. Seventy thousand colored citizens will thank you for the appointment of one, who like Thos J. Durant never proved false. Until Col Williamson, who I learn, has recently sought a mission, shall have contributed to the Republican interest some portion of that activity he lent both to the rebellion and to the Enemies of Republicanism as far down as last fall, I conceive his claims are barren beside those of Mr Pitkin, who began his efforts in 1862 and has never relented since and whose learning and ability are known to other States beside Louisiana. I charged myself specially with this matter in visiting Washington last Winter and gathered from your kind assurances that Mr Pitkin would receive a mission. I am sorry to add that if he is to be cast aside for Mr Williamson you will do the State of Louisiana a great injustice. Let us reward our champions not our tardy recruits." LS and ALS, *ibid.* On April 14 and 17, Pitkin, New Orleans, wrote to Butler. ". . . Grant was manifestly impressed with my papers when Durant & Roudanez presented them and it seems to me that with those documents AGAIN BEFORE HIM and with the supplement to be enclosed by Mr Parker, he (Grant) cannot hesitate. I suppose Fish has the old papers on file,—*Grant* took charge of them about Jan. 1st. The La. delegation all united upon me in Washn—West agreeing not to oppose, although he dislikes me because of my persistent Editorial fusilade a year ago. Mr Parker thinks West's dislike must commend me to Grant. Now as to Williamson. He subscribed a telegram Mch 13th, in my behalf (and without my asking the service) and left forthwith for Wash. to ask a mission for himself He never dreamt of standing by Grant last fall until he saw the Democrats would not stand by his Reform (?) nomination as Governor. Then he shot off in a huff to California and on his return late in Oct. made one speech at Kellogg's instance for K. and *incidentally* for Grant. For this service he demands heavy requital. He is now attorney for the Texas Pacific R. R,—a post he owes, I think, to K. Fellows came to me in haste just after W's late return from Washn and told me W. would not forego this attorneyship; so an intimate of Ws had just told Fellows. I earnestly hope that by the 1st prox a favorable decision may be reached. I don't know how to thank you, General, for all yr kindness." "I was told *confidentially* by Kellogg yesterday that Williamson had asked him for the appointment of Mayor of Shreveport, where Williamson resides. This would indicate that W. foregoes his idea of a mission. . . . Were I less disquieted as to my health, I would annoy you less, General, but a change of climate is *absolutely* needful to me. Do push it as soon as you can,—and I will owe you my life. . . ." ALS, *ibid.* Related papers are *ibid.* On Dec. 8, Pitkin wrote to U.S. Representative Chester B. Darrall of La. withdrawing from consideration for a foreign mission. ALS, *ibid.* On May 29, 1875, Casey, Packard, Kellogg, and John M. G. Parker, postmaster, New Orleans, and others petitioned USG to appoint Pitkin as consul, Rio de Janeiro. DS, *ibid.* Related papers are *ibid.*

On Aug. 31, 1876, Packard wrote to USG. "The fact that I am a candidate for the office of Governor in the approaching election renders it proper that I surrender the office of which I am the incumbent. I therefore tender you my resignation of the office of United States Marshal for the District of Louisiana to take effect as soon as a successor is appointed and qualified. I avail myself of this occasion to express my high personal regard for you and my gratitude for the generous and assuring confidence which you have bestowed on me during my official relation to the Federal Government, extending through a continuous period of more than seven years, much of the time under circumstances of extraordinary difficulty. In view of my relation to the impending canvass in this State I respectfully suggest that the vacancy be filled with as little delay as is consistent with a proper selection." ALS, *ibid.*, RG 60, Letters from the President. USG endorsed this letter. "Atty. Gn Accept." AE (undated), *ibid.* On Dec. 14, USG nominated Pitkin as marshal, La. See *HMD*, 45-3-31, part 1, pp. 399–422, 450–66; *New York Times*, May 29, June 12, 1877, June 26–28, Dec. 31, 1878.

On April 15, 1891, Pitkin, U.S. minister, Buenos Aires, wrote to Frederick Dent Grant, U.S. minister, Vienna. "Pardon an unofficial word. How are you and how do you like your post? B. Aires has its frequent political tempests but New Orleans long since seasoned me for low barometers. The attachment which I bore your noble father has not abated; the paternal interest he felt in my career during the last fifteen years of his life and the confidences we shared together remain precious memories. Will you kindly communicate an expression of profound regard to your mother, if she be with you, and to your wife though the latter lady may not recall me as one of the 'City of Mexico' party that crossed the Gulf in 1880." ALS, USG 3.

To Frederick Dent Grant

Washington, D. C. Feb.y 8th *18~~6~~*71.

DEAR FRED,

I have read your Uncle Wrenshall's[1] letter to you, and now return it. The offer made to you is a splendid one if you can make up your mind to five years of close application to business with very small returns. I advise you not to decide now definitely, but to write to your Uncle Wren and say that you will go out next Summer and decide then. If you can get tickets as proposed in his letter do so.

If you go into stock raising it will be five years before you can have much income from that source. In the mean time you can have Olives, ~~f~~Figs, Almonds and such other fruits growing as are produced there, and can lay the foundation for future independence. But you will have to attend to the business closely yourself. Such business will not do if left to others. You will require necessarily means beside land and stock to start on. If I think well of the enterprise after you go upon the ground and report, I think I might spare you six or eight thousand dollars to start with, and $2500 00 pr. annum thereafter for three or four years.

You should write to the gentleman who makes you the offer as well as to your Uncle.

Yours Truly
U. S. GRANT

CADET F. D. GRANT,
WEST POINT, N. Y.

ALS, USG 3. On [Feb.] 3, 1871, USG telegraphed to Col. Thomas G. Pitcher, superintendent, USMA. "I wish you would give Fred leave from Friday to Monday to come to Washington—this week or next" Telegram received, USMA.

1. George Wrenshall Dent. See *PUSG*, 20, 139–40.

To J. Russell Jones

Washington, D. C. Feb.y 8th *18~~6~~*71.

DEAR JONES:

As I have neither printed cards, nor the vanity to keep on hand my photograph, I cannot reply fittingly to your last enclosure. I accept the rebuke however and confess that I have been a little negligent about writing. If I had enough little Missions like yours to give all my friends I would have more time to devote to private correspondence.

Your friend Sumner has been on the warpath ever since the treaty for the acquisition of Santo Domingo was sent to the Senate, and perfectly rabbid since the removal of Motley. I understand he has a special fondness for you and Washburne. By the way Washburne by his course in remaining at his post through so many trials, and his prudence and ability while at it, has won for himself new lawrels.[1] I have not written to Washburne since he has been shut up in Paris. I must do so now however.

Every thing seems to be working here favorably. The democratic and self st~~i~~yled independent press, are as abusive as ever however. I pay no attention to them and would not know what they say only that there are always *friends* to tell you everything that is disagreeable.

Mrs. Grant talks some of making a visit to Europe before my term expires. If she does you will see her, with the two yougest children, and possibly Fred, then.—My family are all well and desire to be remembered to Mrs. Jones and the children.[2]

Yours Truly
U. S. GRANT

P. S. Dont let my failure to write keep you from writing to me. I am always glad to hear from you.

U. S. G.

ALS, George R. Jones, Chicago, Ill. On Feb. 26, 1871, J. Russell Jones, U.S. minister, Brussels, wrote to USG. "I have yours of the 8th inst, and was glad enough to hear from you. If, by sending you a cheap Photograph occasionally it will bring me a letter in return, I shall lay in a good supply. The only fear I had was that you would mistake it for Bismarck and write to him. I hope your friend Sumner will have his likeness taken, showing the black eye the Senate gave him in Cramers case, and send Sanford and me a lot of them. He is an 'Excellent Citizen', I like him immensly, and highly appreciate his 'fondness for Washburne & myself.' Speaking of Washburne, I think he is getting a good deal more glory than he deserves, and I a good deal less. His duties were simple & easy, as compared with mine, ~~and~~ It has required infinitely more skill and ability to manage the 1200 American grass-Widows I have had on my hands during the war than to discharge the duties of Minister to France, and yet it has never occurred to anyone to speak of me. I am not sure that I could have done as well at Paris as W. has, though I am sure he was better fitted for this post than I am. *If* he has a weakness, it is for American grass-Widows. I am delighted at the bare possibility of seeing Mrs Grant & the children over here. If it is a possible thing I shall get your letter from the Queen before Mrs Grant sees her. The election of Frank Blair to the Senate seems to me to have let you nicely out of the Shurtz Embroglio, and I like immensly the turn you have given to the Alabama and Fishery questions. *I am afraid of Butler. Watch him.* We are all well, and getting along very well. At the first Court ball of the Season, on the 10th, Mrs Jones presented twelve Ladies and I six Gentlemen to the King & Queen, and when Washburne was here, on the 13th, I presented him and Mrs W. I went to Paris with W. when he returned and was there a week. The City is much less changed than I had supposed. With the exception of the Bois de Boulogne, where, for a long distance the trees are all cut down, the City will look as nicely as ever in three months after peace is restored. From all I could learn I think Trochu a first rate match for McClelland. I had made all my arrangements to start this week with Mrs Jones on a little trip of a month or six weeks through Italy, but have just rec'd a line from Harry Wilson saying he would Sail on the 22d and I shall now hold on until he comes. Speaking of Harry Wilson's coming over here, can't you make some excuse for sending old Dr Kittoe over here on some mission which will pay his expenses? I want to see him, and he would come if he was not too poor. I hear poor Old Man Houghton is at home again. His is a _____ tough case. No man in our state has worked longer or more faithfully than he, and it seems as though some younger or less deserving men (like me) should be made to give way to him. I wish he had been made Consul here, though I should not dare say so above a whisper. I liked the way Mr Fish disposed of poor Motley, immensely. Motleys 'protest' gave the Secretary a fine opportunity to get the facts before the people, which was needed, and he did it well. We are to have all the American's here on Monday evening, who can furnish a certificate of good moral character. Washburne requires nothing of this sort. The only trouble I have ever had here has grown out of my refusal to present people at Court who I either knew nothing about or knew that they were not fit persons to be presented. You will, I am sure be gratified to know that you have at least one Representative abroad who runs his machine on high moral principles Washburne will do better as he gets older. His back troubles him a good deal yet. Remember me kindly to Mrs Grant and the Children, Porter, Babcock et. al. Write me whenever you can. It does me good to get your letters. I will give no more of them to the Queen. . . . I hope Parker will come out all right. It will be _____ if it shall turn out that he has been stealing. I can not think it possible." ALS, USG 3. See letter to J. Russell Jones, Nov. 7, 1871.

On Jan. 9, USG had written to Jones. "I take pleasure in introducing to you Gen. Wesley Merritt of the Army, who visits Europe on leave of absence. Gen Merritt distinguished himself as an officer during the late war. Any attention you may be able to show him will be bestowed upon one who deserves well of his government, and one who will duly appreciate the kindness." Copy (misdated 1870), DLC-USG, II, 1. See *PUSG*, 14, 258; *ibid.*, 20, 91–94.

1. On Nov. 17, 1870, John Lothrop Motley, U.S. minister, London, wrote to Elihu B. Washburne. "... I send you herewith the copy of a telegram rec'd yesterday morning from Mr Fish, which I trust will reach you safely. I thought it unsafe to attempt to telegraph to you. Copy: 'FISH SECY OF STATE TO MOTLEY MINISTER LONDON Nov 15th. Send by first opportunity following "WASHBURNE MINISTER PARIS. the President instructs me to say that whenever you & Read or either desire or find it convenient to leave Paris you are at liberty to do so. In that event he or you or both will go to Tours & communicate with the proper official there. Inform Read of this."'..." ALS, DLC-Elihu B. Washburne. On Feb. 21, 1871, Washburne, Paris, wrote to USG. "Mr. Kohn, who is the managing man of Mr. Ruttinger, the celebrated photographer of this city, has sent me a magnificent Imperial photograph of M. Thiers, to be transmitted to you. I send it tonight, by the bag which goes to London, and I hope it may reach you safely. I went to Brussels some ten days ago to see my family, and on my return a few days since I was stricken down by one of my old attacks, and I have been very unwell ever since. I am now on the mend however. Russ Jones came down with me, as did Kreismann from Berlin. They left on their return to day. Russ has not been well all winter. and looks quite feeble. I found my family very well If we can have a peace, I shall bring them back here as soon as things are settled. With kindest regards to Mrs. Grant and the children, ..." LS, *ibid.* On Feb. 28, Washburne wrote to John C. Smith. "I lose no time in thanking you for your long and most interesting letter of the 30th ultimo. You give me a great deal of news that interests me very much. I do not believe the income tax will be repealed, and therefore I expect you will retain your place. I came out of the long and dreadful siege safe and sound, but I have been quite unwell since. I am, however, nearly as well as usual, which, by the way, is not much to brag of. I have too much Fever River malaria in my bones, I fear, to ever again enjoy perfect health. I am glad to hear that old Galena is brushing up a little. I assure you I shall be glad to get back once more among the old friends.... I hope the 'Indian' will come out right. As to the President he always comes out ahead in the end. The curs will bark at his heels as they did after Shiloh, but they will find their Appomattox in 1872. I shall always be glad to hear from you. I hope to bring my family here from Brussels before long." ALS, William J. Prince, East Lansing, Mich.

2. Jones married Elizabeth Ann Scott on Sept. 14, 1848. Their children were Russell Sheldon, Ben Campbell, Frank Ormsby, Lizzie Scott, Rebecca Fulkerson, and Eliza Maria. Jones's niece, Annie Eliza Campbell (daughter of Benjamin H. Campbell of Galena), had married Orville E. Babcock. See *PUSG*, 16, 365–66; *New York Times*, Oct. 2, 1889; *ibid.*, Jan. 24, 1902.

To Senate

To the Senate:

The British Minister accredited to this Government, recently, in compliance with instructions from his Government, submitted a proposal for the appointment of a "Joint High Commission" to be composed of Members to be named by each Government, to hold its session at Washington, and to treat and discuss the mode of settling the different questions which have arisen out of the Fisheries,[1] as well as those which affect the relations of the United States toward the British Possessions in North America.

I did not deem it expedient to agree to the proposal unless the consideration of the questions growing out of the acts committed by the Vessels which have given rise to the claims known as the "Alabama Claims" were to be within the subject of discussion and settlement by the Commission. The British Government having assented to this, the Commission is expected shortly to meet.[2] I therefore nominate as such Commissioners[3] jointly and severally. on the part of the United States: Hamilton Fish, Secretary of State Robert C. Schenck,[4] Envoy Extraordinary and Minister Plenipotentiary to Great Britain Samuel Nelson, an Associate Justice of the Supreme Court of the United States Ebenezer R. Hoar of Massachusetts George H. Williams of Oregon.

I communicate herewith, the correspondence which has passed on this subject between the Secretary of State and the British Minister[5]

U. S. GRANT

WASHINGTON, 9TH FEBRUARY 1871.

DS, DNA, RG 46, Presidential Messages, Foreign Affairs, Great Britain. Related papers are *ibid.* On Dec. 9, 1870, Secretary of State Hamilton Fish had written in his diary. "Read in Confidence a private letter from Sir John Rose dated in London Novr 24—respecting the questions between the two governments, & intimating that the British Cabinet is disposed to enter upon a negotiation &c—he professes to speak without authority—Boutwell remarks that he lately saw a letter from him to Morton Bliss & Co of NY, dated 4th Novr—in which Rose stated that the unsettled condition of the Alabama claims interfered with the funding of the Public Debt—President makes no comment on the letter—but asks if I have any thing else to present—" DLC-Hamilton Fish. See Annual Message, Dec. 5, 1870, note 4.

On Jan. 9, 1871, Fish recorded in his diary. "Memorandum of points taken in a Conversation between Secretary Fish and Sir John Rose at Mr Fishs house. January 9. 1871 Sir John stated that he had been requested by the British Government informally, unofficially and personally, as one half American, half English, enjoying the confidence of both Governments to ascertain what could be done for settling the pending questions between the two Governments; and that he was authorized to say that if it would be acceptable to the Government of the United States to refer all those subjects to a joint Commission, framed something upon the model of the Commission which made the Treaty of Ghent, he could say that the British Government were prepared to send out such a Commission on their part composed of persons of the highest rank in the realm. . . . Some discussion was also had as to the manner in which the questions should be raised. Sir John Rose said that the British Government could not take the initiative in the question of the Alabama Claims and suggested that, in case the way for the settlement seemed clear, the British Govt should propose a commission for the settlement of the San Juan boundary, the fisheries & other Canadian questions, and that the United States should accede provided the claims for the acts of the vessels should be also considered. Mr Fish assented to this." DLC-Hamilton Fish. See J. C. Bancroft Davis, *Mr. Fish and the Alabama Claims: A Chapter in Diplomatic History* (Boston, 1893), pp. 59–64; Nevins, *Fish*, pp. 435–36.

On Jan. 26, Sir Edward Thornton, British minister, wrote to Fish, proposing ". . . the appointment of a joint High Commission which shall be composed of members to be named by each Government, shall hold its Sessions at Washington, and shall treat of and discuss the mode of settling the different questions which have arisen out of the fisheries, as well as all those which affect the relations of the United States towards Her Majesty's possessions in North America. . . ." LS, DNA, RG 59, Notes from Foreign Legations, Great Britain. On Jan. 30, Fish wrote to Thornton. ". . . I have laid your note before the President, who instructs me to say that he shares with Her Majesty's Government the appreciation of the importance of a friendly and complete understanding between the two Governments with reference to the subjects specially suggested for the consideration of the proposed Joint High Commission; and he fully recognizes the friendly spirit which has prompted the proposal. The President is however of the opinion, that without the adjustment of a class of questions not alluded to in your note, the proposed High Commission would fail to establish the permanent relations, and the sincere, substantial, and lasting friendship between the two Governments, which, in common with Her Majesty's Government, he desires should prevail. He thinks that the removal of the differences which arose during the rebellion in the United States, and which have existed since then, growing out of the acts committed by the several vessels which have given rise to the claims generically known as the 'Alabama Claims,' will also be essential to the restoration of cordial and amicable relations between the two Governments. He directs me to say that should Her Majesty's Government accept this view of this matter, and assent that this subject also may be treated of by the proposed High Commission, and may thus be put in the way of a final and amicable settlement, this Government, will with much pleasure, appoint High Commissioners on the part of the United States, to meet those who may be appointed on behalf of Her Majesty's Government, and will spare no efforts to secure at the earliest practicable moment, a just and amicable arrangement of all the questions which now unfortunately stand in the way of an entire and abiding friendship between the two nations." Copy, *ibid.*, RG 46, Presidential Messages, Foreign Affairs, Great Britain. On Feb. 1, after consulting by cable with Earl Granville, Thornton wrote to Fish. ". . . I am now authorised by His Lordship to state that it would give Her Majesty's Government great satisfaction if the claims commonly known by the name of the 'Alabama' claims were submitted to the consideration of the same High Commission by which Her Majesty's Government have proposed that the questions relating to the British possessions in North America should be discussed, provided that all other claims both of British subjects and citizens of the United States arising out of acts committed during the recent civil war in this country are similarly referred to the same Commission. . . ." LS, *ibid.*, RG 59, Notes from Foreign Legations, Great Britain. For more on this exchange of letters between Thornton and Fish, see note 5 below. On Feb. 5, Fish wrote in his diary. "Thornton calls, asks if we will not delay announcement of agreement for High Commission, until Thursday morning, as Parliament will meet on that day, & the Queen will probably announce it in her speech, & it will be more agreeable to the British Govt & People to recive the first intelligence through their own Channels—to which I agree." DLC-Hamilton Fish.

On Feb. 10, following Senate approval, USG formally appointed U.S. commissioners. On Feb. 12, Levi P. Morton, New York City, wrote to USG. "Will you allow me to express my great gratification at the reception by the press and public—almost unanimous—of the appointment of the High Commission and the negotiations which resulted in that agreement. I thought it important that the Herald should take the right stand, and took the responsibility, as soon as matters were finally settled, to send for Mr Bennett Jr to come to my house to receive some confidential information (for his own & Fathers use)—he came and agreed to sustain the Govt in the matter—this he has done. The leader in yesterdays Herald, (except the part referring to Gov Boutwell) was written by our mutual friend Young and is, I think, a splendid article. I have had the curiosity to look up my first cable correspondence with Sir John Rose on the subject & take the liberty of giving the first cables, as I have reason to *know* that it was the private knowledge of your friendly sentiments which laid the foundation for the good results which have since occured. In response to a cable enquiry from Rose as to the state of feeling here on English relations, I replied by cable Nov 18th saying 'Know the President desires settlement when it can be made to satisfy both peoples, and cordial friendly future relations' Leading men of both parties here say that these results to the nation, if they issue successfully, will bring even as lasting fame as the Military events of the past." ALS, USG 3. See letter to Hamilton Fish, March 4, 1871.

1. See Annual Message, Dec. 5, 1870, note 5.

2. The Joint High Commission held its first meeting on Feb. 27, 1871. On March 4, Fish wrote in his diary. "At 1½ PM—Joint High Commrs meet—All present Protocol of last meeting read, & approved & ordered to be signed by the Protocolists—. . . The question then was considered as to the *order* in which the several subjects should be considered, referring to Sir Ed Thornton 1st note to me (in the Protocol) remarks that the subjects proposed seem to divide themselves into two classes I. the questions arising out of the Fisheries—II those which affect the relations of the US. toward H. M. possessions in N. A. . . . The British Commrs then ask what subject shall be first considered—& some conversation arises as to the relative importance of the questions—In pursuance of the understanding reached on Monday, I adhere to the order of precedence as presented in the Correspondence Judge Hoar, speaks of the greater importance of the Alabama question—It is urged that the imminence of conflict, & danger from the Fisheries makes it important to consider that first—The British Commrs seize with earnestness on Hoars suggestion—Hoar & Schenck propose that the Am. Commrs retire to consult which is done—in consultation H. & S. urge their view Nelson prefers holding the Brit. Commrs to their own order, finally agreed that we say to them that we prefer not to propose any change from the order in which the subjects have been presented in the Correspondence, unless requested by the Brit. Commrs Should they indicate a desire to change we are ready to assent—It was then agreed that on Monday we proceed to consider the Fisheries—& the Alabama be the next—Adjourned to Monday at Noon—" DLC-Hamilton Fish.

3. On Feb. 3 and 7, 1871, Fish wrote in his diary. ". . . Question of the Commis-

sioners is considered. I suggest the importance of having the different sections of the Country represented, & if having the South, & the Democratic party represented—& suggest, in addition to Schenck & the Secr of State, Judge Hoar, Williams of Oregon, & Judge Campbell—Delano raises question as to Hoar—President speaks favorably—All approve Williams—question whether Campbell is not disqualified—some doubt by ~~B~~ *all* whether any Democrat should be named—& whether it wd be proper to entrust to one who was interested in the Confederacy the settlement of questions with Gt Britain for acts which were to benefit that Goverment—Hendricks is named I think as a Presidential Candidate he wd be disposed to fillibuster, & to deprive the Administration of the credit of settling these questions—Thurman—but he & Schenck are both from Ohio—Chas O'Connor—Benj R Curtis—Geo T. Curtis, Jas L Orr, are named. Prsdt says Saml Glover of St Louis is a Democrat, & a very able Lawyer—No one else present knows him, except Delano, who has heard of him" "Question of Joint High Commrs (with Gt Britain) coming up President authorizes me to write to Judge Hoar—& to ask Senator Williams, & Judge Nelson of Supreme Court if they will serve—Delano doubts the propriety of Nelson's selection—Robeson—Akerman approve—Boutwell, & Belknap & Cresswell acquiescent" DLC-Hamilton Fish.

On Jan. 21, Governor John W. Geary of Pa. wrote to USG. "I am informed that it is your intention to appoint Commissioners to settle the claims for spoliations by the 'Alabama' and other piratical vessels. Should this be so, permit me to present to your consideration for one of the Commissioners, Ex Governor W. A. Newell, of New Jersey. Who is in every respect eminently qualified and whose services through 'the Union League of America', and otherwise, are such as to entitle him to such a recognition. His appointment will be popular and highly gratifying . . ." ALS, DNA, RG 59, Letters of Application and Recommendation.

In Feb., both Elias H. Derby, a prominent Mass. lawyer who had advised Secretary of State William H. Seward on the fisheries dispute, and Charles B. Norton, a New York City publisher, wrote to Fish applying to be secretary to the Joint High Commission. LS and ALS, *ibid.* See *PUSG*, 18, 384–85. On Feb. 14, Fish wrote in his diary. "Calling yesterday at the Presidents, I found Boutwell & the President signed a designation of Bancroft Davis to act as Secretary to the American Commissioners, on the 'Joint High Commission' about to meet—I mentioned the name of George Bemis as an Assistant Secretary stating that he probably knows more of the 'Alabama Case' than any man in the Country—Boutwell at once remarked, 'I would not have him associated with the settlement of the case—he is the mere shadow of Sumner, and will do whatever Sumner wants—& if as I believe Sumner means "War" upon the Administration, & hostility to the Commission, Bemis will work into his hands—' The President said he thought it would be unwise to have him associated with the Commission, & would not have him appointed—" DLC-Hamilton Fish.

On Feb. 6 and 9, Fish wrote in his diary. "Thornton, calls in the afternoon, has a telegram, announcing the names of British Commrs, Lord De Grey—(President of the Council) Sir John A Macdonald, (or if he declines, Sir John Rose) and Thornton himself—he is not instructed to announce these names, & communicates them Confidentially—Says his Govt has required him to send by Cable, the notes which have passed between us on the subject of the Joint Commission—says they cost £800—" "Thornton, calls in the afternoon, saying he has a telegram announcing that in addition to Ld de Grey, himself & Sir John Macdonald—Professor Bernard & Sir John Rose will be on the Commission & Ld Tenterden, will be Secretary—I reply that 'Prof. Bernard wrote a very bad book about the Alabama Claims—& Ld Tenterden was the Author of the once famous "Notes"—' He remarks 'Oh, that will make no difference—Ld Tenterden is only Secretary—& as to Bernard, we will persuade him' I express some regret that these two are chosen—He says they will sail on Saturday—" DLC-Hamilton Fish. See Nevins, *Fish*, p. 471.

4. On Jan. 10 and 11, Fish wrote in his diary. "Read to the President Curtins private letter to me of Decr 18, from St Petersburg—Also Mac Veagh's private letter from Constantinople Stated to him privately the conversation of last Eveg with Sir John Rose—at first he expressed unwillingness to hasten the negotiation in advance of Schenck's departure—but on mentioning that Schenck should of course be one of the Commrs, & delay his departure, in case the proposal is well entertained he objected that the Commrs would come with instructions, which they could not yield, & that probably more concessions could be obtained by Schenck abroad than from British Commissioners here—I thought not—that if they send Commrs over here, it will be with the determination to settle all questions, & because they will have agreed to admit their liability for the 'Alabama'—He assents, & desire me to see Schenck expressing ~~the~~ a reluctance to agree to any arrangement which might disappoint him." "Genl Schenck called to say that he is disappointed as to his passage for England—the ~~vessel~~ Steamer (Russia) in which he had taken State Rooms does not sail on 25 Jay—& they had sent him tickets for 1 Feb—I mention to him Sir John Rose's proposal, & read to him the Memorandum . . . & ask his opinion both as to the general proposition of Sending Commrs & the question with respect to the Alabama—He thinks there will be more probability of agreement if the Commrs come here, & agrees that there is great doubt of the liability of Gt Britain for the Acts of some of the Cruisers other than the Alabama—& that if Gt B. admits her liability as to the Alabama, the Country will be grateful & the Senate ratify the Treaty I intimate to him that should this course be adopted he of course will be named as one of the Commissioners & that although by the rules of the Dept he is allowed pay for only thirty days while awaiting instructions any additional delay in consequence of this suggested arrangement, will be allowed him—He says that if he can be one of a Commission that will adjust these questions, & sign his name to the Convention for that purpose, it will relieve him from much labor, & anxiety after reaching London, & will doubtless make his service there more pleasant & secure him a more cordial reception . . ." DLC-Hamilton Fish. See Nevins, *Fish*, pp. 436–37; message to Senate, Dec. 21, 1870.

5. On Feb. 3, 1871, Fish wrote in his diary. "Sr Edw Thornton calls before Breakfast—returns the draft of proposed reply which I sent him by Rose last Evening—with entire approval—leaves with me a proposed draft of a further note, accepting terms to include 'the Alabama Claims' in the Commission, provided all other claims of Citizens or subjects of either party against the other Govt be also included—I remark that the terms are broad & enquire what is meant to be covered by it—that it might include claims for the Confederate debt, which by the Constitution, cannot be allowed or paid—He replied that 'of course they could not be presented'—that the Brit. Govt had recognized the Confederates as belligerents but there were cases of seizures & arrests, of distruction of property, which might be presented—He proposes that the several notes be antedated so as to allow an interval sufficient for them to have been transmitted, & considered It is agreed that his first note to me bear date Jany 26—my reply Jany. 30—his second (of which he now shews leaves with me the proposed draft) Feb 1—& my reply to it, Feb 3—He asks for & takes with him the draft of his ~~first~~ proposed first note—& sends me a copy (Official) in the course of the Morning" DLC-Hamilton Fish.

On May 30, Fish wrote to Francis Lieber. ". . . you have asked me whether the transfer of the negotiations on the Alabama question, from London to Washington, originated with me—The idea & the determination were mine *before* even the rejection of the Johnson Clarendon treaty—Soon after I entered upon the office of Secy of State, I saw that that Treaty was foredoomed to be rejected—I then decided, & expressed to the President, the opinion, that we must take pause in the discussion with G. B. & that when the excitement & irritation had subsided (which would ensue on the rejection of the Treaty) we should insist that any renewed negotiations be had here—In my instructions to Mr Motley of 15 May /69 I instructed him to suggest a suspense of the question—on 28 June 69, I instructed him that when the negotiations should be resumed we desired them to be Conducted in this Country—Although this was the first *Official* declaration on the subject of the transfer of the negotiations (a change of venue, the lawyers would call it) it was what I had expressed in conversation in private, & in semi official Correspondence, & in deliberations in the Cabinet, & in ~~discu~~ consultations with the President, from my entrance on office, in March /69—The sending a Special Mission, & some person of high official rank, was suggested by me in May /69 & was the subject of close confidential conversation, & *of correspondence* with influential persons in England, as early as the 1st June 1869 & the Correspondence was continued, in this mode, until the fruit ripened; & the official letters between Sr Edward Thornton & me, (which of course were written & revised, & exchanged & had passed through the Cable, word for word) before they were signed) finally took date & signature in the latter part of January last—Those four letters were the official parturition of twenty months secret Diplomacy—" ALS, CSmH.

To Hamilton Fish

Washington D. C. Feb.y 9th *18*71

HON. H. FISH;
SEC. OF STATE;
DEAR SIR:

Enclosed I send you a letter received some time since from Mr. Francis.[1] I should like to appoint Mr. F. to Greece, but would not do so without giving Mr. Tuckerman[2] a chance to resign, which I understand he desires to do if his place is wanted for another. If you think well of this will you let Mr. Davis so advise Mr. T.

Respectfully yours,
U. S. GRANT

ALS, DLC-Hamilton Fish.

1. John M. Francis, born in 1823 in Prattsburg, N. Y., began work as a printer in 1838 at Canandaigua and by 1844 had obtained an editorial position with the *Rochester*

Daily Advertiser. He then pursued legal work but in 1846 resumed his newspaper career in Troy and founded the *Troy Daily Times* in 1851. Originally a Free Soil Democrat, Francis championed the Republican Party from its formation. On Jan. 24 and April 12, 1871, Francis wrote to USG. "In our recent private interview—(and for the privilege of that interview you have my thanks)—you referred to two missions held by citizens of this state, Berlin and Greece. The incumbents, as was remarked, are by no means influential Republican representative men. I write you this, Mr. President, to say that if in your opinion a change should be deemed advisable in the mission at Athens, I would like to be considered a candidate, promising you that, if appointed, I would endeavor to discharge the duties of the office in a satisfactory manner. I need not tell you how gratified I should be, *under the circumstances*, with the tender of such Executive compliment. Of my deservings you may judge. I only beg as a personal favor in this respect that you will devote a few minutes in glancing over the *brief* of recommendations in my behalf that were filed in the office of the Secretary of State soon after your inauguration. In this matter, too, I think Mr. Conkling & Mr. Fenton will be found in agreement as they were when both originally presented my name for a mission. I *do* feel a sensitive interest in this application, Mr. President, because self-pride if not deserving Republican merit, induces an earnest desire for recognition after all that has been said in the matter." "*Personal.* . . . When I was at Washington Mr. Fish expressed the opinion as I understood him that Mr. Tuckerman's reply would probably be received in the course of four weeks from that time, (March 2d) Forty days have now elapsed, a sufficient time to hear from him by due course of mail, though it was intended I believe that he should reply by cable. I feel some anxiety in this matter with reference to securing action by the Senate, *so that it may be consummated before adjournment.* This is my apology for writing now. Let me say that, in the San Domingo business, you have been proudly vindicated, and the record made will redound to your honor. Accept the congratulations of your earnest supporter, . . ." ALS, *ibid.*

On March 8, 1869, Charles A. Dana, New York City, had written to USG. "I beg respectfully to recommend the appointment of Mr J. M. Francis of this State to one of the diplomatic offices to be filled in Europe. Mr Francis is a man of high character and in every way qualified for such a place. His position as a citizen and as the conductor of one of the ablest and most influential Republican journals of the State also fully entitles him to be considered when the selection of foreign ministers is to be made. His appointment would be received with entire satisfaction by the Republicans of the State." ALS, DNA, RG 59, Letters of Application and Recommendation. On the same day, U.S. Senator Reuben E. Fenton and U.S. Representative John A. Griswold of N. Y. wrote to USG. "We desire to present for your consideration the name of the Hon. J. M. Francis, of Troy, N. Y., and to recommend him as a proper person to represent our country abroad. . . ." LS, *ibid.* On March 13, Speaker of the House James G. Blaine wrote to USG. "The name Mr Jno M. Francis Editor of the Troy Times is before you for appointment to some position in the Diplomatic service—By culture, character, long & devoted & efficient labor in the loyal cause Mr Francis is entitled to the highest consideration—I do not know of any gentleman who would more honorably, ably & creditably represent his country abroad—It would be regarded by myself as a personal favor to have Mr Francis case promptly & favorably considered—" ALS, *ibid.* On Jan. 22, 1870, U.S. Senator Roscoe Conkling of N. Y. wrote to Secretary of State Hamilton Fish recommending Francis. ALS, *ibid.* Related papers are *ibid.* On May 10, 1871, USG nominated Francis as minister to Greece. See *New York Times*, June 19, 1897.

2. Charles K. Tuckerman, born into a prominent Boston family in 1821, attended Boston Latin School. He engaged in business overseas before returning to the U.S. in 1856 and becoming director of the New York Institution for the Blind. He edited Alexander R. Rangabé, *Greece: Her Progress and Her Present Position* (New York, 1867); on Feb. 5, 1868, President Andrew Johnson nominated him as the first minister to Greece. On Nov. 14, Tuckerman, Athens, wrote to USG. "The announcement of your election to the Presidency of the U. S., was received in Athens by telegram and excited much interest, not only among the Greeks, but among the Foreign Representatives resident here. The Ministers of Great Britain—France—Prussia & Italy at once called at the Legation & presented their congratulations. Many prominent Greek Citizens including the Minister of Foreign Affairs have also expressed to me their gratification at the result of the election, for your name & fame are familiar to them, and their sympathy with American institutions has been strengthened by the result of the rebellion. Of him who mainly brought about that result, the Greeks are consequently not unmindful, for they are a liberty loving people however inexperienced they may be in practical self government. Permit me, General, to add to these, my own congratulations at the result of the contest—in which you yourself have taken no part—but which the people in their enthusiasm have carried to a triumphal end. That the era of *real* Union & of *real* peace is about to dawn on our beloved Country, I do not for a moment doubt. May God give you health & strength to meet all emergencies & to accomplish the great results which I believe you have at heart. With kind remembrances to Mrs Grant & with Mrs. Tuckermans & my own sincere regards, . . ." ALS, USG 3.

On March 9, 1869, Maj. Benjamin Alvord, Omaha, wrote to USG. "My object in writing this is to say that I have seen in the papers that an effort will be made for the removal of my friend *Hon Chas. K. Tuckerman* as *Minister to Greece.* I write to urge that he be retained—I feel satisfied that the public service will be subserved by his retention. He has but recently established himself with his family at Athens, and has given universal satisfaction. I feel certain of this; and that he is admirably fitted to perform the duties devolved upon him—He is an accomplished gentleman, thoroughly informed as to our interests in that quarter. But he has not failed to keep up his interest with affairs here and his sympathy with the Republican party. He was warmly interested in our success in the late war, and encountered great pecuniary sacrifices occasioned by the war, by going, at the instance of President Lincoln, into the project of colonization of negroes in the West Indies—The death of Mr. Lincoln, before measures were matured, has as yet prevented a reimbursement to him for these sacrifices. He was unanimously confirmed by the Senate, and my advices from those well informed satisfy me that his retention will please the enlightened friends of Greece in the U. S., who look with great interests to events in that quarter. My personal interest in Mr. Tuckerman & his family has grown out of his being a neighbour at Hasting, on the Hudson, where I was stationed two years ago in New York—I cannot close without offering you my sincere congratulations on your inauguration, and the very auspicious circumstances under which you enter upon your duties." ALS, DNA, RG 59, Letters of Application and Recommendation. On March 20, Marshall O. Roberts, Richard M. Blatchford, and William Cullen Bryant, New York City, wrote to USG. "We respectfully ask of the President that Mr Charles K. Tuckerman, now Minister to Greece, be continued in office, he being not only a loyal citizen, but eminently qualified for the position & very acceptable to the Greek Nation." LS, *ibid.* On the same day, Admiral David G.

Farragut, New York City, endorsed this letter. "I would respectfully say to yr Excellency, that during my recent visit to Greece I was fully impressed with the truth of all expressed in the within letter." AES, *ibid.* Related papers are *ibid.*

Also on March 20, George Gibbs, Washington, D. C., wrote to USG. "I enclose a letter from Mr Henry T. Tuckerman, the author and poet, requesting that his brother Mr Charles K Tuckerman be retained in his present office as Minister to Greece. I beg leave to urge his petition as I know personally of Mr Tuckerman's ability and his successful administration" ALS, Georgetown University, Washington, D. C. Gibbs enclosed a letter of March 17 from Henry T. Tuckerman, New York City, to USG. "Being prevented by indisposition, from paying my respects to you in person, & having been informed by a friend in the Senate of a probable attempt to displace my brother now U. S. Minister at Athens, I beg leave respectfully to state that the office he holds, was bestowed without his personal knowledge or solicitation, partly because of the great pecuniary sacrifices he made during the war, but chiefly because of the high estimation in which his character & capacity were held by leading men in Washington; that he was confirmed by the whole Senate with the exception of Mr Sumner, who, however made no personal objection but thought a friend of his had stronger claims; that the appointment was most cordially received by the Republican press & party here & elsewhere; that my brother has only within a few weeks, succeeded, after great trouble & expense, in establishing himself & his family at Athens; that he has won the respect & confidence of the government, people, educators & missionaries & was most judicious & efficient in conciliating the local antagonisms growing out of the recent warlike threatenings in the East. Having thus auspiciously initiated the new mission, in evidence of which I can refer to his record in the State Department, I submit that any interference with him, on the advent of an administration with the principles of which we are both publicly identified, &, under the circumstances I have mentioned, would be a reflection upon his character & detrimental to the public interest. I have been told, but have no proof of the fact, that statements have been made by interested parties, to disparage him, but I have in my possession ample evidence of the falsity thereof. In consequence of the absence of certain influential friends in Washington, who would promptly correct any misapprehension regarding my brother—political or official—I have ventured to anticipate any attempt to disturb him, by thus appealing to your justice & courtesy, justified, I hope, by my duty to the absent & also by the public interest & the consideration due to a loyal citizen, a gentleman of integrity & a faithful & capable servant of the Republic. I have refrained from citing the testimony offered in the highest quarters—including that of some of your best friends, to my brother's claims, preferring to confide in this plain statement of facts, assuring you that, if deemed requisite, I can command any amount of influence—political or social, here & in Washington, to sustain my statements. With sincere apologies for this trespass upon your time & attention, & every confidence in your kindly consideration, . . ." ALS, *ibid.*

On June 2, Charles K. Tuckerman wrote to USG. "*Private and Confidential.* . . . I had the honor of sending you some months ago, two small photographs of the King and Queen of Greece, signed by their Majesties and forwarded at their request. My friend General Badeau was good enough to inform me, through my brother, that you had received the photographs and would yourself write to me on the subject. This encourages me to say a few words to you with regard to my official position here, believing that you of all men will be most interested to know that my relations with the King and Government of Greece are of the most agreeable character and are calculated to advance the interests of free institutions in this little struggling

Kingdom of Greece. I should be pleased to lay before you the peculiar and trying position which this Kingdom holds towards European Governments in General, and the three 'Protecting Powers'—England, France and Russia—in particular, but I have no right to take up your valuable time with the perusal of such a paper, especially as my despatches to the State Department contain all references of this nature necessary to be made known to our Government. But I do desire to call your attention to the fact that the King has honored me with a degree of confidence which assures me that the influence of our country is quietly and sensibly working good to Greece and moderating that selfish supremacy which, since the birth of her independence, the Powers of Western Europe have not ceased to strive to maintain in Eastern Affairs. From the day of my arrival here I have kept aloof from *party politics* in Athens, in order to exercise an independent influence for good *over the whole.* Perhaps no where in Europe is this so difficult a thing to do as in Greece and I may safely say that I am the only foreign Minister in Athens who is not more or less, directly or indirectly, mixed up with clique movements or party organizations. The jealousy of the European Powers almost necessitates this condition of affairs. As I despise *intrigue,*—which is a chronic political defect in Oriental countries,—so I rejoice in plain outspoken truth, and this has obtained for me the end I sought for,—the confidence of those with whom I come in contact. Especially is this the case in my relations with King George who now sends to confer with me in private, on matters which he never broaches to the representatives of the other Powers. My private despatches to Mr Fish will have illustrated this point. Herein lies the 'political influence' of your representative in Greece and not in noisy demonstrations or underhand party affiliations. If I am honored with your confidence, I have no fear but that with the growth of the principles which it is the Mission of the United States to disseminate in Europe, Greece will disengage herself from European entanglements, as she is now disengaged in sympathy from all nations but our own. I ask your pardon General, for having written so much of a personal nature, but I have had a purpose in doing so. I desire that *you* should know, what it would be manifestly improper for me to communicate officially to others. Yet I would not have ventured to speak of myself if I had not already assurances from you that you are not indifferent to me. My ambition is to continue to merit your esteem which I believe will stand proof against every selfish effort made to impair it. I have the honor to be General, with Mrs. Tuckermans and my regards to Mrs. Grant and yourself, . . ." LS, NHi. See Charles K. Tuckerman, *Personal Recollections of Notable People at Home and Abroad* (London, 1895), I, 136–51, II, 121–48.

To Mary E. Rawlins

Washington, D, C,
Feb.y 13th 1871,

MY DEAR MRS. RAWLINS,

Your letter enquiring if the back rent had yet ~~been~~ on your house in this city had yet been paid was received yesterday. I was about writing you that it had not and enclosing the note endorsed over to you when Mr. S.[1] come in and paid it. I enclose you a draft for the amount; Please write acknowlidging receipt. I would also like to know if your ac~~k~~count for interest, principal due, &c. on the house you live in is satisfactorily arranged.[2]

I should like very much to see you at some time the coming spring to arrange definitely for the future for the trust left in my hand. I do not fee[l] that I can continue to hold it; and am sometimes made to feel that it is not pleasant to you that I should do so. My whole desire has been to be of service to the family of Gen. Rawlins and to that end I have striven.[3]

Please answer soon.

Yours Truly
U. S. GRANT

Photocopy, USGA. On Jan. 4, 1871, Mary E. Rawlins, Danbury, Conn., wrote to USG. "I returned last evening from a visit out of town with the children, and found your very kind letter covering check for $1155 awaiting my arrival I thank you, Mr President, for your very kind thoughtfulness in remitting me this amount before Jan. 1 '71—and although I could not avail myself of it until now, still it does not lessen my gratitude and thanks for your kindness and thoughtfulness—We are getting along nicely, and the children enjoy themselves, and are happy and healthy in our new home. There is one item of business to which I will refer in a future letter. The children join me in love to Mrs. Grant, and kindest regards to yourself." ALS, USG 3. On July 10, Horace Porter, Long Branch, wrote to Governor Henry D. Cooke of D. C. "The President directs me to acknowledge the receipt of your letter of the 9th inst. enclosing check for $1.155. interest on bonds purchased from the 'Rawlins fund'" ALS, CSmH.

On Jan. 12, Porter, Washington, D. C., had written to Mary Rawlins. "The President desires me to enclose you the account for rent of house for Dec. and Jany. with a draft for $64.00 the balance. You will also find enclosed the bills which have been paid. Trusting you will find it all correct, . . ." Copy, DLC-USG, II, 1. On Nov. 27, Orville E. Babcock wrote to Mary Rawlins. "I have, in accordance with the instructions contained in your letter of the 6th. inst. paid the assessment against the house, of $34.27, and taken out a policy of insurance in the 'North British and Mercantile Insurance Co.' for $5,000.00 for one year at a premium of $20.00. The Chairman of the Bureau of Assessments gives me as his opinion that, there will be no more assessments for some time, at least. Below I give a statement of receipts and expenditures as you request. . . . Enclosed please find draft for the amount of balance of 45.69. . . . P. S. Enclosed also please find the receipt for the assessment of 34.27. The policy of insurance I have placed in our safe where it is secure." Copy, *ibid.* Notices of rent, tax, and maintenance payments dated between March, 1871 and Jan., 1872 are *ibid.* See letters to William S. Hillyer, Jan. 31, July 12, Oct. 20, 1872.

1. On Jan. 14, 1871, Babcock had written to Daniel E. Somes, Washington, D. C. "The President directs me to write that he holds D. E. Somes' note, dated Sept. 26. 1870, to Jno. E. Smith; for the Estate of Mrs Rawlings, for the sum of four hundred dollars, and that he would be pleased to have it paid at as early a date as possible." Copy, DLC-USG, II, 1. See *PUSG*, 20, 97–99.

2. On Aug. 17 or 18, 1870, USG wrote to Mary Rawlins. "I have just returned from the West. Gen. Porter has explained to me the character of the different pieces of property for sale in Danbury . . . His views correspond with yours both as to the cheapest property and that which is the most desirable . . . you may close for the $10,000 house. As soon as the deed is made to the 'Widow & heirs of John A. Rawlins' I will pay the $5,000 cash payment, and I think you can well spare $500 from accrued interest. If your Washington house is rented you can pay another $500. by Jany 1st 71. . . ." Dated Aug. 17, Carnegie Book Shop, Catalogue 261 [1962], no. 211; dated Aug. 18, Parke-Bernet Sale No. 2145, Nov. 27–28, 1962, no. 79. On Aug. 23, USG again wrote to Mary Rawlins. *ABPC* (1902), p. 599.

3. On Sept. 17, 1872, James S. Rawlins, Baltimore, wrote "*To the Editors of the Baltimore Gazette.*" "In your edition of last Friday, the 13th instant, appears an editorial headed 'A Dead Friend,' in which you refer to the President's connection with the late John A. Rawlins in a manner calculated to reflect very unjustly upon the former's friendship for the latter. As a brother of General Rawlins, I have to request that you will give a place in your paper for this note, in which I beg to assure you that nothing could be further from the true facts in the case than the statements made in the editorial referred to. The whole course of the President during the illness and since the death of my brother has been so generous, and given such earnest evidence of his great regard for General Rawlins, as to place our whole family under the deepest gratitude. The fund subscribed by the personal friends of General Rawlins was paid over to the President, and fully accounted for in every respect, and was invested for the benefit of General Rawlins' family, in the manner designated by those contributing the fund, to the perfect satisfaction of the family, who are pained more by such an article as your editorial of last Friday than the President can possibly be." *Washington Chronicle*, Sept. 24, 1872.

To Ministers and Consuls

Washington D. C. Feb. 14, 71

SIR:

This will introduce to you Gen. J. H. Wilson[1] late an officer of Engineers and Bvt. Major Gen, U. S. A., who served on my personal staff during a part of the rebellion and afterwards commanded the Cavalry Army of the West with signal distinction.

Since the War he has greatly added to his reputation as an engineer by his success in improving the navigation of the Upper Missisippi and the construction of an important line of rail-road. I take great pleasure in commending him to you and in bespeaking for him during his sojourn in your vicinity such good offices as it may be in your power to afford him.

Respectfully Yours
U. S. GRANT

U. S. MINISTERS AND CONSULS RESIDENT ABROAD.

Copy, DLC-USG, II, 1.

On Dec. 29, 1868, Bvt. Maj. Gen. James H. Wilson, Keokuk, wrote to Hiram Barney, New York City. "... I am gratified as a matter of course, at your kind remembrance of me in your conversation with Genl Grant, and also for the good opinions which you both seem to entertain for me. I saw him at Chicago and had a good deal of conversation with him, at various times. He was as good and plain, and frank, as he always was. I never saw so modest or so unselfish a man—and I am sure he will make one of the best presidents we have ever had. We had a Grand Reunion at Chicago.... I am glad Dana made a good speech at the Banquet for Evarts, and that it pleased Grant, as it ought to have done, for I want Grant to give him a good office, such as requires an honest and capable man to fill.... Whenever you speak of me to Grant Call me plain 'Wilson' or 'Harry Wilson' and then he'll know who you mean." ALS, CSmH.

On March 5 and 17, 1869, Wilson wrote to Barney. "... How do you like the President's Inaugural? I think it the most remarkable document ever issued under such circumstances. Clean, strong, manly, statemanlike and brave. If our people will only receive it and act up to it, we shall make a tremendous moral stride forward, as a people, in all that relates to public affairs. The beauty of it is, that every word of the address is Grant's—Of this I have already had the most convincing evidence...." "I have yours of the 12th and hasten to reply. I like the new Cabinet—and wouldn't change a man of it except Fish. They are all friendly enough to me so far as I know, but I take it that it is a matter of much more importance that they shall be found to be friendly only to the country's best interests. It's one of my principles that no individual is essential to our government, or deserves special consideration except in so far as he may be useful to the public—It is the race and its interests at large which should engage the attention of Statesmen and philanthropists. I accept your congratulations that Grant, Rawlins & Sherman are all my warm personal friends—for I have had abundant reason for believing that they are—but they are also the personal friends of many other persons—many more probably than either of them ever suspected heretofore. I have had no injustice done to me, or at least none that they are responsible for or can in any way repair—To the contrary I regard myself as having been more than unusually fortunate, in escaping private wrongs, & receiving reward for my *desire* to be useful. So you see, I am in a position of considerable independence—too much so at all events, to allow me to ask any favors, for myself. To be sure I am ambitious, and feel a certain amount of professional pride, but these sentiments stand to each other as mutual supports, and neither would permit me to ask for anything, except *work*. I have some apprehension that in the reoganization of the army under the 'Absorption' law, I shall be disposed of as a 'supernumerary' owing to the fact that I am on '*detached duty*,' & that would be disagreeable, as it would probably militate against my advancement when promotions should be again resumed—..." ALS, *ibid.*

On June 21, Wilson wrote to Barney. "... I am sorry that what you say of the President's unpopularity, may be true—but as Rome was not builded in a day—so the public service of a great country can't be systematised & purified in a month. If the President will throw the weight of his influence in favor of the reorganization of the civil service under some such plan as that of Mr Jenckes, he will more than regain the confidence of the public, provided the reorganization is reasonably successful. The faults of his administration so far have not been of that vital character, that they cannot be more than wiped out by such a reform as the public interests now demand & which if Grant don't make, some of his successors, will ride into fame upon.—I am glad Dana has triumphed in the matter of John Russel Young, for I believe he was entirely right—but I am sorry he is so hard upon Grant. I think he is mistaken in the means he has adopted for serving the public—Grant isn't easily driven—& yet he may be goaded into doing what he ought to do of his own freewill. But in this case, like most men, he will probably hate the person who has goaded him. . . ." ALS, *ibid.*

1. See Endorsement, [*Nov. 1870*].

To Congress

[*Feb. 15, 1871*]

If this was a bill for the repeal of the "Test Oath" required of Members of Congress, before assuming legislative duties, I would not interpose an objection. The effect of the law however is to relieve from taking a prescribe oath all those persons who it was intended to exclude from seats in Congress and to require it of all others. By this law the ~~G~~Soldier who fought and bled for his country is to swear to his loyalty before assuming legislative functions whilst the ~~sold~~General who commanded hosts for the overthrow of his Government is admitted to his seat without ~~question~~ it.—~~As well might a woman of nown virtue be required to affirm her chastity before being admitted into society whilst the known unchaste woman was admitted without a question~~.

I can not affix my name to a law which discriminates against against the upholder of his govt. I believe however that it is not wise policy to keep from office, the choise of legal voters, by an oath those who are not disqualified by the Constitution. But whilst releasing them ~~release~~ from an oath which they can not take release those too for whom the oath has no application.

ADf, Illinois State University, Normal, Ill.; DS, DNA, RG 46, Presidential Messages. On Feb. 14, 1871, Secretary of State Hamilton Fish wrote in his diary. "The Bill relieving certain persons from the necessity of taking the test oath, is before the President—the ten days within which he must sign, it, or it become a law, unless vetoed, will expire tomorrow—Prsdt read the draft of a message which he has prepared to accompany the announcement of its having become a law without his signature—he having decided not to sign, & not to veto it—the message is considered, & some alterations mainly of phraseology, suggested—" DLC-Hamilton Fish. On Feb. 15, Orville E. Babcock wrote to Fish. "The President directs me to transmit to your department S. 218 'An Act prescribing an Oath of office to be taken by persons who participated in the late rebellion, but who are not disqualified from holding office by the fourteenth amendment to the Constitution of the United States' which was received by him on February 3d 1871, and not having been returned by him to the House of Congress in which it originated within the time prescribed by the Constitution of the United States has become a law without his approval." Copy, DLC-USG, II, 1. See *SED*, 41-3-42. Debate on this bill in the House of Representatives concerned discrepancies between legislative action on loyalty oaths and provisions of the Fourteenth Amendment and also the effect of loyalty oaths on Ku Klux Klan violence. *CG*, 41–3, 864–66, 880–87.

Endorsement

Respectfully refered to the Sec. of War. Notify as supernumerary to come below those already notified.

U. S. Grant

Feb.y 17th, 71

AES, DNA, RG 94, Correspondence, USMA. Written on papers recommending John W. Drummond for an appointment to USMA, including an undated letter from Thomas Printz to USG. "my Nephew is desirous of entering west Point and I would ask you, for *my Sake*, to give him an appointment if you possibley can. I lost my right leg at the Battle of Peachorched *va* while Serving in the 20th Reg. Ind. Vols and now I am a Cripple for life and draw a pension from the government & it is my desire to See my nephew realize Some of his dreams of glory and I feel Satisfied he will be an honer to his Country, if Successful in receiving the appointment—from you." ALS, *ibid.* On Sept. 5, 1870, Walter Q. Gresham, New Albany, Ind., had written to [USG]. "I earnestly recommend Mr John W Drummond for a cadetship at West Point—Mr D attempted to enter the service in my Regt. 53 Ind. in 1862, but failed on account of his youth—He is a young man of excellent habits and fine promise—and he has the requisite qualifications, physical and mental, to enter the Academy—I hope he will succeed—" ALS, *ibid.* On June 23, 1871, Drummond, Louisville, wrote to USG. "About 6½ o'clock P M. Febry. 17th 1871 Your Excellency honored me with a private interview at the White House when I had the honor to present credentials from Govr Baker of my native State, Jno D Evans, auditor of State, Gen. N. Kimball Treasurer, Col. Jas B. Black Rep. Supreme Court, J G. Grenawault Adj. Gen., A. H. Conner chairman Rep. State Cent. Com. Capt. Silas F. Miller, Edgar Needham Esq., Gen. W. Q Gresham and others, including one from my uncle Thos Printz who lost a leg at Peach Orchard Va. which last, Your Excellency was kind enough to think 'best of all.' My object was to obtain an appointment to West Point. Your Excellency placed my name on the supernumerary list, with the assurance that my chance for the appointment was nearly, if not quite as good as if the appointment had been made. I take the liberty to recall these facts to Your Excellency because my employers make their semi-annual engagements with their employees 1st July and 1st January and as I shall not like to give up a good place on an uncertainty, would ask you to honor me with information regarding the appointment as soon as Your Excellency finds it convenient. It is possible that my employers would release me at any time for Such honors, but it is best to know at the proper time. If it is not within your power to gratify my ambition this year. *may I hope* that you will place my name on the Supernumerary list, 1st 2nd or 3rd for next year? Dear President I have made *truth* my foundation for an illustrious life and can promise Your Excellency faithful and attentive service as a Cadet. I trust your well-known kindness will not fail to appreciate my anxie~~c~~ty to fit myself for the Service of my Country. . . . Communications may be directed Care Capt Silas F. Miller Louisville" ALS, *ibid.*

On Aug. 4, John M. Harlan, Louisville, wrote to USG. "Mr. John W. Drummond of this city, the bearer hereof, desires an appointment to West Point Academy. His name he informs me was upon the supernumerary list of last year, but was not reached. He now desires to be placed on the list for 1872. Mr Drummond comes to me recommended by gentlemen of the highest standing in this community, who are your personal and political friends. Mr D. is a young gentleman of excellent moral character, and I doubt not his appointment to the Academy would meet the approval of the friends of the Administration, and ultimately redound to the interests of the Country. If consistent with your official duty, I *will be glad* to have the name of Mr Drummond placed on the list for 1872." ALS, *ibid.* On Aug. 16, USG endorsed this letter. "This nomination may be made on the supernumerary list next below those already appointed." AES, *ibid.* Drummond did not attend USMA.

On June 16, 1874, Drummond wrote to Secretary of State Hamilton Fish. "Is there a consulate vacant in Italy, France, Prussia, Scicily, or Austria that may be obtained through proper procedure by a person twenty four years of age and qualified?" ALS, *ibid.*, RG 59, Letters of Application and Recommendation.

To William W. Belknap

[Feb. 19. 71]

Indications of a riot in Little Rock Ark. existing ~~the Sec of War~~ [you] may telegraph to the Commanding officer there to keep his troops in hand to suppress and quiet the factions should a disturbance take place The merits of the quarrel between the Govr[1] and the Lt. Govr[2] who claims to be the Executive of the state, Articles of impeachment having been prefered against the Govr, is not well enough understood to justify deciding which of these functionaries should be respected in asking the aid of the Govt.

The troops will not be used to aid either faction but to ~~suppress riot~~ ~~and~~ ~~bloodshed~~ ~~and~~ to preserve order.

[U. S. G.]

[SECTY OF WAR.]

AN (bracketed material not in USG's hand), IC; copy, DLC-USG. On Feb. 19, 1871, Horace Porter, "By order of the President," wrote to Secretary of War William W. Belknap conveying USG's note as if composed by Porter. ALS, DNA, RG 94, Letters Received, 626 1871. On the same day, Belknap wrote to AG Edward D. Townsend. "I found enclosed note at my house, on returning from church. Please telegraph the necessary order and also send the enclosure to Genl. Sherman . . . The telegram had better be full enough to embody the substance of the entire order of the President" ALS, *ibid.* On Feb. 21, Lt. Col. Daniel Huston, Little Rock, telegraphed to Townsend. "Your telegram of the nineteenth (19th) inst just rec'd, I assumed Command of this post yesterday, I have seen no indication of a riot being imminent however should there be one, will act as ordered with the very small number of troops available here," Telegram received, *ibid.*

1. See telegram to Powell Clayton, March 13, 1871.

2. On March 15, 1867, Albert W. Bishop, Ark. AG, *et al.*, Washington, D. C., had written to President Andrew Johnson. "We have the honor respectfully to request the nomination of Hon James M. Johnson late col, First Arkansas Infantry Vols, for the brevet of Brigadier General. Col Johnson served with distinction during the late rebellion and we believe it to be eminently proper that the brevet asked for should be conferred upon him." DS (4 signatures), DNA, RG 94, ACP, J49 CB 1867. On March 27 and April 5, USG endorsed this letter. "Not approved" "Upon reconsideration of this case the recommendations for brevet promotion of Col. Johnson are approved" ES, *ibid.* Born in 1832 in Warren County, Tenn., James M. Johnson attended St. Louis Medical College and practiced medicine. Elected from Ark. to the U.S. House of Representatives (1864), he was not seated. As lt. governor of Ark. (1868–71), he organized a Liberal Republican party in opposition to Governor Powell Clayton. For recommendations for Johnson as minister to Hawaii, see *PUSG*, 20, 83–84.

To Hannibal Hamlin

Washington D. C. Feb.y 21st *18*71.

DEAR SIR:

I have the pleasure to acknowledge the receipt of your note, of yesterdays date, and to comply with your request.

Very Truly yours,
U. S. GRANT

HON. H. HAMLIN U. S. S.

ALS, Broadcast Music, Inc., New York, N. Y. Hannibal Hamlin, born in 1809 at Paris Hill, Maine, served as Democratic U.S. representative (1843–47) and U.S. senator (1848–57). As a Republican, he served briefly as governor (1857), reentered the senate (1857–61), and was U.S. vice-president (1861–65). In 1869, he entered the senate for the third time. See Charles E. Hamlin, *The Life and Times of Hannibal Hamlin* (Cambridge, Mass., 1899), pp. 519–34; H. Draper Hunt, *Hannibal Hamlin of Maine: Lincoln's First Vice-President* (Syracuse, 1969), pp. 208–9, 215.

Hamlin had introduced and strongly advocated a bill eventually passed as an "*Act to provide a Government for the District of Columbia.*" Signed by USG on Feb. 21, 1871, this legislation authorized the president to nominate a governor, a secretary, and eleven councilmen representing districts within D. C. An elected house of delegates consisting of twenty-two members completed the bicameral legislative assembly of D. C., whose acts remained "subject to repeal or modification by the Congress of the United States." The act also created a presidentially nominated board of health and board of public works with particular membership requirements. See *CG*, 41–2, 1555, 3912–14, 41–3, 639–47, 685–88, 1264–65, 1363–65, 1562; *U.S. Statutes at Large*, XVI, 419–29; Alan Lessoff, *The Nation and Its City: Politics, "Corruption," and Progress in Washington, D. C., 1861–1902* (Baltimore, 1994), pp. 44–57.

On Feb. 18, 1871, Alexander R. Shepherd, Washington, D. C., wrote to Henry D. Cooke. "I have just understood that the President is embarrassed as to the appointment of Governor under the new bill. will you do me the favor to say to Genl Grant that if his choice is between Mr Emery & myself I shall withdraw in favor of Mr E. recognizing his magnanimity in supporting the bill which has virtually legislated him out of office" ALS, DNA, RG 59, Letters of Application and Recommendation. On Feb. 23, a correspondent reported: "Quite a spirited fight is being made here now for the appointment as Governor of the Territory of the District of Columbia. Hon. M. G. Emery, Mayor; Hon. Sayles J. Bowen, ex-Mayor; A. J. Magruder, Collector of the port of Georgetown, D. C., and A. R. Shepherd, appear to be the most prominent candidates at present. A delegation of the City Councils and others held an interview with the President to-day and urged the claims of Mr. Bowen for the position." *Philadelphia Public Ledger*, Feb. 24, 1871. On Feb. 24, E. Peck, Georgetown, D. C., wrote to USG. "Feeling much solicitude about the appointment of a Governor for the District of Columbia under the new law, and having moreover a desire that your interests shall be advanced by the selection of a proper as well as popular person for that important and untried office. Having heard very many favorable opinions in favor of Mr Alexander H Shepherd, an old citizen of Washington, as being probably the most suitable and acceptable person that could receive that appointment I take the liberty of suggesting his appointment—Mr Shepherd is a stranger to me, and I only present his name, because I think, it will be satisfactory to the largest number of the citizens. If it were not that I am so much of an invalid, I should have called in person to urge this appointment—I trust you will pardon this intrusion upon your attention" ALS, Columbia Historical Society, Washington, D. C. See *PUSG*, 20, 51.

On Feb. 27, Speaker of the House James G. Blaine wrote to USG. "I hear the name of Col Jno. W. Forney mentioned for the Governorship of the District—I think no name would be so acceptable to the people & none so valuable in a public & party point of view—I had hoped to be able to see you personally on a matter in which I feel so much interest—" ALS, OFH. See letter to John W. Forney, March 22, 1871.

On Feb. 26, Secretary of State Hamilton Fish had written in his diary. "Sunday Evenig—President calls at my House, accompanied by Mr Drexel—taking me aside he says that Genl Dent called this afternoon—to say that if Henry D Cooke were nominated as Governor of the Territory of Columbia he will accept & give up his intended visit to Europe in the Spring—He requests me to nominate him to morrow—(A good escape from a number of embarasments & some perils!)" DLC-Hamilton Fish. On Feb. 27, Monday, USG nominated Cooke as governor, D. C. On the same day, "About 1 o'clock the committee appointed at the Republican meeting held at Union League Hall on Friday evening last, called at the White House and were soon after admitted to the President's room. . . . Mr. A. K. Browne, as chairman of the committee, informed the President that they were a committee appointed at a Republican mass meeting to request the President to withhold the nomination for Governor and Councilmen until after a convention which had been called could express the preferences of the party. . . . The President replied that the nomination for Governor had already been made that morning. This announcement seemed to surprise the committee, and one of them inquired who had been nominated. The President answered that he had selected a gentleman who would be acceptable to all. . . . A short time afterward several members of Congress called to see the President, and having been admitted, they urged the President to appoint Colonel John W. Forney as Governor of the District. The President informed them also that the nomination had been made, and added that he had supposed that Colonel Forney would not accept the nomination if it had been tendered to him. . . . Mr. W. S. Huntington yesterday telegraphed to Mr. Cooke, who is in Philadelphia, informing him of his nomination to the Governorship of the District, and inquiring what he should say to those who asked if he would accept the nomination. Mr. Cooke replied that he could only say now what he had said to the President on Saturday, that he could not accept the appointment if offered to him, as it would place him in an unpleasant position with a large number of friends. . . ." *Washington Chronicle*, Feb. 28, 1871. On March 2, USG conferred with Cooke about appointments. *Philadelphia Public Ledger*, March 3, 1871. See letter to Henry D. Cooke, Sept. 12, 1873.

On Feb. 23, 1871, Amasa Copp, Washington, D. C., had written to USG. "I earnestly solicit the appointment of my son Henry N. Copp to be Secretary for this District under the new Government. Henry is a graduate of Union College New York, has an unblemished moral character and is competant to perform all the duties of the office. He served in the Union Army in the late war and since its close has been engaged as an educator in this city. I think he is well and favorably known here. I ask this appointment for Henry because he is my only dependence since the death of my other son Ensign Charles A Copp on the Oneida" ALS, DNA, RG 59, Letters of Application and Recommendation.

On March 2, Orville E. Babcock wrote to Fish. "The President directs me to say that he has nominated N. P. Chipman as Secretary of the District of Columbia. The nomination was prepared at this Office as the President desired it to go to the Senate to day." Copy, DLC-USG, II, 1. On April 17, a correspondent reported: "The General Republican Committee of the District of Columbia waited upon the President to-day and presented the resolutions adopted by the Republican Convention, in favor of the appointment of Fred. Douglass as Secretary of the new Government, if a vacancy occurs by the election of General Chipman as a Delegate to Congress." *Indianapolis Journal*, April 18, 1871. On May 17, USG nominated Edwin L. Stanton as secretary, D. C., after Norton P. Chipman resigned to become U.S. delegate from D. C. See letter to Edwin L. Stanton, Sept. 22, 1873.

On April 19, 1871, Horace Porter had written to Secretary of the Navy George M. Robeson. "The President will be pleased to have you grant leave of absence to-morrow, to attend the election, to all employees of your department, who have registered." LS, DNA, RG 45, Letters Received from the President. On the same day, Porter drafted a similar letter for "All Cabinet except P. M. G. & Sec'y: of State." Copy, DLC-USG, II, 1. On April 20, voters elected a congressional delegate and the house of delegates. On May 24, "the members of the House of Delegates, by previous arrangement, met at the executive office, corner of 17th street and Pennsylvania avenue, and from thence went to the White House, preceded by Governor Cooke and Mr. Hulse, Speaker of the House, to pay their respects to the President. . . ." *Washington Evening Star*, May 24, 1871.

On Feb. 22, John Bell Adams *et al.*, Washington, D. C., had petitioned USG. "We the undersigned imposing confidence in the ability and integrity of Dr A. T. Augusta, a resident and property holder in the city of Washington District of Columbia; he having served four years as Surgeon of U. S. Volunteers during the late rebellion, and who was the only colored man that held such a position; and was breveted Lieut. Colonel for distinguished services during that period, do most respectfully request, that your Excellency would appoint him one of the Councillors created by the law, to form a territorial government for the District of Columbia." DS (14 signatures), DNA, RG 59, Letters of Application and Recommendation.

On March 3, U.S. Senator George H. Williams of Ore. wrote to USG. "It would afford me pleasure to have George T Bassett nominated for one of the members of the Council for the District of Columbia" ALS, *ibid.*

On March 11, U.S. Representative Luke P. Poland of Vt. wrote to USG. "I desire to recommend to your consideration for appointment as a member of the Council of the new goverment of the District of Columbia, Mr. Henry A. Jones. From my knowledge of him. I believe him every way well qualified for the position, and his previous service for the Country. both military and civil entitle him to consideration.—I know that his appointment is earnestly desired by many prominent Republicans of the District. and I think would give general satisfaction—" ALS, *ibid.* U.S. Representative John A. Peters of Maine and Blaine favorably endorsed this letter. ES, *ibid.*

On April 13, USG nominated Daniel L. Eaton, John A. Gray, A. K. Browne, George F. Gulick, and Samuel Cross, for one year terms; Frederick Douglass, Adolphus Hall, Charles F. Peck, Nehemiah H. Miller, William Stickney, and Daniel Smith, for two year terms, D. C. council. For biographical information, see *Evening Star*, April 13, 1871. On April 15, USG withdrew Miller's nomination "at his own request." DS, DNA, RG 46, Nominations.

On June 6, Frederick Douglass, Washington, D. C., wrote to USG. "I have the honor to resign my seat as the member for the first District, in the Legislative Council of the District of Columbia. I beg also to request that my resignation shall be allowed to take effect ten days after the date of this Communication." ALS, *ibid.*, RG 59, Letters of Resignation and Declination. On June 28, Porter wrote to Fish. "The President directs me to say that he will be pleased to have you make out the appointment of Lewis H. Douglass to be a member of the Council of the District of Columbia, vice Fredk. Douglass resigned." Copy, DLC-USG, II, 1. Lewis H. Douglass was Frederick Douglass's son. On Dec. 14, USG received a petition signed by 213 members of the Republican Club of the first legislative district of D. C. asking him "to recall the nomination of Lewis H. Douglass as a member of the Council of the Legislative Assembly. The petitioners allege that Douglass endeavored to split the republican party in the first district at the late election, and that he is not the choice of the republicans of the district." *Evening Star*, Dec. 14, 1871. See *Life and Times of Frederick Douglass: Written By Himself* (1892; reprinted, New York, 1962), p. 412.

On March 30, 1872, John W. Le Barnes, chairman, Republican General Committee, D. C., wrote to USG. "I desire on behalf of the Republican Party of the District of Columbia to express to you the feeling and sentiment of the Republicans of this District in respect to the nominations soon to be made to fill vacancies in the District Legislative Council. It is a matter of universal comment and criticism that the Council, if appointed exclusively upon the recommendation of the Govenor and other executive officers of the District, cannot and do not represent the people, but only the Official influences which obtain or consent to their appointment. This is one of the chief evils which is felt to exist under the new form of Government adopted for this District.... I also desire respectfully to state to you that the present construction of the Board of Public Works is felt among all classes and parties to be inimical to the public wish and to the general interests of the District.... I beg leave to say to you, that it is my information and conviction derived from intimate acquaintance with the feelings, fears, and wishes of the Republicans of the District, both property-holders and laboring men, that at least three of the present members of the Board ought to be replaced by others by whom the people would be better represented and ~~in regard~~ to whosem ~~official~~ ~~policy~~ the people generally would be more readily satisfied to have their local interests entrusted. If one of these changes should be the detail of an Engineer officer of the Army, without regard to political character, only that he be a competent and faithful officer and a man of irreproachable integrity, I am satisfied that such course would meet with the unqualified approbation of our whole people. As to the other two I beg leave respectfully to suggest that the appointment of two pronounced Republicans, of integrity and firmness, who represent the principles and masses of the party, (one of whom might well be a colored man,) and who are not committed to the policy which now prevails, and who reside in the city proper, would be satisfactory to the Republicans of the District and to the whole people." ALS, DNA, RG 59, Letters of Application and Recommendation. On the same day, Nehemiah G. Ordway, sergeant at arms, U.S. House of Representatives, wrote to USG. "I own property and reside in the Council District now represented by George F. Gulick, whose term of office expires within a short time. The officers of the Republican club in this District have, with great unanimity, recommended, Edward S. Atkinson,—a highly respectable colored man, and a Christain Gentleman, to be appointed in that District. I cordially concur in the recommendation of Mr. Atkinson, and can say that I know of no man in the District, white or colored, in whom all classes of citizens have more confidence than in Mr. Atkinson. I can vouch for his ability and integrity to the fullest extent. I believe this is the first time that I have ever asked or sought an appointment of you as a personal matter, but living as I do in the District referred to, I have decided to recommend Mr. Atkinson for a member of the Council from that District." ALS, *ibid.* A related petition is *ibid.* On April 15, Porter wrote to Fish. "The President directs me to say that, Gov: Cooke recommends the re-appointment of councilmen John A Gray, Danl Eaton, A. K. Brown, Geo. F. Gulick and Saml Cross; and the appointment of Joshua Riley vice Chas Peck, resigned. These he approves and requests that you have the nominations prepared." Copy, DLC-USG, II, 1.

On March 23, Charles L. Hulse *et al.*, Washington, D. C., had petitioned USG. "The undersigned citizens of the District of Columbia being well satisfied of the Wisdom of your selection of the Hon John A Gray as a member of the council of the

District of Columbia, do most earnestly request his re-appointment to the position he has filled with so much satisfaction to his constituency and honor to himself." DS (29 signatures), DNA, RG 59, Letters of Application and Recommendation. On July 5, Gray, Washington, D. C., wrote to USG. "I have been recently appointed (by the Secretary of the Interior) *Trustee* for the colered Schools of the District of Columbia, and have been led to suppose that the acceptance of that position was incompatible with the office I now hold as Councilman of the 5th Council District; in the Legislature Assemble of the District of Columbia and labouring under that misapprehension I tendered my Resignation, which I now ask that it *be not Accepted.* After consulting legal advice—I am creditable informed that the holding of one position do not in the least effect or prohibit me from accepting the other I therefore desire to withdraw my Resignation" LS, *ibid.*, Letters of Resignation and Declination. On July 1, Cooke, Philadelphia, had written to USG. "I respectfully recommend that you appoint Mr J. W. Brooks a member of the Council, of the Legislative Assembly, *vice*, John A. Gray. resigned. Mr Gray's resignation was tende[red] in order that he might accept to position of School Trustee, for which he was named by the Secretary of the Interior; and I respectfully suggest the importance of having Mr Gray's place filled by an intelligent colered man. Mr Brooks, will, I am sure, give general satisfaction. For various reasons, it is important that the vacancy be filled at once—" ALS, *ibid.*, Letters of Application and Recommendation. On July 2, USG endorsed this letter. "Please send apt. for my signature to-day." AES, *ibid.* On Nov. 6, John H. Brooks, chairman, Republican General Committee, Washington, D. C., wrote to USG. "I have the honor to tender the sincere Congratulations of this Committee and the Colored Voters of Maryland among whom (since our local election) we have been working. If we have not succeeded in carrying the state for Grant & Wilson we have made an excellent Fight and greatly reduced their majority" ALS, USG 3. On Dec. 3, USG nominated Brooks to the D. C. council.

On March 12, 1873, Levi P. Luckey wrote to Fish. "The President directs me to say that Governor Cooke has submitted the names of the following gentlemen to be Members of the Council of the Legislative Assembly of the District of Columbia: S. M. Golden, J. W. Baker, Adolphus Hall, Joshua Riley, J. W. Thompson, Wm Stickney and Daniel Smith, and ask if you have any objection to the submission of their names to the Senate." Copy, DLC-USG, II, 2. On Dec. 7, 1870, USG had nominated Stephen M. Golden as a member of the levy court, D. C.

On March 2, 1871, USG had nominated John M. Langston, Nathan S. Lincoln, Tullio S. Verdi, Henry A. Willard, and John Marbury, Jr., to the D. C. Board of Health. On March 22, USG nominated Christopher C. Cox in place of Lincoln. See letter to John M. Langston, Dec. 15, 1870; Langston, *From the Virginia Plantation to the National Capitol* (1894; reprinted, New York, 1968), pp. 318–34.

On April 6, 1869, Cox, Washington, D. C., had written to USG. "Cognizant of the extraordinary pressure to which you are subjected by applicants for position I desire to releive you of all furthur embarrassment in regard to my own—and, therefore, respectfully tender my resignation, as COMMISSIONER OF PENSIONS, to take effect from 1st proxo." LS, DNA, RG 48, Appointment Div., Letters Received. About the same date, Cox wrote to USG. "Having found you too much occupied, yesterday, to obtain an interview, I take this occasion to call your attention to my application for Foreign Appointment. Without desiring to dictate the period of your decision (which I would not for a moment presume to do), you will, I am sure, pardon me for suggesting that the earliest conveniet indication of your purpose will, in view of the unsettled state of my plans, be most acceptable. As I informed you—one object in seeking to go abroad is to complete certain unfinished Literary labors; and especially a '*Philosophical History of the Times*.'..." ALS, *ibid.*, RG 59, Letters of Application and Recommendation. On April 12, Governor Oden Bowie of Md. wrote to USG. "Learning that on his retiring from the Pension Office the friends of Lt Governor Cox of Md. will present his name for a foreign mission I gladly add my request to theirs. I served in the Senate of Md when Gov Cox was its presiding officer as Lt Governor, and had the honor also of being the Democratic Candidate against him when he was elected. I therefore know Gov Cox well, and I am sure his polite address and other qualifications would make his appointment an eminently fit and proper one." ALS, *ibid.* Related papers are *ibid.* On May 24, U.S. Representative John A. Bingham of Ohio wrote to USG. "I beg leave to ask your attention to the fact that the representative men of the United States in the profession of Medicine and Surgery have recommended Dr. C. C. Cox, to be Superintendent of the Government Insane Asylum in the District of Columbia. I do not hesitate to say that I have not seen so imposing and commanding a recommendation for any man for Official position in America. Permit me to add further that I knew Doctor Cox in the darkest hours of our struggle with rebellion—that he had the confidence of *Mr Lincoln* and is entitled to your confidence and to the confidence of the great people who have saved the Republic and carried you into the Presidency I would esteem his appointment as a personal favor to myself, and am sure it would reflect credit upon your administration, and give the best satisfaction to the people." ALS, *ibid.*, RG 48, Appointment Div., Letters Received. On Aug. 31, 1871, USG wrote to U.S. ministers and consuls. "I take pleasure in introducing to you Hon. C. C. Cox, of Washington, D. C. who is about to visit Europe. Mr Cox stands deservedly high at home as a gentleman of literary and scientific merit and I bespeak for him the good offices of all U. S. officials residing abroad." Copy, DLC-USG, II, 1. On Feb. 10 and July 4, 1873, Cox wrote to USG. "Should either the Indian or Pension Bureau be vacant I desire to be considered as a candidate for either position. If appointed it will be my earnest endeavor to do justice to the claims of the office, & reflect credit upon yr administration. The injurious effect upon my health, due to the exposure & irregularities of a rapidly increasing practice, prompts me to seek the position at yr hands. Congratulating you upon the remarkable success of your wise & judicious administration, & the almost unanimous endorsement it has received from the people,..." ALS, DNA, RG 48, Appointment Div., Letters Received. "I have the honor herewith to tender my resignation as Honorary Commissioner to the Universal Exposition, at Vienna, Austria, Upon accepting the appointment it was my intention to visit Europe, and, while contributing my best efforts in furtherance of the special object of the mission, to institute such investigations as might be possible, into the most approved sanitary systems of the old World: Although anticipated in this latter object by another member of the Board, now abroad, (who had secured a commission from the Governor of this District) my purpose to avail myself of the proferred honor remained unchanged, until the appearance of cholera in the Western Cities, and its possible extension to the capitol of the nation, induced me to hesitate, and finally to submit this declination, Deeming it, therefore, a serious duty, in view of the possible advent of the epidemic, to remain at my post in Washington, and in accordance with the judgement and advice of intelligent friends, I feel compelled reluctantly to surrender the trust with which you have honored me,..." LS, *ibid.*, RG 59, Letters of Resignation and Declination.

In an undated letter, U.S. Senator Matthew H. Carpenter of Wis. wrote to USG. "I Respectfully solicit the appointment of Dr Thomas S. Mercer, as one of *the Board of Public Works* under the Territorial Government of Washington Dr Mercer is a gentleman of high character, of perfect integrity and fine abilities. I should be delighted with his appointment" ALS, *ibid.*, RG 48, Appointment Div., Letters Received. On Jan. 28, 1871, Samuel Miller, U.S. Supreme Court, wrote to USG recommending Thomas S. Mercer. ALS, *ibid.* On the same day, David Davis and Noah H. Swayne, U.S. Supreme Court, favorably endorsed Mercer. AES, *ibid.*

On [*Feb. 18*], A. H. Kinney wrote to USG. "I have the honor to apply for an appointment as one of the Board of Public Works, under the recent act of Congress, providing for a form of government for the District of Columbia. I entered the 7th Regiment of Connecticut Volunteers as a private soldier in August 1861, at the age of seventeen, and served until August 1865, when I was discharged, as a Lieutenant. I was appointed to a clerkship in the Treasury Department at the close of the War, and am still employed in that Department. As an earnest Republican I have taken an active part in behalf of the party in the city of Washington, from the date of my appointment. I refer you to the testimonials of prominent men, some of whom are known to you" ALS, OFH. U.S. Senator William A. Buckingham and U.S. Representatives Henry H. Starkweather, Julius L. Strong, and Stephen W. Kellogg of Conn., and nine others, favorably endorsed Kinney. AES, *ibid.* On Feb. 23, E. W. Whitaker, Washington, D. C., wrote to USG. "I desire to especially commend to your favorable consideration the application of Mr. A. H. Kinney of this City for the appointment to the Board of Public Works. Mr. Kinney served his country gallantly in a Conn. regiment during the late war and has since resided in this City taking an active part in politics, always true as steel to republican principles. In Mr. K. you will find a faithful, fearless worker, an honest and energetic official. I trust you will examine his papers." ALS, *ibid.*

On March 8, 1869, Charles H. Cragin, Georgetown, D. C., had written to USG. "the undersigned respectfully recommends ~~J~~Col. James A. Magruder, for reappointment as Collector of Customs for the District of Columbia. Col. Magruder served with credit as an officer in the late War: has been ever a true and patriotic citizen, and, it is understood, has administered the affairs of the office to the entire satisfaction of the Government and persons having business with the Custom House. The Republicans of this Town all earnestly desire the Col.s reappointment, and will be much gratified at the same, as he eminently deserves it." ALS, DNA, RG 56, Collector of Customs Applications. On March 9, James A. Magruder, Georgetown, wrote to USG. "My Commission as Collector of Customs for this district expired on the 16th of January last. The late President nominated for the place John D. McGill, the Senate has not confirmed Said McGill, consequently I am discharging the duties of the office. I respectfully ask to be reappointed Collector of Customs for this district, and beg to refer you to the accompanying papers." ALS, *ibid.* On the same day, Cooke wrote to USG. "I take pleasure in commending Col J. A. Magruder's application for reappointment, as collector of Customs at the Port of Georgetown, to your favorable consideraton.—Col. Magruder served with credit during the war against rebellion, and has since discharged the duties of the office named, with marked ability—He is a most worthy citizen, an excellent business man, and a gentleman of undoubted integrity." ALS, *ibid.* A related paper is *ibid.* On April 6, USG nominated Magruder as collector of customs, Georgetown. On March 2, 1871, USG nominated Magruder, Shepherd, Samuel P. Brown, and Alfred B. Mullett as members, D. C. Board of Public Works.

On Oct. 14 and 18, 1872, Mullett, Washington, D. C., wrote to USG. "I hereby tender my resignation as Member of the Board of Public Works of the District of

Columbia, to take effect from and after this date: And in so doing I desire to thank you most earnestly for the honor conferred upon me by the appointment, and for the uniform kindness and consideration that I have received at your hands. It is but justice to my Colleagues to assure you that my resignation is prompted by no other motive than the inability to find the time necessary for the performance of my duties, without neglecting those of the Office of Supervising Architect, and to say that my relations with them have been of the most agreeable nature, that I have unshaken confidence in their integrity and ability, and that no difference of opinion exists between us, as far as I am aware, and I can but deeply regret that other and more pressing duties compel me to sever the very pleasant official relations heretofore existing between us." "I most earnestly recommend the appointment of Adolph Cluss Esq. to fill the vacancy on the Board of Public Works, caused by my resignation He is a competent architect and engineer and an earnest and sincere republican, and in my opinion a gentleman of the very highest integrity. I know of no person in the District of Columbia whose appointment would in my opinion give more general satisfaction or who is more competent. Mr. Cluss' appointment would, I think, be highly appreciated by the german republicans of this city." LS, *ibid.*, RG 48, Appointment Div., Letters Received. For Mullett, see letter to Ministers and Consuls, May 20, 1875.

On Oct. 17, 1872, Chipman had written to USG. "Learning that Mr Mullett contemplates resigning from the Board of Public Works I beg to suggest as his successor Adolph Cluss Esq of this city. Mr Cluss is an accomplished architect & Engineer: is a man of large acquaintance with the wants of our people and would I believe reflect credit upon the Executive in his appointment." ALS, DNA, RG 48, Appointment Div., Letters Received. On Oct. 18, Shepherd and Magruder wrote to USG. "The undersigned Members of the Board of Public works in view of the resignation of A. B. Mullett Esq from said Board respectfully recommend as his successor. Adolf Cluss for many year's an Archict & Engineer resident in our Midst and thoroughly qualified to perform the duties of the office We further believe that his appointment would give general satisfaction ~~th~~to the people of this District" LS (misdated 1873), *ibid.* On the same day, USG endorsed this letter. "Approved." AES, *ibid.* On Dec. 5, USG nominated Adolph Cluss to the D. C. Board of Public Works.

Proclamation

To all to whom these presents shall come, Greeting:

Know ye, That reposing special trust and confidence in the integrity, prudence and ability, of Hamilton Fish, Secretary of State of the United States, I have invested him with full and all manner of power and authority, for and in the name of the United States, to meet and confer with any person or persons duly authorized on the part of Her Britannic Majesty's Government, and with him or them to agree, treat, consult and negotiate, of and concerning the citizenship of citizens of the United States, who have emigrated or who may emigrate from the United States of America, to the British dominions, and of British subjects who have emigrated or may emigrate from the British dominions to the United States of America, and to conclude and sign a Convention supplemental to the Convention on that subject, signed at London on the 13th day of May, 1870.

In witness whereof, I have caused the seal of the United States to be hereunto affixed.

Given under my hand at the city of Washington, the 22d day of February, in the year of our Lord one thousand eight hundred and seventy one, and of the Independence of the United States of America the ninety-fifth.

U. S. GRANT

DS, DLC-Hamilton Fish. On Feb. 23, 1871, Secretary of State Hamilton Fish recorded in his diary that he and Edward Thornton, British minister, had signed "the supplementary Treaty to the Naturalization Convention with Great Britain." *Ibid.* On March 22, the Senate ratified this treaty. See *PUSG*, 20, 152–53.

Order

February 23d 1871

It having been shown to my satisfaction that the parties named in the foregoing list are adult members of the Pottowatomie tribe of Indians, and pursuant to the provisions of the Treaty concluded November 15th 1861 with said Indians, and also to the provisions of the supplemental treaty with said Indians, concluded March 29th 1866, have appeared before the District Court of the United States for the District of Kansas and have each taken the oath of allegiance provided by law for the naturalization of aliens, and have also made the proof to the satisfaction of said Court, that they are sufficiently intelligent and prudent to control their own affairs and interests; and that they have each adopted the habits of civilized life and have been able to support themselves and families for at least five years and the said persons having applied to me to cause the lands allotted to and held by them under the provisions of the treaty between the United States and the Pottowatomie Indians concluded on the 15th day of November 1861 to be conveyed to them by patent in fee simple with the power of alienation and also cause to be paid to each of them their proportion of the cash value of the credits of the tribe, principal and interest now held in trust by the United States and also their proportion of the proceeds of the sales of lands under the provisions of said treaty. Now, therefore, I. Ulysses S. Grant, President of the United States being satisfied that each of the parties named in said list are sufficiently prudent to control their own affairs and interests; do order and direct that the Secretary of the Interior cause the lands to be patented, and the payment of the proportionate share of each of said parties to the trust and land fund to be made to them in accordance with their request.

U. S. Grant

Copy, DNA, RG 130, Orders and Proclamations. On Feb. 18, 1871, Secretary of the Interior Columbus Delano wrote to USG. "I have the honor to transmit herewith, ~~five~~Six lists of Pottawatomie Indians who, under the treaties of November 15. 1861, March 29. 1866, and February 27. 1867, have become citizens of the United States, and are entitled to patents for the land allotted to them and the payment of their share of moneys to the credit of the tribe. From an examination of the papers submitted with the reports of the Commissioner of Indian Affairs, dated the 28th Oct. last, and the 17th inst., it appears that the claimants have complied with the conditions of the treaties; and I, therefore, respectfully recommend that you sign the order appended to each list, for carrying into effect the treaty stipulations." LS, OFH. On Feb. 23, USG signed additional documents authorizing Delano to make land patent transfers to Potawatomis. Copies, DNA, RG 130, Orders and Proclamations. For the consequences of issuing land patents to Potawatomis, see *HED*, 42-2-1, part 5, p. 912.

On March 10, USG ordered a similar land allotment for the Kickapoos. Copy, DNA, RG 130, Orders and Proclamations. See *HED*, 42-2-1, part 5, 420–21, 896–99; A. M. Gibson, *The Kickapoos: Lords of the Middle Border* (Norman, 1963), pp. 124–40.

To Hamilton Fish

Washington D. C. Feb.y 25 1871

HON. H. FISH,
SEC. OF STATE;
DEAR SIR:

Senator Pratt and Gen. Dunn[1] have just called and request the apt. of David M. Dunn, of Ia. as Consul in place of Scammon[2] resigned. I have no objection to the apt. but favorable action can not be taken in the case of the other Dunn,[3] from the same state.

Respectfully &c
U. S. GRANT

ALS, DNA, RG 59, Letters of Application and Recommendation. On Feb. 25, 1871, U.S. Senators Oliver P. Morton and Daniel D. Pratt of Ind. wrote to Secretary of State Hamilton Fish. "We recommend Col David M Dunn of Logansport Indiana as a proper person to receive the appointment of Consul at Prince Edward Island, and earnestly recommend his appointment," LS, *ibid.* As lt. col., 29th Ind., David M. Dunn fought at Stone's River and Chickamauga. On March 9, USG nominated Dunn as consul, Prince Edward Island, in place of Eliakim P. Scammon.

1. William M. Dunn, born in 1814 in Indiana Territory, graduated from Indiana University (1832) and taught at Hanover College before practicing law. Active in Ind. Whig and Republican politics, he was U.S. representative (1859–63) and then entered the U.S. Army as maj. and judge advocate. His son, William M. Dunn, Jr., served on USG's staff. See *PUSG*, 9, 576; *ibid.*, 13, 358; *ibid.*, 16, 499–500.

2. Scammon, USMA 1837, dismissed from the U.S. Army for drunkenness and disobeying orders (1856), returned as col., 23rd Ohio, and was promoted to brig. gen. (1862). On April 9, 1866, President Andrew Johnson nominated Scammon as consul, Prince Edward Island. On Feb. 5, 1869, Scammon, Charlottetown, Prince Edward Island, wrote to USG. "I trust it may not be amiss to congratulate you on your elevation to the high position of President of the United States. I am very sure that you will give me credit for sincerity in this expression, as, apart from the kindness I have already received at your hands, and other considerations purely personal, I am confident that all my acquaintances will give me credit for some degree of conservatism—And this, it has seemed to me, was the question really at issue in our country. I fear that what I intended as a respectful felicitation may seem like only an awkward prelude to a request—and not to tire you with words, I venture to ask your favorable consideration of an application which I presume will be made by some persons who are favorably disposed in my regard. In the event of a vacancy I have asked my friends to Solicit for me the Consulship at Montreal or in the same event, that of St John N. B. In these cases I have no disposition to solicit another man's place; but if, as I have thought possible, either the first or second of these places should be vacant, I would, respectfully solicit your favor. I had, the misfortune, some six weeks since, to fall upon the ice and break a leg, which, without increasing my claims to favor, makes one the more

solicitous to obtain it. Begging you to pardon me if I am indiscreet or presuming in preparing this letter, which I propose to send through my friends in the States," ALS, DNA, RG 59, Letters of Application and Recommendation. In an undated letter, Scammon's daughter Margaret S. Lockwood, Brooklyn, wrote to Secretary of the Interior Jacob D. Cox requesting help for her father. ALS, *ibid.* Cox endorsed this letter. "Respectfully referred to the Sec. of State—A letter from Gen. Scammon to the Prest has been already placed in the Presidents hands." AES, *ibid.* On March 26, Governor Rutherford B. Hayes of Ohio wrote a recommendation for Scammon. ADS, *ibid.*

3. On March 11, Morton had written to Fish. "I take pleasure in enclosing you the reccommendations of the Hon Moses F: Dunn, of Indiana—for a Consulate to one of the German states—He is a fine scholar and speaks German and French fluently—He possesses all the qualifications necessary to fill the position with credit to both himself and the government—I earnestly desire his appointment" ALS, *ibid.* The enclosures are *ibid.* On Feb. 24, 1871, Pratt wrote to Fish. "I take pleasure in forwarding to you a paper signed by the Entire Republican Delegation from Indiana with one exception—It is in favor of Moses F. Dunn of Bedford Indiana, son of the late George G. Dunn who represented the Bedford District in Congress for several years with distinguished ability—. . ." ALS, *ibid.* The enclosure is *ibid.* No appointment followed.

Veto

To the House of Representatives:

I herewith return without my approval—House Bill No. 2566, entitled, "An Act for the relief of Henry Willman, late a private in the third regiment of Indiana cavalry," for the following reasons:

The records of the War Department show that Henry Willman was mustered into the military service, April 4th 1862, and that he was mounted on a private horse. It appears from evidence presented by himself that his horse died May 18th 1862; that he remounted himself on June 8th 1862, and so continued mounted till October 1st 1862, when his horse was killed by the enemy, and that he was not afterwards mounted upon a private horse.

Upon presenting a claim against the United States for the legal value of the two horses lost by him in the public service, the claim, after investigation, was allowed; but it being discovered that he had erroneously been paid for the use and risk of a private horse from May 18th to June 8th 1862, and from October 1st 1862 to April 30th 1864, during which periods he had no horse in the public service, the amount so over paid was off set against his claim, leaving the latter fully liquidated and the claimant indebted to the United States in an amount not yet refunded.

The person named in the Act is not in law or equity, entitled to the relief therein provided and has no unsatisfied demands against the United States.

U. S. GRANT

EXECUTIVE MANSION,
FEBRUARY 28TH 1871.

DS, DNA, RG 233, 41A-D1. On Feb. 22, 1871, Horace Porter wrote to Secretary of War William W. Belknap. "The President directs me to submit for your examination H. R. 2566. 'An Act for the relief of Henry Willman, late a private in the third regiment of Indiana Cavalry,' and H. R. 2707. 'An Act for the relief of General John C McQuiston and Jeremiah D. Skeen, of Indiana.' and request your report whether any reasons exist why either of them should not receive his approval." LS, *ibid.*, RG 110, Enrollment Div., Letters Received. On Feb. 24, Belknap wrote to USG advising approval of the bill for the relief of John C. McQuiston and Jeremiah D. Skeen. Copy, *ibid.* On the same day, Belknap wrote to USG recommending a veto of the bill for the relief of Henry Willman, supplying text repeated in USG's veto message. Copy, *ibid.*, RG 107, Letters Sent, Military Affairs. On Dec. 19, 1870, U.S. Representative William S. Holman of Ind. had introduced a bill providing Willman with $200 for the loss of two horses and equipment; on Feb. 18, 1871, the bill passed. *CG*, 41–3, 170, 480, 1385, 1414. See *HED*, 41-3-152.

To William Elrod

Washington D. C. Feb. 28th *18*71

DEAR ELROD:

The bull sent to you is a thoroughbred Alderney. If you can get any one to take him to keep for their own use until the calves of the bull y[ou] now have are old enough to serve you might do so, and th[en] either sell the one you have, or change him with whoever keeps this last one.

Some time in Jan. or earlyer, I sent you a pamphlet on agriculture, and particularly on the feeding of stock, and wrote at the same time that you might regard your pay raised to $60 00 pr. month from the 1st of Jan.y. Did you get my letter and the pamphlet? I will be in St. Louis this Spring ~~and~~ or Summer and will be on the farm two or three days and make arrangements for building more stable room and for the repair of your house. I think you are right about buying cows instead of heiffers. When you have the money buy cows as the opportunity occurs. Raise ~~your~~ ~~own~~ the heiffer calves however calved on the place.

AL (signature clipped), Illinois Historical Survey, University of Illinois, Urbana, Ill.

Speech

[*March 2, 1871*]

Prince it gives me much pleasure to receive you in this friendly and unofficial way, and to learn from your lips the amicable feelings of the people of Japan towards the United States. The people of this country reciprocate your wish that the present means of intercourse between the two nations, great and comfortable as you deem them to be, may be increased.

The United States have seen with pride the young men of Japan coming here to receive scientific educations.[1] I shall take great pleasure in contributing to make their residence in this country agreeable and profitable to them, sharing with you the opinion that education is the basis of progress, and the hope and belief that by accquiring it in the United States they will help to cement and extend the friendly relations which now happily exist between the two nations.

Baltimore Sun, March 3, 1871. USG spoke in reply to Prince Mits Fusimi [*Higashi Fushimi*]. "This audience has been sought that I might personally express to you my admiration and interest in the many wonderful works of American enterprise, and I assure you these expressions are not empty words, but the hearty sentiments of our people. Intercourse between our respective countries has been regularly established through a monthly line of American steamships of surpassing excellence, whose trips, in connection with the great Pacific railway, afford us a rapid and agreeable route to Europe. With every modern luxury of speed and convenience across your continent, our travelers and students, like myself, on their way abroad, will hereafter become better acquainted with your country and people. We shall constantly encourage intercourse, and aim to annually increase more intimate and important relations, and sincerely hope for your kind co-operation and assistance, and shall welcome any augmentation of mail and traveling facilities to more closely unite our interests. The government of Japan is well aware that education is the basis of all progress, and therefore sends its young men to receive scientific educations in America and Europe, hoping thereby to fitly prepare them to take a wise and discriminating part hereafter in the affairs of our own government. With this view, my brother, Quache Nomia [*Kachō-nomiya*], was last year sent to this country, under the traveling name of Adzumah Takahico, and I am now on my way to Prussia for a like purpose. In leaving my brother in America I feel confident of kind treatment and certain of your friendly assistance should our charge d'affairs, Ingoi Aunori Mori, request it. Our government has commissioned a diplomatic resident to this country to assure you that it is earnestly seeking for permanent progress in all that is great and good as rapidly as it can acquire these cherished ends, and desires particularly to cement more closely the already friendly relations existing between our respective countries." *Ibid.* On March 2, 1871, Secretary of State Hamilton Fish wrote in his diary. "After receiving the Japanese Chargé this mornig, & naming the appointment with the President, Mr Brooks (the Japanese Consul at San Francisco) shewed me a copy of an Address which the Prince (Mits Fusimi) proposes to make this Evening to the President—The Prince is on his way to Europe only passing through Washington—has no diplomatic functions—I explained to Mr Brooks and Jugoi Arinori Mori (the Chargé) that the introduction to the President would have no political significance, & would simply be a private introduction, of one gentleman of high character to another—" DLC-Hamilton Fish. On the same day, Fish wrote to USG. "I enclose a list of the names of the Japanese Gentlemen who propose to pay you a visit this evening—They will call at 8 o'clock—The Prince proposes to make a complimentary speech (in Japanese), we will try to have a reply in readiness, but possibly may not have time to have it written out in Japanese—if not, will you be content to deliver it in English?" Copy, *ibid.*

On April 22, Fish wrote to Orville E. Babcock. "I learn this morning that Madam de Bille (wife of the Danish Minister) has not received her invitation to the dinner at the President's next week. I presume that it is an accident & suggest that another invitation be sent. It would be unfortunate not to correct the accident & to leave the wife of a Minister from a court with which it is our interest to be on particularly good terms, under the misapprehension of neglect—You will also readily imagine reasons of a personal nature (in connection with our Representative to Denmark) that make it important not to allow the suspicion of any slight to the wife of the Danish Minister. Let me ask if the Japanese chargé has been invited? I fear that the list which the President has of Foreign Ministers was made before Mr Mori was accredited—Pardon my troubling you—but you know how much these little things are considered by these Diplomats & how much they sometimes affect the relations of Governments & the influence of one nation with another—" LS (press), *ibid.* On the same day, Babcock wrote to Fish. "*Personal* . . . I send you a list of those invited &c, as the list now stands. Turenne saved us all trouble by sending a regret, just as I was signing the note to him. Madam de Bille—has this morning been invited (that is since your note was received)—we dated the invitation same as the others. If you have any suggestions—please let me know—I shall be glad to make any corrections you may suggest." ALS, *ibid.* Enclosed is a "List of guests invited to State dinner on 29th Apl." indicating acceptances and regrets. D, *ibid.* On April 19 and 20, Horace Porter had written to Fish. "Thanks for your note of last evening in regard to Turenne. His name was suggested for the dinner, but I reasoned just as you do, and, in making out the invitations yesterday, I had Treillard and wife only, from the French legation, invited. In case they declined no one else will be invited from that legation." "During my absence at the Capitol Treillard's regret came in, and the President ordered an invitation to be sent to Turenne. I have not seen the President to learn what possessed him to do this. My clerk reported that it hasd been done. The President is out at present. However, it is too late to recall the invitation, even if he were here. I regret it exceedingly. An invitation was made out for da Cunha. He has received it, no doubt, by this time." ALS, *ibid.* On April 21, Babcock wrote to Fish. "The enclosed is a draft of a letter I propose sending Count Turenne. If you have any alterations to suggest I should be pleased to know them" LS, *ibid.* The enclosure is dated the same day: "The President directs me to inform you that by an error, an invitation was issued to you to a dinner at the Executive Mansion on the 29th instant. It was issued upon the supposition that you were in charge of the French Legation. As M. de Bellounet holds that position, the President desires to recall the invitation. Regretting the error necessitating this recall, . . ." Df, *ibid.* Also on April 21, Fish wrote to Babcock. "I do not think the letter proposed to be sent to Count Turenne could be improved In haste" ALS, ICN. Fish wrote in his diary that Henry de Bellonnet, 1st secretary of the French legation, had presented his letters of credence as interim chargé d'affaires on April 20. DLC-Hamilton Fish. See *New York Times,* April 30, 1871.

On Oct. 27, Horace Porter wrote to Charles Lanman, American secretary, Japanese legation, Washington, D. C. "The President directs me to acknowledge the receipt of your note of the 20th inst and the accompanying publication, and request you to convey to Mr. Mori his grateful acknowledgements for his polite attention." Copy, DLC-USG, II, 1. See Mori Arinori, *Life and Resources in America* (Washington, 1871); Ivan Parker Hall, *Mori Arinori* (Cambridge, Mass., 1973), pp. 159–60, 209–12.

1. On May 16, James McCosh, president, Princeton College, wrote to USG. "I think I told you when you did us the honor to visit us at Princeton that we had two intelligent Japanese youths at our College—I find that we could teach a dozen as easily and more effectively than two. If some of these Japanese who have lately come to this country could be induced to come to our College we could organize a department for their thorough instruction My only aim in this proposal is to help the East to profit by what we have in the West. You have been helping this cause and I would be glad to aid you As Mr Mori cannot be expected to know any thing about our College is it asking too much from you to beg you to refer this matter to Mr Mori saying what you conscientiously can about our College Hoping you will excuse this liberty . . ." ALS, DNA, RG 59, Miscellaneous Letters. See Draft Annual Message, Dec. 4, 1871, note 5.

Order

March 2d 1871.

It is directed that the results of the re-enumeration of, by Executive Order, of the Cities of New York and Philadelphia, be taken as exhibiting the true population of those cities at the Ninth Census of the United States, and that the same be included in the total population of the States, respectively, of New York and Pennsylvania, and in the total population of the United States."[1]

U. S. GRANT.

Copy, DNA, RG 130, Orders and Proclamations. On March 1, 1871, Secretary of the Interior Columbus Delano wrote to USG. "I have the honor to transmit, herewith, a draft of an Executive Order, prepared in pursuance of the views expressed by you in our interview of yesterday, with respect to the re-enumeration of the population of the cities of New York and Philadelphia, taken at the Ninth Census of the U. S. Should the draft meet your approval, I will thank you to cause it to be returned to this Department, after it shall have received your signature." LS, OFH.

On Sept. 12, 1870, Mayor A. Oakey Hall of New York City had accused George H. Sharpe, U.S. marshal, of undercounting the city's population for political reasons. See *New York Times*, Sept. 13, Dec. 17, 1870. On Oct. 28, USG issued an order. "Whereas, public question is made, by the Mayor of the City of New York, as to the correctness of the census of the City and County of New York recently taken by the U. S. Marshal. It is directed that a new census be forthwith taken of said City and County; that such new census be taken by districts made to conform to the districts recently established by the City Government for election purposes: and that every practicable precaution be taken to make such new census exactly correct and full." Copy, DNA, RG 130, Orders and Proclamations. On Nov. 5, USG ordered that the census of Philadelphia be retaken. Copy, *ibid.*

1. The new counts raised the population total in New York City from 923,944 to 942,292 and in Philadelphia from 657,277 to 674,022. See *The Statistics of the Population of the United States,... from the Original Returns of the Ninth Census,...* (Washington, 1872), I, xx–xxi.

To Hamilton Fish

Washington D. C. March 4th *18*71

MY DEAR GOVERNOR:

The hours named in your note of this date for receiving Sir Stafford Northcote, ~~and~~ Sir John A McDonald and Mr. Lopez Roberts,[1] Spanish Minister, towit: half past eleven on Monday[2] next for the two former, and twelve m on Tuesday for the latter will entirely suit my convenience.

Truly Yours
U. S. GRANT

HON. H. FISH,
SEC. OF STATE.

ALS, DLC-Hamilton Fish. Stafford H. Northcote, born in 1818, long prominent in English politics, and John A. Macdonald, born in 1815, first prime minister of the Dominion of Canada (1867), served as members of the Joint High Commission to settle the Alabama Claims. See *New York Times*, March 7, 1871; Nevins, *Fish*, pp. 446–47; message to Senate, Feb. 9, 1871.

On March 18, 1871, Adam Badeau, London, wrote to USG. "I returned from Spain a day or two ago, and wrote to Gov Fish, who sent me, an explanation of a delay of two weeks or more which was occasioned by a severe fit of sickness I had in Madrid. Strangers are often acclimated there through the stomach, and as that is my weak spot, I was especially liable. I had almost an inflammation of the stomach, and suffered much. I saw a good deal of Sickles, talked a great deal with him, and with his friend Wikoff, who was there (at Sickles's house). Sickles seemed very popular; I went out a few times before I was taken ill, and saw him in Society. The Marshal Serrano and other members of the government seemed greatly impressed by him; and he impressed me more than ever with his ability. He said every thing is agreeable now in Spain, and if the government wanted to accomplish any thing but Cuba, now would be a good time. A naturalization treaty, a Consular convention, a commercial treaty could be easily arranged. The present government he thinks willing to do any thing of the sort, but as for Cuba, the death of Prim removed the only man who dared face the situation. They all know that Cuba must eventually be ours, but no one is bold enough to take the bull by the horns. He thinks the permanancy of the King very questionable. If a republic is maintained in France, the young gentleman must go home to his papa. I was very much struck with the extent of republican feeling in Spain, as evidenced by the newspapers. Many refuse to call the King any thing but the Young Man Amadeo, and so on. Sickles gave a great ball on Washington's birthday, had Spanish & American flags intertwined, your picture and Washington's on the wall &c. &c. I was too ill to go. He and Wikoff talked home politics a good deal with me, separately and together They both seemed very sanguine of your reelection. I think that Sickles is nearly tired of his present post, there seeming to be no chance of Cuba, or any other great *coup*, and that he would like to be home to engage in the Presidential canvas of 1872. He did not say so, however. There is an idea which may have already reached you, of identifying Fisk & Gould and the Erie. railroad, with the Democratic party, which can easily be effected by means of the connexion which really exists between them and Hoffman, Tweed, Judge Barnard and Tammany. The load would certainly be too heavy for the Democracy to carry. If the people were asked whether they wanted Fisk & Gould to run the United States government, I think I know what their answer would be. I saw Washburne as I came back thro' Paris. He was pretty well, talked confidently about home politics, anxiously about France; both he and Sickles thought there was no doubt about the propriety of laying out Sumner. He had made so furious and personal an onslaught on you and on your administration, that the party must choose who should be its chief. Both desired to be remembered to you. Sheridan was in Paris. He agreed entirely with me that all that has been the matter with the French is there lack of pluck. They would have had leaders and organization, if they had been willing to stand fire. I am disgusted with the nation. I saw hundreds of thousands of fine, hearty men as I came thro' France. When I got to London I found your very kind and important letter. I had already heard from Gov. Fish your decision and his about the Froude article, which indeed I had anticipated, and which I beleive to have been the proper one. I thank you for the interest you manifest in my doings however, and for the order you gave the War Office for me. I thank you even more Dear General, for so kind and gratifying a letter. It shows that you have not lost your confidence in me. The two sentences about England were extremely important, and I took the letter to a club that night, and read them to several important people who were highly pleased. Lest you should have forgotten them, I repeat them here, so that you may not think I have been indiscreet. 'You will see before this reaches you that we are in a fair way now of coming to some conclusion with Great Britain in the matter of our differences. I hope sincerely that they may be settled to the mutual satisfaction of both parties.' The English are certainly very anxious to be very friendly with us, and skilful management at Washington will give us all we can want. They would give us Canada tomorrow, if Canada would come. The great growth of Germany the overthrow of France, her alliance with Russia, the recent diplomatic success of Russia—all conspire to leave England weak and solitary her influence is waning and she knows it, and turns to us. The foreign policy of Gladstone's government is miserable in the extreme. He is *very timid*, bear this in mind. He did not dare assist France; he gave way to Russia; he is for abandoning the colonies. You can bring him to terms. Earl de Grey and Sir Stafford Northcote, are amiable men, but not of first rate calibre or importance. Northcote however is a political opponent of Gladstone, and I suspect the ablest Englishman on the commission. I had a note from Lady Northcote today in which she says; 'I have heard from Sir Stafford from Washington, and he seems delighted with all he has seen there and is full of cheerful anticipations of the happy issue of the affair.' I have also seen Sir John Rose, who speaks very hopefully. I congratulate you on the over throw of Sumner. I have heard from various sources that he is insane. It is a charitable supposition, but I hope it will speedily be known to the public. Now if you only could get rid of Butler A man of importance, an American told me recently that Butler had said he was only supporting you till he got a good chance to injure you. His support in deed does that all the time. It brings you no partisan support, because you have the strict party men secure, and it alienates and repels many good men who are not partisan; and these are the men who decide elections. This is what he does, supposing him to be honest in his support. But I had a letter from Wm E. Chandler, who was Asst. Sec of the Treasury for a while under Lincoln & Johnson, till Johnson went over; and who is intimate with Butler. He says Butler says you can't be re-elected, and he tells me that you cant rely on Butler. Chandler himself is a little sore. He says you don't know him; that he has never asked an office or a favor of the administration, (and he never did thro' me, or to my knowledge); but that if he had bored you, you would have known him. What he wants is recognition, I suppose; for people to suppose that he is in favor with the administration. If civility would accomplish this, it would not be wasted, for he is important. I see New Hampshire is lost. He is a New Hampshire man and worked very hard ~~for~~there and two years ago for you. I suspect he has done nothing this year, and I think he could have saved the state. He did not ask me to say a word of this, but I fancy he wrote the letter to show me his feelings Please make my best regards to Mrs Grant and the children, . . ." ALS, USG 3. For Badeau's trip to Spain as a special messenger, see telegram of Jan. 28 from Secretary of State Hamilton Fish to Benjamin Moran, chargé d'affaires, London, and letter of May 17 from Moran to Fish. Copy, DNA, RG 59, Diplomatic Instructions, Great Britain; ALS, *ibid.*, Diplomatic Despatches, Great Britain. On March 18, Lord Halifax, London, wrote to Badeau. "I am glad to hear of your return to England, & am much obliged to you for the books which you have been good enough to send me relating to the United States. I was sorry that you were not here when we determined on sending Lord DeGrey & the Commission to Washington, as I think it would have contributed to the probable success of the Commission that he should have had the advantage of some communication with you. Your account of the Presidents hopes is very encouraging. . . ." ALS, DLC-Adam Badeau.

On March 23 and April 4, Badeau wrote to USG. "There was one matter about which I talked with General Sickles, that I did not mention in my letter of a day or two ago, and which seems to me of importance. It was in regard to the Alabama question. The English as you know, claim that they did all that their law allowed, to stop the Alabama; and we maintain that their law is nothing to us; that if their municipal law failed to carry out the obligations which international law imposed on them, they are responsible. They should have better laws, or take the consequences. Sickles said this very doctrine has been maintained by Gladstone, since he has been Prime Minister, in a speech in the House of Commons, made after Greece had allowed several Englishmen to be captured by brigands and shot, ~~and~~ saying that her law did not allow her to interfere: I looked up the debates to-day, and find in the London Times of May 21, 1870, a report of the speeches made the night before, when Sir Henry Bulwer, Sir Roundell Palmer (who was the Crown lawyer, in the government, when the Alabama escaped, and who was very hostile to us), both maintained the ground we now assume; and Mr Gladstone also declared in so many words that *no municipal law could excuse a failure in international law.* I dont see why this would not be a good authority to quote to the Joint High Commission. There is a file of the Times in the State Dept. Again: Sickles told me of a case paralell to the Alabama, which occurred under Washington's administration, when England and France were at war, and we neutrals. Privateers were fitted out by our merchants, and tho' we had no treaty binding us not to allow this, yet when England complained on the same grounds as we do now, Washington not only allowed the claim and paid the damages, but went beyond the demands of England. There is a very remarkable letter on the subject written by Jefferson when he was Secretary of State, at Washingtons direction, to Mr. Hammond the British Minister. This letter is on Page 132 of Volume 8, United States Statutes at Large—European Treaties. It tells the whole story, and shows that we set the precedent which we ask England to follow; and that she then asked us to do precisely what she has hitherto refused to do herself. If Gov. Fish has not unearthed this letter, it will be worth his while to do so." "*Confidential* . . . I have just seen Mr. J. R. Young, who brought me your messages about my book. I am hard at work on it every day, and very anxious to complete it. I want it brought out immediately *after* your renomination, not before. That act will not depend upon the people directly, or at least your popularity and the remembrance of your great achievements will only act indirectly in accomplishing it. You will be renominated because the politicians will be convinced that no other Republican can possibly be elected; and *then*, after you are nominated, will be the time to remind the people of the great events of that last glorious year of the war. The ~~people~~ men who go to the Nominating Convention wont care a particle for what you have done; their care is for themselves The people of the country *do* care for your record, and consider it, as it is, the record of the country for now nearly ten years past. Young said you had some material ready for me; I suppose it is that of which I wrote to you. I should be glad to have it as soon as possible. I am not certain whether I may not want to be back in America for a month or two during the printing of my book; but if I can possibly escape the misery of two sea voyages, I will. Perhaps I can have the whole work printed here and stereotyped here, and the plates sent over. I may however need to consult you personally about some of my chapters. If not, I shall send either the manuscript, or the first proof for your inspection. Mr Young says he is here to look after the press; and it needs it badly. Of course I will do anything in my power to assist him. I see the rumor that Gov Fish is to come here instead of Gen Schenck. It will be a good thing to have here a full minister, who is supposed really to represent you. Mr Moran is the most faithful of secretaries, and an admirable subordinate; but he is negative and wooden; has no influence whatever; and besides he is a trimmer. His whole aim is to keep his place. The other day, he told me he was afraid your action in the Sumner matter would break up the party. I could see that he was preparing, in Case Sumner won, to be ready to serve under your enemies. He has been ~~for~~ under Buchanan, Dallas, Adams, Reverdy Johnson and Motley, and ~~for~~ as many different Presidents. Every body here says that he was strong for Buchanan, and even for the South, till it was unadvisable; and I have no doubt he would have been as strong for Seymour as he is now for you, if Seymour had won. He wont be false while you are in power, but he will welcome your enemy, if he should be your successor; not out of ill will to you, but from a desire to keep his place. All of which I say not to injure him, but to let you know that you can't count on any self sacrificing personal devotion from him in an emergency. As I don't want his place, and want to see him retained in the Legation I have no motive, except to let you know just how far you can depend on him. I suppose he is not different from most people; but I have always found that the passions of men influence them more than their interests. A man here who loved you, or thoroughly believed in his party, would make a positively powerful minister. Moran is only good for a secretary. Please, dear General, destroy this, and consider it *entirely confidential*. . . . April 28 . . . Please destroy this whole letter . . . I have kept this letter nearly a month, because I was not sure whether I ought to send it; but I conclude to do so, repeating however what I have said that M. will be and is faithful now; he only will not risk his future by any partisanship. He and I are on excellent terms, and I dont want to injure him in your eyes: but I want to see a strong man here. There has been none for a long time now. Motley of course had no weight after it was known that he was recalled, and Moran's ability is not equal to any thing more than his Secretaryship. I was delighted with your St Domingo message. I regretted the necessity, but it had the old ring in it. I knew who wrote every line. It sounded like those sentences I used to admire of old. Short, terse, to the point; full of sense and force and patriotism. I dont know but your course in the matter will be one of the strongest arguments in your favor with the people. You triumphantly vindicated yourself and your friends, and then made it evident how different a man you are from your predecessor. God bless you, General" ALS, USG 3. On May 22, Horace Porter wrote to J. C. Bancroft Davis, asst. secretary of state. "I send copies of all papers on file in War Dep't. necessary to complete Badeau's second vol. of the President's life. Will you please send the package to him in such a manner as to guard against all possibility of loss, . . ." ALS, DLC-J. C. Bancroft Davis.

On April 26, John Russell Young, London, wrote to USG. "I have the honor to enclose you a letter addressed by me to *The Times*, with its reply. The publication is the result of a good deal of earnest patient work,—as *The Times* has been very hostile, and is one of the most powerful, as well as the most difficult journal to reach in the world. The tone of *The Times* is kinder than it has shown for years. This discussion seems to have a good color to the press generally, and I hope people here are coming to a more generous feeling. I have written Mr. Fish and Mr Boutwell at length, especially as to any further instructions. The time for which I promised to stay is coming to an end, and I am anxious to have your further instructions. There is no doubt a great work to be done here. It requires patience and tact, and a clear knowledge of the influences to be reached and the best way to reach them." ALS, USG 3. Young's letter to *The Times*, dated April 18, is signed "R." "I welcome your article of Monday upon the Joint High Commission, and I am sure it will be welcomed by that great part of the American people who have hoped for the best results from the conference at Washington. There are, however, one or two considerations, which, from an American point of view, I trust you will deem worthy of attention. There is a prevailing American sentiment that the settlement of the Alabama question is so much the affair of England that any reasonable proposition from the Washington Cabinet must of necessity be friendly and peaceful. It does not seem to be sufficiently remembered in England that America has a few active and influential public men who hold that an open issue with your Government is a necessary element in American politics. They feel that the best way to settle the 'Alabama Claims' is to leave them unsettled. They contend that the precedent which was created either by the law of England or the administration of its Government is so dangerous that its existence alone is a menace to your naval power. They reason that if in any way, lawfully or unlawfully, it was possible for Admiral Semmes to buy war-ships at Birkenhead, it would be just as possible, lawfully or unlawfully, for the enterprising Admiral of any Power that chanced to be at war with England to buy ships at New York or San Francisco and attack your commerce. When it is further considered that America has shipbuilding ports on the two great oceans, it is argued that the Alabama precedent adds largely to the difficulties which war imposes upon any country, and that, in your case especially, America would be practically in perpetual alliance with any maritime Power that chose to attack your flag. . . . And now that America has no commerce to lose, with no war probable for generations, and with a territory which can scarcely be invaded, there are those, not without power and political dexterity and influence among the politicians, who insist that America would be justified in permitting the Alabama question to rest as a standing menace to England. . . . I am anxious, knowing this, that England should do justice to the President of the United States. His administration means peace. Like your own Wellington—to whom, in fact, his character bears many points of resemblance—he has seen enough of war not to view with horror and deep concern any question that might lead to war. All that military renown can give he has gained. His further renown must come from victories of peace. His administration must be great and successful as he determines the domestic finances and the relations of the Republic with England. His Secretary of the Treasury has met the financial problem by paying off more than 200 millions of the war debt. Mr. Fish has made every advance in the matter of England by his hearty acceptance of the Commission, and by agreeing to a new principle of International Law—a principle which must in time be a precious and cardinal point in the laws of maritime nations. That principle, as your Correspondent telegraphs it, is,—'*That a neutral is responsible for depredations committed on a friendly Power by a vessel manned and fitted out at a neutral port*.' . . . Why should America be looked upon by so many of your journals and statesmen as a truculent, whimsical, uncertain Power, whose very existence is an anomaly and almost a scandal, and whose men in authority have no sincere political emotion but hatred of England? Why should the great Confederation be tempted or permitted to drift into all manner of odd and unnatural 'alliances' and 'understandings' with Russia and Prussia and France, and any country that seeks them, when the true natural alliance is with the mighty people from whose loins she sprang, with whom she is in the closest ties of kinship, and bound by a common jurisprudence, a common language, and a common faith? . . ." *The Times* (London), April 20, 1871. An editorial in the same issue responded. "A gentleman from the United States at present in London has addressed us a letter which deserves to be answered in its own friendly spirit. . . . He claims just credit for the courage and patriotism of the PRESIDENT and his colleagues in pressing on a settlement of the Alabama Question. Why? Because in so doing they have withstood the policy of 'a few active and influential public men'—in another part of our correspondent's letter described as 'many active minds in

America'—'who hold that an open issue with the English Government is a necessary element in American politics.' Here we have the explanation of the English delusion. At this distance we only hear the echoes of the 'active and influential men' in the Union, and when we find them habitually playing on the passions of the Irish constituencies whom they lead to the poll, we are apt to think they mean what they say, and that the sentiments they express are widely, if not universally, held. Let us be specific. We shall not confound the American nation with General BUTLER when he calls for a rupture with England as a means of revivifying the Republican party; but we ask 'R.,' and those who feel with him, to consider what Englishmen naturally thought when they heard that the House of Representatives had passed a Resolution welcoming O'DONOVAN ROSSA and his associates to the shores of the States. The same exiles were subsequently received at the White House. Anybody, it will be answered, can be received at the White House; it is only necessary to attend at certain hours and walk in; but even those Englishmen who know the Republican simplicity of the PRESIDENT's Receptions may be pardoned if they thought that the Chief Magistrate of a great nation would have refused the privilege of an interview to convicted rebels against a friendly Government. . . ." *Ibid.* See Endorsement, March 13, 1871.

1. See *PUSG*, 19, 154–55; Speech, March 7, 1871.
2. March 6.

Speech

[*March 7, 1871*]

MR. LOPEZ ROBERTS: I congratulate you upon the mark of the continued confidence of your Government, which the new credentials presented by you evince. This congratulation may be the more cordial as it confirms the general opinion of your course during your past official residence here, a course distinguished by zeal and fidelity to your own country and by courtesy and consideration toward that to which you have been accredited. The recent changes in public persons and affairs in Spain are understood to have been so amply sanctioned by the popular will that they must be entirely acquiesced in, especially in countries whose governments repose upon a similar basis. I heartily desire that the new order of things there may tend to strengthen the bonds of amity and good will which have always been maintained between our respective countries, and that the United States may never forget that Spain was their useful friend at an early and critical period of their career.

New York Tribune, March 8, 1871. USG spoke in reply to Mauricio Lopez Roberts. "... In a few days it will be two years, Mr. President, since on an occasion like the present, I presented to you the letters which accredited me in the same quality in the name of the Provisional Government formed in Spain after the revolution of September, 1868. During the time which has elapsed since then, the Sovereign Spanish Cortes, elected by universal suffrage, have settled in the most liberal manner the gravest and most important questions, which greatly obstructed social reforms and the development of the material interests of the nation; and they have given to their country a Constitution in which, while it embodies the most liberal political principles, are recognized at the same time all the essential attributes of a monarchy; the rights of the Spanish people, thus being reconciled with the prestige and authority of the throne, on which reconciliation must rest the welfare and happiness of free nations having a monarchical form of government...." *Ibid.* See Hamilton Fish diary, March 2, 1871, DLC-Hamilton Fish.

To Senate

Washington. D. C. March 8. 1871.

TO THE SENATE. OF THE UNITED STATES.

I nominate the persons herein named for appointment under Section 2 of the Act making appropriations for the support of the Army for the year ending June 30. 1872. and for other purposes. *Asa O. Aldis*[1] of Vermont. *James B. Howell.*[2] of Iowa. and *Orange Ferris.*[3] of New York. to be COMMISSIONERS OF CLAIMS, to receive, examine and consider the justice and validity of the claims of loyal citizens, for stores, supplies. etc. take[n] or furnished for the use of the Army of the United States in insurrectionary states. and of which Commission *Asa O. Aldis* is designated as President, as provided in Section 3 of said Act.

U. S. GRANT

DS, DNA, RG 46, Nominations. On March 8, 1871, Secretary of War William W. Belknap wrote to USG proposing these nominations. Df, *ibid.*, RG 94, ACP, 1314 1871. A Southern Claims Commission originally had been the subject of a separate bill. See *CG*, 41–3, 880, 1849–50, 1914–16, 1966–73; *U.S. Statutes at Large,* XVI, 524–25; *HMD*, 42-2-16; Frank W. Klingberg, *The Southern Claims Commission* (Berkeley and Los Angeles, 1955).

1. Asa O. Aldis, born in 1811 in St. Albans, Vt., graduated from the University of Vt. (1829), attended Harvard and Yale Law Schools, and practiced law. He served as judge, Vt. supreme court (1857–65), and consul, Nice (1865–70). On March 8, 1871, Secretary of State Hamilton Fish wrote in his diary. "Judge Aldis (of Vermont) by

appointment—Offered him the position of Arbitrator under the Agreement with Spain for Settlement of Claims of Am. Citizens, for injuries &c in Cuba (see Sickles No 288—Feb 12)—He prefers the appointment on the Board to assess damages for property & supplies taken from loyal Citizens, in Rebellious States—" DLC-Hamilton Fish.

On March 7, Roger M. Sherman, Washington, D. C., had written to Frederick T. Dent. "You are probably aware that at the close of the session just ended an act was passed providing for a commission of three to settle certain Southern claims, &c. It is supposed that of these, one will be chosen from New England, and, as I hear, probably from Connecticut. My uncle Henry Sherman Esq., now residing in this city but whose 'residence' is Hartford, Conn., has been asked to allow his name to be presented to the President for the office and both of the Senators from Connecticut have assured him of their cordial support in the Senate—Senator Buckingham that he would, if possible, see the President this morning on the subject. They both have known him long and well and are well acquainted with his eminent fitness for just that position. My object in writing to you is to ask, if you are at liberty to inform me, whether I am right in the belief that Conn. will receive one of these appointments and whether the President has fixed upon anyone for the office. Also to ask him, in case he has not, and Senator B. has not yet spoken to him about my uncle, to consult the Senators from Conn. as to the propriety of this nomination, before he decides finally. If I may so far trespass on your kindness I will be greatly obliged." ALS, ICarbS.

2. Also on March 7, William B. Allison, Washington, D. C., wrote to USG. "I learn that late Senator J. B. Howell would accept one of the Commissionerships to adjust & collate Southern Claims I take pleasure in commending him as in every way qualified for the position, and it would give me pleasure to hear of his appointment" ALS, University of Iowa, Iowa City, Iowa. Born in 1816 near Morristown, N. J., but raised in Newark, Ohio, James B. Howell graduated from Miami University (1837), practiced law, moved to Iowa (1841), owned newspapers, and served as postmaster, Keokuk (1861–66). An active Republican, he filled an unexpired term in the U.S. Senate (1870–71).

On March 16, 1869, James F. Wilson, Washington, D. C., had written to USG. "The Iowa delegation in Congress have united in recommending James B. Howell, Esqr, of Keokuk, Iowa, for appointment to the post of Minister Resident to Guatemala. We desire to join the delegation in this recommendation; and to express our most earnest interest in this case. Mr. Howell is a high-toned, educated gentleman, qualified for the position, and well deserving favor at the hands of the present admintration. We speak of him from personal knowledge, and put no limitation on our recommendation in this case." ALS, DNA, RG 59, Letters of Application and Recommendation. On March 19, Belknap, Keokuk, wrote to Secretary of War John A. Rawlins. "The first Editor in this state to espouse the cause of Genl. Grant for the Presidency, as far as I know, was James B. Howell, Editor of the 'Gate City' of Keokuk. He is now an applicant for the mission to Guatemala and is capable of filling the place with credit. He is a man of will and resolution, and of first rate education, and if the President should appoint him I am sure he will be satisfied with the result." ALS, *ibid.* Grenville M. Dodge favorably endorsed this letter. AES (undated), *ibid.* On March 23, Governor Samuel Merrill of Iowa wrote to USG. "I desire to join with Iowa Delegation in recommending the appointment of Hon James B. Howell of Keokuk Io. to the Office of Minister resident at Guatemala Central America. That position is now held by a citizen of Iowa who will not I presume expect to retain it under the present administration. Mr. Howell is an old citizen of our State, An Editor for more than twenty yrs. of one of the leading papers, has done much to make Iowa what she is politically was the first to raise the banner for Grant & Victory—He has good ability & a fine education. his appointment would give entire satisfaction to our people—" ALS, *ibid.* On May 1, U.S. Representative George W. McCrary of Iowa, Keokuk, wrote to Reader W. Clarke, Washington, D. C. "I write to you in behalf of our mutual friend, J, B, Howell of the 'Gate City' and because I know that your personal friendship for him as well as for the President will prompt you to appreciate what I want to say, I need not recount to you Mr Howell's services in the Republican Cause, for you know that he has for more than a quarter of a century, fought the democracy, with uncommon zeal and ability, He has now reached his fiftieth year; his health is impaired; he has not acquired wealth; he desires a foreign mission which will enable him to go abroad, release him for awhile from hard work, and enable him at the same time to save some money, The entire Republican delegation from Iowa recommended him, for the Guatemala Mission, It being understood that this appointment would be given to an Iowa man, and no other Iowa man having been recommended for it, all parties in Iowa considered his appointment a certainty, The Republican press of the state endorsed it and rejoiced in it. Silas A. Hudson of Burlington a Cousin of the President was appointed, Now I do not write you to Complain of the President, or to say anything against Hudson, but to assure you that very great and serious dissatisfaction has grown out of Mr Howell's defeat under all these circumstances. . . ." ALS, *ibid.* Related papers are *ibid.* On April 12, USG had nominated Silas A. Hudson as minister to Guatemala.

3. Orange Ferriss, born in 1814 in Glens Falls, N. Y., attended the University of Vt., practiced law, and held numerous local offices. He was Republican U.S. representative (1867–71).

To James G. Blaine

Washington D. C. Mch. 9. 71.

HON: J G. BLAINE
SPEAKER HOUSE OF REPRESENTATIVES.
DEAR SIR:

As I have been waited upon by great numbers of representatives of the two houses of Congress asking my views as to the necessity of lagislation during this session of Congress, and as what I have said might be wrongly interpreted, I write this unofficially, to express exactly what I do think—In the first place there is a deplorable state of affairs existing in some portions of the South demanding the immediate attention of Congress. If the attention of Congress can be confined to the single subject of providing means for the protection of life and property in those Sections of the Country where the present civil authority fails to secure that end, I feel that we should have such legislation. But if Committees are to be appointed and general legislation entered upon, then I fear the object of continuing the present session will be lost. These are about the views I have endeavored to express and are the exact views which I entertain. If it can be agreed upon to take up no other subject but that of passing a single Act of the sort alluded to I would think it wise in Congress to remain for that purpose.

I do not write this to dictate what Congress should do, but write it because my views have been sought by a great number of members; and to prevent any misunderstanding as to what I have said on the subject.

Very respectfully
Your obt: Svt:
U. S. GRANT.

Copy, DLC-USG, II, 1. See letter to Alexander G. Cattell, March 21, 1871; message to Congress, March 23, 1871; James G. Blaine, *Twenty Years of Congress: From Lincoln to Garfield* (Norwich, 1886), II, 468–70. James G. Blaine, born in 1830 in West Brownsville, Pa., rose to political prominence in Maine while a newspaper editor and became U.S. representative (1863) and Speaker of the House (1869). For his public statements concerning USG in 1868 and 1885, see Blaine, *Political Discussions: Legislative, Diplomatic, and Popular, 1856–1886* (Norwich, 1887), pp. 95–103, 472–76.

Speech

[*March 10, 1871*]

Baron Gerolt: The notification which you have conveyed to me, relates to an event of great historical importance.[1] The states of this Union which severally bear a relation to the others similar to that which Prussia bears to the other states of Germany, have recently made such sacrifices and efforts towards maintaining the integrity of their common country for general purposes in peace and war that they cannot fail to sympathise in similar proceedings for a like object elsewhere. The new title which has been accepted by your sovereign may be regarded as the symbol and the fulfilment on its part by Germany of that purpose.

The disposition which you express on behalf of the Emperor of United Germany to maintain unimpaired its friendly relations with the government and people of the United States, is heartily reciprocated.[2]

Washington Evening Star, March 10, 1871. Baron Gerolt, Prussian minister, had transmitted a letter of Jan. 29, 1871, from Emperor William I to USG. "I hereby inform you that, the rulers and free cities of Germany having unanimously requested me to assume the title of Emperor at the close of the war, I have considered it a duty to the Fatherland at large to accept this title for myself, and my successors on the throne of Prussia, with gratitude for the confidence in me which has been manifested by the sovereigns of Germany and my other allies. While I entertain the confident hope of being able, by the gracious help of God, to fulfill the duties connected with the Imperial dignity in such a manner as shall best subserve the interests of Germany, I beg you to feel assured that I shall most sincerely desire the happiness and prosperity of the North American Free States, and shall give you proofs, on every occasion which may present itself to me, of my most distinguished consideration." Copy (translation), DNA, RG 59, Notes from Foreign Legations, Germany.

On March 16, USG wrote to William I. "I have received the letter written to me by your Majesty on the 29th of January last stating that the rulers and Free cities of Germany having unanimously requested you to assume the title of Emperor you had decided to accept that title in deference to their wishes—Permit me to congratulate your Majesty upon this fresh and well deserved mark of the confidence of your countrymen—It may be hoped that the functions incident to the new dignity thus conferred on your Majesty will conduce to the security and prosperity of Germany in which the United States take a lively interest. I I pray God to have your Majesty always in his safe and holy keeping." Copy, *ibid.*, RG 84, Germany, Instructions.

On April 8, George Bancroft, U.S. minister, Berlin, wrote to Secretary of State Hamilton Fish. "This afternoon I delivered to the emperor the president's letter of March 16th congratulating him on attaining the dignity which makes him the representative of German Union and expressing the cordial good wishes of the United States for the most friendly relations with Germany. With reference to his new position he said: I have neither sought for it nor expected it nor desired it. The movement that was manifest in the history of a long period of years could not be unobserved. But I had no thought that the end would be attained unless it might be in the time of my son or of my grandson. With respect to the United States the emperor most cordially reciprocated the good feeling which the president had expressed; and as all the world gives him credit for being a man of his word the president may be certain that the declaration was made with deliberation and sincerity. He expressed particularly his wish that the two nations might continue to cultivate mutually those good and friendly feelings which have been so apparent ever since Germany began to unite itself anew. His expressions to me personally were as friendly as possible." LS, *ibid.*, RG 59, Diplomatic Despatches, Germany. See message to Congress, Feb. 7, 1871.

1. On March 8, Fish had written to USG. "I will thank you to inform me whether it will be agreeable to you to grant an interview to Baron Gerolt on Friday next at 12 M., to enable him to present a letter addressed to you by His Majesty the King of Prussia, announcing his acceptance of the Imperial dignity" Copy, DNA, RG 59, Domestic Letters. On the same day, USG wrote to Fish. "Friday at 12 m it will be entirely

agreeable for me to receive Baron Gerolt." ALS, IHi. On March 10, Gerolt read a letter to USG. "I feel most happy to be the bearer of a letter from my most gracious Sovereign to Your Excellency, conveying the notification that, at the unanimous request of the Sovereigns of the German States and of the free Cities of Germany to assume the ancient title of Emperor, after the German Empire had been reestablished by the union of the German States under one Constituti[on] my August Sovereign has considered it as a duty to the common Fatherland to accept thankfully this dignity conferred, by the confidence of His German Confederates, upon His Majesty and His successors on the throne of Prussia. In having the honor to present ~~Th~~His Majesty letter to Your Excellency it needs no new assurance from me that the Emperor and United Germany desire to maintain as heretofore their friendly relations with the Government and the people of the United States, for whose happiness and welfare they have always entertained their most sincere wishes." Copy, DNA, RG 59, Notes from Foreign Legations, Germany.

2. On April 6, Orville E. Babcock wrote to Secretary of State Hamilton Fish. "If consistent with the public interests, a leave of absence for one day, may be granted to the Germans employed in your department to attend the German 'peace festival' on Monday the 10th instant." LS, *ibid.*, Miscellaneous Letters. On the same day, Babcock wrote similiar letters to Secretary of the Navy George M. Robeson and Attorney Gen. Amos T. Akerman. LS, *ibid.*, RG 45, Letters Received; *ibid.*, RG 60, Letters Received. The peace festival celebrated the end of the Franco-Prussian War and German unification. *New York Times*, April 10, 1871.

Endorsement

Respectfully refered to the Sec. of State with the wish that a proper request may be made for the release of the prisoner named in this petition. I understa[n]d [*that*] Sir John McDonald is acquainted with the father of the prisoner and will probably interest himself in his behalf.

U. S. GRANT

MARCH 13TH /71

AES, DNA, RG 59, Miscellaneous Letters. Written on an undated letter from Thomas Condon to USG. "My son, Edward M. Condon, a citizen of the United States and of the state of Ohio is in prison in England. Years ago I came from Ireland with my family to Canada, and afterwards removed to the states, settled in Cincinnati and became an American. Three of my sons fought for the union, and all were in the battle of Nashville where Edward was wounded. Brought up to my trade as Carpenter and builder, with a fair english and classical education he is an honest industrious and law-abiding man well qualified to be an useful citizen. Having inherited property in Ireland I sent him in 1867 to look after my interests and in Sept. 67 he was in Manchester visiting my relations when the political troubles arose and a riot occurred in which an officer was killed. The officer was in a 'Van' conveying prisoners through the city, the 'van' was assailed by a mob seeking to rescue the prisoners, when the officer hearing the noise looked through the key-hole of the van door. It happened at the moment that one of the mob wishing to shatter the lock, fired a pistol into the key-hole, and without intending it shot the officer in the eye and killed him. As was proven by two respectable disinterested witnesses, my son was not within three miles of the place and had nothing to do with the riot, yet in the prevailing excitement and exasperation on the testimony of a policeman, interested in a reward, and of lewd women, who pretended to have seen him in the crowd he was found guilty. Three other men were convicted of the crime and hanged but in view of the doubts in Edwards case which divided the court on a motion for a new trial his sentence was commuted to imprisonment for life at hard labor. He has endured this punishment for three years and his health is broken so that continued confinement will cause his death. We cannot understand why in the general delivery, which fills so many households with gratitude and joy, this exception should be made against my son. His mother, his wife and all his friends and fellow citizens naturally expected to find him among the liberated. and why should he suffer alone while those innocent, as he is, and many guilty, as he is not, go free? We know not unless it be for a word spoken at his trial. While stoutly and truly protesting his innocence he is said to have exclaimed 'God Save Ireland.' Silence would have been better but must a man perish for a prayer for his native land! Mr President this brave boy has friends, few private citizens have more, and I am proud to be able to say that whereever I am known there are good men who wish me well. Many distinguished americans are aiding us, and in Canada four Cabinet Ministers and Sixty two Members of Parliament have joined in a petition for clemency—and we cannot doubt that if your excellency will exert your influence as you may deem proper your effort will be crowned with success, . . ." LS, *ibid.* U.S. Senators John Sherman of Ohio and Oliver P. Morton of Ind., U.S. Representative Benjamin F. Butler of Mass., and twenty-two others favorably endorsed this letter. ES, *ibid.* On Sept. 18, 1871, Morton, Cincinnati, wrote to USG. "This will introduce to you Mr. Thomas Condon of this City. He has a son in prison in England who was convicted as a Fenian, who has been punished now for four years. He claims that his son is innocent of the offence and the circumstances as he states them, has excited my sympathy. I should be glad to have you hear Mr. Condon's story and to have you do anything for him you can consistent with your duty." LS, *ibid.* The next day, USG endorsed this letter to Secretary of State Hamilton Fish. AES, *ibid.* Fish recorded in a register entry that "Genl Morton's (O P) letter to the President respecting Condon—If I mistake not this is the man in whose behalf I spoke to Earl de Gray & Sir John Macdonald—The Presidents reference of the letter requires an examination again of the case—Please lay aside for consideration (to be brought under notice) on my return to Washington" AD, DLC-J. C. Bancroft Davis. On Sept. 21, 1872, U.S. Representative Job E. Stevenson of Ohio, Cincinnati, wrote to USG. "Edward O'M Condon of Cincinnati Ohio is still in prison in England. It is beleived by his father, and by his friends and fellow citizens who are deeply interested in his behalf—that if another effort were made his release might be accomplished. So far as I know he is the only American citizen yet suffering imprisonment in foreign lands and his liberation would be a most gratifying public event—" ALS, DNA, RG 59, Miscellaneous Letters. On Sept. 23, Rutherford B. Hayes, Cincinnati, wrote to USG. "Edward. O. M. Condon the son of a citizen of this City it is represented is now a prisoner in Portland England. I have to request that this young mans case may receive the attention of our government, and that due effort may be made to obtain his early release from imprisonment. Trusting that this will be done . . ." ALS, DLC-Hamilton Fish. On May 4, 1874, Fish wrote to U.S. Senator Simon Cameron of Pa.,

Committee on Foreign Relations. "I have the honor to acknowledge the receipt of your letter of the 28th ultimo, in which you state that the House of Representatives have passed a Resolution urging the President to intercede with the Queen of Great Britain for the release of Edward O'Meagher Condon, who is confined in prison in Manchester England, for complicity in the killing of a policeman; and requesting any information in regard to the case . . . it may be stated that Mr. Thomas Condon, the father, a most respectable citizen of Ohio, has personally presented the case of his son. He was formerly, as is understood a resident of Canada, and during the sitting in this city of the Joint High Commission which negotiated the Treaty of Washington with Great Britain in 1871, Mr. Condon was in Washington, and enlisted warm sympathy. Learning that while in Canada he had been acquainted with Sir John Macdonald (one of the British Commissioners) I spoke privately and unofficially to him, and also to Lord de Grey (the Head of the British Commission) and obtained from them assurance of their friendly interest in behalf of an application for the pardon of Condon, coupled, however, with an expression of the gravity of his case, and of the embarrassments attending the obtaining of the clemency sought. I have reason to believe that each of these gentlemen exercised his good offices in the direction desired. I have no official information of the result of Mr. Condon's (the fathers) visit to London. It was understood that he had reason to count upon the influence of one or more gentlemen of high official position, connected with the British Government, and that such influence was warmly exercised in aid of the repeated applications made under the instructions of this Department. But I am forced with much regret, to say that the determination of the British Government to adhere to its policy, and not to grant a pardon, has hitherto been unshaken and no indication exists of any change in this respect." Copy, DNA, RG 59, Reports to the President and Congress. Related papers are *ibid.* See *HRC*, 43-3-42; *HED*, 44-2-1, part 1, pp. 176–79, 45-2-1, part 1, pp. 260–63. Edward O'Meagher Condon, alias Edward Shore, was pardoned in Sept., 1878. DNA, RG 59, Diplomatic Despatches, Great Britain; *HED*, 45-3-1, part 1, pp. 283–90, 312–13; William D'Arcy, *The Fenian Movement in the United States: 1858–1886* (1947; reprinted, New York, 1971), pp. 108, 268–71.

On Feb. 12, 1871, Jeremiah O'Donovan Rossa, New York City, had written to USG. "I presume you are aware that Rickard OSullivan Burke, an American Citizen is detained in an English prison because that being considered of unsound mind he is held incapable of understanding the Conditional pardon that is offered to him in the option of leaving the British Islands. Some friends of his in NewYork have come to me to say they will go to England and take charge of him to bring him here if they get him, and with this arrangement I see no difficulty in the way of having him out of prison. If you say the united States will recieve him thro' these friends, he will be given to them. I have told his friends that I would write to you and that I had little doubt of having a favorable reply from you in a few days." ALS, DNA, RG 59, Miscellaneous Letters. On March 18 and April 24, Rossa wrote to USG. "Early in February I wrote to you regarding the case of Rickard O'Sullivan Burke an American citizen detained in an English prison because he was considered of unsound mind and unable to understand the conditions of release offered to him and others. Your secretary replied that the matter would recieve your attention, and your Secretary of State subsequently replied that you had no official information on the subject. A Commission of Inquiry was last year instituted to inquire into the treatment of the 'Irish Treason Felony prisoners' and I have in my possession their printed report in which they declare that Rickard O'Sullivan Burke is of unsound mind. His friends offer to go to England for him, and I am of opinion that by your speaking for Mr Burke and accepting the Conditions of release on his behalf—recognizing his friends as your messengers—he would be given up to them. Indeed I would volunteer myself to go for him as your messenger. John McCafferty is a native born American held in prison, and I would have a question asked as to his detention. Edward O'Meagher Condon is another American citizen, and he has been excluded from the Conditional release for the alleged reason that his offence was not a political one. It was as much political as mine. He fought with you for union in this Country; he was laboring in union with others for the freedom of Ireland, and seeing one of his Companions arrested on a charge of Treason, he was charged with assisting in having him rescued from the police. I bring his case under your notice that you may urge that he is a political prisoner and that he is excluded from the ~~release~~ 'Amnesty' which Mr Gladstone declares includes all the political prisoners I will now submit to you a case of my own for consideration. I do not do so for the purpose of raising any vexatious issue between your Excellency and the English gentlemen of the Commission now sitting in Washington, but if they are troublesome about little matters I may as well give you a trifle to put to account. The Royal Commision of Inquiry into the treatment of the 'Treason Felony' prisoners in England declares *that I have been* ILLEGALLY *treated*: that my hands were tied behind my back for *thirty five* days, whereas the English prison Laws, rules and regulations declare that this punishment cannot be inflicted on any prisoner for a longer term than *three* days I have been thirty two days bound illegally, and I think I have as an America[n] citizen claim to reparation. If your Excelle[ncy] thinks so you will demand thirty two thousa[nd] pounds for these thirty two days of illegal torture which the London 'Spectator' characteri[zed] as a disgrace to Civilization. If any thing in this letter is interesti[ng] to your Excellency and that you require further information I will be happy to afford it, either by laying before you the printed report of the Royal Commissioners, in Conversation if you do me the honor of granting me an audience and Speaking t[o] . . ." "Since your Secretary of State informed me that he had sent instructions to your representative in London to inquire after Rickard O'Sullivan Burke an American Citizen Confined in an English prison, time enough has elapsed to allow you have a reply. I told his friends I would attend to his case; they are pressing me for information and I respectfully request your Excellency to inform me if you are in a position to tell me that Mr Burke will be given up to his friends to bring him to America Mr. Burkes friends authorise you to speak for Mr Burke and to accept for him the Conditions imposed of his leaving the British dominions." ALS, *ibid.*

On June 21, Denis Dowling Mulcahy, New York City, wrote to USG. "Permit me to call your attention to the case of Ricard O Sullivan Burke, late captain of Engineers United States Volunteers, and now an Irish Political convict undergoing a Sentence of Fifteen Years Penal Servitude, in the Broadmoor Convict Lunatic Asylum, England. Captain Burke claims to be a citizen of the United States of America, and Served with fidelity and distinction in the Federal Army during the late War. His claim to citizenship has been admitted by the United States Government, and his Services as a Soldier acknowledged. His case has been more than once brought under the notice of the United States ministers at London, and of the Secretary of State at Washington, both by Captain Burke himself, and by his legal representative Mr Merriman, of London I learn from Mr Benjamin Moran's reply to Mr Merriman, published at pages 32 and 33. Ex. Doc. No. 170 that 'the Case of Captain OSullivan Burke is familiar to the legation, and is perfectly well known to the United States government in all its aspects and details.' This being so, I see no necessity for me to reproduce here facts and details with which your Excellency & the United States Government are so thoroughly conversant already. Besides, the facts and details to which Mr Moran's reply has reference are those relating to Captain Burke's trial. With these I have nothing to do. My object in addressing your Excellency and inviting your attention to the case of Captain Burke has no reference to the legality of his trial at the central criminal Court in London, but to the criminality of his treatment in the convict prison at Chatham. I have now before me a letter dated Punishment Ward, Chatham Prison, Kent, 6th December 1869 written by Captain Burke, and embodying in a Condensed form the Substantial facts of a Memorial written by Captain Burke & bearing date 3rd December 1869 addressed & forwarded by him to the Home Secretary for England. In this important letter, for the genuineness of which I can vouch, Captain Burke charges the British Government with attempting to poison him by administering to him deletereous drugs in his medicine and food.... This letter of Captain Burke is of considerable length, and contains a circumstantial account of the effects of those Drugs upon him, and he States it as his beleif and conviction, that they contained some Salt of Mercury. He gives day & date for what he says & when & where he suffered. So dreadful was their action upon the Brain and Nervous System that he apprehended the loss of his Reason and that apprehension was but too well founded for within less than ten days after he received the last terrible dose he was removed from 'the able-bodied' convict Prison of Chatham to the Invalid Convict prison of Woking a Lunatic & an Imbecil. This occurred on the 10th day of December 1869, and on the 30th day of August 1870 he was taken to the Convict Lunatic Asylum of Broadmoor having been pronounced in a confirmed State of Dementia, by at least half a dozen of the ablest medical men in Great Britain, all of whom had been Specially Selected by the British government lest they should have any Sympathy with the Irish Political Felon.... Before I close this already long letter I feel bound in justice to my friend & late fellow prisoner to say that the American government should not over look the enormity of the crime charged by Captain Burke against the British government Simply because by an accident or rather an effort of nature he survived the effects of the powerful drugs administered to him. Had the vomiting & purging been less violent, the probability is that Captain Burke would have been found in a *dead-house* instead of a *mad-house* on the morning of the 8th December 1869 Had this been so, & had his letter, fully authenticate[d] fallen into the hands of the American Minister at London, or the Secretary of State at Washington would the American government be satisfied, or would it be justified before its own people & the world at large in accepting the contradictory explanations given by the medical officers of the convict prison whom he had charged with poisoning him? or even with the assurance of the first minister of the crown that he died from natural causes by the visitation of god, as cornor's juries invariably find to be the case of all who have the misfortune to die in convict prisons even when they succumb under the cat o'nine tails steeped in brine & loaded with lead. If under the circumstances I have described the American government would have instituted an inquiry into the *cause of death*, I can not well see how it can refuse to demand an investigation into the *cause of the Insanity*, which detains in Penal Servitude a loyal citizen of the United States a gallant Soldier & brave defender of the great Republic of America. Having to the best of my humble ability brought the case under your Excellency's notice, I now leave it in your hands, hoping it will receive ~~that~~ the immediate attention of the American government & that an effort worthy of the United States be made without delay to obtain the absolute & speedy release of Captain Ricard O Sullivan Burke, and ample Satisfaction demanded of the British government if the charges made by Captain Burke be satisfactorily proved." ALS, *ibid.* See *PUSG*, 18, 84; *ibid.*, 20, 115–18.

On Feb. 22, a correspondent had reported from Washington, D. C. "The Fenian exiles, thirteen in number, called at the executive mansion to-day, in accordance with a previous arrangement, and were introduced to the President by a member of the City Council of Washington. After paying their respects a short conversation ensued. The Fenians assured the President that their treatment in the English prisons had told severely upon the health of some of them, and expressed an anxiety to present a written statement of their case to this government. To this the President responded that they could do so, and whatever was proper to be done by the government would be performed." *Missouri Democrat*, Feb. 23, 1871.

On March 27, John Warren, New York City, wrote to USG. "I had the honer of calling on your Excellency on Tuesday the 21st. inst., on which occasion I called your attention to a former interview with reference to my claim aginst the English Goverment for false imprisonment, which claim was printed by order of the senate, and referred to you by a vote of the House *for action.* The papers at that time were not submitted to your Excellency; but you promised me to give immediate and personal attention to it. Since then I have received a communication (which I hope was urged by your Excellency), in answer to one of mine of the 10th inst. seeking information bearing on the above subject. Ernestly concluding that your Excellency means to forthwith remove the charge from your administration, of giving precedence to the question of a personal, pecunary, loss in cod fish cotten &c., by overlooking the important principal involved in the case of the humble writer of this note, and thereby apparently ignoring the sacred rights of the American Citizen—I herewith enclose for your Excellency's observation an abstract of the points in my case as follows:—1st—According to the naturalization laws of the United States I am an American Citizen, entitled to all the previleges and protection thereof. 2nd I landded in Ireland on the First day of June 1867., and in a few hours afterwards was arrested while peacably riding along a public road. I had committed no overt act; had no documents or weapons of any kind in my possession. 3d After said arrest, I was kept in prison for four and a half months; treated as an ordinary convict, having no charge of any kind preferred aginst me. 4th At the end of the above period I was indicted and con~~vic~~mmitted and tried a few days after a victim to the old Fudal Dogma 'On~~e~~ce a subject and always'; claimed as a British subject; and under the law of constructive treason as a co-conspiritor convicted for an *overt act* committed by others three months before my arrival in the country. 5th That the English Officials admitted that I was in NewYork City when the *overt act* was committed for which I was tried and convicted. 6th That according to the laws of England a mixed jury is awarded to aliens. That I claimed by virtue of my naturalization to be an alien; filed my plea as such, which was indignantly, insultingly, and defiantly repudiated, and the offecial answer given was *'That I did not have the right to change my allegi~~e~~ance neither did the United States have the right to confer theirs on me'* 7th That I in my turn indignantly ignored the jurisdiction of the court; dismissed my counsel; left the case go by default; was convicted and sentenced to 15 years penal servitude; two years of which I served with all its indignities, degradations and hardships, 8th That at the end of the last mentioned period I was with a number of other prisoners of the same class discharged by an act of clemency on the part of the Queen, yet styled and claimed as a British subject. 9th After my arrival in this country I placed my claim before your Excellency, and you promptly and kindly gave me a note of recommendation to the Sec. of State, to whom I submitted facts bearing on the case in question. 10th That I concluded from the interview with the sec. of state that it was my imperative duty to give publicity to my case, and seek redress thro. Congress. That I accordingly prepared a memorial compiled from the English Offecial report of my trial, which I had presented in the senate by senator Wilson, and in the House by Gen. Banks—*which Memorial is now in the hands of your Excellency for final action.* 11th That the obligation rests now entirely with your Excellency, and millions wait with intense anxiety the result viz:—If the soldier President will give precedence to private, individual, pecuniary, cod fish claims, to that of the *sacred violated rights of the American Citizen Soldier.* . . . 12th My friend Col. Wm Roberts M. C. will place this note in your Excellency's hands, and I humbly pay you will give him an answer" ALS, DNA, RG 59, Miscellaneous Letters. A printed copy of Warren's memorial to Congress is *ibid.* On April 17, Edward McPherson, clerk, U.S. House of Representatives, forwarded a resolution passed on motion of U.S. Representative William R. Roberts of N. Y. "That the President of the United States be requested to intercede with the Authorities of the Dominion of Canada for the release of American citizens now confined in Canadian Prisons." DS, *ibid.* On July 7, Roberts, New York City, wrote to USG. "On the 17th of last April, I had the honor [o]f presenting in the House of Representatives, a resolution, which passed the House Unanimously—requesting the President of the United States, to interceede, with the proper authorities of the Dominion of Canada, for the release of American Citizens, held as political pris[o]ners, in the Dungeons of Canada. May I ask if your Excellency, has taken any [S]teps, to carry out the purpose of the resolution, and [if] So, with what result. The deep interest which I take in the fate of [t]hese prisoners, & the desire of their relatives, & of their friends [t]hroughout the United States, to see them, enjoying, once more, the freedom of their Country, will I trust, be sufficient excuse for my anxiety, to learn the result of your efforts in their behalf; Hoping for an early reply. . . ." ALS, *ibid.* See *CG*, 42-1, 736; *New York Herald*, April 30, 1871.

On April 14, Fish had written in his diary. "*Cabinet* all present—. . . On 10 April a letter was sent to the State Department ~~from the~~ (referred by the President) addressed to him by Col John Warren, dated NewYork March 27, in which Warrens claims the intervention of the U. S. to recover damages against G. Britain, for his arrest—trial, conviction & imprisonment, for 'Treason Felony'—the letter was referred without instructions—I ask what he desires to have done with it—he replies that he scarcely read it, but seeing to what it referred had sent it to the State Dept—I enquire whether he wishes it to be answered—he says 'no'—I then ask if it will be sufficient to file it—to which he replies 'yes' file it'—Previous to the introduction of this subject, Atty Genl—had alluded to a letter he had recd from D Wemys Jobson—whom the Prsdt said 'he knew & that he was crazy'—I introduced the subject of Warren's letter, as 'from another troublesome fellow'—" DLC-Hamilton Fish. See *HED*, 40-3-66; *SMD*, 41-2-141; Brian Jenkins, *Fenians and Anglo-American Relations during Reconstruction* (Ithaca, 1969), pp. 237–50, 295–96.

On March 4, 1875, Warren wrote to Fish. "I received yours of the 2d instant with the enclosed copy of the Treaty between Great Britain and this Country for which please accept my thanks Seeing your kindly feeling towards me I will ask of you to interest yourself in another proposition. I have not been successful in business lately, and also have had some *domestic troubles*, both of which forse on to me the necessity of a change. I have in consequence come to the conclusion to make application to you and the President for an appointment to some Consulship or foreign mission, and take this oppertunity to aske your advise with reference to it.

I can obtain the influence of Tom Murphy, Gen Aurther, Gen Sharp, Gen. Jones, Col. James, and hundreds of others if necessary, but prefer this my first application to you" ALS, DNA, RG 59, Letters of Application and Recommendation. No appointment followed.

In a letter docketed June 16, 1871, John C. Tiffany had written to USG. "Ear this i Pray has given notice to the Partition intrusted to your Venarable Father to Present to you in regard to a Fenian Prisonar Confined in Kingston Penitentiary Canada. One word from your Excellency to. Sir John. A. McDonnial would secure said Owen Kennedys release. Others as i Pray you may give this Subject Notice and interfear in his behalf He has been confined Five Years and has an aged Father and feable. Sirter who would be gratley benefited by his sirvices at home Have Mercy and grant you may make glade and happy thoes on the Virge of the Grave" ALS, *ibid.*, Miscellaneous Letters.

To Hamilton Fish

Washington D. C. March 13d *18*71

DEAR GOVERNOR:

If no apt. has been promised for the Consulship, made vacant at Pernambuco[1] by the declention of Mr. Houghton,[2] you may appoint Jas. M. Wilson,[3] of Mo.

Yours Truly
U. S. GRANT

HON. H. FISH,
SEC. OF STATE

ALS, DLC-Hamilton Fish.

1. On Feb. 8, 1871, George Opdyke, New York City, wrote to USG. "Jos. W. Stryker of this State has made application to the State Department for the Consulship at Bahia or at Rio Grande du sul in Brazil. He informes me that the former is now filled by a democrat, and that the latter is vacant His application is well endorsed, and I have pleasure in adding the assurance that he is a gentleman of good character, ability and education, and also a firm supporter of your Administration. His appoint to either position would be gratefully appreciated by me" ALS, DNA, RG 59, Letters of Application and Recommendation. On Feb. 13, USG endorsed this letter. "If Mr. Opdyke can be accomodated in this matter I will be pleased." AES, *ibid.* Related papers are *ibid.* On March 31, Orville E. Babcock wrote to Secretary of State Hamilton Fish. "The President directs me to say that he will be pleased if you will have Mr. Jas W. Stryker of New York, who is recommended by Mr. Opdyke, nominated for the Consulate of Pernambuco." Copy, DLC-USG, II, 1. Joseph W. Stryker was Opdyke's nephew.

On Feb. 28, U.S. Senators John Pool and Joseph C. Abbott of N. C. had written to USG. "Mr Geo. B. Bergen applies for the Consulship at Odessa. I believe him fully qualified to discharge the duties of the position, & his services in the Army during the rebellion were such as to intitle him to high consideration from the Governmt. He is a lawyer by profession & has seen considerable practice in the City of Philadelphia, as acting Solicitor of the City, & in private causes." LS, DNA, RG 59, Letters of Application and Recommendation. On March 1, USG endorsed this letter. "If vacancy exists I would like this appointment to be made." AES, *ibid.* Dating his letter March 16, Pool wrote to USG. "Col. Bergen informs me that he has been given hopes of appointment as a Consul to Pernambuco, Brazil—but is uneasy at the delay—Unless there be some reasons to the contrary, may I ask that action be taken in the case, at some early time?" ALS, *ibid.* USG endorsed this letter. "No objection to this apt." AES (dated March 15), *ibid.* On March 17, USG nominated George B. Bergen as consul, Pernambuco. On March 27, Israel G. Lash, Salem, N. C., wrote to Robert M. Douglas. "The nomination of Burgin as Consul to Pernambucco I fear has been a mistake and if confirmed by the Senate will have a damaging effect Can you not intimate to the President that the withdrawell of his name would be very satisfactory to a large portion of the inteligent & influential Republicans in this State. I am at a loss to know what kind of influence was brot to bear in this Case. The President certainly did not know that he is the notorious Burgin referred to by Witnesses before the Outrages Committee" ALS, *ibid.* On March 29, Douglas endorsed this letter. "Respectfully referred to the Hon. Secretary of State. Hon. I. G. Lash, late Member from the 5 Dist. of N. Carolina, is one of the most prominent, reliable, and influential Republicans in the state." AES, *ibid.* On the same day, Babcock wrote to Fish. "The President directs me to say that from what he has learned of Mr Geo. B. Bergen of N. C., since his nomination as Consul at Pernambuco, on the 17th. inst. he does not believe him to be a proper person for that position and requests that you have prepared a withdrawal of his name from the Senate." LS, *ibid.* On March 30, Pool wrote to USG. "The recommendation of Col. Bergen for appointment to a consulship was made after he had sworn that the charges against him, for conduct in North Carolina, were false, . . . I now beg leave respectfully to request that the nomination be withdrawn" LS, *ibid.* See message to Senate, Jan. 17, 1871; *SRC*, 42-1-1, 150–57.

2. Horace H. Houghton, born in 1806 at Springfield, Vt., a printer in New York City, Boston, and Vt., began his long association with the *Galena Gazette* in 1835. See *PUSG*, 18, 394. On April 2, 1869, USG nominated Houghton as consul, Lahaina, Hawaii. On March 20, 1871, Houghton, Galena, wrote to USG. "I take the liberty of enclosing to you with this a letter from Dr. J. S. McGrew, Physician and Surgeon of the U. S. Marine Hospital at Honolulu, H. I. When last there I had a knowledge, by personal observation, of the present good condition of the Hospital, referred to in the letter of Dr. McG., and I learned by report, of the uncomfortably disgraceful condition in which he had previously found it, on taking possession. He has been at considerable expense in fitting up the premises, and they are now extensive enough, cleanly, comfortable, and in every way proper. Further, I was credibly informed that the doctor was reaping no adequate regard for his highly skilful services under the present arrangement. I think he is losing money by it. His withdrawal from the post would be a severe loss to the unfortunates of the class whom he so well befriends, and many of whom owe to him the salvation of their lives. Dr. McGrew is highly regarded in Honolulu, is an honor to American citizenship, and has a large private practic[e.] If any thing can be done for his relief, in legal propriety, I have no doubt it will receive from you due consideration." ALS, DNA, RG 59, Miscellaneous Letters. The enclosure is a letter of Feb. 27 from John S. McGrew, Honolulu, to

Houghton. "Your very welcome letter of Jan 11th came to hand pr last Steamer—but too late for an answer on her return—I hope that you have found things more to your satisfaction on your arrival, and that our 'mutual friend,' in Washington has changed the 'situation' of affairs to your general liking—. . . It is a well known fact that my Hospital is far superior to any thing of the kind ever upon these Islands. When Dr Judd sold out to me, the place was not actually fit for a *pig-pen.* I went to large expenditures to make it a fit place for American Seamen, after which it seems some fatality had to follow, as I have not had enough men to pay the interest on my out lay—Dr Judd had it under contract—which saved him from loses, if he was compelled to keep it open, with only one or two in it—he was paid for it—Enclosed I send you a copy—If I could get an agreement of a similar kind it would save me from loses and enable me to keep a respectable place, as I now have here, for the accommodation of American Seamen who are destitute and thrown upon the hands of the Consul—I have addressed a letter to Major Mattoon, the US Consul here, embracing all the points laid down ~~here~~, which I suppose he will forward to Washington, in a dispatch, with his own views in regard it—Any thing you will do for me will be ever remembered as a great kindness" ALS, *ibid.* For McGrew, see *PUSG*, 19, 239.

On Nov. 5, 1870, Babcock had written to Elijah Jones, Galena. "The President directs me to acknowledge the receipt of your letter and to inform you that the consulate of Lahaina, at which Mr. Houghton has been for the last year, has been discontinued and Mr. H. was transferred to Pernambuco." Copy, DLC-USG, II, 1. On Dec. 28, McGrew, Honolulu, wrote to Babcock. "Mr H. H. Houghton our late U. S. Consul at Lahaina being about to return to Washington on business, I embrace th~~ise~~ opportunity of sending you this hastily written note by him—I have learned from Mr Houghton that he will not, in all probability, accept the appointment of Consul to Pernambuco, in that case he will present the name of a young friend of mine, Mr J. S. Christie—of New Jersey—Mr Christie is competent is of good family, a good Republican, a firm friend of our mutual devotions, President Grant, and I sincerely hope that you will aid him with your influence for the place. New Jersey deserves something now that she has done so nobly—" ALS, DNA, RG 59, Letters of Application and Recommendation. On Feb. 10, 1875, Jonathan S. Christie, Jr., Washington, D. C., wrote to USG. "I respectfully solicit the appointment of United States Consul at Hong Kong, . . ." ALS, *ibid.* Related papers are *ibid.* On March 5, Babcock wrote to Fish. "The President directs me to say that you are authorized to appoint Mr J. S. Christie, Marshal of the Consular Courts of Japan and if you have no other views you may nominate Mr Buckalow to the small Consulate in Germany which you spoke to Mr Frelinghuysen of yesterday" LS, *ibid.*

On Dec. 13, 1872, Babcock wrote to Houghton, Galena. "The President desires me to acknowledge the receipt of your letter of the 19th ultimo and say that he has intended to appoint you to the position you desire, when the time came, and that it will afford him pleasure to do so." Copy, DLC-USG, II, 1. On March 10, 1873, USG nominated Houghton as postmaster, Galena.

3. On March 20, 1871, USG nominated James M. Wilson as consul, Nuremberg.

To Powell Clayton

Washington, D. C. March 13 1871

GOV. P. CLAYTON,[1]
LITTLE ROCK, ARK.

I will be glad to aid any way in my power to heal differences in your state, but can make no absolute promises.

U. S. GRANT

Copy, DLC-USG, II, 5. On March 14, 1871, John A. Joyce, Little Rock, wrote to Orville E. Babcock. "*Personal.* . . . You will have learned long ere this reaches its distination that Hon. Powell Clayton has been elected to the United States Senate from Arkansas for six years. *This result is an Administration triumph,* and secures the electoral vote of the state for the Republican party and General Grant in 1872! You can depend on what I say, and I tell you now that Clayton will work with the President if he gets half a chance! I send an opinion of Judge Caldwell in the Tobacco cases &c. I am on the look out for Genl. Grant." ALS, ICN. On March 25, Babcock wrote to Joyce. "Your letter is at hand. I read it to the President. I think Clayton will have no trouble, you know how we all stand on that subject. . . ." ADf (initialed) and LS, *ibid.* On Jan. 25, 1872, during a meeting with "anti-Clayton men from Arkansas," USG "said he had never intended to interfere in the case of Senator Clayton, and had no feeling in the matter. It was true that he had made some changes in the Federal offices in the State, but where they were shown to be bad he would gladly annul them. It was also his desire that the charges against Clayton should be thoroughly investigated." *Philadelphia Public Ledger,* Jan. 26, 1872. For Governor Powell Clayton and Ark. political factions, see note to William W. Belknap, Feb. 19, 1871; letter to Amos T. Akerman, April 13, 1871; *PUSG,* 19, 111–13; Clayton, *The Aftermath of the Civil War, In Arkansas* (1915; reprinted, New York, 1969); Orval Truman Driggs, Jr., "The Issues of the Powell Clayton Regime, 1868–1871," *Arkansas Historical Quarterly,* VIII, 1 (Spring, 1949), 1–75.

1. Clayton, born in 1833 in Bethel County, Pa., attended Partridge Military Academy in Bristol, Pa., and studied civil engineering at Wilmington, Del. Elected city engineer and surveyor as a Douglas Democrat in Leavenworth, Kan. (1859), he served in the 1st Kan. and 5th Kan. Cav. and won promotion to brig. gen. for his defense of Pine Bluff, Ark. (1864). Becoming a cotton planter and Republican in Ark., he won an unopposed election for governor (1868). On March 25, 1870, USG had telegraphed to Clayton. "Immediately upon confirmation" Telegram sent, Arkansas History Commission, Little Rock, Ark. On Aug. 30, Clayton wrote to USG. "I have [t]he honor to foreward herewith, a [c]ommunication from Judge Stephenson in relation to the establishment of the Land Office at Huntsville. Ark and requesting the appointment of James S. Shrigly and U. H. H. Clayton as Register and Receiver in that Departmt I have deemed it proper heretofore to leave the question of Federal Appointments to our delegation in Congress, but as one of the Parties recommended is my Brother I have been reluctant to ask others to intercede in his behalf and feel that the relations existing between Your Excellency and myself, are such as to permit me to ask his appointmt as a personal favor at your hands" ALS (press), *ibid.*

To Amos T. Akerman

Washington D. C. Mch. 15. 71.

HON: A. T. AKERMAN
ATTORNEY GENERAL
DEAR SIR

Understanding that a Judge[1] in Idaho Territory has resigned I would designate Mad. E. Hollister of Ills. to the vacancy if no promise has been made to another

truly yours
U. S. GRANT.

Copy, DLC-USG, II, 1. Madison E. Hollister, born in 1808 in Cayuga County, N. Y., studied law, and settled in Ottawa, Ill. (1836). A Democratic presidential elector (1848) who became a Republican, he served as judge, 9th judicial district (1855–66), and consul, Buenos Aires (1866–69). See *PUSG*, 20, 396.

1. Joseph R. Lewis. See Endorsement, Dec. 21, 1871; Ronald H. Limbaugh, *Rocky Mountain Carpetbaggers: Idaho's Territorial Governors, 1863–1890* (Moscow, Idaho, 1982), pp. 89–90.

To George S. Boutwell

Washington D. C. March 15. 1871

HON: GEO: S. BOUTWELL
SEC'Y: OF THE TREASURY.
DEAR SIR:

Enclosed I send you the resignation of Mr. Moore,[1] Collector of Customs Phila. Pa.

Before there is strife for the place I suggest nominating John Tucker[2] for the vacant place

Truly yours
U. S. GRANT.

Copy, DLC-USG, II, 1. See telegram to John W. Forney, March 22, 1871.

1. Henry D. Moore, born in 1817 in Goshen, N. Y., worked in New York City as a tailor, and prospered in Philadelphia in the mahogany and marble business. He served as a Whig U.S. representative (1849–53), lost a bid for mayor of Philadelphia

(1856), and held office as Pa. treasurer (1861–63, 1864–65). On March 17, 1869, USG nominated Moore as collector of customs, Philadelphia. On Feb. 8, 1873, Matthew Baird & Co., J. Gillingham Fell, J. Edgar Thomson, and Thomas A. Scott, Philadelphia, wrote to USG. "We have the honor to recommend the appointment of Hon. Henry D. Moore, who is now residing at St. Petersburg, Russia, as one of the Commissioners to the World's Fair at Vienna. Mr. Moore was a former resident of Philadelphia, and a member of the House of Representatives from this city. Subsequently, for a short time, he was Collector of the Port of Philadelphia. We have been personally acquainted with him for some twenty-five years, and know him to be a gentleman whose character, both in public and private life, has been, in the highest degree, exemplary and above reproach. He was, for many years, connected with the industrial interests of our State, and is thoroughly informed upon all subjects connected therewith. We believe that he is, in every way, qualified to represent his country worthily at the approaching Exposition; and we cordially commend him to your favorable consideration." DS, DNA, RG 59, Letters of Application and Recommendation.

On March 15, 1869, Robert K. Wright, Philadelphia, had written to USG. "Having had considerable business intercourse as an Importer, with our Customs Authorities, it afford me sincere pleasure to testify to the uniform kindness & courtesy of our present Collector Col Ja W Cake—The business interests of our community would undoubtedly be promoted by his retention in his present position and his integrity and capability are undoubted." ALS, *ibid.*, RG 56, Collector of Customs Applications. Related papers are *ibid.*

On March 10, Horace Porter had written to John F. Hartley, asst. secretary of the treasury. "The President directs that the Commission of James N. Marks as Collector of Customs for the District of Philadelphia be mailed to his address." LS, *ibid.* On March 15, James N. Marks, Philadelphia, wrote to USG. "A commission (bearing date March 4, 1869) having been issued by your direction, conferring upon me the appointment and powers of Collector of the Port of Philadelphia I desire respectfully to decline acting under the same, and hereby resign all rights and powers of said appointment or office." ALS, *ibid.*

On March 10, William Cummings, Philadelphia, had written to USG. "Permit me to present myself, an applicant for the Position of Collector of Customs, for the Port of Philadelphia. Herewith I enclose you some testimonials, from my friends, who have been kind enough, to reccommend me for the Office. I also respectfully refer you, to the Hon. Secretary of the Navy, and Aubrey H Smith Esqr. If appointed, my best efforts shall be devoted, to the interest of the Government," ALS, *ibid.* The enclosures are *ibid.*

On March 12, William B. Thomas, Philadelphia, wrote to USG. "Upon the accession of Abraham Lincoln to the Presidency, through *his* partiality and that of my old personal & political friend Gov. Chase, I was appointed Collector of Customs of this Port, This appointmt was unsolisited by me, although the Republican Club (the first in the county) which I had organized, and of which I was President claimed it for me as the Representative of the Radical wing of the successfull party, The Rebelion having already broken out, I very soon perceived the importance of strengthing the government by the organization of our citizens into military companys, And assuming that it was the special duty of those having charge of public property to defend it when attacked, I commenced the organization of the Custom House officials into a 'Revinue Guard,' removing from office such as refused to lend their aid to its defense. In pursuance of this policy I recruited the (1st) & (2nd) companys of 'Revenue Guards,' The governmt being at this time destitute of arms and clothing I supplyed both at an expense of over $6.000 in the aggrigate. Scarcely had I completed these organizations when our state was invaded by Rebels, and I at once March to Harrisburg upon the call of the Governor at their head as Cap. of the 1st Co, Upon my arrival their, the 'Revinue Guards were made the bases of the 20th Regt P. M. of which I was commissioned Colonel. We were ordered down the Cumberland Vally into Maryland and remained in the service of the state untill the rebels were driven from the state, and were then ordered to Phila and mustered out of the service. Upon the 'assumed' invasion of our state, I again offered my services to the govermt was again accepted with with the 20th Reg. mustered into the service during for the 'Emergency' (a verry indefinite period) during which the Regiment performed much severe service, being engaged almost constantly in the construction of fortification, block houses, and rifle pits, when not on the march. But very few Regimts performed more constant and severe labours during the war than did the 20th on this occasion. When the President, in that dark hour of 1864 called for additional troops for 100 Days, I again offered my services to raise one or more Regiments was accepted, and in less than 10 Days was ready to march with the 192 Reg. P. G ranking 1500 men. As on former occasions I again asked leave of absense from my duties as Collector, of Hon the Secy of the Treasury, tendering my resignation of that office in the event the Secretary declined to grant the leave of absence, ~~feeling~~ because I felt that at this critical moment, when the destiny of the Union seemed to be trembling in the balance, ~~that~~ it was the duty of every able bodyed man to enter the army and serve his country in its hour of need, The Secretary refused to accept my resignation but granted leave of absense and instructed me to nominate for his approval a Depty. Collector, which I did and left Phila with my Reg. for Baltimore on the 7th July was ordered to Ft. McHenry for garrison duty, thence to Johnsons Island Lake Erie, to guard the prisoners confined there, whose liberation was threatened, ~~and~~ from thence to Gallipoliss Ohio. and from thence to Western Va. After performing every duty (as we have reason to know) to the satisfaction of our superior officers we were mustered out on the 15th Nov. at Phila having been in service about 5 months. Being engaged in private business which yielded me all the money which my necssities required, I resolved when I accepted the post of Collector, not to retain any part of the public moneys received as salary, but to expend it for patriotic and benevolent purposes. I therefore appropriated all my ~~receipts~~ salary as Collector my pay as colonel—and receipts from ~~this~~ office source to charitable purposes, encouraging enlistments, and raising Regiments. I have now in my possession the recepts ~~for receipts~~ of the diferent soldiers refreshmt saloons and charitable accounts covering all the samples of sugars. liquors. molases &c. drawn during my administration and which usually constitute the valuable perquisites of the Collectors office. Uppon my return from the Army I found, upon an examination of the Custom House accounts, that my Cashier had embezzeled $80.000 of the funds of the Goverment. Seeing that the hour for his exposure had come, he pretended that his dwelling had been entered, the Customs vault keys stolen, the vault entered and the mony stolen. He was arrested and after remaining in prison about eight months he was released on bail and is now a fugitive from Justice. Notwithstanding I was absent with the permission of the Secy. of the Treasury in the service of my country, and the Custom house in charge of another officer approved by the secretary upon whom devolved the duties as well as the responsibilities of the Collector. So anxious was I that, our political enemys should not say that the peoples money's were lost by a Republican office holder that I resolved to pay ~~the~~ whatever deficency should be found to exist with my private funds and did so pay over $70.000 about

$10.000 having be~~ing~~en recovered from the Cashier, although there was no moral, ~~if there was~~ or legal obligation resting upon me to do so. These statements will be verrified by Secretary's of the Treasury Chase & McCulloch. When Andrew Johnson resolved to antagonizing Congress & organizing a party of his own, I was urgently entreated to give the movemt my support, and was offered the controll of his entire patronage in Pa. if I would doo so. This I indignantly refused to do in a published card, and this was (as I believe) the first instance of a Federal office holder under him opposing his contemplated project. I should have said that I was reappointed by Prest Jonhson upon the expiration of my term office at the urgent request of the Merchants of Phila without regard to party. When the question of a successor to Prest. Johnson was being agitated by the Republican party, I was in favour of my life long personal and political friend Gov. Chase. Entertaining an ardent admiration for him as a statesman and a sense of deep gratitude for his partiality in recommending me for an honourable position to Prest Lincoln, and for the confidence he always reposed in m~~y~~e as expressed in many kind letters to me. So strong was & is my regard for him, that, I should have sustained his election even though he should have been the nominee of the Democratic party, *if uppon a platform which I could have approved.* Upon the nomination of Seymour & Blair, I at once expressed my determination to support the Chicago nominees, and thereafter exertoned myself to the Extent of my ability (and I think with some effect) to promote their election. I do not claim to have been one of your E[xcellencys o]rigina[l] supporters for the Presidency, and candidly admit that I should have much prefered, that the 'great Captain' of our political salvation, would have remained for life at the head of the army which he led to so many victories, and which he had also rendered so glorious in the eye of all the nations of the earth. rather than to have become the target of political attack for four or at most eight short years. I do not intend to approach you in person or by proxy as an applicant for office. Indeed I have refrained ~~from participating~~ from participating in deminstrations intended to doo you honour lest selfish motives ~~should~~ be ascribed to me. I am sure however that 90. pr ct. of the Merchants and citizens of Phil without regard to party in view of my losses and services & sacrifices for the Union whilst in office, and ~~o~~if the satisfactory manner in which my former administration was conducted. and of the further fact that of all those who now aspire to the office of Collector of Customs, none can present a higher claim than mere *party feality*, desire my re-appointmt and would urge it, if I should publicly avow myself a candidate, In conclusion allow me to say that, my present purpose in addressing to your Excellency, this long letter, which I would have made shorter had it been practicable, is to place within your knowledge all the facts in my case so that, if there is merit in my claim, your keen perciption of the right may detect it. and to say that, should you consider my claim to the office of Collector of Customs of this Port, paramount to others, (all things considered) I shall consider myself highly honoured and as being placed under obligation beyond my ability to repay. As to my qualifications for the office I will refer with great confidence to Secretarys McCulloch & Chase as well as to a large number of testimonals on file in the Treasury department, Whilst occupying the office under Prest Lincoln. I assumed the position that Members of Congress were elected by the people to make laws for them, and not appoint officials in the Custom houses for the proper performance of whose duties the Prest. Secry. of the Treasry & the Collector were responsible, and that whilst I would give their recommendations due consideration they must not expect me in all cases to comply with their requests, An attempt was made by them to effect my removal on this account, but my action was so thorougholy sustained by our merchants, the people and the press including the Tribune of NewYork, that their defeat was overwhelming I notice that they are now demanding the same controll over subordinate appontmts and it is not likely that they could be induced to favour one opposed to their pretentions, although our personal relations are quite friendly," ALS, *ibid.*

On March 15, James H. Orne, Philadelphia, wrote to USG. "I desire to present for your favourable Consideration the name of John E. Addicks for collector of the Port of Phila. I have known Mr Addicks for many years and think him capable in every way to fill the office. He has been a most loyal citizen during the war, aiding and assisting in every way to support the goverment, and I think his appointment will give general Satisfaction to all parties, and I should consider myself under obligations if you can entertain it favourably." ALS, *ibid.* Related petitions are *ibid.*

2. John Tucker, a railroad official and entrepreneur from Philadelphia, received an appointment from Secretary of War Simon Cameron as general agent of transportation on May 8, 1861. On Jan. 23, 1862, President Abraham Lincoln nominated Tucker as asst. secretary of war. Tucker was asst. secretary of war until Jan. 21, 1863. See *HRC*, 37-2-2, part 2, pp. 306–26; *Senate Executive Journal*, XII, 99–100; *PUSG*, 15, 354–55; *O.R.*, III, i, 175; *ibid.*, iii, 1199; John Tucker to Simon Cameron, Jan. 23, 1865, DLC-Abraham Lincoln; Samuel Richey Kamm, *The Civil War Career of Thomas A. Scott* (Philadelphia, 1940), pp. 83–84.

To Charles W. Ford

Washington D. C. March 15th *18*71

Dear Ford:

I have neglected to answer your question as to whether I would compromise any of the Carondelet land at $50 pr arpent! I will not compromise any more at less than $100. As soon as I can get out of my office I will have the deed which you sent to me executed. If Congress adjourns any time before the 10th of Apl. I shall start immediately for St Louis and spend three or four days there looking after my affairs.

Yours Truly
U. S. Grant

ALS, DLC-USG. On March 2, 1871, Charles W. Ford, St. Louis, wrote to USG. "I enclose you a quit Claim deed to Geo T Hulse. for your signature, if it is all right. You will have to fill up the blanks in the deed—I told Mr Hulse that I thought you might be out here during the month—and possibly retain this until you came—If you execute it & send to me—I will attend to it and remit the proceeds or otherwise as you may direct." ALS, USG 3. On Feb. 27, George T. Hulse, cashier, Mechanic's Bank, St. Louis, wrote to Ford. "Enclosed please find deed filled in part, (to be completed at

Washington) for the land included in the compromise between Genl. Grant and myself, which you will please forward to be signed stamped and acknowledged. I will also expect with the return of the deed, such papers as are necessary, to a dismissal of the suit against me free of cost. I am not advised whether the land referred to is claimed by the elder Mr Dent, or his sons, or by them jointly. I enter upon this compromise on the supposition that Genl. Grant is fully authorized to convey for either or all claiming an interest in the land, and that his authority is a matter of record in St. Louis County." LS, *ibid.*

To Alexander G. Cattell

Washington D. C. Mch. 21[3?]./71.

HON A. G. CATTELL
DEAR SIR:

Your letter of yesterday, saying that you observe reports that I desire an extension of the present Session of Congress to push through Santo Domingo Annexation; also that at the opening of the present session of Congress I desired a reconstruction of the Senate Committee on Foreign Relations for the purpose of securing favorable action upon the question of annexation is received.

Both these statements are unequivically and unqualifiedly untrue. I did not want a March term of Congress for any other purpose whatever than to provide better means of protection for life and property in disturbed Sections of the Country. So doubtful was I about Congress agreeing upon a measure to secure that end, and so fearful that other legislation might be entered upon, that I hesitated about making any recommendation on the subject as much as I felt the necessity for congressional action upon the subject referred to. In regard to the second slander, as I deem it fair to call it, I had no expectation that the Santo Domingo matter would come before the Senate at this Session of Congress. My views upon that subject, of the annexation of Santo Domingo, were formed from the report made by gentlemen in whose ability, integrity and judgement I have the most unbounded confidence. These views were honestly laid before the Senate in a special message and in my message to Congress last December. I never wished to make the annexation of Santo Dominga a party question, or the support of it a party test. I never asked to have any particular person put upon any one of the Senate standing Committees. All that I have asked is that the Chairman of the Committee on Foreign Relations might be some one with whom the Secretary of State and myself might confer and advise. This I deemed due to the Country in view of the very important questions, which, of necessity, must come before it.

I will add here that the treaty for the annexation of Santo Domingo, honestly entertained by me as for the best interests of the two people was not only rejected by the Senate of the United States but insinuations of fraud, corruption, crime and a catalogue of Sins were attributed to all concerned in negotiating it. This reasons and my belief that the Country would demand the admission of Santo Domingo if the question were thoroughly understood, let me to ask for a commission to visit that republic. My desire was to vindicate myself and the gentlemen whom I had selected to visit that country. Also to get all the light I could for the people, Congress and myself on the subject.

Further action on my part will be determined by the report that will be made by the eminent gentlemen selected by me to serve on that commission. All that I ask is the same liberality on the part of the public and Congress.

"I have no policy to enforce against the will of the people".

I have the honor to be with great respect

Your obt: Svt:
U. S. GRANT.[1]

Copy, DLC-USG, II, 1. On March 22, 1871, Alexander G. Cattell, Philadelphia, wrote to USG. "I do not fail to observe statements made in many of the newspapers of the Country and which statements are extensively repeated by individuals, that you desire an extension of the present Session of Congress for the purpose of Submitting the report of the San Domingo Commissioners with a view to the Action of Congress on the question of Annexation at this Session—~~a~~And Coupled with this I observe also the Statement that at the opening of the present Congress, you desired a reconstruction of the Senate Committee on Foreign ~~Affairs~~ relations—for the purpose of securing favorable Action upon the question of Annexation—From what I have gathered in Casual interviews with you, I am Sure these reports are wholly erroneous, and believing they are being used to mislead the public mind, I have taken the liberty of addressing you on the Subject, and would be glad if Consistent with your views of propriety to have an Authoritative Statement touching these points—" ALS, USG 3.

In 1872, Cattell wrote to USG. "The 'bloody chasm' show don't seem to take with loyal people, and I guess it will be withdrawn. Exit Greely, Brown, Shurts, Trumble & Co." William Evarts Benjamin, Catalogue No. 27, Nov., 1889, p. 6. Cattell had also written to USG in 1871. *Ibid.* See *PUSG*, 16, 554; *ibid.*, 20, 349.

Cattell, born in 1816 in Salem, N. J., eldest son of a leading merchant and banker, moved to Philadelphia (1846), where he served on the common council (1848–54) while rising to business prominence. Establishing a residence near Merchantville, N. J. (1855), he became an active Republican and U.S. senator (1866–71). On Oct. 29, 1866, Cattell, Camden, N. J., had written to USG. "My young friend Cap William P. Robeson, who was appointed as you will doubtless remember on my recommendation has just passed his examination, and received orders to report without delay at Fort Riley Kan He desires if possible to be allowed a week to make preperations for his departure, and his brother Gen Geo. M Robeson left at your Head Quarters, on Saturday an application for this time—If this can be allowed without any detrement to the Service, I will be greatly obliged if you will Kindly grant the request—If however the Service will in your opinion Suffer by his delay, he will leave for his post at once" ALS, DNA, RG 94, Letters Received, 430R 1866. On Nov. 2, George M. Robeson, Philadelphia, telegraphed to Maj. George K. Leet. "Has Leave certainly been granted Captain Robeson, 7th Cavalry as you informed Col Allison? Order not received—Please telegraph me at Camden" Telegram received (at 4:40 P.M.), *ibid.*, RG 108, Telegrams Received. On Nov. 3, Leet telegraphed to Robeson. "Permission to delay for seven days has been granted Capt. Robeson" Copies, DLC-USG, V, 47, 60; DNA, RG 108, Letters Sent.

On Oct. 14, 1867, Cattell, Philadelphia, wrote to USG. "My friend Mr William Coffin who will present this letter, is interested in Edward C. Shinn a private in the 34th U. S Infantry, and hopes to be able to Secure a Commission for him—Mr Shinn is from my County and is of highly respectable family—I have know his Father for many years, lived in the Same town with him, and take great pleasure in vouching for him as one of the most respectable Citizens of our County I will only add that I Shall be much pleased if you Can grant Mr Coffins request" ALS, *ibid.*, RG 94, ACP, S1345 CB 1867.

On Dec. 19, 1870, Horace Porter wrote to Alexander G. Cattell & Co., Philadelphia. "I enclose you the Presidents' check for $236 98, the amount of your bill of the 17th. inst. for oats. I return herewith the bill, which please receipt and return." Copy, DLC-USG, II, 1.

On June 16, Cattell, Philadelphia, wrote to USG. "My young friend Charles Clifford Heisley, whose name you kindly added to the list of Alternates for West Point, was not reachd—Nine out of the ten of your appointmts passed—If Heisley's name could be placed among the ten for the next class I would be very much pleased You will remember, that he is the son of a chaplain who served with great credit, for three years and the boy himself was in the Army as Drummer Boy for a year and a half—Mr Heisley is a popular Minister in the Methodist Church, now Stationed at New Brunswick N. J and would feel the appointmt of his son to be a great favor" ALS, DNA, RG 94, Correspondence, USMA. On Jan. 27, 1873, Charles W. Heisley, New Brunswick, wrote to USG. "I beg leave to have the honor of this personal address. Through the kind offices of Hon A. G. Cattell, you honored my Son last year with appointment, as an alternate to any of Your appointees to cadetship at W. P. M. Academy; and since then, as Mr Cattell informed, to any vacancy that might occur; and in case there were none, then to cadetship as one of your ten at large. Will you please to honor him with appointment to fill one of the vacancies made by two cadets recently?—My Son was enlisted as a musician in the 28th Regt. Pa of, Col. J. W. Geary Ex Gov of Penna, myself being Chaplain for three years. My son was a little over eleven years old, and remained until the Regimental Bands were mustered out just after '2nd Bull Run' Genl. Geary and others who know us well have heretofore sent sufficient commendations through Mr Cattell to you. Please remember that unless my son receive his appointment soon he may be past age. He is abundantly qualified to enter, having applied himself closely since he received the assurances last season. He is a soldier by choice. . . ." ALS, *ibid.* On Jan. 29, Orville E. Babcock wrote to Secretary of War William W. Belknap. "The President directs me to say that he wishes Charles Clifford Hiesley, whose application & recommendations for a military cadetship are on file in your department, designated as one of the cadets to be appointed when the appointments come to be made." LS, *ibid.* On May 26, 1874, Belknap wrote to Cattell. "The Superintendent of the Military Academy, has just reported that Charles Clifford Heisl~~e~~y who was last year appointed a cadet at large by the President, and in whom you are interested, was admitted a cadet to West Point from the First, District of New Jersey in June 1868, at which time he reported his age as eighteen years and eight months. He failed at a subsequent examination in June 1869, and was discharged. According to his statement in 1868, he would now be over the age at which cadets may be admitted to the Military Academy, but besides this fact, which would necessitate the cancelation of his appointment, he now states his age as twenty three years and nine months, and thus makes himself a year younger than his former statement would make him. For this reason the President has directed the cancelation of his appointment, and instructions have been given the Superintendent to that effect." LS (press), *ibid.* On the same day, Charles W. Heisley telegraphed to USG. "Senator Cattell will show that a mistake was surely made at West Point causing your revoking yesterday my son's appointment. Please wait to hear from him" Telegram received, *ibid.* Also on May 26, Belknap wrote to Col. Thomas H. Ruger, superintendent, USMA. "Personal for Gen'l. Ruger—The President has, without remark, sent me a telegram from this man's Father . . . Thus the matter stands" AN (initialed and press), *ibid.*

1. In an undated letter, U.S. Senator Oliver P. Morton of Ind. had written to USG. "Confidential . . . I suggest a letter embracing the following points: ~~That in reply~~ That you do not desire the annexation of San Domingo unless it be in accordance with ~~public~~ the sentiment of the Country. That the Commission ~~of~~ was appointed with the understanding that if they reported against ~~the~~ annexation it would be dropped; that their report would be laid before Congress and the country, and if after full deliberation the sentiment was in favor of annexation you would ~~press it~~ again favor it. That all reports that you desired to ~~Congress~~ hold Congress here to act on it at this session or would call back the Senate back for that purpose are without foundation That all reports that you had attempted to manipulate committees in the Senate to secure favorable action on the annexation question, or had appointed any one to office, or removed any one from office on that account are without foundation. That you have never made it a test question in your intercourse or dealings with members of the Senate as many members can testify. That your own opinion from the first has been that annexation of St Domingo would be of great ad- to the country, ~~and~~ but that you desired the appointment of the Commission to obtain accurate information which would satisfy the country one way or the other. That you thought the investigation was due to you after you had been charged with corruption on the floor of the Senate. That you have only the same interest in it with every other Citizen, and are

sorry systematic efforts have been made to forestall the action of the Commission I think your letter should embrace the substance of the above points and such others as may occur to you." ALS, USG 3.

To John W. Forney

Washington, D. C. March 22d 1871

COL. JNO. W. FORNEY
PHILADELPHIA, PA

I have sent your name to the Senate for Collector. If you prefer the mission to Brazil[1] I shall name you for that office

U. S. GRANT

Copy, DLC-USG, II, 5. On March 22, 1871, U.S. Representative Alfred C. Harmer of Pa. wrote to USG. "I telegraphed Col. Forney urging his acceptance of the Collectorship of the Port of Philada and have received the enclosed reply. Judge Kelly has also just received one of similar import" ALS, PHi. On the same day, a correspondent reported: "Senator Cameron called on the President today, and during his presence there the President had made out the nomination of Colonel John W. Forney as Collector of the Port of Philadelphia, and it was immediately transmitted to the Senate. The Chronicle of this morning is mistaken in stating that Judge Kelley favors Mr. Southworth for this place. He heartily endorses Colonel Forney." *Philadelphia Public Ledger*, March 23, 1871. John W. Forney replaced Henry D. Moore as collector of customs, Philadelphia. See *PUSG*, 20, 164; letter to George S. Boutwell, March 15, 1871; letter to John W. Forney, Feb. 12, 1872.

On March 16, 1871, U.S. Representatives Harmer, Willam D. Kelley, Leonard Myers, and John V. Creely of Pa. had written to USG. "We respectfully recommend D. P. Southworth of Philad, for the Collectorship of that Port. Mr. Southworth is a business man—for years connected with the mercantile interests of Philadelphia and commanding the confidence of all who were brought into connection with him—As Assessor of one of the Phila Districts under President Lincoln his fitness & worth were generally recognized, & appointed afterwards to the Supervisorship of the Eastern District of Pennsylvania he discharged the duties of that office most acceptably until relieved at his own request. Mr. Southworth is honest and competent, and his excellent business qualifications, and sound record will make the selection a popular one" DS, DNA, RG 56, Collector of Customs Applications. On March 8, 1869, Galusha A. Grow, Glenwood, Pa., had written to USG. "D. P. Southworth Esq Supervisor of Internal Revenue for the Eastern District of Pennsylvania is a worthy gentleman of good business habits an early devoted Republican, who has rendered efficient serice to the party His appointment as Consul to Cuba I should regard as a special personal favor" ALS, *ibid.*, RG 59, Letters of Application and Recommendation. About the same time, Kelley and sixteen others petitioned USG to nominate Delos P. Southworth as consul, Havana. DS (undated), *ibid.* A related paper is *ibid.* No appointment followed.

On Feb. 14, 1871, Alex T. Lane, Philadelphia, wrote to USG. "Believing that perhaps you would select a merchant for Collector of Port of Philada I take the liberty of applying for the position I have been a resident of Philada for more than 33 years and in business over 20 years My business at present is Commission in Foreign & Domestic Woolens am favorably known to the merchants & Citizens of Philada & a staunch Republican & during the wars *I subscribed liberally to the cause* Can give Undoubted reference as to character, Integrity & Business qualifications, . . ." ALS, *ibid.*, RG 56, Collector of Customs Applications. On March 1, 1873, Lane wrote to USG. "I called this afternoon on Hon A E Borie supposing he would go to Washington on Monday, desiring him to bear me in mind and speak to you on my behalf—in relation to the Geneva Award, provided the Conference Committee of the Senate and House of Representatives, decided there should be Commissioners appointed Hon Borie is complaining of not feeling very well and thinks it is doubtful whether he will be there on Inaguration day—but perhaps would be—in a few days after I write to say, if it is decided in favor of Commissioners being appointed, and you should honor me with an appointment, I shall be happy to serve as one of the Commissioners. On 17th of January the State Department acknowledged receipt and filing of my testimonials, which you were kind enough to suggest, I should have filed" ALS, *ibid.*, RG 59, Letters of Application and Recommendation. Related papers are *ibid.* No appointment followed.

On March 18, 1871, Seth J. Comly & Co. and others, Philadelphia, petitioned USG. "We, the undersigned citizens and Merchants of the City of Philadelphia, having enjoyed a long and familiar intercourse with E. Harper Jeffries, Esq. can confidently bear testimony to his high order of merit as a gentleman of large mercantile experience, varied intelligence, sterling integrity, and strict adherence to the principles of the Republican party.— . . ." DS, *ibid.*, RG 56, Collector of Customs Applications. On Feb. 13 and 21, 1872, William Brice, Philadelphia, telegraphed to USG. "As President of the Commercial Exchange permit me to say that E Harper Jeffries is the unanimous choice of our Business men for Collector of the Port." "Our Commercial exchange adhere to the almost unanimously expressed preference for E. Harper Jefferies for Collector" Telegrams received (the first at 5:21 P.M.), *ibid.* On Feb. 14, James Steel, Philadelphia, wrote to USG. "I have the honor to commend to you, for appointment as collector of the Port of Philadelphia, E Harper Jefferies late President of our Commercial Exchange, and take leave to say that no one who has been named for this place, in so eminent a degree possesses the Confidence and esteem of Philadelphia Merchants and business men, or who is better qualified for the place—. . ." ALS, *ibid.* Related papers are *ibid.*

On March 21, 1871, F. A. Godwin, Philadelphia, wrote to USG. "This is my first application to you for office I now desire to place myself before you for the Office of Collector of the Port Philada—I will not trouble you much, but only wish to refer you to. Hon A Borie, A J Drexal, Esq. Hon Geo Robeson, Secy Navy, Hon H D Moore, present incumbent; & to the Merchants of Philada *in general.* I have been 25 years engaged in Mercantile pursuits in the city, have had much to do with the Customs & think I am competent I have not seen any of our Congressmen, or either of our Senators, they all me well. Perhaps you honor may give my application a favorable consideration I am *needy*, & have a large family, & have been for many years supporting an aged, & afflicted sister—Any reference you may require can be given May I ask you to take into favorable consideration my application—Hon Geo Robeson can tell you who I am . . . *Please bear me in mind.*" ALS, *ibid.*

1. On May 16 and 18, Secretary of State Hamilton Fish wrote in his diary after a Cabinet meeting. "The filling of the Brazilian Mission is mentioned & I urge the importance of doing so without delay—that the party now acting as Chargé, is represented to have been an open Rebel during the late Civil War—He states that Willard Warner has been recommended—but he thinks it ought to be given to some person from the Valley of the Mississippi—" "He was writing a letter to me as I entered his room, proposing to recall Markbreit, minister to Bolivia, on account of the political attitude of his half brother Fredc Hassaurek who is engaged in organising the third Party, in Ohio—his note proposed Wm A. Pile for his place in Bolivia, & Willard Warner, as Govr of New Mexico, in place of Pile—the note was unfinished; & after showing me what he had written, he tore it up—I told him that Markbreit had lately been doing a very good act in saving the life of (see PS on opposite page) the late President of Bolivia, & had rcd approval therefor—I suggest that Partridge be nominated for Brazil—& Pile for Venezuela, which leaves New Mexico, for Warner—President approves & I send him nominations accordingly—. . . PS—I find that I was mistaken in saying to the Prsdt. this morning that Markbreit had saved the life of the late President of Bolivia—It was Torbert, who saved the life of Genl Duenas—late President of that Republic" DLC-Hamilton Fish. For Willard Warner, see letter to Charles W. Buckley, Nov. 21, 1870, note 2; for James R. Partridge, see letter to Hamilton Fish, Dec. 21, 1870, note 1.

On March 3, 1871, Isaac F. Shepard, Chauncey I. Filley, Elias W. Fox, and two others, St. Louis, had written to USG. "Understanding that there is, or is about to be, a vacancy in the Brazilian Mission, now or lately occupied by Hon Henry T. Blow of Missouri, we most respectfully suggest to you the name of Hon. John H. Stover, and earnestly solicit~~ed~~ from your Excllency the nomination of Col. Stover for that position. We are well acquainted with the gentleman, and believe the appointment to be eminently appropriate on both personal and political grounds." LS, DNA, RG 59, Letters of Application and Recommendation. On Nov. 25, 1872, John McDonald, supervisor of Internal Revenue, St. Louis, wrote to USG. "I have the honor to recommend to your consideration Col. John H. Stover, late candidate for the office of Lieutenant Governor of this state on the Republican ticket. Col. Stover rendered valuable services to the party and the Administration in the campaign just closed. Col. Stover is a gentleman of fine ability, and would honor the service and himself in any position you might bestow upon him." ALS, *ibid.*, RG 60, Records Relating to Appointments. Related papers are *ibid.*

On Dec. 7, Robert A. Vance, Gallatin, Mo., wrote to USG. "I understand Mr Smith U. S. Marshal for the Western District of Missouri is going to resign his position on the 1st of March 1873—and in that case there will be a Vacancy in the office, and I desire the position myself if I can honorably obtain it . . ." ALS, *ibid.* On Dec. 23, Joseph W. McClurg, Linn Creek, Mo., wrote to USG. "Understanding there may be a vacancy in the office of U. S. Marshal for the Western District of Missouri, I beg leave to respectfully recommend for that position Robert A. Vance Esqr of Gallatin, Daviess County, this state, who is qualified, worthy and eminently deserving. He was an officer, during the late war of the rebellion, was wounded in the line of duty, has remained true to his principles and never, at any time, deserted the Republican party." ALS, *ibid.* On Jan. 18, 1873, Benjamin F. Loan, St. Joseph, wrote to USG. "Capt Robert A Vance of Gallatin Mo. is an applicant for appointment as Marshal of the Western District of Mo. I know Mr. Vance well and I take pleasure in saying that he is a gentleman and a lawyer of good standing. He was a soldier on the Union side in the war of the rebellion;

He served in the Army under Gen Thomas He entered the Army as a private and was promoted to the office of Captain for meritorious Conduct. . . ." ALS, *ibid.* Related papers are *ibid.* On March 8, USG renominated George Smith as marshal, Western District, Mo. See *PUSG*, 19, 428.

On March 17, 1871, W. A. Price, Savannah, Mo., had written to USG. "Having observed in yesterdays St Joseph Union that a tender had been mad by your Exilency of Minister to Brazil to the Honl B. F. Loan of St Joseph and that the Honl B. F. Loan had kindly declined your friendly consideration, I was sorry to be compeled to think that Genl Loan was under the necesity of declineing your magnanimous and kind offer for the Genl is worthy of most any position you might feel disposed to confer upon him. If then I am correctly informed through the medium befor named that the Honl B. F. Loan has ~~has~~ declined this Honl position may I as a fast friend and supporter of Your Administration be permitted to ask that this appointment may be confered upon the Honl A. J. Harland You no doubt are aware that Mr Harland ran for Lieut Govr on the regular Republican ticket in connection with Govr McClerg which ticket was unfortuneatily defeated to the lasting shame of the bolting wing of our party Mr Harland has represented this County (Andrew Co) two Sessions in the General Assembly of the St of Mo having been chosen Speaker of the House at both Sessions and received much commendation for his presiding qualities. Mr Harland is a mild affible Gentleman and has heretofor hild honorabl positions and I have no doubt would dignifie the position herein solisited for him. Mr Harland is a resident of our plesent little City Savannah" ALS, DNA, RG 59, Letters of Application and Recommendation.

On March 27, Frank Adams, Barnesville, Ohio, wrote to USG. "Please excuse my intrusion, for I have but a few words to say.—I notice that the Mission to Brazil is still vacant, and as I would be very much pleased to visit that Country, I ask whether it could be possible for me to receive the appointment of Minister?—I am no politician.—Have been a Union Soldier during the war.—Am a printer and a poor man.—Never have used malt or intoxicating liquors.—Think I can [a]ttend to the duties of the position as Minister to ~~Brazile~~ Brazil with satisfaction to our government.—My age is 37. Would endeavor to discharge the duties of the office with promptness and honesty.—As to my honesty, sobriety and capability, I can refer to George McClelland, editor of the *Enterprise*, Barnesville, Ohio; G. S. Newcomb & Co., Cleveland, Ohio; Sanford & Hayward, Cleveland, Ohio. If my application is inappropriate, or not worthy of consideration, please hold this letter *confidential* and destroy it.—" ALS, *ibid.*

On April 17 and May 27, William W. Ivory, St. Louis, wrote to USG. "The writer of this late a Capt in 1st Nebraska, Service from 61 to 66. A. A. A Gen Gen Thayers staff shortly after Shiloh, also for short time with Gen Davidson, (and on Present duty in this City on account of good conduct in the field in various battles South) and still harder service on the frontier last 2 years of war I would most respectfully ask the appt of Secty of Legation to Brazil, particularly would I press my claim in case the minister is appt from any other state and if my old friend and Genl. should get the mission I would be still more anxious to go with him. I will forward with this on to the Secty of State such recommendations as to character ability &c as will satisfy the Department I served with the 2nd Penna in war with Mexico and was promoted to Lieut when only 17 year age for good conduct after Chepultepec. When I left Mexico I could speak very fair Spanish have no doubt I could get the language in few weeks In 1860 I was appt Receiver of the Land Office at Dakota Nebraska, out of forty applicants: but war troubles looming up &

coming on did not make a dollar and Democratic proclivites when Regt organized at Omaha prevented me getting Commission, though I done more I think than any one man to fill up and organize, Col afterwards Gen Thayer done all he could for me after we got to know each other. I have been since 1861 and am now a thorough loyal Republican, and have acted at all times since in this state with the friends of your Adminstration." "Hope that we can find some plan to unite the party here. how to do this and fix the Offices to suit without any loss to the Public. Great many of the best of your friends think that some changes necessary. they say Gen Smith keeps in Democrats and Catholics why their religion is brought in I dont know, dont suppose that the Gen knows of the religion of any nor need he, in this City. But this is certain that to make the party efficient none but sound Republicans or such as will work and act with us should be appt to any office here, Gen Soloman I understand wants the P. O, and he has some friends want him to have it. He never was friend of yours, tho I believe he would work for you when nominated. he would be pretty strong man If Ferd Meyer Braun and the West Post influence goes for him, and the New World & Democrat could be satisfied it would be pretty strong appt I worked hard spoke and wrote letters for your election, Not paid much attention since that to politics my hope was to get along as a business man. But the little success of the Democrats make them so overbearing and insulting, that in my opinion the very safety of what we all fought so hard for lies in your reelection I felt it my duty at the late Mayors election to stay at the Polls with tickets in my hands from daylight to near evg ~~with tickets in my hands~~ working for the success of our party, it was very aggravating to find that many of these gentlemen in Public offices. took no intrest in it and many I understand did not vote, While the Conduct of many Republicans (giving as part of reasons because the offices were not distributed for benefit of Republican.) through a fatal inactivity made us lose the City" ALS, *ibid.* A letter of May 31 from Ivory to USG on the same subject is *ibid.*, as are related papers.

On June 12, Richard C. Shannon, New York City, wrote to USG. "I have the honor to state that my formal application for the Post of Secretary of Legation with the new mission about to set out for Brazil is now before the proper department for consideration. I would respectfully invite your attention to the enclosed note from the Hon. Jas R. Partridge the new minister to Brazil and especially to that part of it where he says; 'That place however is not at my disposal although I have no doubt the Pres't. would if the person I recommended were *acceptable to him* favorably consider it.' In this connection may I take the liberty of referring to Lewis B. Brown Esq. a gentleman who I believe is your neighbor at Long Branch who has known me for several years, especially during the war period and the whole time I resided in Brazil." ALS, *ibid.* The enclosure is *ibid.* On June 21, Fish telegraphed to USG, Long Branch. "Shannon has not produced some papers, promised, and required—If appointed he must receive a Commission under seal, and take & file an oath; & receive instructions before he sails—This cannot be done in time for him to sail with Minister—Mr Partridge has been informed of Shannons failure to produce promised papers" ALS (telegram sent), DLC-Hamilton Fish. On the same day, U.S. Representative John A. Peters of Maine, Bangor, telegraphed to Fish. "*Personal* . . . I most cordially vouch for the reliable political character of Richard C. Shannon, who asks to be Legation Secretary at Brazil." Copy, DNA, RG 59, Letters of Application and Recommendation. On June 23, U.S. Senator Hannibal Hamlin of Maine, Bangor, telegraphed to Fish. "I recommend Col. Richard C. Shannon for Secretary of Legation, Brazil. He is a gentleman of Cultivation, well qualified, and an earnest Republican. He speaks the language of the Country." Copy, *ibid.* Related papers are *ibid.* On Dec. 6, USG nominated Shannon as secretary of legation, Brazil.

To Congress

THE THE SENATE AND HOUSE OF REPRESENTATIVES.

A condition of affairs now exists in some of the States of the Union,[1] rendering life and property insecure,[2] and the carrying of the mails, and the collection of the revenue dangerous.

The proof that such a condition of affairs exists in some localities, is now before the Senate.[3] That the power to correct these evils, is beyond the control of the State authorities, I do not doubt. That the power of the Executive of the United States, acting within the limits of ~~present~~ existing laws, is sufficient for present emergencies, is not clear.

Therefore, I urgently recommend, such legislation, as in the judgment of Congress, shall effectually secure life liberty and property, and the enforcement of law, in all parts of the United States.

It may be expedient to provide, that such law as shall be passed in pursuance of this recommendation shall expire at the end of the next session of Congress.

There is no other subject, on which I would recommend, legislation during the present session

U. S. GRANT

WASHINGTON D. C.
MARCH 23D 1871—

DS, DNA, RG 46, Presidential Messages. For the perfunctory reception of USG's message in the Senate and its partisan reception in the House of Representatives, see *CG*, 42–1, 236, 244–49. The House appointed Republicans Samuel Shellabarger of Ohio, Benjamin F. Butler and Henry L. Dawes of Mass., Glenni W. Scofield of Pa., Austin Blair of Mich., Charles R. Thomas of N. C., and Democrats George W. Morgan of Ohio, Michael C. Kerr of Ind., and Washington C. Whitthorne of Tenn., as a select committee to consider USG's message. On March 23, 1871, a presidential secretary wrote to Secretary of the Treasury George S. Boutwell. "The President desires me to say that he will visit the Capitol to day at twelve O'Clock and will be pleased to have you call here and ride up with him in his carriage." Copy, DLC-USG, II, 1. On the same day, a correspondent reported: "The President came to the Capitol to-day, accompanied by all the members of his Cabinet, except Postmaster-General Cresswell.

He immediately sent for the Southern Republican delegation in Congress, and also for Judge Mercur, of Pennsylvania, Judge Shellabarger, of Ohio, Senators Morton, Rice and Chandler. The brief of his message, relative to the Southern States, was laid before them and discussed in all its aspects. The President had no suggestion to offer at this time as to the character of a bill upon this question but preferred to leave the matter wholly with Congress. The points submitted by the President were satisfactory to all present, and after a session of about an hour the message was sent into both Houses of Congress." *Philadelphia Public Ledger*, March 24, 1871. See letter to James G. Blaine, March 9, 1871; George S. Boutwell, *Reminiscences of Sixty Years in Public Affairs* (New York, 1902), II, 252; George F. Hoar, *Autobiography of Seventy Years* (New York, 1903), I, 204–6.

On March 23, 1871, U.S. Representative James A. Garfield of Ohio had written to Jacob D. Cox, Cincinnati. "Yours, of the 20th inst, is received. Public Affairs are growing about as bad as the devil could wish, if he were arranging them his own way. You have interpreted the Sumner difficulty exactly as I understand it. I was in favor of an early adjournment, and joined in a movement to refer, the whole Ku Klux question, to a Committee of Investigation, during the Recess, and have them report, to the House, in December. I took this view, in part because our laws, on the subject of outrages, in the South, are stringent, and comprehensive, and the President has sent us no message, asking for any further legislation. I do not think that Congress ought to take the initiative, in thrusting upon the Executive more tools, when there is no evidence, from him, that he needs them. But, the debate has gone on, until the popular mind is fully aroused, to the difficulties of the situation. All these three weeks, the President has made no communication, to Congress, on any subject. During that time he has been away to Philadelphia, on a pleasure excursion, and the papers are filled with the particulars, of his preparation, for a trip to California, and his Summer Residence, at Long Branch. But, not one word comes to us, touching public affairs[.] Within the last day or two, it has been said, that he has, all the while, very much desired, that we should legislate, on the state of affairs, at the South; that he had a message ready to send in, at the beginning of the Session, but that Cameron, and the High Tariff Leaders, made a raid upon him, dissuading him from sending it in, for fear that the Session should be prolonged; that Coal and Salt would get on the Free list. He gave way to their solicitations, and here we are, quarreling among ourselves, mad at each other, and mad at him. It is understood, that he has now concluded to send in the message, and we shall probably receive it some time to day, but he is very anxious, that Congress shall do nothing else, but legislate, concerning the Ku Klux. Of course, this means that the Tariff shall not be touched. But, about the Ku Klux business itself, I am greatly perplexed. Shellabarger, and Bingham have bills ready, which rest on an interpretation, of the 14.th Amendment, which I cannot yet see my way to adopt. They assume that the 14th Amendment, empowers Congress to provide, by law, that the President may with out the invitation of the State Legislature, or its Governor, send the Army into any State, and assume control of affairs, whenever, in his judgement, the State Laws, are not so administered, as to give that equal protection, to life and property, which the 14th Article requires. This interpretation is based on the word 'deny' in this clause: 'No State shall deny to any citizen the equal protection of the laws. They say that if the State neglect to enforce the laws of the State, which grant equal protection, such neglect will constitute a *denial* of equal protection, and will authorize the President to interfere. It seems to me, that this will virtually empower the President to abolish the State Governments. I am in great trouble about the whole matter, and I hope you will find time to write to me, in regard to it. . . . I ought to have added, in another place, that the impression is gaining ground, that the election of Grant is impossible, but it is feared that his nomination is inevitable. . . ." ALS, Cox Papers, Oberlin College, Oberlin, Ohio. See Mary L. Hinsdale, ed., *Garfield-Hinsdale Letters: Correspondence Between James Abram Garfield and Burke Aaron Hinsdale* (1949; reprinted, New York, 1969), pp. 171–72.

On March 25, Governor Edmund J. Davis of Tex. wrote to USG. "In view of the information by telegraph today, that Congress will probably give you plenary powers in the way of suppressing lawlessness in some of the Southern States, I have thought I might to some extent promote the object in view by drawing your attention to Lieut. Col. Geo. P. Buell of 11th Infy. in connection with the selection of officers to command Districts to be placed under martial law. Previous to the reorganization of the State Government, Col. (and at that time Genl.) Geo. P. Buell commanded a large sub. District in the N. Eastern part of this State. It was the most lawless part of all this very lawless State, when he took command, but his administration was so effective that I now find less trouble there than any where else. I passed through the District in the Fall of 1869 and his system of management then impressed me very favorably. I think if you try him you will find the work done effectually." LS, PHi.

On March 28, Ethan A. Allen, New York City, wrote to USG. "As we are *personally* to each other strangers you may deem my letters to you as a liberty on my part with which you can dispense. I am induced Mr President to *volunteer* advice to you, as chief Executive from the kindest motives when I see you surrounded by advisers whom you trust, & in whom you doubtless have the most unlimited confidence leading you to inevitable *political if not personal ruin.* be assured Sir had better halt. look carefully around & drop the political advisers by whom you are now surrounded. The Ku-Klux bill which has been passed is designed by Sherman & its advocates. backed by Morton is a *conspiracy against your re-nomination for the Presidency* I am really surprised that you should be blind to the movements of your *professed* friends—I beg of you Mr President to pause in your career until you can at least, look around & satisfy yourself of the fact which I state. viz. that *your political death* is what the party now in power are aiming at. The *true* condition of affairs at the South is *unknown to you.* & I *could* sugjest to you a course which should you pursue would extricate you from the net work in which you are *now entangled.* I should like to have a private interview with you when I would *fully* convince you that you now slumber upon a tremendous volcano. to which the match is almost ready to be applied. I should much dislike to see you stripd of your laurels. & your Military glory become sadly tarnished. I fully understand the Southern people, & could give you certain ideas on which you could not fail to act. on reflection The whole Machinery of your Government is sadly out of order. & requires vigor & *prompt* action to restore it to a harmonious working. & prevent your overwhelming defeat. You have no time to lose. I as a private citizen holding *no* political Office can & do look carefully on the conflicting parties. & not being *pecunarily* interested in the success of each as a a matter of personal Office I am of course enabled to form an *unbiased* judgment. again. In the first place I never to my knowledge saw Mr Thomas Murphy the Collector of this Port but *once* & that was about two months ago when I called on him at the Custom House for the purpose of imparting to him some well founded reports or suspicions that a certain firm in this City were defrauding the U S Government. by smuggling Murphy looked at me in surprise & said 'If you have positive *proofs* & *affidavits* of the fact to lay before me I will listen to you' This kind of a man Mr President at once proves himself to be unworthy, of & incompetent. to discharge so important a trust as Collector of this or any other Port. A business man. or Gentleman who knows the concomitant relations in which he stands toward his imployees would have heard all I had to say & caused some investigation to be made into the circumstances attending my report. I told Murphy 'I was not an employe of the Government.' and turned on my heel leaving him in *disgust.* You had decidedly better *dismiss* this man Murphy *at once.* take the wind out of the sails of the cliques here. inaugerate a decided & independent course. & send an appointment to a man in this City who is a most *sound Republican.* who has the entire confidence of the Mercantile Community. is a Gentleman of unimpeachable character & a man who will fully & solidly *consolidate* the party here. Permit me again to say that I again write you in *your own* interests. & without the knowledge of the best man you could place at the head of the Custom House this Gentleman is *Edward C. Johnson* of. Bridge Street, in this City." ALS, OFH.

Also on March 28, Shellabarger reported a bill from the select committee "to enforce the provisions of the fourteenth amendment to the Constitution of the United States, and for other purposes." *CG*, 42–1, 317. On the same day, Shellabarger spoke. "I enter, Mr. Speaker, upon the consideration of this measure with unfeigned reluctance. The measure is one, sir, which does affect the foundations of the Government itself, which goes to every part of it, and touches the liberties and the rights of all the people, and doubtless the destinies of the Union. And more than that, Mr. Speaker, it involves questions of constitutional law of importance absolutely vital. . . ." *Ibid.*, Appendix, 67.

On March 30, U.S. Representative James B. Beck of Ky. spoke. "Many of you would rather see the President dictator to-day than to see the Democratic party come into power and expose the outrageous acts your party has committed. That is at the bottom of it all. I do not know that General Grant is as bad a man as some of his leading party friends say he is. They know him better than I. But if he was the best man on earth, if he was General Washington himself, the power this bill proposes to give should not be conferred on him. . . . If these States of the South would only continue to be Radical, if they would only agree that they would vote for General Grant again, you would never hear anything about the Ku Klux, you would never more hear of any reconstruction acts. . . ." *CG*, 42–1, 355, 357.

On the same day, U.S. Representative Fernando Wood of N. Y. spoke. "Now, sir, I say that in no portion of our history has any such power been delegated; in no free Government anywhere in the world has any such power been delegated by the people. Nor is there any despot for the past century who would attempt to exercise it. Napoleon, in the day of his imperial strength, never attempted to exercise it; and even the life of the present emperor of Russia, with all his great personal authority, holding in his hands not only the Church but the State, not only the sword but the purse, whose subjects are vassals, would not be safe for twenty-four hours if he attempted to exercise the power now proposed to be given to the present President of the United States. And, Mr. Speaker, in whose hands do we propose to place this monstrous supremacy? Is there anything in the military or civil history of the present President of the United States which will justify our placing it in his hands? Are his knowledge and estimate of our institutions in keeping with the liberties of our people? Has he not recently told us what is his idea of the Government of the United States? Has he not recently sent a message to Congress, in which he declared that the present German empire had a form of government and a theory of political institutions very like and quite similar to our own; that in consequence of this analogy he recommended the raising of the present American embassy to Berlin to a full mission on the par or pay of those to France and Great Britain? I cannot see that the empire of Germany has a Government similar to our own as stated by the President. . . . He did not appreciate the difference between despotism and republicanism; and this, doubtless, accounted for his admiration of Germanic imperialism, which subordinated political opinion to the edicts of the State. Is it to such a man, who has this conception of our Government, that we are to intrust a power like this? Shall we give it to a man who deems it to be his right to exercise the war-making power over peaceful communities, as he did in New York and Philadelphia when he sent the military there to overawe and subdue them, and to use the naval forces of the United States to despoil a neighboring republic in the Caribbean sea? Is it into the hands of such a man we are to place supreme authority, who, since we have had experience of his incumbency of office, has never shown the least patriotic spirit, nor announced one single principle of republican government, nor shown a single conception of the Constitution of the United States or the Government over which he presides?. . ." *Ibid.*, Appendix, 75.

On March 31, U.S. Representative Thomas Swann of Md. spoke. "Mr. Speaker, why the urgent necessity for this bill, converting us from a free into a military government?. . . If the appeal to this House was so imperative why did he find it necessary to visit the antechamber of the Senate to prepare the message upon which this action is founded? Could he not act for himself, without the aid of the Radical junta by which he was surrounded, and to whose counsels he yielded? No, sir, there are other reasons for this sudden movement on the part of General Grant. He saw that his own star was waning. He saw that his party had fallen into a state of anarchy and disorganization. He saw that his outrageous conduct in the San Domingo job was about to assume proportions, under the scathing lash of a member of his own party, whom he had been instrumental in degrading. He saw that there must be a diversion, that the current must be turned back, that the old prejudices and issues of the war must be revived as his only hope of recovery; and he conceived the magnanimous idea of recommencing the war upon the poor down-trodden South. . . ." *CG*, 42–1, 362.

On April 1, U.S. Representative John B. Hawley of Ill. spoke. "We are told by gentlemen on the other side of the House that if the power be granted to the President of the United States proposed by this bill he will be a despot, a dictator; that he will override the liberties of this great people. Why should he do so? Not because he shall execute the laws, but, if he shall do this thing, it will be because he will disregard the law and override the law. Sir, why shall we say this great chieftain, who marched at the head of more than a million men, will seek for a pretext to call out the militia in one or two or more States in order to subvert the liberties of the American people, when we know there was a day when he stood at the head of an army composed of a million veteran soldiers, and yet at the behest of the civil power this great army melted away like the dew before the morning sun?. . ." *Ibid.*, p. 383. See also the remarks of U.S. Representatives Philadelph Van Trump of Ohio, Daniel W. Voorhees of Ind., and Horatio C. Burchard of Ill. *Ibid.*, p. 409; *Ibid.*, Appendix, 180, 315–16.

On April 6, Shellabarger spoke. ". . . That the revenues of the Republic cannot be collected, because a mastering conspiracy forbids it, we are told by him whom the Constitution makes to swear that he will take care that the laws shall be executed; that the mails of this Government cannot be safely carried, because this incipient treason forbids it; that the States cannot defend the people, because this treason is so strong as to forbid it; that that race—their men and their women and their little ones—become, by act of God, the wards of the nation as well as its citizens, is perishing away under this new and immense murder; that the armies of the Republic are marching back to Sumter! And, then, you are told by the President that the sufficiency of the laws for the appalling emergency is not sure. Can you go off and not make it sure?... We also hold the bolts which the nation has for the blasting of the returning treason, and, in the name of your again defied and insulted country, I demand that you give the President power to strike the conspiracy instantly—dead." *CG*, 42–1, 519. On the same day, the House passed an amended bill. *Ibid.*, p. 522.

On April 7, the Senate referred to its Judiciary Committee the bill from the House. *Ibid.*, pp. 523–24. On April 10, U.S. Senator George F. Edmunds of Vt. reported the bill from committee "favorably, with certain amendments." *Ibid.*, p. 538.

On April 12, U.S. Senator Eli Saulsbury of Del. spoke. "... You are afraid the southern States will cast their electoral vote against your party in 1872; and you wish to interfere in their internal affairs that you may control their elections by military power and prevent such a result. This scheme has been concocted for that purpose...." *Ibid.*, p. 603.

On April 13, U.S. Senator Garrett Davis of Ky. spoke. "... The annexation of Dominica and the whole island, and the passage of this bill are the pet measures of the President, and of much the most interest of the few that he has ever recommended to the consideration of Congress. Their first origin was not in either House of Congress, but the Grant Radicals of both have been brought by him to their strenuous support. No previous Administration approximated the weakness of the present one, the number and length of its absences from Washington city, the frequency of its election excursions and speeches, its general neglect of duty, and its unremitting and energetic exertions to bring the powers and patronage of the United States Government into conflict with the freedom of the suffrage of the American people. Two years of deplorable failure have demonstrated the incompetency and unfitness of the President for the great and difficult duties of his office...." *Ibid.*, p. 649.

On the same day, U.S. Senator Francis P. Blair spoke. "The bill substantially declares that if certain offenses are not punished to the satisfaction of the President he may proclaim that rebellion exists and assume the government of such of the States as he proclaims in rebellion. He is invited to become *dictator*. It is proposed to confer this unlimited power upon a man whose history is wholly military, except for the two years of his Presidency, which has been signalized by utter disregard of law, as admitted by his own friends on the Judiciary Committee in reference to his conduct in Georgia, and by the late chairman of the Committee on Foreign Relations in reference to San Domingo." *Ibid.*, Appendix, 231–32. On April 14, the Senate passed an amended bill. *CG*, 42–1, 709.

Between April 15 and 19, the House and Senate authorized two conference committees and passed the second conference report. *Ibid.*, pp. 716, 723–28, 749–79, 787–810, 819–31. On April 19 and 20, Horace Porter wrote to George C. Gorham, secretary, U.S. Senate. "President will be at Senate quarter before five oclock. Please let this be known in Senate." "President will be at Senate by eleven o'clock. Please retain bills for his signature there" Copies, DLC-USG, II, 5. On April 20, a correspondent reported: "President Grant, accompanied by Secretary Robeson and General Porter, came to the President's room, at the Capitol, at noon to-day, and the Ku-Klux bill was presented to him at one o'clock and he signed it...." *Philadelphia Public Ledger*, April 21, 1871. See *CG*, 42–1, 838; *U.S. Statutes at Large*, XVII, 13–15; Everette Swinney, *Suppressing the Ku Klux Klan: The Enforcement of the Reconstruction Amendments 1870–1877* (New York, 1987), pp. 124–79.

On April 13, Secretary of State Hamilton Fish had written in his diary. "Called upon the President, . . . He has given up his California trip for this spring—hopes to go in August or Sept—assigns as a reason for not going now, in addition to the uncertainty of having the British negotiation disposed of that the absence of himself & Cabinet, & of the General of the Army, immediately after the enactment of the 'Ku-klux' Bill, would not be proper." DLC-Hamilton Fish. See letter to George W. Dent, March 27, 1871.

1. On [*March 22*], U.S. Senator Roscoe Conkling of N. Y. wrote to USG. "*Private* . . . Shall we be right in acting today on the expectation that some communication touching Southern troubles will come in from you? Will something come *today*?" ALS, ICN. See *Cincinnati Gazette*, March 9, 1871.

On April 1, U.S. Representative Joseph H. Lewis of Ky. spoke. "From the 4th to the 23d of March Congress remained in session, at the public expense, contrary to public expectation and against the public will, doing literally no business whatever, the whole time being consumed by a discussion between the more moderate and conservative Republicans who favored an adjournment and the ultra members of that party who demanded more legislation, that there may be more strife and more persecution of the unhappy South. When it became manifest that the conservative Republicans, aided by the Democrats, had the power to force an adjournment, and the country began to feel assured no further mischief would be done this session, the President, hitherto profoundly unconscious of or else profoundly indifferent to the existence of any facts worthy to be communicated, unexpectedly to all, on the 23d of March favored us with a message, . . . Sir, as it is not pretended any new or startling event has occurred since the 4th of March important for Congress to know, or that any sudden emergency has arisen, the question is, why the delay on the part of the President in regard to a matter of the magnitude he states the subject of his message to be? The President asks Congress for more power. Did he ever before delay or hesitate to ask that? Sir, these circumstances authorize me to say that if this bill is passed at all it will be the result of executive dictation, made to further the schemes of the ultra wing of the Republican party, . . ." *CG*, 42–1, 384–85.

On April 4, U.S. Representative Job E. Stevenson of Ohio spoke. "The President asks for legislation to enable him lawfully to suppress Ku Klux outrages. He has been slow in reaching the conclusion that extraordinary measures are requisite. So have we all. . . . It was natural for the President and for every Republican to be reluctant and unwilling t[o] admit the deplorable condition of the South[.] It is the only blemish on our record, the only imperfection of our work, of Union, liberty, and equality. When we can proclaim peace throughout the land, history will pronounce upon the Republican party the grandest eulogy ever awarded to men. But we now see and acknowledge the condition of affairs and are uniting on a remedy. Necessity closes our divisions and brings us into line. . . ." *Ibid.*, Appendix, 298.

2. On Jan. 28, Governor Harrison Reed of Fla. had written to Secretary of War William W. Belknap. "The presence of ~~the~~ two companies of Infantry under Major Cochrane, which you did us the honor to assign to Florida, have been of signal service in restraining premeditated violence & bloodshed. Their arrival was most opportune as sedition & treason was rampant & threatening. The armed bands of outlaws have for the time hid themselves & a well-grounded fear of federal power holds them in awe. It is of the first consequence to the security of republican government here that we have the continuance of a small U. S. force here & I therefore ask that you will establish this as a military post under command of Major Cochrane & that the two companies now here may be ordered to remain here during the present year & until

republican government is acquiesced in & rendered secure." ALS, DNA, RG 94, Letters Received, 506 1871. On Feb. 8, Belknap endorsed this letter. "The President desires the troops to be kept at Tallahassee for the present" AE (initialed), *ibid.*

On March 25, a correspondent reported: "Among the visitors to the Executive Mansion to-day was Governor Lindsay, the Democratic Governor of Alabama, who called to pay his respects to the President. The interview was satisfactory and courteous, Governor Linday assuring the President that his State was thoroughly peaceable, except the usual crimes that pervade everywhere. He also declared his ability to repress and check all outrages without appealing to the President for protection, and declared his intention to maintain the laws at all hazards. He further assured the President that, should occasion require, he would not hesitate to call upon the federal authorities for assistance. The President expressed his satisfaction at these assurances." *Philadelphia Public Ledger*, March 27, 1871. See Endorsement, June 9, 1871, note 1.

On March 27, Robert W. Burns, Lexington, Ky., wrote to USG. "As a peace loving and a law-abiding citizen I write you to know if there is a law in this free land of ours that will protect and guarrentee safety against the Rebel prowlers that infest evry nook an corner, better known as K. K. K's, who are armed and ready to take the life of any one if they do not endorse treason, and rebellion. No matter what business one may be in, if he is known as a law abiding citizen and even expresses himself that treason is wrong, and leaves it at that, he is pointed out and ee'r the morrows sun has risen his life is in jeopardy Grand Jurys, and laws in this state do not protict any one from violence that is known as a Republican; and evry man carries a revolver, in fact the war must soon be resumed if these prowling bands are not delt with to the full extent of any law that will reach them; and Martial law is now all that will reach such mean an contemptable Democrats, as they are pleased to term themselves; but better known as Rebels or K. K. K. Rebellion & treason is all the go, and one would think, from the indications that wa~~s~~r was sure. The people spend their time in working on the feelings of the masses, recounting the wrongs that they have suffered, and how the North has stolen their rights, and an ignorant people beleives it, and from the present indications of things war is all that will satisfy a treason loving people. I appeal to you as the President of the United States & as a peace loving & law-abiding citizen and ask protiction from violence, at the hands of these prowling rebels known as K. K. K; I ask protection because I have a right to it, and because I have faith in the present administration, and beleive that Your Excellency will grant protection to a peace-loving & law-abiding Citizen. This does not come from my self alone, but from many. Hoping that you will force armed Rebels to become law-abiding citizens . . ." ALS, DNA, RG 48, Appointment Div., Letters Received. See *Cincinnati Gazette*, Nov. 25, 1870.

On April 12, 1871, William H. Irwin, Cleveland, wrote to USG. "In submitting to you the following facts I am placing my fortune & my life in your hands, & I do this with implicit confidence in your Honor, Patriotism & Wisdom—In 1867–8 I was Attorney for Civil Affairs at Hd Qrs 5th Mil. Dist. New Orleans, then commanded by Maj. Genl W. S. Hancock, U. S. A. The importance of this position, & the deep depression of business, with the very low rates of Real Estate in Texas & Louisiana &c brought every kind of property to the hammer, & much of it to my notice, with the most admirable offers for investment—Rejecting all speculative offers I purchased the famous Iron Mountain in 'Cherokee Alabama', known as 'Round Mountain' & probably familiar to your Excellency, as the Iron Works there were burned by *Genl. Blair*, they being in possession of the Confederacy—& used in the making of Iron for Ordnance, under the supervision of the Secretary of Ordnance Dept, C. States. I knew that if the representations in regard to this Iron Mtn were correct it must be intrinsically of immense value, & it was available at once by its position within the route of the Coosa River, navigable for Steamers to Rome, Georgia, at all seasons. A short leave from Genl Hancock enabled me personally, & critically to examine the Rd Mtn Estate, & I found it to be far more valuable than any representations had made it. A Mountain 300 ft high, 2½ M. in circumference & covered from base to summit with a powerful, persistent Stratum of lenticular, fossiliferous Red Oxide of Iron, *5 to 10 ft thick*, with a very light cover, requiring neither hoisting, propping, pumping, or blasting in mining it, but can be, & was mined & delivered at the furnaces at the foot of the Mtn for *seventy five cents* per ton gross! The Ore is specifically adapted to the making of 'Bessemer' Steel, & by the concurrent testimony of all familiar with it yielded the best Ordnance Metal in the South—To preserve this magnificent Estate I abandoned the control of large mining interests in Pennsylvania, & have successfully carried the whole property since 19th March 1868, & had just completed, as I supposed, my arrangts to blow in a new, and Excellent furnace when the infamous treachery of Revd Herman C. Duncan of New Orleans, my partner, destroyed all my well arranged plans, & overwhelmed me in misfortune: *Treachery*, Your Excellency, not only to me, but to our common Country—To my amazement I learned from his letters, written at New Orleans, that he was offered $50.000—fifty thousand dollars! to have me displaced from the Superintendency of Our Iron Works. Neither J. L. McConnell Esqr of Centre, Cherokee County, Ala. my Counsel, nor myself could divine what such an offer meant, altho' I was startled to find Duncan in close communication with the late Secty Confed. States, who assured him 'that no words could exaggerate the value of Rd Mtn' & I found, too, that a late Confed. Staff Officer was a confidl friend & adviser of Duncan—But when Duncan boastfully assured me that he himself, preacher as he was, had been offered a Colnelcy in a secret politico-military Organization in the South, numbering 500,000 men, ready at a moment to take the field, & that another War between the North and South was 'inevitable'—his very words—I saw that I had a dangerous person to deal with—either a Fanatic, or a Traitor. His extreme bitterness towards Genl Longstreet—(for whom I inquired, having known him by reputation in Mexico, in the Army, in 1847, & hearing much of his soldierly qualities from my Cousin Capt. R. P. Maclay 8th U. S. Inf'y, even at that early day, & admiring, as every one must, his splendid fighting reputation, & his noble acknowledgt of error in taking up Arms against this Government)—convinced me that Duncan's heart was not right toward our Country, & all his subsequent villainy confirms this opinion. I myself saw him salute with his hand a mounted, disguised man who, early in the morning, was returning to the stable near our cottage at Rd Mtn a horse which he had taken thence a day or two previously & had severely ridden. I heard him repeatedly applaud this, secret organization, declare that the South was a unit in all future movts & boast of his willingness to accept the position offered him in this organization *whenever it was ready to take the field*!! He made *no secret* of his opinions in Alabama, or New Orleans, or on the steamer between that City & Mobile! I must confess, Your Excellency, that I regarded Duncan more as a boaster, & braggart than any other character: I could not believe it possible, either, that a half million of men in the South were banded together to uproot our Government, and plunge us into all the horrors of another Civil War, or that, even if this should take place, ~~that~~ an important military command wd be tendered a Preacher of the Gospel! Yet certain it is, that immediately on obtaining a Deed from me for ¾s of Rd Mtn he instantly put it on record, and then disclaimed all partnership with me, altho' our agrts were clear & full, & in duplicate, & tested, and his confidential correspondent an ex-confederate, is using every means to destroy all possibility of my resuscitating the Iron Works, & the instant Duncan denounced me the whole pack of rascals joined, 'like fiends & wolves' in the words of McConnell. When I connect the ominous words of Duncan, with the menaces made against Republicans, in my own room at Rd Mtn by armed, disguised men, at midnight; with the declaration which I heard from an ex-officer Confed. Navy ~~ofr~~ '*When we fight the damned Yankee dogs again it will not be alone*', and when I *know* that the oath required of the members of this secret organization is paramount to *all* obligations—my information is from a thoroughly reliable source, a person who refused the oath on this very account—and when I was warned by a Southerner not to bring South a Northern Republican Founder for my furnace *because he would be hung*! when I learned from a Southren Agt of a Northern Ins. Co. that this organization was spread all over the South, when I have heard a prominent Lawyer of Ga. declare, that if he was young he would join the Ku-Klux to carry out his hostility to the Yankees, & have heard a Kentuckian in Rome, publicly declare, that the only way to rid the South of Yankees was to Ku-Klux them, & witnessed the cordial approval which this infamous remark met with, when, in Rome I was informed by one of the employes of Government there, that if the U. S. Soldiers were removed he could not remain, when I have heard, on all sides from leading Southren men, the most bitter, public, & insolent denunciations of our Government, I confess that I lately give more credence to Duncan's declarations than I had before done. There is a preciseness in what he said that does not savor of lying impromptu; he assured me that the plan of the organization was, to rise at a given order, armed, & ready for a march northward & to strike at the northern sea-board cities at once. This to be done if the election of 1872 should go against the South, altho' Duncan declares another war 'inevitable,' under any circumstances—The possession of the key to the Valleys of the Coosa & Tennessee which is the low depression in Lookout Mtn 3 miles West of *Rd Mtn*—(it is there only 250 ft high)—would be a matter of immense moment to any insurrection in Alabama, Mississippi, & Georgia—as no one better understands than Your Excellency—Coal & Iron, abound there, & supplies of all kinds are cheap & abundant, & Lookt Mtn & its foothills are natural fastnesses almost impregnable—Both Rivers are navigable, except at the Shoals, in all Seasons, & ~~two~~ Railways now traverse both valleys—I am sure that Duncan, altho' full of duplicity, has not the sagacity or Military Knowledge to appreciate a great strategic point, but he may be prompted by those who ~~do~~ understand & appreciate it, & those are the dangerous men in the South; Wily, silent, yet desperate, men, who are leading the masses of the people, into a false position, feeding their imaginations with ~~false~~ wicked insidious hopes of military aid from the Northern Democracy, assuring them of payment for their slaves lost during the War, & urging a War of Races by insisting that it will come—Your Excellency, I need not enter further into details in this matter. No doubt cumulative & irresistible testimony in regard to the condition of the South is before you: I add only a *peculiar phase*, which may or may not have a special significance, but I could not but think that it *might* be the index of a powerful, concentrated movt against which early preventive measures ought to be taken. I *know* that it is the opinion of Majr D. A. Banks of Genl Jos. Johnston's Staff, a highly intelligent Officer, that another war is extremely probable, & I am sure that he deeply regrets it—I *know* also that arrangts were being made in N. Orl's to organize a Co. with an immense capl to sweep the mineral region of the Coosa, & I have heard the terrible declaration boldly announced, that if a conflict occurred between the two great parties in the North, every male negro in the South would be killed in 48 hours, &

Southren Troops would march against the Republican Army. *Beyond all doubt* some desperate Northern men are stimulating the wild hopes of The South with the assurance of material aid from The Northern Democracy—a vain & desperate hope! a cruel & immeasurably wicked political expedient of a few demagogues not the Democratic Party which has done, & will do infinite mischief. At first I regarded the Ku-Klux as no more than a party of 'Regulators,' & doubtless the better portion of them were acting as a police, but if I may judge from what I have heard uttered by one of their number in my own room, & what I have learned from a friend who was partly initiated into The Klan, 'Death to ~~Republicans~~ Radicals & Negroes' is part of their design now—most certainly of the more desperate portion of them—I will not disgust Your Excellency with a repetition of the base language utterd by the disguised & armed ruffian with whom I conversed. I calmly & firmly warned him & his comrade that such midnight visits would compel every Northern Man to leave The South: they assured me of their friendship for me, but denounced Negroes & Radicals—These miscreants are The *Sepoys of The South,* bloody, fanatical, remorseless as the grave, & if taken with arms in their hands they should *be blown from our guns*—What must be the demoralization of part of The South when an Episcopal Preacher, The Secretary of The Diocese, the intimate friend of his Bishop will be leagued with assassins & traitors? Duncan's social position, his religious associations, the high standing his family—(he is the grandson of Herman Cope of Philade a very eminent Quaker merchant, & the son of _____ Duncan of N. Orl's, a distinguished Lawyer)—& his reputed wealth give great weight to his opinions among his class—the governing class of the South, & he is therefore *doubly dangerous,* and should be under strict surveillance—*He will do all the harm he can do*—I shall not be in the least surprised to find in his hands the thread of a formidable conspiracy against The Government of The United States, altho' I am convinced that the *very best* people in The South cannot again be dragged into a Civil War—But, Your Excellency, the danger is that politicians in The South, if defeated in 1872, will spring an insurrection on the country & sweep willing or unwilling all The South into the vortex. The Ku-Klux is a military organization, with a terribly severe discipline—Small arms they have in abundance, & ordnance they will have if they are not dispersed. The South is full of young men who were boys at the Surrender, ardent spirits are universally used, & to an extraordinary excess, almost every male is armed constantly, life is of little value—all the elements of an outbreak are collected, & a spark may kindle it—Kentucky is in a *very dangerous* condition & must be carefully observed. A firm, menacing yet kind attitude toward the insurgent spirits of The South is demanded by every consideration moral & political. Temporary measures, *half measures* will only aggravate the evil. I found myself much more respected & influential by never declining, in proper occasions, to declare my sentiments as a Union Officer, & citizen, & urging on all submission to The Laws. The South must know that we are ready, & that another War with us will insure their destruction. Traitors who denounce The Government, & counsel rebellion should be summarily dealt with, be they in The South or in The North—In a word, Your Excellency, *the power & dignity* of this Government must be asserted *promptly & to the full. For fifty years hence* it will be dangerous to place much power in the hands of Southren *Leaders.* Our RailRoads leading to the Gulf of Mexico must be built & largely managed by Northern Capitalists, the whole South must be covered with RlRds & Emigration turned thither; Yankee towns, Yankee manufactories, Yankee farmers, Yankee miners must be found all through The South, and these will secure us against conspiracies, but if the political & ~~moral~~ social isolation now initiated in The South is not broken up, insurrection will become the normal condition of that

Section—neither Life, nor Property can be safe—A few more words, Your Excellency, & my duty is done—I have purposely kept aloof from all party connections in this communication to the President. I have long acted with the Democratic Party, but in The South have avoided politics & devoted myself to business, & have counselled Northern men there to do likewise. My statements are those of a gentleman, and a Soldier, given, under a deep sense of duty, to The Executive of this Government, at a very critical period in our history, when The Truth must be told, at all hazards. I have lived since last May, until January, in the heart of The South. I have kept my own counsel—'a silent tongue & a listening ear,' have never worn arms, & discouraged the practice, by prudence & good humor have succeeded in business & avoided insult & injury, yet I knew that *Death was ever at my side.* At last I had to interfere to save an inoffensive, industrious workman from being mercilessly beaten only because he was a mulatto; one of my workmen, known to be a Ku Klux, killed his companion in broad day without provocation, near the works. Duncan denounced me, and broke up all our highly important business arrangements, covering himself with ignominy as a Liar, a Hypocrite & a Traitor, and to crown all, that malignant arch traitor Davis in his reported Selma speech insolently, & defiantly gave the signal of Treason. I instantly wrote to Majr. Genl. W. S. Hancock, at St Paul denouncing that incendiary speech & warning him against Duncan who is an active, unscrupulous politician, & a strong writer. I found that I must either countenance Barbarity & Treason or sacrifice a magnificent Estate, and abandon my House in one of the most beautiful, healthful, & charming regions on this Continent—Your Excellency, I have not hesitated; Now, as in 1860 I give my adhesion to The Government; Now as then The Union of these States is paramount to all personal considerations—In conclusion Your Excellency, permit me to say that there is a very large body of kind, good, true people in The South, *probably the majority*, who will rally to the cause of Peace & Good Will between The North & South, it is *the active desperate minority* which is to be feared. If Your Excellency desires any information as to myself I most respectfully refer to Genl. W. S. Hancock, or to my War Record—My Brevet Majority in U. S. A. was won in Mexico under the eye of Lt Col. William Montrose Graham, at 'Contreras, Churubusco, & El Molino Del Rey.' My Brevet Brigr Genl. I won at 'Antietam' in Command of Smith's 3d Brigade of Franklin's Corps—" ALS, DNA, RG 94, Letters Received, 1686 1871. A related paper is *ibid.* See Ethel Armes, *The Story of Coal and Iron in Alabama* (1910; reprinted, Birmingham, Ala., 1972), pp. 186, 195, 320.

3. The Select Committee of the Senate to Investigate Alleged Outrages in the Southern States. See *SRC*, 42-1-1; William Dudley Foulke, *Life of Oliver P. Morton* (1899; reprinted, New York, 1974), II, 189–93.

Proclamation

Whereas it is provided in the Constitution of the United States, that the United States shall protect every State in this Union, on application of the legislature or of the executive (when the legislature cannot be convened) against domestic violence; and

Whereas it is provided in the laws of the United States, that in all cases of insurrection in any State or of obstruction to the laws thereof, it shall be lawful for the President of the United States, on application of the legislature of such State, or of the executive, (when the legislature cannot be convened), to call forth the militia of any other State or States, or to employ such part of the land and naval force as shall be judged necessary for the purpose of suppressing such insurrection or of causing the laws to be duly executed; and

Whereas I have received information that combinations of armed men unauthorized by law are now disturbing the peace and safety of the citizens of the State of South Carolina and committing acts of violence in said State of a character and to an extent which render the power of the State and its officers unequal to the task of protecting life and property and securing public order therein; and

Whereas the legislature of said State is not now in session and cannot be convened in time to meet the present emergency, and the executive of said State has therefore made application to me for such part of the military force of the United States as may be necessary and adequate to protect said State and the citizens thereof against the domestic violence hereinbefore mentioned, and to enforce the due execution of the laws;[1] and

Whereas the laws of the United States require, that, whenever it may be necessary in the judgment of the President to use the military force for the purpose aforesaid, he shall forthwith by proclamation command such insurgents to disperse and retire peaceably to their respective abodes within a limited time:

Now, therefore, I, Ulysses S. Grant, President of the United States, do hereby command the persons composing the unlawful combinations aforesaid to disperse and retire peaceably to their respective abodes within twenty days from this date.[2]

In witness whereof I have hereunto set my hand and caused the seal of the United States to be affixed.

Done at the City of Washington this twenty-fourth day of March in the year of our Lord eighteen hundred and seventy-one, and of the Independence of the United States the ninety-fifth.

U. S. GRANT

DS, DNA, RG 130, Presidential Proclamations. On March 24, 1871, Secretary of State Hamilton Fish wrote in his diary. "Cabinet—All present Attorney General reads draft proclamation relating to the unlawful combinations &c in South Carolina—which is approved, & signed—" DLC-Hamilton Fish.

On Nov. 7, 1870, a correspondent reported from Washington, D. C. "Col. C. C. Baker, Aid-de-Camp on the staff of Gov. Scott of South Carolina, arrived here today, and had interviews with the President and Secretary of War, in reference to the condition of affairs in that State. He states that murder and other acts of violence are constantly occurring, and that the offenders go unpunished in consequence of the inertness or want of power of the civil authorities. These offenses have been constantly on the increase since the election, and Col. Baker is seeking the retention of troops in certain localities, who are now under orders to leave for Georgia. An attempt was made a few days since to assassinate Col. Baker, and three shots perforated his clothing, luckily without injuring him." *New York Tribune*, Nov. 8, 1870.

On Jan. 17, 1871, Governor Robert K. Scott of S. C. wrote to Brig. Gen. Alfred H. Terry, Atlanta. Scott sent a copy to USG. "The outrages in Spartanburg and Union Counties in this State have become so numerous, and such a reign of terror exists that but few Republicans dare sleep in their houses at night. A number of people have been whipped and murdered, and I see no remedy, other than the stationing of U. S. Troops in those Counties. At 1. Oclock. Thursday morning the 5th inst, a party of disguised men visited the town of Union, took five men to the woods and shot them, killing three, I would attempt the Suppression of this violence by the State Militia, and am only deterred by the knowledge that their inefficiency in drill &c, would necessarily. fail in accomplishing any good, and that their presence would be a signal for a general uprising and slaughter of those not in sympathy with the marauders. I am satisfied that a large portion of these turbulent men are from North Carolina. As an example of these Outrages I enclose you an extract from a letter written by a man who has been a prominent leader of the republican party in Union County. 'I would have written you sooner, but the opportunity was not good, as I have not slept in my house since I came home from Columbia. and I know many others who have not. The Ku-Klux. have been through my house since I came home, and came the second time, but did not enter.'... I hope, therefore, General, that you will feel disposed to send troops to those Counties with a view of having them remain there for a length of time, or at least until confidence and quiet is rëestablished," Copy, DNA, RG 46, Reports Submitted to Senate. On Feb. 14, Scott telegraphed to USG. "I would request that a detachment of U S. troops be sent to Union CH S C The legislature has made a request of protection which will come by mail" Telegram received (at 4:25 P.M.), *ibid.*, RG 94, Letters Received, 555 1871. On Feb. 15, Gen. William T. Sherman telegraphed to Maj. Gen. Henry W. Halleck, Louisville. "The President orders that a Detachmt of troops be sent to Union Court House South Carolina. I suppose a single Company will be ample." ALS (telegram sent), *ibid.*

On Feb. 8, the S. C. legislature had adopted a "*PREAMBLE AND CONCURRENT RESOLUTION*." "*Whereas*, a state of *domestic violence*, to an alarming extent, exists in this State, especially in the upper Counties thereof, *And Whereas*, murders and punishments of the most barbarous and indecent character, have been, and continue to be inflicted upon the citizens by organized bands of lawless persons.—*And Whereas*, the civil authorities have failed and are altogether unable to arrest and bring to trial the perpetrators of of the murders and outrages above referred to. *And Whereas*, under the existing state of affairs, both life and property are altogether insecure: Be it therefore *Resolved* by the House of Representatives, the Senate concurring, that the Legislature hereby call on the Government of the United States, to give to the citizens of the State, that protection against *domestic violence*, guaranteed to them, by the 4th Section, 4th Article of the Constitution of the United States. *Resolved*; That the foregoing Preamble and Resolution, be sent to the Governor, with the request, that he will transmit the same to the President of the United States, together with the request that it be laid before Congress." DS, *ibid.* On Feb. 14, Scott wrote to USG. "I have the honor to transmit herewith the accompanying preamble and concurrent Resolution of the General Assembly of this State, and respectfully recommend it to your immediate attention. The condition of things in the Counties alluded to is of the most fearful and alarming character, and earnestly demand the interposition of the Federal Government for the protection of the lives and persons of our people from the armed bands of lawless and turbulent men by whom they are threatened, and from whose assaults the forces at the disposal of the State, are utterly incompetent to protect them. To attempt to surpress these organized bands by undisciplined Militia, would only be to inaugurate a war in which the loyal people would be sacrificed. I hope garrisons will be stationed in the upper part of the State, strong enough to create a wholesome influence." LS, *ibid.* On Feb. 18, Orville E. Babcock wrote to U.S. Senator John Scott of Pa. "The President directs me to forward to you the enclosed copies of a Preamble and Resolution of the General Assembly of South Carolina, and of a letter from Gov. Scott, which he has just received and which he desires you to submit to your committee." Copy, DLC-USG, II, 1.

On Feb. 24, Secretary of State Hamilton Fish wrote in his diary. ". . . President refers to the condition of affairs in the South especially in S. Ca Reads the report of the State Constable, of the conditions in several Counties—Murders, Whippings & of Violence—he expressed a determination to bring a regimt of Cavalry, & perhaps one of Infantry, from Texas, where (he says) they are protecting from the Indians a population who annually murder more Union men, merely because they are Union men, than the Indians would kill of them—The Question of bringing Colored troops is considered—on the one side it is urged that the presence of Colored regular soldiers will encourage, the negro population, & give them more confidence & self reliance: on the other it may irritate the white population, & provoke collisions, in which case many at the North will say it was unwise to provoke a prejudice—I present the latter views—Robeson & Delano incline to the former" DLC-Hamilton Fish.

On March 2, S. C. Representatives Warren D. Wilkes and Samuel Nuckles, Washington, D. C., wrote to USG. "About the 18th day of February last, the House of Representatives of the Legislataure of South Carolina, upon the verbal suggeston of Gov. R. K. Scott adopted a Resolution directing the appointment of a Committee of three discreet members of its body irrespective of party, to proceed to Washington City, and lay before the President, a fair and truthful statement of the recent outrages committed in Union and other Counties of said State, and to ask him in the name of the Representatives of the entire people, to immediately send troops into those disturbed Counties, to maintain order, and to protect the lives and property of the citizens. Under said resolution, the speaker appointed Messrs William J. Whipper, Warren D. Wilkes and Samuel Nuckles, as the Committee, who came on to this city, on the 21st day of February last, to discharge the duty assigned to them as aforesaid. Having learned that the Committee probably, would not be able to communicate with your Excellency, for several days, Mr. Whipper felt impelled as Chairman of the Committee of Ways and Means, to return to the Legislature of South Carolina, to perfect and present the General Appropriation Bill. He carried with him the certified copy of the Resolution, expecting to return to this city after the lapse of a few days As he has not arrived, Messrs Wilks and Nuckles having waited thus long, feel it due to themselves and to the body which they in part represent, to ask leave of your Excellency to present the foregoing epitome of said Resolution, which is correct in every respect, the original having been draughted by Mr. Wilkes. The undersigned respectfully urge your Excellency, to comply with the request contained in the resolution, upon a consideration of the following impartial statement of facts. Just prior to the 25th day of last December, a white man named Matt Stevens, of Union County, was killed in a row at a contraband Whiskey waggon. The crime was charged upon a body of colored Militia, commanded by a colored captain Ellick Walker. Walker and some eleven colored men were immediately arrested and lodged in Union Jail. Walker was arrested while on his way to see the Governor in referance to the viollent seizure of the arms of his Company. The others, in defending their guns from violent seizure, got into a conflict, and were induced to surrender and go to Jail, upon the promise of the Intendant and other prominent citizens of Unionvill, that their lives should be protected. Yet in face of this promise of protection Walker and f~~our~~ive of the others were taken in a few nights thereafter, from the Jail, by an armed band of men, said to belong to the Ku-Klux-Klan. Walker and one other were shot dead, and three others left for dead on the ground. Afterwards about the 14th day of February last, learning that the remaining eight colored men who were accused of complicity in the death of Stevens, were likely to by taken to Columbia, on a writ of Habeas Corpus issued by Judge Thomas, seven hundred of the Klu-Klux-Klan, again assaulted the Jail of Union County overpowered the Jailer and by fource took the eight colored men from thence and deliberately murdered them. For a detailed statement of this last outrage, we refer your Excellency to an account thereof written by the Editor of the Unionvill Times and copied into the 'Enterprise' dated the 22nd Feberuary 1871; here-with submitted and marked Exhibit A. The statement of the Editor we suppose to be true, except that the presence of the writ of Habeas Corpus, had been kept a profound secret, It was proven before the undersigned as members of a special Committee to investigate this very outrage, that the Deputy Sheriff exhibited the writ to every lawyer in the town, who pronounced it informal, and left the impression upon the mind of the Sheriff that he was not obliged to obey it. And we charge, that this extraordinary conduct of the Deputy Sheriff and members of the Bar, not only produced the delay in obeying the writ, but gave that notice to the Ku-Klux-Klan, that resulted in the murder of the prisoners—Strange conduct on the part of two sett of officials, solemnly sworn to observe the law! For a statement of the reasons that actuated the Klu-Klux-Klan in perpetrating these outrages, we refer your Excellency to a letter contained in the 'Columbia Phoenix,' of February the 23rd 1871, written from Union Court House, herewith submitted, and marked Exhibit B. The letter is a remarkable one, and exhibites a deep seated hostility to the entire administration of the Government of South Carolina. We call your attention to the fact, that those men murdered in Union, were in the Jail, in the custody of the Law, and ameanable to the law. They had a right to demand, justice did demand that the guilty or innocence of those men should be tested in open Court, by an impartial Jury, and according to the strict rules of evidence, and if found guilty, the measure of their punishment under the law should have been awarded by an authorized Judge. Was this course pursued? So far from it, the spirit of injustice, more than anarchy triumphed, and a band of Klu-Klux, acting as prosecutor, Judge, Jury, and executor, determine, that they are guilty and proceed to inflict, under cover of the night the highest penalty known to the law. The fact stands out that the Courts are closed practically, and night and secrecy is the measure of right. The effect of such a condition of things is seen in the fact, that two hundred colored people have since fled from Union County, in terror for their lives. More recent acts of lawlessness in York, ~~Chester~~ and other counties demonstrate the appalling fact, that in a large scope of South Carolina, the Government thereof is powerless to preserve law and order, to protect life, liberty and property; and the constituted authorities invokes the strong arm of the United States to do so. If it will not, then we declare to your Excellency our solemn conviction as Legislators that violence, encouraged by impunity from punishment, will rapidly extend over the entire state, and culminate in a bloody war of extermination, We trust it will be your pleasure to avert such a calamity, by a prompt intervention of your authority." DS, DNA, RG 94, Letters Received, 4569 1871. The enclosures are *ibid.* Nuckles added a supplement. "The undersigned, as a citizen and Representative of Union County, begs leave to make a statement of facts, coming more immediately within his knowledge. 1st Matt Stevens was a desperate character, he was at a whiskey waggon when killed—that Captain Walker was not present, for his wife was confined on that night and he was at home—that it is well known there were no colored men present in the character of Militia—the meeting at the whiskey waggon was accidental, so far as any colored men were concerned—that Stevens went to raid the whiskey waggon in his character of a Ku-Klux, which is proven by the fact, that his wife it is said, when she heard of his death, exclaimed, Yes! I told him to stay at home—I knew what he would get when he went Ku-Kluxing! When A. S. Wallace candidate for Congress, spoke at Union last year, Matt Stevens tried openly to persuade Al. Buckner to kill him. On saturday night 31st Decr. last, Stevens was killed 4 miles from Union on the Spartanburg road. On the next day a crowd of white men in, and around Union, ranged the country demanding, and taking the State guns in the hands of Walker's company, when they got to Union on Sunday evening, Walker came up and demanded the guns, they refused, and threatened him, this was the reason he made off for Columbia to see the Gov, The crowd came to Joe Vanleu, who lives in Union: his brothers, Button and Henry, one Gordon, and Vanleu's mother were in his house. The crowd demanded their guns, they refused to give them up, the mob then fired into the house some thirty rounds, and wounded Button Vanlue, and Gordon, the latter died of his wounds, The fire was returned from the house, and Dan Smith wounded. The assailants then left and carried Smith off. The Intendant of the town, and two other prominent citizens of Union, came down a pursuaded Joe, Henry, and Button Vanlue, to surrender, promising if they would do so that their lives should be protected, They did so, were carried to Jail, locked up and these men put the keys into their pockets. A few nights there-after, the Jail was entered by the Ku-Klux and Walker, and another killed. The second time the Jail was entered by the Klu-Klux, anong the colored men taken out and killed were Joe and Henry Vanlue. Prior to these murders, on North Pacolet River in Union County,—Owens (white) was killed by the Klu-Klux; Jim Peeler, was killed by the Klu-Klux on Broad river. Strab Jeffers, colored was in like manner killed near Cherokee ford on Broad river. A colored man, Rufus Norton, was also stripped and whipped with thorns on account of his Republican principles. For this reason Giles White (colored). was whipped and forced to leave the County. D. D. Goings elected last year Probate Judge, Union County was whipped until he resigned the office. I know of many more who were whipped on account of their Republican principles, and driven from my section of the County" DS, *ibid.* On July 20, Nuckles testified in Columbia, S. C., before a subcommittee of the Joint Select Committee to Inquire into the Condition of Affairs in the Late Insurrectionary States. "I am a refugee from Union County.... *Question.* Are you afraid to go back to Union County to live? *Answer.* I am, at this time, unless there is an alteration. The reason I am so now is because they became so bitter against me because I went to Washington as one of the committee on account of the whippings and outrages in my county.... *Question.* You are still a member of the legislature? *Answer.* Yes, sir. *Question.* Were you called upon to resign? *Answer.* Yes, sir;... *Question.* How many members are there from Union? *Answer.* Four—three in the house and one in the senate. *Question.* How many of them have resigned? *Answer.* None of them, for they are all here—myself, and Samuel Farr, Junius Mobley, and H. R. Duncan. There are three colored men of us and one white man.... I am about fifty-seven years old.... I can read a little and write my name.... I never was at school.... *Question.* You were a slave? *Answer.* Yes, sir; a hard-down slave.... *Question.* You say the Ku-Klux became bitter against you because you went to Washington; how do you know that? *Answer.* When I came back from Washington I got into conversation with Mr. Dunn, our sheriff, at Union Village, and he told me I had better not go up there in Union County. I was very well known in Union Village, because I used to live there. I used to be a citizen of that town, and had a blacksmith shop there...." *SRC*, 42-2-41, part 4, pp. 1158–61, 1163.

On March 9, Governor Scott had telegraphed to USG. "I must call for more troops. an actual state of war exists in York & Chester Counties fighting for four days by KuKlux from North Carolina & this state I will be compelled to declare martial law legislature not in session" Telegram received (at 9:50 P.M.), DNA, RG 60, Letters Received, S. C. On March 10, USG telegraphed to Scott. "Troops will be sent to South Carolina" ALS (telegram sent), *ibid.*, RG 107, Telegrams Collected (Bound). On March 13, AG Edward D. Townsend telegraphed to Halleck. "Your despatch of 12th recd—Genl Sherman sent you a despatch the 11th Four comps of Cavalry in North & South Caro ~~He has no farther order, use your own discretion~~—The President wishes you to send troops immediately from those now under your command to York and chester Counties So. Ca there to be replaced by the new ones as they arrive, at your discretion." Df (initialed), *ibid.*, RG 94, Letters Received, 767 1871.

On April 19, Mrs. S. E. Lane, Chesterfield District, S. C., wrote to USG. "I do not know that any Apology is necessary for my addressing you, for nothing but the extreme urgency of the case induced me thus to take the liberty of trespassing, even by a few lines, upon your time & patience,—I write to ask your help, your protection for us, a few families located in Chesterfield District S. C. the immediate locality known formerly as 'Old Store'—Post Office address Oro—a few miles from here—Staunch & loyal to you Sir, we are as the head & Administrator of our National Affairs & interests—true & hearty Republicans, & as individuals & families, kind & friendly to all around us—but Sir, we are in terror from Ku-Klux threats & outrages—there is neither law or justice in our midst,—our nearest neighbor—a prominent Repub'can now lies dead—murdered, by a disguised Ruffian Band, which attacked his House at midnight a few nights since—his wife also was murdered—she was buried yesterday, & a daughter is lying dangerously ill from a shot-wound.—my Husband's life is threatened—a northern man who has bought a Plantation here—a friend's also,—a northern man—Revd Dr Fox, formerly of N. Y,—only because they are Republicans—we are in constant fear & terror—our nights are sleepless, we are filled with anxiety & dismay.—Ought this to be?—it seems almost impossible to believe that we are in our own Land,—thus to be left without protection or redress,—letters, have several times been Sent from here to Govr Scott for aid, but no help has come—not even Arms, nor as much as a reply to the letters. Now Mr Pres't, I appeal to you,—in the strength & power with which you are invested, in the high & honorable, & responsible position you hold toward us,—& as a Husband & Father too,—have compassion, & send *at once* Troops, to protect us, & enforce law—" ALS, *ibid.*, 1414 1871. On the same day, Henry J. Fox, Oro, S. C., wrote to John P. Newman. "We have tried all means of obtaining releif and have failed—we try now, a womans expediant. The writer of the enclosed letter a Mrs Lane, the wife of a presbyterian clergyman has not overstated our terror. She does not know as I do, all the grounds of alarm. I have to sleep out in the woods. We beg you to read the letter to the president. Help us if you can. I have just come from the scene of blood and death. We are marked as the next.... Our mails are tampered with, & it would set our minds at rest, if we can know this reaches you. One line is enough" ALS, *ibid.* Related papers are *ibid.*

On May 12, C. F. Jones, Glenn Springs, Spartanburg County, wrote to USG. "I am a clergyman, superannuated, dwellin[g] on my plantation, having a number of coloured tenants and hired labourers. On Thursday night, the 4th inst, my farm was invaded by a gang of disguised ruffians, who went from house, dragging the inmates out, beating them, firing pistols at them &c—a bullet has since been extracted from the head of one—another aged, upright, christian man, was slaughtered, in his own yard, while begging them to spare him. I applied to the nearest trial justice. He could do nothing. Enclosed is his reply—afterwards I applied to the Sheriff—with the same result. Enclosed is his reply—Then I applied to Capt Myers, commander of the Cavalry—his orders had not arrived and he could do nothing. Thus we are left totally helpless, und[er] a reign of terror. If we knew the murderer, and were to denounce him to the authorities our lives would be forfeited. What is remarkable is that the republican newspapers, are perfectly silent in regard to these weekly occurring murders and outrages, playing into the hands of Gov Scott, a weak, vacillating man, who blows hot and cold—I have read your proclamation to the poor trembling people and told them when president Grant says, he will exhaust the powers of the government for their protection it is sure to be done—He is a man of action, not words. To prevent this letter from being intercepted, it will be enclosed to the Post master at Washington. *Please not to publish my name, or I might suffer—*" ALS, *ibid.*, 1831 1871. The enclosures are *ibid.* On May 23, Secretary of War William W. Belknap endorsed these items. "Copies of these papers to be sent to Chairman of Congressional Committee now in session" AE (initialed), *ibid.*

On May 23, Joseph Crews, Columbia, S. C., wrote to USG. "I understand that thier is some brobibility of the Troops being removed from Laurensville in this State I hope you will not allow it done as the County has been the scene of a great many ottrages and I am confident I can not return to Laurens (my house) if the Troops are removed I hope you will have Gen Terry requested to keep Laurens garrisoned until after our next Election as it is highly important that our People should not be under any more danger than they are now" ALS, *ibid.*, 1997 1871. On July 1, Belknap wrote to Crews. "Your comn relative to the removal of troops from Laurensville, S. C., has been received from the President; and as, on investigation, it appears they were removed on the report & recommendation of the Adjutant General of the State, who should be aware of any sufficient reason for their remaining, if such existed, the Department does not consider it either advisable or expedient to rescind the order." Copy, *ibid.* On July 26, 1872, Crews wrote to USG complaining that troops had not been returned to Laurensville. ALS, *ibid.* See *SRC*, 42-2-41, part 5, pp. 1314–15.

On July 26, 1871, Maj. Lewis Merrill testified in Yorkville, S. C., before a subcommittee of the Joint Select Committee. "*Question.* Are you the officer in command of the post at this place? *Answer.* Yes, sir. *Question.* At what time did you come here? *Answer.* Within a few days of the 26th of March, 1871. I assumed command on the 26th. *Question.* What is your rank in the Army? *Answer.* Major of the Seventh Cavalry, and brevet colonel. . . . At the date of my arrival, the people, both white and black, of this county, were still very much excited; but the condition of affairs was better than it had been for some time previous, and the excitement and bitterness, exhibited in acts of violence appeared to be rapidly subsiding. The hope that this state of things would continue, and even decidedly improve, proved to be delusive. Within a week or two the Ku-Klux organization renewed their acts of outrage and violence, which for some time became nightly more aggravated and numerous. This state of affairs continued until some few weeks since, since which time the number and aggravation of acts of outrage have decreased, and are now few. I do not, however, consider this the result of the abandonment of the organization, but believe it comes from other and transient causes, and that the outrages and violence will, in the near future, be renewed with more vigor than ever. My duty here was to aid the civil authorities of both the State and the United States, should they call upon me for assistance, and I was instructed by my commanding officer to exercise all the moral influence possible to bring about a better state of things here, and in any case to protect individuals against mob violence or illegal arrest, should they seek the shelter of my camp. . . . [I]n the course of my official conversation with General Terry, commander of the department, I asked him how much truth there was in the newspaper stories. He replied, 'When you get to South Carolina you will find that the half has not been told you.' Still, I came here with the idea that they were sporadic instances of mob violence, fully impressed with the notion that they were a few occasional cases that might be regarded rather as vigilance committee matters than anything else. When I first came here I was impressed for a number of days with the idea, from my conversation with the principal people here, and from the appearance of things, that there was every probability, and I so reported, of a speedy termination of these acts. But very soon, from the facts brought to my notice, I had occasion to change my mind, and I became convinced that the Ku-Klux organization was not only a very large one and exceedingly well organized, but a very dangerous one, and that their purpose was to persist in this whenever opportunity favored them. I am now of opinion that I never conceived of such a state of social disorganization being possible in any civilized community as exists in this county now. Although quiet, it is now very little better than it has been previously. There appears to me to be a diseased state of public sentiment in regard to the administration of justice. . . ." *Ibid.*, pp. 1463–64, 1470, 1481–82. See Proclamation, Oct. 12, 1871; note to William W. Belknap, Jan. 30, 1872, note 1; Allen W. Trelease, *White Terror: The Ku Klux Klan Conspiracy and Southern Reconstruction* (New York, 1971), pp. 369–76.

On July 18, Horace Porter, Long Branch, N. J., had written to Secretary of the Treasury George S. Boutwell. "The President has received a letter from Luke P. Poland, John Pool, and John Coburn, of the Committee on Southern outrages, asking whether there are any funds in the Treasury ~~of~~ or State Departments which can be applied to assisting them in continuing their labors. It seems that they have exhausted the Congressional appropriation. The letter was referred to the state Dep't, and the Sec. of State requested to inform these gentlemen in regards to its means of assisting them. The President requests that you will furnish them similar information in regard to your Department." ALS, DNA, RG 56, Letters Received.

1. On March 16, Governor Scott had written to USG. "I am under the painful necessity of informing you that combinations of armed men unauthorized by law are now disturbing the peace and safety of the citizens of this State, and committing acts of violence of a character and to an extent which render the power of the State and its Officers unequal to the task of protecting life and property and securing public order. The Legislature is not now in Session, and it will be impossible to convene it in time to meet the present emergency. I, therefore, make application to you for such Military force of the United States as may be necessary and adequate to protect this State and the Citizens thereof agains[t] the domestic violence hereinbefore mentioned and to enforce the due execution of the Laws" LS, *ibid.*, RG 59, Miscellaneous Letters. On the same day, Daniel H. Chamberlain, S. C. attorney gen., wrote to Attorney Gen. Amos T. Akerman. "His Excellency Governor Scott requests me to acknowledge receipt of yours of the 11th, instant, and to inform you that he has this day forwarded an application to the President in accordance with your suggestion." LS, *ibid.*, RG 60, Letters Received, S. C.

On March 21, "Senators Robertson and Sawyer accompanied D. H. Chamberlain, Attorney General of South Carolina, and L. D. Carpenter, to the Executive Mansion, the last two named having been delegated by the Governor of that State to visit the President on the subject of affording protection to the people in the upper part of South Carolina, near the North Carolina line. Mr. Chamberlain represented the condition of affairs in that section, and desired to know how long the four companies of cavalry, now on their way thither, would remain there, for he said if their sojourn were only for a brief period it would do more harm than good. The President listened patiently to the representations made to him, and assured the gentlemen that the troops should remain there long enough to restore peace and secure obedience to the laws, even if they should be thus employed during the remainder of his administration. The gentlemen expressed themselves satisfied, and will to-morrow leave for home. . . ." *Philadelphia Public Ledger*, March 22, 1871.

In late May, Governor Scott met USG in Washington, D. C. Scott indicated that "there was no necessity for putting the State under martial law, and that there was a good state of feeling among the better classes of citizens to put down Kuklux organizations." *New York Times*, May 27, 1871.

2. On June 14, Reuben Tomlinson, former S. C. auditor, testified in Washington, D. C., before the Joint Select Committee. "*Question.* What is your belief as to the efficacy of the law of Congress recently passed for the purpose of bringing offenders of that class to justice? *Answer.* I am scarcely lawyer enough to decide that question. I confess I have had some want of faith as to the efficacy of that law; I do not know that there is any law that can better things in South Carolina. . . . I think the effect of the President's proclamation under that law has been good. There has been only one case of outrage that I know of since that proclamation was made; that occurred at Newberry, about two or three weeks or a month ago. . . . *Question.* Do you think these outrages are committed by property-holders? *Answer.* No, sir; I think they are committed mostly by young men. There is a class of men who have nothing to do but loaf about taverns and bar-rooms; I think the outrages are committed mainly by that class

of men, but I think they are countenanced to a lamentable degree by the intelligent people of those counties. In my judgment, they could not occur if the intelligent people of those counties set themselves against it. *Question.* You mean the old white property-holding element? *Answer.* Yes, sir. I do not think it is at all certain but what these bands may get the better of everybody in those counties before they get through. *Question.* Do you suppose they are increasing in the upper part of the State? *Answer.* I think they are thoroughly organized, and simply lying quiet now, as the result of the proclamation of the President based upon this law. My opinion is that unless something is done between now and next year, there will be a great deal of trouble in South Carolina. . . ." *SRC*, 42-2-41, part 3, pp. 88, 93. See also *ibid.*, part 4, pp. 941–43.

To Joseph H. Dixon and Charles Rehm

TO JOSEPH H. DIXON AND CHARLES REHM, GREETING:

Whereas, it appears by information in due form by me received, that Alfred Ziegenmeyer, charged with the crime of murder in Cook County in the State of Illinois, is a fugitive from the justice of the United States and is now believed to be in the City of Bremen, Germany;

And whereas, application has been made for the extradition, by the authorities of the North German Union, of said fugitive, in compliance with existing treaty stipulations and laws, enacted for giving effect to such stipulations;

And whereas, information has been received that, in compliance with such application the necessary Warrant is ready to be issued by the authorities aforesaid for the delivery of the above named fugitive into the custody of such person or persons as may be duly authorized to receive said fugitive and bring him back to the United States for trial.

Now therefore, you are hereby authorized and empowered in virtue of the treaty aforesaid and in the execution thereof, to receive the said Alfred Ziegenmeyer as aforesaid, and to take and hold him in your custody and conduct him from such place of delivery in Germany, by the most direct convenient means of transportation to and into the State of Illinois, there to surrender the said Alfred Ziegenmeyer to the proper authorities of the State of Illinois.

For all which these Presents shall be your sufficient warrant

In testimony whereof, I have hereunto signed my name and caused the Seal of the United States to be affixed.

Done at the City of Washington, this Twenty seventh day of March, A. D. 1871, and of the Independence of the United States the Ninety fifth.

U. S. GRANT.

Copy, DNA, RG 59, General Records. On March 27, 1871, Secretary of State Hamilton Fish wrote to George Bancroft, U.S. minister, Berlin. "You are instructed to apply for the issue of a Warrant, in conformity with the stipulations contained in the Convention of June 16th 1852, between the United States and Prussia and other States of the Germanic Confederation, a copy of which is herewith enclosed for the extradition of one Alfred Ziegenmyer, charged with the commission of the crime of murder in the State of Illinois, and who is supposed to be now under arrest at Bremen. Messrs Jasper H. Dixon and Charles Rehm, who will probably present themselves at your Legation, are in possession of the evidence in the case, and are entrusted with the necessary power to receive the criminal and bring him back to the United States for trial." Copy, *ibid.*, Diplomatic Instructions, Germany. On April 24 and May 8, Bancroft wrote to Fish. "Alfred Ziegenmeyer to escape extradition denies his American citizenship; first he said he had never made application for citizen papers and that assertion being proved false he asserts that he was in America but three years and a half and that therefore under our treaty we have no right to claim his delivery. . . ." L (incomplete), *ibid.*, Diplomatic Despatches, Germany. "The authorities at Brunswick with the approbation of the German government have delivered up Alfred Ziegenmeyer. It appeared incontrovertibly that he had not been five years in the United States and that his naturalization paper was fraudulent. Nevertheless he had made use of his American passport and was on record with the police as an American citizen; and they declined to go behind the record. The extradition is made on the assumption that he is an American citizen" LS, *ibid.* Alfred Ziegenmeyer, born about 1850, had been accused of murdering and then impersonating his friend William Gumbleton, an Irish businessman. Tried in Chicago, Ziegenmeyer was convicted and sentenced to life imprisonment. See *New York Times*, May 4, July 18, 1871; *Chicago Tribune*, July 25, 28, 1871.

To James F. Casey

Washington D. C. March 27th *1871.*

DEAR CASEY

I advise that you make no removals from the Custom House merely because of adherence to this or that wing of the Republican party.[1]

Every man holding place should be reliable and equal to the duties he has to perform and should be a republican. I would not enquire however whether he belonged to this or to that wing of the party.

Above all I would not make removals on such such grounds.

your truly
U S. GRANT

Copy, USG 3. On March 26 and 27, 1871, U.S. Senator J. Rodman West of La. wrote to Governor Henry C. Warmoth of La. "Your two letters of the 19th & 20th have reached me since I last wrote. We might just as well understand the matter at once—the President is not with us—he is a political coward—After my argument before the Committee the chairman was instructed to call on Grant and ascertain whether he desired that Blanchard should be confirmed. The President's reply was—'I leave the matter to the Senate—to do as they think best for the Republican party' Did you ever hear of such a political Bimsby? Nearly all the colored city delegation who endorsed Blanchard have revoked by telegram to Kellogg. I have not ⅚th of the delegation—Sheldon is the only one who stands square and manly—Morey cannot meddle in the fight—Darrell belongs to Kellogg and Sypher is standing on his dignity about the President—But I am not discouraged—though standing nearly alone I am giving them the best fight I have got on hand, and from all appearances the enemy don't feel very comfortable. Now taking the chances of Blanchard's rejection, and the open and avowed hostility of every federal officer in the State, with Dunn's mighty influence among his color, can we carry next State Convention? Meantime we must make no war on Grant—let that matter sleep until we have had the Convention fight. All my energies now are directed to having the Committee report favorably on Blanchard's case—but K. and I are bound to have it out in the Senate any way I suppose—I shall go for him—rest assured—" "I was too unwell to go to the White House to-day—so I sent Longstreet's letter (tell him) to the President. The annexed note from Babcock implies that Grant has telegraphed to Casey to hold up—The rehearing of Blanchard's case will take place before the Committee in a day or two—I think we are going to win—am working under my friend Kg—do nothing until I get back to N. O." ALS, Warmoth Papers, Southern Historical Collection, University of North Carolina, Chapel Hill, N. C. On the same day, Orville E. Babcock had written to West. "Your note is at hand. The President has read the letter. and I think acted upon it, You will never be considered 'intrusive' when sending anything you may ~~have~~ wish me to attend to." ALS, *ibid.* On March 17, James Longstreet, surveyor of customs, New Orleans, wrote to USG concerning the appointment of a postmaster at New Orleans. Parke-Bernet Sale No. 2235, Dec. 3, 1963, no. 155. On March 29 and 30, West wrote to Warmoth. "I have your two notes of the 25th Inst: Lowell has been to the President and expressed willingness to resign if not 'Kicked out' as you say—Yet having witnessed the President's vacillation I doubt even with this invitation he will remove him after Congress adjourns, should Blanchard fail. As well as I can comprehend Kellogg's plan it is to prevent action on the Blanchard case, and then to have Lowell retained on the magnanimity plea—Ramsey chairman Com'te has promised me another hearing, but he is very loth to decide either for or against me, and in fact outside influence will do more to decide the matter than any hearings—I am working hard in this way myself—Kellogg's game is to smother everything—I can beat him before the Committee and hope to ~~be~~ before the Senate—Old Hamlin is working hard for Lowell. I don't think Kellogg will quote Mark's paper—I would be very much obliged to him if he would There is no telling what Grant will do, but I believe he is afraid to withdraw Blanchard's name. In response to Longstreet's letter Grant wrote to Casey on the 27th to keep out of our fights, and not to remove any man because he was your friend. But there are events transpiring that will show us the way out of our fights much easier than by having Grant with us—in fact I do not kn[o]w whether we want him or not—ponder over this—and when I get back we will see how the land lays—Meantime I will continue my fight for Blanch[a]rd—if we win it, remember we a[r]e under no obligation to Grant as he renders no aid whatever—" "I am convinced that we have no prospect of effectiveness in the organization of our party matters in N. O. as long as Casey remains Collector—I think it very probable that I can get Sheldon and Sypher to join me in a personal presentation of this view to the President. Unless we can get wholesale endorsement (and we cannot have that as long as Casey is there) of our views by the President, we can do better by avowed opposition to Grant, than by temporizing with him. Give this consideration and and if you agree with me telegraph 'make the move on Jones', as our time is growing short here—Remember that our failure will be war with Grant but it seems to me that it must come sooner or later. Of course I shall do nothing as long as Blanchard's case is undecided. I fancy that Kellogg's game is to foster dissension within our party—I infer this from having had Frank Blair sounded—he is square against me and will hurt me with the Democrats—Kellogg is very thick with him—It would be well to have Hatch write him" ALS, Warmoth Papers, Southern Historical Collection.

On Nov. 17, 1870, Longstreet had written to USG. "The impression seems to be general, *amongst your earnest friends* that a change in the Offices of Marshall and Post Master would be of great advantage to the party in the State. I have just learned that efforts are being made in favor of Col Wm Roy and Mr B. P. Blanchard for the positions, and avail myself of the opportunity to make the same recommendation. There seems to be a disposition on the part of the gentlemen, who are objected to, to create dissension, and serious apprehensions are felt of a party divided against itself, unless a change which will insure concert of action is made. The late election will satisfy you of the political character of the State, and I believe that I may safely assure you that with proper support the state will secure increasing majorities. Gov Warmoth is your staunch friend and supporter and feels the necessity of the change suggested." ALS, DNA, RG 60, Records Relating to Appointments. A copy of this letter, dated Nov. 18 and with variant text, is in the Warmoth Papers, Southern Historical Collection. On Nov. 17, Frank Morey and two others, New Orleans, wrote to USG. "We respectfully ask the immediate removal of Chas W. Lowell, Postmaster of New Orleans and S. B. Packard, U. S. Marshall of the District of Louisiana, We are constrained to make this request of your Excellency, because these gentlemen are factionists and dissentionists and are seeking to disturb and divide the Republican party on unnecessary issues and impracticable measures, During the late Canvass and election they used the influence derived from their official positions against Republican party measures and for the gratificiation of personal animosities and the attainment of personal advantages to the neglect of party interests and the hazard of our party success in this City and State. There is no reason to believe their conduct in the future will differ from what it has been in the past. We consider it unquestionable that the immediate removal of these gentlemen will greatly promote the peace and future success of the Republican party in Louisiana." Copy, *ibid.* On Nov. 25, M. A. Southworth, New Orleans, La. member, National Republican Executive Committee, wrote to USG. "I respectfully recommend the immediate removal of Chas. W. Lowell Postmaster at New Orleans, and of S. B. Packard U. S. Marshall for Louisiana for the reasons given in the petition of the Republican Auxilliary Committee," Copy, *ibid.*

On Nov. 19, U.S. Representative Lionel A. Sheldon of La., New Orleans, had written to USG. "Col. Charles W. Lowell Post Master of NewOrleans during the late canvass in this State has pursued a cou[rs]e tending to distract and disrupt the republican party, He has incurred the displeasure of many of our most active and efficient and leading republicans and there has been given by him much cause for this displeasure, If Col. Lowell is displaced by the appointment in his place of Mr. Brainard P. Blanchard; the change shall receive my approval and support and I recommend that this change be made. Mr. Blanchard is a young man of extraordinary capacity, unexceptionable in his habits and character and is entitled to the greatest favors for his labors in the republican cause and especially in the State Campaign just ended. This appointment would give general satisfaction to the party and people." Copy, *ibid.* On Dec. 17, Babcock wrote to U.S. Senator William P. Kellogg of La., Willard's Hotel. "The President will be pleased to see Gov. Dunn on Monday at noon. He says *noon* for the members of the House and Senate will be at the capitol at that time. If the Govr is to leave before Monday, he says he will see him tomorrow after dinner. He wants to see the Govr before he leaves." Copy, DLC-USG, II, 1. On Monday, Dec. 19, USG met with Kellogg and Lt. Governor Oscar J. Dunn of La. to discuss the appointment of postmaster at New Orleans. *New Orleans Picayune*, Dec. 20, 1870. On Dec. 20, Horace Porter wrote to U.S. Senator Alexander Ramsey of Minn. "The President directs me to request you to with-hold action in your committee upon the nomination of B. P. Blanchard to be P. M. at New. Orleans until you hear from him further concerning it." Copy, DLC-USG, II, 1. On Dec. 22, Warmoth wrote to USG. "*Confidential* . . . I enclose you two telegraphic dispatches, dictated by Senator Kellogg and clipped from the New Orleans Picayune.—He also telegraphed, a day or two ago, to gentlemen here, that you had directed Mr. Blanchard's commission to be delayed until the Senate takes action on his confirmation; and yesterday, he caused to be telegraphed to this city, that you had directed Mr. Blanchard's name to be withdrawn from the Senate. Mr Creswell also told Genl. Sheldon there would be delay in sending the commission. I send you these clippings and give you this information that you may know of the course that the Postmaster General and Senator Kellogg are pursuing in the matter." LS, OFH. On Dec. 7, USG had nominated Brainard P. Blanchard as postmaster, New Orleans; the Senate rejected this nomination.

On Jan. 19, 1871, Longstreet, Washington, D. C., wrote to Warmoth. "I arrived last night. Had an extended interview with the President to-day and explained your views as to the political prospects of La. and your apprehension that designing parties might have misrepresented you, to him, and stated that you only needed his confidence and support to insure satisfactory results in the future. He says that such reports as have reached him have been made in such way as to indicate intentions to prejudice your purposes and interests, and that therefore they have made no impression upon him. That your recommendations will have great weight, and probably controlling influence. Particularly after you are in condition to aid his recommendations in the senate. Meanwhile it may be better to defer other nominations.

He seems fully prepared to renew his nomination of your choice for P. M. as soon as it is probable that the nomination will be confirmed. In short he only asks that you, or those who make recommendations will only select the best men for the positions. He expressed the hope that Gen West will not come here pledged against San Domingo. If the Commission reports favorably upon it, he will probably do so, too, but the matter will not receive further consideration if an adverse report is made. I hope to start back on 24th or 25. Sooner if I can have our business in the sugar seizures, and compromises arranged. Unless you have other suggestions. If you have I hope that you will telegraph me to remain until your instructions are received . . . The Prest asked me why we did not telegraph him when the rumor was started that he intended instructing Federal Officers to oppose the election of your favorite candidate for the U. S. Senate." ALS, Warmoth Papers, Southern Historical Collection. On Feb. 16, Kellogg wrote to USG. "If it is desired that the nomination recently sent to Senate for Post Master at N. Orleans be left before the Senate this can be attained by withdring the *message* of *withdrawl.* This last did not take effect eles the nomination would have been returned by order of withdrawl entered upon Calander of Senate. Such is not now the case for when the Telegram from Babcock to Porter come in though not strictly official the message of withdrawl was by common consent laid on Table to await whatever further action you might desire to take in the premises. I have consulted the oldest Senators & all agree with me in this" ALS, OFH. On March 10, Babcock wrote to Postmaster Gen. John A. J. Creswell. "The President directs me to say that, he will be pleased to have you have a nomination prepared to go to the Senate to day of B. P. Blanchard to be Deputy Post master at New Orleans." Copy, DLC-USG, II, 1. On March 13, Porter wrote to Creswell. "The President directs me to request that the name of Henry S. Gibbons to be Deputy Post Master at St. Johns Michigan and that of B. P. Blanchard, to be Deputy Post Master at New Orleans, La. be withdrawn from the Senate to day. Both of these nominations went in on the 10th instant." Copy, *ibid.* On the same day, Babcock telegraphed to West and to Porter, Senate Chamber. "President has left office. Cannot do anything to-day." "Keep that withdrawal of P. M. in New Orleans." Copies, *ibid.*, II, 5. On March 14, West wrote to Warmoth. "Our web has been so tangled the past few days that I doubt my ability to describe the events. The President sent in Blanchard's name on Friday—Saturday we had no session—Kellogg interviewed the President on Monday morning—a friend over-heard the President tell him that he would withdraw Bs appointment—this news reached me at 12 30 in the Senate—I immediately went to the White House and Porter had left for the Senate with the withdrawal—got the Prest to telegraph to Porter at the Senate to withhold the withdrawal—the message failed to reach Porter in time and when I returned to the Senate the withdrawal was in the hands of the Vice President, and although I fell heir to the telegram that did not reach Porter, it was not official and I could do nothing more than get the matter laid over. This morning the fully signed telegram signed by yourself, Judges, administrators, Senators and members reached me and Sheldon accompanied me to the White House—we had a very pointed talk with the President and *he agreed to send in to-day another message withdrawing the withdrawal*—thus putting the nomination back in the hands of the Senate. I went up to the usual session, saw Ramsey and enough of the Committee on Post Offices who agreed to report favorably on my assurance that the President would do as I said he would—Kellogg found out what I had done, and he brought pressure enough to bear upon Ramsey to induce him to say that he would report the case without recommendation. Then K. commenced electioneering with Hamlin, Stewart, Nye,

Stewart &c using entreaties with some and making bargains with others—I was not idle and we had the field about even—I was prepared for a bitter fight in executive session and still think I would have won. What was my astonishment at 1 30 P. M. when Porter came in with the daily budget, to find that *Grant had not done as he agreed to, two hours before.* Kellogg was quick to discern this and used it—*what answer could I make?* the case was ruined by Grant's vacillation—first he nominates—then he withdraws—then he attempts to get that back—then he agrees to recall withdrawal and finally he ignominiously peters out as Mrs Deane says—What kind of a fight could I make with such backing? Casey, Dunn, Lowell and Carter are all here or will be shortly and we need never expect to hear of Grant's support again—It is all gone, or rather never was worth a cent—Bottle your wrath, draw your own inferences—lay out your plans and *stand alone* for you have got to—We must carry the next state convention at all hazards—Be cautious in what you say—events will loom up—make themselves and we must adapt ourselves to them for" AL (incomplete), Warmoth Papers, Southern Historical Collection. On March 17, USG again nominated Blanchard; he was not confirmed.

On March 15, 1872, West wrote to Warmoth. "... Blanchard will be renominated to-morrow as the telegraph will have told you I believe the matter was referred to the Cabinet—and the decision come to to send his name in once more—but I believe the President will not urge his friends to vote for his confirmation—With the ramifications of K's venality he can pull powerful strings—If I can get the case fairly before the Senate in Executive Session I believe I could carry it, and shall not mince matters in ventilating it—But very many artifices can be resorted to to prevent this, and a confirmation can be defeated ~~to prevent this~~ by a motion to reconsider at this late day. So meagre do the chances look that the House delegation thought that I ought not to let Blanchard's name go in again, but I Wanted the prestige of the *President being against Lowell.* I shall not allow B. to be rejected, but if his confirmation fails he cannot be appointed after adjournment: Grant is determined to remove Lowell and if we can't win under Blanchard now, we shall encounter the same difficulties next winter—So we must look out for a new man—how will C. H. Merritt answer? John Lynch is not eligible as P. M, but I have him in my mind for something else. If necessary ie—Blanchard's failure and early adjournment—telegraph me who is your preference—..." ALS, *ibid.* USG did not renominate Blanchard. See *HMD*, 42-2-211, 327–29, 434–53. On March 1, 1873, USG nominated Charles W. Ringgold as postmaster, New Orleans, replacing Lowell.

1. On March 5, 1871, James F. Casey, collector of customs, New Orleans, telegraphed to USG. "I would urge the two names recommended by myself and others for appraisers, you can rest assured they are the best men proposed. if the change is made it should be done at once." Telegram received (on March 6), DNA, RG 56, Appraiser of Customs Applications. On March 8, Stephen B. Packard, U.S. marshal, New Orleans, telegraphed to USG. "State Committee & Collector Casey are in entire accord upon changes in appraisers Department & agreed upon names submitted we earnestly hope the Collector will be sustained in this matter as party interest will thus be subserved" Telegram received (at 6:10 P.M.), *ibid.* On March 13 or 14, Porter telegraphed to Casey. "Secretary has telegraphed you about appointments. If you insist on appointment of Dunn I think it will be made." ALS (telegram sent), *ibid.*, RG 107, Telegrams Collected (Bound). That same month, Casey, Dunn, Packard, and John Ray wrote to USG. "Should a vacancy arise in the Appraiser's department here, no appointee thereto could be more vigilant and scrupulous in behalf of

the Government than Fabius McK. Dunn, Esq of this city. Mr Dunn is one of our most pronounced independent and active Republicans and as warm in the faith as his distinguished relative our Lieut: Governor. In his selection, the government would not only requite signal though modest merit but assure itself a reliable servant." DS, *ibid.*, RG 56, Appraiser of Customs Applications. Kellogg endorsed this letter. "I know Mr McK Dunn to be a young man of ability & as I believe of undoubted ~~ability~~ integrity. he was formerly an officer in this N. O. Custom House & proved himself both faithful & efficient, Mr Darrall & Mr Morey M. C. of La also give him a high character." AES (undated), *ibid.* On March 9, USG nominated Fabius McK. Dunn as appraiser of merchandise, New Orleans, replacing Henry P. Sampson.

On Dec. 29, Longstreet wrote to USG reporting his place threatened by "some prominent Federal Officers here . . . It is true that that does not affect my duty to yourself, nor will it effect my zeal in your service, nor my appreciation of your noble character. . . ." Parke-Bernet Sale No. 2235, Dec. 3, 1963, no. 155. On March 12, 1872, USG nominated John M. G. Parker as surveyor of customs, New Orleans, after Longstreet's resignation. On April 9, USG withdrew this nomination at Parker's request and nominated James H. Ingraham. See *PUSG*, 19, 469. On July 2, Ingraham, New Orleans, wrote to USG. "A committee will wait upon your Excellency, and request the removal of Marshal Packard and myself, ostensibly for an improper use of our official positions, but really that we may be humiliated for the overwhelming defeat of venal and corrupt political aspirations, of which the committee is but the representative and tool. Failing in the lavish and unblushing expenditure of money, and profiting but little from the patent and very questionable support of Govr Warmoth, Mr Billings, and his friends intend to visit with sore displeasure all who have labored to preserve the purity of the Republican party, and were true to Louisiana's best interests. It is impossible to anticipate with certainty what charges may be brought against me. Certain it is that I have been guilty of no dereliction of official duty. I have not officially attempted to coerce in any manner, any political organization, nor any individual, with whom I have had official relations. I beg leave to assure you that I have done nothing as an officer that you will disapprove, nor anything as a gentleman that will cause my friends to be ashamed. I therefore respectfully request that you will suspend action in the matter, until I shall have had an opportunity to answer my traducers." LS, DNA, RG 56, Appraiser of Customs Applications. On March 5, 1873, USG nominated Parker as surveyor to replace Ingraham.

On Feb. 16, 1871, Ray, New Orleans, had written to USG. "When at Washington in Decr in an interview, you were kind enough to grant me, I explained to you the circumstances that at that time disturbed or was likely to disturb the harmony of the Republican party in this State—those causes operated so as, at the commencement of our present session of the Legislature, to create considerable feeling, but I am gratified to be able to say to you that much progress has been made in healing those difficulties, and I confidently expect that by the close of this session the party will be perfectly harmonious and as strong and possibly stronger than at any period in this state. I think that your prudence in leaving the parties to settle their own differences has had much to in bringing about this result Permit me to say to you that I feel confident that at the next Presidential election the Republican party will be a unit for you in this state if you should allow your name to be used" Copy, Warmoth Papers, Southern Historical Collection.

To George W. Dent

Washington D. C. Mch 27. /71.

SIR:

I have to acknowledge the receipt of your letter and to inform you that I hope to leave here by the 10th or 15th of May; If my public duties prevent my leaving by the 15th of May, I shall not be able to enjoy, this season, the great pleasure the visit would afford me. Should I go I will be very glad to see the fine stock of California, and will notify you of my movements, that you may inform the gentlemen.

I wish you to communicate my sincere thanks to Mr. Du[*n*]can for the very kind offer to afford me an opportunity to see the fine stock of the Pacific Coast

Very truly yours
U. S. GRANT.

GEO: W. DENT ESQ. SAN FRANCISCO. CAL.

Copy, DLC-USG, II, 1. See letter to Frederick Dent Grant, Feb. 8, 1871. On March 13, 1871, Orville E. Babcock wrote to W. E. Brown, Sacramento. "The President requests me to acknowlege the receipt of your letter and to communicate his sincere thanks for the very kind expression it contains. He wishes me to say that he hopes to go to California this Spring, but is not yet certain that his official duties will permit. He says however that should he go, and the plans settled upon permit of the plan you propose he will avail himself of your kind offer. He request me to assure you that the pleasant remembrance of the social evening are reciprocal." Copy, DLC-USG, II, 1. On March 16, John P. Usher wrote to USG inviting him to use the Kansas Pacific Railroad on his proposed trip to Calif. Parke-Bernet Sale, Oct. 13, 1964, no. 150. On March 17, this letter was endorsed: "Thanks for Kindness. He cannot tell positively when will go. If makes the trip would be pleased to return over Kansas Pacific RR." *Ibid.* On March 27, USG wrote to Darius O. Mills *et al.*, San Francisco. "I have the honor to acknowledge the receipt of your very flattering invitation to visit the Pacific Coast. I beg that you will accept my sincere thanks for the warm interest shown. I hope to visit the Pacific Coast this Spring. If my public duties will permit I shall start about the 10th or 15th of May. Should my official duties be such that I can[n]ot leave by that time, I shall not be able; this season, to enjoy the great pleasure a visit to the Pacific Coast would afford me. Should I be able to go, timely notice will be given you by telegraph." Copy, DLC-USG, II, 1.

On April 14, Babcock wrote to Mills *et al.* and to George W. Dent, San Francisco. "The President desires me to inform you that he is now certain that his public duties will not permit him to make his contemplated visit to California this Spring. He regrets that he is deprived of the pleasure the visit would afford him but hopes to be able to make the trip in the Fall." "The President desires me to inform you that he is now certain that it will be impossible, on account of his public duties, to visit California this spring. He wishes you to notify Mr. Duncan who so kindly offered to show him the Stock of Cal. He hopes however, to be able to make the trip in the Fall." Copies, *ibid.* For USG's reasons for postponing his visit to Calif., see message to Congress, March 23, 1871.

On June 1, Maj. Gen. John M. Schofield, San Francisco, wrote to Babcock. "I have just received your enclosure of the President's Message communicating the report of the Santo Domingo Commission, and an admirable likeness of the President. Please accept my thanks and congratulations. The Presidents language in reference to you is like himself, true as steel to those who deserve his confidence. Give my warmest regards to the President with the hope that he will not fail to make his promised visit here in the Fall." Copy, DLC-John M. Schofield. On July 1, Babcock wrote to Andrew S. Hallidie, president, Mechanics Institute, San Francisco. "The President directs me to thank you for the very kind invitation extended to him, to be present at the inauguration of the Industrial Exhibition to be held in San Francisco on the 8th of next month; and to state that while he regrets that his engagements will deprive him of the pleasure of being in your City in time for the 'opening', he still hopes to visit it later in the season." Copy, DLC-USG, II, 1.

On July 29, a correspondent reported from Long Branch: "President Grant and family will remain here at his cottage the remainder of the season, and will, on leaving here, proceed to Washington. The President has abandoned his trip to the West and California, he having been advised by Generals Phil. Sheridan, Sherman, and many others, that it is now too late in the season for a satisfactory visit through the West, the crops having all been gathered and the country being in a bare condition. He has, accordingly, concluded to postpone his trip until the latter part of the spring of 1872." *Missouri Democrat*, July 30, 1871.

To Allan McLane

Washington D. C. Mch 29./71.

DEAR SIR:

I have the honor to acknowledge the receipt of your very kind offer to afford me an opportunity to visit China and Japan during the coming Summer.

I appreciate you liberal kindness and if it were possible, it would afford me great pleasure to avail myself of it, but my public duties will deprive me of the pleasure of such a trip.

Please accept for yourself and convey to the Directors of your Company, my sincere thanks.

I am Sir
Very respectfully
U. S. Grant

Mr. Allan McLane
Prest: P. M. S. S. Co.
New York

Copy, DLC-USG, II, 1. Son of Andrew Jackson's secretary of state Louis McLane, Allan, born in 1823 at Wilmington, Del., left Princeton College (1842) to become a midshipman, participated in the Mexican War, and graduated from the U.S. Naval Academy (1848). He resigned from the navy (1852) to command vessels for the Pacific Mail Steamship Co., became co. agent, and was elected president (1861).

Order

The act of June 15, 1852, section 1 (10 U. S. Stat., p. 10), provides "that whenever any officer of either of the territories of the United States shall be absent therefrom and from the duties of his office, no salary shall be paid him during the year in which such absence shall occur, unless good cause therefor shall be shown to the President of the United States, who shall officially certify his opinion of such cause to the proper accounting officer, to be filed in his office."

It has been the practice under this law, for the territorial officers who have desired to be absent from their respective territories, to apply for leave to the head of the proper Department at Washington, and when such leave has been given the required certificate of the President has been granted as a matter of course.

The unusual number of applications for leave of absence which have been lately made by territorial officers, has induced the President to announce that he expects the gentlemen who hold those offices to stay in their respective territories and to attend strictly to their official duties.

They have been appointed for service in the territory, and for the benefit and convenience of the territorial population. By personal presence they identify themselves with the people, and acquire local information without which their duties cannot be well performed. Frequent or long absence makes them, in some degree, strangers, and therefore less acceptable to the people. Their absence, no matter with what substitution, must often put the people to inconvenience. Executive officers may be required for emergencies which could not be foreseen. Judges should be at hand, not only when the courts are in session, but for matters of bail, *habeas corpus*, orders in equity, examination of persons charged with crime, and other similar business which often arises in vacation.

These and similar considerations no doubt induced Congress to pass the law above quoted.

It is, therefore, directed that, in future, the heads of Departments shall grant leaves of absence to territorial officers only for reasons of the most urgent character, and then only for the shortest possible time.

By order of the President.

HAMILTON FISH
Secretary of State.

WASHINGTON, MARCH 31, 1871.

DS, DNA, RG 59, Miscellaneous Letters.

To George W. Childs

Washington, D. C. Apl. 2d *18~~6~~*71

MY DEAR MR. CHILDS;

Mrs. Grant wants me to acknowledge the receipt of the books which you were so kind as to send her, and to thank you for them—She wants me to say too how much she regrets the termination of Mrs. Childs visit to us, which she had hoped would not only be pleasant to her but that the change might have benefited her health instead of causing illness.[1] I hope she is better now and that we may yet have a visit from her when you can come along. I know the Ledger could run alone for a week and if you will leave it for that length of time, and spend it with us; I will promise to make the time pass as pleasantly as I know how. I would ~~allmost~~ all most promise to write an editorial for the Ledger.

Mrs. Grant and Nellie send their love to Mrs. Childs, Mrs. Drexel and daughters,[2] and I do not know but she means to include you and Mr. Drexel[3] also but does not feel at liberty to ask me to write it. I will send my love to both of you however and include your families, which divided, would make two very respectable families, in numbers, and all that go to make up happiness and contentment in this world. I know Mr. Drexel since my visit[4] and can say, if I am any judge of men, that your high confidence in him, and appreciation of him, is not misplaced; that he is one of a class of men that it is a pitty we have not more of.

Tell my good *old* friend Mr. Borie[5] that he need not flatter himself that I am going to give him the chance to do all the oratory on our trip to California[6] because I gave him the chance to do my talking at the little dinner party we attended in Philadelphia.[7] This will be a disappointment to him I know and therefore I want to prepare him beforehand. Give my love to Mr. and Mrs. Borie.[8]

Yours Truly
U. S. GRANT

ALS, DLC-USG. See *PUSG*, 9, 339–40. George W. Childs married Emma Peterson, daughter of his early employer, Robert E. Peterson, bookseller. Childs dedicated *Recollections of General Grant:*... (Philadelphia, 1890): "To Mrs. Julia Dent Grant, whose devotion as a wife was only equalled by the affection of her illustrious husband, . . ." See *New York Times*, Feb. 3–4, 1894.

1. On April 3, 1871, Julia Dent Grant wrote to Emma Childs. "Your letter my dear Mrs Childs, was read with great pleasure, as it assured me, that you were well enough to sit up & write. We were very anxious about yu you, indeed, after Genl Porter returned as he told us how very much dabilitated you were, be fore you reached home—I really feared to hear from you—But now that you are well agin suppose you come on with Miss Emily & Fannie Drexel & spend the Easter Holey days with us—cant you? Miss Kitty left us on Friday last—we miss her. Nellie & I have been highly entertained, however in reading one of those nice books Mr Childs sent us—Jessie exihibits his Bear to evry one that calls. It is a wonderful little thing is it not? Nellie is stile ~~wearing~~ enjoying her smelling bottle, & wearing her braceletts & ring. She is a young lady that enjoys all she posseses After again expressing my great pleasure

over your convalesence Let me send many thanks & kind regards to Mr Childs . . ." ALS, DLC-USG, IB. On April 18, 1870, Julia Grant had written to Emma Childs declining an invitation and thanking Childs for a "fine photograph of Mr. Borie— . . ." "Letters of Presidents of the United States and 'Ladies of the White House,'" *The Pennsylvania Magazine of History and Biography*, XXVI, 2 (1902), 275.

2. Anthony J. Drexel's wife Ellen was the daughter of John Rozet, a French merchant. The Drexels had three daughters.

3. Drexel, born in 1826 in Philadelphia, entered his father's brokerage office, Drexel & Co., when thirteen, became a partner in 1847, and expanded its size and scope. In 1864, he purchased the *Philadelphia Public Ledger* with George W. Childs. In Feb., Drexel and his wife had stayed as guests at the White House. *Washington Evening Star*, Feb. 21, 1871.

On March 25, 1869, Drexel, Philadelphia, had written to USG. "Mr G Henry Horstmann of Munich, but a native and Citizen of the United States is an applicant for the position of Consul at that City. I think his appointment will give great satisfaction as he is a gentleman of high character thouroughly acquainted with the German language and customs and therefore most suitable for the position" ALS, DNA, RG 59, Letters of Application and Recommendation. Related papers are *ibid.* On April 12, USG nominated G. Henry Horstmann as consul, Munich. See G. Henry Horstmann, *Consular Reminiscences* (Philadelphia, 1886), p. 194.

4. Between March 17 and 19, 1871, USG visited Philadelphia as Drexel's guest. *New York Times*, March 18–20, 1871. On March 20, a Washington correspondent reported. "There is a good deal of unfavorable comment among Republican politicians here at the President being the guest of so prominent a Democrat while in Philadelphia as A. J. Drexel. They think, that with everything else, it will tend to demoralize the rank and file—who cannot understand how the President can affiliate with Democrats in a city where there are so many prominent Republicans." *Boston Transcript*, March 20, 1871.

5. See *PUSG*, 19, 145–46. From Feb. 7 to 13, 1871, Adolph E. Borie and his wife visited the White House. *Evening Star*, Feb. 7, 9, 11, 14, 1871.

6. See letter to George W. Dent, March 27, 1871.

7. USG received a special invitation to the annual dinner of the Hibernian Society held at the St. Cloud Hotel on March 17. *New York Times*, March 19, 1871. USG spoke following the toast: "The President of the United States." "Gentlemen of the Hibernian Society, I am most happy to be with you on this pleasant occasion, but not being given to speech making, you will excuse me if I decline making any protracted remarks. I expected something of this kind, however, and came provided for the occasion with my friend, Mr. Borie, who will now address you." *Philadelphia Public Ledger*, March 18, 1871. On Feb. 19, 1872, Horace Porter wrote to Robert Patterson, Philadelphia. "The President directs me to reply to your note of the 14th inst, and convey his regrets that the certificate of Membership of the Hibernian Society was not acknowledged before. It was received from the Express Co. by the Steward and his attention was not called to it, or it would have received earlier attention. He wishes me to convey his thanks to you and to the Society for the compliment, which he accepts with much pleasure." Copy, DLC-USG, II, 1. See *PUSG*, 20, 393; John H. Campbell, *History of the Friendly Sons of St. Patrick and of the Hibernian Society* . . . (Philadelphia, 1892), pp. 226–27, 418.

8. See *PUSG*, 19, 219.

To Congress

[*April 5, 1871*]

To the Senate and House of Representatives.

During the early months of the present Administration two separate agents, (and at two separate times) of the President of the Republic of San Doming called on me, with verbal propositions from President Baéz, to receive into the Federal Union that Island, with its people and great resources. It was explained that the proposition was only verbal because the Govt. of San Doming was weak, and if the proposition should be rejected it would be the occasion of great embarrassment if it became known that an unsuccessful proposition had been made to change the allegiance of the people of the island.

To these propositions I made no reply, nor did I indicate to either of the Agts. of President Baéz the course I should pursue. In view however of the long proclaimed "Monroe doctrine" I did not believe that a President of the United States could look idly on and reject such propositions without investigation, and good grounds upon which to reject. The resolve was instantly made therefore, (though not communicated to either of the agents of President Baéz) to send an Agt. to San Domingo to ascertain whether Annexation to the United States was the will of the people of San Domingo or only of a few officials. As such agent I selected Gen. Babcock,[1] an officer who has served close to me for a period of six years, and in whos capacity, judgment and integrity I feel the most unbounded confidence.

Gen. Babcock remained upon the Island of San Domingo long enough to thoroughly satisfy himself that there was scarsely a dissenting f voice there to the proposition of Annexation. (Evidence is now before the Senate of the United States that this feeling extends to the enemies as well as the friends of the present administration upon the Island.)[2] Being satisfied upon this point he had, very properly, a full free talk with President Baéz, and his Cabinet, upon the terms under which they would expect admittance into our Union;

the nature and amount of their liabilities; the sessions and grants the Dominican government had made, &c. and, very properly, had the replies to all these querries reduced to writing. Nothing that he did bound this government in the slightest degree. But, should we reject the proposition which the people of San Domingo have made, in good faith, to come into the American Union; accompanied, as it was with their declaration that they are weak in numbers, without the ~~the~~ wealth or the power to give protection whilst developing the vast resources of their country? ~~h~~How ca[n] we then say to any other country to whom they may offer themselves, "we cannot permit territory on this continent to pass into the hands of any foreign power not now in possession"?[3]

Republican institutions, like the Christian religion, ~~is~~are broad enough and strong enough to to extend their benefits wherever voluntarily received. I would not force our institutions upon unwilling peoples not now forming a part of our government, but I would not withhold them from any people on this continent voluntarily seeking them. San Doming is now, unanimously, seeking them, and sooner or later, without a struggle, and without any derangement of the industries or monitary affairs of this country, they are bound to extend over every foot of this Continent.

The United States emerged from the War of the Revolution with the elements in it of becoming a calossal power, bound to occupy the entire Continent of America, though it was then hemmed in at the North, South and West, occupying its self but a strip upon the Atlantic seaboard whilst European powers possessed all the rest, or ~~they~~ it was occupied alone by the aborigines. The United States entered at once into the occupation of her rightful possessions Westward to the banks of the Mississippi. Since that, by the purchase of La. and its right of extension North to the line of the treaty demarkation between France & Great Britain, and West to the Pacific Ocean; by the purchase of Florida; by the annexation of the independent state of Texas and the purchase of New Mexico, Arizona, ~~and~~ California a Alaska, the United States has only been following out the destiny predicted for her by our earlyest statesmen. Not one of these acquisitions were made without strenuous opposition from statesmen of the day. Who now would part with one foot of our acquisitions? Out of the La. purchase has been carved great and flourishing state, capable of sustaining vast populations. But its purchase was fought with as much bitterness, and more reason, than the acquisition of San Domingo now is. In the former instance the Uniteds States were extending the area over which slavery could be carried. In the present instance we are saying that the institution of Slavery can no longer exist on this continent.

In the acquisition of Texas, and with it our valuable possessions through to, and on, the Pacific, the opposition was so great that a treaty ~~for its~~ failed to receive the requisite a two thirds vote of the Senate, and the method had to be resorted to of admitting the state by "Joint Resolution" of the two houses of Congress. ~~The~~ I now ask the concurrence of the two houses of Congress in the acquisition of that portion of the Island of San Doming embracd in the Dominican government, on the terms of the treaty, (as amended,) which has ~~been~~ failed to receive the requisite two thirds vote of the Senate.—It seems but fair that the ~~lower house~~ most numerous branch of Congress, who are chosen directly by the people whom they represent, should be consulted in matters of National policy like that of adding to the public domain, and particularly when the necessary appropriation to carry out the terms of the treaty must be allowed by them, or fail.

I do not favor the acquisitions of territory, no matter how desirable, at the cost of strict justice to all parties concerned. But if ~~the~~ acquisitions, by honorable means, pave the way for other acquisitions let them come. San Domingo once in the American Union I do not doubt but it will make the very existence of Cuba & Porto Rico depend either upon their independence or their following the example of their neighbor.

Our Commerce with the Islands of Cuba & Porto Rico is greater than with all the British North American possessions, notwithstanding the exlusion of so much of our produce~~ed~~ts by ~~us by~~ high duties. For the year ending June 30th 1869, our imports from all British North American possessions, including Britsh West Indies, amounted $38.772.705, and our exports to them, including re-exports, to $33.441.336, or a total commerce with British North America of $72.214.041, whilst with Cuba & Porto Rico, for the same year, our total commerce amounted $88.102.017. Owing to foreign domination over these islands but little o[v]er Twenty-two Millions of this commerce was exports, and of the exports about one third was re-exports, or export of articles not produced in the United States. These figures[4] show at what pecuniary cost to the United States these islands are legislated for by a Nation separated from us, and them, by the Atlantic Ocean. Independent, or in the American Union, our imports would probably be paid for by our exports. Free Cuba & Porto Rico, a vast trade profitable to them and us and the abolition of Slavery in the West Indies, is the sequence to the Annexation of St. Domingo.

ADf, DLC-USG, III. Phrases and themes from the first three paragraphs of this draft recur in the following draft.

1. See *PUSG*, 19, 209–10.

2. See message to Senate, Jan. 11, 1871. This statement indicates that USG drafted this message after Jan. 11.

3. Another reference to the Monroe Doctrine.

4. See *PUSG*, 20, 443.

To Congress

[*April 5, 1871*]

To the Senate And House of Representatives

I have the honor to submit herewith, to the two houses of Congress, the report of the Commissioners appointed in pursuance of joint resolution approved [(Insert date) Jan 12 1871] ~~and to ask such action, and at such time, as Congress the representatives of the people may approve of~~ [~~deem proper~~].

It will be observed that this report more than sustains all that I have heretofore said in regard to the productiveness, and healthfulness of the island [Republic] of San~~to~~ Domingo, ~~and~~ of the unanimity of the people for annexation to the United States, and of their peacable character.[1] ~~I do not recommend at this time any further action upon this report than to have it printed and placed before the public for its~~ [(~~consideration and deliberate~~)] ~~judgement~~. "~~I~~ "~~I have no policy to enforce against the will of the people~~."

It is (~~probably~~) due to the public, ~~and~~ [as] it certainly is to ~~me~~ [myself], that I should here give all the ~~incidents~~ [circumstances] which first led to the negociation of a treaty for the annexation of the republic of San~~to~~ Domingo to the United States. ~~I will say first that w~~When ~~I was installed in~~ [I accepted] the arduous and responsible position which I now hold I did not dream of instituting any steps for the acquisition of insular possessions. I believed however that our institutions were broad enough to extend (~~protection~~) ~~of~~ (~~an~~) [over the] entire continent as rapidly as other peoples might desire to bring themselves ~~within their~~ [under our] protection. I believed further that we (~~could~~) [should] not permit any independent government within the limits of North America to pass from a condition of independence to one of ownership or protection ~~by~~ [under] an European power.—Soon after my inauguration as ~~p~~President I was waited upon by (~~a gentleman representing himself as~~) an agent of President Baez, with a proposition to annex [the republic of] San~~to~~ Domingo to the United States. This gentleman represented the capacity of the island, the ~~will~~ [desire] of the people, their character and habits about as thay have been described by the Commissioners whos report accompanies this [message]. He ~~represented~~ [stated] further that being weak in numbers, and poor, [in purse] they were not capable of developing their great resources; that the people had no incentive to industry ~~because~~ [on account] of lack of protection for their accumulations; and that if not accepted by the United States, with institutions which they loved above those of any other nation, they would be compelled to seek protection elsewhere.

To (~~all~~) these statements I made no reply, [and] gave no indication of what I thought of the proposition.

In the course of time I was waited upon by a second gentleman from San~~to~~ Doming who made the same representations (~~as the first~~) and who was received in like manner (~~with him.~~) ~~Such repre-~~

~~sentations having been made however~~, ~~and in view of the oft declared~~ [In view of the facts which had been laid before me, and with an earnest desire to maintain the] "Monroe doctrine," I believed that I would be dirilict in my dut~~ies~~[y] if I did not [take measures to] ascertain the the exact wish of the government and people of [the Republic of] San~~to~~ Domingo in regard to [its] annexation to the United States. Accordingly after ~~selecting~~ [having appointed] a Commissioner[2] to visit the island who declined [on account of sickness] I selected (~~General O. E. Babcock, of the U. S. Engineer Corps,~~) a [Second] gentleman in whos capacity, ~~J~~judgement and integrity I had, and have yet, the most unbounded confidence. He visited San~~to~~ Domingo not to secure or hasten annexation, but unprejudiced and unbiased to learn all the facts about the government, [the] people and [the] resources of that ~~island~~ [Republic] ~~or that part of it presided over by President Baéz~~. He went (~~just~~) [certainly] as well prepared to make an unfavorable report as a favorable one if the facts warranted it.

His report ~~was such as to con~~[~~con~~]~~vince me~~ [fully corroborated the views of previous Commissioners and upon its receipt I felt] that [a sense of] duty and ~~interest both and~~ [a due regard for our] great National intersts (~~of both nations~~) compelled me to negociate a treaty for the acquisition of the republic of San~~to~~ Domingo. ~~It is a clear Constitutional privilege right~~ [~~of~~] ~~the Executive~~ (~~has~~) ~~to negociate any treaty with other nations he may deem proper. It is for the Senate to ratify or reject. A treaty which at first I supposed would receive~~ [~~in the Senate a support in the Senate~~] ~~almost as unanimous~~ (~~support in the Senate~~) ~~as it had received of the people of Santo Domingo not only was rejected by that honorable body but~~ (~~all~~) [~~those~~] ~~concerned in n~~[e]~~gociating it were stigmatized as corrup, venal and guilty of a catalogue of crime. Had the treaty been discussed fairly upon its merits, and then rejected, as much as I might have differed with the Senate as to the wisdom of their action, it is not likely that the subject of annexation would have come up again during this Administration. Certainly it would not unless some new phase had presented itself making it a new subject.~~ [~~But~~] ~~The subject~~ (~~being~~) [~~was so~~] ~~treated~~ (~~as it was~~) ~~both in the Senate~~

and in the public press of the country [that] I deemed it due to thos[e] whom I had sent to Santo Domingo, and to myself that we (should) [might] be vindicated if innocent of the charges alleged, and that it was due to the country that it should be fully informed upon a subject which so vitally effects its interest. [& its destiny)] For these reasons I asked Congress at the begining of last session to authorize me to send these commissions to Santo Domingo to examine and report upon such points as it was desirable to have information upon.[3] The authority was given and the Commission was selected with reference to their high character and capacity for the work before them. Their report is now before you. (May) (I ask that it receive careful and dispassionate consideration,) believing that a thorough understanding of the subject will bring the great Majority [of the people & their representatives] to the same conclusion upon it that I came to after a careful study of it. [I ask that it receive careful despationate & deliberat consideration]

ADf (bracketed material in another hand), DLC-USG, III. On March 28 and 31, 1871, Secretary of State Hamilton Fish wrote in his diary. "In the Evening call upon the President—. . . He says he proposes with the report of the San Domingo Commrs to send it to Congress with a short Message, refering to the confirmation it furnishes of his views of the facts alleged in favor of Annexation & as the vindication of the agents he sent against the charges & insinuations against them, & to submit the question to Congress—without further recommendation—This being what I wanted him to do, I simply express my gratification—He thinks that he will be able to submit the report & message to the Cabinet on Friday—" "Cabinet—Robeson & Delano absent—the latter represented by Otto—President reads draft of proposed message communicating the report of San Domingo Commrs to which is some amendments & alterations are suggested—In the main it is right—it submits the whole question to Congress & the Peoples—asks no action—recounts his action with regard to it & claims that the report justifies his views & expressions—" DLC-Hamilton Fish. For a synopsis of USG's message based on this draft, see *New York Times*, April 3, 1871.

On March 21, Secretary of the Navy George M. Robeson wrote to USG. "I am at this moment, 3.30 P. M, in receipt of the following telegram:—'Tennessee arrived at Key West at one o'clock this day—now coming to anchor.'" LS, OFH. On March 26, the Santo Domingo Commission landed at Charleston, S. C. *New York Times*, March 27, 1871. On March 28 and April 3, a correspondent reported: "Hon. Ben Wade and the other members of the San Domingo Commission called on the President to-day, but only paid their respects and indulged in casual remarks. The opinion prevails among Senators to-day that the report of the San Domingo Commissioners, whether for or against annexation, will be submitted to the Senate and appropriately referred. No action of the Senate upon the subject is expected this session." "The only visitors the President saw to-day were Hon. Ben Wade and Judge Burton, Secretary of the San Domingo Commission." *Philadelphia Public Ledger*, March 29 and April 4, 1871. On March 30, USG had hosted a White House dinner for Benjamin F. Wade, Andrew D. White, Samuel G. Howe, and Allan A. Burton. *New York Times*, March 31, 1871. For discussion of the absence of Frederick Douglass, see Merline Pitre, "Frederick Douglass and the Annexation of Santo Domingo," *Journal of Negro History*, 62, 4 (October, 1977), 394; William S. McFeely, *Frederick Douglass* (New York, 1991), p. 277.

On March 13, John Danforth, New London, Conn., had written to USG. "We are anches to here the report from our San Demengo Committee, hoping it will be in favour of having that Island under the Laws of the United States. The amount we Shall have to pay had, not better be named I, would go in for the Island of Cubia. we Shall want both of those Islands, Soon," ALS, DNA, RG 48, Appointment Div., Letters Received.

On April 7, Ebenezer R. Hoar, Washington, D. C., wrote to Jacob D. Cox. "Washington seems very empty without you, and not attractive as a place of residence. You will not hastily conclude that I mean it was very attractive, even with you, for you know how much I preferred Massachusetts, or Ohio, or any other place not infested by men in office. But it seems hardly the same place without you to fall back on when I want a little strengthening in the way of solid sense and sincerity. I have called on the President twice only, in the five weeks that I have been here, beside attending his State dinner—He seemed very friendly and cordial; and we met much as we used to—but I cannot help feeling the shadow of San Domingo, & Mc Garrahan, and the abandonment to Conkling, and Cameron and Chandler; in short, that things are on a lower level. So, without any intention about it, I have kept away from the White House. Neither Robeson nor Creswell have called on me—though I have met them at various places. Gov. & Mrs. Fish are as agreeable as ever, and speak of you with much affection. But the Governor & Sumner are in a high state of mutual exasperation, and accuse each other of treachery and lying, with a freedom that is very trying to an innocent third person who is inclined, after a fashion, to believe in them both. I think, on the whole, that I have had as much solid satisfaction in seeing Belknap and Gen. Sherman as any body that I have found here. I was much obliged to you for the report from Mr. Scammon; but Gov. Fish was aware of his report, and we had been fully possessed of the facts about P. E. Island from various sources. I think we are likely to make a treaty that the country *ought* to be satisfied with; and if we do, it looks likely to be accomplished in the course of a week or two. We have got over what seemed at first the greatest difficulties, but there are some various points that are troublesome, and on which we may yet make shipwreck. The English gentlemen are very kindly and cordial, as agreeable persons to deal with as any one could desire; and yet, I think, very able and clear headed, and extremely wary and cautious. Our side you know all about. It is very hard work, something like playing chess or fencing for several hours a day, with all your faculties on the stretch. The secrets of the Commission are well kept, what you see about it in the newspapers being the invention of correspondents or the speculations of editors, without the slightest foundation in fact.... I was glad to see your Cincinnati political association's action—though not quite agreeing with it all—But I think the hope of the Country is in the independent announcement and discussion of principles and purposes, to shew that there is something for parties to do beside scramble for offices. The New York meeting of last night, at which Evarts spoke, seems an important and hopeful move in the same direction. The Ohio resolution on St. Domingo was capital—witty as well as wise. But I feel very confident that that little operation is dead and buried. Your state of mind about the Sumner business is very much like mine—but the relation of the parties is such that nothing can be done about it at present, except to let things take their course—. . ." ALS, Cox Papers, Oberlin College, Oberlin, Ohio.

1. On Feb. 13, William McMichael wrote from Santo Domingo City. "On the evening of February 9th, a large crowd of natives, both Spanish and negroes, led by two or three societies of the city of Santo Domingo, and band of music, serenaded the United States Commissioners. After the music had ceased, Don Juan M. Tejera, Justice of Supreme Court of Dominica, addressed the Commissioners as follows: Gentlemen: We have done ourselves the honor of calling upon you, the Commissioners named by the President of the United States to investigate the question of the annexation of Santo Domingo, and we desire that our call and this music may be taken as an expression of our respect for you, our affection and admiration for the great Republic, and our earnest hope that the negotiations pending may have the happy result we all desire, namely, annexation to the United States. Hon. B. F. Wade then responded, saying: Gentlemen: It gives me great pleasure to hear from the people of this republic. We do not come here, however, to persuade the people of this country to come under the flag of the United States, but rather to ascertain what their opinions and wishes are. We commend your judgment and good sense in wishing to come under that flag. . . ." *Philadelphia Public Ledger*, Feb. 24, 1871. On Feb. 24, McMichael discussed Santo Domingo with USG and "reported the Commissioners and large number of the people in favor of annexation." *Ibid.*, Feb. 25, 1871. On March 20, R. Curiel, "Secretary of War of the Dominican Republic," Santo Domingo, wrote to Burton, Washington, D. C. "I received in due time your note from Azua, saying good-bye, for which I pray you to accept my best thanks. The country is entirely tranquil, and is every day more anxious that our anticipated annexation to the great Republic be speedily and favorably accomplished. I can see no other means of salvation from the insidious intrigues of our Western neighbors. . . ." *New York Times*, April 5, 1871. On April 13, Orville E. Babcock wrote to Gen. José Caminero, Santo Domingo. "The President desires me to acknowledge the receipt of your note enclosing your photograph, and in reply to convey to you his thanks for your very polite attention. He wishes me to enclose you a photograph of himself in return and beg you to accept his kind regards." Copy, DLC-USG, II, 1. See letter to Samuel G. Howe, June 9, 1871, note 1; *SED*, 42-1-9, 11–13, 50.

On Feb. 25, Gen. José María Cabral, San Juan, Santo Domingo, wrote to Wade, Howe, and White. "Being informed that the Senate of your nation, in sending you to the territory of our republic, has done so with a view of your ascertaining if it be true that the Dominican people desire to be annexed to the republic of the United States of America, it is my duty, as a good citizen and as chief of the revolution which I head, to make known to you, that the Dominicans are opposed to carrying out the scheme of said annexation; that the majority of them desire only to preserve the political sovereignty of their nation; to be free and independent; preserving at the same time good relations of peace and harmony with all civilized nations of the world, and chiefly with the enlightened and grand republic of the United States of America. In representing the contrary, the government of Señor Baez has been wanting in truth, and the means that have been used to make the cabinet at Washington believe that annexation is acceptable to the Dominicans has been the result of the arbitrary conduct, the tyranny and the terrorism which he has exercised over the inhabitants of the country, by imprisoning, expelling from the country, shooting all those who have heretofore spoken out, or that now speak out, against the idea of annexing our republic. Availing himself of bad faith, he has attempted to cause it to be believed that the revolution, which I have the honor to lead, is without principles of order, and that it is made up of people without conscience, calling us robber chiefs and utterly demoralized and powerless. The falsity of all this is palpable when it is remembered that it is now three years since the revolution was proclaimed in this the southern province, and far from his being able to suffocate it, he has not been able to make it recede a single step. . . ." *Ibid.*, pp. 54–55. See *ibid.*, pp. 55–56, 174–76; *CG*, 42–1, 86–88; message to Senate, Jan. 11, 1871.

2. On June 2, 1869, Fish issued a passport to Benjamin P. Hunt "traveling abroad as a Special Agent of the United States to the Dominican Republic." DS, DNA, RG 59, Consular Despatches, Santo Domingo. On June 10, Hunt, Philadelphia, wrote to Fish. "I telegraphed you on the morning of the 7th inst, that illness would prevent me from going out to St. *Domingo*, by the Steamship 'Tybee', which vessel accordingly left New York without me. The return of a chronic complaint in my chest, to which I have, at intervals, long been subject, and which is only to be suppressed by quietness, care and the entire command of my own movements, made it clear to me that I could not attend to the business with which you had intrusted me, and I reluctantly gave up the voyage. I most sincerely regret the necessity which compelled me to do so, as, had my health permitted; I think I should have been able to obtain information, useful in its results both to this country and to St. Domingo. Old acquaintances, whom I saw in New York, just arrived from Port au Prince, represented the condition of the Haytien part of the island as critical, to the last degree. Mr Oliver Cutts, my former partner in business at Port au Prince, informs me that when he left the island on the 23rd ultimo a special envoy from Salnave was preparing to visit Washington, and that in all probability he would arrive at New York by the next Steamer. The purpose of his visit is to obtain assistance from the United States by means of the cession to us in some form of the Mole-St. Nicolas, one of the strongest maritime positions in this hemisphere. Mr Cutts represents Salnave and Baez as on friendly terms, disposed to support each other, both exceedingly poor and both eager to obtain money on territorial security. He also says the people were never so poor as at present and in Port au Prince there is a growing feeling in favor of a[nn]exation to the United States. As Mr Cutts relations are very intimate with Salnave who obtains most of his government supplies through the commercial house of the former these representations are likely to [be,] if not entirely disinterested, at least worthy of consideration. My instructions not having been carried out, I suppose it to be proper to return them; I therefore forward them, with my unused passport, enclosed." LS, *ibid.* Born in Mass., Hunt had lived in Haiti and studied its history. While a resident of Philadelphia, he gained a reputation as an advocate of equal treatment for blacks. See Charles C. Tansill, *The United States and Santo Domingo, 1798–1873: A Chapter in Caribbean Diplomacy* (Baltimore, 1938), p. 357; Margaret Munsterberg, "Manuscripts on the West Indies," *More Books: The Bulletin of the Boston Public Library*, IV, 8 (Oct., 1929), 313–21.

3. On Feb. 1, 1871, Wade, Santo Domingo, wrote to Caroline Wade. ". . . There is no more fruitful Country on Earth and they are so far all without exception crazy to be annexed—All that Grant said about it is true—all that Sumner said is false—This is the first time I have had to write home, nor have I heard a word from the states since I started—" ALS, DLC-Benjamin F. Wade. On March 4, Babcock wrote to J. C. Bancroft Davis, asst. secretary of state. "I send you two letters from Mr Wade, to read. May I ask you to return them by the bearer as the President has not seen the one of the 6th—The Secty of State has not seen that letter. it came in the 2nd Mail yesterday. Please hand it to him to read. Colfax has seen both as you will see by his note" ALS, DLC-J. C. Bancroft Davis. On March 7, Charles C. Fulton reported from Port-

au-Prince: "Mr. Wade is preparing a short preliminary report which he hopes to get off on the steamer this evening. He has also sent a short letter to the President." *Baltimore American*, March 17, 1871. A letter from Wade to USG, 1871, from Port-au-Prince, supporting annexation is listed in William Evarts Benjamin, Catalogue No. 27, Nov., 1889, p. 10. On March 17, John McGarigle, *Baltimore American*, telegraphed to Babcock. "If Mr Wades preliminary report, is to be made public will you please furnish us with advance copy," Telegram received, DNA, RG 59, Miscellaneous Letters. Babcock referred the telegram to Fish. AES, *ibid.* On the same day, Babcock telegraphed to McGarigle. "Have not seen such report. Shall comply with your request—is such report is published." Copy, DLC-USG, II, 5. On March 21, Fulton reported from Key West: "The Commission arrived here to-day on the Tennessee, having sailed from Kingston, Jamaica, on Thursday. The Commissioners have agreed on Mr. Wade's report with some elaborations by the other Commissioners. The report is about as prefigured in my Puerto Prince letter, closing with an earnest appeal for immediate annexation as a measure of justice to the Dominicans. . . ." *Baltimore American*, March 22, 1871. On March 24, Horace Porter telegraphed to McGarigle. "We have no information. Must have been left by mistake." Copy, DLC-USG, II, 5. On March 27, Fulton reported while at sea en route to Baltimore: ". . . Mr. Wade took the ground that it would not be proper to return to Washington without a report signed and prepared for presentation. That any other course would subject them to the charge of being tampered with, or with having been influenced by the friends or opponents of annexation at Washington. He at first proposed to leave the preparation of the report to Professor White, but on reaching Peurto Prince, and receiving the assurance that he did not intend to commence it until their return to Washington, Mr. Wade at once began the preparation of a series of answers to all the questions embraced in the resolutions of inquiry. The report is a plain and concise statement of facts, such as could only be given even by Senators Sumner and Schurze had they as thoroughly investigated the subject in all its bearings as the Commissioners have. Indeed, it was the impression of every one on the Tennessee that Messrs. Howe and White entered upon their labors strongly inclined to the views of these two distinguished Senators, expecting to sustain rather than refute their charges. They now throughly agree with the views of Mr. Wade. . . ." *Baltimore American*, March 30, 1871.

On March 29, a correspondent reported: "Mr. Frederick Douglass had an audience of the President today, at which were present Secretary Robeson and Attorney-General Akerman. In reply to an inquiry of the President, Mr. Douglass gave his impressions of the republics of Dominica and Hayti. He said that in his judgment the Dominicans are a far superior people to the Haytians; that there is no republicanism whatever in Hayti, and that the Government there is an absolute despotism of the most oppressive character. Mr. Douglass expressed his regret at the course which Senator Sumner has seen fit to pursue, but he said that he had strong hopes that Mr. Sumner would change the opinions which he now holds on the subject as soon as he had read the report of the Commissioners. 'If Mr. Sumner after that,' said Mr. Douglass, 'shall persevere in his present policy, I shall consider his opposition fractious, and regard him as the worst foe the colored race has on this continent.'" *New York Times*, March 30, 1871. On April 3, Douglass wrote to Fish. ". . . I had the honor to accompany the Commissioners as directed during their whole tour of observation in the West Indies and returned with them to the united states landing at Charleston. Regretting that my services in the capacity authorised by the terms of my appointment were inconsiderable and unimportant, I can nevertheless assure you that such other services in connection with the objects of the mission as the honorable Commissioners ~~saw fit~~ were pleased to require at my hands were promptly and cheerfully rendered." ALS, DLC-Frederick Douglass. See letter to Buenaventura Báez, Jan. 15, 1871.

To Congress

To the Senate and House of Representatives:

I have the honor to submit herewith, to the two houses of Congress, the report of the Commissioners appointed in pursuance of joint resolution approved January 12, 1871. . . .[1]

In view of the facts which had been laid before me, and with an earnest desire to maintain the "Monroe doctrine," I believed that I would be derelict in my duty if I did not take measures to ascertain the exact wish of the government and inhabitants of the Republic of San Domingo in regard to annexation and communicate the information to the people of the United States. Under the attending circumstances I felt that if I turned a deaf ear to this appeal I might in the future be justly charged with a flagrant neglect of the public interests and an utter disregard of the welfare of a down-trodden race, praying for the blessings of a free and strong government and for protection in the enjoyment of the fruits of their own industry.

Those opponents of annexation who have heretofore professed to be pre-eminently the friends of the rights of man I believed would be my most violent assailants if I neglected so clear a duty. Accordingly after having appointed a commissioner to visit the Island, who declined on account of sickness, I selected a second gentleman in whose capacity, judgement and integrity I had, and have yet, the most unbounded confidence.

He visited San Domingo, not to secure or hasten annexation, but unprejudiced and unbiased, to learn all the facts about the government, the people and the resources of that Republic.

He went certainly as well prepared to make an unfavorable report as a favorable one, if the facts warranted it. His report fully corroborated the views of previous commissioners, and upon its receipt I felt that a sense of duty and a due regard for our great National interests required me to negotiate a treaty for the acquisition of the Republic of San Domingo.

As soon as it became publicly known that such a treaty had been negotiated, the attention of the country was occupied with allegations calculated to prejudice the merits of the case, and with aspersions upon those whose duty had connected them with it. Amidst the public excitement thus created, the treaty failed to receive the requisite two thirds vote of the Senate and was rejected; but whether the action of that body was based wholly upon the merits of the treaty, or might not have been, in some degree, influenced by such unfounded allegations, could not be known by the people, because the debates of the Senate in secret session are not published. Under these circumstances I deemed it due to the office which I hold, and due to the character of the agents who had been charged with the investigation, that such proceedings should be had as would enable the people to know the truth. A commission was therefore constituted, under authority of Congress, consisting of gentlemen selected with special reference to their high character and capacity for the laborious work entrusted to them, who were instructed to visit the spot and report upon the facts. Other eminent citizens were requested to accompany the commission in order that the people might have the benefit of their views. Students of Science and correspondents of the press without regard to political opinions were invited to join the expedition, and their numbers were limited only by the capacity of the vessel.

The mere rejection by the Senate of a treaty negotiated by the President, only indicates a difference of opinion between two coordinate departments of the government, without touching the character, or wounding the pride, of either. But when such rejection takes place simultaneously with charges openly made of corruption on the part of the President, or of those employed by him, the case is different. Indeed, in such case, the honor of the nation demands investigation. This has been accomplished by the report of the commissioners herewith transmitted, and which, fully vindicates the purity of the motives and action of those who represented the United States in the negotiation.

And now my task is finished, and with it ends all personal solicitude upon the subject. My duty being done, yours begins; and I gladly hand over the whole matter to the judgement of the American people, and of their Representatives in Congress assembled. The facts will now be spread before the country, and a decision rendered by that tribunal whose convictions so seldom err, and against whose will I have no policy to enforce. My opinion remains unchanged—indeed, it is confirmed by the report—that the interests of our country and of San Domingo alike invite the annexation of that Republic.

In view of the difference of opinion upon this subject, I suggest that no action be taken at the present session beyond the printing and general dissemination of the report. Before the next session of Congress the people will have considered the subject and formed an intelligent opinion concerning it; to which opinion, deliberately made up, it will be the duty of every department of the government to give heed, and no one will more cheerfully conform to it than myself. It is not only the theory of our Constitution that the will of the people, constitutionally expressed, is the supreme law, but I have ever believed that "all men are wiser than any one man"; and if the people, upon a full presentation of the facts, shall decide that the annexation of the Republic is not desirable, every department of the government ought to acquiesce in that decision.

In again submitting to Congress a subject upon which public sentiment has been divided, and which has been made the occasion of acrimonious debates in Congress, as well as of unjust aspersions elsewhere, I may, I trust, be indulged in a single remark. No man could hope to perform duties so delicate and responsible as pertain to the Presidential office, without sometimes incurring the hostility of those who deem their opinions and wishes treated with insufficient consideration; and he who undertakes to conduct the affairs of a great government as a faithful public servant, if sustained by the approval of his own conscience, may rely with confidence upon the candor and intelligence of a free people, whose best interests he has striven to subserve, and can bear with patience the censure of disappointed men.

U. S. GRANT

EXECUTIVE MANSION
APRIL 5TH 1871.

DS, DNA, RG 46, Presidential Messages, Foreign Relations, Santo Domingo. *SED*, 42-1-9. The "Report of The Commission of Inquiry to Santo Domingo" is *ibid.* On April 5, 1871, a correspondent reported: "The San Domingo report is at last before the public, swollen from the four modest columns which comprised its proportions when the Commissioners returned here, to fully ten columns, as finally completed this morning, which everybody will say is unfortunate, since its number of readers is reduced in proportion as its length is increased. . . . In the House, the report was received at about 4½ o'clock, and, when the accompanying Message was read, Mr. DICKEY moved that it and the accompanying documents be referred to the Committee on Foreign Relations; and Mr. KELLEY submitted a resolution to print 25,000 copies, which was referred to the Committee on Printing. The reception of the President's Message by the Republican members of the House was very cordial indeed. . . . The Democrats received it with angry scowls, and Mr. BROOKS, of New-York, could not repress the ebullition of a spiteful remark or two, at its conclusion. The wide contrast between the temper of the Message and the temper in which the President has been assailed, is especially remarked. Some think it would have been wiser had there been no allusion, even indirect, to the disappointed men. . . . After the Senate doors were opened at the close of the Executive Session, the report of the San Domingo Commission came in. Quite a lively scene followed. Mr. HARLAN moved that it lay on the table and be printed, but the restrictive rule which ties the hands of the Senate came up to bar this out, or at least the proposal to print. Mr. MORRILL, of Vermont, then stated that he had a speech prepared which he desired should go to the country, along with the report. . . . It was first decided to lay the report on the table; next, not to consider the Message at this session; and then the differences were averaged, not with a very yielding grace to be sure, and it was unanimously agreed that the Message and report should be printed, that Mr. MORRILL should have the opportunity afforded him on Friday to read his speech, and that no more speeches on the subject should be made at this session." *New York Times*, April 6, 1871. See *CG*, 42–1, 469–74, 492.

On April 7, U.S. Senator Justin S. Morrill of Vt. spoke. "Mr. President, let me say in the outset that the message from the President, accompanying the report of the commissioners, has my cordial approval. If a partisan press has heretofore assailed his character, that, in the face of the report, will be no longer possible. The President wisely remits the question to the voice of the people, and stands, as at his inauguration, with no policy to enforce against their wishes. This I regard as an end of a vexed question; and I should not have trespassed upon the patience of the Senate only that I think it just and fair that some of the reasons for regarding the annexation of Santo Domingo with disfavor should be allowed to have utterance at the same time with the dissemination of a report which is likely to attract more or less the attention of the country. . . . The annual message of the President brought into one golden sheaf the heads of a large number of arguments in behalf of Santo Domingo annexation, strong enough to stand while closely huddled together, but doomed to bend and fall one after another when standing alone and examined separately and apart, or when the rhetorical band holding them so snugly together has been once broken. . . . It is useless to disguise the fact that the people of a portion of our present territory have not become assimilated with the American people and American institutions, and the time when they will do so must be computed, not by years, but by generations. To say nothing of our lately acquired Siberia, commonly called Alaska, it must be conceded that Arizona, New Mexico, Utah, and that portion of Texas bordering upon Mexico are yet not only essentially un-American, but they have no overwhelming attachment to our form of government nor to the Anglo-Saxon race. . . . One of the arguments in behalf of annexation is that we need the bay of Samana as a harbor for the protection of our commerce. Why do we need it? Certainly not for a coaling station unless we first carry coal there. . . . The fact that the Tennessee, sent out on a national mission, with five hundred men and nine alert newspaper reporters on board, was as much lost to the world for the long period of thirty-three days as though she had been navigating in the open Polar sea, exhibits in the strongest light the absence of trade and ships in the route to Samana, and also its useless remoteness as a harbor for us or any other nation. . . . We are asked to buy the site, next to improve and fortify it, and then to occupy it with a naval fleet, with the vain idea that we might thus fire the languid brains and torpid muscles of the Dominicans to make sugar, grow coffee, and hack down the mahogany trees in such incredible quantities as to glut the world with their exports. We are asked to launch one expenditure which drags after it numerous others of greater and constantly increasing magnitude, and all for the desperate purpose of establishing a permanent commerce and American institutions where nothing has been permanent but failures and revolutions, or for the even more desperate purpose of finding security for our Republic by making fast to a tropical island, whose foundations have been often shaken by earthquakes, and which is scarred all over with the political as well as atmospherical hurricanes of previous centuries. . . . A people wholly without education, led in factions by unprincipled and desperate chiefs, destitute of all ambition which a high civilization inspires, reeking in filth and laziness, regardless of marriage or its binding power, who never invented anything nor comprehended the use of the inventions of others, whose virtue is indexed by a priesthood elevated by no scrap of learning and wretchedly debauched in morals, would prove a serious political and moral as well as financial incumbrance. . . . The possession of Santo Domingo would heavily increase national taxes, as it would be absurd to suppose that a country without an acre of public lands, of one hundred and twenty or one hundred and sixty thousand poor Dominican men and women, unaccustomed and unwilling to labor, could or would make even the smallest contribution to the payment of the public debt or even to their own defense. The tracks would all be outgoing from the Treasury, and none incoming. . . . There is a question of some gravity as to the salubrity of the climate in Santo Domingo. If it is really healthful why is it that its population has been forever on the wane? Its colored population, without thrift or fertility, steadily diminishes in number, and whites never go and stay there with any purpose to make it a family home. Concede that the soil is fertile and hot in its fecundity, then may it not be asked whether it is not true everywhere under a tropical sun that a country, rank to rottenness in its vegetation, is equally rank in its malarial diseases?. . . But were all other circumstances as favorable to Dominican annexation as they are in fact repugnant to the scheme, there still remains one more vital consideration, namely, do the people of Santo Domingo really desire to sink their independent existence and be permanently stitched to the mere selvage of the United States? Decidedly no! The ruling passion of the people, mainly descendants of Indians and forty different African races, is a hatred of the white race. Smothered it may be for a time, but it is sure sooner or later to crop out. . . . It will not be pretended that there has been any enlightened public judgment in favor of the annexation of Santo Domingo. There has been all that in favor of President Grant; and his well-earned popularity, in spite of his Dominicanism, constitutes the entire strength, the back-bone of the measure. Unindorsed by him, may I not venture to say it would not have had or have a corporal's guard of supporters?. . ." *Ibid.*, pp. 524–26, 530–31, 533–34.

On April 19, U.S. Senator Cornelius Cole of Calif. summarized views favoring Santo Domingo annexation. *Ibid.*, pp. 814–17. On the same day, the Senate tabled a resolution to print "fifty thousand copies of the message of the President and the report of the commissioners, relating to San Domingo." *Ibid.*, pp. 814, 817. See *ibid.*, pp. 598, 643. Congress took no further action on the report or any related proposition to annex Santo Domingo. See letter to Samuel G. Howe, June 9, 1871; Charles C. Tansill, *The United States and Santo Domingo, 1798–1873: A Chapter in Caribbean Diplomacy* (Baltimore, 1938), pp. 436–40.

On April 14, Orville E. Babcock had written to Almon M. Clapp, congressional printer. "The President directs me to say that he would be pleased to have 100 Copies of the Message and report on San Domingo. Be kind enough to send the Bill for them in duplicate, & against the Executive Mansion." Copy, DLC-USG, II, 1. Related correspondence is *ibid.*

On April 14, Babcock had written to Martin B. Anderson, Rochester, N. Y. "The President desires me to acknowledge the receipt of your letter of the 6th inst, which he read with much pleasure. He wishes me to convey to you his thanks for the kind expressions contained therein, and say that he is gratified to be assured, by gentlemen who view from so fair a stand point, that his actions meet their approval,—which approval he hopes to continue to merit." LS, NRU. In March, Anderson, president, University of Rochester, had written to USG. "I have just read with pride & admiration your late Message to Congress on the Santo Domingo Treaty. For clearness, point, conclusiveness & dignity it will take rank among the ablest state papers which our country has produced. In my humble sphere, I have sought to vindicate your motives & action throughout this whole controversy. So strongly have I felt on the subject that, contrary to my usual custom I gave to my students a lecture covering the entire ground ~~ground~~ of the controversy, showing as I thought the gross injustice done you by those, who from every consideration which should influence honorable men, ought to have been among your staunchest defenders. There are differences of opinion among patriotic men regarding the policy of annexing foreign territory, but I do not see how there can be differences of opinion among fair minded men regarding the factious & dishonorable course of Senator Sumner & his few followers in the Senate. I have been constantly reminded during this debate of the excitement on the 'Jay Treaty, during Washington' administration. Washington' letter to the citizens of Boston in reply to their animadversions on his conduct in connection with that Treaty, is familiar to all. The abuse heaped upon the President on that occasion was more general & hardly less severe than that which has been showered upon you through the vituperative & turgid Rhetoric of Mr Sumner. This letter as much as any act of his public life exhibits the moral courage and calm wisdom of Washington I spontaneously compared your late message with that celibrated letter The two documents will go down to ~~posterity~~ history ~~with~~ together and will be equally honorable to those who wrote them The late course of Mr Sumner is entirely in harmony with his past action His ~~policy~~ whole policy as a statesman ~~is~~ has tended to reduce the constitutional powers of the Executive on the one hand and that of the States on the other and enlarge at their expense the power of Congress especially that of the Senate During his administration Mr Lincoln patiently endured the arrogance of Mr Sumner in view of the common peril During the administration of Mr Johnson circumstances gave full play to Mr Sumner political tendences and personal characteristics. It is clear that he expected to continue the same course after your accession to the Presidency. I am gratified, that in the interest, of sound constitutional doctrines you have maintained ~~the~~ and asserted the just power and dignity of the office which you hold This controversy seems to me to have a grave constitutional significance. The issue involved is; shall the powers and duties ~~which~~ devolved by the constitution on the President be usurped by senatorial committees. Mr Sumner policy would soon destroy the balance of powers among the departments of our government and its whole force would be absorbed by a powerful oligarchy represented by the Senate and the head of committees for the time being. Contrary to the opinion of most I believe that the Executive is the department of our gov't. most in danger of losing its just ~~force~~ power under the constitution The History of England illustrates this tendency Under the ~~the~~ British constitution the Executive has lost its power completely and exists only in name The House of Commons selects the Prime Minister who is the real King but dependent for the term of his offise upon the will of the House We have been moving in the same direction and in this action Mr Sumner has taken the lead As chairman of the Com. of Foreing Relations he has assumed to have the powers of the Secretary of State independent of the choice of the President He has evidently sought to control the most important diplomatic appointments and has shown a desire to appear to the European govts as the power behind the throne in all matters relating to diplomacy. This was shown in his tenacious efforts to retain Mr Motley in office after he had ceased to have the confidence of the Executive Mr Motely is a tolerable historian but he has proved himself even while at Venna to be by no means fit for a diplomatist. You did right in removing him It is true that the Harvard College clique were annoyed at your action and that Mr Sumner wished he represented in London rather that you or the country should Intelligent Americans abroad are well aware that Mr Motley received three several orders orders to remonstrate with the Austrian govt for permitting the enlistment of soldiers for Maximilian in Mexico before he discharged his duty He showed himself more anxious to secure favor with the social forces at court than than to obey ~~the~~ instructions or do his duty The whole matter of controlling the ~~executive~~ Executive by irresponsible committees or caucuses is dangerous and unconstitutional It is only among animal organisations of the lower orders that the tail moves the head The worst govts on Earth have been those controlled by an oligarchy whether hereditary or elective. The system works practically like the old Austrian method of governing a general in chief in the presence of an enemy by an Aulic council of politicians I know that the opinions of so humble an individual as myself can be of little moment to you but I trust that you will pardon me for what may seem an intrusion . . ." ADfS, *ibid.* See Asahel C. Kendrick, *Martin B. Anderson, LL.D.: A Biography* (Philadelphia, 1895), pp. 169–70.

On April 8, a correspondent reported: "Garritt Smith to-day had a long interview with the President, the principal topic being San Domingo. Mr. Smith expresses great satisfaction over the course of the President in turning the whole matter over to the people, and thinks the late message will renew and add to the strength of General Grant among large numbers of old line Republicans who have differed widely with him upon the question of annexation." *Missouri Democrat*, April 9, 1871.

On April 11, John A. Joyce, St. Louis, wrote to Babcock. "*Personal.* . . . I enclose herewith an article from the pen of the undersigned published in the 'Herald' a few days since. Everybody sees the point of the article; and Sumner & Schurz for the first time are shown up in their true light. During our recent trip *three daily papers* have come out in favor of the San Domingo question. Let me hear from you." ALS, ICN. On April 17, Dennis H. Mahan, USMA, wrote to Babcock. "I have yours Ap. 14, with the Presidents Message and the San Domingo Commissioners Report. The contemptible attacks made upon you by Sumner has only recoiled upon himself. Like most politicians, *with aspirations,* from civil life, he has a bitter fear and hatred of the army; and any opportunity of showing it is more than his prudence can withstand. The honest nonpoliticians, fortunately, know that there is a class in the land, however small, whose integrity and loyalty to duty can be counted upon, however great the trust committed to their care; and upon whom bribes, come in what guise they may, can make no impression. A West Point ~~graduate~~ diploma to these men is a patent of entire confidence. Thus far it has been merited. I wrote, and sent over a week ago, an article to the N. Y. Times, intended as a reply to Schurz' poor attempt to place the General's administration in the same category as that of the Duke of Wellington's in England. The parallel was not what Mr Schurz' proposed. In both the difficulties were enormous, in the public problems to be solved, and in the unscrupulous opposition to be encountered. The Duke had Huskisson and Earl Grey, who deserted their party and turned upon him. The General, Sumner and Schurz. I also defended the General's statesmanship in this step, showing the military value of the acquisition; and calling attention to Jeff. Davis' attempt to make an entering wedge there, in the interests of the Slaveocracy of that day The *Times,* for some reason, perhaps because the article was somewhat strong in flavor, has not published it. At some opportune moment I shall return to the charge. In a private note to the Editor, I told him not to be mealy mouthed about San Domingo; that our people had more than an Ostrich's stomach for digesting such food; and that, after swallowing Alaska, San Domingo would go off as easily as a Soft boiled egg. I hear nothing yet of Den's leave. I suppose it will come in good time. Fred's translation in the Army and Navy Journal will repay your perusal of it." ALS, *ibid.*

On April 24, Charles C. Fulton, Baltimore, wrote to Benjamin F. Wade. ". . . I also have had several talks with the President relative to the Santo Domingo Commission and yourself, in which he alluded to the letter you remember I wrote to Mr Delano, from Peurto Prinse, which he told me he had ~~kept~~ in his possession. He spoke in the kindest terms of you, and said that although you had positively declined the nomination for Governor he was gratified to see so much unanimity in your favor throughout the State. Putting all these things together it is my impression that you will be tendered the position of Secretary of State, and that the movement from Washington to bring out popular feeling in Ohi[o] is to popularize such an appointment. . . ." ALS, DLC-Benjamin F. Wade.

On Nov. 8, John Bell Hepburn, Port-au-Prince, wrote to USG. "In perusing your message of the fifth of April, of this present year, on the occasion of sending the report of the St Domingo Commissioners to Congress, wherein your Excellency was pleased to state, summarily, the motives by which your Excellency were guided, in recommending the annexation of St Domingo to the United States. In one of the benefits alluded to, your Excellency was pleased to mention that which would accrue to a *down trodden race.* This pathetic and sympathetic expression alludes to my race and from the promptings of the heart the mouth hath spoken. I must humbly apologize for trespassing on your valued time and on your patience, but as one of that down trodden race, I take the liberty of breaking through the bounds of courtly etiquette to arrive, by this, to your Excellency, to offer my heartfelt thanks, my gratitude, for all that you have accomplished and are still doing for the 'down trodden race.' President Lincoln, directed by an invisible hand and under the force of circumstances, gave freedom to the slaves of the United States, but emancipation without political privileges would cause the emancipated to be but a little removed from their former condition. Then to you, President and to the great party which you head, are due all those estimable privileges that they constitutionally possess this day, and and that there should be one who can rise and speak and write volumes antagonistic to the teachings of a whole life time spent in behalf of all measures beneficial to the african race, is truly painful. The transition of Mr Sumner is a new evidence that man, to carry a point, pushed on by vengeance and self aggrandizement, will seek to demolish exalted positions and calumniate the most virtuous. To say that your noble efforts to annex St Domingo is an insult *to the african race* and that the race should be left to work out its own civilization, are sentiments devoid of sound reflexion, for the first is absurd, and the second impossible. President, your plan is the only one, the only sure one, that can save this this remnant of the race, from becoming their own caterpillas and the tigers of their own destruction. At this moment there are twenty two persons in prison here, for eating human flesh! Where then will Mr Sumner find, in this island, the elements necessary to work out that civilization to which he alludes. Without the aid of another race, having the Bible in one hand, and the necessary means to civilize in the other, nothing can be accomplished. Annexation will not only be a blessing here but to thousands in the West Indies. It will in a certain measure put an end to the Ku Klux Klan cruelties of the South of the United States, by offering a new home to the despise—a home where they can really under their own vine & fig tree, enjoy the blessing of Liberty and a free expression of their social and political privileges, and under a *Govenor of their own color*, in less than one year, thousands will flock around its standard. I had the honor and satisfaction of making the acquaintance of General Sigel, Judge Burton, and Frederick Douglass Esqres, and at my House I introduced them to the President of Hayti. The last sitting of the St Domingo Commissioners Dr Howe, Professor White &c, was at my House. I had the honor to address your Excellency in July 1870, and then brought to the notice of your Excellency my claim against the Haytian Government for indemnity, for injuries done to me under the Government of Salnave. I have received several letters from the Honorable Hamilton Fish, but it seems that this high functionary was misinformed as regards my case, probably by some person inimical, here, to my interest. Mr Fish intimates that because I have lived for many years out of the United States, I can not claim the protection of the American Government, and that he can not make any discrimination between a native of Hayti and myself, but adds that Mr Basset may give me his friendly aid, *but not officially*, the fact of my having lived a long time in Hayti does not of necessity make me a Haytian without my consen[t.] My case as a colored american affords an exception to the rule laid down by Mr Fish. When I was in the United States, as a man of color, I was considered *a chattel and by a judicial decision* had *no wrights that a white man ought to respect.* Being a man of sensibility and honor could I be blamed for VOLUNTARILY EXPATRIATING myself to another country and from the cruel injustice of my native land? Now she has become just and equitable to all her children can it be otherwise but wright that I claim her protection to obtain a just indemnity for injuries done to my person and property in a foreign state? If the rule laid down by the the Honorable Secretary of State is to be obligatory to all persons who are similarly situated as in my case, would it be any thing but wright to ask its Abrogation? In conclusion, permit me, President, to request your acceptation of the sincere regards of one who *is of the down trodden race* and who will never cease to love and respect you and most sincerely pray to Almighty God for a success of your second presidential term and for the welfare and prosperity of yourself and family" ALS, DNA, RG 59, Miscellaneous Letters. See *PUSG*, 20, 13–14.

1. The omission repeated text in the second through fifth paragraphs of the preceding draft.

To Senate

To the Senate of the United States:

I transmit confidentially for the information and consideration of the Senate, a copy of a despatch of the 25th. of February last, relative to the annexation of the Hawaiian Islands, addressed to the Department of State by Henry A. Peirce,[1] Minister Resident of the United States at Honolulu. Although I do not deem it advisable to express any opinion or to make any recommendation in regard to the subject at this juncture, the views of the Senate, if it should be deemed proper to express them, would be very acceptable with reference to any future course which there might be a disposition to adopt.

U. S. Grant

Washington, April 5. 1871.

DS, DNA, RG 46, Presidential Messages. On March 21, 1871, Secretary of State Hamilton Fish wrote in his diary. "*Cabinet*—All present except Delano who is represented by Judge Otto—. . . I read Peirces No 101—from Honolulu, on the subject of prospective arrangements for the annexation of the Hawaian Group to the U. S. and suggest whether it will not be well to communicate it confidentially to the Senate for their opinion & advice—President directs that to be done without expressing any opinion of the Administration, but leaving the subject within the discretion of the Senate" DLC-Hamilton Fish. On Feb. 25, Henry A. Peirce, U.S. minister, Honolulu, had written to Fish. "(No 101.) . . . Impressed with the importance of the subject now presented for consideration; I beg leave to suggest the enquiry, whether the period has not arrived; making it proper, wise and sagacious, for the U S. Government to again consider the project of Annexing the Hawaiian Islands to the Territory of the Republic. That such is to be the political destiny of this Archipelago; seems a foregone conclusion, in the opinion of all who have given attention to the subject; in this country, the U. States, England, France & Germany. A majority of the Aboriginees, Creoles and naturalized foreigners, of this country, as I am credibly informed; are favourable, even anxious for the consummation of the measure named. The event of the decease of the present sovereign, of Hawaii, leaving no heir or successor to the Throne; and the consequent election to be made by the Legislative Assembly, of a King and new Stirpe for a Royal family; Will produce a Crisis in political affairs; which, it is thought will be availed of, as a propitious occasion to inaugurate measures for Annexation of the Islands to the U. States. The, Same to be effected as the manifest will and choice of the majority of the Hawaiian people; and through means proper, peaceful & honorable. It is evident, however no steps will be taken to accomplish the object named, without the proper sanction or approbation of the U S Government in approval thereof. The Hawaiian people, for Fifty years have been under educational instruction of American Missionaries, and the civilizing influences of New-England people—commercial & maritime. Hence they are Puritan & Democratic in their ideas & tendencies—modified by a tropical climate. Their favourite songs & airs are American. 'Shermans March through Georgia', & 'John Browns soul is marching on' are daily heard in the Streets and in their school rooms. The Fifteenth Amendment of the Constitution of the U. States; has made the project of Annexation to our Union, more popular than ever; both here and in the U. States. The native population is fast disappearing—The number existing is now estimated at 45.000 Having decreased about 15000 since the Census of 1866.—The number of Foreigners, in addition is between 5000 & 6000—Two thirds of whom are from the U States—and they own more than that proportion of foreign capital; as represented in the Agriculture Commerce, Navigation & Whalefisheries of the Kingdom. This country and soverignty, will soon be left to the possession of Foreigners. 'To unlineal hands, no son of theirs succeeding'—To what foreign nation shall these islands belong, if not to the Great Republic? At the present, those of foreign nativities, hold all the important offices of government, & control legislation, the judiciary &c. Well disposed as the Government now is, towards the U States and its resident citizens here; in course of time, it may be otherwise—as was the case during our civil war. I now proceed to state some points of a more general character; which should influence the U States Government in their decision of the policy of acquiring possession of this Archipelago. Their geographical position: occupying as they do an important, central strategetical point in the North Pacific Ocean; Valuable; perhaps necessary to the U States, for a Naval depot and coaling station—and to shelter and and protect our Commerce & Navigation; Which in this hemisphere is destined to increase enormously from our intercourse with the 500 Million—population of China, Japan and Australia. Humbolt predicted that the Commerce on the Pacific, would in time rival that on the Atlantic. A future generation no doubt, will see the prophecy fulfilled. The immense injury inflicted on American Navigation & Commerce, by Great Britain in the war of 1812–14, through her possessions of Bermuda & other West India Islands—As also that suffered by the English, from French privateers from the Isle of France, during the wars between those nations; are instances in proof of the necessity of anticipating & preventing when we can, similar evils that may issue from these Islands if held by other powers. Their proximity to the Pacific States of the Union; fine climate & soil; and tropical productions of Sugar, Coffee Rice, Fruits, Hides, Goat Skins, Salt, Cotton, fine wool &c; required by the West in exchange for Flour, grain, lumber, shooks and manufactures of of Cotton, wool, iron & other articles; Is Evidence of the commercial value of one to the other region. Is it probable that any European power, who may hereafter be at war with the U S; will refrain from taking possession of this weak Kingdom; in view of the great injury that could be done to our Commerce through their acquisition of them—? It is said, that at a proper time the U States may have the sovereignty of these Islands, without money & without price—Except perhaps for purchase of the Crown & Public Lands; and moderate annuities to be given to the five or six high chiefs now living; with uncertain claims as successors to the Crown. His Hawaiian Majesty, although only in his 41st year, is liable to a sudden decease—owing to frequent attacks of difficulty in breathing, and danger of suffocation by congestion; Caused by obesity—His weight is 300#. He is sole survivor of the Royal race of Kamehameha.—unmarried.—No heir, natural or adopted.—Possesses the Constitutional prerogative of naming his successor; but it is believed he will not exercise it; from a superstitous belief his own death would follow, immediately the act. Prince Alexander, & Lott Kamehameha; (the former subsequently became the Fourth Hawaiian King & the latter the Fifth); and Dr G. P Judd my informant; visited England in 1850 as Hawaiian Commissrs Lord Palmerston, at their interview with him;—said in substance, 'That the British government desired the Hawaiian people to maintain proper government & preserve National independence—If they were unable to do so; he recommended receiving a Protectorate Government under the U S. or by becoming an integral part of that nation Such, he thought was the destiny of the Hawaiian Islands; arising from their proximity to the States of California & Oregon. And natural dependence on those markets for exports & imports. Together, with probable extinction of the Hawaiian aboriginal population; and its substitution by immigration from the United States.' That advice seems sound & prophetic. . . ." ALS, DNA, RG 59, Diplomatic Despatches, Hawaii; *SRC*, 53-2-227, 29–32.

1. Born in 1808 in Dorchester, Mass., Peirce went to Honolulu as a young man and prospered in merchant ventures. Returning to Mass., he acted as Hawaiian consul for New England, financed recruitment for the U.S. Army, and incurred heavy losses from privateers and an investment in a Miss. plantation. See *PUSG*, 20, 85.

On Dec. 15 and 20, 1871, Fish wrote in his diary. "*Cabinet*—All present President wants to find a place for Sayles J Bowen & not having any other wishes to recall H. A Peirce from Hawaii—he has heard from old Mr Houghton, who was Consul at Lahaina, which Consulate Peirce recommended should be abolished—that Peirce at a dinner party made some indelicate remarks & admissions of former lewdness—The appointment is staved off, for the present—" "PRESIDENT . . . He speaks of Peirce (minister to Hawaii) & wishes to send Bowen there—I tell him that Peirce is personally indifferent to me but I think it to be unwise to remove him—he is well acquainted with the relations of the two Governments, & has much influence in Hawaii, both with the Govt, & with foreign Representatives He asks if there is any place to which Bowen can be sent. I mention the Argentine Republic, ~~& that~~ as vacant, & that Mr Settle tells me it is doubtful if he will return to Peru He proposes to appoint Bowen to the Argentine—to which I remark that possibly that may be throwing away a place which might be better filled—" DLC-Hamilton Fish. See letter to Hamilton Fish, March 13, 1871, note 2.

To Nathan Patten

Washington, D. C. April, 6th. *18~~6~~*71.

Sir:

This will introduce to you Capt. J. Sanford Barnes,[1] whom I have known intimately for some years and for whom I entertain a very high regard.

I take pleasure in commending him to you and bespeaking for him such good offices as it may be in your power to afford him.

Yours respectfully
U. S. Grant

Mr Nathan Patten
Collr Customs. Galveston, Texas.

LS, NHi. On Dec. 7, 1869, USG nominated Nathan Patten as collector of customs, Galveston, Tex. See Carl H. Moneyhon, *Republicanism in Reconstruction Texas* (Austin, 1980), p. 116.

1. Born in 1836 at USMA, John S. Barnes, son of James Barnes, USMA 1829, graduated from the U.S. Naval Academy (1854) and resigned as master (1858). Resuming service during the Civil War as act. lt., he rose to fleet capt., North Atlantic Blockading Squadron, and to lt. commander, commanding *Bat* and other ships. He taught ethics at the U.S. Naval Academy after the war and resigned as of Feb. 4, 1869, to pursue a career in law and banking. See *PUSG*, 20, 58; *O.R.* (Navy), I, xxiv, 194.

To William W. Belknap

Washington, D. C., April 7. 1871

Gen. W. W. Belknap
Cincinnati, Ohio.

Give my congratulations to the gallant Society of the Army of the Tenn. and regrets that public duty prevented me being with them on the anniversary of one of the hardest fought battles of the rebellion. The battle of Shiloh though much criticised at the time will ever be remembered by those engaged in it as a brilliant success, won with raw troops over a superior force and under circumstances the most unfavorable to the Union troops.

U. S. Grant.

Copy, DLC-USG, II, 5. See *Report of the Proceedings of the Society of the Army of the Tennessee, at the Fifth Annual Meeting,* . . . (Cincinnati, 1877), pp. 487–88. On March 29, 1871, Secretary of War William W. Belknap had telegraphed to Andrew Hickenlooper and to Manning F. Force, Cincinnati. "The President cannot be present. He regrets it exceedingly. I shall be there without fail." "The President regrets that he is unable to be present. I shall be there without fail." Telegrams sent, DNA, RG 107, Telegrams Collected (Bound).

To Amos T. Akerman

Washington, D, C
Apl. 13th 1871

HON. A. T. AKERMAN;
ATTY. GN.
DEAR SIR:

Please see Senator Clayton[1] and after hearing him please telegraph to Judge Caldwell[2] for advice as to instructions which should be given to the Mar.[3] and Dist. Atty.[4] or whether they, or either of them, should be removed and more faithful officers aptd.

Respectfully
your obt. svt.
U. S. GRANT

ALS, DNA, RG 60, Letters Received. On April 24, 1871, this letter was filed with an endorsement conveying a message from U.S. Judge Henry C. Caldwell, Eastern District, Ark. "Says there is no offici[al] unfaithfulness in the Marshal or Attorney & n[o] cause for their removal—" E, *ibid.* On May 31, Horace Porter wrote to Attorney Gen. Amos T. Akerman. "The President directs me to request that a Recess appointment may issue for U. S. Marshal and U. S. Dist. Atty. in Arkansas, and that the commissions be sent to him for signature this morning." Copy, DLC-USG, II, 1.

On July 22, U.S. Senator Benjamin F. Rice of Ark., New York City, telegraphed to Akerman. "HAVE THE PAPERS IN THE CASE OF CATTERSON AND WHIPPLE BEEN FORWARDED TO THE PRESIDENT." Telegram received, DNA, RG 60, Letters Received, Senate. On the same day, Akerman wrote to USG. "Senator Rice and Mr. Whipple, the late District Attorney, and Mr. Catterson, the late Marshal, of the Eastern District of Arkansas have laid before me very voluminous papers intended to show that these officers should be reinstated. I intended to send you an abstract; but after making out one as condensed as possible, I find it occupies eighteen pages, and I suppose it is hardly worth while to trouble you with it. The substance of the representations is, that these officers did only their strict legal duty in the prosecutions for election frauds; that they took no personal or partisan interest in the prosecution against Governor Clayton. These representations are sustained by their own sworn statements, by the statement of most of the Grand jurors, and by affidavits of various parties. Judge Caldwell writes to you that his letter to Governor Clayton complaining of Mr. Whipple was hastily written and was *ex parte*, and asks that the case may be disposed of by you unprejudiced in the slightest degree by any opinion contained in that letter. Many officials set forth that Messrs Whipple and Catterson are efficient and competent officers, who command the respect and confidence of the members of the bar, the suitors and all others interested in the United States courts. Ex Senator McDonald gives them a strong endorsement. Those gentlement have urged me to give to you my impression of the case, I will add that their personal appearance, bearing and conversation have impressed me favorably, and from all that I can learn. I believe they are competent officers and have served the Government well in their general duties. But their action in the prosecutions of which Governor Clayton complains is so entangled with the snarls of Arkansas politics that I am not able to form a positive opinion as to whether or not they have been moved in these matters by party feeling or by a strict sense of duty. If you wish to make the matter a subject of personal investigation, I will forward to you the abstract or the original papers or both as you may desire. I should apprise you that the papers are exceedingly Voluminous." Copy, *ibid.*, Letters Sent to Executive Officers. Earlier in June, USG had received affidavits from Jerry Gray, and Zura L. Colton, president, Board of Registration, taken on April 6. "I am a resident of Hot Springs in Hot Springs County Arkansas and was one of the Judges of Election for Hot Springs Precinct at an election held in November 1870. I was arrested in the month of February 1871 by one E M Jennings a Deputy United States Marshall and taken to Little Rock, was taken to the Pacific Hotel and to the rooms of Charles J Peshall and there was told by the United States Attorney Wm G Whipple that if I did not Swear concerning the elections in Hot Springs County as one Charles Thomas had sworn he would send me to Jail and when the Courts came on would send me to the Penetentiary but that if I would swear that the statements set forth by the aforesaid Thomas were true I should be released and could return home to my wife and children for whom he felt pity and further that he would not prosecute me before the United States Grand Jury I told him I would tell the truth. I was then required to give bond in the sum of Fifteen hundred dollars for my appearance at the April term of the US Court. I am a colored man and a carpenter by trade and dependent upon my trade for a living for myself and family" D (signed by mark), *ibid.*, Letters from the President. "On or about the 25th day of February AD 1871 I was by one E M Jennings a Deputy United States Marshall arrested on an Alias Capias issued from the United States Court at Little Rock Arkansas while at my house at Mount Ida Arkansas . . . I came into Little Rock and went to the rooms of the said Dist Attorney who told me if I would turn States evidence in the matter of elections in Hot Springs County under the provisions of the enforcement act, He would release me on my personal recognizance and that he was going to prosecute one D P Beldin to the utmost extent of the law that he was pledged to that effect and that he would send him to the Penetentiary He then informed me what certain men had told him about the matter and I informed him that the ~~facts~~ Statements as told by these witnesses were not true and that he was misinformed I then gave recognizance in the sum of Fifteen hundred dollars for my appearance at the April term. D P Beldin was in no ways connected with the registration of Hot Springs County nor did I appoint him to any position connected with the election. . . ." DS, *ibid.* USG endorsed both documents to Akerman. AE (undated), *ibid.*

On Sept. 23, Edward Wheeler testified before the Joint Select Committee to

Inquire into the Condition of Affairs in the Late Insurrectionary States investigating election frauds in Ark. "*Question.* Where do you reside? *Answer.* In Little Rock, Arkansas.... I am connected with the Little Rock and Fort Smith Railroad, as one of the directors, representing the financial interests of certain parties.... *Question.* Were you a member of the grand jury of the United States court last spring? *Answer.* Yes, sir; and its foreman.... It commenced on the 10th of April last.... There were six or seven different parties indicted in Hot Springs County; judges, and clerks of elections, and registrars; also some six or seven in Clark County for frauds in elections; and Governor Clayton, of Pulaski County, was indicted. *Question.* What was the offense for which Governor Clayton was indicted, and what was the evidence upon which he was indicted? *Answer.* The evidence was entirely documentary, being the returns in the office of the secretary of state. The witnesses were the ex-secretary of state, and the deputy secretary of state. They brought the returns, or a tabular statement of them sworn to, and laid it before the grand jury.... *Question.* Immediately after this indictment was found there was a change made by the President in the offices of marshal of the State and district attorney? *Answer.* Yes, sir; some few weeks after—... it was generally considered that it was on account of this indictment against Governor Clayton. It was claimed that Governor Clayton had caused the removal of those parties on account of that indictment; there was no other reason known; there could have been none. The governor had for some time been making a strong effort to have those two officers removed, on the ground that they were making a personal fight upon him. He tried to influence Judge Caldwell to give his influence for their removal, which Judge Caldwell declined to do at the time, according to his statement to me, stating that he believed them to be efficient and competent officers; that he was perfectly satisfied with them, and did not care to have them removed, and did not think they should be. The judge told me that, at the time of his first conversation with Governor Clayton, he assured the governor that those officers would not do anything to injure him. But after this indictment was found, the judge wrote a letter to Governor Clayton withdrawing the assurances he had previously given him. It was claimed that the removal was made upon that letter; that the letter was laid before the President and he removed them at once.... Mr. Harrington was appointed in the place of Mr. Whipple, and Mr. Mills in place of Mr. Catterson. Mr. Mills was the old marshal, some two or three years ago; Mr. Catterson succeeded Mr. Mills.... Mr. Harrington was an aid on General Clayton's staff during the whole war, I believe, and also adjutant of his regiment at the beginning of the war, I believe. Mr. Mills was an old citizen of the State; took no part in the war, either way; was a Union man, and has always been regarded as a warm personal friend of Senator Clayton.... *Question.* I understand you to say that the letter of Judge Caldwell was laid before the President? *Answer.* The letter that he wrote to Senator Clayton, so I have understood; I know nothing about that, only what I have learned from rumor. I think the President told General Catterson that he had seen the letter. It was written as a private note to Governor Clayton, and marked 'confidential.' Judge Caldwell read a copy of it to me...." *SRC*, 42-2-15, 2, 8–9, 11. On Sept. 25, William G. Whipple testified. "*Question.* How long have you lived in the State of Arkansas? *Answer.* Since September, 1868.... I was attorney for the United States for the eastern district of Arkansas from the 1st of October, 1868, until I was suspended in June last.... *Question.* What do you understand to be the reason for your suspension from office? *Answer.* The President states that it is on account of a letter written by Judge Caldwell, the United States district judge for that district, to Senator Clayton.... I have never seen the letter; but I know what

Judge Caldwell says is its purport and substance. He stated to me that in that letter he desired to retract the assurance he had previously given to Senator Clayton that he was satisfied I would not use the office of district attorney unfairly against him; and he wrote that if he were in the place of Senator Clayton he would do all he could to have me removed from office. . . . I think if I had done anything less than I did, in regard to the prosecution against Senator Clayton, I ought to have been suspended. . . . *Question.* Upon your suspension you came on here and saw the President, did you not, you and Marshal Catterson? *Answer.* Yes, sir. . . . we called upon the President, at Long Branch, and stated the case to him and referred him to the affidavits on file in the Attorney General's Office. He assured us that he would investigate the case, but said that he would take no final action until his return to Washington. *Question.* Did the President say he had suspended you from office on account of representations to him by Governor Clayton? *Answer.* He said he had done it on account of the letter which Judge Caldwell had written to Governor Clayton, and which Governor Clayton had shown to him. . . . *Question.* Now, Judge Caldwell having disavowed the motive attributed to him by you for discharging that grand jury, do you wish us to understand that you say that disavowal is not to be believed, and that he was influenced by his feelings in favor of Governor Clayton? *Answer.* I believe he is influenced by his feelings in favor of Governor Clayton; I have reason to believe it, and do believe it. I omitted to state that he subsequently wrote a letter to General Grant—it was quite a long letter, and is on file with the Attorney General—in which he stated that I was of the impression that his former letter had had some influence in working my removal; that I had offered to lay before him facts in the case; that parties favorable to my removal had also proposed to furnish him evidence; that he did not desire to look into the facts at all, but wished to keep out of the matter; and he therefore wished to have his letter withdrawn from the consideration of the President, as he did not intend to make any recommendation for my removal. *Question.* The question whether your suspension shall continue is still pending before the President?. . ." *Ibid.*, pp. 13, 19, 30–31. For related testimony from Whipple, see *ibid.*, 42-3-512, pp. 193–96.

On Jan. 29, 1872, Porter wrote to Attorney Gen. George H. Williams. "The President directs me to request you to give Senators Rice and Clayton from 10 A. M. to 12 M. tomorrow, at your office, to hear and examine the claims of the contesting Ark. officials for the places of Marshal, Dist. Attorney and Postmaster at Little Rock. The Postmaster General has been requested to join you." Copy, DLC-USG, II, 1. On Feb. 12, Orville E. Babcock wrote to Williams. "The President directs me to say that, in the matter of the cases of the Arkansas officials, he will be pleased to have your report for submission to the Senate at your early convenience." Copy, *ibid.* On the same day, Williams wrote to Rice. "I have conferred with the President as to the nominations for District Attorney and Marshal of the United States for the Eastern District of Arkansas, now pending before the Senate, and, upon my report to him of the facts in respect thereto, he is of the opinion that the objections to such nominations are not of such a nature as to require their withdrawal from the Senate." Copy, DNA, RG 60, Letters Sent to Executive Officers.

On Jan. 19, 1871, USG had telegraphed to Governor Powell Clayton of Ark. "J. L. Hodges was confirmed and commissioned Postmaster at Little Rock, December fifteenth" Copy, DLC-USG, II, 5. On Oct. 21, 1870, USG had suspended James S. Pollock as postmaster, Little Rock, and designated James L. Hodges as successor. On Dec. 7, USG nominated Hodges as postmaster. On Dec. 11, 1871, Porter wrote to Postmaster Gen. John A. J. Creswell. "The President wishes me to request you to send, to go to the Senate today the nomination of Pollock, appointed in Oct. as P. M. at Little Rock Ark" Copy, DLC-USG, II, 1. Pollock's nomination went to the Senate on Dec. 12.

1. See telegram to Powell Clayton, March 13, 1871.

2. Caldwell, born in 1832 in Marshall County, Va., began to practice law in Iowa (1852), served in the state legislature, and was a delegate to the 1860 Republican convention. While col., 3rd Iowa Cav., he received President Abraham Lincoln's nomination as judge, Ark., on May 2, 1864. Caldwell acted as judge for both judicial districts in Ark. until March, 1871. On March 3, 1871, U.S. Senators Rice and Alexander McDonald and U.S. Representative Logan H. Roots of Ark. wrote to USG. "We respectfully recommend William Story for the position of US district judge of the Western District of Arkansas. He has had much experience as circuit judge in said state and is well qualifed for the place." LS, DNA, RG 60, Records Relating to Appointments. On the same day, USG nominated William Story as judge, Western District, Ark.

On Feb. 6, 1872, Caldwell testified before a select committee investigating allegations against Clayton. "Question. State your residence.—Answer. Little Rock, Arkansas. Q. How long have you resided there?—A. In that city, about eight years.... I am judge of the district court of the United States for the eastern district of Arkansas. Q. Were you in Little Rock in the winter of 1870-'71?—A. I was. Q. Residing there?—A. Yes, sir. Q. Were you there at the time of the organization of the legislature of that State?—A. I believe I was at home at that time.... Q. Were you in the habit of attending the sessions of that body?—A. I was not.... I think I was in the general assembly as often as two or three times, probably, during the session; not oftener. Q. Have you any personal knowledge of the difficulties that obtained during the session of that general assembly, which have been referred to by other witnesses?—A. None on earth; I presume I know less about those affairs than almost any gentleman in the city. Q. Are you connected in any way, to use the word that has been used here often, with either of the factions in the republican party in that State?—A. I am not; I carefully abstained from taking any part with either faction. Q. Have you any knowledge of any bargain of any kind or description between Governor Clayton and General Edwards with reference to the giving of a certificate of election to General Edwards?—A. None at all; I never heard of it until I read the testimony of Mr. Whipple and Mr. Wheeler before the ku-klux committee." *SRC*, 42-3-512, 115–16.

3. On April 20, 1869, McDonald and Rice wrote to USG. "We most respectfully ask that Robert. F. Catterson be appointed U. S. Marshall for the Eastern district of Arkansas to take effect Oct 25th 1869—he is peculiarly qualified for the position was a General in the Army and did much toward reconstruction in our state" LS, Duke University, Durham, N. C. On Oct. 20, Clayton telegraphed to USG. "I desire to recall my recommendation for the appointment of R. F. Catterson for the position of U S Marshal for the Eastern District Arkansas I request that no change be made until I can communicate by mail" Telegram received (at 3:35 P.M.), DNA, RG 107, Telegrams Collected (Bound). On March 18, 1870, USG nominated Robert F. Catterson as marshal, Eastern District, Ark. On May 31, 1871, USG suspended Catterson in favor of Isaac C. Mills. On Dec. 6, USG nominated Mills.

On Feb. 26, 1872, Catterson testified. "... At the time I went to Arkansas, I was in the United States Army with the rank of brigadier-general. I had not been mustered out at the time I went to Arkansas.... I was a member of the first legislature that assembled in Arkansas after reconstruction. I was afterward appointed United States marshal for the eastern district of Arkansas. At present I hold the position of mayor of the city of Little Rock. Q. When did you cease to be United States marshal, and how?—A. I was suspended from that office, the suspension, I think, to take effect on the 1st day of June, 1871 . . . I think at the instance of Senator Clayton. . . . I never have voted any ticket excepting as a republican. I never belonged to any other party. I belong to that party now." *SRC*, 42-3-512, 252.

4. On April 12, 1869, USG had nominated Whipple as attorney, Eastern District, Ark. On May 31, 1871, Akerman wrote to Secretary of State Hamilton Fish. "I am directed by the President to request you to issue a commission appointing Stephen R. Harrington to be Attorney of the United States for the Eastern District of Arkansas, in place of William G. Whipple suspended, agreeably to the enclosed executive order." Copy, DNA, RG 60, Letters Sent to Executive Officers. On Dec. 6, USG nominated Stephen R. Harrington.

On May 7, 1869, Harrington, Washington, D. C., had written to Fish seeking a consular appointment. ". . . I served the government nearly four years, during the late war, during which time I never had one day's leave of absence,—was in many battles and several times wounded. I enlisted as a private soldier and was mustered out as Major in same Regiment,—would respectfully call your attention to complimentary orders and letter from my superior Officers filed with my application. Since the close of the war I have ever been actively engaged in support of the principles for which I fought and in behalf of the orphans of my fallen comrades, as shown by letters on file in your office. I was a delegate to the National Republican Convention which nominated U. S. Grant for President; and devoted my entire time to the party from that day until after the election, for which I never received one dollar. . . ." ALS, *ibid.*, RG 59, Letters of Application and Recommendation.

To the Emperor of Japan

To His Majesty, The Tenno of Japan,
Great and Good Friend,

I have made choice of Charles E. De Long, one of our distinguished citizens to reside near the Government of Your Majesty in the quality of Envoy Extraordinary and Minister Plenipotentiary of the United States of America. He is well informed of the relative interests of the two countries and of our sincere desire to strengthen the friendship and good correspondence between us, and from a knowledge of his fidelity, probity and good conduct, I have entire confidence that he will render himself acceptable to Your Majesty by his constant endeavors to preserve and advance the interest and happiness of both nations. I therefore request Your Majesty to receive him favorably and to give full credence to whatever he shall say on the part of the United States, and most of all when he shall assure Your Majesty of their friendship and wishes for your prosperity, and I pray God to have Your Majesty always in his safe and holy keeping.

Written at Washington, this seventeenth day of April in the year of our Lord, one thousand eight hundred and seventy-one.

Your Good Friend
U. S. Grant.

Copy, DNA, RG 84, Japan, Instructions. On July 12, 1870, U.S. Senator William M. Stewart of Nev. wrote to Secretary of State Hamilton Fish. "By a provision in the recent Deplomatic and Consular Appropriation bill the rank of our Minister to Japan was raised to that of Envoy Extraordinary and Minister Plenipotentiary. I beg to request that a new appointment for Hon. Charles E. De Long, in accordance with this change, be transmitted to the Senate at an early day that action may be had thereon before adjournment." ALS, *ibid.*, RG 59, Letters of Application and Recommendation. On July 14, USG sent the desired nomination for Charles E. De Long. See *PUSG*, 19, 378–79; *CG*, 41–2, 4659.

On Jan. 27, 1871, USG wrote to Congress. "I transmit, herewith, for for the consideration of Congress a report from the Secretary of State, and the papers which accompanied it, concerning Regulations for the Consular Courts of the United States in Japan." DS, DNA, RG 46, Presidential Messages. *SED*, 41-3-25. On Jan. 26, Fish had written to USG enclosing a copy of regulations issued by De Long in Sept., 1870, and suggesting ". . . for the consideration of Congress, the propriety of limiting the power of Ministers to make decrees and regulations . . . 'to acts necessary to organize and give efficiency to the Courts created by the act.'" DS, *ibid.* Related papers are *ibid.*

On Nov. 7, 1871, Thomas Walsh, New York City, wrote to USG. "In accordance with the wish expressed by you, at the interview with which you honored me last week, I now submit to you some observations on American relations with Japan. Our commercial intercourse with that country began in 1858. At that date, and for some years afterwards, foreigners knew but little about the country, the peculiarities of its Government, or the character of its people. It may be said therefore that all the Western Powers entered Japan equally ignorant on their own part, and equally under suspicion on the part of the Japanese. The United States had, however, the advantage of priority among those to whom that long closed land was opened; and as the Japanese learned that our nation had no other aim than to cultivate profitable commerce with them, and that intercourse with us involved no danger to their independence, they soon manifested a special good will towards Americans. This disposition our first Minister, Mr. Townsend Harris, endeavored to foster, and he was so far succesful that, up to the time of his retirement (1862), his counsel was preferred to that of any other foreign representative; and American influence surpassed that of any foreign nation. The Japanese learned to trust him and his countrymen, and to feel that in them they had friends who were, as a rule, honorable and considerate, both in their dealings, and in their conduct. The result of this cordiality of feeling was that American Commerce grew rapidly, and although our commercial establishments were soon outnumbered by the English and other Europeans, who controlled more capital, and supplied a greater variety of useful imports, than we could furnish, yet American merchants succeeded, by means of intelligent enterprise, and friendly behavior, in acquiring a larger proportion of the foreign trade of Japan, than their numbers, or their capital alone would have enabled them to command. Had our Government fairly appreciated the importance of maintaining this state of things, we should not now have to deplore the decline of American influence in a country where alone, amid all the vast and populous East, that influence had ever been distinctly felt or acknowledged. But our civil war, and the concentration of attention upon domestic affairs, which it required, led to a neglect of American interests in Japan, which afforded our European rivals, an opportunity that they were not slow to seize. England and France, fresh from the conquest of China, had quickly followed the United States to the doors of Japan, and had easily obtained entrance there on the same conditions. Jealous of each other, and anxious to extend their commerce and their influence, they soon perceived the necessity of nourishing in every way, their relations with a land which was known to be the most populous, the most productive and the most highly developed of any country on the pacific, and which was likely, at no very distant day, to become of serious importance to whoever should seek to dominate that great ocean. Accordingly, these Powers hastened to induce their great steamship Companies, by liberal subsidies, to establish mail lines to Japan, and took care to send there, as Ministers and Consuls, able and earnest men, instructed both by special training and by special orders, to advance their nation's interests on every occasion, and to obtain the greatest possible power and influence in that rich and virgin field. Great Britain showed special energy in this effort, and through her efficient Consulates at every port, and her liberally appointed Legation at the Capital, diligently investigated the nature of the Government, the character and habits of the people, and the resources of the country. Each Consulate had its students, whose duty it was to learn the language, and explore the productions of the Consular District. The frequent and elaborate reports of these agencies guided the Minister in his action, and enabled him continually to enlighten his Government in regard to the organization, capacities and disposition of the Japanese nation. The Legation itself was also furnished with a numerous corps of highly educated and ambitious attachés, required to study the language, and acquaint themselves with the character and customs of the people, and stimulated to diligence therein by promises of preferment, and the hope of permanent employment. A numerous and active Naval Squadron came to aid the civil officers by explorations of the coast, by observations at ports not open to Consuls or to merchant vessels, and by the impression of power and interest which such a force, and such a use of it, were certain to produce on the Japanese mind. Some exceptional attacks upon Englishmen were also availed of to debark at Yokahama a strong military force, which not only contributed to deepen this impression, but by the excursions, investigations and reports of its officers, rendered valuable aid to the Minister in his efforts to understand and influence the politics of the country. By means of such agencies, all of which are still in full activity, and by the operations of a numerous and wealthy body of merchants, having the great advantage of being able to import many useful articles, not purchasable in America, on account of the high cost of production there, Great Britain has steadily gained ascendency in a country which, of all others in the Eastern world, most leaned towards the United States; which is our nearer neighbor; and which is destined herself to be a great Naval and Commercial Power on the Pacific Ocean Thus has Great Britain profited by the absorption of American energies in our civil war; by the burdens which that struggle imposed on our exporting power; and by the resulting decline of our Eastern commerce, to take precedence of us in the most inviting foreign field which has ever been opened to American enterprise. It was but a natural consequence of the possession of such advantages, that, at the crisis of the Japanese Revolution of 1868, which reestablished in that country a pure monarchical government in place of the feudal organization that had previously existed; the intelligence and power of the British Minister succeeded in turning the scale in favor of the party which he preferred; and in fastening upon it an obligation to advance the interests which he so ably represents. France has hitherto failed, through her national peculiarities, to attain the same advantage in Japan as England. But nevertheless, her position there is superior to that of the United States by reason of the more ample representation which she maintains. What she may lack in her commerce or her consulates, is compensated by the energy, ubiquity and devotion of her missionaries and protegés, and she has not omitted to imitate her great rival in lodging a considerable military force ~~i~~on Japanese territory; in maintaining a formidable fleet in Japanese waters; and in furnishing her Legation at Yedo with an efficient staff, who keep it fully informed of all that occurs. Germany also has not neglected her opportunity, but, even during her recent great war, kept at Yedo a well appointed Legation, led by a most astute and accomplished Minister, and supported by an active and patriotic corps of attaches and consuls. Italy, Holland, Belgium, Spain and other European nations, are also now in the field; and, though they do not pretend to vie with the three Greater Powers, and have but little commerce to protect, yet they maintain Legations, and, having naturally more sympathy with European than with American interests, frequently combine adversely to the latter, rendering the efforts of the U. S. representatives so much the more difficult and laborious. It is, Sir, as you may readily conceive, no slight mortification to an American citizen, anxious that his country should occupy in Japan the position to which, for so many reasons, she is clearly entitled, to find himself obliged to declare that, having had so fair an opportunity to ~~serve~~ secure it, she has well nigh lost it by sheer indifference. Yet such must be the conviction of every one who has traced American intercourse with that rising and well disposed nation. It is true that the Japanese continue still friendly to Americans; that, when they feel free to choose, they like to employ Americans to aid them in their efforts to acquire consideration among the nations; that they send many of their youths to study in American schools; and that they desire to extend their commerce with us. But it should be remembered that they are still feeble in force, inexperienced in international affairs, and dependent in a large measure upon the knowledge and good will of Western nations for assistance to attain the position to which they aspire. Under such circumstances, the qualifications and status of the Western representatives in Japan, have a peculiar weight and value. It is far from my intention to reflect, in the least degree upon the present representative of the United States, in that country. On the contrary I think Mr. de Long well qualified for his post, thoroughly in earnest in the discharge of his duties, extraordinarily industrious, and of a temperament and character which entitle him to the esteem of all who know him. And I am assured that the Japanese like and respect him, while I have had personal experience of his zeal to promote and defend American interests. But he is under great disadvantages compared with his principal colleagues. While they have attachés who are familiar with the Japanese language, and therefore qualified to interpret correctly and skilfully; who mingle freely with the more intelligent Japanese, and thereby obtain valuable information; who study the literature and laws of the country, and so become acquainted with the ideas and institutions with which they have to deal;—the U. S. Minister has, or very recently had, neither Secretary, clerk, interpreter nor attaché to aid him in the duties of his office, but was obliged to do every part of those duties himself, even to the copying of his own despatches. It is evident that a Minister so situated, charged with the various interests of a great nation, and having often to act not only as a magistrate in respect to his fellow citizens, but also (owing to the peculiarities of Japanese tribunals) as their only defender in their controversies, cannot possibly perform the duties of his office with any satisfaction to himself, and cannot possibly equal his colleagues in diplomatic affairs. Mr. de Long feels this very keenly, and has written to the Government about it. His desire to serve his country has hitherto sustained him in a position which is not less painful to him than it is unworthy of the American nation. But he is obliged to recognize the fact that day by day his colleagues, by means of their better information and better service, gain precedence of him, and that he cannot cope with them. Private interests are not here in question. They suffer, with all other American interests, by the disabilities of the Legation; but our citizens in Japan and elsewhere have a habit of overcoming difficulties which has thus far enabled them to maintain their commercial position despite their disadvantages. Nor shall I dwell upon the fact that the Japanese, in constructing their railroads, coast lights, telegraphs, arsenals, docks, and other improvements, in all which they require foreign assistance, have found themselves almost obliged to employ Europeans, when they might have preferred Americans. It matters little what may be the nationality of the men who thus promote progress in Japan. But these employés serve as sources of information, and as active political missionaries, for their own countries, and are of no small consequence in these respects. It is therefore of moment that our country should be fairly represented among them. But the greater question is—Can the United States afford to maintain their present attitude of indifference to a nation consisting of nearly thirty five millions of civilized, ingenius, and productive people, our nearest Oriental neighbors, with whom we have already a trade of many millions per annum, and who are inclined to develope commercial and friendly relations with us? Is it not important to us, in view of our future on the Pacific, to convince this people that we are interested in them, and sincerely desirous to understand them, and to cultivate their good opinion? Ought not the Republic to feel and manifest an earnest concern in the awakened activity of so numerous and highly organized a nation, dwelling in the only Ocean where the American flag is still eminent? It is but twelve years since our commerce with Japan commenced, and it has had to contend with many hindrances. Yet today that commerce, deprived though it is of any aid from American exports, exceeds in value our whole commerce with either Russia, Austria, or Portugal,—countries where we maintain tolerably well-equipped Legations, though we have neither reason nor desire to obtain special advantages among their people. I recognize the wisdom of Congress in recently raising the American Mission in Japan to equal rank with the Missions of the European powers. But much more is requisite to enable us to recover the ground which our indifference has ceded to our ever watchful competitors. The Minister of the U. S. should not have to depend for his information upon what he can gather from his colleagues, or from the local newspapers (all under British management) or from his mercantile friends, or from his native servants (often but spies). Nor should he have to rely for his interpreters, as he does now, upon Missionary volunteers, who know little of diplomatic language, nor upon chance scholars in merchant's offices, nor upon the timid and obsequeous native employês of the Japanese Government, who may betray him. He should have a staff of his own whose members he could trust, and through whom he could conduct his business in an intelligent and efficient manner, which would impress upon the Japanese that this Republic is not less concerned in its foreign affairs, than are the Monarchies of Europe; that it is jealous of its reputation, and careful of its interests in Japan, and that it can afford to maintain its dignity there. And this amelioration would not cost much. Young Americans of good character and complete education, could be gathered from our colleges and schools, who would be glad of the chance of a career which Government employment would open to them. Merchants obtain such men without difficulty, and think them indispensable to their business. By the appropriation of not over twenty thousand dollars annually for student assistants to the Legation and Consulates in Japan, and the selection of young men of suitable character and ambition, a corps of useful attachés would be provided, whose acquirements and service, would soon be worth to our national interests and influence, far more than the small sum required to maintain them. If possible, some assurance should be given, (as is done in Great Britain) that attainments and services would be appreciated and rewarded by promotion in office in Japan. But even if so just and stimulating a measure should be impractible at present, the plan proposed would secure to the Government some very useful servants, and would ere long redeem our legation in Japan from its present unfortunate and discreditable condition. It will probably be objected to these suggestions that the United States desire no special political influence in Japan; that our interests there are purely commercial; and that, if our merchants there contrive to prosper under existing circumstances, no change is necessary. But the obvious answer to these narrow objections is that the progress which Japan is now rapidly making, her important position and probable future influence on the ~~p~~Pacific, and her vicinity to us, require us at least to understand her institutions and her policy, and to cultivate her friendship; and that we are not likely to do this by adherence to our present system nor without some such improvement as I have suggested. I regret, Sir, that even this imperfect statement of the case, should have obliged me to occupy your attention with so long a letter. But I have desired to avail myself of your invitation to describe the condition of American interests in Japan as clearly and as fully as possible, feeling that the moment is critical, and that unless something be soon done to increase the efficiency and improve the standing of our representation in that country, most of the advantages of our geographical relation to it, and most of the fruits of the costly Expedition from the United States, which opened it to the world, will be irretrievably lost." Copy, DNA, RG 59, Miscellaneous Letters. See Walsh, *A Letter, Addressed to the President of the United States, on the Existing Diplomatic Relations with Japan* (New York, 1871).

On Feb. 15, 1872, George Webster, San Francisco, wrote to Fish. "for your information I enclose some printed matter which will doubtless be of interest. The subjoined is a heading of one of the many letters written to the *Sacramento Union* the leading journal on this coast in which you have invariably been abused by the very man who you have always supported in Japan, and who now taking advantage of his Official position—is emblazoning his name all over the world as the great man who has succeeded in opening up the far East to Civilization This correspondent is one Frank C. Farrington a low bred hanger on of DeLongs and a fit companion of the Honr: Minister DeLong took this Farrington from a gambling Hell in Virginia City Nevada, and paid his passage to Japan as his private Secretary, and after arriving in Japan De Long tried to have you *pay* this Farrington as such, but you declined, and from that day to this a torrent of abuse has flowed from Farringtons pen every Steamer centering upon you, . . . De Long brags of having no education & brags also that he once kept a low doggery and is acquainted with all the roughs on this coast, which is a fact, and they are his friends He is *all gab*, and got himself into some notoriety here in 56' by leaving the Democratic party and hiring to the Knownothings to stump the state—swinging on to the tail of the lamented Colo Baker,

He then went back to the Demcts and finally run out in California, when he made for the state of 8000 Voters, where he gave Nye & Stewart so much trouble that they besieged President Grant to get him away out of the Country, Hence Charley's greatness by getting puffed up to the skies in consequence of the Great Japanese Embassy, Now a moment as to Charley's financing you raised his salary to more than 12.000 Dollars in Green backs (gold is 10 per ct discount in Japan) I suppose expected some of this money would be expected in *keeping up a house,* Not a dollar *has has he spent,* in that line. Gov. Ito, left Japan more than a year ago, Ito is the ablest man in Japan and a great friend of yours, Some of you ~~the~~ at Washington a year ago treated this man Ito *handsomely,* Ito came ~~bag~~ back to Japan *perfectly delighted* with his treatment in W—, I know all about it, I was in Japan (Yeddo) when the party left, and when they came back, and ~~It~~ know many of the party well Ito at once set about *getting up this embassy,* Ito *never said a word to De Long* about it De Long found it out of Course, and he determined *to make Capital out of it,* It is all *bosh* about De Long inducing the Embassy to Come first to the U. S. *That was a foregone Conclusion* as soon as Ito came back The truth is De Long and his wife have *Crowded themselves* on this Embassy, No matter what Ito may say to you, he *despises* De Long The Japanese are the most courteous and diplomatic people in the world, and you will never hear anything from them as against a Gov. officer . . . I expect soon to come to Washington thence to Europe and then back to china and Japan, I expect to take back to Japan some 75,000 or 100.000 Dollars to invest in an enterprise, and Should this man De Long know that I have paid some attentions to him in this way, it would be impossible for me to get on in Japan at all, for you must know that your Ministers and Consuls in the East are a set of *Small Gods,* They have more absolute power than the Zar of Russia or Emperor of Japan, So *woe woe* to the man who falls under their displeasure. So you will see the importance of this Communication being held *strictly Confidential* between yourself and family, and the Presidents family if you choose I have written something similar to this which President Grant may hear something of. As to my veracity I Respectfully refer you to Honr Lyman Trumbull, Hon Eugene Casserly Senator from this State, and Colo R. McKee 1329. F. St. Washington D. C. I mail to you the 'Overland Monthly' which contains an article on Japan written by me, which if I do say it myself Contains more real information in a few lines about that interesting Country than has ever before appeared in print Please bear in mind Sir that I have not the slightest difficulty with your Minister De Long, I might criticise his official acts many of which are entirely Covered up from you, but I am not disposed to, for I believe you and the President ~~is~~ are satisfied with him, I do not belong politically to your party, and I have no disposition to cry down your subordinates but that you are being shamefully imposed upon by this man De Long there is no doubt whatever, Why Sir I heard De Long say that 'Genl Grant was not a fit man for President, that no man who had accepted presents as Grant had ought ever to be President of the U States, and that the Rep party would never elect him again' Now does not decency call for this man who talks thus shamefully about the President of the U. S. to resign, Sir I honor the President and Sec of State too much to talk in this way, although I am a democrat I shall probably reach Washington by Steamer in 30 days" ALS, *ibid.,* Letters of Application and Recommendation. See "A Few Facts About Japan," *The Overland Monthly,* 7, no. 5 (Nov., 1871), 459–64; *New York Times,* April 23, 1872.

On March 8, 1873, Governor John A. Dix of N. Y. wrote to USG. "The enclosed letter to me is from my son-in-law, Thomas Walsh, from whom you received a communication on Japanese affairs in 1871 and did him the honor to notice officially. You are aware, I believe, that he is at the head of one of the chief commercial houses at Yokohama & has extensive connexions in Europe, to which he is giving his personal attention. As he has no motive in any suggestion he makes but the public welfare, I venture to ask Your attention to his letter, . . ." ALS, DNA, RG 59, Letters of Application and Recommendation. On Feb. 19, Walsh, Berlin, had written to Dix. "While waiting here to meet our Russian Agent, I learn from Japan that a rumour had reached there that Mr de Long, the U. S Minister in Japan, would probably be replaced shortly by some new man—. . . As you know something of the importance of my interests in Japan, and how anxious I have been that my country should be honorably represented there, and enjoy the advantages which belong to her, you will understand with how much regret I should learn that, at such a critical moment, we were to lose the services of a trained and experienced Minister, and to see our Legation replaced, perhaps, in the same unfortunate circumstances in which Mr de Long found it four years ago. And I fear that it would be so; for the suggestions which I made to H. E. the President in 1871 have not yet borne fruit, and the Legation is without any such staff as that which enables one Minister in Europe to replace another without serious derangement of affairs—Everything in Japan is now, as formerly, dependent on the Minister himself, and for this reason, if for no other, Mr de Long could hardly be replaced by any other without detriment to our national interests, particularly at so important a juncture—It is not merely private interest in Japan, but much more the dictate of my duty as a citizen, which impels me to ask you to use your influence to procure such consideration of the matter at Washington as may be necessary—The President has shown, in other cases, that he can disregard party claims when the national welfare is concerned; and, were the circumstances of the present case fairly before him, he would be certain to recognize the importance of retaining Mr de Long in Japan, at least for the present, and until the new Treaties shall have been completed. And even party claims should be satisfied by such a decision, for Mr de Long has been always a staunch supporter of the Administration—" ALS, *ibid.* On March 17, Elihu B. Washburne, Paris, wrote to USG. "I have written the Governor at the instance of Mr. Walsh in regard to the retention of DeLong as Minister to Japan. He Walsh is the largest American merchant in Japan and a most intelligent and accomplished man—the son-in-law of Genl Dix. As I have said to the Governor, I think his judgment in the matter is deserving of consideration—We are all very well. Buck and Hempstead are in correspondence about returning to the United States next month together. With kindest regards to all, . . ." ALS, *ibid.* On Dec. 2, USG nominated John A. Bingham as minister to Japan in place of De Long, affirming an appointment made on May 31.

On June 24, Bingham, Washington, D. C., wrote to Fish. "Upon your suggestion made this morning, I addressed a note to young Mr Stevens, and received a reply thereto, which I have the honor to enclose for your perusal. I have only to repeat what I said this morning, that Mr Stevens would, in my opinion, meet fully every just expectation, as I know him to be a young man of pure life & fine ability" ALS, *ibid.* The enclosure is a letter of the same day from Durham W. Stevens, Washington, D. C., to Bingham. "I have hitherto expressed to you my desire to obtain the position of Secretary of the U. S. Legation in Japan, and I take this occasion to make formal application for the office. You have been so kind as to request a statement, somewhat in detail, as to my age, place of nativity, general education &c. &c. In answer to your enquiries, I have the honor to make the following statements: I was born in this City on the first of February, 1851, and am, consequently, twenty two years of age.

After studying for some time at Oberlin, Ohio, I entered, in 1867, the College at that place, and, having pursued the course of studies laid down in the College curriculum, was graduated in 1871. In the Fall of that year I came to this City, and entered upon the study of law, graduating from the Law Department of Howard University in February, 1873. In this connection, I take great pleasure in referring you to the Dean and Faculty of that Institution for information as to the manner in which I discharged my duties while a student there. With regard to my attainments in the modern languages, I have only to say, that, like most American students, I suffered, while at College, from a surfeit of Greek and Latin, with little or no relief from a study of French and German. I managed, however, to obtain a tolerably fair knowledge of the latter language, to the extent of reading and writing it, indeed, which knowledge has been improved to the best of my ability since leaving College. I am naturally fond of the study of language, and my training in Greek and Latin, unfortunate as it may have been in the 'sin of omission', was positively beneficial in that it gave a special aptitude for, and something of skill in, the pursuit of philological knowledge. With many thanks for the kindness, which prompts your enquiries, and only regretting the haste with which, necessarily, they have been answered, . . ." ALS, *ibid.* On Dec. 2, USG nominated Stevens as secretary of legation, Japan.

To Cyrus B. Comstock

Washington D. C. Apl. 19th *18*71

DEAR COMSTOCK:

Yours of the 15th inst. is received. A change will be made of the Supt. at West Point at the close of the Summer Camp exercises. Of course no one will be appointed who does not desire the position I think it more than probable that Ruger[1] will be the person selected.

Mrs. Grant and the children join me in sending our kindest regards to Mrs. Comstock[2] and yourself. We have been expecting to see you and Mrs. C. soon, having the impression that you would bring your wife here to pay a vist while you go up the lake.

Yours Truly
U. S. GRANT

ALS, WHi. On April 15, [*1871*], Cyrus B. Comstock, Detroit, wrote to Frederick T. Dent. "Will you give the enclosed letter to the President & very much oblige" ALS, ICarbS.

1. Thomas H. Ruger, USMA 1854, resigned as bvt. 2nd lt. and asst. engineer (1855), then practiced law in Janesville, Wis. (1856–61). Appointed lt. col., 3rd Wis., he fought at Antietam, Fredericksburg, Chancellorsville, Gettysburg, Atlanta, and

Franklin, mustered out of the vols. as bvt. maj. gen. (1866), and was appointed col., 33rd Inf. He served as provisional governor of Ga. (1868), transferred to the 18th Inf., and replaced Col. Thomas G. Pitcher as superintendent, USMA, on Sept. 1, 1871.

2. Comstock had married Elizabeth Blair, daughter of Montgomery Blair, on Feb. 3, 1869. She was "Betty" to relatives and friends. See letter to Cyrus B. Comstock, Aug. 13, 1872; Virginia Jeans Laas, *Wartime Washington: The Civil War Letters of Elizabeth Blair Lee* (Urbana and Chicago, 1991).

Proclamation

Whereas objects of interest to the United States require that the Senate should be convened at twelve o'clock on Wednesday the tenth day of May, next, to receive and act upon such communications as may be made to it on the part of the Executive:

Now, therefore, I, Ulysses S. Grant, President of the United States have considered it to be my duty to issue this my proclamation, declaring that an extraordinary occasion requires the Senate of the United States to convene for the transaction of business at the Capitol, in the City of Washington, on Wednesday, the tenth day of May, next, at twelve o'clock on that day, of which all who shall at that time be entitled to act as members of that body are hereby required to take notice.

Given under my hand and the Seal of the United States, at Washington, the twentieth day of April, in the year of our Lord one thousand eight hundred and seventy-one, and of the Independence of the United States of America the Ninety-fifth.

U. S. GRANT

DS, DNA, RG 130, Presidential Proclamations. On April 18, 1871, a correspondent reported. "The President and Secretary of State, in view of the probable result of the negotiation of the Joint High Commission, and the probable necessity for action by the Senate, have been quietly sounding Senators through the members of the Committee on Foreign Relations, to ascertain what time would best suit them for an extra Executive Session. Thus far a majority of Senators have expressed themselves in favor of a meeting in the early part of June." *New York Times*, April 19, 1871. See letter to Elihu B. Washburne, May 17, 1871, note 7; *New York Times*, May 11, 1871.

On March 20 and subsequently, Secretary of State Hamilton Fish had written in his diary. "*President*—returned this morning from Philadelphia—I represent to him the position of the negotiation with the British Commissioners respecting the San Juan Boundary & ask his advice as to offering to the Brit. Commrs to neutralize the

Haro Channel, by stipulating that it shall not be fortified by either Govt He approves—& thinks it may be offered & authorizes our doing so—I then enquire, whether in case of need we are forced to make some further concession, it will do to stipulate on our part not to fortify & leave G. B. at liberty to fortify her side of the Channel—he says we may offer that if absolutely necessary—but he thinks the prohibition ought to be mutual—Practically, from the middle of the Channel, there can be but little object to G. B. in fortifying their side—" "March 28 Tuesday . . . In the Evening call upon the President—tell him what was done yesterday in J. H. C. with respect to the Fisheries He authorizes in the matter of San Juan, in case of necessity, in addition to an agreement to neutralize (not to fortify the Haro Channel) to agree to recognize the rights of property of individuals, who have actually occupied any land on the Islands—" "March 31—Friday . . . I mention in detail the proceedings up to this time of the Joint High Commrs on the Fisheries—the Navigation of the St Lawrence—San Juan—& the Alabama—& read the proposed Articles on Neutrality—President & Boutwell seem to think that these Articles, are possibly more stringent than the U. S. wd like to have them in the future—" "April 13, Thursday Called upon the President, & shewed him the English draft of their Expression of regret for the Escape & depredations of the Alabama & other vessels—Explain present condition of negotiations—& the probable inability to arrive at a conclusion of the San Juan question without Arbitration—He is strongly disinclined to Arbitration—I suggest that if arbitration is resorted to we may be allowed to put in evidence the despatches of our Ministers, &c which tend to shew that the *sole* object of deflecting the 49th parallel before it reached the Ocean was to give to G. B. the possession of the Southern part of Vancouver Island—I ask his opinion as to the purchase of the right of the Inshore Fisheries, at a price to be named by arbitrators—~~he~~ ~~thin~~ without any trade priveleges—he thinks favorably of it, provided the St Lawrence navigation be settled satisfactory—& as a last ~~resort~~ resort will consent to arbitration of San Juan, in a separate treaty—I tell him that the English Commrs have insisted that all the questions be united in one treaty—he then advises me to consult with my Associate Commissioners, & with some leading Senators—. . . I call upon Senator Chandler, shew him the British expression of regret for the Alabama &c, which he says is all that could be asked—He approves the purchase of the right of Inshore Fisheries at a price to be determined by Arbitrators, & will consent to arbitration of San Juan if nothing better can be had—but suggests that Bancrofts letter & 'protest' (as he calls it) should form part of the submission—He promises any aid he can render to help through the House & Senate, any legislation that may be required." DLC-Hamilton Fish.

Endorsement

Respectfully refered to Sec. of State. This recommendation is now transfered to the State Dept. for the office of Govr. of a territory.

U. S. Grant

Apl. 20th /71

AES, DNA, RG 59, Letters of Application and Recommendation. Written on papers including a letter of April 14, 1869, from U.S. Representative Benjamin F. Butler of Mass. to Secretary of State Hamilton Fish. "I desire to present to you, enclosed herewith, the applicat[ion] of Bvt. Maj Genl J Burnham Kinsman, formerly of Maine, now in this District, for Commissioner under the Mexican Treaty Gen Kinsman graduated at Harvard Law School, & was in successful practice in Boston at the breaking out of the war. He volunteered without any commission to go into the war; rose to Lieutenant Colonel in the Army on Gen. Wool's staff for meritorious and gallant services; was detailed to me at New Orleans, and in the absence of Major Bell was at the head of the Provost Court, the only court deciding civil causes in the State of Louisiana during that time, and afterwards at the head of the Commission of Sequestration of rebel property, which commission executed its duty so well and thoroughly as to place more than a million in the United States treasury. I have no doubt of his fitness, intelligence and capacity for the place he seeks. He was candidate for Sergeant-at-Arms of the Senate, received a very large support of Senators, and, except that he was unfortunately prostrated by sickness at the time of the caucus, so that he could make no canvass for it would have been elected to that position. I believe the public service would be promoted by his appointment." LS, *ibid.*

On Dec. 23, 1867, John W. Shaffer, Washington, D. C., had written to Bvt. Maj. Gen. John A. Rawlins. "I enclose you letter of General Weitzel asking that Col J. B. Kinsman be appointed Brevt Brigd Genl I have known Col Kinsman scince May 1862 served with him nearly three years and I do not hesitate to say that he most eminently deserves the Brevt asked for. His service in either Louisiana or Virginia would entitle him to it. I would suggest it be done for services in Army of the James." ALS, *ibid.*, RG 94, ACP, K425 CB 1867. On Dec. 26, USG approved this application. ES, *ibid.* On June 16, 1868, U.S. Representative Halbert E. Paine of Wis. wrote to Secretary of War John M. Schofield. "I have the honor to recommend Gen J. B. Kinsman for the brevet commission of Maj Genl Vols. I became acquainted with in the army of the Gulf in Apl 1862 and know him to be worthy of this promotion." ALS, *ibid.* On June 26, USG approved this application. ES, *ibid.*

On March 17, 1870, George B. Loring, chairman, Republican Committee of Mass., Salem, wrote to USG. "Allow me to recommend Brevet Major Gen'l J. Burnham Kinsman for appointment as minister resident at Constantinople. General Kinsman's service in the war is well known. He entered the service early in the war as a volunteer on the staff of Gen. Butler, without pay & served in that way until after the taking of New Orleans, when Pres't Lincoln without application sent him a Commission of Lt Col. for meritorious service in leading an expedition from N. Orleans through the swamps to Mississippi & capturing Steamer Grey Cloud, & a sailing vessel of great value, in the Bay of St. Louis. He was afterwards promoted to Col. Brigadier General & Major Gen'l, serving with Gen'l Butler until that officer was mustered out;—then in Texas until 1866, when he was honorably discharged. Such service as this deserves reward, & I trust it may be considered by the Administration. The appointment of Gen Kinsman will secure a valuable officer to the Government, & will gratify his numerous friends." ALS, *ibid.*, RG 60, Records Relating to Appointments. Governor William Claflin of Mass., chairman, and William E. Chandler, secretary, Republican National Committee, favorably endorsed this letter. AES, *ibid.* On March 31, U.S. Senator Frederick A. Sawyer of S. C. wrote to Fish recommending J. Burnham Kinsman as minister to Constantinople. ALS, *ibid.* See *PUSG*, 19, 437; *ibid.*, 20, 282.

On Jan. 28, 1873, Governor Edmund J. Davis of Tex. wrote to USG. "If the circuit of Texas is created, I would recommend that Mr. J. B. Kinsman now in Washington be appointed circuit Judge therefor. I knew Mr. (then Col.) Kinsman during the war, and from my observation of the gentleman during those years, I am satisfied he will make a firm, reliable, and safe Judge. We are very much in want here of a Judge who will enforce the laws of the U. S. and to protect the colored people in their lately acquired privileges. The two Dist. Judges we now have here, lamentably fail in these respects." ALS, DNA, RG 60, Records Relating to Appointments.

On March 10, 1875, USG nominated Kinsman as judge, Western District, Ark.; on March 18, USG withdrew this nomination in favor of Isaac C. Parker. On March 9, Parker, Washington, D. C., had written to USG. "I hereby make application for the appointment of United States District judge for the Western District of Arkansas. In doing so I desire for reference to refer you to my standing in my own State as a lawyer and citizen and to my standing in Congress. I desire also to remind you that I was Circuit judge in my own state at the age of thirty years, having been elected in a Circuit which was second in importance in the state for the term of six years and after serving two years I resigned the same to accept a seat in Congress. My knowledge of Indian affairs ~~ob~~ obtained by reason of my connection with the Indian appropriations while on the Committee of appropriations I think will give me some advantages in the way of qualifications over others who may live farther east since the five civilized tribes of Indians come within the jurisdiction of this court Trusting you will give this application consideration and make such disposition of the same as you may deem best." ALS, *ibid.*

On Aug. 4, 1871, B. G. Barrow, Macon, Mo., had written to USG. "I was introduced to you at Macon when you were here, have no intimate personal acquaintance with you, but in the great republican cause which you have espoused and have endeavored to promote, I have been a co-worker with you, and hence there would be a sympathy of a fraternal character with you. I desire to get from you, (if thought consistent with your duty) an appointment as Judge of some court in one of the territories Washington preferred. I am getting a good legal practice here but the health of my wife suggests as I think that a new country with ~~b~~mountain & sea breezes would be ~~better~~ of great benefit to her. I do not feel able financially to travel to afford such benefit, and I thought it barely possible that you might as the lamented Lincoln said 'have an extra hole in which to put a peg in' and knowing that the good book says 'ask & you shall receive' I thought I would 'ask' ~~with~~ which was but little trouble to do, and could only be refused at most, as to my qualification integrity and soundness of Political faith I can refer you to none better that the late Gov. McClurg, who I think will vouch for me. If you think me worthy of being answer, please do so—an accept my apology for what might be a breach of Etiquette for making so free with you but we Missourians take that freedom with each other as brothers, and do not consult Etiquette in Cold formalities, . . ." ALS, *ibid.* On Nov. 18, 1874, Barrow, Washington, D. C., wrote to USG and Attorney Gen. George H. Williams requesting appointment as judge, Western District, Ark., or for Washington Territory. ALS, *ibid.* On the same day, John F. Benjamin, Washington, D. C., wrote to USG introducing Barrow. ALS, *ibid.* On Dec. 4, 1875, George R. Smith, Sedalia, Mo., wrote to USG. "B. G. Barrow is an applicant for the office of chief justice of the Supreme Court of Arazonia—Mr Barrow is in every way qualified for the office—He is capable and honest. He is a thorough Republican and in full sympathy with your administration. His appointment would give much satisfaction to his many friends in Missouri" ALS, *ibid.*

On Dec. 14, 1874, U.S. Senator Henry R. Pease and U.S. Representatives Jason Niles, Albert R. Howe, and John R. Lynch of Miss. had written to USG. "We respectfully recommend the appointment of Judge Greene C. Chandler, of Shieldsboro, Mississippi, to the District Judgeship now vacant in the State of Arkansas. Judge Chandler has earned for himself, since he has been on the bench in Mississippi, the reputation of being an able, impartial, incorruptible and unswerving Judge in the discharge of his duties. He will be remembered as the Mississippi Judge who arrested the Louisiana duelists, and by his firmness and decision effectually cut off the long-standing practice of making the soil of his District the scene of the bloody meetings of the New Orleans hot bloods. In addition we beg leave to refer the President to recommendations of Judge Chandler filed with an application made for him for the Alabama Judgeship." LS, *ibid.* On Nov. 7, Governor Adelbert Ames of Miss., Shieldsboro, had written to USG. "Permit me to recommend to you, as a suitable person to fill the vacancy on the U. S. District bench occasioned by the resignation of Judge Busteed, Judge G. C. Chandler one of the circuit judges of this state. The judge is a native of Alabama but has been residing in this state for a number of years. He is an able man and an upright judge and I have no hesitancy in saying that he will reflect credit both on the appointment and the appointing power. As one of his many friends I join in the expression of the hope that his application for such an appointment may meet with success." ALS, *ibid.* On Nov. 10, John F. H. Claiborne, New Orleans, endorsed this letter. "I beg to say to the President that he could appoint no truer & more zealous friend, no better lawyer & no more influential republican than Judge Chandler. He would redeem & recover all that has been lost by the conduct of Busteed & other party leaders in Alabama. The disasters that have affected the republican cause in so many states are mainly due to such men as Durell, Kellogg & Busteed. They have no *firmness* & no *independence,* & cannot command the confidence of a party." AES, *ibid.* Related papers are *ibid.* No appointments followed for Barrow or Greene C. Chandler.

On May 15, 1876, U.S. Senators George S. Boutwell and Henry L. Dawes of Mass. wrote to USG. "We respectfully recommend J. Burnham Kinsman Esq., as a suitable person to be appointed Judge of the Territorial Court of New Mexico in place of Judge Johnson deceased." LS, *ibid.* No appointment followed.

Speech

[*April 22, 1871*]

Ladies and Gentlemen:—I thank you heartily for this cordial greeting, for I assure you it is entirely unexpected. When I left Washington it was with the view of going to St. Louis without stopping by the way, but on meeting your distinguished Senator Governor Morton,[1] at Pittsburg, he requested me to remain here during this day. That I consented to do, expecting to see you people of Indianapolis turn out to greet your Senator, and not expecting a greeting to me, and I leave him to thank you in more appropriate terms than I could do if I were to try.

Indianapolis Journal, April 24, 1871. USG had arrived in Indianapolis in the early morning of April 22, 1871. In the evening, Governor Conrad Baker of Ind. introduced USG to an audience at the Academy of Music. U.S. Senator Oliver P. Morton of Ind. spoke following USG on Republican policies and politics and closed: ". . . Let us reflect for one moment what the probable condition of our country now would have been had it not been for Donelson, Shiloh, Chattanooga, Vicksburgh, 'fighting-it-out-on-this-line,' and Appomattox, and then rise and give three cheers to our President, and send him on his way to-night rejoicing. Are you ready?" *Ibid.* USG left Indianapolis for St. Louis on a 10:30 P.M. train.

1. On April 22 and 23, Secretary of State Hamilton Fish wrote in his diary. "Speaker Blaine urges me not to withdraw from the Cabinet—Expresses great apprehension of Senator Morton being my successor—& of his influence over the President Expresses great mistrust of him—thinks him a demagogue extremely ambitious, & selfish & does not accord to him much principle, either political, or moral—mentions the statement made to him by 'a lady from Indiana'—'a discreet, matron' &c, that 'no lady in Indianapolis having any regard for her reputation would be seen walking or riding alone in company with him'—also other remarks affecting his character in other respects—Blaine says, that a very general mistrust of M. exists among the Republicans in the House of Reps." "Senator Chandler calls at my house, & remains with me upwards of two hours—Says his object in calling is to speak of Senator Morton, whom he calls 'his friend' but says that he is not a safe adviser, nor of fixed principles, & that he with others are alarmed at the idea which he says M. is giving publicity to, & endeavoring to have believed by the public, that he has the confidence of the President, & a controlling influence over him—'damn it' (says C) 'Morton wants the Public to think that he owns & runs Grant—& G__ d__n him, *he* is succeeding in making them believe it—& nothing could be more injurious to Grant or to the Republican Party'—He says that Morton causes the publication of all the statements that so frequently appear, of his being about to come into the Cabinet—& that he also publishes the constantly appearing paragraphs of his visits to the President, & 'his long conferences with him' & his 'being received in this Parlor or that Parlor'—He says that 'he is carrying water on both shoulders' & endeavors to maintain his intimacies with Schurz & Sumner, & at the same time with the President—that in no debate, & in nothing that has been said or done by him, can it be told on which side he is—that he is putting himself in position to go with whichever may seem the strongest—Says that he is on record on both sides of all the great questions that have lately been discussed—refers to a speech on the redemption of the Public Debt, which he says lost us 10,000 votes in Indiana—& that he has equivocated, & been doubtful on all the reconstruction & other questions—He says he wishes me to repeat what he has said, to the President—To my enquiry why he does not do so himself, & my suggestion that it wd have more effect, & be more proper for him to say these things directly to the President, than for me to repeat them, he replies that he would do so, if the President were here, but he is going away (to Michigan) before the President returns, & 'it is important that the President be cautioned, at

once' & that I can talk to him more freely, & with more influence than any other member of the Cabinet, & he wishes me to use his name, & say that he requested me to make the Communication—and adds that Senator Carpenter authorized him to give his name also, as concuring in the opinions he had expressed—He deprecates the idea of my resigning—& says that should M. succeed me, or come into the Cabinet, it would be impossible for the Republican party to carry the next Presidential Election—'for (said he) no one has confidence in him.' Senator Conkling dined with me—& Robeson—after dinner I explain the points in the negotiation with Gt Britain in which we have come to an agreement—Subsequently Conkling speaks of Morton, & very much in the same terms that Chandler did this morning. . . . (I ask myself the question. What is the meaning of these several parties thus unbosoming themselves with respect to Morton—Several others within a few days past have made similar allusions & remarks)" DLC-Hamilton Fish.

To Julia Dent Grant

St. Louis Mo,
Apl. 23d /71

Dear Julia,

We arrived here this morning and after getting breakfast Porter[1] and I drove to the farm from which we have just returned. Every thing ~~loo~~ looks well but very dry. There has been but little rain here since last Feb. Peaches are all killed again, making four seasons out of five since I have been farming. Last night was a very cold night and killed the grapes. The milk house has not been torn away, but on the contrary Elrod has been working on the Spring to get it to run again so as to make the spring house available. He thinks he has succeeded. The ice house is very neat and is in the sidehill between the house and milk house.—The stock all looks well and is doing well. There is surplus corn on the place sufficient to keep my present stock through another year.

I will be home, barring accidents, on Friday[2] morning. Kiss the children for me.

Yours affectionate
U. S. Grant

ALS, USG 3. On April 21, 1871, USG, Pittsburgh, telegraphed to Julia Dent Grant. "Have been detained here three hours by breaking of engine Will not reach St Louis until Sunday," Telegram received (at 12:55 A.M.), *ibid.* On April 24, Monday, USG visited his farm, lunched at the country residence of William H. Benton, and dined in the evening with Robert Campbell before holding a reception at Benton's. *Indianapolis Journal*, April 25, 1871. On April 25, a correspondent reported from St. Louis that USG and others "went on an excursion to-day to Jefferson Barracks. Thomas Allen, Esq., president of the Iron Mountain road, furnished a special train. In the afternoon the company stopped at South St. Louis and dined with Hon. Henry L. Blow, ex-Minister to Brazil. From 7 to 9 o'clock the President gave a reception at the residence of Mr. Burton [*Benton*], and at 10 he left for Lafayette, . . ." *Washington Chronicle*, April 27, 1871. See letter to Charles W. Ford, May 3, 1871, note 5; *Missouri Democrat*, April 25, 26, 1871.

1. On April 15, Horace Porter telegraphed to James D. Cameron, Harrisburg, Pa. "Thanks for your letter. We cannot leave till Wednesday night." Copy, DLC-USG, II, 5. On April 19, Porter wrote to J. C. Bancroft Davis, asst. secretary of state. "I am terribly crowded today, as we are trying to get off tonight. Babcock and I have a good, safe cipher. Will it do as well to communicate anything to him, in my absence, and let him telegraph it? He and I can arrange to send anything in regard to the Commission in such a manner as not to use distinguishable names of persons or things. There will probably be little occasion for telegraphing at all. As we shall return in a week." ALS, DLC-J. C. Bancroft Davis. On the same day, Porter telegraphed to William S. Forbes, pension agent, Philadelphia. "We have heard nothing of a raid on you. President and I leave for St. Louis to-night. Letter received." Copy, DLC-USG, II, 5. On April 20, Porter telegraphed to Samuel S. Blair, superintendent, Northern Central Railroad, Baltimore. "Congress did not adjourn: President now expects to start at 5.40 this evening" Copy, *ibid.*

2. On April 25, USG, St. Louis, telegraphed to William W. Smith. "It will be impossible for me to stop must be home on Friday." Telegram received (at 10:45 A.M.), Washington County Historical Society, Washington, Pa. On April 27, USG, Pittsburgh, telegraphed to Julia Grant. "Will be home at eight A. M. tomorrow." Telegram received, USG 3.

To Hamilton Fish

Washington D. C.
Apl. 28th 1871.

DEAR GOVERNOR:

Mrs. Grant and Nellie are preparing to attend the party at Earl de Grey's[1] this evening, and as I cannot accompany them they wish to ask if Mrs. Fish is going, and if so if it will be convenient for all to go to-gether.

Mrs. Grant will go to your house and start from there if Mrs. Fish should be going.

Yours Truly
U. S. GRANT

ALS, DLC-Hamilton Fish. On April 28, [*1871*], Secretary of State Hamilton Fish wrote to USG. "Mrs Fish will be most happy to accompany Mrs Grant & Nellie. She will be ready & not detain them—" ALS, Nellie C. Rothwell, La Jolla, Calif.

1. Born in 1827 in London, George Frederick Samuel Robinson entered the House of Commons (1852), became Earl of Ripon and Earl de Grey after the deaths of his father and uncle (1859), gained high standing in the Liberal Party, and served as chairman of the British delegation to the Joint High Commission to settle the Alabama Claims. See letter to Hamilton Fish, March 4, 1871.

Proclamation

TO ALL WHO SHALL SEE THESE PRESENTS, GREETING:

Know Ye, That, reposing special trust and confidence in the integrity and Ability of Daniel J. Morrell,[1] and on his nomination by the Governor of the State of Pennsylvania as delegate from said State, I do appoint the said Daniel J. Morrell, a Commissioner on the Commission authorized to be constituted under and by virtue of the act of Congress "to provide for celebrating the one hundredth anniversary of American independence, by holding an international exhibition of arts, manufactures, and products of the soil and mine, in the City of Philadelphia, and State of Pennsylvania, in the year eighteen hundred and seventy-six," approved March 3, 1871.[2]

In testimony whereof, I have caused these Letters to be made patent, and the Seal of the United States to be hereunto affixed.

Done at the City of Washington, this Twenty-ninth day of April, in the year of our Lord one thousand eight hundred and Seventy one, and of the independence of the United States of America the Ninety-fifth.

U. S. GRANT.

Copy, DNA, RG 59, General Records. The text of this proclamation was followed in appointing other commissioners. Also on April 29, 1871, USG issued a similar proclamation appointing Asa Packer as "Commissioner substitute" for Pa. Copy, *ibid.* The text of this proclamation was followed in appointing other commissioner substitutes.

On April 22, Governor Harrison Reed of Fla. wrote to Secretary of State Hamilton Fish. "In reply to your favor of 15th inst. I have the honor to nominate for appointment as Commissioners to represent the state of Florida . . . J. S. Adams, Jacksonville Duvall Co. . . . Genl J. T. Bernard, Tallahassee Leon County." ALS, *ibid.*, Letters of Application and Recommendation. On May 11, Jesse T. Bernard, Tallahassee, wrote to Fish. "Your favor of 3d inst. enclosing Commission as Commissioner substitute, . . .

is received. While it would afford me much pleasure to accept of the appointment, (and my desire is to accept) I am barred from doing so, by the enclosed oath. If the usual substitute can be furnished me—I mean the modified oath for those whose disabilities have been removed—I will take pleasure in forwarding my formal acceptance, with the oath modified as aforesaid. Hoping that my request is not incompatible with the public interests . . ." ALS, *ibid.* On Nov. 1, 1875, Governor Marcellus L. Stearns of Fla. wrote to USG nominating Thomas W. Osborn as commissioner to fill the vacancy caused by the resignation of John S. Adams. LS, *ibid.*

On Aug. 31, Governor Richard Coke of Tex. wrote to USG. "I have the honor to recommend Messers J. W. Jennings, of Grayson County, and A. M. Hobby of Galveston County, both citizens of Texas, for appointment as Centennial Commissioners, vice W. H. Parsons, and J. C. Chew, heretofore appointed, who more than two years ago removed from the State of Texas, and are now citizens of another State, thus creating vacancies." LS, *ibid.* On Oct. 25, J. W. Jennings, Sandusky, Ohio, wrote to USG. "Your humble Sevt having received notice from home 'Texas' that our Govr Hon Rich Coke, had recommended me to your Excelency for commissioner to the centennial exposition for the state of 'Texas' I would respectfully refer you to the Hon. Z. Chandler, Gov Shepard, and Henry. D. Cooke Ex. Govr of the district who will recognize me as the Post Master of the US. Senate during the first administration of Prest Lincoln. I am assured by our legislature if my appointment is made they will appropriate sufficient money to have Texas well represented at Phila personally I have no particular desire for so empty an honor only that I have a pride in our national exposition being the bigest show ever made—something that will astonish the World, and place 'America' as he is at the head of Nations—I am authorized to use other names as references, but hold these quite sufficient, . . ." ALS, *ibid.* Related papers are *ibid.*

On May 24, 1871, Governor George L. Woods of Utah Territory wrote to USG nominating "John H Wickizer of Salt Lake City Utah Territory a COMMISSIONER to represent said Territory of Utah in making preparations for and celebrating the One Hundredth Anniversary of American Independence in the City of Philadelphia, and State of Pennsylvania in the Year Eighteen Hundred and Seventy Six. And in case that the said John H. Wickizer shall be unable to attend the meetings of the Commission I do hereby Nominate William H Pitts AS ALTERNATE" ALS, *ibid.* On May 6, 1872, Woods wrote to USG. "I wrote to you some time ago of the Resignation of W. H. Pitts as Alternate-Delegate to the Centennial Commissioner from Utah Territory and reccommended for appointment to fill the vacancy Oscar G. Sawyer, of Salt Lake City—now, and for a long time connected with the *New York Herald.* He is anxious to go on, has waited for Commission to come I advise him to apply to you in person He, therefore, will present this to you. He is in every way worthy of your confidence and consideration. I hope you will Commission him He has done much valuable service here in the past and I have no doubt will in the future. . . . P. S: There is much anxiety, here, for the early passage of the much-needed Congressional Legislation. Without it nothing can be done; with it much can be accomplished. I hope every power will be used to secure it *very soon.* We must put down this 'relic of barbarism' Teams have already started South, to the new Post Troops will be here tonight & go tomorrow. I am highly gratified at the movement. The thanks of every patriot in Utah are heartily given you for the noble support which you have given us in this terrible Struggle against this abomination" ALS, *ibid.* See letter to John P. Newman, Nov. 6, 1871. On May 16, 1874, Woods wrote to USG. "Oscar G. Sawyer Esqr, heretofore nominated by me, and appointed by you as an *Alternate Commissioner* to represent Utah Territory at the Centennial Celebration of American

Independence to be holden at the City of Philadelphia State of Pennsylvania in the year A D 1876, having removed from this Territory and taken up his residence elsewhere, I Geo. L. Woods Governor of the Territory of Utah, deeming it proper that the Territory should be represented in full by its own Citizens, do hereby Nominate William Haydon Esqr of Salt Lake City, for the office of Alternate Commissioner, *vice* Oscar G Sawyer Esqr and submit his name to you for further action" ALS, DNA, RG 59, Letters of Application and Recommendation. On March 5, 1875, Oscar G. Sawyer, San Francisco, wrote to U.S. Senator Roscoe Conkling of N. Y. "Shortly after the organization of the U. S. Centennial Commission, I was appointed and commissioned Alternate Commissioner from the Territory of Utah, and have attended every meeting of the commission since, and performed the duties of the Office with zeal, if not with the greatest success. These duties have taken up a good deal of my time, and have cost me a large amount of money, as I had to go to Philadelphia several times, from my home in Salt Lake City. The 'hard times' in Utah and the disastrous ending of my newspaper enterprise compelled me, temporarily, to leave Utah, and seek a living elsewhere, until an improved state of affairs in the Territory should permit me to return there, and go on again with my business. All the interests I have in the world, are in Utah. My home is there, and I have never relinquished my intention to return there and take part in the reorganization of the political and social affairs of the Territory. Under these circumstances you may judge of my surprise, when, unofficially, informed that Ex-Gov. Wood, upon representation of some one unadvised of the true state of matters, that I had gone to Japan with the intention of taking up my residence there permanently, had nominated Mr. William Haydon my successor, and he had been appointed. It was only this morning that this report was confirmed. Gov. Woods was misinformed & seemed to have taken no pains to get at the truth, from me, as he knew I was temporarily sojourning in this City. I still claim to be a citizen of Utah, and feel that Gov. Wood's action was unjust and wrong. I write this to beg of you to do me the great favor to lay these facts before the President, and to request him to take such action as shall leave my commission valid and in full force. . . ." ALS, *ibid.* Conkling endorsed this letter. "Respectfully submitted to the Honorable the Sec. of state, with the remark that Mr S. is a man of talent & respectability whose word I would take." AES (stamped March 16), *ibid.* On March 20, 1876, Governor George W. Emery of Utah Territory wrote to USG. "I herewith send you the names of William Haydon and C. R. Gilchrist, both of whom, I believe you are acquainted with, as Commissioners to the Centennial Exhibition Judge Haydon resigns, as Comr *Substitute,* to be appointed Comr Col. Wickizer the Comr for Utah, has resigned and left the Territory." ALS, *ibid.* Related papers are *ibid.*

On July 15, 1871, Governor Rufus B. Bullock of Ga. wrote to USG nominating "Hon Thomas Hardeman, Junior, of Bibb County" as commissioner and "Louis Waln Smith of Philadelphia, Pennsylvania," as commissioner substitute. LS, *ibid.* On June 15, 1872, Thomas Hardeman, Jr., Macon, wrote to Fish. "Enclosed you will find The Commission—tendered me by His Excellency Prest Grant—as The Commissioner from Georgia, to the Centennial Celebration of the Declaration of American Independence. Upon its reception I notified The Department—I could not accept the Same—on account of The oath required of me—I was requested to await the action of Congress on the Disability bill—Congress having adjourned and having excluded me in their bill of Amnesty—from the benefit of its provisions—I now return ~~that~~ The commission—That His Excellency may appoint Some other person to represent Georgia on that occasion—hoping—that before that day—The animosities of the past, may be forgotten and that we may again—be one people, one in feeling, one in interest, one in destiny" ALS, *ibid.* The enclosure is *ibid.* On Feb. 28, 1874, Governor James M. Smith of Ga. telegraphed to USG. "I have the honor to nom. Hon George Hillyer of Fulton County in this states as Commissioner of Georgia to the international Exhibition of Eighteen seventy six at Philadelphia in place of Hon Thomas Hardeman resigned" Telegram received, *ibid.* On July 27, Lewis Waln Smith, Philadelphia, wrote to USG resigning as "Alternate Centennial Commissioner from Georgia." ALS, *ibid.*, Letters of Declination and Resignation. On Aug. 25, Smith wrote to USG nominating "Mr Richard Peters Jr. of the County of Gordon, in this State, as Alternate Commissioner from Georgia of the International Exhibition of 1876, . . ." LS, *ibid.*, Letters of Application and Recommendation.

On Feb. 10, Benjamin P. Kooser, Santa Cruz, Calif., wrote to Gen. William T. Sherman. "It has been my good fortune to be nominated, by Governor Newton Booth, as Centennial Commissioner to represent California in the Celebration and Exposition to be held July, 1876, in Philadelphia. I ask, as an old friend and Pioneer Companion in Arms, that you would see the President, (Gen. Grant,) and ask him to confirm the nomination made by Gov. Booth. . . ." ALS, *ibid.* On Feb. 21, Sherman endorsed this letter. "The writer of this was a soldier of Company F. 3rd artillery who went around Cape Horn with us in 1846—he was a good sober young man, and has since prospered in California. I recommend him to the Courtesy of the Presdt & would like to communicate a favorable answer to Kooser" AES, *ibid.* On Feb. 16, U.S. Senator Aaron A. Sargent of Calif. had written to USG. "I have received several indignant letters from gentlemen of Santa Cruz of California, the residence of Benjamin P. Kooser, nominated as Com. Cent. Exposition at Philadelphia by the Governor of California, vice Middleton deceased, which nomination by law is effective only by your appointment. These gentlemen declare that Kooser is totally unfit for the place, that he is a vile and abusive fellow, that his associations during the war were traitorous, that he has disgusted that community by filthy abuse of you and others through the columns of a local paper that he has controlled, and they ask to be spared the shame of such an appointment. Knowing much of the man whom they describe, I concur in this estimate of him, and second their request" ALS, *ibid.* USG appointed Kooser.

On Dec. 28, 1871, Governor Ozra A. Hadley of Ark. wrote to USG. "I have the honor to nominate, for appointment by your Excellency, as delegate from Arkansas on the Commission authorized under the Act of Congress providing for celebrating the 100th. Anniversary of American Independence, *Hon. Alex. McDonald, vice* Powell Clayton, U. S. S. declared ineligible." LS, *ibid.* On Jan. 7, 1875, Governor Augustus H. Garland of Ark. wrote to USG. "The Hon A T Goshorn of Philadelphia, Superintendent of the International Exhibition for 1876, has written me several letters urging attention on the part of Arkansas to this highly important and very worthy object. Some weeks since, I addressed you a letter requesting the appointment of Geo W Lawrence of Hot Springs, commissioner for this state, in place of E W Gantt deceased. I have not heard from you on the subject, but I presume your varied & onerous duties have prevented you from attending to this recommendation. I now respectfully renew it for your consideration & action. The Hon A McDonald was also alternate commissioner, & he is no longer a resident or citizen of the state; and I would ask the appointment of Geo. E Dodge of this place in his stead. I am very desirous of bringing this matter, in proper shape before our present Legislature and have such action taken as will do credit to Arkansas in this noble work, and I hope it will be your pleasure to act, at an early day, favorably upon these recommendations:—Before closing this, I beg leave to report, that we are all quiet & orderly in this state, and our people are peaceably & earnestly at work in their legitimate callings. The information of Genl Sheridan that there is terrorism here, and that there are White Leagues I can assure you is erroneous. The Genl. has been imposed upon as to this, and I would be glad indeed for any one to make inquiry into this, & we will show as orderly and law abiding people, as can be found anywhere—and a state in which all classes are protected & secured in their rights:" ALS, *ibid.*

On Feb. 2, 1872, Governor Robert K. Scott of S. C. wrote to USG. "I have the honor to nominate, . . . the Honorable James L. Orr, of Anderson as Commissioner from this State, and Mr Archibald Cameron, of Charleston as Alternate." LS, *ibid.* On May 12, 1873, L. Cass Carpenter, *The Daily and Weekly Union*, Columbia, wrote to USG. "If your Excllency has not already made the appointment to fill the vacancy ion the Board of Commissioners of the Centennial Commission caused by the death of Hon James L. Orr, late Minister to Russia, it would be very gratifying to the undersigned to receive the appointment. I was informed by the late Minister the day he left this city for his post of duty, that I was the 'Alternate' vice Archibald Cameron who refused to serve, but as I had no other notification of the appointment I took it for granted that it was a mistake on his part." ALS, *ibid.* On June 11, Governor Franklin J. Moses, Jr., of S. C. wrote to USG. "I have the honor to nominate for appointment as a commissioner on the part of the State of South Carolina to represent it in the centennial celebration to be held in Philadelphia in 1876, General William Gurney, of Charleston, S. C., *vice* Hon. James L. Orr, deceased." LS, *ibid.*

On Feb. 8, 1872, Governor Tod R. Caldwell of N. C. wrote to USG. "I have the honor to nominate Honl Alfred Dockery of Rockingham, Richmond County North Carolina as Commissioner and Honl Jonathan W. Albertson of Hertford, Perquimans County N. C as alternate to represent the State of North Carolina at the Centennial Anniversary of American Independence . . ." ALS, *ibid.* On April 6, 1871, U.S. Senator John Pool of N. C. had written to Fish. "I take great pleasure in recommending Mr. A. V. Dockery for some consulship that he may be qualified to fill. He is a young gentleman of decided talent & good education, & of the very best family connections in North Carolina. He is the son of Hon. O. H. Dockery, a Representative in the last Congress, & his whole family are Republicans. I ask for him your favorable consideration—" ALS, *ibid.* U.S. Representatives Charles R. Thomas and Clinton L. Cobb of N. C., Joseph C. Abbott, and Robert M. Douglas favorably endorsed this letter. AES, *ibid.* Related papers are *ibid.* On April 15, USG nominated Alfred V. Dockery as consul, Stettin; on Jan. 13, 1873, USG nominated Dockery as consul, Oporto. On Nov. 20, 1872, Caldwell wrote to USG. "Having been notified by the Secretary of State of the United States, that Genl Alfred Dockery has tendered his resignation as Commissioner for the State of North Carolina, to attend the celebration of the international exposition at the City of Philadelphia in 1876, I have the honor to name as his successor Honl Samuel F. Phillips of Wake County N. C.—. . . P. S. Mr. Phillips is now in Washington City—." ALS, *ibid.* See *PUSG*, 15, 424.

On Feb. 12 and March 1, Governor Ridgley C. Powers of Miss. wrote to USG nominating "Hon. O. C. French of Natchez" as commissioner and "Mr Joseph H. Livingston of Philadelphia, Pa." as commissioner substitute. ALS, DNA, RG 59, Letters of Application and Recommendation. On Dec. 22, 1873, Powers wrote to USG. "In conformity with the terms of 'an Act to provide for Celebrating the One Hundredth Anniversary of American Independence' &c, I had the honor to recommend Hon. O. C. French for the appointment as Commissioner from this State. The appointment was duly made by you and Mr. French has accepted the position. Within the last few days my attention has been called to a report submitted to Congress by the Secretary of War in which he represents that Hon. O. C. French is a defaulter to the U. S. Government to the amount of several thousand dollars on account of certain transactions while he was an officer in the Freedmens' Bureau. Other statements damaging to the character of Mr. French have also lately been made upon what seems to be good authority. I therefore desire to withdraw my recommendation on account of these blots which now rest upon his character and disquallify him for the honorable position to which you were please to appoint him. As I have not before this time named a person to be appointed alternate Commissioner, I would respectfully recommend Mr. M. Edwards of Macon, Miss." ALS, *ibid.* On March 18, 1876, Governor Adelbert Ames of Miss. wrote to USG. "Permit me to request a commission for Col. E. D. Frost as Alternate Commissioner to the International Centennial Exhibition for this State *vice* M. Edwards, resigned." LS, *ibid.* Related papers are *ibid.*

On Feb. 29 and March 1, 1872, U.S. Representative James B. Beck of Ky. wrote to USG. "His Excellency P. H. Leslie Governor of Kentucky wrote me a letter recd today saying that he had recommended Robert Mallory of Oldham Co. & Smith M Hobbs of Spencer Co. Ky, as Comrs on behalf of the State to attend the Convention at Philadelphia which meets to celebrate the Centennial Anniversary of American Independence He says no response has been made & he desired me to see you & learn what had been done with his recommendation. I did not think it proper to trouble you with a personal visit, & hoping an answer will be sent to me, so I can advise the Governor." "The enclosed Telegram from the Governor of Ky. shows how anxious he is for an answer to the letter I wrote to you yesterday. He says *'Answer quick'* I would be greatly obliged for an answer which I could telegraph to the Governor" ALS, *ibid.* The enclosure is *ibid.* On March 1, Governor Preston H. Leslie of Ky. telegraphed to USG. "On the eighth Dec last I wrote you nomination Robert Mallory as commissioner & Smith M Hobbs as Alternate under the act of Congress providing for Centennial Celebration they both live here in Kentucky. if you should see proper to send their commissions to me I for my State will feel obliged to you" Telegram received, *ibid.* On the same day, USG endorsed this telegram. "Respectfully refered to the Sec. of State. I have no recollection of seeing the letter refered to by Govr Leslie and if I did see it certainly refered it to the State Dept. to secure the apts ~~recom~~ submitted" AES, *ibid.*

On March 2, Governor John M. Palmer of Ill. telegraphed to USG. "I have nominated F. L. Matthews & Lawrence Weldon Esqrs. Commissioners to represent Illinois at the Centennial anniversary to be held at Philada Communications sent you by mail" Telegram received, *ibid.* On March 5, Fish wrote to USG asking whether Palmer should be advised that notice of his appointments had arrived too late for designation. Copy, *ibid.*, Domestic Letters. On March 7, Orville E. Babcock wrote to Fish. "The President directs me to say in reply to your note of the 5th inst. in relation to the gentlemen named by Govr Palmer of Illinois, by telegraph, as comrs. Cent. Celebration, that the telegram was recd in time and mislaid, but that a reply was sent to Gov. Palmer, upon receipt of the despatch, that the gentlemen named by him would be appointed." LS, *ibid.*, Letters of Application and Recommendation. Related papers are *ibid.* Similar documents for other states and territories are *ibid.*

1. On March 10, 1871, Governor John W. Geary of Pa. had written to USG. "I have the honor to inform you, that, in conformity with the recent Act of Congress; 'to

provide for celebrating the one hundredth anniversary of American Independence,' &c., I have made the following appointments, which I submit for your approval. Hon. Daniel J. Morrell, Johnstown, Cambria County, Pa., to be United States Commissioner for Pennsylvania, in accordance with the provisions of the 2nd Section of the Act. Hon. Asa Packer, Mauch Chunk, Carbon County, Pa., to be the alternate United States Commissioner for Pennsylvania, in accordance with the 4th Section of the same Act." LS, *ibid.* Born in 1821 in Berwick, Maine, Daniel J. Morrell worked as a merchant in Philadelphia, moved to Johnstown (1855), became prominent as an iron manufacturer, gas and water supplier, and bank president, and served as Republican U.S. representative (1867–71). Packer, born in 1805 in Groton, Conn., moved to southeastern Pa., and prospered from canal and railroad management and coal mining. He had been Democratic U.S. representative (1853–57) and candidate for governor (1869).

2. Introduced in the House of Representatives on March 9, 1870, debates over the propriety of holding a centennial celebration in Philadelphia and liability for expenses preceded passage of an amended bill. Morrell and U.S. Senators Simon Cameron and John Scott of Pa. guided the measure against vigorous opposition led by Conkling. The law gave the president one year to appoint commissioners. See *CG*, 41–2, 1813, 41–3, 103–8, 419–23, 448–50, 1293, 1681–82, 1762–63, 1910; *HMD*, 42-3-99; James D. McCabe, *The Illustrated History of the Centennial Exhibition,...* (Philadelphia, 1876), pp. 167–76. See also Proclamation, July 3, 1873; message to Congress, Feb. 25, 1874.

On Aug. 16, 1871, David K. Hitchcock, Boston, wrote to USG. "I shall not be able to see you at Long Branch as I intended. But I write to suggest to you the propriety of appointing Rev Alexander King, D. D. of London Commissioner for the Centennial which is to take place in 1876. Dr King is a very earnest and zealous frind of America & has in his speeches fully appreciated you A few weeks since I forwarded to you his address delivered in this city. Judge Russell presided. This appointment is purely an honorary affair & would be of service to Dr K in England. And I may add, Dr K is in every respect worthy of the compliment." ALS, DNA, RG 59, Letters of Application and Recommendation.

Proclamation

TO ALL TO WHOM THESE PRESENTS SHALL COME, GREETING:

Know ye, that whereas by my power bearing date the tenth day of February, last, Hamilton Fish, Secretary of State, Robert C. Schenck, Envoy Extraordinary and Minister Plenipotentiary to Great Britain, Samuel Nelson, an Associate Justice of the Supreme Court of the United States, Ebenezer R. Hoar, of Massachusetts, and George H. Williams, of Oregon, were authorized to meet the Commissioners appointed or to be appointed on behalf of Her Britannic Majesty, and with them to treat and discuss the mode of settlement of the different questions which should come before them.

And whereas that meeting and discussion have taken place, and the said mode of settlement has been agreed upon:

Now therefore, I Ulysses S. Grant, President of the United States, do hereby appoint the said Hamilton Fish, Robert C. Schenck, Samuel Nelson, Ebenezer R. Hoar and George H. Williams, jointly and severally Plenipotentiaries for and in behalf of the United States, and do authorize them, and any or either of them to conclude and sign any treaty or treaties touching the premises for the final ratification of the President of the United States, by and with the advice and consent of the Senate, if such advice and consent be given.

In witness whereof, I have caused the seal of the United States to be hereunto affixed.

Given under my hand at the city of Washington, the second day of May, in the year of our Lord, one thousand eight hundred and seventy one; and of the Independence of the United States of America the ninety-fifth.

U. S. GRANT

DS, DLC-Hamilton Fish. On April 22 and subsequently, Secretary of State Hamilton Fish wrote in his diary. "Joint High Commission, meet nominally at 12 *M* but from that hour until after 4 *PM* the interviews are between Ld de Grey & myself, each reporting to his colleagues & ~~the~~ several questions respecting the Fisheries—St Lawrence & San Juan, are thus reduced to shape to be agreed upon in the Commission. at 4½ the Commission meet & remain in Session until 6½—during which the several questions referred to are considered, & several agreements reached—" "Apr 28/71 . . . Lord de Grey brings me the revised British proposition [*for*] amendment to the Preamble of the Alabama Articles & their other proposed Amendments—Also the declaration or explanation which they propose to insert with respect to the rules as to neutral rights—He tells me 'confidentially that the reason for objecting to the words in our preamble 'during the recent rebellion &c &c' is that some persons in the Brit. Govt positively refuse to admit the word 'rebellion', & says if we choose to substitute 'civil war' there will be no objection—I reply that we have not officially recognised it as 'civil war'—it was a 'rebellion'—He says the resistance to that word is insuperable—I claim that if the assertion of non admission of the Alabama Claims by G. B. is made in the Treaty, a corresponding statement (such as was proposed) must be inserted with respect to the Fisheries—that Judge Hoar when leaving for home mentioned that he (de Grey) had assented thereto—He said he had told Hoar, that personally he would not object to it, but now the Article had been sent home & agreed to, & this after great trouble He hoped it would not be insisted upon. I tell him that Judge H. was very tenacious respecting it—Subsequently, seeing Schenck, he thinks it must be urged—Schenck will assent to the omission of the words 'during the rebellion &c.'" "May 2, Tuesday . . . *Cabinet.* Belknap absent, Boutwell represented by Richardson, all others present—. . . Read several of the Articles as agreed upon in the Treaty negotiating with Great Britain, viz the San Juan, Navigation Claims, Fishery Articles—. . . In the evening Judge Hoar mentions that on arriving here this afternoon, he was met by Senator Sawyer who mentioned that Judge Richardson (Act'g Secy of the Treasury) had told him that a Treaty with Great Britain had been prepared & read this day in Cabinet." *Ibid.*

To John W. Garrett

Washington. D. C., May 2d *18*71

J. W. GARRETT.
PRES. B & O. R. R.
DEAR SIR:

Your favor of yesterday inviting myself and family to join Mr. G. W. Childs and party in a~~n~~ trip over your road on the 9th inst. is rec'd. I wrote to Mr. Childs yesterday that I should be delighted to go, but that as the Joint High Commission is about closing its labors,[1] and the senate meets in Ex. session on the 10th inst. it will be impossible for me to leave. I thank you nevertheless for your invitation and regret that I can not avail myself of your kindness.

Yours Truly
U. S. GRANT

ALS, DLC-Garrett Family. On May 9, 1871, a newspaper reported. "At the invitation of John W. Garrett, Esq., President of the Baltimore and Ohio Railroad Company, a large party from Philadelphia, New York, Baltimore and Washington, will leave Baltimore to-day on a special train of four Pullman palace cars, embracing two sleeping cars, drawing-room car and commissary car, for an excursion over the beautiful mountain region traversed by the Baltimore and Ohio road. . . . President Grant met the party in Baltimore, but is prevented from joining in the excursion, as was originally designed, by the meeting of the Senate tomorrow." *Philadelphia Public Ledger*, May 9, 1871.

On Jan. 4, Horace Porter had written to Garrett. "The President directs me to convey to you his thanks for your kindness and thoughtfulness in tendering him a complimentary ticket over the B. & O R. R, for the present year. I beg that you will accept my warmest thanks for a similar favor." ALS, DLC-Garrett Family.

1. See preceding Proclamation.

Proclamation

The Act of Congress entitled "An Act to Enforce the Provisions of the Fourteenth Amendment to the Constitution of the United States, and for other Purposes," approved April 20, A. D., 1871, being a law of extraordinary public importance, I consider it my duty to issue this my proclamation calling the attention of the people of the United States thereto; enjoining upon all good citizens, and especially upon all public officers to be zealous in the enforcement thereof, and warning all persons to abstain from committing any of the acts thereby prohibited.

This law of Congress applies to all parts of the United States, and will be enforced everywhere to the extent of the powers vested in the Executive. But inasmuch as the necessity therefor is well known to have been caused chiefly by persistent violations of the rights of citizens of the United States, by combinations of lawless and disaffected persons in certain localities lately the theatre of insurrection and military conflict, I do particularly exhort the people of those parts of the country to suppress all such combinations by their own voluntary efforts through the agency of local laws, and to maintain the rights of all citizens of the United States, and to secure to all such citizens the equal protection of the laws.

Fully sensible of the responsibility imposed upon the Executive by the act of Congress to which public attention is now called, and reluctant to call into exercise any of the extraordinary powers thereby conferred upon me, except in cases of imperative necessity, I do nevertheless deem it my duty to make known that I will not hesitate to exhaust the powers thus vested in the Executive, whenever and wherever it shall become necessary to do so for the purpose of securing to all citizens of the United States the peaceful enjoyment of the rights guaranteed to them by the Constitution and laws.[1]

It is my earnest wish, that peace and cheerful obedience to law may prevail throughout the land, and that all traces of our late unhappy civil strife may be speedily removed. These ends can be easily reached by acquiescence in the results of the conflict, now written in our Constitution, and by the due and proper enforcement of equal, just, and impartial laws in every part of our country.

The failure of local communities to furnish such means for the attainment of results so earnestly desired, imposes upon the National Government the duty of putting forth all its energies for the protection of its citizens of every race and color, and for the restoration of peace and order throughout the entire country.

In testimony whereof, I have hereunto set my hand, and caused the seal of the United States to be affixed.

Done at the City of Washington, this third day of May, in the year of our Lord one thousand eight hundred and seventy-one, and of the Independence of the United States the ninety-fifth.

U. S. GRANT

DS, DNA, RG 130, Orders and Proclamations. On May 2, 1871, Secretary of State Hamilton Fish recorded in his diary. ". . . Akerman reads draft of a Proclamation to be issued with respect to the enforcement of the Ku Klux Bill—which is approved." DLC-Hamilton Fish. On May 9, a correspondent reported: "The Cabinet were in session to-day about two hours. All of the members were present except Secretaries Robeson and Belknap. The mode of procedure in the execution of the Ku-Klux law was not considered, as it was the opinion of the members present that the existing state of affairs in the Southern States do not warrant any hasty action in the premises." *Philadelphia Public Ledger*, May 10, 1871. See message to Congress, March 23, 1871.

On May 15, AG Edward D. Townsend issued General Orders No. 48. "The President directs that whenever proper occasion shall arise, the regular forces of the U. S. stationed in the vicinity of any locality where offences described by the aforesaid act approved April 20, 1871, may be committed, shall in strict accordance with the provisions of the said act, be employed by their commanding officers in assisting the authorized civil authorities of the U. S. in making arrests of persons accused under the said act; in preventing the rescue of persons arrested for such cause; ~~and~~ in breaking up and dispersing bands of disguised marauders; and ~~persons~~ of armed organizations against the peace and quiet, or the lawful pursuits of the citizens in any State, III—Whenever troops are employed in the manner indicated in this order, the commanding officer will at the earliest opportunity make a full report ~~to the~~ of his operations to the proper superior authority," ADf (initialed), DNA, RG 94, Letters Received, 1705 1871.

On May 1 and 3, Robert W. Flournoy, Pontotoc, Miss., wrote to USG. "There is a Ku Klux organization in this county, who have recently closed a colored school, and are now taking steps to close others. I am threatened with personal violence. I edit a paper here called 'Equal Rights' which I have been sending to your address for several months, If you have ever examined any of the numbers, you will have seen that ~~my~~ it is intensely loyal, and a strong advocate of your administration, and of your realection. In the defense of Republican principles I have brought down upon me the heavy hand of Gov Alcorn, a man who is using all his influence to crush down Republicanism, and advance Democracy, in other words to aid the spirit of rebellion now rampant in this state. I am an officer of the United States Government—holding the position of Deputy Post Master. I see by the late act of congress, that protection is given to officers or persons holding office under the United States. I therefore claim protection under that law. It is not for me to point out how that protection shall be afforded. But I feel that unless protected; I cannot remain in safety here. Mine is the only paper that in this state that assumes independent ground—hence it is determined to suppress its publication. I believe if a company of United States soldiers were sent here to remain, officered by the right kind of men, that it would have a very good effect in bringing about order and respect for the laws. The act above refered to and the threats of violence have occured since the passage of the law above ~~refered to~~ mentioned. It is simply impossible for me to seek any redress or security as matters now stand. I would but hasten the catastrophe by attempting it, unless the government give me protection, I have none. I have very unfavourable reports of the proceedings of the Military, sent to Aberdeen. Rebels say they have fraternized with them, and that they have beaten many loyal men. The result so far judging from the expression of rebel Democrats, has been injurious to the cause of loyalty. Nothing but the strong arm of the government firmly administered can prevent very serious consequences to the integrity of the Union. All the hopes of the loyal people are fixed on you, every day loyal men come to me, and enquire will any thing be done for them. I tell them I have the utmost confidence in you, and that I believe you will see that they are protected. Much of the difficulty in state has its origin, from the course of Gov Alcorn, who in his anxiety to be President, is doing every thing to ingatiate himself with the rebel element. The Presidency is his aim, though failing in that he would be willing to be run as vicpresident. The loyal people have nothing to expect from Alcorn but what they have received, oppression. The government will have to act distinct from and outside of the Gov, or all is lost in this state. He has removed and is still removing, loyal Republicans and filling their places, with the bitterist rebel Democrats. And his whole course is intended to weaken loyalty and exalt treason. He has become the eulogist of Gen Lee, and denounced me because in my paper, I defended the course of Mr Boutwell in preventing the flag of the United States from being prostituted to honor Lee. Excuse me if I have departed from the regular mode of bringing before you my grieviances. It is with no desire on my part to be presumptious, but it proceeds from an abiding confidence that you will protect, the down trodden loyal people, who have incured the vengeance of the disloyal, because they sustain the government and your administration. I sincerely hope that this appeal will reach you, and find favour in your judgement." "Since I wrote you before I have evidence that I think will convict some Ku Klux. My life is very insecure here. If consistent with your sense of duty, you will order a detachment of military here, with the right kind of officers. We will put things through Alcorn will do nothing, and I will have to cease publishing my paper unless I am protected. Give me protection and I will make a case. Please do something immediatly . . . P. S. Will President Grants, secretary do me the favour to lay both of my letters before him." ALS, *ibid.*, 1688 1871.

On May 18, Flournoy and C. C. Culling, Pontotoc, telegraphed to Secretary of War William W. Belknap. "The Ku Klux attacked us on Friday night. We drove them off Killing one & wounding others. They threaten to return & burn the town. Can we have troops immediately to protect us." Telegram received, *ibid.* On May 19, Townsend telegraphed to Brig. Gen. Alfred H. Terry, Louisville. "Send troops to

Pontotoc, Mississippi, to protect citizens against disguised marauders. Acknowledge receipt." Copy, *ibid.* On May 25, Flournoy wrote to U.S. Senator Oliver P. Morton of Ind. "Excuse me for troubling you with this letter. A few days since a body of Ku Klux at night visited this place to offer me personal violence, and to destroy my press, upon which is published 'Equal Rights' They were met, and several killed. They now now say they will have revenge. And the people of our town having assurance of their intention to burn it and kill some of the inhabitants have kept out a guard evry night, until they are exhausted. Can the government do nothing for us. I have written our Senator Gen Ames. The strongest kind of a case I think can be made out. Gov Alcorn sent a detachment of troops here, who remained but one day, and returned though I protested against it. Their coming done an injury, for did nothing did not even attempt to arrest any persons although several were in the country wounded. The officer in command affiliated with the rebels, and through their instrumentality they left. The effect is, that our people who are the most credulous in the world, now say the government is afraid of them, and that it does not intend to do any thing with the Ku Klux. Unless we are protected, I at least cannot remain here and publish my paper, which is loyal as probably you have seen. Should I leave the negroes will become completely demoralized. It seems to me if the government would act decisively, and promptly, much could be done towards the restoration of peace and order, And a strong point made in favour of the Republican party. Gov Alcorn cannot be depended upon, he has aspirations for the Presidency or vice presidency, and is doing all he can to concliate rebels. If troops are sent here which should be immediately, for the safety of this town, they should come to remain, and they should be commanded by reliable officers, determined to put down the lawless Ku Klux. Will you use your influence in our behalf. I Telegraphed to the War Department but I received no reply. The state of things here are terrible. I have confidently relied upon protection from the government, as assured in the Presidents Proclamation. If something is not done the cause of loyalty is crushed in this state. Persons are leaving rapidly, and the negroes are very much frightened. This is a very important matter, no matter how received in Washington. After the passage of the law by congress our hopes were bouyant Now evry thing is dark. The Ku Klux came into this town nine days after the President issued his Proclamation, and after it was known here." ALS, *ibid.*

On May 27, Belknap wrote to Townsend. "Please return this letter. Were troops sent to Pontotoc. If not, the President desires a Company sent there" AN (initialed), *ibid.* On the same day, Townsend responded. "All Mr. Flournoy's letters, which were referred to this office, have been sent to the Division commander for proper action—There is no report yet received of troops having been sent there, but Genl Halleck will be telegraphed to in accordance with the above memorandum." AN (initialed), *ibid.* On May 29, Maj. Gen. Henry W. Halleck, Louisville, telegraphed to Townsend. "Telegram received Troops were sent to Pontotoc immediately on receipt of information of disturbance there" Telegram received, *ibid.* On June 8, Flournoy wrote to Secretary of the Treasury George S. Boutwell. ". . . You mentioned in your letter that the Secretary of War informed you that he had directed a company of troops to this place; they have not arrived, nor have I any intelligence of their movements farther than indicated in your letter. I am receiving indecent, threatening and abusive letters professing to be from members of the *Klan* through the Post office informing me of their determination to take my life and destroy my property by burning my house. My friends are worn out and exhausted in their efforts to protect me—and the necessity for troops is just as great now as it has ever been. I hope to be up in a few weeks, and propose then a series of investigations of these lawless bands of cutthroats, if I have assurance of protection. . . ." LS, *ibid.* On June 14, Townsend telegraphed to Halleck. "Report recd. from Pontotoc Miss June 8th shows that troops have not arrived. See your telegram May 29th Acknowledge receipt" Copy, *ibid.* On the same day, Halleck telegraphed to Townsend. "A detachment of twenty four men sent to Pontootac Pontotoc may fifteenth (15th) Another ordered today," Telegram received, *ibid.* Related papers are *ibid.*

On June 28, Flournoy, Washington, D. C., testified before the Joint Select Committee to Inquire into the Condition of Affairs in Late Insurrectionary States. ". . . I moved to Pontotoc County in 1856; I have resided in Pontotoc town about four years. . . . I have been editing a paper in Pontotoc about sixteen months. Sometimes I take law cases. I am not a regular practitioner; I abandoned the practice after I went to Mississippi; but I sometimes take cases. . . . I have been what is called county superintendent of education, appointed by the State superintendent, for the purpose of establishing schools. Ours is a large white county; the negro population there is small compared with the white. I established, I think, about fifty-two white schools, and twelve colored schools. After these schools had been in operation some time, the teachers of a portion of them informed me that they were called upon by disguised men, and required to cease teaching, or they would be 'dealt with;' that was the phrase used. Of course the committee will understand that as to some things which I relate I speak from hearsay; other portions of my testimony will be what I know myself. . . . There has been some feeling against me to a considerable extent in the county of Pontotoc. In the town of Pontotoc, where I live, that feeling has measurably worn away, and I have a good many personal friends there among the democrats and some in the county. But the charge they make in the country is that I want to put the negro over the white man. Of course I need not say to this committee that that is false; I never in my life thought of such a thing as putting one citizen above another in any way; but that is the charge they made in the country. There was a feeling against me growing out of my political opinions. This feeling exists there not only against me, but against all other republicans; and there are some white republicans in my county. . . . *Question.* . . . [H]ave you any doubt as to the existence of an organization known as Ku-Klux? *Answer.* None in the world. They not only exist there, but they exist in other counties. I understood that they had reorganized since this difficulty, and they were riding again in the county a few nights before I left home. After this difficulty on the 13th of May, there had been no riding there until a few days before I left home. *Question.* Are there any instances, so far as you know, in which persons belonging to the democratic party have been visited by them or threatened, except these teachers of colored schools? *Answer.* No, sir; none. *Question.* You stated you went to Mississippi in 1856. Where had you lived before that? *Answer.* In Georgia; I was born there. Howell Cobb, who used to be Speaker of the House of Representatives, was my cousin. . . ." *SRC*, 42-2-41, part 11, pp. 82, 88, 91, 95. On July 7, U.S. Representatives Joseph L. Morphis and George E. Harris of Miss. wrote to USG. "We have the honor to recommend to you, for Minister to some Foreign Court, (South American prefered) our friend R. W. Flournoy of Pontotoc Mississippi Col Flournoy is a stanch and uncompromising Republican of good abilitity, having edited the 'Equal Rights' for some time, has been compelled by the political proscription of Miss. to sell out & leave the State, . . ." LS, DNA, RG 59, Letters of Application and Recommendation. Flournoy contended for a U.S. Senate seat in 1871, lost a congressional election to Lucius Q. C. Lamar in 1872, and withdrew from the Miss. gubernatorial race in 1873. William C. Harris,

The Day of the Carpetbagger: Republican Reconstruction in Mississippi (Baton Rouge, 1979), pp. 265–66, 457, 463–65. See *PUSG*, 17, 144–45; *ibid.*, 19, 371–72.

On May 21, 1871, Miss. Representative J. Aaron Moore had written to USG. "pleas bear with me as a on egeoth man: I. am droven frome home: ane gote my House bount: ane my feartear Take or. bount. I. dont know—I. have a lote ane sume outher things in meridian I hear that theay say if I. come to meridian theay will cill me. I. asks you what shald I doy I have a wife ane thee littel Childs. I. ant dome any thing to eany Pearson: thear is ote. a. chage brought a gance me: all theay have a geane me is my pearlick veews: you will pleas to call the artante of senators A. Anms ane he can tell you how I. am. I. am liveing in Jackson Miss at the preasent I want to go home. O ant it hard to have a home ane cant go to it my Lord help me: will you pleas lete me hear from you:" ALS, DNA, RG 94, Letters Received, 1912 1871. On Aug. 7, Capt. James Kelly, 16th Inf., Jackson, endorsed this letter to Hd. Qrs., Dept. of the South. "I called on the within named *J. Aaron Moore* and requested to be furnished with the names of some responsible persons who could confirm his statements, He referred me to Mr. *J. R. Smith,* Postmaster and Mr. *Mosley,* the Sheriff of Lauderdale County, both residents of *Meridian* Miss, who he said would certify to all he had said in his letter. I proceeded to *Meridian* and found that *J. A. Moores,* statement was well founded. *Smith* and *Mosley* informed me that *Moore* would not live one week if he returned to *Meridian* I enclose the written opinion of the Postmaster which is also the opinion of all others I have spoken to on the subject. On my return I called on *Moore* and informed him if he wished to return to Meridian he would be protected as long as troops were there; he then informed me he would not return under any circumstances; that he will remain in *Jackson Miss,* where he thinks he will be more safe at present" AES, *ibid.* The enclosure is *ibid.* See *SRC*, 42-2-41, part 11, pp. 72, 221.

On June 15, John Allen and four others, Monticello, Miss., petitioned U.S. Representative Benjamin F. Butler of Mass. "Your undersigned petitioners respectfully ask that you will together with Genl A Ames (our former Governer) get Some action on the part of Congress to Suppress the Coming November Election in this State, The Bill of Congress Enfranchising and permitting all males over 21 years of age to vote in this State was a bad Law in our opinion—and the result of the K K, doings all over the State at the present time will warrant us in Saying that if the Election is permitted to come off this fall, we may lose the State to the Radical party. Either this must be done by the Influential members of the Party in power, or have Troops distributed all over the State So as to Secure a fair Election. If the tactic is done we have no fears of the result—hoping to have the honor to hear from you Soon and also to Send you other petitions of this kind from other Counties in this State, . . ." D, DNA, RG 94, Letters Received, 2382 1871. Enclosed is an anonymous letter of the same day to Butler. "Your speech of April last in the H R. comes nearer bringing matters up in a true light than any I have seen, If your Suggestions are not adopted the Coming November Election in this State will result in a victory for the K. K, alias Democracy, as the Colored people who represent the majority of the Republican Party in this State will be So intimedated that they will Either not go to the Polls or after getting there will be afraid to vote. Sir I live here in Miss, and I see these outrages going on, while the Executive of the State stand 'idly looking on'. Cant Congress relieve us? Cant Soldiers wearing 'the Blue' be Sent to the County Sites of the 67 Counties of this State, or at least to those most needing them. If the Democracy Succeed in the Coming Election, no Republican Can have a fair trial before any Court in the State when the position is filled by a Democrat, . . .

I do not dare to give my name for if this fell in the hands of the K. K, I would be a dead man in 24 hours; But believe me when I say you are trying to do what is right—. *Send Bayonetts down South.* Send Genl Ames back here—Keep Miss from voting in the Election of 1872 & you will do right—" AL, *ibid.* On June 27, Butler, Lowell, Mass., endorsed these papers. "Respectfully referred to the President of the United States for his information and action" ES, *ibid.*

On April 7, Allen P. Huggins, Washington, D. C., had written to USG. "It being impracticable for me to perform the functions of my Civil Office under the Government, I have the honor to request a Commission in the Army and to be assigned to duty in the State of Mississippi" ALS, DNA, RG 94, Applications for Positions in War Dept. U.S. Senators Zachariah Chandler and Thomas W. Ferry of Mich., Powell Clayton of Ark., John Scott of Pa., Frederick T. Frelinghuysen of N. J., and U.S. Representative Samuel Shellabarger of Ohio favorably endorsed this application. ES (undated), *ibid.* On May 10, Huggins wrote to USG. "I have the honor to submit the following that something of the disorder in Monroe County Miss. may be conceived of and would ask that the Government act as soon as possible to restore order—The first appearance of Ku Klux in Monroe County was in the month of August 1870. About fifty in number at that time visited the jail at Athens 7 miles from Aberdeen and forcibly took therefrom a Colored man by the name of Saunders Flint and his two grown sons Joseph and Moses—I think were their names—who were in jail for defending themselves against an assault made upon them by 3 white men—The Father Saunders Flint escaped the two sons were found about a week after in the woods torn in pieces by shot—upon the affidavit of Saunders Flint several parties were arrested and tried in Circuit Court—Saunders and two prisoners of the jail swore positively that the parties on trial were present at the jail and assisted in forcing the three men away—but the jury—all white men—found them not guilty—from that time to this the county has been one continued scene of persecution—and horror to union men white and black—but the desperadoes seemed satisfied with beatings, scourgings, and warnings, up to about the commencement of March 1871—about that time a colored man living in the S. E. portion of the county was taken at night and hanged in the buttahatchie swamp—near the Alabama line—a few night after Jack Dupree living about seven miles from Aberdeen was taken from his house about twelve oclock at night by the out laws his only garments shirt and drawers were left in his own yard and nothing more has been heard of him—he of course was murdered but how or where his remains are is not known to any of his friends—on 29th March in the Same neighborhood another Colored Man Alex Page was hanged the murderers burrying him with the rope about his neck—About same time a thrifty Colored man Levi Sykes and a man of influence among his race—was most inhumaly beaten, his injuries were so serious that his life was despaired of for some time—the whipping of Sykes occurred on the west side of Tombigbee river near the western boundary of the county—during April Tom Hornberger Col'd—Jack Lorie Col'd—and one Durham Colored—were murdered ~~near~~ in the north part of the county not far from Okolona—a white Lady living near the scene of Durhams murder & it being supposed she might have been aware of some of the facts connected with it the ruffians called her out the night after and gave her a severe beating—more recently during this present month another Colored man has been litterally shot in pices nearer to okolona but in Monroe County—and Richard owen Col'd was beaten about same time having his neck placed a fence and the beatings administered upon the bare back which is the usual mode—he was scourged until he would say that he was a democrat—The Free

Schools have received a full share of the displeasure of these barberous men as the following list of Schools closed in the County will show—The number of white Schools that have suffered at their hands where many of their own children must have been in attendance will show that their war is in a large measure upon Civilization—and general intelligences—I will give the number of Sub Dis't, the name of teachers—and whether white, or colored, schools—The Teachers of the white schools were all Southern men or women the Districts having chosen their own teachers—. . . The Post master at Aberdeen has been notified to change his politics, the mayor of the City of Aberdeen Mr Jno F. Lacey a man of great personal courage and a firm, true, Republican and good officer was forced to leave his office during the month of March and is now exiled from his home—The board of Supervisors have been threatened if they attempt to Assess the Taxes for State and county purposes and at this time long past the date that they should have been collected no assessment even has been made—it is near the time for some of the Schools that have gone on to close and no provision has been nor can be made by the County Authorities for the payment of the teachers. Two Justices of the peace who have tried to justly administer the law have been notified to resign or suffer the penalty—My own experience with the band of 120 of these out laws you are familiar with I have no hesitancy in placing the number of these desperate characters alone in the County of Monroe, under masks, and Arms, at from three to four hundred—" ALS, *ibid.* For testimony by Sanders Flint, see *SRC*, 42-2-41, part 12, pp. 803–8.

On July 19, Huggins testified before the Joint Select Committee that U.S. troops had quelled the Ku Klux Klan in Monroe County, Miss. *Ibid.*, part 11, pp. 265, 285–87, 297–98. On Nov. 13 and 17, Huggins, Columbus, Miss., gave related testimony to a subcommittee. *Ibid.*, part 12, pp. 820–28. On July 21, Attorney Gen. Amos T. Akerman had written to John Potts, chief clerk, War Dept. "The bearer, Mr. Huggins, is a deputy U. S. Marshal in Northern Mississippi, He is a credible person, as I have every reason to believe, and can give important information about his district. Mr. Bristow, the Solicitor General, has just returned from an official visit to Mississippi, and his report agrees with Mr. Huggins' statements. Mr. H. will acquaint you with the need of military aid there." ALS, DNA, RG 94, Letters Received, 2527 1871. On [July 27], Townsend endorsed this letter and related papers. "Telegraph to Genl. Pope The President directs him to send the company heretofore ordered to be held in readiness, to Aberdeen." AES, *ibid.*

On Aug. 12 and 14, Terry telegraphed to Townsend. "Your dispatch relative to the cavalry sent from Dep't of Missouri is received It was not sent on my application and I have never been informed of the special services for which it was required. I cannot well therefore determine when it should return. I have called on the Commanding Officer for report whether he has been called on to aid Civil Authorities" "The Captain of the troop of Cavalry at Aberdeen Miss, reports that he has not been called upon to aid the civil authorities since he has been there A company of infantry has been at that place for several months" Telegrams received, *ibid.* On Sept. 11, Huggins, Aberdeen, Miss., wrote to Orville E. Babcock. "I have the honor to submit the following statement for your consideration. During the latter part of July last Senator Pool of N. C. called with me and arranged with you to send a company of cavalry to this point for the purpose of making or assisting in making two hundred or three hundred arrests of KuKlux. The cavalry company came from Fort Hays, Kansas and the officers are exactly the men for the business. The company is however under orders to leave for Kansas on Oct. 1st 1871. If the order is not revoked it will leave us in a very unpleasant position as I shall not have the work more than half done by October 1st and the excitement caused by the arrest of so large a number of men with the already excited State of public feeling owing to the approaching election will be more than we as Republicans can stand up under without some aid from United States troops I would respectfully request that the order removing the cavalry be revoked." LS, *ibid.* On Sept. 21, Babcock forwarded this letter to Belknap. AES, *ibid.* On Sept. 30, Belknap wrote to USG. "In the matter of the application of the Deputy U. S. Marshal for the Northern District of Mississippi, Allen B. Huggins, for the revocation of the order removing the company of cavalry now at Aberdeen, Mississippi, therefrom, from the 1st proximo, I have the honor to state that in July last, upon the application of Mr Huggins, and at the instance of the Attorney-General, Company H, 6th Cavalry, was by your direction ordered from the Department of the Missouri to Aberdeen, Miss., for temporary duty. On the 11th August, General Terry, Commanding the Department of the South, was directed to return the company to its proper station. in the Department of the Missouri, as soon as the temporary duty for which it was required was performed. August 19th he reported that the U. S. Marshal for Northern Mississippi desired that the company be kept at his disposal through September, having 200 arrests to make, and recommended that request be granted. In reply the General of the Army telegraphed General Terry, August 21, 1871, that if a company of the 7th Cavalry could not be spared he could keep the company of the 6th Cavalry at Aberdeen through September, and then send it to Kansas. General Sherman is opposed to detaching the company of the 6th from the Department to which it belongs, and where the rest of the regiment is." LS, *ibid.*, RG 60, Letters from the President.

On Sept. 27, U.S. Senator Adelbert Ames of Miss., Sardis, had written to Belknap. "It is rumored that the Cavalry in the Eastern part of this State are to be ordered out of the State about the first of Oct. Our election will take place on the 7th of Nov. We deem it essential in fact indispensible that they should remain here. I sincerely hope our request can be complied with. This will be hand you by Col. Huggins who holds an official position in this state under the U. S. marshall." ALS, *ibid.*, RG 94, Letters Received, 2527 1871. On Oct. 3, Belknap endorsed this letter. "The President directs that a Company be sent to ~~take~~ post at Aberdeen, in lieu of the company recently ordered from there." AE (initialed), *ibid.* On Oct. 6, Halleck telegraphed to Townsend. "Gen Terry reports that there is now one company at Aberdeen is it desired that another be sent to that place." Telegram received, *ibid.* Townsend endorsed this telegram. "ansd. Oct. 6 /71 another compy not deemed necessary at Aberdeen" AE (undated and initialed), *ibid.* On Oct. 12, Huggins, Washington, D. C., wrote to USG. "I have the honor to request that Two Companies of U. S. Troops be sent to North East Mississippi. One to be stationed at Starkville in Oktibaha County and the other a portion at West Point and a portion at Columbus in Lowndes County." ALS, *ibid.* On the same day, James H. Pierce, U.S. marshal, Corinth, wrote to Akerman. "I have learned that Mr. Huggins, a deputy of mine, is now in Washington, urging the Hon Sec. of War to order more troops sent to this District. I would state that I am succeeding well in arresting parties charged with violating the 'Enforcement Act.' I have been out two weeks in the business, and have met with success. Under the circumstances, and knowing that the demand for troops from different quarter's is great, I could not ask for more troops. The company now stationed at Aberdeen, so far as I can now see, is sufficient. I would further state that Mr. Huggins is not authorized by any of the Government officials of this District to make representations as to the condition of affairs, here, to the Department."

Copy, *ibid.* On Oct. 16, Benjamin H. Bristow, solicitor gen. and act. attorney gen., forwarded Pierce's letter to Belknap. LS, *ibid.* On the same day, Huggins, Corinth, wrote to Townsend. "I have the honor to submit the following with the request that I be informed at Aberdeen if there was any Change of Orders issued in this Case—While in Washington recently the Company of 6th Cavalry stationed at Aberdeen Miss was ordered to rejoin its Regiment in Kansas I saw the Secretary of War and he assured me that another Company of Cavalry should be immediately sent to take its place. I saw you and you told me that a company had already been ordered to Aberdeen—I find upon arriving at this place that no cavalry is at Aberdeen and as it places us in a dead lock as far as making the arrests of the great great number of desperadoes I make the above request for information" ALS, *ibid.* On Oct. 24, Ames, Jackson, wrote to Belknap. "I would most respectfully urge that the company of cavalry taken from this state may be replaced before the approaching election—which will take place on the 7th of next month—As in North and South Carolina we here in the eastern part of the State are subject to the Ku Klux bullet—One and the same organization extends over the whole South—We need—we want protection." ALS, *ibid.* On Oct. 26, Ames, Sardis, wrote to Blanche Butler Ames. ". . . Had it not been for the Ku Klux law which we fought for and which the governor fought against, we would not have had any showing at this election. At one time, just previous to the passage of that law, the K. K. organizations were being perfected in every county in the state. It is believed by our friends that had the law not been passed, not one of them would have been safe outside of a few of the larger cities. As it is, the K. K.'s, cowards as they are, have for a time at least suspended their operations in all but the eastern parts of the state. Recent convictions in North Carolina and the President's action in putting a part of South Carolina under martial law has had a very subduing effect all over the South. It is perceptible here. . . ." Blanche Butler Ames, comp., *Chronicles From the Nineteenth Century: Family Letters of Blanche Butler and Adelbert Ames, Married July 21st, 1870* (1957), I, 344–45. On Oct. 28, Belknap wrote to USG. "Acknowledging the receipt, by reference from you, of the requisition of A. P. Huggins for two companies of U. S. troops to be sent to N. E. Mississippi, I have the honor to say that, by your direction, orders were given on the 3rd instant for a company of troops to be sent to Aberdeen, Mississippi, in place of the company recently ordered from there. On the 16th inst., the Atty Gen'l enclosed to this Dept copy of a letter from the US Marshal for the Northern Dist. of Miss., stating that his assistant (Mr Huggins) had no authority from any official of his Dist, to ask for additional troops; which, in his opinion, were not needed ~~to enforce~~ for the successful performance of his duties, in making arrests, &c. Mr Huggins has been informed that this Dept is in direct communication with his superiors on this subject. In connection with this subject, I would respectfully invite attention to a previous communication from this Department of the 30th ultimo, to the effect that General Terry Commanding Department of the South, having, on the 11th August, been ordered to return to its proper station in the Department of the Missouri, as soon as the temporary duty for which it was required, was performed, the company of the 6th Cavalry, which, by your direction, had been stationed at Aberdeen, Mississippi, reported that the U. S. Marshal for Northern Mississippi desired that the company be kept at his disposal through September, having 200 arrests to make, and recommended that request be granted. In reply, the General of the Army telegraphed General Terry, August 21st, 1871, that if a company of the 7th Cavalry could not be spared, he could keep the company of the 6th Cavalry at Aberdeen through September and then send it to Kansas. &c, &c. This latter company has been ordered back to its station." L (initialed), DNA, RG 94, Letters Received, 2527 1871. See Harris, *Day of the Carpetbagger*, pp. 328–30, 396, 399–400.

1. On May 8, C. S. Middlebrook, Trumbull, Conn., wrote to USG. "Your Proclamation of May 3rd in which you say that 'the act to enforce the 14th Amendment to the Constitution applies to *all* parts of the U. S. and will be enforced *everywhere* to the extent of the powers vested in the executive'—'that you will not hesitate to exhaust the powers thus vested in the executive whenever it shall become necessary to do so, for the purpose of secureing to *all citizens* of the United States a peacefull enjoyment of the rights Guaranteed to them by the Constitution & Laws' It appears to me Mr President that one of the particular rights which this act is intended to enforce is the right of suffrage by 'all persons who are born in the United States and subject to its Jurisdiction.' Therefore most respectfully would I call your attention to the following case—which is only one out of manny which occurred in this state this spring A. M. Middlebrook resideing in this town born in this state a tax paying citizen applied Feb 22 1871 to the board of registration and was duly registereed—March 20th appeared before the board of Selectmen & Town Clerk to be qualified as a voter—was refused, on the Ground, that they sat there as Officers of the *State of Conn.* and not of the United States—and as the statutes of Conn. read—'none but white male Citizens could become electors' they could quallify no others. An affidavit was made before L. G. Beers a Justice of peace and one of the Registerrs who was present—stateing the above facts—which affidavit was presented by the Said A. M. Middlebrook to the moderator of the meeting on april 3rd 1871 with the request to vote—which after consultation and under the advise of the Town Clerk & said justice of the Peace—was denied—Notice was given to the District Attorney Calvin G. Childs of Stamford Conn. who refused to give any hearing to the complainent, altho, solicited personally & by letter—Mr President as one of the people and a tax paying citizen of the United States—who has never knowingly transgressed any law of the same I appeal to you for redress—That you order Calvin G Childs to the give the Complanent a fair and candid hearing at some early day—or put some ~~o~~Officer in his place who will do justice acording to the Constitution & Laws of the United States—" ALS, DNA, RG 59, Miscellaneous Letters. On May 14, Middlebrook wrote to Fish arguing for more vigorous enforcement of the Fourteenth Amendment. ALS, *ibid.*

On Nov. 16, Robert A. Griffith, chairman, Union League, Baltimore, wrote to USG. "The Committe instruct me to solict your Excellency's kind offices in obtaining from his honor the Atty Genl an early reply to the enclosed communication. We confidently assert that but for the frauds perpetrated by the State officers at the late election Maryland would now have a Republican Legislature. Defrauded—but not dismayed! we accept these frauds as a confession of weakness on the part of our adversaries. And we hopefully believe that in 1872 Maryland will cast her vote for Ulysses S. Grant and the Republican ticket." ALS, *ibid.*, RG 60, Letters from the President. On the same day, Griffith wrote to Akerman. "The executive comittee of the State Grand Council of U. L. A of Maryland instruct me to ask your opinion on the following questions. 1st Do the provisions of the Law, entitled 'An act to enforce the right of Citizens of the United States to vote and for other purposes,' usually called the enforcement act, apply to state elections in general or are they restricted in their operation to those elections in which members of Congress and electors for President and Vice President are chosen? 2d Do the provisions of the Law comprehend all electors or are they restricted in their operation to electors of African descent only? I am instructed to solicit your opinion on these questions in consequence of the diverse opinions existing among our people on the subject. The opinion obtained very generally with our State Officers at the late election, that the enforcement act so called is inoperative except when members of Congress and Presidential electors are chosen. Our State officials acting upon this hypothesis disfranchised Citizens by wholesale. . . ." ALS, *ibid.*

Proclamation

TO ALL WHO SHALL THESE PRESENTS, GREETING:

I have named and hereby appoint Caleb Cushing, to be Advocate on the part of the United States, to appear before the Arbitrators or Umpire, charged with the settlement of claims of Citizens of the United States or of their heirs against the Government of Spain, under the arrangement made between D. E. Sickles, the Envoy Extraordinary and Minister Plenipotentiary of the United States, and Mr. Cristo Martos, the Minister of State of the Government of Spain, on the twelfth day of February, 1871.

In testimony whereof, I have hereunto signed my name and caused the Seal of the United States to be affixed.

Done at the City of Washington, this Third day of May, in the year of our Lord, one thousand eight hundred and Seventy-one, and of the Independence of the United States of America the Ninety-fifth.

U. S. GRANT

DS, DLC-Caleb Cushing. See *Foreign Relations, 1871*, p. 791. Caleb Cushing served as U.S. representative (1835–43) from Mass., brig. gen. in the Mexican War, and U.S. attorney gen. (1853–57). He was a Democrat until 1861, a Republican thereafter. In 1874, USG nominated Cushing for chief justice. See Claude M. Fuess, *The Life of Caleb Cushing*, 2 vols. (1923; reprinted, Hamden, Conn., 1965).

On Oct. 20, 1871, James F. Casey, collector of customs, New Orleans, and U.S. Senator William P. Kellogg of La., wrote to USG. "Information having reached us, of the contemplated resignation of the Hon. Caleb Cushing as U. S. Advocate before the Commission charged with the settlement of the claims of American citizens against Spain, we venture to prefer a request that the Hon. Thos. J. Durant be in that event selected to fill the vacancy thus created. We ask this without having conferred with Mr. Durant, but are led to believe that he would not decline the appointment and are satisfied that no finer legal talent and judgment could be enlisted in the interests of

American citizens in the line of controversy mentioned—" LS, DNA, RG 59, Letters of Application and Recommendation. On Nov. 22, USG appointed Thomas J. Durant as U.S. advocate before the U.S.-Spanish Claims Commission.

On May 25 and 26, Secretary of State Hamilton Fish had recorded in his diary. "Mr Roberts (Spain) wishes the conference of South American Representatives &c convened next week, . . . He refers to an article in the N. Y. Tribune of 23rd (a correspondent from here) headed 'Cuba.'—He says he inquired of the Associated Press Agents as to the authorship, & was told that it came from the 'White House'—it really is from Paige & Dent as I understood yesterday from Cushing—Roberts says that Dent is in the habit of writing to parties in New York, interested in Cuban Claims saying they must apply to Sidney Webster, Caleb Cushing who are corrupt & will obtain their claims for money—says Paige called on him some time since about the same claim referred to in the newspaper article and abused me ~~so~~ violently so that he Roberts had to tell him he must desist or leave the House." "*Cabinet—All* present—President shews me a communication addressed to him by Dent & Paige, complaining of Caleb Cushing, & the Spanish Minister, in connection with the case of—Garcia Angorica—Without reading the paper through I denounce Dent & Paige & their attempt to influence the President, & to present to him a matter which should only come to him through the State Department—I explain the case to him—that it has been carefully watched & protected—more so perhaps than any of the Cuban Cases—it is provided for under the Claims Arbitration, provided Angorica be as he professes to be, An American Citizen—but mention what Roberts says that the Spanish Govt claim to have evidence of fraud in his pretended naturalization, & that he is in fact a Spanish Subject—I propose to return the paper to Dent & Paige, with a copy of Executive order of Octr 1869 The Prsdt says he has not read the paper—takes it & reads—says he had known nothing of the case—that the night before last, Louis Dent was at the White House—spoke to him about it, & he had requested him to make a statement in writing—I tell him that Dent & Paige are speculating upon claimants, on the ground of their pretended influence, & of Dents connection with him—that they appeal to the Public, through the Press, & make false representations—he says, that is Paige, who has been a newspaperman—I mention, that I have understood & believe, that they have caused the publication of articles in newspapers, & have written letters, accusing different parties, of corruption, & endeavoring to connect me with the charges,—that neither of them has been near me, to speak of the 'Angorica' case, for a year—mention, & shew him the article to the Tribune . . . and that the Spanish Minister has brought it to me, complaining of its injustice, & said that he had enquired at the office of the Paper, & been told that the article 'had been sent there, from the White House'—He says he had never seen nor heard of it, or of any thing connected with it, until night before last—I reply that I supposed not, & had expressed that conviction to the Spanish Minister but I wished him to notice how these men ~~presumed~~ presumed, & what unjustifiable liberties they took with him on account of the connection of one of them with him—He retains Dent & Paiges paper, & when I was coming away I asked if I should take it—he said 'no'—" DLC-Hamilton Fish. See Nevins, *Fish*, pp. 586–88. On Oct. 19, 1869, USG had issued an executive order. "All communications in writing intended for the Executive Department of this government and relating to public business of whatever kind, including suggestions for legislation, claims, contracts, employment, appointments and removals from office and pardons, must be transmitted through the department to which the care of the subject matter of communication properly belongs. Communications otherwise transmitted will not receive attention." *New York Herald*, Oct. 28, 1869.

On Jan. 27, M. Deidamia West, New York City, had written to USG. "Will you do me the favor to recommend the settlement of a Claim long since made by my husband Mr James H West against the Spanish Govt, thus far it has reached the Comee of Foreign Affairs & this Comee have passed it into the hands of a Sub Comee of three who have thoroughly investigated the Claim & pronounced it a just one & were ready to make their report, as soon as the Comrs appointed by the Govt of the United States & Spain should fix a day for the settlement of Claims between the two Govts Wishing you much prosperity—" ALS, DNA, RG 59, Miscellaneous Letters. See *SED*, 33-1-46; *SMD*, 33-Special Session-3.

On May 26, a correspondent reported from Washington, D. C. "The President submitted a mass of documents to the Cabinet to-day relating to seizures of property of American citizens in Cuba. From them it appeared that, in spite of denials made in various quarters, Spain possesses no power in Cuba, but that the Captain-General and the volunteers have absolute control, and not only defy Spain but insult the United States. The seizures of plantations belonging to Americans have rapidly increased in number of late. The one case laid before the Cabinet, for illustration, was the seizure of a plantation worth between $1,000,000 and $2,000,000, nearly two years ago. Fifteen months ago an order was sent from Spain for its release, but the Captain-General did not make any response. Six months ago Mr. Fish sent a note of inquiry concerning it to the Spanish Minister here, coupled with a demand for the restoration of the property. . . ." *New York Tribune*, May 27, 1871. On June 9, 1870, Fish had written to Mauricio Lopez Roberts to complain that Spanish authorities in Cuba had arrested U.S. citizens and seized property; he enclosed a list of names that included José Garcia Angarica and Joaquin Garcia Angarica. *Foreign Relations, 1871*, pp. 698–700. On Oct. 14, Daniel E. Sickles, U.S. minister, Madrid, wrote to Fish enclosing a Spanish government "*Memorandum of citizens of the United States whose property has been embargoed.*" "No. 1.—*Don José Garcia Angarica.*—Does not appear to have been embargoed;. . . No. 2.—*Don Joaquin Garcia Angarica.*—His property was embargoed because he was in connivance with the individuals forming the Cuban Junta of New York. Admiral Poor having addressed a communication, on the 14th of January of the current year, concerning the removal of the embargo on his estate, answer was made that if proof were shown of the inaccuracy of the data in possession of the government, the recommendation of the United States minister would be complied with, and no notice taken of the conspiracy and double citizenship. In February, 1869, this individual passed for a Spanish subject, according to the documents presented in applying for a passport, and in January, 1870, he claimed to be an American citizen." *Ibid.*, p. 714. In 1874, Joaquin Angarica won the release of his estates along with a settlement. See *HED*, 48-1-1, part 1, p. 784.

On Dec. 26, 1876, Postmaster Gen. James N. Tyner wrote to USG. "Nathaniel Page, whom I have appointed a Special Agent at your request, desires an advance of two or three hundred dollars on his salary. It is unusual to grant such applications, but I will do as you wish about it. You can, if you please, address me a *private* note by my messenger who carries this to the Executive Mansion." ALS (facsimile), USGA. On the same day, USG endorsed this letter. "If the advance asked can be made without inconsistency I wish you would make it. If not Mr. Page should borrow the money and leave his act. with the Dept in settlement." AES (facsimile), *ibid.* For Nathaniel Paige, a Washington, D. C. lawyer and former journalist, see *New York Times*, Aug. 10, 1892; *Eminent and Representative Men of Virginia and The District of Columbia of the Nineteenth Century* (Madison, Wis., 1893), pp. 237–38.

To Charles W. Ford

Washington, D. C. May 3d *18~~6~~*71

Dear Ford:

I enclose you a package which I promised McKee,[1] of the Democrat, when I was in st. Louis, and which I wish you would deliver in person. I send it to you because I do not want it opened by any one but himself.

My visit West was a most agreeable one. I thought I saw a very healthy feeling throughout. My own convictions are that it would have been better never to have made a sacrifice of blood and treasure to save the Union than to have the democratic party come in power now and sacrifice by the ballot what the bayonet seemed to have ac[o]mplished—have acomplished if we are true to ourselves.[2]

When going West I had no idea of stopping by the way at any place. I went purely to visit my farm in which I have great interest because it is largely what I must depend on for a support when retired from public duties. That day is near at hand and I hail it as the happiest of my life, except possibly the day I left West Point, a place that I felt I had been at always and that my stay at had no end. But meeting Gov.r Morton in Pittsburg, and going West by the same train, I concented to stop over the day in Indianapolis[3] and thus arive in St. Louis in the morning instead of the evening. I did not suppose there would be a political meeting but expected there would be a reception to meet the Govr. enhanced possibly because a President, a personage who the world thinks ought to be happy, but the most persecuted individual on the Western Continent certainly, was along. I had promised Judge Orth[4] that I would stop over a day at his home on my return.[5] That was a meeting however of the Odd fellows, not political, and an order of which I was a member when you first knew me at Sackets Harbor. That was so long ago that I will not remind you of it in view of your celibacy.

Please give my kindest regards to all enquiring friends in St. Louis.

Yours Truly
U. S. Grant

ALS, DLC-USG.

1. Born in 1815 in New York City, William McKee learned the publishing business, moved to St. Louis (1841), and operated various newspapers, including the *Barnburner* (1849), the first Free Soil paper in Mo. He inaugurated another Free Soil newspaper in 1852 that emerged the following year as the *Missouri Democrat.* He later supported the Republican party and entered into partnership with George W. Fishback, friend of USG. See *PUSG*, 20, 110; Lincoln, *Works*, VI, 325–27; *Missouri Democrat*, Dec. 21, 1879.

On June 29, 1871, Orville E. Babcock wrote to McKee, St. Louis. "The President directs me to acknowledge the receipt of your telegram of to-day and say that the removal has not been contemplated." Copy, DLC-USG, II, 1.

2. On March 18, Gen. William T. Sherman had written to Brig. Gen. Edward O. C. Ord, San Francisco. ". . . The Secretary of War seems jealous of any suggestions from me and I let him work out these problems in his own way . . . The truth is Politics have again gradually but surely drawn the whole country into a situation of as much danger as before the Civil War—The Army left the South subdued—broken and humbled. The Party then in power, forgetful of the fact that sooner or later the People of the South must vote, labored hard to create voters out of Negroes & indifferent material, and when at last these States became reconstructed . . . the prejudices of the past resumed Control. And now the Negro Governments, aided by a weak force of Republican Whites have been swept aside and the Union People there are hustled, branded and even killed. Such is the Nature of our Government . . . All Crimes must be tried by Juries on the spot who of course protect their comrades . . . any Southern Citizen may kill or abuse a Negro or Union Man with as much safety as one of our Frontiersmen may kill an Indian. The memories of the War are fading fast and even our own men are dividing . . . General Grant's personal popularity seems to be waning and the opposition to his administration is such that if they can unite they will surely prevail . . . I keep out of all these controversies because all parties will use the Army alike. If they can use us to advantage it will be done but if more votes are to be made by attacking us, that will be the policy . . ." Western Hemisphere Inc., Books and Manuscripts, *The New World*, Autumn, 1968, p. 26.

On April 16, John A. Joyce, St. Louis, wrote to Babcock. "I send you herewith an article written by me while at St. Joseph: and which the 'Democrat' of its own volition copies. How do you like the ring of the article? We will make the 'Cops' of this state 'hump' themselves in the Campaign of 72. *True hearts* & *hard work* will save this state to the Republicans." ALS, ICN. Joyce perhaps alluded to "Third Partyism," an article that denigrated the "anti-reconstruction" position of the Democrats and warned against a split among Republicans. *Missouri Democrat*, April 13, 1871.

On April 18, Horace Porter wrote to Governor John M. Palmer of Ill. "Confidential. . . . I received your letter of the 25th ult. and read its contents to the President, who fully appreciates the kind interest you take in his success, and the anxiety you feel in regard to holding the party together until it has accomplished the great work which it still has before it. You have always spoken like a prophet upon *one subject*, and everything you said last Summer has been more than verified. I shall not attempt to go over the situation in the Senate. You have of course watched the course of all the republican Senator's, and can tell from their acts who feel sore and who do not. Four or five of them lately had great hopes of inaugurating a third party movement, but they got such a set-back in the Presidents last message that they are terribly demoralized, though they still mean mischief. Everything looks bright now, and I have never seen the party more thoroughly united, but we cannot tell when another cloud may arise. Congress is adjourning under very favorable auspices, The attempt was of course made to remove Bluford Wilson, but the President positively refused to make the change, though Wilson in a very manly letter, urged the President to remove him at any moment he thought it might tend to harmonize matters in the state. I ~~haved~~ hoped we might have had the pleasure of seeing you here this winter. I should have enjoyed a good square talk with you over the general situation." ALS, IHi. See letter to Charles W. Ford, Oct. 26, 1871, note 4.

3. See Speech, April 22, 1871.

4. See letter to Hamilton Fish, Dec. 12, 1870, note 2.

5. USG arrived in Lafayette, Ind., on the morning of April 26, 1871. Escorted by Vice President Schuyler Colfax and Godlove S. Orth, he attended a meeting of the Odd Fellows at 1:00 P.M. USG left for Washington, D. C., on a 5:00 P.M. train. *Indianapolis Journal*, April 27, 1871.

To Senate

TO THE SENATE OF THE UNITED STATES.

I transmit to the Senate, for consideration, with a view to ratification, a "Treaty between the United States and Great Britain for the settlement of pending questions between the two countries, signed at Washington, on the 8th instant, by the Commissioners of the United States and Great Britain, respectively."

Copies of the powers and instructions to the Commissioners on the part of the United States,[1] and of the Protocols of the Conferences, are also transmitted.

U. S. GRANT

WASHINGTON MAY 10, 1871.

DS, DNA, RG 46, Presidential Messages, Foreign Relations, Great Britain. Related papers are *ibid.* See Nevins, *Fish*, pp. 490–91.

On May 11, 1871, Adam Badeau, London, wrote to USG. "*Confidential* . . . I met Mr. Gladstone at dinner last night, and after leaving the table had quite a long and interesting conversation with him. If you notice the date of this, you will observe that yesterday you sent the treaty to the Senate. Mr G. said he had not received the completed text of the treaty but supposed he was acquainted with its various provisions as they had been sent to him from time to time. He was apparently very anxious that it should be ratified by the Senate; and spoke with great earnestness of his desire for complete accord with America. He spoke of your position on the matter with great respect. Of course I took pains to assure him that you were animated by friendly feelings towards England. The dinner was at Lord Halifax's, who you may remember, is a member of Mr Gladstones cabinet. He also took great pains to say that he thought it would be a sinful thing for America and England to disagree. I could not help thinking that if they had thought about the sinfulness before they let the Alabama out, it would have been as well. Later in the evening I met two other members of the government, Mr. Forster and Mr. Goschen, each of whom wanted to know what I thought would be the action of the Senate; and their manner indicated that the inquiry was not a mere passing remark, but sprang from a genuine earnestness—indeed an anxiety. This peculiar anxiety doubtless proceeds from the fact that the government has been so repeatedly defeated within the last two or three weeks. Its very existence has been in danger, and if it should suffer a rebuff at our hands it might be fatal. This is very important for you to know, in case it becomes necessary, because of what may occur in the Senate, to make any changes in the treaty. I think you may count upon the concurrence of the English government. They will yield much before they risk another failure ~~like~~ such as it would be to them, if the treaty fell through There is evidently a disposition on the part of all here to accept the treaty, though it is supposed there will be provisions a little difficult for England. Mr. Gladstone said he thought all parties in England were ready to come to terms; and I said I had noticed that disposition in the Standard, the leading opposition paper. He concurred with me in this. But of course if we again absolutely reject what England agrees to, the reaction here will be very great. I think it may be worth while to let Gov Fish and Gen Schenck know about the evident anxiety of the British cabinet. I am very sure they will yield even more than they have done, rather than let the treaty fall through. They cannot afford another defeat from any quarter, *just now.* I ~~should~~ consider this suggestion so important that I should telegraph it to you if I had the cipher I regret that I have not the right of access to the Legation papers; as I am sure if I knew continuously the state of the negotiations, I could be of great use here. If General Schenck should not object to my reading his despatches as I did when Secretary of Legation, I could be of use to him, as his assisnt. I merely suggest this to you, and of course desire only to be of service to your administration in any way you think best. Please tell Mrs Grant that I took Mrs. Gladstone in to dinner, and am of opinion that the chief of the American state has a wife who is better looking better dressed and better bred than the ~~English~~ head of the English government has. Ask her please not to say this to Lady Thornton. Mrs Gladstone however was an agreeable woman, and what I admired in her was her evident admiration of her husband. He is certainly a great man, but I like my own chi[e]f best." ALS, USG 3.

1. On Feb. 21 and May 9, Secretary of State Hamilton Fish had written in his diary. "Genl Schenck calls, & I read to him the draft of the proposed 'instructions' to the American Commissioners—He remarks that 'they as delicate as could be' Take them to the President to whom I read them, & shew him the 'proofs' of the Memorandum to be forwarded to the Commissioners—He approves them" "I bring up the question of the Amount of Compensation to be allowed to Hoar & Williams, as Commissioners on the Joint High Commn The Prsdt evidently had not considered the question. his first reply was that they might be paid out of the Secret Service fund—being informed of the Appropriation, made for Compensation & expenses of the Commrs he observed—'oh, it is the question of amount', & says they may be paid at the same rate as Cabinet Ministers are paid—I tell him that that will only give them $2.000 each—that I have reason to believe that Judge Hoar has lost much more than that in professional fees, during his attendance on the Commission—& remind the Prsdt that they have been, 'Plenipotentiaries' &c he then says—why not pay them at the rate of the salary of Minister to G. B. I remark that that wd

give each of them about $4375—& that seems scarce sufficient to compensate, at least Hoar. he then say $5.000—to which I remark or $6.000. yes, he said that will not be too much—The subject had previously been spoken of between the Members of the Cabinet present, but the Prsdt was reading & had not heard the Conversation Boutwell had named $5.000, or $6.000, & the others assenting, we had come to the conclusion of $6.000 as a fit sum and so it is determined—" DLC-Hamilton Fish.

To Ministers and Consuls

Washington, D. C. May 12, 71

SIR:

This will introduce to you Mr Franklin B. Gowan President of the Reading Rail Road Company of Pennsylvania. He has achieved an eminent reputation as a lawyer and is held in high esteem by those who are permanently connected with railroad interests in this country.

I take great pleasure in commending him to you and in bespeaking for him during his sojourn in your vicinity such attentions as it may be in your power to extend to him.

Very truly yours
U. S. GRANT

MINISTERS & CONSULS OF THE U. S. RESIDENT ABROAD.

Copy, DLC-USG, II, 1. Born in 1836, Franklin B. Gowen began practicing law (1860), became counsel for the Philadelphia and Reading Railroad (1864), and was named its president (1870).

On Sept. 1 and Oct. 9, 1871, USG wrote letters of introduction for U.S. Senator William M. Stewart of Nev. "who visits Europe during the recess of Congress" and for George L. Hartsuff, "late Assistant Adjutant General of the Army who has retired from active service on account of wounds received in the line of duty, and now visits Europe." Copies, *ibid.* On Oct. 23, USG wrote to "U. S. Officials residing abroad." "The bearer, Mr Browning, of N. Y. visits Europe on pleasure. Mr Browning is a merchant of very high standing in N. Y. and is entitled to kind consideration from all U. S Officials abroad to whom he is commended." LS (facsimile), Nate's Autographs [Nov., 1991], p. 40.

To William W. Belknap

[*May 13, 1871*]

Order the troops in S. C. to aid in making such arrests as the U. S. Com.[1] for S. C. may ask, and in all cases to arrest and break up disguised night marauders.

AN, DNA, RG 94, Letters Received, 1670 1871. AG Edward D. Townsend endorsed USG's note. "The following order of the President handed me by Secretary of War, May 13 /71" AE (initialed), *ibid.* Written on the back of an unsigned memorandum in Attorney Gen. Amos T. Akerman's hand. "In the County of Spartanburgh in the State of South Carolina domestic violence, unlawful combinations and conspiracies have so obstructed and hindered the laws of that State and of the United States, as to deprive a large portion of the people of that County of their rights privileges and immunities and of the protection secured to them by the Constitution and laws of the United States; ~~and by the laws of~~ in this viz that large numbers of persons white and colored have been taken from their homes by ~~persons~~ bands of men in disguise, some of whom have been murdered, others have been subjected to the most violent personal assaults by scourging and shooting, and the constituted authority of the State have been unable or have failed to protect such injured citizens in their rights—Under these circumstances the President has ordered into the County U S. troops, the commanding officers of which say that unless specially authorize so to do, they cannot arrest any persons who may be found organized & proceeding through the County in disguise, for the commission of such offences or even when engaged in their commission. It is the desire of the citizens that such order shall be given if the President considers himself authorize by law to give them." D (undated), *ibid.* On May 13, 1871, Townsend telegraphed to Brig. Gen. Alfred H. Terry, Louisville. "The President directs that the U. S. troops in So. Ca be ordered to aid in making such arrests as the U. S. Commissioner for So. Ca—may ask of persons ~~enga~~ accused of unlawful, and violent acts against peaceable citizens; and in all cases to arrest disguised night marauders and break up their bands: acknowledge receipt." LS (telegram sent), *ibid.* On the same day, a correspondent reported: "Senator Scott, accompanied by a United States Commissioner from South Carolina, had an interview with the President this morning. The commissioner stated that the military in his State had refused to respond when called upon by the civil authorities to make arrests, without an order from the President. The commissioner said he desired such an order from the President, and his request was complied with." *Philadelphia Public Ledger*, May 15, 1871. On May 25, Governor Robert K. Scott of S. C. "had a long interview with President Grant, and said there was no necessity for putting his State under martial law, as the better classes of citizens there were well disposed to suppress the Ku-klux organization." *Ibid.*, May 27, 1871.

On Nov. 19, a correspondent reported: "At the last Cabinet meeting, Attorney General Akerman reported that he had two thousand prisoners in South Carolina alone, captured under the Ku Klux act. A debate followed as to the ability of the courts, or of the general government, to take care of so large a proportion of the population, and a general disposition was manifested to have the arrests somewhat restricted, and, if possible, confined to those ascertained to be active in the Ku-Klux order." *Missouri Democrat*, Nov. 20, 1871. On Dec. 2, Akerman wrote to USG. "The number of arrests in South Carolina by the military without warrant, under the Enforcement Acts, officially reported, is One hundred and sixty eight, (168). This number does not include four Cases of mistaken identity, which it is immaterial to notice. Governor Scott, in his message, puts the number at Six hundred, (600.) This probably includes the arrests under warrant." Copy, DNA, RG 60, Letters Sent to Executive Officers. See Proclamation, Oct. 12, 1871.

1. U.S. commissioners, officers of the circuit and territorial courts, were authorized to proceed against violators of the Civil Rights Act (1866) and the Enforcement Act (1870). *U.S. Statutes at Large*, XIV, 27–29, 343; *ibid.*, XVI, 140, 142–43, 433, 435–38.

To Senate

TO THE SENATE OF THE UNITED STATES.

I transmit for consideration with a view to its ratification, a Convention between the United States of America and the United States of Mexico, signed on the 19th. ultimo, for extending the time limited by the Convention of 4 July 1868, for the termination of the proceedings of the Joint Commission provided for by the latter instrument.

It is understood that telegraph information has been received of the approval of the Mexican Congress of the Convention now transmitted.

A copy of an instruction on the subject, of the 25th of March, last, from the Secretary of State to Mr Nelson,[1] the Minister of the United States at the City of Mexico, is also transmitted for the information of the Senate.

U. S. GRANT

WASHINGTON, MAY 16, 1871.

DS, DNA, RG 46, Presidential Messages. On April 19, 1871, Thomas H. Nelson, U.S. minister, and Manuel Aspiroz, Mexico City, signed a convention "for the settlement of outstanding claims that have originated since the signing of the treaty of Guadalupe Hidalgo on the 2nd of February 1848, by a mixed Commission . . ." Copy, *ibid.* On March 25, April 29, and May 10, Secretary of State Hamilton Fish and Nelson exchanged related correspondence. Copies, *ibid.*; *ibid.*, RG 59, Diplomatic Instructions, Mexico; LS, *ibid.*, Diplomatic Despatches, Mexico. On Dec. 11, the Senate ratified this convention. See *Senate Executive Journal*, XVIII, 92, 102, 147; *HED*, 40-3-98.

On April 18 and 27, 1871, Fish had written in his diary. "Mr Mariscal (Mexico) has recd Powers to negotiate an extension of the Claims Convention Commission—He is informed of the Instructions & Powers sent to Mr Nelson Says that he has been appointed Min of For. Affairs, will leave for Mexico on 8 May—will be there in time for the ratification of a treaty, (if signed) by their Congress which will adjourn about the end of May—He suggests four points to be embraced in the new treaty I to reaffirm & recognize the present treaty II to extend the time III to Authorize the Commission to consider & act upon claims which were presented after the time limited by the existing treaty, & up to the time of the new treaty IV that the Commrs may sit either here or in NY, & shall not adjourn over for more than one week, without the consent of the two govts He alludes to Mr Wadsworths frequent absence—that only 28 cases have been decided—& to the distance & difficulty of presenting claims within the time limited by the existing treaty—I object to the ~~extension~~ admission of claims not presented within the time already limited—& question the propriety or expediency of allowing the Commrs to sit in NY—or to provide a prohibition against Adjourning" "Mr Mariscal (Mexico) enquires about negotiating for an extension of time of the Claims Convention. Is told that the U. S. are quite ready to enter into such a treaty but cannot consent to admit claims which had not been presented within the time, to which the opportunity for so doing had been already extended—. . ." DLC-Hamilton Fish.

1. Born about 1823 near Maysville, Ky., Nelson practiced law in Rockville and Terre Haute, Ind., promoted the Republican party, and served as minister to Chile (1861–66). Returning to the U.S., he actively supported ratification of the Fourteenth Amendment. See *PUSG*, 19, 379.

On March 21, 1871, U.S. Senator William P. Kellogg of La. wrote to USG. "I see by dispatches from Mexico that it is quite possible our minister at Mexico Mr Nelson may resign his position. Should he do So I respectfully Suggest that Mr Edward Lee Plumb is a Gentleman well adapted to fill this important position, his intimate acquaintance with the habits & language of the Mexican people would at this juncture be of especial Service to the Govt." ALS, DNA, RG 59, Letters of Application and Recommendation. On March 22, U.S. Senator Henry B. Anthony of R. I. wrote to USG. "If the report be correct that our Minister at Mexico has asked to be recalled, I take pleasure in adding my testimony to the more valuable recommendations that have been offered in favor of Edward Lee Plumb for that important position Without knowing what further considerations may enter into the selection; or what political necessities may be involved; I think that for familiarity with the country the people, the language, for an honorable record in similar service and for the estimation in which he is held by the Spanish American people Mr. Plumb stands in the front rank of those citizens from whom the selection will naturally be made" ALS, *ibid.* In March, U.S. Delegate Richard C. McCormick of Arizona Territory wrote to USG. "I take the liberty respectfully of commending to the attention of the President the name of Edward Lee Plumb, Esq of New York, formerly chargé d'Affaires of the United States in Mexico and late Consul General of the United States at Havana, Cuba, as a desirable person for appointment to such mission as may be vacant where a thorough knowledge of our relations with Spanish America can be made available—I have known Mr Plumb well for many years—Of the most intense republican principles, earnest and loyal as a Union m[a]n throughout the war, Mr Plumb has made for more th[a]n sixteen years past a special study of our relations with Spanish America and especially with Mexico and Cuba—His long residence in those countries and familiarity with the Spanish language has given him a knowledge of Spanish American Character and of the condition and people of those countries which could not but be of the highest utility in an official position—I know of no one who surpasses Mr Plumb in thorough knowledge of our wants in that direction or the genius and peculiar character of the people there with whom we have to deal—Our relations with Spanish America cannot but increase in importance and delicacy, and just such qualifications as Mr Plumb possesses are wanted for the due advancement of our interests in that quarter—" LS, *ibid.* U.S. Delegate José Francisco Cháves of New Mexico Territory and Governor Edward M. McCook of Colorado Territory favorably endorsed this letter. AES, *ibid.* On July 12, Governor Henry D. Cooke of D. C., New York City, wrote to USG recommending Edward L. Plumb for appointment as governor of New Mexico Territory. ALS, *ibid.* Related papers are *ibid.* No appointment followed.

To Hamilton Fish

Private *Washington D. C.* May 17th *18*71

DEAR GOVERNOR;

Senator Conkling told Gen. Porter this morning that the whole question before the Senate, which interfered with the consideration of the treaty, was closed at 4.45' yesterday, and that the treaty would be taken up to-day.

Yours Truly
U. S. GRANT

HON. H. FISH
SEC. OF STATE

ALS, DLC-Hamilton Fish. Beginning on May 9, 1871, Secretary of State Hamilton Fish wrote in his diary. "Lord de Grey, is asked by Ld Granville whether this Govt intends to make public the text of the Treaty is Is told that the Executive Dept feels itself bound to keep the text of the Treaty secret, until after it shall have been sent to the Senate—That we should be glad to let the public know the full text—but are keeping it back, out of deference to the Senate, & shall not feel at liberty to give it to the public—but that most probably, if the Senate do not authorise its publication, it will be obtained in some way, within two or three days." "May 10. Wednesday . . . I read to the Prsdt an extract from the editorial of the NY Herald of this Morning (which has been telegraphed to me) urging that the text of the Treaty be made public—& suggest that it will probably be of service to have it published—He directs Genl Porter, when he takes the Message to the Senate, to intimate to Cameron that it may be well to authorize the publication of the Treaty—I read to him the letter to Thornton (dated May 8) as finally drawn & actually signed, on the subject of our arrangement for the Fisheries for the coming season—which he approves, & says 'it is exactly right' retiring to the Office I send the note to Thornton" "May 13—Saturday—. . . The publication of the Treaty with G. B. is subject of inquiry by a Special Committee of the Senate. A careful examination shews that it must have been printed from the revise of the Treaty printed on 5 inst. for the use of the Jt Commission—The previous copy ~~differed~~ used by the J H C. was very different—&

this revise differs from the Treaty as signed, & as sent to the Senate, by a misprint, in the 34th Article—the words 'of America' occuring after 'United States' in the early part of the Article, & a transposition of the order of naming the two parties, in the latter part—It appears that two copies of this revise of 5 May, were given by Mr Davis on the Evenig of that day, to Senators Cameron & Morton—befŏre the typographical errors in 34th Article were discovered—Mr D— states that the correction was made, in all the other copies before they were given out—He stated to Cameron this morning this fact—Cameron produced his copy—Morton said that his had been used to send to the Public Printer, & that it had been burnt after being thus used, in presence of the Post Master of the Senate—In the Evening Senators Carpenter & Conkling of the Select investigating Comm. call at my House & make several enquiries—I give them generally the information above, except that I make no reference to what is said of Morton's copy being burnt—& I am under the impression that the third copy was given out, but am not certain, & do not remember to whom, if such were given—They mention that the copy published in the 'World' contained the '40' Article which was omitted in the 'Tribune'" "May 16 Tuesday ... In the Evenig, Davis has learnt from Senator Anthony that the Senate has spent the whole day, discussing the question of the publication by the NY Tribune, of the Treaty—I go to see the President, who had seen Cameron & Conkling this afternoon, & had expressed the wish that no amendment be made to the Treaty, & that it be disposed of & ratified as soon as possible He will send for Carpenter in the Mornig, & request him to suspend the Publication investigation, & have the Treaty considered as soon as practicable" DLC-Hamilton Fish.

On May 10, an editorial had argued for publishing the treaty. "... Why have both the British Commissioners and our own, as well as the government at Washington, been so careful that the text of the treaty should be kept secret? Do they fear newspaper discussion? True, England and Englishmen are not yet emancipated from the old time mysteries of diplomacy. This remnant of feudalism, monarchy and class government still clings to them; but it is out of place—is incompatible in our free country, where the voice of the people is the governing power. While delicate negotiations may be pending, and an interruption of them might prove injurious to the public welfare, there might be some reason for withholding information for a time; but as soon as anything is accomplished, any conditions agreed upon, the people ought to know the facts...." *New York Herald*, May 10, 1871.

Also on May 10, a correspondent reported from Washington. "The Senate went into Executive session a few minutes after 1 o'clock to-day. The first thing done was the reading of the Treaty of the Joint High Commission, which occupied about an hour. This was merely for information. Senator Cameron, Chairman of the Committee on Foreign Relations, made a brief statement to the effect that the Treaty was honorable to both countries, and negotiated in the interest of peace. He hoped, therefore, that the Treaty would receive the approval of the Senate, and suggested that it be given to the press of the country. To this several Senators interposed objections, as they could see no reason for departing from the uniform practice of the Senate.... A majority of the Senate are in favor of removing the injunction of secrecy, so that the Treaty may be now made public, and this would have been the result had the question been pressed to a vote this afternoon. It may come up in the session of Friday, to which time the Senate has adjourned." *New York Tribune*, May 11, 1871. On May 11, the *Tribune* printed the treaty.

On May 12, the Senate passed a resolution approving a committee of five Senators to investigate the treaty's publication. On May 17, "The Sergeant-at-Arms appeared at the bar of the Senate having in custody Z. L. White and Homer J. Ramsdell, arrested by order of the Senate and brought to its bar to answer for contempt in refusing to answer certain interrogatories propounded to them, . . ." *Senate Journal*, 42–Special Session, p. 164. On May 18, Zebulon L. White, chief Washington correspondent of the *New York Tribune*, testified before the Senate. "I have already testified before the special committee of the Senate that I did not receive what purports to be a copy of the treaty of Washington from any Senator or officer of the Senate; that it was printed on folio pages, a single column on each page; and that I first saw it at or about ten o'clock on the night of May 10, instant. I have since been informed that the copy which I thus described was not a Senate document, but was one printed by order of the State Department, of which, I am also informed, forty or more copies were printed for the use of the Department and for distribution. . . ." *Ibid.*, p. 169. On the same day, Hiram J. Ramsdell, also a *Tribune* reporter, gave similar testimony. *Ibid.*, pp. 174–75. See Mark Wahlgren Summers, *The Press Gang: Newspapers and Politics, 1865–1878* (Chapel Hill, 1994), pp. 95–97, 104–7; Donald A. Ritchie, *Press Gallery: Congress and the Washington Correspondents* (Cambridge, Mass., 1991), pp. 90–91.

On May 20, Oliver H. French, New York City, wrote to USG. "Failing to elicit a reply from ANY officials I have written, I respectfully inquire whether the pending 'Treaty of Washington' covers the claim of Ex. A. V. Lt. Commander Chas. A. French against our Government or Gt. Britian for the loss of his Brig 'B. T. Martin' that was burned by the Gunboat 'Union' after having been beached by the U. S. Frigate 'Susquehanna' for having been captured by the rebel Privateer 'Gordon' off Cape Hatteras early in 1861. At your convenience, please direct my inquieries . . ." ALS, DNA, RG 59, Miscellaneous Letters. On June 9, Fish endorsed this letter. "When the Treaty shall have been ratified & exchanged—it will be proclaimed & Mr F. will be able to judge—" AE, *ibid.*

To Hamilton Fish

Washington D. C. May 17th *18*71

MY DEAR GOVERNOR:

It will be agreeable for me to meet the English Commissioners on Saturday,[1] but if equally convenient for them to call at 12 m instead of 1 p. m. I would prefer it. I will remain in however until they do call.

Yours Truly
U. S. GRANT

HON. H. FISH
SEC. OF STATE.

ALS, DLC-Hamilton Fish.

On May 15, 1871, USG wrote to the Senate. "I transmit to the Senate in answer to their resolution of the tenth instant a report from the the Secretary of State, and the papers which accompanied it." DS, DNA, RG 46, Presidential Messages. On May 10, the Senate, in special session, had passed a resolution requesting "a copy of all reports made by Hon. Wm. Whiting, as solicitor of the War Department, upon any claims made by the subjects of any foreign nation for damages in consequence of the War against the rebellious States from 1861 to 1865 inclusive, and which are supposed to be now on file in the State Department" DS, *ibid.*, RG 59, Miscellaneous Letters. See *SED*, 42–Special Session-2.

On May 15, the Senate passed a resolution requesting information on all claims "on the part of corporations, companies or private individuals," against either the U.S. or Great Britain. DS, DNA, RG 59, Miscellaneous Letters. On May 17, Secretary of State Hamilton Fish wrote in his diary. "I take to the President a message to the Senate in Answer to a resolution (in Executive Session) calling for information as to Claims which may be presented under the 12th & subsequent Articles, of the Treaty with Gt Britain, now pending—" DLC-Hamilton Fish. On the same day, USG wrote to the Senate. "In answer to a Resolution of the Senate, of the 15th instant, I transmit herewith a Report from the the Secretary of State." DS, DNA, RG 46, Reports Submitted to the Senate. Fish's report, also dated May 17, categorized claims for personal injury and property damage against the U.S. and Great Britain. DS, *ibid.*

On May 12, Augustus J. Pleasonton, Philadelphia, wrote to USG. "I deem it to be of sufficient national importance to trouble you with this communication, in order to inform you if you are not already aware of the fact, that in the autumn of the year 1860 when the cotton growing States were threatening Secession from the Union there appeared in the newspapers of Birmingham and Manchester in England, very serious cautions to the people of those States against a Severance of the Union,—in which it was stated that as the Manufacturers of Birmingham and Manchester for their previous advances of money to the planters on their crops of cotton had taken mortgages on their slaves as collateral security therefor, to the full extent of three fourths of all the Slaves of those States, which said mortgages would be jeopardised by civil war, they the manufacturers would not in the future, lend the Southern planters a single dollar if they should persist in their mischievous designs—Now as the Slaves at that time were computed to be about four millions in number with an average value of five hundred dollars per head; the aggregate value of them would have been some 2 thousand millions of dollars, three fourths of which would be one thousand five hundred millions of dollars according to the statements in the said newspapers—If the treaty of Washington shall be ratified without amendment, these claims would doubtless be preferred against the Government—which might not be able to have them rejected—" ALS, *ibid.*, RG 59, Miscellaneous Letters.

On May 18 and subsequently, Fish wrote in his diary. "Senator Trumbull enquires whether an amendment to the Treaty ~~p~~with Gt Britain, pending before the Senate, will jeopard it—& is told that any amendment however trivial, will probably inevitably destroy it entirely—as it will enable G. B. then, either to recede entirely, or to propose other amendments—& there appears to be a strong feeling in England to have the Treaty rejected" "May 21 Sunday—Sr Ed. Thornton, refers to an objection said to be taken by Senator Trumbull, to the 2d of the Rules of ~~International~~ Neutral duties as laid down in the Treaty with Gt Britain that the language may be construed to prohibit the sale of Arms, by a neutral, in the course of ordinary Commerce &c He disclaims any agreement in this view, but says that strangely the same question has been raised in Gt Britain, and by Sr Roundell Palmer—He ~~hands~~ shews me a paper which he says is the substance of a telegram recd by him as follows 'the objection taken is that the 2d Rule might extend to any systematic exportation of Arms or other military supplies from the neutral' he suggests that an agreement be signed by him & me explainig the rule & denying this interpretation of its meanig. I think it will be better that the Senate adopt a resolution declaratory of their understanding of the rule, & request the Prsdt to obtain the agreement of the Brit. Govt thereto—that he & I may agree upon the form of the Resolution &c—& I undertake to consult with Judge Hoar & some others, as to the form & terms of the Resolution—I call upon Senator Trumbull, & submit to him the following as the basis of the explanatory resolution,—'that the 2d of the Rules &c—does not prohibit the exportation from the Neutral Govt of Military Supplies, or Arms purchased sold and shipped in the ordinary Course of regular Commercial transactions'—He is uncertain of the meaning of the words 'Military supplies' & thinks that Coal &c, might be refused to a belligerent—& he ~~G~~gives me the following words as embracing an idea or principle which he wishes to have embraced in the explanatory resolution or notes—viz 'nor does the term "Military supplies" as therein used include any other than such as are solely applicable to war purposes'—Dined at the Presidents—Judge Hoar, Vice President—Boutwell Belknap & Carpenter—Carpenter presents same objection to the Treaty that Trumbull had (to the 2d ~~Art~~. Rule). I suggest a resolution defining the understanding of the Senate &c—which he warmly commends—" "May 22 ~~Tuesday~~ Monday—Sir Ed. Thornton sends me a copy of the resolution as suggested by me last Evenig—& I send it—(by Mr Davis) with a further resolution (as follows), to the Comm. on For. Rels' of the Senate 'Resolved that the President be requested to Communicate to H B M. Govt this understanding of the Senate & Govt of the U. S. & obtain their assent to the same'" DLC-Hamilton Fish. On or about May 26, Fish wrote to U.S. Senator Simon Cameron of Pa. "The Resolution explanatory of the understanding of the Scond rule in the 6th article of the Treaty with Great Britain has the approval of the Commissioners of both Governments and may be important to define the meaning when the rules come to be presented to other governments, and shall be translated, into other languages. It is deemed important to have the contemporaneous interpretation of both Governments to avoid questions being raised by other Powers who may become belligerent against the sale of arms &c by the people of the United States as neutrals and to submit this interpretation with the rules. It is also of importance that the Treaty with Mexico extending the claims commission be acted upon by the Senate before its adjournment, otherwise the work of the Commission may all be lost I have seen Governor Morton and removed his doubts" Copy, DNA, RG 59, General Records. The Senate took no action on the resolution. See Adrian Cook, *The Alabama Claims: American Politics and Anglo-American Relations, 1865–1872* (Ithaca, 1975), pp. 202–3.

On May 24, the Senate ratified the Treaty of Washington by a vote of 50 to 12. On May 25, Horace Porter wrote to Fish. "Will you be kind enough to return the Treaty, sent herewith, designating the place for the President to affix his signature." LS, DNA, RG 59, Miscellaneous Letters.

On May 30, Fish wrote to Cameron. "*Personal* . . . I beg to tender to you my very sincere & earnest thanks for the generous & very efficient & effective aid & support you have rendered to the various subjects which have gone from the Department of State to the Senate, since you have been at the head of the Committee on

Foreign Relations—& particularly to the Treaty with Great Britain—Since you took charge ~~of~~ in the Senate of the business from this Department, I have felt that important measures, & Treaties negotiated were no longer to be smothered, & pigeonholed in the Committee Room—& the Country owes to you that a number of Treaties which had thus lain buried for weeks & months, were readily & easily passed, & the nation saved the discredit of negotiating & then neglecting to act upon solemn Conventions with other Powers—Personally I desire to make my thanks for your warm support of the Treaty with Great Britain—" ALS, DLC-Simon Cameron. On July 17, William Hunter, 2nd asst. secretary of state, wrote to Horace Porter, Long Branch. "I have to acknowledge the receipt of your letter to Mr Davis of the 14th instant, and in his absence to enclose to you in compliance with the President's wish a list of the treaties before the Senate while Mr Sumner was Chairman of the Committee on Foreign Relations, and not acted upon previously to his removal. The dates of the Senates Action on those disposed of while Mr Cameron was Chairman, are noted in red ink." LS (press), DLC-Hamilton Fish.

1. On May 20, Fish recorded in his diary. "At Noon, the British Joint Commissionrs, met by appointment at the Presidents, to take leave prior to their return to England—" *Ibid.*

To John Sherman

Washington D. C. May 17th *18*71

DEAR SIR:

Your favor of the 15th inst. inviting me at the instance of prominent citizens of Sandusky, Ohio, to visit there on the 4th of July is only this minuet received.

It would afford me great pleasure to accept the invitation thus extended but my arrangements for the Summer will not admit of my acceptance. I shall not be able to go West more than once during the Summer and on that occasion I want to visit Cincinnati for two or three days, and Chicago about the same time, which will leave me no time to spare, or at least not beyond a few hours at a time, at other places.

Please express my regrets to the gentlemen who have been kind enough to extend this invitation.

Very respectfully
Your Obt. svt,
U. S. GRANT

HON. J. SHERMAN, U. S. S.

ALS, DLC-John Sherman. USG spent July 4, 1871, at Long Branch.

On Dec. 17, 1870, and May 14, 1871, U.S. Senator John Sherman of Ohio wrote to his wife, Cecilia S. Sherman. "... We are independant in property—in good health—I have been remarkably fortunate in business & politics and you have the hearty good will of all in social life—with these and many other blessings it seems ludicrous for you to be troubled because Mrs Grant has not been courteous enough—and for me to worry because Grant does not yield always to my desires—In every respect you are the equal of Mrs Grant if not her superior—while in point of morals I know well enough that while I am not a model—yet Grant and most of those whose opinions you fear do not come up to my standard by many degrees. This is true not only in point of fact but in point of reputation: I confess I was annoyed ~~that~~ when I finally really wished for the English Mission and was not selected upon the mere suggestion that I would accept it—but I am not sure but it is better that my wish was not granted—We always underestimate present possessions—Most persons would be surprised that I would have exchanged my seat in the Senate & future prospects for any Executive Office. But 2 or 3 persons knew that I even contemplated it I am now entirely content. The field is reasonably clear for my reelection I have had more hopeful indications of this within two weeks than at any time since I entered political life—I have no doubt that Grant not only expects it but will aid it. Delano does not now contemplate any other result. Schencks appointment even enures to my benefit and indeed is foolishly & falsely attributed to me—to get him out of the way. Under these circumstances I want nothing to occur to indicate an indifference on your part to social obligations or an undervaluation by you of your social position...." "... We will be in Session until about June 1st & some think longer. There is much opposition developing to the Treaty—but I have studied it carefully & will vote for it but will not engage in the debate It is the general impression here that I am to be reelected: Delano it is said positively declares I am at a loss to discern his real purposes but it is apparent that the controlling powers here do not care much to aid me but will put no obstacles in my way. I had yesterday a long & friendly interview with the President & I think he anticipates my election & will not allow any Govermental opposition to me...." ALS, Mansfield-Richland County Public Library, Mansfield, Ohio. See letter to John Sherman, June 14, 1871; letter to William T. Sherman, Jan. 26, 1872.

On Feb. 18, 1871, John Sherman wrote to USG "in behalf of 'Carpetbaggers.'" William Reese Co., Catalogue 76, no. 77.

To Elihu B. Washburne

Washington, D. C. May 17th *18~~6~~*71

DEAR WASHBURNE:

Your favor of the 20th of Apl. with enclosure, as all your other very welcome letters, was duly received. I have not written to you whilst shut up in Paris because I did not know that any thing but purely official dispatches were proper, or would be so considered by the Prussians, to send through the lines. I thought none the less frequently of you however, and the relief from care and anxiety which you sought in a foreign Mission. Your time will come I trust for relief. Already you have the reward of your services in the gratitude and pride the American people feel for the glorious course you pursued in standing at your post which all others, like situated, had deserted.

My trials here have been considerable but, I believe, so far every tempest that has been aroused has recoiled on them who got ~~them~~ it up. First, San Domingo; but you have read all that has been said about that matter in Congress and out of Congress, and what I have had to say, and probably know the present status of the question? I ~~will only~~

I will only add that a great many professedly staunch republicans acted very much as if the wanted to outdo the democracy in breaking up the republican party. Every thing looks more favorably now though, for the party, than it did in /63, when the war was raging.

Sumner[1] and Schurtz[2] have acted worse than any other two men, and not far behind them is Ferry[3] of Conn. and Tipton[4] of Neb. John Logan[5] is paving the way to be just as bad as he knows how to be; but out of full fellowship with the rep. party he will amount to but little. He is effected with that "Maggott' Mr. Lincoln used to speak of.[6]

Before this reaches you the Senate[7] will have acted upon the Alabama treaty! It looks now as if there would be but very little opposition to it. If however a single amendment is adopted there is no telling when the matter will end. Such a course would undoubtedly result in long debate, and as the treaty would have to be returned to England no doubt it would be amended there in such a way as to force us to reject it. I hope a better result.

My family are all well and send a greatdeal of love to Mrs. Washburne and the children. Please give my kindest regards to them also, and believe me, as ever, your friend,

U. S. Grant

ALS, ICHi. On July 24, 1871, Elihu B. Washburne, "Carlsbad, Bohemia," wrote to USG. "I had the pleasure to receive your last letter sometime before I left Paris. I wonder, how amid all your labors and responsibilities, you could find time to think of me, and much more, to write me. It is a source of immeasurable gratification to know that my course as our representative in Paris during the unprecedented events of the last year meets with your approbation. Could I have foreseen what was to fall upon me, I would have never dared to have undertaken the mission. But looking back I am amazed to think I got along so well. I cannot see that I made any material blunders in all the responsible and delicate matters upon which I was constantly called upon to act. It seems almost impossible for me now to realize how I was enabled to perform all the functions of a Prussian Minister, for eleven months among a people bearing the fiendish hate which the French bear towards the Germans. But I managed to get along through it all with nothing more serious than an idle threat of an irresponsible club, made during the Siege, to hang me, and the miserable slanders of a scurrilous Paris paper, partly edited by a New Orleans rebel, that I had been in compromising correspondence with the 'Commune'. Yet it must be said that my acting as Prussian Minister has been the cause of a good deal of prejudice toward our Legation. The Paris people understand very well well that our sympathies in the United States were nearly all with the Germans and they seize hold of everything to prove it. They made a big howl over your message in regard to raising the importance of the Berlin mission. But I hope things will quiet down after a little time and that we may run along smoothly. I am away from Paris since the second of July on a leave the Governor was kind enough to grant me. I always have a great deal of the Seine River ague hanging about me, [—] and I was determined to try these waters here, and afterwards some celebrated b[a]ths not far off. I was in hopes Mrs. W. would have joined me before this time, but I am sorry to say that her trip has been delayed by a severe illness. My family have been in the country, out some thirty miles from Paris, since Old Papa Thiers shelled us out of our house in Paris. But as some four hundred soldiers have been quartered at the chateau near which our cottage is, we have got to move again—the *seventh* time in little more than a year. I shall, however expect Mrs. W. here at a later date. Our second son, Hempstead came over about a month ago, and so I have my entire family on this side. I see by the papers that Fred is coming abroad, and when in Paris I shall insist that he stop with [u]s. The only thing is I am afraid the young man will think we live a little too far away from the grand centre of the city I read the home papers very thoroughly and have a good idea of the situation. The political horizon looks much brighter than it did six months ago. You have had your troubles which always come to an administration at the middle of the term, but they were not so great as Mr. Lincoln had. When he had been in as long as you have now been in, he had reached a degree of unpopularity without parallel. Indeed, to my certain knowledge, there were not a dozen members of the House, who were his friends and who favored his re-nomination. I can now see nothing in the way of your triumphant nomination and re-election. The people fully understand the Sumners, the Squirtz (Schurz) the Trumbulls the Jack Logans and the Tiptons and Ferrys. But is it not rather hard to see our noble state crucified by such a representation in the Senate. Next year comes the tug of war. We shall both have to go to Galena to vote. Suppose we both agree to spend the month of October there. The people will like to see you there. That reminds me, is it possible for you to do anything for that true hearted old friend of yours, Mr. Houghton? He is in want, and I feel a great sympathy for him. My kindest regards to your family . . ." ALS (press), DLC-Elihu B. Washburne. For Horace H. Houghton, see letter to Hamilton Fish, March 13, 1871, note 2.

1. See letter to Oliver P. Morton, Dec. 9, 1870. On March 19 and 21, 1871, Secretary of State Hamilton Fish wrote in his diary. "Govr Morton calls—see him in his carriage at the door—he wishes me to write an article for Harper's Weekly—or the American Monthly—or a letter, presenting the true statement of Sumner's attitude toward the Administration—& the causes leading to the necessity of not reappointing him as Chairman of the Comm—on For—Relations—I doubt the policy of any public discussion—it will continue the subject in the public mind, which otherwise will gradually forget—it—but he seems urgent—while talking Creswell passing stops. he expresses the same opinion which I had done—without having heard my opinion—Conkling subsequently joins & expresses the same opinion—Morton says Sumner applied yesterday or the day before to Pomeroy, for information as to some alleged remark of Babcock, intimating an intention to assault Sumner—that Pomeroy declined giving any statement, & Sumner said he should have occasion to use the information On Friday Crounse told me that he learnt from some reporters who were in the habit of frequenting Sumners house that he threatened a speech in which he intended to attack me violently—saying that 'he excused Grant for his ignorance—but that Fish was the Mephistopheles who entrapped & led him astray &c &c' Boutwell in the Evening, tells me he has seen Sumner today (he frequently does) & he seems more tranquil apparently pleased & satisfied with the newspaper response to his failure of reappointment—" "*Cabinet*—All present except Delano who is represented by Judge Otto—President reads copy of letter from Sumner to Dr Francis Vinton, on the publication of his letter to the President about San Domingo, & Vintons reply—He then remark that he understands that Sumner has said to several persons that he intends to oppose every thing the Administration proposes—Boutwell takes no notice, & seems to be reading something—I call his attention to what the President said & ~~remark that I think that~~ ask whether Sumner did not say something of the sort to him—He answers shortly, 'no he did not say that,—to me'—" DLC-Hamilton Fish.

On Feb. 3, Francis Vinton, Trinity Church, New York City, had written to USG. "I have just returned from Nassau, N. P., where I escorted Mrs. Vinton for health, leaving her there for the winter and spring months. This voyage has occasioned reflections and conversations on the question of acquiring San Domingo Island as a sanitarium. The universal wish of the Americans at Nassau was for a resort on American soil in the West Indies for the benefit of invalids, expressed in a longing for the success of your efforts to secure the Island of San Domingo. But this motive is secondary to the great political and commercial advantages. In conversing with her Britannic Majesty's Governor (Walker) of Nassau, he said to me that he earnestly hoped that the United States would secure the Island of San Domingo for the twofold reason: First. That our civilization and culture would redeem the society of the West Indies, and, Second. That the soil and productions of that island, surpassing those of any other, not excepting Cuba, would enrich our country beyond any cost that its acquisition would demand. Governor Walker has been forty-one years in the West Indies, and is about to return home to enjoy retirement on his pension. His eulogy on San Domingo was qualified. Another view of the importance of securing the island was suggested by a talk with an intelligent sea captain, with the chart before us, with soundings, etc. He pointed out that, supposing the ship canal be made through the Isthmus of Panama, the direct route from Asia to Europe *must* be through the channels on either side of San Domingo, which accordingly must become the great entrepot between these quarters of the world. I beg you to examine the chart with this view, and it will strike you forcibly that an island so rich, so fertile, so badly ruled, and so carelessly cultivated, will certainly fall into the hands of some people of the Caucasian race, of some government wise enough to hold it. I wish my old friend and school-mate at the Dane Law School, Cambridge, Mr. Sumner, would cease to oppose the measures set on foot by the President and Congress, and see the matter with the eyes which have revealed to me the immense importance of obtaining San Domingo; and in this hope and opinion I feel assured the masses of our fellow-citizens, who are not blinded by party nor by ignorance, coincide. I pray that God's blessing may prosper your plans in this regard for the benefit of universal man, the good of our dear country, and the happiness of the inhabitants of the island." Clipping, *ibid.* On Feb. 13, Orville E. Babcock wrote to Vinton. "The President directs me to acknowledge the receipt of your letter of the 3d inst. for which he desires me to convey to you his thanks. It gratifies the President very much to see that, such men as yourself, whose whole lives are disconnected from politics and devoted entirely to benefitting and improving mankind, hold the same views concerning San Domingo as himself. He wishes me to ask you if you have any objection to your letter becoming a portion of public record." Copy, DLC-USG, II, 1.

On March 24, U.S. Senator Charles Sumner of Mass. introduced "Resolutions regarding the employment of the Navy of the United States on the coasts of St. Domingo during the pendency of negotiations for the acquisition of part of that island." *CG*, 42–1, 253. On March 25, a correspondent reported: "In course of conversation to-day with a Republican Senator, the President took occasion to deprecate the anticipated debate in the Senate next week over Sumner's San Domingo resolutions. He thinks that the opposition to the annexation scheme should be willing to wait the return of the commissioners, and until the report of the same has been officially submitted before again opening up their rhetorical batteries. He suggested that the friends of the scheme should not be drawn into any discussion on the subject, at least during the present session, unless to answer some gross misstatements or insinuations, but to let the report speak for itself. . . ." *Missouri Democrat*, March 26, 1871. On March 27, Sumner spoke. "The question which I present is very simple. It is not, whether the acquisition of the island of San Domingo, in whole or part, with a population foreign in origin, language, and institutions, is desirable; but whether we are justified in the means employed to accomplish this acquisition. . . . Never before has there been such Presidential intervention in the Senate as we have been constrained to witness. Presidential visits to the Capitol, with appeals to Senators, have been followed by assemblies at the Executive Mansion, also with appeals to Senators; and who can measure the pressure of all kinds by himself or agents, especially through the appointing power, all to secure the consummation of this scheme? In harmony with this effort was the Presidential message, where, while charging the Senate with 'folly' in rejecting the treaty, we are gravely assured that by the proposed acquisition 'our large debt abroad is to be ultimately extinguished,' thus making St. Domingo the pack-horse of our vast load, or perhaps, copying Don Quixote when he imposed upon the shoulders of Sancho Panza the penitential stripes which belonged to himself. . . . I need not remind you that the Senate is now occupied in considering how to suppress lawlessness within our own borders and to save the African race from outrage. Surely our efforts at home must be weakened by the drama we are now playing abroad. Pray, sir, with what face can we insist upon obedience to law and respect for the African race, while we are openly engaged in lawlessness on the coasts of St. Domingo and outrage upon the African race represented by the Black Republic? How can we expect to put down the Ku Klux at the South, when we set in motion another Ku Klux kindred in constant insubordination to law and Constitution? Differing in object the two are identical in this insubordination. One strikes at national life and the other at individual life, while both strike at the African race. One molests a people, the other a community. Lawlessness is the common element. But it is difficult to see how we can condemn with proper, whole-hearted reprobation, our own domestic Ku Klux with its fearful outrages while the President puts himself at the head of a powerful and costly Ku Klux operating abroad in defiance of International Law and the Constitution of the United States. These are questions which I ask with sorrow, and only in obedience to that truth which is the requirement of this debate; nor should I do otherwise than fail in justice to the occasion if I did not declare my unhesitating conviction, that, had the President been so inspired as to bestow upon the protection of Southern Unionists, white and black, one half nay, sir, one quarter of the time, money, zeal, will, personal attention, personal effort, and personal intercession, which he has bestowed on his attempt to obtain half an island in the Caribbean Sea, our Southern Ku Klux would have existed in name only, while tranquillity reigned everywhere within our borders. . . ." *CG*, 42–1, 295, 304–5. U.S. Senators Oliver P. Morton of Ind. and Timothy O. Howe of Wis. spoke in defense of USG. *ibid.*, pp. 305, 307; *ibid.*, Appendix, 40–46. On March 29, the Senate tabled Sumner's resolutions. *ibid.*, p. 329. See Edward L. Pierce, *Memoir and Letters of Charles Sumner: Period 1860 to Death* (London, 1893), IV, 483–88; David Donald, *Charles Sumner and the Rights of Man* (New York, 1970), pp. 509–15.

2. On March 28 and 29, U.S. Senator Carl Schurz of Mo. defended Sumner's opposition to annexation of Santo Domingo and attacked USG for usurping congressional power. "To-day I read in a newspaper that my only object in stepping forward in this debate was to injure the President in the opinion of the people. Sir, I am too well aware of the peculiar position which General Grant holds in this country, not to know that his Administration cannot be broken down, unless it breaks down itself; and what it has accomplished in that direction falls upon its own responsibility. . . . I do not speak of the President without that respect which is his due. Nor do I put upon the things he has done a harsh construction. The President's education was that of military life. He was unused to the operations of the checks and balances of power which constitute the rule of civil government. If the habits of peremptory command on the one side and of absolute obedience on the other impressed themselves strongly on his mind, it was not his fault. So he was elected President, and suddenly transferred to the complex duties of the most responsible civil position of this Republic. If his temper is not such as to shake off the force of life-long habits with ease; if it is not supple enough to accommodate itself to a position no longer one of undivided power and responsibility, it may be called his misfortune; but let it not, by a confidence beyond reasonable bounds, become the misfortune of the American people. . . . Sir, it was with astonishment and mortification that I heard the just criticism passed by the Senator from Massachusetts upon the President's act denounced as a blow struck at the Republican party. The Republican party! What, sir, is Ulysses S. Grant the Republican party? Is the San Domingo scheme the Republican cause? Is that most preposterous and dangerous doctrine, that the President may acquire the war-making power by a sleight-of-hand, the Republican platform? Republican Senators would do well to pause before they commit themselves on so fatal a position. If it has come to this, if you really could make the people of the country believe that fidelity to the Constitution and republican government, that hostility to the San Domingo scheme and to usurpation, means hostility to the Republican party, then you will find that presidential party uncomfortably small. I warn my Republican friends not to identify the cause of their party with one man and with the acts of one man. . . . Our disapproval of a presidential act of

General Grant will not encroach upon our appreciation of the capture of Vicksburg and the victory of Richmond; but the laurels of Vicksburg and Richmond cannot make his acts now under discussion constitutional, nor can they turn a presidential blunder into an act of wisdom. . . ." *CG*, 42–1, Appendix, 60–62. On April 14, Schurz accused USG and other Republicans of political designs in their support for the measure commonly known as the "Ku Klux" bill. *CG*, 42–1, 687–88. See message to Congress, March 23, 1871; Hans L. Trefousse, *Carl Schurz: A Biography* (Knoxville, 1982), pp. 185–88, 191–95.

On April 4, Schurz had written to Jacob D. Cox. ". . . Unless I greatly mistake the signs of the times, the superstition that Grant is *the* necessary man, is rapidly giving way. The spell is broken, and we have only to push through the breach. As for *San domingo,* I am confident that no treaty of annexation can pass this body. The President may try to press the treaty for the lease of the Bay of Samana, a comparatively innocent thing. We shall resist that also and I think we can defeat it too. The Pres., as I understand, is as *stubborn as ever,* and seems determined to risk his all upon that one card. He seems to have a genius for suicide. I suppose you have already thought of spreading your organization all over your State. Perhaps you might take care of Indiana too. . . ." ALS, Cox Papers, Oberlin College, Oberlin, Ohio. See *PUSG*, 20, 189; letter to George W. Childs, Nov. 28, 1871, note 1.

On April 13, Christopher C. Andrews, U.S. minister, Stockholm, wrote to USG. "The Minister for Foreign Affairs Count Wachtmeister yesterday handed me a copy of the Daily Globe containing Senator Schurz speech of Jan'y 11 on the San Domingo question remarking that it was a 'remarkable speech'. He no further expressed his opinion of the speech but I inferred he thought it important. I have since read the speech and find the Senator's theory to be that civilization, or in other words free government, cannot prosper in a tropical climate. On this point I thought I would venture to make a suggestion to you. Two thousand years ago and more the civilization of the world was located in the mild and hot climates. Egypt one of the most civilized countries that has existed has a climate about the same as tropical. We can on the other hand turn to many northern countries like Scotland for examples which though now civilized were less than a thousand years ago embroiled in almost constant warfare and in a scarcely half civilized condition. As late as the eleventh century human sacrifices and as late as the thirteenth century the pagan custom of exposing children prevailed here in Sweden. The great writer Buckle in summing up the agencies which affect civilization says: . . . History of Civilization in England vol. 1 (2d London ed.) p. 207 It appears to me this is an authority against Senator Schurz" ALS (press), Andrews Papers, Minnesota Historical Society, St. Paul, Minn.

3. On June 8, 1870, U.S. Senator Orris S. Ferry of Conn. spoke about the imprisonment of Davis Hatch, his constituent, in Santo Domingo, condemning Babcock for "intervening against the release of the prisoner, upon his own avowed declaration to the American commercial agent that if the prisoner was released he, after his release, would interfere with and be an obstacle in the way of the project of the annexation of San Domingo, which General Babcock had then in charge." *CG*, 41–2, 4194. Sumner and U.S. Senator Thomas W. Tipton of Neb. sustained Ferry. *Ibid.*, pp. 4194–4201. See *PUSG*, 19, 209–10; *ibid.*, 20, 166–67; *CG*, 41–2, 1774–75.

4. On March 10, 1871, Tipton spoke in support of Sumner and Schurz. "When the San Domingo question came here originally, when the Senator from Missouri [Mr. SCHURZ] moved an investigating committee in regard to the imprisonment of a citizen of Connecticut, the charge was distinctly made here that it was a war upon

the President of the United States that those men were attempting who asked for that investigation. I knew then that the intention existed to array the President against the men who should signalize themselves in leading off against the San Domingo iniquity. We were warned then. We met you then; we meet you now; and we will meet you at all times triumphantly on a question of this kind. You then tantalized us; for it was in no ordinary language that the intimation was made here that the men who asked for the investigation in regard to Hatch were making a war upon the President of the United States. You failed to overawe the Senators who made that investigation. You failed to overawe the Republicans of the country. . . ." Brackets in original; *ibid.*, pp. 47–48.

5. Also on March 10, U.S. Senator John A. Logan of Ill. spoke in favor of Sumner. "I differ and have differed, as is known by the Republicans here, with the majority in reference to the action taken by them in the change of the chairman of the Committee on Foreign Relations, and I differ with the gentlemen who have discussed this question in the Senate with regard to the reasons for it. I do not believe that this change has been made merely because the Senate has a right to change its committees, or has a right to form committees as it pleases. . . . I believe the legislative department of this Government to be an independent department of the Government, independent of the Executive; and the Executive has no right to dictate who shall be chairman of a committee or who shall form any portion of a committee. . . ." *Ibid.*, p. 46. See James P. Jones, *John A. Logan: Stalwart Republican from Illinois* (Tallahassee, 1982), pp. 56–59.

6. See Ida M. Tarbell, *The Life of Abraham Lincoln* (New York, 1900), II, 186–88.

7. See Proclamation, April 20, 1871. On May 10, 12, and 14, Fish wrote in his diary. "President signs message sending to the Senate the Treaty with Great Britain—Also several nominations of small Consuls, & also that of John M Francis as Minister to Greece While in his room, a Committee of the Senate, (Sns Anthony & Casserly) announce that the Senate has organized, & is ready to ~~proce~~ receive any Communication's from him—&c He replies that he will within a few minutes send a message with a Treaty, to which he will ask their favorable consideration—He adds that he hopes the Comm. to which he supposes it will be referred will not keep it long under consideration—Anthony, remarks that if they do he will be inclined to move to discharge them from its consideration &c—. . . Carl Schurz called this morning—read the protocol & looked at the Treaty—gave him a copy of each—He is reserved as to his opinion & action on the Treaty" "Cabinet—Belknap & Akerman absent—nothing done, except a discussion of the Treaty with Gt Britain, & the probabilities of its approval by the Senate—& the position of individual Senators, towards the Administration, & with respect to the Treaty—" "Judge Hoar says that now he feels sure that all will be right—That Sumner intends to make a speech & openly declare his intention to vote for the Treaty—In the Evenig John V. L Pruyn who has been dining with Sumner & comes from his house to mine, says that S— criticises the Treaty & will offer Amendments—" DLC-Hamilton Fish.

To William W. Belknap

Washington D. C. May 18th *18*71

Hon. W. W. Belknap,
Sec. of War;
Sir:

Please name John T. Broadhead[1] as third supernumerary for West Point this year.

Respectfully &c.
U. S. Grant

ALS, DNA, RG 94, Correspondence, USMA. Another hand underlined "third" and noted at the bottom "Above means 4th." Filed with a draft of a War Dept. form letter, dated May 26, 1871. "The President having been pleased to name you as an alternate in anticipation of the possible failure of one or more of the appointees to the Military Academy at West Point, for 1871, to pass the requisite ~~m~~Medical & ~~a~~Academical examinations, you are requested to ~~to~~ report to the Superintendent of the Academy by the 31st of May, for examination before the Acedemic & Medical Boards, with other candidates for admission. This letter will be presented to the Supt." Df, *ibid.* Four alternates are listed at the top, in order: Hugh L. Scott (see *PUSG*, 20, 426), William Maynadier (*ibid.*, p. 384), John L. Clem (*ibid.*, 19, 186–87), and John T. Brodhead.

On May 17, a reporter wrote that "The President has appointed as cadets at large to West Point Military Academy, Francis H. Hardie, son of Inspector-General Hardie; Hamlin Spiegel, son of Col. Spiegel of Ohio Volunteers; John Pitcher, son of Gen. Thomas G. Pitcher, Colonel of the First Infantry; Francis Preston Fremont, son of Gen. John C. Fremont; Eben Swift, son of Surgeon Swift of the Regulars; Wm. Reeve Hamilton, Wisconsin, son of Gen. Charles S. Hamilton of Volunteers; Almer H. Wells, Michigan, a United States volunteer who distinguished himself in the rebellion; Hamilton Rowan, Maryland, son of Vice-Admiral Rowan; John R. Williams, Michigan, son of Brigadier-Gen. Williams of Volunteers, killed at Baton Rouge." *Boston Transcript*, May 18, 1871. On May 13, Secretary of War William W. Belknap had suggested the appointment of Eben Swift, Jr., to USG. D (initialed), DNA, RG 94, Correspondence, USMA. Swift, John Pitcher, and William R. Hamilton graduated from USMA in 1876. Hamlin Spiegel and Almer H. Wells did not graduate from USMA. See *PUSG*, 20, 394, 397–98.

On May 20, 1870, Francis H. Hardie, Chicago, had written to USG. "I have the honor to request an appointment of Cadet (at large) to the U S Mil Acady at West Point for the Class to be appointed this June to enter next June I am sixteen years of age in Sept next My father is an officer of the Army Gn. James A Hardie" ALS, DNA, RG 94, Correspondence, USMA. On Jan. 27 and Feb. 10, 1873, Col. James A. Hardie, inspector gen., wrote to USG. "My son, Francis, whom you were good enough to appoint Cadet has failed in his Jany examination in Mathematics. But he has been recommended by the Academic Board for reappointment. During the year previous to his entry to the Mily Academy his preparation for the institution had been measurably frustrated by the Chicago fire, which disturbed school instruction for a time and so deranged my special plans as that he did not study Algebra at all. Mathematical studies had never engaged his attention which had been exclusively devoted to the Classics. So his method of study for his new position was left to be acquired. He was just learning the mathematical processes, when his examination occurred. In general intelligence, I have many proofs of his superiority. I know he cannot be behind the average of West Point boys in that. Another chance, with the special education he will be afforded mean time will I feel confident ensure him success. I therefore entreat of you to reappoint him Cadet for the year 1874." "I have the honor to request that the late order accepting the resignation of Cadet Francis Hunter Hardie, of the U. S. Military Academy, be rescinded and that he be ordered to report to the Superintendent on the 30th day of June next, to join the next succeeding Fourth Class, as recommended by the Academic Board." ALS and LS, *ibid.* On Feb. 10, USG endorsed the second letter. "Approved." AES, *ibid.* On July 6, 1875, Orville E. Babcock, Long Branch, N. J., wrote to Margaret Hardie. "I have submitted your request, as also the request of Gen Ingalls for the appt of your son in the Army, to the President, who directs me to say in reply that he cannot do so without violating a rule, that would have grieved his father to have been violated, when he was a Cadet, viz—to appoint the son a Lieut before the class with which he entered the Academy graduates, and thus place him ahead of all his classmates, and thus make a failure a reward—The President thinks Gen Hardie will see this matter in the same light that he does, and fully appreciate his feelings—" ALS, DLC-James A. Hardie. On Sept. 8, Babcock wrote to James Hardie, Philadelphia. "Your letter received I have communicated your message to the President relative to your Son—The President knows young Stevenson or his family and has ordered his appointment.... P. S. Your letter destroyed" ALS, *ibid.* On March 4, 1876, Col. Rufus Ingalls, Washington, D. C., wrote to James Hardie. "I have only time now to say that I saw the President—He said he could not appoint your Son until after next July—I am sorry, but will see he does then" ALS, *ibid.* On May 26, 1875, Francis Hardie had been dismissed from USMA; on July 28, 1876, USG nominated him as 2nd lt., 3rd Cav.

On Jan. 14, 1871, Vice Admiral Stephen C. Rowan, Baltimore, had written to USG. "I have the Honor to forward herewith an application of my Son for an appointment to the military academy at West Point. If you can, consistently with the claims of others—give my boy the appointment he so much covets; you will make a young heart joyous, and add to the grateful acknowledgements of, . . ." ALS, DNA, RG 94, Correspondence, USMA. On Jan. 15, Hamilton Rowan, Baltimore, wrote to USG. "I have the honor to make an application for an appointment to the U. S. Military Academy, for the month of June 1872, at which time my age will be seventeen years and two months. I am very anxious to be a soldier and hope you will grant my request." ALS, *ibid.* On Jan. 17, USG endorsed these papers. "Special attention invited." AES, *ibid.* Rowan graduated from USMA in 1876, last in his class.

On Feb. 18, 1871, Jessie B. Frémont had written a note. "Francis Preston Frémont born May 17th 1855—in Washington D. C—will be sixteen this May 17th '71—I send the President the name and age of my son with my renewed thanks for his very courteous and agreeable manner of making the appointment." ANS, *ibid.* On the same day, Frederick T. Dent endorsed this note. "refd to the Hon sec of War with the request of the President that when the appntmt of Cadets is to be made the Presidents specia[l] attentn be called to this" AES, *ibid.* On Sept. 8, 1874, John C. Frémont, "Pocaho," N. Y., wrote to Francis Frémont. "I am spending the day at home. Your mother has told me of her visit to the Point and of the condition of your health. Dr Van Buren's letter led me to expect it, but I had not thought it would be so soon. I am sorry for it but I think there is no longer any room for hesitation. You should not expose yourself to any chance of illness or of running down to a point you might find it hard to recover from. Nothing would be gained by it, but something might be lost. You should resign immediately and come home, and you have our full consent to do so. I am told it will be sufficient for Genl Ruger if you will shew him this note that he may know we approve of your action in resigning." ALS, *ibid.* Jessie Frémont endorsed this letter. "You have my thorough consent too, dear Frank" AES, *ibid.* On Sept. 8, Frémont resigned from USMA. LS, *ibid.* On Sept. 20, 1879, Jessie Frémont, Prescott, Arizona Territory, wrote to USG and Julia Dent Grant. "I have asked my friend Mrs Shillaber, who has also been a guest of the Viceroy of India, to give you this 'Welcome home' from me,—and with it some violets—which go to say how very sorry we were when that mistaken telegram told us of the sorrow which would have changed your lives. Now we know nothing breaks the perfect round of your journey which ends as happily as it has been carried through. I wish also to say that two very kind acts commenced some years ago by you General, have ripened into completed and useful lives for the two young men you were good enough to notice specially through me. Mr Guy Huse to whom you gave a substitutes number (5) as all your cadetships were filled, had the good fortune to go into West Point upon it and has graduated high and is now, thanks to you, in Texas on duty. And my son to whom you so graciously offered a cadetship and whose illness obliged him to resign after a year at West Point, is now thoroughly and soundly restored to health and is, after a very high examination, restored to his profession, having just been commissioned. So you see many a good and kind act of yours continues growing and in this case gives me double reason for wishing Mrs Grant and yourself the continued health and family happiness we are so glad was not broken." ALS, USG 3. On Nov. 14, 1883, USG and Julia Grant attended Francis Frémont's wedding in New York City. *New York Times*, Nov. 15, 1883.

On April 24, 1871, Mary Bailey Williams, Newburgh, N. Y., had written to USG. "Having learned that it is necessary for a boy wishing to enter the West Point Military Academy to have his appointment a year in advance—I write to remind you of your kind promise thro' Mr. Brush of Detroit to appoint my son. John R. Williams to a cadetship—He passed his sixteenth birthday in February—will therefore be of suitable age to enter next year—Hoping to hear from you soon—with kind remembrances & best wishes for the health & happiness of yourself, Mrs. Grant & family, . . ." ALS, DNA, RG 94, Correspondence, USMA. On May 1, USG endorsed this letter. "Let special attention be called to this application." AES, *ibid.* John R. Williams, son of Brig. Gen. Thomas Williams, graduated from USMA in 1876, first in his class.

On May 27, 1871, Francis Vinton, USMA, wrote to USG. "My Son Arthur Duley Vinton whom you appointed Cadet at large has been rejected as of '*feeble Constitution* & *muscular tenuity*, by the Board of Surgeons. While these defects could be cured by the bodily discipline of West Point, yet I am bound to submit to official judgment. I write to beg you to fill the Vacancy immediately with the name of my other boy *Frederic Betts Vinton* with an order to report on or after the 1st of June. To relieve my mind will you send me a Telegram, at Trinity Church New York that, if possible, Fred may report by June 1st" ALS, *ibid.* On May 28, Babcock endorsed this letter. "Respectfully referred to the Secty of War. The President will be pleased to have the request of the Rev Dr Vinton complied with and Frederick Betts Vinton appointed a Cadet, and directed to report as requested." AES, *ibid.* On June 17, Babcock wrote to Francis Vinton, Trinity Church, New York City. "Your letter came to me yesterday, and I read it to the President. He desired me to say that he had already directed the Secretary of the Navy to appoint him to the Naval Academy for next year. He says that two supernumeraries have been appointed of the West Point list, and that if he is put on that list he will have to be third on the list. Should you wish this changed, please to let me know and I will attend to it. It would afford me pleasure to meet with you at West Point but I cannot leave the City just now. The new duties imposed upon me, viz the charge of the Public Buildings and Grounds &c. will keep me here the most of the Summer." Copy, DLC-USG, II, 1. On Dec. 27, 1872, Louise C. Hoppin, Brooklyn, wrote to USG. "Being on a visit to my Uncle, Dr. Francis Vinton who is just recovering from a severe illness, he has employed me to write the application herewith enclosed, for an appointment at large to my son Howard—I beg to add my personal wish to his request and to plead the martial services of my Father and his glorious death, as a motive to your favorable response to this application—" ALS, DNA, RG 94, Correspondence, USMA. On the same day, Vinton wrote to Babcock. "will you please say to the President, that the promise he made me of an appointment of my son as Cadet at West Point for 1873, I wish that he would transfer to my nephew Howard O. Hoppin, grandson of my brother John R. Vinton, who was killed while commanding the trenches at Vera Cruz—The President knows all about my brother's military history & fame—My brother's daughter, mother of this boy is a widow, with five children—and she wishes to devote her son to the service of his Country—. . ." LS, *ibid.* Frederick B. Vinton graduated from the U.S. Naval Academy in 1875; Curtis B. Hoppin graduated USMA in 1877. Francis Vinton had supported USG's position on Santo Domingo. See preceding letter.

1. On April 25, 1870, John M. Brodhead, second comptroller, Treasury Dept., had written to USG. "The only son of my brother, Col. Thornton F. Brodhead, 1st Michigan Cavalry, who was killed at the 2d Bull Run battle, desires to enter West Point Academy. His name is John Thornton Brodhead, and by both parents he comes of good military stock, his mother, formerly Miss Macomb, being the niece of the former General-in-chief of the Army. I took him immediately after his father's death, and have kept him at school ever since. He is a remarkably fine youth in appearance, manners and intellect, and unknown to me had been recommended for the appointment by the Michigan delegation in Congress. My brother did not leave his family in easy circumstances, and if you would designate young Brodhead as one of the cadets at large, it would relieve them much, though neither they nor I would press the request, if it should cause you the slightest embarrassment." ALS, DNA, RG 94, Correspondence, USMA. On April 6, 1872, USG nominated John T. Brodhead as 2nd lt., U.S. Marine Corps.

To Frederick Dent Grant

Washington, D. C. May 21st *18~~6~~7*1

Dear Fred:

In the Vicksburg campaign I crossed the Mississippi river with less than 41.000 men. Johnston had 58.000 of whom 50.000 were directly under the command of Pemberton, and occupied Hayne's Bluff, Vicksburg, Grand Gulf and the R. R. Bridge across the Big Black, East of Vicksburg. ~~In no engagement~~ About 8.000 men were with Johnston at Jackson, Miss. In no engagement in the rear of Vicksburg, or after crossing the Miss. river, had I near all my troops in any one battle. At Port Gibson none of Sherman's command was present: indeed had not more than left Youngs Point when that battle was fought. At Raymond only ~~as~~a portion, two divisions I believe, of McPherson's Corps were engage or even very near. At Jackson none of McClernand's Corps was present, or nearer than Raymond, and Blair's Div. of Sherman's Corps had not yet joined the Army East of the Miss. At Champion Hill, and the Big Black Sherman was absent with two Divisions of his Corps seeking a crossing of the river (the Big Black) some miles above.—As soon as Vicksburg was invested I brought 21.000 more men of my own command into the intrenchments, and was re-inforced by Halleck until the troops there numbered about 75.000 men. Of this number, after we were well intrenched, Sherman had 40.000 given to him to occupy a line running from Hayne's Bluff to the Big Black on to form a line of countervalation. This left about 35.000 men in the line of investment. My lossess were slight, numbering probably less than 1800 men, from all causes, in all the engagement before the assault on Vicksburg, exclusive of losses at Champion Hill. There I think our lossess, from killed and wounded, numbered about 3.000.—We captured from the enemy, and sent North in the Campaign, in round numbers 6.000 men. Johnston was driven North from Jackson with his 8.000 men. At Champion Hill Loring's Division was cut off from its retreat into Vicksburg, and I think the enemy lost in killed and wounded, in all the engagements, about as many men as we did. The number of men surrendered at Vicksburg was 31.600.

I started from Culpepper with 123.000 men. Lee had about 85.000 men including Longstreets Corps. Longstreet was some twenty miles away from where I crossed the Rapidann but got up quite as soon as as the most distant of my troops did.[1] Considering that I was in the enemy's country, and had an immense train to guard, the number of men that each could bring into action was about the same. For further particulars you must consult history.

Yours affectionately
U. S. GRANT

ALS, USG 3.

On May 16, 1871, Dennis H. Mahan, West Point, had written to Frederick T. Dent. "Will you be kind enough to put the accompanying note in the Presidents' hands. It contains no request, and nothing that will give him any trouble but the reading of it Please say to Mrs Grant that Fred is doing very nicely with me." ALS, ICarbS.

1. See *PUSG*, 10, 233–39, 273–76, 388–89, 397–401; *Memoirs*, II, 129–45.

To Joshua S. Valentine, Henry DuPont, and Samuel M. Harrington

WASHINGTON, D. C., May 24, 1871.

J. S. Valentine,[1] *H. DuPont,*[2] *S. M. Harrington:*[3]

GENTLEMEN: Your letter of the 20th instant, inviting me to be present on the occasion of the unveiling of the Soldiers' and Sailors' Monument by the Soldiers' and Sailors' Association of Delaware, on the 30th instant, is received. I regret that I cannot be present with you on that interesting occasion, as I should like to be, because of similar ceremonies in commemoration of the same patriotic services by our departed soldiers and sailors taking place here on that day. I do not feel that it would be proper for me to leave at such a time. The 30th of May is set apart as Decoration Day, and I expect to attend the ceremony of that day over the graves of the departed who have found their last earthly resting-place at Arlington, Va.

I have the honor to be, very respectfully, your obedient servant,

U. S. GRANT.

New York Times, June 3, 1871. On May 30, 1871, USG, Secretary of War William W. Belknap, and Secretary of the Navy George M. Robeson attended the ceremonies at Arlington National Cemetery sponsored by the Grand Army of the Republic. *Ibid.*, May 31, 1871. On May 18, Robeson had written to USG. "The Grand Army of the Republic, Department of the Potomac, has applied to me to order the attendance of the Marine Band during the ceremonies attending the decoration of soldiers' graves on the 30th inst. I have the honor to refer their request to you for such order as you may desire to give." Copy, DNA, RG 45, Letters Sent to the President. See John W. Blassingame and John R. McKivigan *et al.*, eds., *The Frederick Douglass Papers. Series One: Speeches, Debates, and Interviews Volume 4: 1864–80* (New Haven, 1979), pp. 289–92.

1. Joshua S. Valentine, born in 1811 in East Marlboro, Pa., moved to Wilmington, Del. (1838), and worked as a clerk, school principal, and railroad agent. Elected as a Whig to the Del. legislature (1853), he subsequently held many local offices in Wilmington as a Republican. He served as capt., Co. K., 4th Del. (1862–65), and was elected mayor of Wilmington (1866).

2. Born in 1812 in Wilmington, Del., Henry DuPont, USMA 1833, resigned (1834) as bvt. 2nd lt., 4th Art., to join his family's gunpowder manufacturing business. Appointed maj. gen. of Del. troops (1861), he supported the federal government and Republican party.

3. The eldest son of prominent jurist Samuel Maxwell Harrington, Samuel M. Harrington was born in 1840 in Dover, Del., graduated from Delaware College (1857), and practiced law. An active Republican, he served as Del. AG (1862) and secretary of state (1863–65).

To Charles W. Ford

Washington D. C. May 28th *18*71

DEAR FORD:

I have no objection to your entering any of my stock you choose at the Fair next Fall. My Alderney bull and three of the heiffers are as pure blood as there is in the country. The same is true of the Holstein cattle. The three year old colt too is worth shewing. What did you do with the buffalo calves?[1] It is too bad if you put them off on Benton.[2] He can however invite some friends to his farm and have a buffalo chase when they get a little larger, and get rid of them in that way. That is about what I shall do with them the first time I go to the farm if they are at my place.

I received a letter from Shepley[3] a few weeks ago which I intended to answer immediately by am not sure whether I did. suppose you ask him and if I did not say to him that in the matter of the compromise which he spoke of I will leave it entirely to his judgement. If he thinks our chances are enhanced by compromising for the lands which are defended by pleading the "statute of limitation" tell him to do so. His judgement in this matter is much better than mine and I will be guided by it.

Yours Truly
U. S. GRANT

ALS, DLC-USG. See letter to Charles W. Ford, Sept. 24, 1871.

1. On [*April 13*], 1871, USG telegraphed to Col. John E. Smith, 14th Inf., Fort Laramie. "Send the cattle to C. W. Ford U. S. Express office St. Louis Mo." Telegram sent, DNA, RG 107, Telegrams Collected (Bound). On April 17, Porter wrote to Smith. "The President received your letter of the 27th ult. and telegraphed you to send the buffalo calves to C. W. Ford at St. Louis. He wishes me to send you many thanks for your kindness" LS, Smith Papers, Trinity College, Hartford, Conn.

2. William H. Benton.

3. John R. Shepley, born in 1817 in Saco, Maine, graduated from Bowdoin College (1837) and Harvard Law School (1839). He practiced law in St. Louis and earned distinction from cases involving land titles. See letter to William S. Hillyer, [*Jan. 1873*]; *St. Louis Globe-Dispatch*, Oct. 12, 1884.

Calendar

1870, Nov. 1. Alfred Voisin, Cayenne, French Guyana, to USG. "Excuse an humble planter of Guyana for addressing to you the present letter and disturbing you in your high occupations. French Guyana, Your Excellency, suffers much from the disastrous war now going on between France, its mother country, and the Kingdom of Prussia, and the inhabitants of the poor colony expect nothing good for themselves. Guyana, a country which is essentially rich, but still unknown on account of its vast extent, would not like to become Prussian; and we are here persuaded that Prussia, which does not possess a foot of ground outside of Europe, covets this beautiful country, and that she will require of France, if conquered, the cession of our vast territory. Your Excellency, if we cannot remain Frenchmen, our most ardent desire is to become Americans; that is the nation for which we have the most sympathy, and into whose arms we desire to throw ourselves; our interests, the situation of the two countries, which are on the same continent, tell plainly enough that we neither can nor will have other protectors than the great American nation. The object of this letter, ~~y~~Your Excellency, is, in case of disaster to France, to know whether we can solicit from your high benevolence the powerful protection of your flag, which will secure us against the ambition of Prussia, which we all abhor here. In case of acceptance, an address signed by the whole population of Guyana will be sent. Once more, Your Excellency, if we cannot remain Frenchmen, we wish to become Americans, and we greatly desire to see our wishes realized."—ALS (in French), DNA, RG 59, Miscellaneous Letters; translation, *ibid.*

1870, Nov. 1. "Petitioners, of Cape, Palmas," Liberia, to USG. "your humble petitioners of the undersgned douth humble pray That your Excelency Will Take In consideration your humble petitioners Case as it is lade before, you at this time, Our Condisions are these We Emigrated Out in the year of 1866 and 1867, by the exspence of the Colonization Socity and after we where out here for a Short time We find Ourselves not Safe, and nor are we Satefide Whith Our Condisions. we have no Meain or no Money, by Witch We Can help ourselves. after trying for ~~fore~~ fore years, to Select apland by Witch we Might be able to Make our excape from this land, to the land that give us Birth, we cam to the Conclusion to Write to your Excelency, as the President of the United States, because we are the People of the united States, Any ade that We Would receved from your Excelency toward getting back hom it will be thankfully Receved by your humble petitioners. We pray your Excelency, please to answer this as Soon as possible, please your Excelency think of Us all, and remember all the Emigrants here at Cape, Palmas, Liberia. please your Excelency if your Hon. see fit to Write Dirict to Mr James Gadsden)"—AD, DNA, RG 59, Miscellaneous Letters.

1870, Nov. 2. Secretary of the Interior Columbus Delano to USG.—LS (press—largely illegible), Illinois Historical Survey, University of Illinois, Urbana, Ill.

1870, Nov. 5. USG endorsement. "Respectfully refered to the Sec. of State."—AES, DNA, RG 59, Letters of Application and Recommendation. Written on a letter of Oct. 24 from E. D. Webster and Silas B. Dutcher, Brooklyn, to USG. "We cheerfully recommend Mr Christopher C. Wust for the position of Consul at Rotterdam, knowing him to be eminently well qualified for the position and satisfied that his appointment would be gratefully received by the Dutch and German residents of Kings County and would be highly beneficial to the Republican party in this County and in the State at this particular juncture"—LS, *ibid.* No appointment followed.

1870, Nov. 5. John Kayrahoo and four others, Quindaro, Kan., to USG. "We have been informed that two thousand dollars was appropriated by congress in the Indian appropriation bill, approved July 15, 1870, to be expended under the direction of the President. As all these tribes except the Wyandottes have been settled upon their respective reserves for the last two years, and most if not all of them, have received annuities or other moneys from the Government within the year, we respectfully ask that at least one half of the sum appropriated as above stated be used or expended for the benefit of the poor and destitute Wyandottes, a considerable number of whom will go to their new home within the next two weeks and will greatly need the relief we ask for them. We also respectfully ask that you direct the Agent to extend the relief asked for to such persons as shall be indicated by the Wyandotte council, as these charities are too often thrown away upon undeserving objects. As the present Chief and councillors all served in the armies of the United States during the late war for the Union, we respectfully ask that you will order a flag of the United States to be presented to us to be suspended over our council House on occasions of special public interest."—D (signed by mark), DNA, RG 75, Letters Received, Wyandot Agency.

[1870, Nov. 6]. To U.S. Senator Roscoe Conkling of N. Y. "one. I will drop Garfield a line myself, but I shall not be able to say more than that I think this would be well received by all parties."—ALS (fragment—date in another hand), DLC-Roscoe Conkling.

1870, Nov. 8. James F. Casey, collector of customs, New Orleans, to USG. "J R Beckwith a citizen will be strongly recommended for District Attorney he is a good lawyer perfectly honest conversant with the business of the Office good republican and worthy of the appointment"—Telegram received (at 5:30 P.M.), DNA, RG 60, Records Relating to Appointments. On Dec. 7, USG nominated James R. Beckwith as U.S. attorney, La. Papers recommending Beckwith's dismissal are *ibid.* On March 22, 1872, T. Morris Chester, Harrisburg, Pa., wrote to USG. "Enclosed are the papers to which I referred on the occasion of my presentation to Your Excellency, with reference to Mr. Beckwith, the U. S. District Attorney, at New Orleans. Mr. B. is the counsel for the Board of Metropolitan Police at a salary of $4000 per year, and Administrator of the Charity Hospital under Gov. Warmouth, which will explain his indisposition to do us justice. Robert H. Shannon, the U. S. Commissioner, named in the enclosed papers is the gentleman whom I recommended as a suitable person, should a vacancy occur."—ALS, *ibid.*

1870, Nov. 8. Anthony Higgins, U.S. attorney, Wilmington, Del., to USG. "Colored voters have been driven from the polls at Odessa and Smyrna by Clubs bludgeons and revolvers the democrats have taken possession of the polls, Will you please order, a company of marines from Navy Yard at Philadelphia to report by special train to J M. Dunn United States Marshall at Wilmington Del, to proceed to above places,"—Telegram received, DNA, RG 60, Letters Received, Del. On the same day, Attorney Gen. Amos T. Akerman telegraphed to Higgins. "Yours to the President received. It is too late to bring up the Marines before the election closes. Gather evidence of the outrages promptly."—Copy, DLC-USG, II, 5.

1870, Nov. 8. Sidney Perham, Paris, Maine, to USG. "I transmit herewith copy of a Resolution adopted at a meeting of the Board of Trustees of the U. S. General Convention of Universalists held Nov. ~~8~~2. 1870—I also beg to ask whether, if a suitable man connected with the denomination should be recommended, you will be at liberty to appoint him—The General Convention through its Board of Trustees has charge of the general missionary work of the denomination—We would also be glad to be informed as to the duties and compensation of the Indian Agents—The desire of some of the leading men in the denomination to co-operate with you in your policy in regard to the Indians, has prompted this action ~~of~~ on the part of the Board—"—ALS, DNA, RG 48, Appointment Div., Letters Received. The enclosure is *ibid.*

1870, Nov. 9. USG endorsement. "If Mr. Brunner can be aptd. to some other Consulate near where he now is I have no objection to its being done."—AES, DNA, RG 59, Letters of Application and Recommendation. Written on a letter of Nov. 5 from Capt. Daniel Ammen to USG. "I take the liberty of enclosing information asked by me at the State Dep't. I find that Mr Bruner after getting to Talcuhuano at about the espense of a year's pay is now without any pay as is shown by this note. Mr Bruner could not be justly rejected on any political ground, or upon a want of respectability or fitness. He served throughout the War faithfully as a Volunteer officer of the Navy and was honorably discharged in april '69.—His rejection under all the circumstances will I feel sure appeal to your active sympathy. He is actually without the means of living or of returning to the United States with a wife and four children seven thousand miles away from his friends or acquaintances and his country and is so without any fault of his own or any one connected with him."—ALS, *ibid.* The enclosure and related papers are *ibid.* On Dec. 6, 1869, USG had nominated Elias D. Bruner as consul, Talcahuano, Chile, but the Senate rejected the nomination.

On May 14, 1864, President Abraham Lincoln had endorsed papers recommending Capt. Edmund Johnson. "If the Secretary of State can find a consulate for Capt Edmund Johnson, bearer of this, which he will accept, I shall be glad to give it to him."—AES, *ibid.* On March 14, 1870, U.S. Representative Nathaniel P. Banks of Mass. wrote to USG. "Permit me to ask the privilege of an interview with you for Mrs. E. Johnson, the wife of Captain Johnson, who was an honorable officer of the army, and is now suffering from the wounds he received in the service. I have great sympathy for Captain Johnson, and his family, and hope that you may be able to comply with the request they have to make, believing them to be worthy of the favor of the Government."—LS, *ibid.* On April 12, USG nominated Johnson as consul, Ghent, withdrew the nomination, and, on July 14, appointed him consul, Talcahuano. On Dec. 21, USG nominated Bruner to replace Johnson, who had resigned because of poor health. On May 23, 1871, Mrs. D. H. Johnson, Louisa County, Va., wrote to Julia Dent Grant asking a consular appointment in Europe for her husband.—ALS, *ibid.* On May 14, 1872, Banks and U.S. Senator Henry Wilson of Mass. wrote to USG. "This morning we had the honor to leave with you a letter of Senator Pool and Mrs. Johnson relating to the appointment of Captain Johnson to the consulate at Tampico. Mr. Pool, to whom this appointment had been promised, signified his willingness to defer his request if he could have the assurance that his friend might be appointed to the consulate at Scio, which would give him an opportunity to remain in this country until after the coming election. The other letter will show the distress which weighs upon the family of Captain Johnson, who has been deprived by wounds received in the service of the means to support his family. He was of the command of General Banks, who knows him to be a most deserving man. This situation, it is believed, will restore him to health. He is master of the Spanish language, and well qualified, we believe, for this post; and we earnestly hope you will give his application early and favorable consideration."—LS, *ibid.* On June 3, USG nominated Johnson as consul, Tampico, Mexico.

1870, Nov. 10. Adam Badeau, London, to USG. "I beg to introduce to you the Hon R. B. Dennis who has recently been inspecting by your direction and that of the Secretary of the Treasury, the Consulates in Great Britain. He has done this very thoroughly and efficiently, and has derived some views in regard to the Consular system in this Kingdom, which seem to me very important. If you could spare time for a little conversation with Mr Dennis, I am sure you would be greatly interested in what he can tell you, and you could judge of the value of the suggestions he has to make, and which he thinks will result in a very large increase of the internal revenue"—ALS (press), NjR. On the same day, Badeau wrote on the same subject to Secretary of the Treasury George S. Boutwell, to J. C. Bancroft Davis, asst. secretary of state, and to Horace Porter.—ALS (press), *ibid.* See *PUSG*, 20, 215.

1870, Nov. 11. George B. Upton, Boston, to USG. "I respectfully represent that I have a large claim for losses of property upon the Ocean during the late rebellion, and known as the 'Alabama Claims'. According to my view of this matter, my losses grow out of a National breach of faith upon the part of the Government of Great Britain, by permitting their subjects to fit out armed vessels to prey upon our Commerce, under the shadow of a Flag which they had set up for that purpose. With these views, I respectfully submit, that these claims are not to be arbitrated or mixed up with ordinary claims for losses as between citizens of the several Countries;—and as the Government of Great Britain has failed to make proper reparation for them and for the stain inflicted upon the Honor of this Country by these acts, and as it is now nearly eight years since my losses were incurred,—I respectfully ask of you to bring the subject before Congress, and if there are reasons of State why the payment should not now be demanded of the Goverment which permitted the outrage, that I may be allowed to have my claim audited before the Court of Claims, and if approved by said Court, that thereupon upon the assignment of it to the Treasury Department of the United States,—Bonds may be issued to me for the amount, bearing such rate of interest as may be equitable, and styled 'the Alabama Claims Bonds—and for other losses by British Cruisers,'"—ALS, DNA, RG 59, Miscellaneous Letters. A printed letter of March 23 from Upton to Lord John Russell is *ibid.*

1870, Nov. 14. William T. Bennett, Washington, D. C., to USG. "I am compelled to submit the accompanying letters relative to a suit pending against me for the past year in the U. S. Dist Court for North Carolina to your Excellency for the reason that the Acting Commissioner of Int Rev declines to recommend a discontinuance of the case. I attended trial at the June term in Raleigh where no case was made out—the Jury however failing to agree. Upon a careful examination of the records of the trial (accompanying this) Senators Chandler, Sawyer, Abbott with Gov Austin Blair, Gov Holden & Judge Duryea recommended the dismissal of the case with result as aforsaid—The annoyance and Expense attending this case which was brought against me by the Tobacco & Whisky men of N. C. to justify their misrepresentations through I. T. Deweese and through which I was unjustly removed by Mr Delano, as Supervisor, have been of incalculable injury to me and my family, and I earnestly trust, for the sake of justice I may not again be subjected to a trial in a District notorious for its rebel sympathies and especially for its antagonism to Northern men and ~~r~~Revenue officers. There is scarcely a man in the District whose antipathy to me has not arisen through siezures of illicit Tobacco and Whiskey and I trust my reports to the Department—Showing the gross violations of law at the time I held office, may be investigated—Not one of them were permitted to be read at the trial."—ALS, DNA, RG 60, Letters from the President.

1870, Nov. 17. Edward S. Wheeler, Washington, D. C., to USG. "Your avowed and established Policy of honesty, humanity and peace, in relation to Indian affairs, instead of robbery and 'Extermination', removes a public disgrace; and while creditable to you as the Executive of a great Nation confers an eternal honor upon you personally since it manifests a love of the immortal principles of Justice. The dreadful circumstances of rebellion and war made necessary your military career which has placed you upon the page of history as an honorable, successful and magnanamous Soldier. Your administration will give you the fame of the Statesman; while your defence of the Indian, as well as others liable to spoliation and wrong wins for you the transcendent and happy reputation of a just majistrate a noble humanitarian and wise philanthropist. . . . John Y. Mason, Esqr of Conn., a noble English emigrant, secured through the British Parliment the return of certain lands to the Mohegans; thus was formed the first Reservation. They were my playmates upon their own domain. In common with very many others of my own way of thinking, as a Spiritualist I have deplored the course pursued toward the Indian which no Administration seemed able to restrain. With painful feelings as citizens and well-wishers to mankind we have watched *all* that has been done well aware that to act for practical good we must encountre the hostility of a sett of thieves, to whom murder was pastime when they were balked in their purpose. We knew the Indian was considered *game* to be hunted for his value, and his friends as so many interlopers to be made unlucky in life, and harmless even in death. Aware of the power and desperation of this banditti and the impotence of the Department we felt hopeless of good to the wards of the Nation. It seemed absurd to us to begin Theological teaching among those who had every reason to believe the ethics of the White man inferior to their own sense of right. We had no confidence in miraculous agencies which would 'convert' a hungry murderous savage who knew he had been imposed upon into a Christian gentleman before we had acquired his confidence in our disposition to treat him at least as well as he treated us. Neither did we see much chance for secular education until a way could be opened by slow degrees to attach the population to the soil; believing that to show the tribes the practical advantages of civilized life was the surest way of leading them into its comforts and making education *possible.* We could see no way but to break up the 'Indian Ring,' educate the people and reform the Government. A Stupenduous task, but knowing we were right, we began the work. We were told even by the Spirits of those immortal men to whose patriotic wisdom and large humanity our Nation owes its existence and character that the way would open and there would be a man raised up—a man with a heart of human flesh, but a will of iron. Then we could work and not see our improvements destroyed; our efforts wasted because there would be a stable mind a just comprehension, a settled purpose in command. This was more than twelve years ago. We see that man in our President. All this time we have not rested—we have been a growing people. But twenty two years ago unknown, we now number by millions, among all classes of citizens, in all manner of positions. We have a National and several state, as well as hundreds of local Societies; one in this city. We have an extensive literature, and publish a dozen or more well conducted papers; and magazines in this country as well as abroad. They are located in Boston, New York, Cleveland.

O. Chicago. Ill. and one in Washington printed in German. We have over three hundred active Speakers and thousands of media. All these means of influence we have had at work. The Indian has become one of the articles of our creed; justice to him a principle of our Religion. On the floor of the Senate, no less than before the people, Spiritualists have made themselves heard on this question. Spiritualism has increased in the United States as in no other country. We believe this due no more to our mental freedom under the never to be amended impartiality of the Constitution in matters of Religion or *no Religion* than to the presence and influence of Indian Spirits among us. We know them as our friends, and believe they are our immediate helpers in sickness and many affairs of life. Some of our Media have been among the Indians, and although made captives were set at liberty out of regard for their characters as inspired persons. In our Conventions we have discussed this matter, and I will by permission leave with Commissioner Parker documentary evidence of our action. True we have done nothing but talk write and agitate, but we could see no chance for anything else, and so labored to develop a public sentiment which would support a policy of justice if a great and good Statesman inaugurated it, or *demand* it in due time if it were forgotten. In making your Indian Policy known as a *fixed purpose* you have given us the assurance we have hoped and waited for—you have enlisted us anew upon the issue. But we are not satisfied. We would avail ourselves of the same opportunity which has been given others. We are aware you have no Sectarian bias in the matter, only anxious to secure the honest and faithful carrying out of such regulations and provisions as the Government and people have been, and are ready to make. It was wise to place the business of the Indian Agencies in the hands of those who had shown themselves interested in their welfare by establishing their missions among them. Thus you have secured the co-operation of different denominations and made even Sectarian rivalry and ambition a power for good. . . . It is my opinion, and that of some others, that if Spiritualists could be assured that there was an opening for us to establish ourselves where circumstances were at all favorable, under the same endorsement aid and encouragement given those who have missions already among the Indians we could soon so focalize and concentrate the feeling of the people that we could not only have proper persons selected for the duties imposed upon them as agents of the Government, but could also add to the provision made by the Dep't. considerable sums of money to be expended for their benefit. . . ."—ALS, DNA, RG 48, Appointment Div., Letters Received.

1870, Nov. 20. Orville E. Babcock to John G. Foster, Boston. "I received your note this morning. I spoke to the President about the matter and he says he has heard no mention made of leaving Gordon out and that he should suppose he would be just the one to retain, so I guess it is all right."—ALS, Foster Papers, New Hampshire Historical Society, Concord, N. H. George H. Gordon continued as collector of Internal Revenue, 7th District, Mass. See *PUSG*, 16, 226.

1870, Nov. 21. E. Philip Jacobson, U.S. attorney, Vicksburg, to USG. "Captain M. Shaughenessy, a gentleman residing at Columbus, Miss., is an applicant for a position under the government. He is entitled by reason of faithful service in the late war, excellent moral character, good ability and sound political principles to your especial consideration, and I would most respectfully recommend him to you."—ALS, DNA, RG 94, Applications for Positions in War Dept. Letters recommending Michael Shaughnessy as paymaster are *ibid.* On Dec. 14, USG nominated Shaughnessy as marshal, Southern District, Miss. On June 23, 1874, USG nominated him as collector of Internal Revenue, 2nd District, Miss.; on Dec. 10, as collector, 1st District.

1870, Nov. 25. To G. Washington Warren, president, Bunker Hill Monument Association. "I have the honor to acknowledge the receipt of the copy of the proceedings of the Monumental Association at the annual meeting in June last which you were kind enough to send me, and return to you my thanks for the kind remembrance."—Copy, DLC-USG, II, 1. On March 4, Warren, Charlestown, Mass., had written to USG. "The Bunker Hill Monument Association having at its last annual meeting made you an Honorary Member, I have the honor to forward to you a Diploma. The Association bears upon its roll the names of several of your predecessors, & of other illustrious citizens;—but, believe me, no name among them all will be more cherished than your own."—ALS, USG 3.

1870, Nov. 26. Charles C. Fulton, *Baltimore American,* to USG. "*I* take great pleasure in recommending to you for retention in the *Revenue Service,* in case of any consolidation in the Baltimore Districts, '*Samuel M. Evans, Esqr,* at present *Collector* of the *Second District. In* so doing I confidently beleive that *I* express the wish of *nine-tenths* of the tax payers, and business men of Baltimore, irrespective of *Party,* as well, as of the great mass of the *Republicans,* of the City and State. *Mr Evans* character as an efficiant, energetic and capable Officer I understand ranks *No 1,* with the Department, and his courteous treatment of tax payers, has been a marked feature of his administration of the Office. *Laws* that are unpopular should not be made more objectional, by an offensive manner of enforcing them, hence the general desire for the retention of *Mr Evans. As* Chairman, of the *State Centrail Committee* in a *State* like *Maryland, Mr Evans,* has political claims that are certainly superior to those of any other applicant."—LS, Maryland Historical Society, Baltimore, Md. Related papers are *ibid.* Samuel M. Evans, nominated by USG on April 12, 1869, as collector of Internal Revenue, 2nd District, Md., continued in office.

1870, Nov. 28. Jessee Roberts, Anna, Ill., to USG. "In July 1863, while you were in command of the U S. forces around Vicksburg Miss, you called for volunteers from the command to go upon transports and pass the Rebel Batteries at that place. Among those who responded to your call were Wm. T. Roberts, (my son) and myself; I was commanding a company in the 31st

Ill. Regt. These men who volunteered in that dangerous adventure were to be paid from Eight to twelve hundred Dollars. They were all paid off except my son who died in the Army and my self, we never received anything for our dangers and truble. I have written to Mr E, B, French, 2nd Auditor and he tells me that there is no Authority by which a claim of this nature can be paid. You are fully acquainted with the nature of the claim, as you ordered them paid. Please to give me information."—ALS, DNA, RG 56, Letters Received. On Feb. 2, 1871, William Elstun, DuQuoin, Ill., wrote to U.S. Representative John A. Logan. "There are some soldiers here who run the blockade at Vicksburg, and claim that Genl Grant made an order that the couton used on the boats for breastworks: Should be Sold: and the proceeds divided among the volunteer crus, And one of them says he drew $700. as his part. Was there any such order or arangment. And if so can the money be drawn now? And if so how? and where?"—ALS, *ibid.*, RG 94, Letters Received, 463 1871. On Feb. 16, Secretary of War William W. Belknap wrote to Logan. "... nothing is known by this Dept concerning any arrangement by which the cotton used as breastworks on the vessels that ran past Vicksburg during the late war was to be sold and the proceeds divided amongst the volunteer crews of the vessels—"—Copy, *ibid.* Related papers are *ibid.*

1870, Nov. 30. John F. Simpson, Benton, Maine, to USG. "My object in bringing before you, The following Subject, Is that I understand, you, are about to appoint a New Minister to the Court of Saint James 'England' As soon as Congress meets, It appears to me, by the reports of Newpapers, both in England and the United States That both Governments are anxious, to have all National Questions that are now pending, Settled in an Honorable and Amicable manner, The perplexing Question of the Alabama Claims in particular My proposed Condition and mode of Settling the above Claims are as follows Viz That the United State, And Her Britanic majesty's Governments, make a new Boundary Line, between Her Majestys North American possessions and the United States,... I do sincerely believe that the British government feels in honor, duty bound to pay the above Claims, And I think it the most ~~the~~ Concilitory manner, and lest Self Sacrifying to the feeling of the Crown of any way, at the present time, And State of public feeling, both in England an in the United states. Sir if I have trespassed on your prescious time at this busy season, you will please to pardon ..."—ALS, DNA, RG 59, Miscellaneous Letters. An undated letter from Simpson on the same subject is *ibid.*

1870, Nov. 30. J. F. Whipple, New York City, to USG. "Refering to the conversation I had the honor of having with you & the rifle I I showed you on the 23d inst; I beg to submit the following, relative to the ordnance board lately convened at St Louis. Mo. That board was directed to report 'in order of relative merit' on the six best rifles offered. Herewith please find report of that board. My object in writing is to call your attention to the marked injustice done the Ward-Burton Rifle and also to see if you will have, simple honest justice done in this matter. The records *plainly show* it to have performed the best of the six selected To more fully show the injustice let me call your attention to the comparative records of No 1 *Remingtons* and No 6 *Ward-Burton* . . ."—ALS, DNA, RG 156, Letters Received. Related papers are *ibid.*

1870, Nov. James R. Ludlow *et al.* to USG. "The undersigned Memorialists appointed for the purpose by the *San Francisco Baptist Association of California,* and representing that body as convened at Sacramento Cal on the 11th Inst. As citizens of the Great Republic, and as christians we earnestly desire to cooperate with the general Government for the elevation of the *Indians of this State.* At our late meeting in Saco this subject came before us in connexion with the 'Report on Missions.' An entire evening was devoted to its consideration. Delegates from all portions of the State spoke earnestly on behalf of the remnants of once powerful tribes now rendered homeless & hopeless wanderers through the encroachments of the white races squatting upon their lands—robbing them of their Stock—burning their rude homes—and crowding them into the inhospitable mountain regions of the State We do not complain of the government—. It has done much to mitigate the evils of their condition. We are more disposed to blame ourselves for past apathy in not assisting the government to provide for their instruction and moral culture, by assisting you with good and faithful teachers and Missionaries of the Gospel of the Prince of Peace. We are appointed by your fellow citizens whom we have the honor to represent to give to the subject of the moral condition and wants of the Indians our special and minute attention during the coming year; to visit if necessary the Reservations; to recommend what may best be done for their religious culture; & particularly to urge upon the *Executive of the United States* the great importance of establishing permanent schools for the instruction of the young in all the Indian Reservations of California. . . ."—DS (4 signatures—docketed as received on Nov. 26), DNA, RG 75, Letters Received, Calif. Superintendency.

1870, [Nov.]. Standing Hawk and 45 others to USG, Secretary of the Interior Jacob D. Cox, and Ely S. Parker, commissioner of Indian Affairs. "We, the undersigned Chiefs, members of Police, and head men of the Omaha tribe of Indians, respectfully represent, That having been for a long time past encouraged by the Government to have our lands allotted to us in Severalty, agreeably to the terms prescribed in the fourth article of the treaty of March 6th 1865 and to adopt the pursuits of agriculture and the habits of civilized life, and whereas, the said lands have now been so allotted to us, and we are desirous to proceed promptly with the building of houses for our people, and the breaking up and fencing of our lands, as well as for the purchase of teams, agricultural implements, seeds &c, and for the support of schools amongst us, but have not the necessary funds at our disposal for these purposes, and whereas only a little more than 50.000 of the 205.000 acres of our lands have been required to allot to us a sufficiency of land for our easy support, we are therefore united in the respectful request that the most western portion of our Reservation amounting to as near 50.000 acres as can be separated from the remaining portion of our lands by a line running along the Section lines from North to South, may be offered for sale, at as early a day as practicable, and that the said sale may take place under the direction of the President of the United States, and 'under such laws rules and regulations as may hereafter be prescribed' by him: agreeably to the provisions of the 6th article of the treaty of March 16th: 1854, believing that the said sale may thereby be effected at an earlier day than if delayed for the action of Congress, and we also respectfully request that the Chiefs of our tribe, or so many of them as may be required for the occasion; together with our Agent, may be invited to proceed to Washington for the purpose of conferring with the constituted authorities of the Government in relation to the aforesaid procedure."—D (signed by mark), DNA, RG 75, Letters Received, Omaha Agency. On Nov. 8, Samuel M. Janney, superintendent of Indian Affairs, Omaha, wrote to Parker enclosing this petition.—ALS, *ibid.* See *HED*, 41-3-1, part 4, pp. 714–16; Clyde A. Milner II, *With Good Intentions: Quaker Work among the Pawnees, Otos, and Omahas in the 1870s* (Lincoln, 1982), pp. 160–63.

1870, DEC. 1. Mayor John F. Torrence of Cincinnati to USG. "The bearer of this, Gen. Peter J. Sullivan of this city, was a staunch and active Union man during our civil troubles, and was mainly instrumental in raising four regiments for the field. His health having become precarious, he is desirous of being appointed to some position of trust under the Government, a foreign mission, or something of the kind. The General is an old and respectable Lawyer, and deserve well of your Administration."—LS, DNA, RG 59, Letters of Application and Recommendation."—Related papers are *ibid.* No appointment followed for Peter J. Sullivan, minister to Colombia, 1867–69. See *PUSG*, 9, 597–98.

1870, DEC. 3. Daniel E. Marvin, Fredericksburg, Va., to USG. "I write to as you to help me to the appointment of superintendent of the National Cemetry at Fredericksburg Virginia by doing so you will help a disabled Solder to a lucrative employment. I was a member of Co D 3rd Regt. N. J. Vols, & since I was discharged have received a Pension of four Dollars a month so it is difficult for me to obtain a living not being able to do heavy work on account of the wound I received"—ALS, DNA, RG 94, ACP, M306 CB 1870.

1870, DEC. 5. To William Hiss, Baltimore. "I have the honor to acknowledge the receipt of your very cordial invitation to attend the Jubilee to be given by the Sabbath School children on the evening of the 8th inst. I regret that my public duties will not permit my acceptance."—Typescript of framed original in Omaha Public Library, USGA. See *Baltimore Sun*, Dec. 7–9, 1870.

1870, DEC. 5. To Alfred Pleasonton, Duncan A. Pell, and George H. Hopper, New York City. "I am in receipt of your letter requesting permission to use my name as manager of the fair of the Union Home and School for Soldier's and Sailor's orphans. It will afford me great pleasure to be associated with an enterprize which has in view such a worthy object. The liberality of the people of New York in their care of the sufferers from the late war is proverbial and I shall be most happy to contribute in any manner to the noble cause in which they are laboring."—Copy, DLC-USG, II, 1. See *New York Tribune*, Dec. 14–16, 20, 23, 27, 1870; J. F. Richmond, *New York and Its Institutions, 1609–1872* (New York, 1872), pp. 449–51.

1870, DEC. 6. To Congress. "I herewith transmit to Congress a report, dated the 5th instant, with the accompanying papers, received from the Secretary of State, in compliance with the requirements of the 18th section of the Act entitled 'An Act to regulate the diplomatic and consular systems of the United States', approved August 18. 1856."—DS, DNA, RG 46, Presidential Messages. *HED*, 41-3-10. On Dec. 5, Secretary of State Hamilton Fish had written to USG transmitting records of fees collected by U.S. consular officials.—DS, DNA, RG 46, Presidential Messages.

1870, DEC. 6. To Congress. "In pursuance of the provisions of the second section of the Act approved June 20th 1864, entitled 'An Act making appropriations for the Consular and Diplomatic expenses of the Government for the year ending thirtieth June 1865, and for other purposes',—I inform Congress that Louis W. Viollier, a Consular Clerk, was, on the 26th day of September last, removed from office for the following cause, namely: for disobedience of orders, and continued absence from duty after orders to proceed to his post."—DS, DNA, RG 46, Annual Messages. Related papers are *ibid.*, RG 59, Letters of Application and Recommendation.

1870, DEC. 7. Griffin Terry, Roanoke Island, N. C., to USG advocating improved navigation of Albemarle Sound.—ALS, DNA, RG 77, Explorations and Surveys, Letters Received.

1870, DEC. 8. To Senate. "In answer to a Resolution of the 5th instant, I transmit to the Senate a report from the Secretary of State."—LS, DNA, RG 46, Presidential Messages. *SED*, 41-3-3. On the same day, Secretary of State Hamilton Fish had written to USG. "The Secretary of State, to whom was referred the Resolution of the Senate of the 5th instant requesting the President, if not incompatible with the public interest, to communicate to the Senate all the correspondence between the Minister of the United States at Paris, and the Secretary of State, from the breaking out of the war between France and Prussia, so far as the same relates to political subjects and to matters connected with the said war, as [we]ll as to the question of the protection of the subjects of the North German Confederation in France with which the Legation of the United States at Paris has been charged, has the honor to report that all the correspondence called for by the said Resolution was communicated, with other Diplomatic correspondence accompanying the President's annual Message, to the Senate and House of Representatives on the 5th instant."—LS, DNA, RG 46, Presidential Messages.

1870, DEC. 8. To House of Representatives. "In answer to their resolution of 1st of July 1870, I transmit to the House of Representatives a report from the Secretary of State."—Copies, DNA, RG 59, General Records; *ibid.*, RG 130, Messages to Congress. *HED*, 41-3-36. On Dec. 8, Secretary of State Hamilton Fish had written to USG. "The Secretary of State, to whom was referred the Resolution of the House of Representatives of the 1st of July 1870, relating to the arrest and detention of American Fishing vessels in the Straits of Canso by armed vessels flying the British flag, has the honor to report that all the correspondence on the subject referred to by said resolution was communicated to Congress with the President's Message of the 5th instant."—Copy, DNA, RG 59, General Records.

1870, DEC. 8. William Mattox, Florence, Mo., to USG. "I will inform you that I have invented a new motive power, a 'Magnetic Engine' which will supersede Steam on Railways, and in the 'Navy' &Co—I have a model mover in my possesion which will convince any one that it is practical beyond cavil or dispute."—ALS, DNA, RG 45, Subject File, Div. EM.

1870, DEC. 10. Governor Joshua L. Chamberlain of Maine to USG. "Lt. Col. E. B. Knox, late of the 44th Regt. New York Vols, and now 1st Lieut in the Regular Army, was recently retired on a lower grade than he and his surgeons think right. He was commanding his Regiment when he received the wound from which he suffers most disability. I knew him well in the service, & can testify to his high character as a man & his remarkable merit as an officer. I have before written the War Department in his favor; but the case appeared to be closed there & the only resort is now to the President. It would seem to me an act of well-placed favor—not to say of *justice*—if he might be allowed a further examination. Mr Knox is now in *Albany New York.* He sends me the certificate which I beg to enclose as the basis of this request."—ALS, DNA, RG 94, ACP, 61 1871. Related papers are *ibid.*

1870, DEC. 10. Josiah Slick, Washington, D. C., to USG. "I served from the beginning to the end of the late war, as an enlisted man in the 55th Pa. Vols. and as an officer in the 107th U. S. Colored Troops; was wounded three times and was promoted three times for 'gallant and meritorious services during the war.' I respectfully request the appointment of member of the Levy Court of the county of Washington D. C. now held by Mr. R. C. Belt an aged and feeble man, and is considered by every interested citizen in the portion of the county which he represents wholly incompetent to fill the position and was only appointed because no one opposed him, He is not a supporter of the present administration and his nearest relative (a nephew) was in the rebel army ('Mosbys guerillas'). I own property and reside in the county of Washington D. C. and in consideration of the facts set forth above, I earnestly request the appointment."—ALS, DNA, RG 60, Records Relating to Appointments. On July 21, 1866, USG had approved papers recommending Slick as bvt. capt.—ES, *ibid.*, RG 94, ACP, 827S CB 1866. On Feb. 20, 1873, Slick wrote to USG. "I most respectfully request the appointment as Member of the Council of the D. C. made vacant by the death of Col. D. L. Eaton. I reside and practice medicine in Tennallytown. D. C. was born and raised in Pennsylvania, have been a resident in the county of Washington. D. C. for over five years. I was recommended to you for the position as Member of the Board of public works, by Genl. *Butler*, Senator Scott. Hon. John Cessna. and other prominent men. In addition to my official duties within the last five years as clerk in the Qr. Mr. Genls. office, where I am now employed as clerk, I have studied and graduated as a Physician. I served in the Volunteer Army from July 4th 61. to Dec. 4th 66. entered the service as an enlisted man and was honorably discharged as a Captain. I desire to leave the civil service if I can do anything else to support my family until I can be warranted a sufficiant practice in medicine to live on comfortably. I am over twenty five years old and am a member of the county school board."—ALS, *ibid.*, RG 48, Appointment Div., Letters Received. No appointment followed.

1870, DEC. 10. George Thomas, Plymouth, Pa., to USG. "Having purchased a tract of Land (Containin 80 acrs) from the H. & St. J R. R. Co. for the purpose of Settling on, and Improving the Same, but on Account of the iregularity of the Coal Mines in this vacinity I Cannot Save money to make a Start on farming. So If it will Please you to lend me One Thousand Dolars $1000 on Mortgage on the above tract on Legal Interest it will be a favour to me and I will Consider myself Indebted to you to the Utmost of my ability . . ."—ALS, DNA, RG 48, Miscellaneous Div., Letters Received.

1870, DEC. 12. To Senate. "I submit to the Senate for their consideration, with a view to ratification, a Convention relating to naturalization between the United States and the Austro-Hungarian Empire, signed at Vienna, on the 20th of September, 1870, which is accompanied by the papers mentioned in the subjoined list."—DS, DNA, RG 46, Presidential Messages, Foreign Relations, Austria-Hungary. The enclosure is *ibid.*

1870, DEC. 13. To Senate. "I transmit in answer to the Resolution of the Senate of the 14th of June 1870, a report from the Secretary of State, and the papers by which it was accompanied."—DS, DNA, RG 46, Presidential Messages. *SED*, 41-3-5. On Dec. 12, Secretary of State Hamilton Fish had written to USG. "The Secretary of State to whom was referred the Resolution of the Senate of the 14th of June, 1870, requesting the President 'if in his judgment not incompatible with the public interest, to inquire into the charges made by the International Ocean Telegraph Company upon messages passing over their lines, and report to the Senate, if they are in excess of the rates allowed by the Act of Congress, approved May, 5 1866,' has the honor to lay before the President the papers mentioned in the subjoined list, which contain all the information upon the subject in the possession of this Department—"—LS, DNA, RG 46, Presidential Messages. The enclosures are *ibid.*

1870, DEC. 14. Lt. Col. Samuel B. Holabird, St. Paul, to USG. "I have the honor to petition your Excellency for the appointment of my son William Holabird to a Cadetship at large at the United States Military Academy at West Point. He is now sixteen years of age; I wish the privilege of filing hereafter, with this, application, such evidences of Character, Scholarship and fitness, as the case warrants, in order to satisfy your Excellency, that should you entertain this application favorably, your executive Confidence will not be misplaced."—LS, DNA, RG 94, Correspondence, USMA. On March 2, 1872, U.S. Senator Alexander Ramsey of Minn. wrote to USG. "Allow me to again call your attention to the nomination of Wm Holabird Son of Genl. S. B. Hobird Asst Q M Gnl. as a cadeet to West Point, of which you will recollect I had a conversation with you some two weeks since: . . ."—ALS, *ibid.* William Holabird, who entered USMA in 1873, resigned in 1875. See Carl W. Condit, *The Chicago School of Architecture: A History of Commercial and Public Building in the Chicago Area, 1875–1925* (Chicago and London, 1964), pp. 116–26.

1870, DEC. 15. To House of Representatives. "In answer to the resolution of the House of Representatives of the 9th of April 1869 I herewith transmit a report from the Secretary of State."—Copies, DNA, RG 59, General Records; *ibid.*, RG 130, Messages to Congress. *HED*, 41-3-14. On the same day, Secretary of State Hamilton Fish had written to USG. "The Secretary of State, to whom was referred the Resolution of the House of Representatives of the 9th of April 1869, requesting the President to transmit to that Body 'if not incompatible with the public interest, in addition to the correspondence already transmitted upon the condition of affairs in Paraguay, the letter of General Webb & Admiral Godon in answer to a letter of Mr Washburn, dated October 1, 1866; and also a letter of General Webb to the Secretary of State concerning his alleged interference in defense of of Admiral Godon, and any other correspondence not heretofore transmitted which may, consistently with the public interest, be communicated', has the honor to report that all the correspondence upon the subject adverted to which is believed to be required by the public interest, has already been made public"—Copy, DNA, RG 59, General Records.

1870, DEC. 15. To House of Representatives. "In answer to the resolution of the House of Representatives of the 20th January last I herewith transmit a report from the Secretary of State with accompanying documents."—Copies, DNA, RG 59, General Records; *ibid.*, RG 130, Messages to Congress.

HED, 41-3-13. On the same day, Secretary of State Hamilton Fish had written to USG. "The Secretary of State, to whom was referred the Resolution of the House of Representatives of the 20th of January 1870, requesting the President 'if compatible with the public interest, to furnish to the House all the correspondence between our late Minister to Brazil, General Webb, and the Brazilian Government, from the 26th of March to the 27th of May 1869, relating to a claim for indemnity in the case of the ship "Canada", wrecked on the coast of Brazil in 1865, and which led to a suspension of diplomatic relations by our Minister and the restoration of the same, together with a copy of our Minister's despatch to the State Department on the subject; and also copies of any correspondence between this Government and the Government of Brazil or its representatives, on the subject of said suspension of diplomatic intercourse, and copies of any letters or instructions from the Secretary of State to our present Minister at the Court at Brazil on the same subject', has the honor to report that the case of the 'Canada' has been disposed of by reference to the British Minister as arbiter. A printed summary of the case and of all of the material correspondence connected with it, together with a copy of the award of the arbiter, is herewith transmitted."—Copy, DNA, RG 59, General Records.

1870, DEC. 16. To U.S. Representative Aaron F. Stevens of N. H. "I have the honor to acknowledge the receipt of your kind invitation to attend the annual re-union of the New Hampshire Officers, on the third of Jan'y. next. It would afford me great pleasure to be present upon so interesting an occasion, if my public duties would admit of my leaving the capital at that time; but I shall be unable to do so. Please accept my thanks for the kind remembrance."—LS, Vermont Historical Society, Montpelier, Vt. The Veterans' Union met in Concord, N. H.—*Boston Transcript*, Jan. 3, 1871.

1870, DEC. 16. Orville E. Babcock to W. Crafton, Humboldt, Kan. "The President is in receipt of your letter of Dec 5th. and wishes me to say in reply that you are mistaken about his having hired horses and buggies from you while at Camp Yates in 1861. That he did not hire a horse and buggy from any stable while there."—Copy, DLC-USG, II, 1.

1870, DEC. 16. William McLain, American Colonization Society, Washington, D. C., to USG. "The 16 Dec. 1858 the Senate of the U. S. adopted a resolution requesting the President to 'Communicate, if not in his opinion, incompatible with the public interest, any information in his possession in relation to the landing of the barque Wanderer on the Coast of Georgia with a Cargo of Slaves.' The President Sent to the Senate in reply a Message dated the 11 Jan. 1859, inclosing the opinion of the Attorney General J. S. Black on the subject, in which he Says, 'I have to state that at this stage of the proceedings it would, in my opinion, be wholly incompatible with the public interest to communicate the steps which have been taken therein. The fact a vessel of that name did land a Cargo of upwards of 300 negroes from the Coast of Africa, in Geo. is well known, & there is official information of that fact. It is also true that the most effective measures have been adopted by this Government, & by the local Authorities of the U. S. in Georgia, to execute the laws which forbid Such importations, & to punish the offenders. The Correspondence of this office & of the Treasury Department with the Collector, District Attorney, Special Counsel, Marshal & other officers at Savannah, is in My possession'. We have sent to Africa two of the negroes brought into Georgia by the said Wanderer. We have lately been applied to send back a Company of about *Thirty* of them now living near Mobile, Ala We are very anxious to get a copy of the letters referred to by Mr. Black, and will take it as a great favor if you will order it for us. We suppose that at this time there cannot be any objection 'to vindicating the truth of history,' as it is found in that Correspondence—"—ALS, DNA, RG 60, Letters from the President. See *SED*, 35-2-8.

1870, DEC. 16. U.S. Senator John Sherman of Ohio to USG. "Gen. R. Hastings now Marshall of the Northern Dist. of Ohio is an applicant for reappointment—his term being out in the Spring—I hear of no dissatisfaction with him—and his fidelity in his office & his military services and wound entitle him to your favor—I join in recommending his appointment"—ALS, DNA, RG 60, Records Relating to Appointments. On Dec. 17, Gen. William T. Sherman endorsed this letter. "Col Hastings lost his leg in battle at Winchester Va—under Sheridan—I know from my Brother Chas T Sherman Judge of the Northn Dist of Ohio that this officer is Eminently qualified for his office and fully merits reappointmt."—AES, *ibid.* Related papers are *ibid.* On Feb. 14, 1871, USG nominated Russell Hastings as marshal, Northern District, Ohio.

1870, DEC. 18. Cornelia Williams, Saratoga Springs, N. Y., to USG. "Although an utter stranger to you, I entreat your forbearance for a few moments. My deceased Father, James C De Camp was a friend of yours some years ago, and I, his daughter, feel that in writing to you, may be listened to, for his sake. My Husband, Lt. Constant Williams, is a first Lieutenant in the U. S Army 7th Infantry now stationed in Dakota Territory, and I with my young child, am. visiting my Mother, Mrs. James De Camp, at this place, Saratoga Springs. In the recent Army Bill my Husband is liable to be transferred to the list of supernumeraries, to be discharged; what I earnestly beg of you, is not to let him be transferred, if he *should* be reccommended. He has no property besides his pay and a family to support—Therefore, my earnest petition to you, and should you listen to it, I would ever be most grateful. Hoping that I have not trespassed too long on your time and attention, and most earnestly desiring some answer to this request, . . ."—ALS, DNA, RG 94, ACP, 1490 1873. On March 5, 1875, Williams, Louisville, again wrote to USG. "As you have signed the act authorizing appointments in the Pay Dept. U. S. A., I earnestly beg that the applications for such an appointment made by My Husband, (Capt. Constant Williams, 7th Inftry—

U. S. A.—now serving in Montana) and myself, may be favorably considered by you. . . ."—ALS, *ibid.* Capt. Constant Williams, 7th Inf., remained with his regt.

1870, DEC. 19. To House of Representatives. "I transmit to the House of Representatives a report of the Secretary of State and the papers by which it was accompanied, in answer to their resolution of the 7th instant."—Copies, DNA, RG 59, General Records; *ibid.*, RG 130, Messages to Congress. *HED*, 41-3-19. On the same day, Secretary of State Hamilton Fish had written to USG submitting papers concerning seizure of the schooner *Granada* by a British cutter.—Copy, DNA, RG 59, General Records.

1870, DEC. 19. Lt. Col. August V. Kautz, Fort Stanton, New Mexico Territory, to USG. "The bearer of this, Major Lawrence G. Murphy of the firm of Fritz &. Murphy, Post Traders at this post, is seeking the reappointment of Post Trader under the recent Law. They have been superceaded by Mr. Stevens of Santa Fe, a man not at all suited to the position; he is well known in the Territory as a professional Gambler and is very objectionable to the officers of the Post. Fritz & Murphy have given satisfaction in every respect and deserve to be continued, on accont of their record as officers of our army in the late war. Both Col. Fritz and Major Murphy served two enlistments in the Regular army before the war, and subsequently attained the grade of Field officers, in the Volunteer Service. I should be very sorry to see them superceded by such a man as Stevens."—ALS, NNP. Lawrence G. Murphy and Emil Fritz continued as post traders, Fort Stanton, New Mexico Territory. On April 2, 1869, USG had nominated Richard M. Stephens as postmaster, Santa Fé, but suspended the appointment on May 31. Papers denouncing Stephens as a professional gambler are in DNA, RG 46, Papers Pertaining to Nominations. See *HRC*, 44-1-799, 90, 273; Darlis A. Miller, *The California Column in New Mexico* (Albuquerque, 1982), pp. 146–47; Robert M. Utley, *High Noon in Lincoln: Violence on the Western Frontier* (Albuquerque, 1987), pp. 14–16.

1870, DEC. 19. Edwin R. Ross, Neosho Falls, Kan., to USG. "I am in want of information regarding Soldiers' Land and as you are our chief Commander, I thought you could post me. I was in the Service of my Country for awhile, am Sorry that I could not Stay longer and Serve better. I was a Member of Co. (C.) 83rd Ohio, V. I. Commanded by Col' F. W. Moore of Cincinnati I was enrolled on the ninth day of August 1862 to serve three years or During the War Was Discharged the first day of July 1863 at Camp Dennison Ohio, By reason of Surg ctf & G. O. 36 of 1862. Was Born in Madisonville Ohio. Tinner by Trade when enrolled. Was TwentySix Years of Age. Sir I have came to the State of Kansas to get me a Home, have found Land to Suit Me in Sedgwick County, had to leave My Family at the above-named place as I went out on account of delicate Health got a Log Cabbin partly finished but had not enough Money to finish it So as My

Family were here I came here to get Work to procure means to go ahead on the Land as soon as I can get back to it, and Sir if as I am told a Soldier is allowed one hundred Sixty Acres of Land I would be well pleased to have it allowed me in Sedgwick County Kan's where My old Fatherinlaw has Setled with me, and as he is geting Old I want to be near him to help him through if he needs. he lost a Son in the Service. will you Sir, be so kind as to post me in regard to the Matter as soon as convenient by doing so you will confer a lasting Favor on a Man who has *Love* of Country at *Heart.* I have never before asked for Aid from my Government in the way of Pension allthough I perhaps deserved it as much as a great many that draws Pension. I have been told several times I could get it, but I told them as long as I could get along without I would not ask it, as the Country was far enough behind without Me adding more expense to it."—ALS, DNA, RG 48, Lands and Railroads Div., Miscellaneous, Letters Received.

1870, DEC. 20. U.S. Representative William B. Stokes of Tenn. to USG. "Inclosed find a letter addressed to yourself, which I take pleasure in forwarding. The Same was inclosed to me by Captain, Bowden. a gallant Officer in the Union Army, & is the Clerk and Master for Fentress County Tennessee & is therefore entitled to Consideration."—ALS, DNA, RG 94, Letters Received, 92 AGO 1871. On Dec. 12, Baley O. Bowden, Jamestown, Tenn., had written to USG. "I believe the Chief Executive of a nation should know the condition of his subjects in evry part of his government, so that he could afford them protection. I write to inform you of the condition of your subjects in these parts. The condition of the union men, those who were loyal through the war, especially those who fought to sustain the government and have voted the republican ticket since, is very bad, worse than it was in 1861 and they have almost given up all hopes of seeing better days. The men, who gave up all for their country, left their homes and dear ones and hid themselves in the coverns of the earth until there was an opportunity to escape to the federal lines, are now being hunted up and driven from their homes, by the very men who fought for four years to destroy the government, to whom the government has been so merciful after they had forfeited their lives and property. Union men are forbidden to move to or be allowed to live on their own farms they have come by honestly, they are taken from their houses and frightened wives and children and whiped or shamefully treated. The men who fought for the government are in a worse condition than those who fought to destroy it—The loyal men and conquerers are those that suffer and are driven from their homes by the rebels and the conquered. The condition of the rebel is as good as could be wished, while the union man is afraid to sleep in his bed at night, fearing he will be run on by a band of masked men and either killed or cruelly beaten. I had purchased a very rich little farm in Overton County in this State and had commenced moving to it. I had no inclination to meddle ~~in~~ in politics, I asked no office; but, only, wished to improve my farm, raise fine stock and help build up the country—I was willing to allow the rebels to be equal to me in every respect. I did not wish to oppress any one, because he had been a rebel; but after having moved a part of my effects and a few days before I was going to move my family, I received the following letter which I enclose to you so you can see what is going on here. What did they mean when they said 'nor none of your sort?' I was at college at the commencement of the war. The faculty and most of the students went off with the South, I remained firm to the union, and after the battle of Fishing Creek, being afraid to stay in the South any longer I went to the State of Illinois. In August 1862 I enlisted in the 122nd Illinois regiment commanded by Col. John I. Rinaker in which I seved duering the war, I was discharged at Springfield Illinois, returned home—was appointed assistant assessor for Fentress County, which I resigned after a few months. I was appointed Assistant Marshal to take the census of a part of this county. As to my character I am willing for the rebels to testify. The records at Washington will show what I have said is true—as having served in the 122nd Illinois regiment, being assistant assessor, and having worked in taking the 9th census, hence, it seems that they mean union men or federal soldiers The other day two families were notified to leave their homes in Overton County—A very old man by the name of Samuel Boman who was in the war of 1812, has an honorable discharge and has been duering and since the war a true union man, was run on beaten most shamefully, and they hung three times a negro boy living with him until he was nearly dead trying to make him tell where the old man's money was. Other families have been compelled to leave and come to Fentress County. Under the existing state of affairs I think there is danger of trouble here—There is some talk of the Ku Klux making a raid into this county and if they do the work will commence. I do hope there will be none of this, for I want peace and quiet. Yet I want to be in life, liberty and property and in safety permitted to go and live where I please and I am willing to grant the same to every one. I think it is the duty of a government to protect every one of its citizens however humble they may be and when a government fails to do this it fails to do that for which it is established. And as an humble citizen of the United States I would ask for protection. I write not for the purpose affording evidence for the 'Reconstruction Committee,' for I am not much of a reconstructionist—I advise no measures leaving that for wiser heads I ask pardon for being so bold as to write you"—ALS, *ibid.* In an undated letter, "K. K. K.s, Headquarter Den Num 1," wrote to Bowden. "information having wreacht the moon that that you are going to chnge plases of residen and Ocupy the Sproul plce, Sir we woul advise you to stay wher you ar Or go som wher els for we have no earthley use for you nor non of your sort her, please tak this as advis from One who would advise you write,"—AL, *ibid.*

1870, Dec. 21. USG endorsement. "Payment of the within account allowed under the special taxation of the circuit court of the United States for the southern district of New York, in which district the services were rendered, and is to be paid from the appropriation for defraying the expenses of the judiciary. An advance of an amount sufficient to pay the same is authorized."—*HRC*, 44-1-800, 335. Written on papers pertaining to the accounts of George H. Sharpe, U.S. marshal, Southern District, N. Y.

1870, DEC. 22. To Secretary of the Treasury George S. Boutwell. "If there is no special reason for retaining the present assistant collector, Jersey City, I should like to have Gen. B. Vickers, Sussex, N. J. appointed."—Copy, DLC-USG, II, 1. On May 4, George T. Cobb, Morristown, N. J., had written to USG. "I learn General Kilpatrick is about to resign the position of US. Minister to Chili with a view of returning to the United States and that his brother in law, General Vickers, is solicitous of obtaining the office . . ."—ALS, DNA, RG 59, Letters of Application and Recommendation. Related papers are *ibid.* On June 13, James F. Meline, Washington, D. C., wrote to USG. "I have the honor to apply for appointment to the office of Assistant Collector of the Customs in the District of New York to reside at Jersey City. an office created by Act of Congress February 21st 1863. In support of this application I beg leave to submit a letter from M. H. Grinnell Esq Collector of the Port of New York, and one from General Pleasanton."—Copy, *ibid.*, RG 56, Collector of Customs Applications, N. Y. Related papers are *ibid.* On July 16, USG appointed Meline as asst. collector of customs, Jersey City, in place of Phineas C. Dummer.

On Dec. 29, Alexander H. Wallis *et al.* wrote to USG. "The undersigned residents of Jersey City, New Jersey, respectfully represent that the removal of Phineas C. Dummer from the position of Deputy Collector ~~of~~ residing in Jersey City, was received by all the leading and influential Republicans of Jersey City with feelings of deep regret and disapproval and they have ever since expected his restoration to the place from which he was without any sufficient reason removed but have hitherto been disappointed yet they must respectfully submit that the restoration of Mr Dummer to his former position is absolutely essential to the maintenance of the integrity of the Republican party in Hudson County New Jersey—"—DS (8 signatures), *ibid.* On Jan. 31, 1871, Ellen E. Sherman, Washington, D. C., wrote to USG. "I beg your personal attention for one moment. Last Spring Mr. Meline was appointed by you to the Office of Asst. Collector in Jersey City. He is in miserable health or he would not need the position. He is an old acquaintance & friend of mine, is a man of unimpeachable character *and Served throughout the War.* I learn that there is an effort being made to restore the old incumbent, who was occupying that berth during a part of the time at least, that Col. Meline was in the field. I earnestly beg that you will allow my friend who has every claim Military *& Political* upon the Administration to remain where you so kindly placed him."—ALS, CSmH. Because USG did not make a formal nomination of Meline on the opening day of the next session of the Senate, Dummer regained the position.

1870, DEC. 28. Speech. "CHEVALIER: I am happy to receive you as the diplomatic representative of a sovereign with whom the United States have always maintained, and desire uniformly to preserve, the most friendly and cordial relations. It is to be hoped that you may find your abode here agreeable, and you may be assured that nothing shall be omitted on my part toward contributing to so desirable a purpose."—*Washington Chronicle*, Dec. 29, 1870. USG responded to Oluf Stenersen, minister from Sweden and Norway. On Dec. 27, Secretary of State Hamilton Fish wrote to USG. "Mr O. Stenersen, the newly arrived Minister from Sweden and Norway, having asked for the appointment of a time to deliver his credentials, I have taken the liberty to say that you would receive him tomorrow, the 28th instant at eleven o'clock. If therefore, I should not have been mistaken in supposing that that hour would be convenient for you, I shall then introduce that gentleman."—LS, OFH.

1870, Dec. 28. Memorandum to Culver C. Sniffen, USG's clerk, instructing him to compose a letter.—Parke-Bernet Sale No. 2235, Dec. 3, 1963, no. 104.

1870, Dec. 28. Col. James H. Simpson, Mobile, to USG. "The enclosed letter is from my young friend, Mr. Dana Borup, at the present time an under graduate of De Veaux College, Suspension Bridge, N. Y: but a citizen of St Paul, Minnesota. It will be seen that he is anxious for an appointment to a cadetship at the military academy at West Point; & thinks I may be of some assistance to him in this matter: and it would indeed be very gratifying to me, could I have influence enough to induce the President to grant him an appointment *from at large* . . ."—ALS, DNA, RG 94, Correspondence, USMA. A related letter is *ibid.* Henry Dana Borup graduated USMA in 1876.

1870, Dec. 29. Orville E. Babcock to Margaret Toos, Sioux City, Iowa. "The President directs me to say that he received your note of the 2nd instant and the quilt. He appreciates the kind motives which prompted you to send him the work of your own hands—but feels to accept it would be robbing you of a much needed comfort this winter. Therefore he returns it to you by express and encloses herein $10. with which he hopes you will be enabled to avert some of the hardships of this cold season."—Copy, DLC-USG, II, 1. On Feb. 4, 1871, Babcock wrote to Toos. "The President directs me to say that your letter of the 31st ultimo, has reached him and that he regrets that his letter mailed on the 29th. December—the same day on which the quilt was returned—had not yet come to your hand. Herewith you will please find a copy of that letter, by which you will see that he was actuated by only the kindest motives in repossessing you of that household comfort."—Copy, *ibid.*

1870, Dec. 30. Governor Rutherford B. Hayes of Ohio to USG. "I know Judge Ichabod Corwin well, and am acquainted with his reputation as a lawyer, judge, and public man. He is a gentleman of purity of character, sound judgment, and superior talents. His legal learning and ability are of a high order, and his qualifications for the office of judge are excellent in al[l] respects. He is a patriotic Republican, and possesses the confidence of good men. His reputation is of the best sort and I believe he deserves it."—ALS (press), OFH.

[1870, Dec.]. Horace Porter to Secretary of War William W. Belknap. "The President says he gave Fletcher the card upon the principle that it is a good thing for young officers to go into civil life, and he thinks they ought to be granted leaves to encourage this, but he recalls the card so far as it may conflict with [an]y rule you may have established You can now deal with Fletcher in your own way"—ALS, DNA, RG 94, Letters Received, 308F 1870. On Dec. 28, Belknap wrote to AG Edward D. Townsend. "On a re-examination of the application of Lieut Robt. Fletcher for leave for six months to enable him to occupy a Professorship at Dartmouth College—I am satisfied that my action was wrong in granting that leave *for that purpose*—Hence the order granting the leave must be revoked."—AN (initialed), *ibid.*

1870, Dec. U.S. Senator Frederick A. Sawyer of S. C. *et al.* to USG. "We, the undersigned, having full assurance that Col. Wm. L. Long, formerly and for many years Naval Store-keeper at Spezia, and afterwards U. S. Vice Consul at that place, is, and has always been, a man of ardent patriotism, of zealous devotion to duty, of strict integrity and of a chivalrous sense of honor, would beg leave to recommend him for the appointment of U. S. Consul at Carrara—if possible, or if not, to some other place, where the official income will secure him against absolute want in his declining years after so long a period of faithful service to the country. . . . The present Consul at Carrara, Mr. Franklin Torrey from Mass, is a very worthy gentleman, but he is engaged in the marble business, and it is stated, resides permanently in Leghorn, leaving the duties at Carrara to an Italian clerk. . . ."—DS (11 signatures), DNA, RG 59, Letters of Application and Recommendation. Related papers are *ibid.* On Dec. 21, USG nominated William L. Long as consul, Carrara, Italy.

1871, Jan. 4. To House of Representatives. "I transmit to the House of Representatives in answer to their resolution of the 12th of December 1870, a report from the Secretary of State, with accompanying documents."—Copy, DNA, RG 130, Messages to Congress. *HED*, 41-3-38. On Dec. 21, 1870, Secretary of State Hamilton Fish had written to USG. "The Secretary of State has the honor to report to the President that a Resolution adopted by the House of Representatives on the 12th instant, was received at this Department on the 13th instant, the text of which is as follows: 'Resolved that the Secretary of State be requested to communicate to this House, if not in his opinion incompatible with the public interests, so much of the correspondence of Hon. Samuel Shellabarger with the State Department, while Minister to Portugal, as relates to public documents or libraries in the care of foreign ministers, with any recommendation he may deem proper to make in relation thereto.' The Secretary of State has the honor to lay before the President a copy of a despatch of the 24th of July, 1869 from Mr Shellabarger, late Minister of the United States to Portugal and, as further illustrative of the subject of the Resolution, a copy of the correspondence with certain other Ministers of the United States upon the same subject, and it is submitted that the suggestions contained in these papers are entitled to the serious consideration of Congress."—Copy, DNA, RG 59, General Records. The ministers desired law books with diplomatic uses in lieu of congressional documents.

1871, JAN. 4. To Leonora Jones. "I am in receipt of your letter enclosing the proposed Constitution of the Dispensary and Hospital Society of the Woman's Institute of New York City, and other papers. I think it is a noble enterprise. I have no objection to your including my name in the list of managers, and regret that my public duties will prevent my exercising any active part. Wishing you all success . . ."—Copy, DLC-USG, II, 1. See *New York Times*, Feb. 7, 1871.

1871, JAN. 5. Orville E. Babcock to American Merchants Union Express Co., New York City. "The President is in receipt of your letter transmitting a renewal of his 'Frank' on your company for 'personal and family packages.' He wishes me to communicate his thanks for your renewed expression of kindness."—Copy, DLC-USG, II, 1.

1871, [JAN. 5]. Senator Edmund G. Ross of Kan. to USG. "I am in receipt of information from Kansas, that Gen. Merrill is at La Cygne, a town in the Miami Indian lands, with an order from the Sec'y of War, to remove all the settlers from those lands. If that order is executed, more than a thousand white people will be turned out upon the prairie, & subjected to very great suffering & injustice. I have called to ask you to order a temporary suspension of th~~at~~e order for their removal, until an investigation into the merits of the case can be had. I am confident that such an investigation will show that these settlers are in no just sense trespassers upon the rights of the Indians or any body else, but on the contrary, that this order has been procured at the instigation of parties who are themselves engaged in a conspiracy to plunder the Indians All I ask, & all the settlers desire, is a temporary suspension of the order for their removal, to the end that the facts may be shown, & justice done between them & the Indians"—ALS, DNA, RG 94, Letters Received, 186I 1870. On Jan. 16, AG Edward D. Townsend wrote to Ross "that orders were issued on the 29th ult. suspending the removal of settlers from the Reservation in question."—Copy, *ibid.*, Letters Sent.

1871, JAN. 6. USG endorsement. "I approve the within ~~change~~ recommended change of Dist. Atty. for Western Dist. of Mo"—AES, DNA, RG

60, Records Relating to Appointments. Written on a letter of Jan. 5 from U.S. Representatives Samuel S. Burdett and Robert T. Van Horn of Mo. to USG. "We very respectfully and confidently commend to you for appointment to the Office of District Attorney for the Western Dist of Missouri—Mr James. S Botsford a citizen of the city of Sedalia Missouri—Mr Botsford is a Lawyer of excellent repute and attainments in his profession—of spotless character—and faithful in all the relations of. life—During the late canvass in Missouri as well as previously he was actively identified with the Administration—and with the interests of the National Republican Party: . . ."—LS, *ibid.* On Jan. 23, USG nominated James S. Botsford as U.S. attorney, Western District, Mo.

1871, JAN. 6. George A. Aaron, Glen's Fork, Ky., to USG. "Wee desire thate you Maye Now oure Condition Ate this time oure lande is in A Moste Miseable Conditon Ate this time there is A ~~Can~~ Clan of Clu clucks ore Rebells they Are treting the Rattical party bade they say the Raticle party And the Negro has to leave heare Wee do Note Wante to leave oure homes And sacryfise oure propity to plese them if there is Note somthing done Wee will hafe to leave heare son Wee Wante you to helpe us this oure time of Neede Wee Wante soldiers here Will you please sende us soldiers ore Give us permiton to Make two upe fore state troopes fore two years till Ater the Naxte presidential Electin Wee Will prove oure loyalty Wilst thou Give us Consolation thate We May Singe Columbia Columbia the home of the Brave. lande of the free"—ALS, DNA, RG 94, Letters Received, 226 AGO 1871.

1871, JAN. 7. To Governor Edmund J. Davis of Tex. "Mr. Moore Assessor of Internal Revenue, Third District of Texas, goes to the Mexican frontier on public business. I would respectfully request the co-operation of yourself and officers should he need any counsel or aid from the State authorities."—Copy, DLC-USG, II, 1. On the same day, USG wrote to "U. S. Officials" in Tex. "The bearer W. B. Moore, Assessor of Int. Rev. 3d Dist. Texas, goes to the Mexican frontier on official business. The commanding officer of the United States forces in Texas will furnish him such transportation, escort &c. as may be needed in the Execution of the duties entrusted to him."—Copy, *ibid.*

1871, JAN. 7. Bernard Hess, New York City, to USG. "On or about the 22nd day of April last, I send to you a letter paying for the release of one Jno. D. McHenry, then at Albany Pennitentary, to which place he was innocently sent & has been made a *Victim* of the so called corrupt Revenue Ring men who robbed the U. S. Govt. out of Millions of Dolls though they are unmolasted & unpunisshed, yet, you granted him his Pardon soon afterwards, for which I offer indivitually my thanks to you. I said letter I stated, that you are imposed upon, & surroundet by dishonest officials some of which are now out of office, & some of the gang you have elevated to higher office with out asking me, for any explanation, of my allegations. No doubt you thought me too insignificient, but behold Mr President, I am fearless & ready to lay all my matters before you, or befor the Public, & let mass of the American People pass their Judgement, in 1872—! For my honesty & fidellity while a Revenue Officer, I was persecuted, & reduced to poverty by dishonest U. S. Dist Attys, & Revenue Commissioners . . . P. S. I have enough information & facts, respecting corruption committed in the Custom House of this Port—!!!"—ALS, DNA, RG 56, Letters Received. On April 28, 1870, USG pardoned John D. McHenry, convicted of perjury at the "May term '69 US Circuit Ct. So. Dist. N. Y. Recommd by Gen. Slocum—Hon Horace Greeley—Gen. Banks M. C.—H. B. Claflin Esqr.—& many other prominent men."—Copy, *ibid.*, RG 130, Pardon Records.

1871, JAN. 9. To Senate. "I transmit for consideration with a view to its ratification, a Treaty of Amity, Commerce and Consular privileges between the United States and the Republic of Salvador, signed at the City of San Salvador on the sixth of December last. A copy of the official correspondence relating to the instrument, is also herewith transmitted."—DS, DNA, RG 46, Presidential Messages, Foreign Relations, Salvador. Related papers are *ibid.*

1871, JAN. 9. Orville E. Babcock to Secretary of the Navy George M. Robeson. "The President directs me to say that, as the 'Saginaw' has been lost he thinks that some other vessel should be sent out at once to take the place on the survey."—LS, DNA, RG 45, Letters Received from the President. See *HED*, 42-2-1, part 3, pp. 6–8, 203–38.

1871, JAN. 9. F. L. Price, Independence, Kan., to USG. "May the blessings of an allwise God fall upon you if you will but heed these few lines. I can hardly make myself believe that I will gain anything by writing this letter. In 1861 I took up arms against a Rebelion. I served three years in the federal army under our brave Gen Sherman lost the use of my left arm at the battle of Altoona and not long after I came home although crippled for life I have braved it through up to this time. I came to Kansas 18 months ago from Min and took a claim and done very well for some time, but it was not long until I found out that I had a man to contend with and as I had but very little money it soon run throug. Now my contest comes off before long and I cannot hire any lawyer for want of money. for the last two months I have not been able to do a days ~~b~~ work and my three little chrildren are too ragged to go to school and are actually suffering for want of cloths. the land I claim is a very valuble piece. my opponent is a man of means, and, I cannot borrow any money for I have nothing to secure a man with. I am a penniless unfortunate man—union man. You can find my name in the records. My last cent nearly went to pay my taxes but, I will not grumble at this. My neighbors have given me all they can to eat and my little ones are crying half of the time for something to eat. For Gods sake, and for suffering humanities sake I, beg of you to give me a little money . . . If I had not lost my power physically in serving my country I would not make this appeal to you. I will look for it that is some money for ten or twelve days at the P. O. or a letter from you. Could the cry of my children in their distress reach your ear I am sure it would melt your heart and touch your benevolence. Oh for Christ's sake do hark unto this."—ALS, DNA, RG 48, Miscellaneous Div., Letters Received.

1871, Jan. 11. Secretary of the Interior Columbus Delano to USG. "I have the honor to return, herewith, House Resolution No. 188—'Joint Resolution for publishing specifications and drawings of Patent Office, and to state that I am aware of no reason why the same should not receive your approval."—LS, OFH.

1871, Jan. 12. Orville E. Babcock to Mrs. E. B. McMullin, Philadelphia. "The President directs me to acknowledge the receipt of your letter and to say that he had given instructions to order your husband before the retiring board, when the Secretary of War informed him of the fact that your husband's pay had been stopped and that charges had been preferred against him in New Mexico, and that a request had been made by his commanding officer to have him returned for trial. On receiving this information he withdrew his instructions."—Copy, DLC-USG, II, 1. See *PUSG*, 18, 478–79.

1871, Jan. 12. Brig. Gen. Oliver O. Howard to John Taylor, London. "I saw the president of the United States today—Your suggestion with regard to aid in furnishing seed corn for the poor people impoverished by the war touched his sympathies, but he saw nothing he could do officially. Should you petition our Congress for aid in this matter through the President I believe he would warmly second your appeal. I need not say that I would do all in my power to further any effort, public or private, to help you—"—ALS (press), Howard Papers, MeB.

1871, Jan. 13. To Senate. "In answer to the Resolution of the Senate of the 5th instant, I return herewith a certified copy of the resolution of the Senate of the 22d of December last advising and consenting to the appointment of Jacob Corlies as Deputy Postmaster at Red Bank, New Jersey. As the resolution contains notice of other confirmations, it is retained as evidence as to the commissions which have been issued thereupon. Should it be necessary, however, the original will be sent."—DS, DNA, RG 46, Papers Pertaining to Certain Nominations. On Jan. 12, Postmaster Gen. John A. J. Creswell had written to USG. "Upon the receipt of the Resolution of the Senate calling for the return of the confirmation of Jacob Corlies as Deputy Postmaster at Red Bank, N. J., the original being filed in the State Department, application was made to said Department for its return. The Hon. Secretary of State furnishes a certified copy, which together with his explanatory letter is herewith sent"—LS, OFH. On Dec. 14, 1870, USG had nominated Jacob Corlies as postmaster in place of Emeline H. Finch.

1871, JAN. 14. USG endorsement. "Respectfully refered to the Sec. of War. I think this case should be refered to the Atty. Gn. for his ~~views~~ opinion."—AES, DNA, RG 94, ACP, 1889 1871. Written on a letter of Jan. 5 from Ann B. Brevolt, Norristown, Pa., to USG. "I have just learned that Major John P. Sherburne asst Adjt Genl has been dismissed the Service principally on account of a bill of long standing which he owed me.—I wrote to the Secretary of War some time ago concerning it, but I never thought or intended that my action should be the cause of his being turned out of the Service—I have since learned the causes of his embarrasments, and the reasons for his not paying.—I am satisfied with his explanations, and that he will properly and honorably settle the account.—I hope your excellency will overlook this matter in his case, and not let him suffer on account of any action of mine.—Major Sherburne with his family, boarded at my house for a long time and paid his board all to a balance of about $400—for which he gave me his note which however remains unpaid but doubtless will be paid should he be reinstated—My only object in calling the attention of the Department to my claim was to secure its payment and not with any object or desire of having him dismissed the Service.—"—LS, *ibid.* Attorney Gen. George H. Williams later wrote to USG. "I would most respectfully invite your attention to the case of Major John P. Sherburne who has been mustered out of the ser[vice on] the recommendation of the Board of which Gen. Hancock was President. . . . Maj. Sherburne has been about sixteen years in the Army, and was at one time during the war Military Governor of the City of Washington. His record it is believed, will c[ompare] favorably with that of many other officers, who are justly honored while he is humiliated and disgraced. Several causes of complaint were stated to the Board but it is understood that the only one that availed anything related to the non payment of a debt. Maj. Sherburne's explanation of this charge it seems to me ought to be accepted, but if it should appear that his conduct in that matter is not above criticism it would certainly be dangerous to good morals to hold that poverty in the Army of the United States is to be punished as a crime. I earnestly ask that Maj. Sherburne upon legal grounds if upon no other be reinstated as Ast. Adjt. General of the Army."—DS (undated), *ibid.* Thirteen congressmen endorsed the recommendation. No action followed.

1871, JAN. 16. M. A. Smith, Olive Branch, Ohio, to USG. "I take the priveleg of wrighting a few lines for the purpus of laying befor your magesty the wrongs outrages that has bin committed on the person ~~of~~ and propity of Timothy Smith, formaly Hawsville, Hancock Co, Ky, by the citizens of that place. he is an natuerlized Englishman; he took the oath of alegence when he came to this country to support this goverment, and to abide by her laws, and not to take up arms agnst it, and because he was true to his oath and the goverment he was made to indure all of thoes outrages; he was robed of every thing they could take away; his wife knocked down; the money taken out of his pockett, and taken out of bed to be hung for voating for Mr Lincolen, and his life threttend, and a thousan other outrages to tegest to mention, [and] years befor the war they took f a child from him and sent her up to Pitsburg and they put her in the poor house, for their she was destitute and he has never seen her since, and he proved at the time she was well taken care of and well provided for, and they made him pay all the expences. they took every dust of flower and meal out of the house; even his diner out of the pot, and now they have driven him from his home that he has worked hard for, and destroyed it, so he can neither live their ore go to it. they would take his life if he was even to go over their to see it and he has bin and applied at every place in Ky wher he thought he could get redress for his wrongs, but all to no avale, for all the offices are filed with rebels, frome the govener down to a constable and all protect a theefe and cutthroats and last summer he walked and beged his way to Washington city to lay his case befor th attorney Generel, he was not at home but the clurk gave him a letter to destrick atturney at Louisville; and he went their but he would do no thing, and now he says he cant get no justice ore protection He will go back to Englan and publish his wrongs and the outrages he has met with in all the public gournels and speaches throuout Englan, and, swar his life aganst the united states and lay a damage of a not les then a hundred thousan dolers; but I beg and implor of you as the president of the United states who promesed protection to all citizens of the united states, to put and see that the laws in Ky are put in forse, and to gave him some athority ~~to~~ and a few words to know that he can still be proteted. their has bin severel letters wroate to you on this subject but no ansur reseved, but I hope this will meet with better success. pleas to address a few lines to Mr Timothy Smith Olive Branch, Clermont Co, Ohio. I beg and implor you to do some thing for this man, and you will ever reseve the thanks and blessing, and prais of a his devoted wife.... P. S.—wright back imedetly ore send some dispach, so that we may know that our petician is granted."—ALS (corrections in another hand omitted), DNA, RG 46, Reports Submitted to the Senate. See *SED*, 41-3-28.

1871, JAN. 18. USG endorsement. "Refered to the Sec. of State. If Govr Wood does not accept this Consulship it may be well to consider this application."—AES, DNA, RG 59, Letters of Application and Recommendation. Written on a letter of Jan. 17 from U.S. Representative Horace Maynard of Tenn. to USG. "It gives me pleasure to suggest the appointment of Gen. Witcher, now a member of the House from W. Va. as Consul to Melbourne. During his service in the House he has secured the respect & confidence of all parties. And I am sure he would represent our interests abroad acceptably & creditably."—ALS, *ibid.* Related papers are *ibid.* On Feb. 24, USG nominated John S. Witcher as collector of Internal Revenue, 3rd District, West Va. For George L. Woods, see letter to John P. Newman, Nov. 6, 1871.

On Feb. 27, William L. Hall, Melbourne, wrote to USG. "Having been appointed Acting Consul of the United States for Melbourne, at the request of the resident American Merchants by D. S. Pinnell Esq late Consul, who has resigned his appointment and returned to America—I have the honor to request that your Excellency will be pleased to confer the appointment of Consul upon me for the remainder of the term, or during your Excellencys pleasure. Herewith I enclose a memorial to your Excellency in my behalf signed by the American residents of this city, together with a copy of the recommendation to the late Consul from the American Merchants"—ALS, *ibid.* The enclosures are *ibid.* On Jan. 31, USG had nominated Thomas Adamson, Jr., as consul, Melbourne. See *PUSG,* 20, 87–88.

1871, JAN. 18. Orville E. Babcock to Secretary of War William W. Belknap. "The President says Mrs Bower is to remain and take a family dinner with them and wants you to join them. To dine at 5oclock (five oclock). No other guests: 'No swallow tails or kid gloves'."—ALS, NjP. Amanda T. Bower, a widow, was the sister of Belknap's second wife, Carita, who had died on Dec. 29, 1870. Belknap and Amanda Bower married on Dec. 11, 1873. See *New York Times,* Dec. 30, 1870, Dec. 12, 1873.

1871, JAN. 18. Orville E. Babcock to Jacob B. Graw, Long Branch. "The President directs me to acknowledge the receipt of your circular and to say that he will be pleased to have you put his name down for one hundred dollars and to send him word when you wish the money."—Copy, DLC-USG, II, 1. On April 13, Babcock wrote to Graw, Mount Holly, N. J. "The President desires me to acknowledge the receipt of your letter of the 10th instant and enclose you his check drawn to your order for one hundred dollars the amount of his subscription to the fund for erection of a Cottage for Bishop Simpson at Long Branch.—The President is glad to hear that the house will be so soon completed. He desires me to convey to you his thanks for the kind expressions contained in your letter."—Copy, *ibid.* See A. C. Graw, *Life of Rev. J. B. Graw, D. D. 1832–1901* (Camden, N. J., 1901), pp. 80–90.

1871, JAN. 18. Orville E. Babcock to Corwin J. Holmes, Waterford, N. Y. "I am directed by the President to return your letter and to say that he cannot give an order, for a position, on any of the officials."—Copy, DLC-USG, II, 1.

1871, JAN. 18. William F. Mallory, Petersburg, Va., to USG. "A few days ago I wrote to Capt Platt who is the Member of Congress from this District, he replied and wrote me that I could get the appointment if I had not held the office of Sergeant Well General I was Sergeant for a short time, and the reason I do not still hold the office is, that our Legislature passed the Enabling Act and the Judge who was appointed for this City being a rank Secessionist, and I being a Union man his first act was to remove me from my office, and appoint a Secessionist, but I thank God I am not a defaulting Sheriff, as I settled up in three days after my removal. Now General, this Mr Carr the present Collector of Customs here, has no claim whatever to the office. In the first place he does not live in the district, constituting the collection of Customs. In the second place he is State Senator from Dinwiddie Co. I applied for the office long before Mr Carr made an application, There are not five merchants in Petersburg who would not say I ought to have it. My first application is in the office at *Washington.* I am *very poor,* else I would not trouble you. Please let me know if you can do any-thing for me and I will forward you any papers you may ask. . . ."—ALS, DNA, RG 56, Collector of Customs Applications. No appointment followed.

1871, JAN. 19. USG endorsement. "Respectfully refered to the Sec. of the Navy."—AES, DNA, RG 45, ZB, William H. Varney. Written on a letter of the same day from Cyrenius B. Denio, Washington, D. C., to USG. "There is but *one* Naval Constructor in the United States who is a *Republican*—I desire and respectfully request that Mr. Wm H. Varney (now acting as Naval Constructor) at Mare Island California may be promoted as full Naval Constructor and be continued at said place."—ALS, *ibid.* See *PUSG,* 14, 448. On Jan. 18, Secretary of the Navy George M. Robeson had written to USG. "I have the honor to submit, herewith; the nomination of Isaiah Hanscom, to be Chief of the Bureau of Construction and Repair of the Navy Department. This appointment is to fill a vacancy now existing in the office, which occurred by expiration of the term of the last incumbent, some time since. After a great deal of consideration I recommend the appointment of Isaiah Hanscom. Mr. Lenthall, the old incumbent, is a retired officer, who has been for a long time (21 years) in the Bureau, and has at last been retired by reason of age. To reappoint him for a fixed term would be entirely contrary to the policy and practice of the Department at this time, and to its written declarations with regard to the other Bureaus. It is also, I think, contrary to the spirit, if not the letter of the law. Moreover, I think there should be changes in the heads of Bureaus from time to time, as after long occupancy they get into fixed habits and modes of doing business which at last tend to impede improvement. Mr. Lenthall can still be usefully employed in matters connected with his branch of the profession, but should no longer be at the head. This appointment can only be made from the corps of Naval Constructors, and Mr. Hanscom, who is next but one to the head of the list (the other at the head to be retired in a short time) is the only Naval Constructor now in the service, of proper age, in accord with the administration. He has had long experience, has built several of our best and largest vessels, and is very strongly recommended by senators, representatives, merchants and ship-builders."—Copy, DNA, RG 45, Letters Sent to the President. On Jan. 19, USG nominated Isaiah Hanscom as chief, Bureau of Construction and Repair, Navy Dept.

1871, JAN. 19. D. H. Brumburgh and M. V. Carpenter, Panora, Iowa, to USG. "It Being almost a matter of impossibility to ascertain to a certainty—the *facts* in reference to *Land Grants* to Soldiers who served in our late war—We have concluded to take the liberty of asking *you* to enlighten us on this subject. What we want to know is *How Much* land is a Soldier entitled to and what is necessary to be done to get it, &c. We address you believing that *you will not* refuse to answer this simple petition of two who have followed you to victory on the field of Battle—Sory to troubl you with this . . ."—LS, DNA, RG 48, Lands and Railroads Div., Miscellaneous Letters Received.

1871, JAN. 20. Carman A. Newcomb, Charles W. Ford, Elias W. Fox, and Isaac F. Shepard, St. Louis, to USG. "There being a vacancy in the Office of Recorder of Land Titles in this District occasioned by the appointment of the present incumbent (Albert Seigel) to the Office of Adjutant General of Missouri by Gov. Brown. We respectfully recommend Wm J Drumhill as a Suitable Man to fill Said Office Mr. Drumhill is a man of high character every way qualified to fill the Office, devoted to the Republican party Served as a Soldier through the War was wounded in the Service disabled for life his appointment will be satisfactory to all our friends here."—DS, DNA, RG 48, Appointment Div., Letters Received. On Jan. 21, Newcomb wrote to USG on the same subject.—ALS, *ibid.* On Feb. 22, Christopher Rall, St. Louis, wrote to USG. "I hereby apply for the Office of United States Recorder of Land Titles for the District of Missouri. I am familiar with the french language in which most the archives of said Office is written and have been a Clerk in said Office ever since the middle of the year 1865, and have become familiar with duties thereof. From the beginning of the Rebellion in 1861 to the end thereof in 1865 I was a soldier in the United States Army. I learned the french language in Europe from which Country imigrated twenty five years ago. I refer you to the recommendations herewith sent you."—ALS, *ibid.* On March 14, USG nominated Stillman O. Fish as recorder of land titles, St. Louis. See *O.R.*, I, x, part 1, 167.

1871, JAN. 21. Orville E. Babcock to Joseph P. Wilson, New York City. "Your letter is at hand. I have read it to the President, who wishes me to say in answer, that he will be pleased to have you do as you suggest with the Sherry, and forward to him as soon as prepared. The President will be pleased to have you 'bottle one of the 1830 "Harriet", and a small one of the "1832" "Amantillado",'"—Copy, DLC-USG, II, 1.

[1871], JAN. 21. Brig. Gen. Oliver O. Howard to USG. "I heartily join with others in recommending for pardon Jared M. Davis, now in prison at Manchester N. H. for robbing the mail. He has served fifteen months of a sentence of two two years, and with six months previous to his trial has in all been in prison twenty one months. It is his first offence: he has been a faithful soldier; has lost an arm in his country's service and is now suffering from the wound; and I believe his intentions for the future are good and well founded. It will be an act of mercy not only to him but to his suffering family."—ALS (press), MeB. On Aug. 21, USG pardoned Jared M. Davis.—Copy, DNA, RG 130, Pardon Records.

1871, [JAN. 23]. Secretary of the Interior Columbus Delano to USG. "I have the honor to submit herewith, a copy of a report, dated the 13th instant, from the Commissioner of Indian Affairs, and the accompanying papers, therein referred to, in relation to Indian Affairs on the Tule River reservation in California. I am informed by the Commissioner that the General of the Army, to whom the subject has been mentioned, is prepared to send the requisite military force to the reservation to protect the Agent in the discharge of his duties, and to maintain order thereon. I, therefore, recommend that such instructions in the premises may be given, as, to the Executive, may seem proper."—LS (misdated July 23), DNA, RG 153, Military Reservation Files, Calif. On Jan. 23, Secretary of War William W. Belknap wrote to Delano. "I have the honor to inform you that the request in your communication of the 23d July (January?) '71 to the President, relative to sending a military force to the Tule Indian reservation in California has been referred to the General of the Army with orders to comply with the request."—Copy, *ibid.*, RG 107, Letters Sent, Military Affairs. See *HED*, 42-2-1, part 2, p. 70, part 5, pp. 743, 755.

1871, JAN. 23. Orville E. Babcock to Secretary of War William W. Belknap. "The President will be pleased to have 'a delay' of sixty (60) days to join his regiment, given to 1st Lieut. D. H. Kelton of the 10th Infantry—now at Newport Barracks. Ky"—LS, DNA, RG 94, ACP, 1038 1873.

1871, JAN. 23. Horace Porter to Secretary of the Treasury George S. Boutwell. "I am directed by the President to submit for your consideration, S. No. 53, entitled; 'An Act to pay two companies of Oregon Volunteers,' and to ask whether any reasons exist why it should not receive his approval?"—LS, OFH. On Jan. 24, Ezra B. French, auditor, endorsed this letter.—AES, *ibid.* Boutwell endorsed this letter. "The above is respectfully communicated to the President with the statement that I can not learn that the Dept has any information upon the subject."—AES (undated), *ibid.* On Feb. 2, this bill, related to the Rogue River Indian War in 1854, became law without USG's signature.—*CG*, 41–3, 906. See *ibid.*, 41–2, 2949, 4308, 4958, 41–3, 498; *SRC*, 41-2-37.

1871, JAN. 24. To Senate. "In answer to your Resolution of the 21st December 1870, requesting the President 'to furnish the Senate with the amount of money expended by the United States for freights and passage to the Pacific Coast by way of the Isthmus and Cape Horn during the twelve months now last past'—I herewith transmit Reports from the Secretary of the Treasury, of War and of the Navy, to whom, respectively, the Resolution was referred."—DS, DNA, RG 46, Presidential Messages. *SED*, 41-3-24. Related papers are in DNA, RG 46, Presidential Messages.

1871, JAN. 24. Secretary of the Interior Columbus Delano to USG. "A treaty concluded with the Chippewas and Munsee or christain Indians, on the 1st June 1868; is now pending in the Senate for the constitutional action of that body thereon, The Commissioner of Indian Affairs, is in receipt of a communication, bearing date the 17th inst. from Edward McCoonse, and Ignatious Caleb, the duly authorized representatives of said tribes, asking that the treaty referred to be withdrawn from the Senate, In view of this disire of the Indians, and of the fact that they hope to make other arrangements, for the settlement of their tribal affairs, through the medium of Congressional legislation, I respectfully recommend that the President request the withdrawal of said treaty from the consideration of Senate, to be returned to this Department,"—Copy, DNA, RG 48, Indian Div., Letters Sent. On Jan. 25, Orville E. Babcock wrote to Delano. "The President directs me to forward to you the accompanying Senate bill No. 610 'An Act for the relief of the Stockbridge and Muncee tribe of Indians in the State of Wisconsin.' and ask your examination and report whether any reasons exist why it should not receive his approval."—Copy, DLC-USG, II, 1. On Jan. 30, Delano wrote to USG. "I have the honor to return herewith, Senate Bill No 610, . . . While I cannot advise that the Executive approval be withheld from the Bill, some of its provisions do not fully accord with the views of the Department,"—LS, OFH. On Feb. 6, the bill became law without USG's signature.—*CG*, 41–3, 988. See *ibid.*, pp. 587–88, 615.

1871, Jan. 24. Secretary of the Interior Columbus Delano to USG. "I have the honor to return, herewith, H. R. No. 2355, entitled 'An act for the relief of Pierpont Seymour, of East Bloomfield, New York', and to state that I know of no just reason why the same should not become a law."—LS, OFH. This bill extended a patent on agricultural machinery.—*CG*, 41–3, 593.

1871, Jan. 24. Henry H. Johnson, Louisville, to USG. "I can scarcely expect you to remember me but in the hope that you will excuse the liberty I take and that I may be instrumental in doing some good for our party I thus intrude on you, Since the close of the 'war of the rebellion' I have made this city my home and have been identified with the Republican Party in all its workings and as I am not an office holder or seeker, I think can give an unpredjudiced statement of facts pertaining to the party. Our Offices in this city are no doubt well filled, but at the same time they give very general dissatisfaction to our friends at large. nor do I believe there is a single *true* Republican in the city outside of what is known as the 'Custom House ring' that does not earnestly pray for a radical change therein. When our competent and deserving soldiers are indignantly turned away when applying for some minor place and Ex-Rebels, boasting Democrats and Foreign Subjects, given the places, it certainly presents poor encouragments to others to become members of the party and thereby be prescribed in all business and many social circles. All this is generally known and freely talked over the city and the other party approach our men and tell them that no one cares for them and they cannot even dislodge *boasted Rebels*, from government places, Many of our truest friends are now anticipating a speedy change and none more heartily than myself. It was not my intention to speak for or against any applicant for these offices but in asmuch as we have an original vacancy here, 'Appraiser of Merchandise' I beg to offer my testimony in favor of Capt Robert Johnson, a true and tried officer during the war, and certainly in every way qualified for the position. I am at least certain that whatever of good has been done for the Republican Party here, is due to no one *more than to him*—I am greatly in favor of those who spent some years of prime of life, protecting their country; now having whatever of good is left. This is only natural of course as I spent over over four years there myself, being long a member of 4th Cav. Reg. Ills. Vols. and some time a member of your escort. This is my great claim to your indulgence. With many wishes for your happiness and success of the Party, . . ."—ALS, DNA, RG 56, Appraiser of Customs Applications. On Feb. 9, Alvin P. Hovey, Mount Vernon, Ind., wrote to USG. "At the request of Col McQuiddy, I forward to you in person his application for the position of Appraiser in the Custom House at Louisville Ky, which I hope you will be willing to grant. You no doubt remember him as one of my Aids in the glorious Vicksburgh Campaign. For his gallantry and ability, he rose from 1st Lieutenant of the 23d Indiana Vols to the Command and rank of Col of Vols of an Indiana Regiment. A braver, better, or truer Man never served under my command, and let me add, no Kentuckian nor Northern Man is a better Republican. Remembering his past services and sacrifices, and as I have no personal favors to ask for, I trust that you will give to him this small Office—which I shall add to your many personal favors to myself"—ALS, *ibid.* On the same day, Governor Conrad Baker of Ind. favorably endorsed this letter. AES, *ibid.* Papers recommending Richard R. Bolling and William Cash are *ibid.* On March 23, USG nominated Jeremiah F. Huber, formerly capt. and bvt. maj., commissary of subsistence, as appraiser of merchandise, Louisville.

1871, JAN. 25. Orville E. Babcock to Secretary of War William W. Belknap. "The President directs me to submit for your consideration, H. R. 1357. entitled: 'An Act for the relief of Shadrach Saunders, Daniel Moore, Alexander Forbes and other citizens of Petersburg Va.' and to ask whether any reasons exist why it should not receive his approval."—Copy, DLC-USG, II, 1. On Jan. 26, Max Bock, clerk, War Dept., wrote a memorandum. ". . . The com'y Genl states that his records do not show anything with regard to the services of these men &c.—but it appears from the records in *A. G. O.* that on the 20th Feby 68 Hon. J. M Thayer, U. S. S. forwarded 6 vouchers (pay rolls) furnished by Capt W. P. Martin, Com. Sub. of certain colored men of Petersburg, Va, for services rendered in the Subce Dept. in 1865—. . . From what I remember these men were ordered to be employed by Genl Grant only for the purpose of receiving rations but no pay, in order to keep them from starving"—ADS, DNA, RG 94, Letters Received, 316 1871. On Feb. 2, Belknap wrote to USG. "I have the honor to return, herewith, the Act of Congress for the relief of Shadrack Saunders and other citizens of Petersburg, Virginia, and to state that there is no evidence in possession of this

Department to show that the persons named in the act rendered service in the commissary department of the army at Petersburg between the dates mentioned therein—Some of the beneficiaries designated are parties to a claim for compensation for services rendered in the commissary department at Petersburg between dates subsequent to those named in the act, but the claim has been disallowed for the reason that during the time for which compensation is claimed there was an order of the military commander which, though it authorized the acceptance by military officers of the labor of destitute able-bodied citizens in return for rations to be issued to them and their destitute families, expressly forbade the payment or allowance of any money compensation for such labor. The period named in this act is prior to the date of the military order just cited, and if the services were actually rendered and at the time named, there appears to be no objection to the bill."—Copy, *ibid.*, RG 107, Letters Sent, Military Affairs. On Feb. 4, Horace Porter wrote to Secretary of State Hamilton Fish. "The President directs me to transmit herewith H. R. 1357, . . . which was received at the Executive Mansion on the 24th of January last, and not having been returned to the House of Representatives within the ten days prescribed by the Constitution, has become a law of the United States."—Copy, DLC-USG, II, 1. This law gave each claimant $16.80. See *CG*, 41–2, 4593.

1871, JAN. 25. U.S. Senator George F. Edmunds of Vt. to USG. "I suppose we shall very soon pass a joint resolution for certain scientific investigations into the subject of our coast and lake fishes, & their dimunition &c. I write this to suggest that Prof. S F. Baird of the Smithsonian Institution has been pursuing investigations into the matter for some time and it is at his proposal that this official proceedure is considered &c. And I think, and therefore venture to hope, that he ought to be named for the commissioner. His character and attainments are pre eminent, and he will be enabled with the authority of the proposed law to carry on the inquiry with much benefit to important interests of the country."—ALS, DNA, RG 59, Letters of Application and Recommendation. On Feb. 7, Edmunds wrote to USG on the same subject.—ALS, *ibid.* On Feb. 14, USG nominated Spencer F. Baird, asst. secretary, Smithsonian Institution, as Commissioner of Fish and Fisheries. See *CG*, 41–3, 584–85, 683, 1092; A. Hunter Dupree, *Science in the Federal Government: A History of Policies and Activities to 1940* (Cambridge, Mass., 1957), pp. 236–38.

1871, JAN. 26. Mattie Green, Jackson, Tenn., to USG. "This letter will be handed you by Genl Smith, Member of Congress from our District, together with some papers in reference to the case I am going to speak of—I hope you will remember me—my name was Mattie, McRee, & you knew me very well during the war, when I told you Good bye you said to me 'any thing I can ever assist you in just let me know,' I never forgot it and now I am in great need of a little assistance from you, Occupying as you do such a high & honorable position I feel as though I am quite bold in addressing, but I hope you will excuse me when I relate you my position & will lend me a helping hand in time of *need* and, Any thing I can ever do for you on earth will cheerfully be performed Genl Smith can reccommend my husband and my self to you as being *True* now and during the whole War, I am now married, I married Lieut Green of the, 7,th Wisconsin Battery, Hon. M. H. Carpenter of Wisconsin is personally acquainted with him—Lieut Green was stationed at Memphis, Tenn with his command & was tried by Court Marshal for a trivial & unjust offence for which he never was guilty, just some envious enemies of his performed the whole plot and carried it out, he was not *relieved* of *duty* or *put under arrest at all, during trial,* he continued on duty as 1st Lieut until Janry 15th 1864, at which date he received an order signed by you dated at Vickburg, Miss, dismissing him from Service to take effect, Sept 30,th, 1863. You see by this he done duty 3½ months after date of order as is shown also by certificate of Lieut Wheelock who commanded Battery at time he was on Service and the order receved. The certificate refered to you will see in papers with this letter, on Settling his accounts with Department in order to draw ~~my~~his pay, the Second Auditer has ruled that he cannot be paid for services rendered from the date of order of dismissal 30 Sept. 1863 to date of recieving order Jan. 15, 1864 without an order from you as President of the, U. S. States, After Lt. Green, was dissmissed he went to Washington immediately and his disabilities were removed by President Licon as ~~is~~ shown by the accompayning letter of Ajt Genl dated May 17, 1864, Ther are other papers relating to the case I send also, & if any thing more is required let me know I only ask you President Grant to give us *justice* in this matter, Genl Smith can tell you our condition here, and how my husband has been treated, it is all we can do to make a living, We have two little ones & we need all we can get—You will see there is near $400,00 due my husband as a Soldier, which would help us greatly now—In fact I depend largely upon it, we are owing debts which must be paid, and you can have this just money allowed us—I hope and trust you will decide this matter in our favor, we have been trying faithful to get it for a long time now—& this is our last hope—If you please send us the required order for the pay which I am quite sure you will decide is justly due him, and it is in your power *only* to grant this request and have the money allowed us—"—ALS, DNA, RG 233, 42A-D1. The enclosures and related papers are *ibid.* On March 10, Secretary of War William W. Belknap endorsed these papers. "Respectfully returned to the President with the required report, as contained in the preceding endorsements of the Judge Advocate General and the Adjutant-General of the Army. Under the circumstances, it is recommended that the claim be submitted to Congress and commended to favorable consideration—"—ES, *ibid.* On Feb. 4, 1873, Belknap wrote to USG recommending that he sign a bill securing payment to Galen E. Green.—Copy, DNA, RG 107, Letters Sent, Military Affairs; *CG*, 42–3, 1092. See *SRC*, 42-3-272.

1871, JAN. 27. To Senate. "I transmit for consideration, with a view to its ratification, a Treaty of Friendship, Commerce and Navigation between the United States and the Oriental Republic of Uruguay, which was signed at

Monte Video it is presumed in the course of last month, though the precise date has inadvertently been omitted. A copy of the correspondence relating to the instrument is also herewith transmitted. From this it will be seen that the treaty is substantially the same as one between the same parties which has already been approved by the Senate and ratified by the President of the United States, but the ratifications of which have never been exchanged. If the Senate should approve the new treaty, it is suggested that their Resolution to that effect should include authority to insert the precise date, when that shall have been ascertained."—DS, RG 46, Presidential Messages. Related papers are *ibid.* On March 31, the Senate ratified this treaty.

1871, Jan. 27. To Secretary of the Interior Columbus Delano. "The Military and Wood reservations at Fort Colville, Washington Territory, as described in the accompanying map, report and papers, are made for military purposes, as recommended by the Secretary of War; and the Secretary of the Interior will cause the same to be noted in the General Land Office."—Copy, DNA, RG 107, Letters Sent, Military Affairs.

1871, Jan. 27. U.S. Senators Matthew H. Carpenter and Timothy O. Howe of Wis. to USG. "We earnestly recommend George C. Stevens, Esq. of Milwaukee Wisconsin, to be appointed Collector of the Port of Milwaukie. Mr Stevens is well known to us; is a sound Republican, a man of integrity and ability, and we respectfully ask for his immediate appointment"—LS, DNA, RG 56, Collector of Customs Applications. On Feb. 6, USG nominated George C. Stevens as collector of customs, Milwaukee.

1871, Jan. 28. Secretary of the Interior Columbus Delano to USG. "I have the honor to return, herewith, enrolled bill—H. R. 1549—entitled 'An Act to enable Ann M. Rodefer, Administratrix of Joseph Rodefer, deceased, to make application for the extension of letters patent for an improvement in bedstead fastenings,' and to state that I am aware of no just reason why the same should not become a law."—LS, OFH.

1871, Jan. 31. U.S. Representative John Coburn of Ind. to USG. "The bearer, Mr Silas Shoecraft of Greencastle Indiana, desires a short interview with you. Mr Shoecraft has for many years lived in central Indiana where he is known as an honest, industrious and excellent man. When the enlistment of Colored troops was allowed he at once went to work and by his general acquaintance and influence did very much in filling up that branch of the military service. We had in our region no more active or efficient Colored man in this work than Mr Shoecraft. He was afterwards employed by the General Government at the same work in the South. He made sacrifices and incurred losses which cannot be repaid. It may be that there is some position which he can obtain, but such a thing is beyond my control. I most cordially endorse him in all respects and ask for him your favorable consideration."—ALS, In.

1871, JAN. Charles P. Bailey, "Kannawha Station Wood County," West Va., to USG. "having decended or Come down as it were from a former Generation, pardon me for rehearsing what You must or should assuredly know, that the government of the U. S. as brought into being by the Sovreign head the people of the Respective states was and was to be a Civil Government. Yet we the people of the respective states have a Military force for the Especial purpose and none other to support pr~~otect~~eserve protict, defend and purpetuate the Civil authorities (both state & Federal), and that Millitary force or power cannot be used by the Legislative branch of the government for Only three specific and distinct Object, as we infer from the power vested in that brance of the government, which reads to provide for Calling fourth the Millitia to Execute the Laws of the Union suppress insurection and repell invasion, (not a word about reconstruction.) this being one of the granted powers to Congress the enquiry now arises as to what Constitutes the Laws of the Union. In answer we the people do say the Laws of the Union Covers and imbraces all the mutual agreements of the sovreign head the people of the respective states as set fourth and defined by their Constitution the Ordained and Established Constitution of the U S. leaving out the reconstruction acts of Congress, but not leaving out the Legislative Executive and Juditial branches of the government:. . . hence Mr President having never taken the Oath to preserve protect and defend the Constitution of the U. S. I do not feel Competent or Justifiable in making any other suggestion than that made in a former Communication. If that measure should be rejected by the Congress you will no doubt apply and use all the remedies placed in your hands for the preservation protection and defence of the Constitution of the U. S. In conclusion I will now say what my solemn Convictions are without any desire to offend or mislead you in the discharge of your solemn Obligation to the high god of heaven and the people of the United States—had such a state of things been brought about by the Congress as now exists, in the days of President Jackson what that Constitutional Iron willed President would have said by the Eternal the Juditial branch of the government must and shall be sustained in the discharge of all the powers conferd upon it"—ALS, DLC-Salmon P. Chase.

1871, FEB. 1. Horace Porter to Secretary of the Treasury George S. Boutwell. "The President directs me to call your attention to the appointment of Saml Coulter as Collr of Int. Rev. for the District of Washington Territory on the 27th of Oct. 1870, and whose name has not yet been sent to the Senate for confirmation."—Copy, DLC-USG, II, 1. On Feb. 2, Boutwell wrote to USG. "I transmit herewith the nomination of Samuel Coulter as Collector of Internal Revenue for the Collection District of Washington Territory, vice Hazard Stevens to be removed. In explanation of the fact that Mr. Coulter's nomination was not submitted for transmission to the Senate with other temporary appointments (Dec. 6th 1870) I have respectfully to state, that his temporary designation bears date of October 27th 1870, and since that date the Department has not been notified or been aware of any steps being taken with a view to his qualification. The terms and conditions of a temporary appointment or commission not having been complied with I request that the enclosed—prepared for Mr. Coulter and the suspension of Hazard Stevens may be cancelled and returned to this Department."—Copy, DNA, RG 56, Letters Sent. On the same day, USG nominated Samuel Coulter as collector of Internal Revenue, Washington Territory.

1871, FEB. 1. Olivia D. Adams, Clinton, Iowa, to USG. "do please listen to me for I do not no to hoom I can go for aid if not to you and I come on my bended nees as to the father of us all and ask you to aid me in this my time of great nead on acount of my three little children not for my self I have praid to the God who rules over us all to assist me in the wright way to do and something seems to say to my heart consult the President altho it may be an eval genious I feal at heart it is rite to obey it when the rebellion broke out me and my dear husband lived in missoura and he inlisted in the servise on the 21 day of Jan and I was left at home with two little children the yongest 6 months old in that land of rebels I shal not atempt to disscribe what I suffered then and their alone choping and carying my own wood from the woods but it was my duty as a true union woman to do so and to bair all with courage and hope for the future but O the future has come when my husband had bin in the servise near 2 years he was discharged on acount of chronic diare the rebels still raged whair we wair for my husbands safety we came north he has bin sick with the same complant till last august he died and left me with three little children the youngest 4 years old one boy and two girls and then what am I to do funeral expenses and doctor bill has taken all most the last remaning cent I have bin told to go and try if my little children could not draw a pension and if they can whair am I to go too to find out I have no money to give a lawyear and they no it therefore they will not aid me I want to give my children some learning so they may learn to take care of them selves when they are older for they may not long have a mother to aid them for cair and trouble has nerely wore me out my boy is twelve but no learning his father has had to keep him at home in somers to help on the farm for we wrented and had to do all we could earn a living and in the winter me and the boy had to git most of the wood and do the chores for we was not able to hire O my hart aches for that dear boy we had forty achers of land in adair co mo, before the war but the taxis has eat it up O is nothing left me but to beg cant I draw back pension for him I can git the doctors that has docterd him to sertify to the truth of his case and now ~~mr grant~~ Mr G Grant do please do something for me if nothing more refer me too to the man in washington that will attend to my case O Sir think if your little ones was in the plase of mine it is not finery nor extravigense that has put me here but this dreadful dreadful war for our close are limited to ten cent calico sickness and death and trouble almost makes me crasy O sir I beseach you to aid me some if I but had the old close you thro a way it would be a great help for me if I could git 500 or 600 dolars to bild me a house I have the offer of a lot in the out age of town and if I can git money enuf to go their I can wash and work hard to earn a living and send my children to school I wish you would aid me as I hate to raise my childre[n] in ignuranse I will now close hoping the blesings of good to sest upon you and yours O I prey you to aid me in this my time of great nead if you will be as good as to aid me whitch I hope you will here is my adress, . . ."—ALS, DNA, RG 48, Miscellaneous Div., Letters Received.

1871, FEB. 2. USG endorsement. "If the Minister appointed to Liberia does not accept, and leave for his post with but little delay, I am willing that this apt. should be made."—AES, DNA, RG 59, Letters of Application and Recommendation. Written on a letter of Nov. 12, 1870, from Edward S. Rowse, St. Louis, praising J. Milton Turner.—ALS, *ibid.* On April 26, 1869, Governor Joseph W. McClurg of Mo. had written to USG. "It affords me pleasure to be able to recommend *James Milton Turner*, a citizen of African descent, for the appointment of Minister to *Liberia.* He is now a teacher in Boonville, in this State. He was educated at Oberlin, Ohio, and has distinguished himself as an Orator. He is unquestionably a man of ability, sustains a fine moral character and would honor the position. I sincerely hope he will receive the appointment."—ALS, *ibid.* On Nov. 10, 1870, McClurg wrote a similar letter to USG.—ALS, *ibid.* Related papers are *ibid.* On Feb. 17, 1871, USG nominated Turner as minister to Liberia. J. Randolph Clay, Francis E. Dumas, and James W. Mason had declined to succeed John Seys in this post. Papers related to these nominations are *ibid.* On March 7, Secretary of State Hamilton Fish wrote in his diary. "J Milton Turner, lately appointed Minister to Liberia calls in Company with Mr Burdett M. C. from Missouri says he is poor & unable to pay his expenses to Liberia unless the Department can aid him"—DLC-Hamilton Fish. See Gary R. Kremer, *James Milton Turner and the Promise of America: The Public Life of a Post-Civil War Black Leader* (Columbia, Mo., and London, 1991), pp. 40–54.

On Dec. 31, 1872, Stephen B. Packard, U.S. marshal, La., *et al.*, New Orleans, wrote to USG recommending Thomas de S. Tucker as minister to Liberia.—DS (14 signatures), DNA, RG 59, Letters of Application and Recommendation. No appointment followed.

On Jan. 13, 1873, Frederick Douglass, St. Louis, wrote to USG. "Having learned that the mission to Liberia is soon to be vacated by the resignation of Mr. J. M. Turner; and believing that you will fill his place by some competent and deserving colored man, I take the liberty to recommend for that position Mr C. L de Randamie. I do this because I consider him a gentlemen in all respects qualified to discharge the duties of that position in a creditable manner. Mr De Randamie is well known in St Louis as an *honest, industrious and capable man*—a faithful supporter of the Republican party and of your administration. I am quite sure, from all I have heard and learned here, that his appointment, will be gratifying to the colored citizens of the U. States."—ALS, *ibid.* On Jan. 18, Lewis H. Douglass, managing editor, *New National*

Era, Washington, D. C., wrote to Constantine L. de Randamie. "It having come to my knowledge that my father (Frederick Douglass) recommends you for the position of Minister Resident and Consul General to Liberia and the New National Era having indorsed William Craft Esq: for the same position it might possibly occur to you that his indorsement of you was incincere. I feel it my duty to state to you that my father had no knowledge of the attitude of the 'New National Era' in relation to the position mentioned above owing to his absence from the City. And I also wish to assure you that had I known my father's wishes in this matter the publications in the New National Era would have been made to conform to them. . . ."—ALS, *ibid.* In an undated letter, de Randamie wrote to USG soliciting "the appointment of Consul General to Liberia; vacated by the Hon: J. Milton Turner. Your petitioner begs to say that he has resided in Liberia, for a period of ten years and was for many years agent of the American Colonization Society in Grand Bassa County; is well acquainted with the public and business men of that Country, and of the United States who do business in that Country. It may perhaps be proper to also state that he is familiar with the English, Dutch, French and German languages."—ALS, *ibid.* On Jan. 11, Carman A. Newcomb, John McDonald, Charles W. Ford, and others, St. Louis, favorably endorsed this letter.—ES, *ibid.* On Jan. 18, de Randamie, Washington, D. C., wrote to U.S. Representative Horace Maynard of Tenn. "Without any claim upon your assistance in promoting my aspirations to the Liberian Mission, I feel nevertheless encouraged by the attention you have been pleased to vouchsafe me, during my late intrusive call at your residence, to again solicit your kind services near Secretary Fish Senators Conkling, Morton (who knows of me) and such other officials, whose countenance & advocacy of my pretension near the President may promote the success of my present effort—The unfortunate attitude of the Senators from my own State toward the administration, forces this alternative upon me, . . ."—ALS, *ibid.* Related papers are *ibid.* No appointment followed.

On Jan. 26, U.S. Representative George F. Hoar of Mass. wrote to USG. "I commend to your most kind and favorable consideration the desire of William Crafts to be appointed minister to Liberia. I have no personal knowledge of Mr Crafts but I am satisfied from the statements of persons in whom I have confidence that Mr Crafts is capable of rendering eminent service to the country—"—ALS, *ibid.* On Jan. 13, William Craft, Washington, D. C., had written to Fish. "In the event of its being deemed desirable to make a change in the Liberian mission I beg to offer the Government my humble services as Minister to that country. I was born in the State of Georgia (in 1826) where I now reside. The following are a few reasons that induce me to aspire to the honorable & responsible position of representing the Government abroad In 1862 I was residing in England & was there commissioned by a number of enfluential gentlemen to the King of Dahomey & other chiefs on the West Coast of Africa with the view of getting them to turn their attention more fully to legitimate commerce in the hope that it might supersede the Slave-traffic. I was well received & have cause to believe that my duty was discharged satisfactorilly to those interesed. I became acquainted with President Roberts & other promenant men of Liberia, & were I appointed there, have no doubt that the commercial & other experiance gained in Europe as well as in Africa, would enable me to be of service to my country. On the occasion of my leaving England for the United States—a few of the gentlemen with whom I had the privilige of being associated, ~~with~~ for some time, especially during the Rebellion, in keeping alive public sentiment favourable to the Union—kindly sent me the accompaning testimonial which I have the honor to submit with this application for your kind consideration"—ALS, *ibid.* The enclosure is *ibid.* No appointment followed. See *New York Times*, Dec. 8, 1874; Craft, *Running a Thousand Miles for Freedom; or, the Escape of William and Ellen Craft from Slavery* (1860; reprinted, Miami, 1969); L. Maria Child, *The Freedmen's Book* (Boston, 1865), pp. 179–204.

On Feb. 1, 1873, Governor John L. Beveridge of Ill. and many others petitioned USG to appoint as "Minister to the Republic of Liberia, our respected and esteemed fellow citizen, Rev. James W. H. Jackson, of Springfield, Illinois. His age is about 42 years. He has long been a resident of Springfield. He is a man of unblemished reputation and of the strictest integrity and would be an honorable representative of our Government in the position referred to. His appointment would be received and looked upon by our colored fellow citizens (as well as by all others) as another step towards recognizing the fitness of colored men to fill, with honor and credit to themselves and to the country, certain positions of responsibility and trust."—DS, DNA, RG 59, Letters of Application and Recommendation. On July 20 and 26, James W. H. Jackson, Springfield, wrote to USG. "By the request of my friends Sir I consented to petition your Excellency for the appointment as Minister to the republic of Liberia not that we desired the removal of Hon. J. Milton Turnner in our favor but if he was removed that we might fill the place. now Sir: it seems to me that the office of consul both in Hayti and Liberia is of Sufficient important to demand the attention of a consul and if in your judgment that an agent would subserve the best interest to the Government in a commercial point of view then sir I would desire to be the appointee however this is for your consideration" "in view of the fact that I have called your attention to my petition and the desire that I have to fill the office of Minister or Consul of Liberia permit me to State what seems to me to be the facts in the case now sir. in the first place it seems to me to be impossible for the Ministers give the attention that each office does require for instant in Liberia there are four hundred 400 miles of sea board with six ports to ship from Monrovia Sierre Leone and Sherbro and also in Hayti there are three or more there is Port-au-Prince Cape Haytien and Jereimie these are the principal ports in each place now sir in Liberia th Territory is vary large to travel over by one man and in Hayti the business is vary large for one man to attend to and in the second place with these facts in view it does seem to me that the Commercial interest must unavoidably Suffer for want of a special agent both in Liberia and Hayti to look more a specialy after the Commercial interest of each of the republics it will require a consul in each besides the Government would be better represented with these agents"—ALS, *ibid.* Related papers are *ibid.* No appointment followed.

On March 11, U.S. Senator George E. Spencer of Ala. forwarded to USG a letter recommending Jeremiah Haralson for minister to Liberia.—AES, *ibid.* Related papers are *ibid.* No appointment followed. Haralson served as Republican U.S. representative from Ala. (1875–77).

1871, FEB. 2. Secretary of the Treasury George S. Boutwell to USG. "I have the honor to suggest for your approval, the appointment of the following gentlemen as Special Commissioners for the annual Assay at the Mint of the United States at Philadelphia, on the 13th day of February inst. in accordance with the 32nd Section of the Act of January 18th, 1837, viz: Professor Joseph Henry, Smithsonian Institute, Professor John Torrey United States Assay Office, Rev. F. A. P. Barnard, Presd't Columbia College N. Y. J. E. Hilgard Asst. Supt. Weights and Measures. Hon. H. R. Linderman, Philadelphia. Professor Fairman Rogers Philadelphia. John Jay Knox Deputy Comptroller of Currency. Hon. John P. Putnam, Boston, E. B. Elliott, Esq. Washington Horace Thompson Esq. St. Paul Minn. M. C. Read, Esq. Hudson, Ohio."—Copy (tabular material expanded), DNA, RG 104, Letters Sent to Mint Directors. USG endorsed this letter. "Approved."—Copy (undated), *ibid.* On Feb. 4, Boutwell wrote to USG recommending Robert J. Stevens of San Francisco to replace Horace Thompson, who declined the appointment.—Copy, *ibid.*

1871, FEB. 2. Elias W. Fox, surveyor of customs, St. Louis, to USG. "Mr Wm B. Baker (the gentleman in whose behalf this is written) has resided in St Louis for many years and occupied prominent positions on the Editorial Staffs of both the 'Democrat', and 'Republican': he has also been Sect'y of the 'Union Merchants Exchange', and of the 'St Louis Board of Trade'. Mr Baker is a gentleman of culture, learning, ripe experience and integrity, and is in my judgement well qualified to make an excellent and efficient officer in the position he seeks—viz 'Indian Inspector'. At one period of his life he resided in New Mexico, and I think him well acquainted with the administration of Indian affairs in that locality. He is (and has been) an ardent supporter of the Administration and has promoted its interests and those of the Republican party in no small degree, with his pen. His appointment will be regarded with favor by Republicans generally throughout the State."—LS, DNA, RG 48, Appointment Div., Letters Received. On Jan. 7, William B. Baker had written to USG. "In case the Bill of Senator Wilson, making provision for six Indian Inspectors, receives the favorable consideration of the Senate and the Executive, I respectfully present myself as an applicant for a position on said Commission. Of my ability to perform the duties of the office, permit me to refer you to the accompanying letter of Hon: E. W. Fox, of this city, and to Hon: C. D. Drake, of the Court of Claims."—ALS, *ibid.* The bill did not pass.

1871, FEB. 5. James L. Prouty, Clintonville, Mo., to USG. "knowing the troubles by which you are beset, on account personel malice or of men who seek their own personel agrandizement. Like the renegade Brown and his adherents. Men whose only aim is to destroy or the mation if the Republican party. They do not care which. You still have friends in this part of the country who hope for your reelection in 72 and among them is your humble servant. But my chief object in writing this letter was not only to let you know my political views, but another matter which I consider of some importance to myself. Several years ago during Mr Lincoln's administration Col J. E. Burbank (through the influence of Gov Morton) was allowed to choose a cadet for the military academy from Nebraska. I was chosen but on finding my Education not sufficient. and I was not the required age some one else was chosen but a wild fancy had taken hold of me and I have improved every chance of gaining education I had not the ~~use~~ advantage of schools and so had to get my learning the best I could. My aim was one day to be a member of the Military Academy. I applied (last June) in the regular way to the Secretary of War, but received information that there was a member from this district. My only chance now is in your bounty I can procure good recomindations of character from my former place of residence Nebraska, and from this place. My age is 19 years 2 monts 22 days My place of residence 1½ miles north of east of Clintonville My full name is James. Lester Prouty. If you should see fit to appoint me you would do me the greatest favor in your power and I should one day hope to repay you. . . . P. S. My only deformity was the result of accident when I was quite young by it my thumb on my right hand ~~is~~was made stiff in the first joint & was misshapen as considerable but it is as sound as ever if you think this would not pass examination I frankly say I donot want the appointment"—ALS, DNA, RG 94, Unsuccessful Cadet Applications.

1871, FEB. 6. Orville E. Babcock to Secretary of the Treasury George S. Boutwell. "The President directs me to write you and ask if you do not think he had better send in the name of Mr Gooch for Collector of the Port of Boston, to take effect upon the expiration of the term of office of the present incumbent, and thus anticipate the pressure of applications. . . . P. S. If sent this morning the nomination will go to the Senate today."—Copy, DLC-USG, II, 1. On Feb. 21, USG nominated Thomas Russell for reappointment as collector of customs, Boston and Charlestown.

1871, FEB. 6. Samuel M. Janney, Omaha, to USG. "I purpose retiring from the position I now occupy as superintendent of Indian affairs for the Northern Superintendency, at the close of the third quarter of this year. Being now in my seventy first year, I wish to be relieved from the care & labor attendant on this office. I therefore tender my resignation to take effct on the 30th of the ninth month 1871."—ALS, DNA, RG 48, Appointment Div., Letters Received. On Jan. 5, Orville E. Babcock had written to Janney. "The President directs me to acknowledge the receipt of your letter and the very interesting photographs of Indians and indian scenes. He wishes me to communicate his thanks for the photographs and for the very kind assurance of your support to the present Indian policy. He will be pleased if you will communicate his thanks to those associated with you in sending the photographs."—Copy, DLC-USG, II, 1. See *HED*, 42-2-1, part 5, pp. 854–55; *Memoirs of Samuel M. Janney* (2nd ed., Philadelphia, 1881), pp. 250–87.

On July 24, William Dorsey, Philadelphia, wrote to USG. "We herewith hand thee the resignation of our friend Samuel M Janney Superintendent of Indian affairs for the northern Superintendency—and also present to thee the name of Barclay White of Juliustown New Jersey whom we designate as a person well qualified to succeed him in his responsible position—on behalf of the executive committee of the Six Yearly meetings of Friends"—ALS, DNA, RG 48, Appointment Div., Letters Received. On Dec. 5, USG nominated Barclay White.

1871, FEB. 7. Governor Rutherford B. Hayes of Ohio to USG. "I urgently request the appointment of Henry N Eastman of Zanesville. O. as a Cadet at West Point. He belongs to a family conspicuous for talents and public services; and I am led by representations, that I b[e]lieve trustw[or]thy, to believe that Henry will be a creditable student and officer."—ALS (press), OFH. Henry N. Eastman did not attend USMA.

187[*1*], FEB. 7. Carie E. Loop, Washington, D. C., to USG. "after calling at the White House three times, and could not see you, I take this opportunity of writing to you through the Mail mearly asking a favor of which I hope you will grant, My Husband is a Marine Soldier at the Navy Y D and he is sick nearly all the time, his Diseas being Chronic Liver Complaint, and his Lungs are consideraby affected, and he is not fit to do the Duty of a Soldier, and besides he cannot Support his Family of 16 per Month as he is not allowed Rations for them, they tell him they have more marred men, then they are allowed, and ~~it~~ is utterly Imposible for me to get along without his help, he has the Prosspect of a Situation at the Treasury, soon as I can get his Discharge out . . ."—ALS, DNA, RG 127, Letters Received. On Feb. 16, 1871, Francis M. Loop, Washington, D. C., wrote to Secretary of the Navy George M. Robeson requesting his discharge from the Marine Corps.—ALS, *ibid.*

1871, FEB. 8. To Congress. "I transmit herewith an extract of a paper addressed to the President, the Secretary of the Interior and the Commissioner of Indian Affairs, by the Committee, of Friends, on Indian Affairs, having charge of the Northern Superintendency, in relation to a desire of certain Indian tribes to sell a portion of the lands owned by them, with a view of locating on other lands that they may be able to purchase; together with a report of the Commissioner of Indian Affairs thereon, and a letter of the Secretary of the Interior Department, approving the report of the Commissioner. I submit the draft of a bill which has been prepared and which it is believed will effect the object desired by the Committee, and request the consideration thereof by Congress."—DS, DNA, RG 46, Presidential Messages; Df, ICarbS. *SED*, 41-3-35. On Feb. 2, Secretary of the Interior Columbus Delano had written to USG transmitting a letter of Jan. 25 from Henry R. Clum, act. commissioner of Indian Affairs, enclosing draft legislation for Indian tribes to sell or purchase land.—LS, DNA, RG 46, Presidential Messages. The bill did not become law.

1871, FEB. 8. To Lt. Col. William D. Whipple. "I have the honor to acknowledge the receipt yesterday, through you, of Mr David B. Hoffman's deed for ten acres of land in the City of San Diego, Cal. I herewith return it and beg that you will say to Mr Hoffman that while I appreciate his kindness I cannot accept his offer. Mr Hoffman will appreciate the motive which necessitates my returning this and thereby rejecting his kind offer."—Copy, DLC-USG, II, 1.

On July 8, 1874, David B. Hoffman, San Diego, wrote to USG. "*Confidential* . . . Col Finnegass Treasury detective, and U. S. Marshal, for the District of California, informs me that there will be a change made in the Custom House, here, in consequence of the recent robbery of the safe of that place. If you can do so with propriety I wish you would give me the appointmt. My record is good at home, and abroad. I have been twice Deputy Collector of this Port, and have never had any trouble; always giving good satisfaction to all concerned. I was one of the Presidentil Electors, in 1868., and traveled and worked hard for you then, and in your last campaign. During the recent rebellion, I held a comn as Asst Surgeon, of Volenteers, in the army for over four years, with it has been said, by my superior officers, 'honor to the service, the country and myself.' My personal character, is well known to Senators Jones, Sargent, Hager, Stewart, Booth, and Representatives, Houghton, Page, Clayton, and McCormick. Also Judge Field's, of the Supreme Court, to whom I have the pleasure as well as the permission to refer. Finally, I am in straightened circumstances, with a large and growing family, on my hands, and need the position refered to very much. If you desire it, I can forward recommendations, *ad libitum*, but I am not able to visit Washington, and attend to the matter in person. Hoping that you may give me a favorable hearing, . . ."—ALS, DNA, RG 56, Collector of Customs Applications. On July 10, Hoffman wrote to USG on the same subject.—ALS, *ibid.* No appointment followed.

1871, FEB. 9. W. J. Q. Baker, New Orleans, to USG. "A bill to create a Dist Court, in North Louisiana has passed the House of Representatives, and will probably become a law—I am an applicant for the Judgeship in that event. In 1863, the day you broke up your head quarters at Vicksburg, I was there—On that occasion we had a conversation in regard to the war and in regard to Reconstruction—You then did me the honor to write a letter of introduction to Dr Cottman—in which you state your belief as to my loyalty—That letter is in the archives of the U. S. court here—I enclose a copy—Judge Chase did me the honor to appoint me Register in Bankruptcy of the 5. Cong Dist of La. which office I now hold—to take it required to take the Oath of July 1862—I was a Union man before and during the war, have favored reconstruction and voted for you for President—I should be proud of your nomination to the office of Judge of the new District if formed."—ALS, DNA, RG 60, Records Relating to Appointments. On March 16, Walter Q. Gresham, Indianapolis, wrote to USG. "Hon Charles Case, now and for some five years past a resident of New Orleans, where he is practicing law—will be an applicant for the District Judgship of Louisiana—Mr C formerly resided in this state, and represented his district two terms in Congress—. . ."—ALS, *ibid.* On Aug. 20, Wade H. Hough, Niagara Falls, N. Y., wrote to USG. "The writer is the man who called on you at your Cottage at Long Branch, about the 1st Inst.—And I really wished to have seen and conversed with you for a few moments again before I left Long Branch, but you did not say to call on you again, and I did not wish to intrude farther on your Valuable time.—You will perhaps better recollect me by the circumstance of my introducing myself to you by means of a letter of introduction from Lieut Govr Dunn of La, & a letter to Genl Dent as Judge of the 13th Judicial District Court of the State of Louisiana—and as an old resident of that State.—And I must say Mr President that considering the great ~~of~~ amount of persecution & proscription that I sufferred in my State for espousing your cause and Republican principles in 1868 & since that time I was somewhat mortified and chagrinned at my ~~short~~ reception on my short visit to you, Yet without a knowledge of these facts, the reception you gave me was friendly and cordial enough.—I now take the liberty of giving you a Succinct history of my political course. In 1860 I was a Union Man, and opposed with all my zeal & ability the Secession of my State from the Federal Union. I was myself a Senatorial Delegate in the Secession convention of La in 1861, and I was one among the few who would not & did not vote for nor sign the Ordinance of Secession—but after the war was inaugurated, being largely interested in the South I could not well leave the country, and I took an unwilling part in the Rebellion but after the war closed, and the 14th Amendment was declared adopted, my political status was so well known that Congress immediately removed my political disabilities—I accepted and advocated the adoption of the reconstrunction measures of Congress adopted 1867. And I was the first man among the old citizens of the country of any political Standing that openly & avowedly advocated your Election 1868. and for which I had to arm myself and a party of friends composed of both Races for a few weeks before the Election ~~from~~ to avoid being assassinated or driven out of the Parish where I had resided for more than a quarter of a century—I have ever since been a consistent Republican, though not extremely radical.—For the course I thought proper to pursue politically my old friends abandoned me, and nearly all my old clients left me—Now my Dear sir I have never called for nor received any favor or office from the General Goverment—And if there is anything I do abhor more than another it is the professional officer seeker,

And I felt so senitive on this subject when I saw you, that I did not muster up enough courage to ~~ask~~ tell you what I wished for you to do for me in the future. And I ask it now before hand for the reason that when the occasion arises my official duties ~~sh~~will preclude me from calling on you— It is this. There is a Bill now pending before Congress to create a Federal Judicial District in North La. which will probably become a Law, and as I am getting old, & dont wish to make a political scramble for a Judicial office I want the Appoint of Judge for the District should it be created, and my object in thus presenting my claim so early is that you may know & learn who your real and tried Friends are in Louisiana And who was so when it required a man of moral courage there to stand by you and that you may know in time the moral character & legal qualifications of the man that you may nominate—I am a Lawyer of over 20 years standing and for the last 3 years Judge of the 13th Judicial District of the State—I have no doubt but that I can give you satisfactory testimonials of my capacity & political status. I belong at present to neither of the Republican factions of the State, but hope to see them harmonized—My address is Natchez Miss. as we have no P. O. at Vidalia La where I live—I would be pleased to have a few lines in answer to this—Execuse me for the liberty I have thus taking in writing you so extensively—"—ALS, *ibid.* Congress did not create a second judicial district in La. See *CG*, 42–1, 15, 42–2, 3865–66.

1871, FEB. 10. To Congress. "I submit [h]erewith, for the information of Congress, the second annual report, of the Board of Indian Commissioners, to the Secretary of the Interior."—DS, DNA, RG 46, Presidential Messages. *SED*, 41-3-39. On Feb. 9, Secretary of the Interior Columbus Delano had written to USG conveying this report.—LS, DNA, RG 46, Presidential Messages.

1871, FEB. 11. George W. Currin, Ladiesburg, Md., to USG. "As it has been some time since I seen you or had any conversation with you since the surrender of Lee at Farmville I being a member of Company A 3rd Maryland Infantry and served under you through the Virginia Campaign. My object in writing is to find out how the soldiers who have an honorably discharge is to get the land which the Government promised to give them or if the government would pay anything for it and how much. As I am ignorant about the matter and dont know who to see about it so I thought I would write to you and try and learn if I could not get something for it. If you will give me a reply, I will be greatly indebted to you for your kindness"—ALS, DNA, RG 48, Lands and Railroads Div., Letters Received.

1871, FEB. 11. Gustavus A. Smith *et al.*, Santa Fé, to USG. "In case of a vacancy in the office of U. S. Dist. Attorney for New Mexico the undersigned republicans most earnestly request the appointment of Thomas B. Catron Esq to the position, and in support of the request urge the following reasons, *First.* Mr Catron speaks fluently and understands well the Spanish language, a knowledge of which is indispensably necessary to the success of a prosecuting officer in New Mexico. in addition to this he has been a resident of the Territory for five years and is largely and intimately acquainted with the people. *Second.* Mr Catron is an able energetic and experienced Prosecuting Attorney, having been for the last two years Attoney General for New Mexico, which office he has filled with marked ability, and to the entire satisfaction to the people. in addition to this he has often represented the interests of the U. S. in the various U. S. Courts, as substitute U. S. Attoney. *Third.* Since the arrival of Mr Catron in New Mexico, he has been an active and faithful member of the Republican party and in perfect harmony with the admistration."—DS (16 signatures), DNA, RG 60, Records Relating to Appointments. Related papers are *ibid.* On Feb. 5, 1872, USG nominated Thomas B. Catron as U.S. attorney, New Mexico Territory.

1871, FEB. 13. Horace Porter to Secretary of State Hamilton Fish. "The President directs me to transmit to your department S. 849. entitled 'An Act to authorize the sale of certain lands reserved for the use of the Menomonee tribe of Indians in the state of Wisconsin.'—which was received at the Executive Mansion on the first instant and not having been returned to the House in which it originated within the ten days prescribed by the Constitution has become a law of the United States without his signature."—Copy, DLC-USG, II, 1.

1871, FEB. 13. U.S. Senators William M. Stewart and James W. Nye and U.S. Representative Thomas Fitch of Nev. to USG. "We respectfully request and reccomend that Hon J Neely Johnson of Nevada be appointed one of the Board of Visitors at the West Point M A for this year Mr Johnson was formerly Governor of California, was President of the Nevada Constitutional Convention and more recently one of the Supreme Judges of that State"—LS, DNA, RG 94, USMA, Board of Visitors. On Feb. 27, U.S. Representative-elect Lewis Tillman of Tenn. *et al.* wrote to USG. "We respectfully suggest and recommend Col James L. Scudder of Shelbyville Bedford county Tenn. a suitable person to be appointed one of the Board of Visitors to the Military Academy at West-Point for the present year. Col—Scudder was a Lieut. in the Mexican war, was severely wounded at Montery and mentioned favorably by Gen. Taylor in his report of that battle."—LS (6 signatures), *ibid.*, Unsuccessful Cadet Applications. USG appointed J. Neely Johnson to the board of visitors, USMA, for June 1871, and James L. Scudder for June 1872. See *Calendar*, Nov. 15, 1871; *HED*, 42-2-1, part 2, pp. 434–43.

1871, FEB. 14. J. B. Gilliland, Emporia, Kan., to USG. "I beg leave to call your attention to the Kaw Indian reservation. The citizens of this State are generally very anxious that said Indians be removed from said resevation this comeing Spring, & that said land be opened to settlement as it is one of the best tracts of land in the State. I have been informed that their will be a certain amount of money raised from said reservation to be paid these

Indians If so I would suggest that the lands be appraised so as to cover the amount of said money due, And that the settlers be allowed to have their lands not exceeting ¼ of a section to each settler by their paying the amount due on said land. Some think it will go to the R. R. & be sold as other R R lands in payments. others that it will come in at sealed bids. & by the way this last course is the least satisfactory. We have seen the evil affects of this mode of disposeing of the Public lands. Whol sections of as good land as is in the State is n[o]t occupyed by man f[r]om 5 to 10 miles square. owned by large land Spiculators. others think it will come in to the higest bidder That I dont think best. The provisions of the homestead bill should be carried out as near as possible. giving the poar, & the landless soldier some Show, . . ."—ALS, DNA, RG 75, Letters Received, Kansas Agency.

1871, Feb. 14. James A. Murray, Buffalo, to USG. "(Confidential.). . . A year ago I had the pleasure of addressing you in reference to a certain Bill introduced in Congress, providing for the division of the present judicial District of Northern New York into two Districts—one to be called the Northern and the other the Western. I see by the telegraphic dispatches, that the Judiciary Committee have decided to report in favor of the Bill at the present session of Congress. I beg to say that if the proposed Bill is allowed to become a law, it will be a fraud upon the people of the United States. No division of the District is necessary, except to provide offices for ambitious politicians. The Bill provides for the appointment of a Judge, Marshal &c. for the new District,—thereby imposing additional burdens and taxes upon the people. If a division of this District was ever required, the time for doing so has past. From 1862 until 1868 there was sufficient business to keep two setts of officers fully occupied; but since that time there is no more than enough for one sett of officers. I believe, however, that the District Judge has too much labor. An Act of Congress, providing for the appointment of a Judge to transact *Bankruptcy business* would remedy all defects in that respect. It would relieve the Dist. Judge from so much laborious work—the new appointee to vacate his office on the repeal of the Bank'cy Act. But, inasmuch as Congress intends to increase the salary of the Dist. Judges to $5,000. per annum, it is questionable whether any action should be taken. I beg to state that a *veto* would have the desired effect in this matter; and I hope that it will be interposed."—ALS, DNA, RG 60, Letters Received, N. Y. On Feb. 9, 1874, Murray, asst. U.S. attorney, Lockport, wrote to USG on the same subject.—ALS, *ibid.*, Letters from the President.

1871, Feb. 15. USG endorsement. "The within recommendation of the Secretary of the Interior is hereby approved."—ES, DNA, RG 75, Letters Received, Central Superintendency. Written on a letter of Feb. 13 from Secretary of the Interior Columbus Delano to USG. "At the request of the Commissioner of Indian Affairs I have the honor to recommend that the Osage River Indian Agency in Kansas, be discontinued under the authority vested in the President of the United States by the 4th section of an Act of Congress, approved June 30th 1834 (4th Stat. at large page 735) and that the services of James Stanley as Agent be dispensed with. I also recommend that the Peoria, Kaskaskia, Piankeshaw, and Wea tribes of Indians be transferred from the Neosho Agency, and assigned to a Special Agency,—in connection with the Senecas, Mixed Senecas, Shawnees, Quapaws, and Ottawas,—to be established by this Department."—LS, *ibid.*

In March, Louis P. Chouteau (Sho-to-Shin-ca), Indian Territory, wrote to USG. "Will the Great Father pardon one so humble, so remote, an Osage Indian, for addressing him?—But my heart is full; and why should I not speak? Does not the Christian white man, carry his joy, and grief, and gratitude, to *his* Father?—claiming that he is even higher! I can only bring to you, My Father, a most grateful heart. How grateful, none can tell, without some knowledge of the history, traditions and condition of my race. These I have, from my own memory, and from old men who still are. We were a mighty people;—had undisputed ownership and sway, over an almost boundless country. The Mississippi, the Missouri, the Rocky Mountains and Texas, were on our borders. Our young men were strong and brave; our young women chaste and beautiful. Who was there to molest or make us afraid? Men are still on the earth, who were living, when these things were true: Men are among us still, who *remember* our first treaty with the white man; when our nation was solemnly pledged to perpetual friendship with him and his Government. We have kept that pledge. At what cost? Did our white brother ask us for land; we yielded it to him, piece by piece, until now We knew little or nothing of values, and trusted him. Often have we been forced to feed ourselves and little ones on promises. At last, a little strip of land was left us in Kansas. Portions of this strip were conveyed by treaty. But in no treaty, within the knowledge of any Osage living or dead, was there any stipulation conveying our title to the 'Neutral-lands'. If such a stipulation is on record, it was not read to us,—it was not talked to us,—it is a fraud. Some other portions of territory, are in the same condition. Let that pass. From the home still remaining, we would go onto the plains, to seek food and clothing. We had but few horses,—they had been stolen. No tents; no blankets,—no flour,—no coffee. We would meet tribes of our red bretheren,—who perhaps had just been warring upon the whites—rich in all these things. They jeered at our poverty,—taunted us with it, as the price we paid for our friendship for the white man. Wars ensued,—for we are not cowards. Our numbers wasted. And returning home, with heavy hearts, for the dead that were left, we would often find those homes occupied by whitemen, and ourselves homeless. Through all this, our father, we remembered that we were 'Wa-Sha-Sha',—trustworthy. Our name; and almost all that was left us. We knew that our 'great father' had bad children, who wronged us. But we blamed him not. True, we began to think, in our poverty and sorrow and feebleness, that he had forgotten us; and our hearts sunk.—But when you became our great chief, we soon felt that we were not forgotten. The men you sent to us, to speak your words, were our friends. We trusted them. We sold our home cheerfully, because you said it was best for us. Our new home, though not all we could wish—there is too little ground for corn—is still our home. We feel secure in it; feel certain that the men you have placed over us, will protect us. We have also heard of the good words you have spoken of us. And, now, though but a feeble remnant of a once powerful nation, we are no longer a heart-sick and despairing one. For all this 'Our Father' we thank you. I write this at the instigation of no white man. I learned his language, and something of its literature, but my heart is wholly with my people,—and I have no higher hope than to live and die, 'Wa-Sha-Sha.'"—ALS, *ibid.*, Letters Received, Neosho Agency.

On Nov. 3 and 8, reports came from Washington, D. C. "Francis T. King, member of the Orthodox Society of Friends, and Mr. Gibson, agent for the Osage Indians, had separate interviews with the Secretary of the Interior and President Grant to-day, also with the Board of Indian Commissioners, on the subject of the present condition of the Osage Indians. Agent Gibson represents that there are over 800 white trespassers from Kansas on the new Osage reservation, which was recently set apart for those Indians by the Government under the most solemn pledges that white intruders should be kept away, the Indians having been forced to sell their lands in Kansas about a year ago owing to similar encroachments." "The President and Secretary of War have had a conference relative to the squatters on the Osage lands. If they shall not remove in compliance with the notice of the Secretary of the Interior, they will be ejected by military force."—*New York Tribune*, Nov. 4, 9, 1871. See Message to Senate, Jan. 19, 1874; *HED*, 42-2-1, part 5, pp. 899–908, 42-3-1, part 5, I, 629–31.

1871, FEB. 15. Orville E. Babcock to U.S. Representative Benjamin F. Butler of Mass. "I return to you Gen Browne's letter with many thanks for your kindness—Please thank him for me when you write and greatly oblige. I have conversed with a number on the Post Master of Boston, and feel certain he can be confirmed with Senator Sumner's opposition. Would it not be well for Gen Burt's friends to bring his case up, so that if we have any fight we can commence early?"—ALS, DLC-Benjamin F. Butler. On March 1, USG renominated William L. Burt as postmaster, Boston.

1871, FEB. 15. Orville E. Babcock to George N. Eaton, Baltimore. "The President desires me to ask you to request Miss Purveyance to send him the name age and place of birth of the orphan he promised to send to the Naval Academy."—Copy, DLC-USG, II, 1. On Feb. 17, Babcock wrote to Eaton. "The President directs me to acknowledge the receipt of your letter of yesterday, and to say in answer that he supposed the boy was an orphan, the son of either an enlisted man or officer, and that he is sorry to say that the boy Smith does not come within the list from which he wishes to select cadets. He regrets that any misunderstanding has occurred. With thanks for your kindness, . . ."—Copy, *ibid.*

1871, Feb. 16. Henri Masson, Washington, D. C., to USG. "There is, I understand, a Vacancy in the Department of languages, at West-Point The appointment of a Professor of French, to fill that vacancy resting in your hands, I beg the honor of your choice . . ."—ALS, DNA, RG 94, Correspondence, USMA. On June 22, 1870, Horace Porter had written to Masson. "The President directs me to acknowledge the receipt of your letter and to say in reply that, you are at liberty to use his name, as a reference, as you request."—Copy, DLC-USG, II, 1.

On Feb. 16, 1871, Col. Thomas G. Pitcher, West Point, N. Y., telegraphed to Mary B. Pitcher. "Say to the President if he asks, Professor Coppeé first and Col Dubarry second."—Telegram received, DNA, RG 107, Telegrams Collected (Bound).

On Feb. 17, U.S. Representative Luke P. Poland of Vt. wrote to Secretary of State Hamilton Fish. "You will remember that nearly two years ago Gen. Henry A. Smalley was an applicant for a consular appointment, which I tried to help. In aid of his suit, he filed in your Dept. a large number of recommendations and among them one from the Professors at West Point, where he was educated and where he was for some time the Asst. Professor of French.—Gen. Smalley, is now an applicant for the vacant place, at West Point, caused by the death of Prof. Agnel. . . ."—ALS, *ibid.*, RG 59, Letters of Application and Recommendation.

On Feb. 21, E. W. Shore, Louisville, wrote to USG. "I would respectfully present to you the name of Charles Saffray M. D. as Professor of French in the Military Academy at West Point to fill the chair made vacant by the death of Professor H. R. Agnel. Dr Saffray is a native of France—finely educated—having graduated with great honor—in the University of Paris both in the Medical and Literary Departments. He has resided for a number of years in South America and was there engaged in the active duties of his profession and as a Professor of French. He came to NewYork in 1864—where he soon gained enviable distinction in his profession. He is now a Professor in the Medical College of Louisville. and also fills the chair of Professor in French of the Louisville Female College. . . ."—ALS, *ibid.*, RG 94, Correspondence, USMA.

In [*Feb. 1871*], Eugéne Subit wrote to USG. "The fact has just fallen under my notice that a vacancy exists at the military Academy of West Point in the Professorship of French. From my advantages in one of the first Universities of Europe, together with an experience of fifteen years in teaching in this country, I feel confident that I should be able to fill the position vacated, with advantage to the Institution and credit to myself. Besides the French (my native language) I am thoroughly acquainted with ancient languages and most of the modern European languages. Before becoming a citizen of this country I enlisted in the Army of the Union where I served for three years as an officer—I was at City Point and took part in the battles around Petersburg. I have always been identified with the Republican party and have always used my influence with the foreign population in behalf of the Administration—By giving this your kind consideration you will ~~have~~

~~done~~ do an act of justice to a staunch supporter of your Administration—" —ALS, *ibid.*

On April 6, 1870, Sidney Bartlett *et al.* had petitioned USG. "The undersigned members of the Bar respectfully request that Gen. George L. Andrews may be retained in his present office of Marshal of the District of Massachusetts, he having discharged the duties of that office to the entire satisfaction of the bar and the public generally."—DS (117 signatures), CtY. On Feb. 19, 1871, Edward B. Dalton, Boston, wrote to USG. "May I take the liberty of saying a word to you regarding Genl. Andrews, U. S. Marshal of this district, whose high character & public services have created the strongest feeling here Especially among those who are not politicians, that you may retain him in office—It is only because I know this, & because I know how great and general would be the disappointment in his removal, that I venture to address you in such a matter—Please accept this as my excuse . . ."—ALS, *ibid.* On Feb. 27, USG nominated George L. Andrews as professor of French, USMA, and, the next day, nominated Roland G. Usher as marshal, Mass.

1871, FEB. 17. To Senate. "In answer to your Resolution of the 19th of December last, requesting the President 'to furnish the Senate with the entire cost of transportation of mails and freights of every description to the Pacific Coast, also to all intermediate points west of the Missouri River from the annexation of California to July 1st 1864; and also the expenses of the War Department and Indian Bureau during the same period in guarding the overland route from the Missouri River to California against Indians and Mormons and the cost of the Indian service on the same line including in all cases freights and all other expenditures'—I transmit herewith reports received from the Secretary of the Interior; the Secretary of War and the Postmaster General."—DS, DNA, RG 46, Presidential Messages. On Jan. 17, Secretary of the Interior Columbus Delano had transmitted to USG a report of Jan. 12 from Henry R. Clum, act. commissioner of Indian Affairs, stating transportation costs to the dept. as $162,109.91 and Indian service costs as $8,761,757.91.—LS, *ibid.* On Dec. 22, 1870, Secretary of War William W. Belknap had written to USG. "The Secretary of War has the honor to report to the *President of the United States,* with reference to the Resolution of the *United States Senate* of December 19, 1870, that it is regarded as wholly impracticable, with the available clerical force of the Department, and with other present facilities, to furnish, within a reasonable time or with sufficient accuracy, the desired information concerning the *cost of military transportation and of guarding the overland route, from the Missouri River to the Pacific Ocean, against Indians and Mormons,* including all expenditures, from the annexation of California to July 1, 1864. Estimates can however be made from the best information now available, but it will consume much time and will require an appropriation for expenses; the clerical force of the Department being now actually below the current demands of the public service."—DS, *ibid.*, RG 107, Letters Received from Bureaus. Related papers are *ibid.*

On Feb. 15, 1871, Belknap wrote to USG. "The Secretary of War has the honor to report to the *President*, . . . that the entire *cost to the military service of guarding the overland route from the Missouri river to the Pacific ocean*, between the date of the annexation of California and July 1, 1864, so far as can be ascertained within a reasonable time and without an unreasonable expenditure of labor, was about one hundred millions of dollars. It is proper to state that, all things considered, the sum named is below rather than above the true cost of the service—"—DS, *ibid.*, RG 46, Presidential Messages. On Jan. 16, Postmaster Gen. John A. J. Creswell had written to USG. "The cost of the transportation of the mails to the Pacific coast, . . . is ascertained to have been not less than fourteen millions five hundred and eighty three thousand, nine hundred and eighty eight dollars and and sixty eight cents. ($14,583,988.68) as shown by the inclosed statement. As there is no continuous record in the department of expenditures for this service, the items making this aggregate had to be obtained (except the sum of $5,551,674.24 furnished by the Navy Dept paid under contracts made with that dept. in pursuance of law) by a laborious examination of the books and records for sixteen years past, aided by the memory of persons long in the public service; it is possible, therefore, that some expenditures of small amount may have escaped notice, but the total amount is believed to be substantially correct."—LS, *ibid.* The enclosure is *ibid.* See *SED*, 41-3-44.

1871, FEB. 17. Henry Hopkins, warden, Kan. State Penitentiary, Leavenworth, to USG. "Among those confined in this Prison who have been convicted of crimes against the General Government and sentenced to imprisonment by the United States Courts and Military Courts Martial—there are many who are *very* desirous to have their 'Rights of Citizenship' restored by Pardon at the expiration of their imprisonment I feel fully convinced to so restore them their 'Rights' would aid materially their future efforts to live correct lives I would respectfully ask is it in the power of the Executive to restore such as have obeyed all the Rules of the Prison and on such recommendation from the Warden would it be granted? I am pleading now Mr President for the fallen—those who need every assistance and encouragement to regain their Manhood This course is practiced with our State Prisoners and has been a great stimulus to live as they should both in and out of Prison"—ALS, DNA, RG 60, Letters from the President.

1871, FEB. 18. Samuel Shellabarger, Springfield, Ohio, to USG. "It is my desire, should the bill now pending to create a third Judicial district in Ohio become a law, to recommend the appointment of Hon Wm White of the Supreme Court of Ohio as judge of that district. I desired the privilege of doing so in person upon my going on to the meeting of the 42nd Congress; but did not wish to make any recommendation until *after* the bill became law. I am admonished by letters from influential friends of Judge White that such applications are now being pressed for this appointment as may make applications for *him* too late, if not made soon. I am therefore induced *now* to say to the president that I think the appointment of Judge White one, on *every* account, eminently fit to be made . . ."—ALS, DNA, RG 60, Records Relating to Appointments. On Feb. 20, Moses M. Granger, Zanesville, wrote to USG. "I venture to address you directly because there is no Member of either House of Congress to represent me, and yet I am one of the candidates for appointment as Judge of the proposed Middle District of Ohio. The Hon. G. W. Morgan member from this Cong. Dist. is a Democrat, and all my acquaintances from other Districts are as I am informed either candidates themselves or advocates of some local friend. Senator Sherman the only Republican Senator from Ohio, declines to make any recommendation for the office named, but under the circumstances abovestated has kindly consented to receive such papers as may be forwarded on my behalf and present them for consideration. . . ."—ALS, *ibid.* Related papers are *ibid.* In Feb., Joseph M. Trimble, Columbus, wrote to USG. "Believing you will seek for the proper man for the Judgeship of the Middle District of Ohio, created by the recent action of Congress—I would name to you Mr L J Critchfield of Columbus, Ohio former partner of Judge Swain . . ."—ALS, *ibid.*

On March 8, U.S. Representative William P. Sprague of Ohio wrote to USG recommending "Hon. T. W. Ewart of Marietta O. as Judge of the Middle Ohio District Court of U. S. (when Constituted), . . ."—ALS, *ibid.* Related papers are *ibid.* On Feb. 27, 1873, James W. Robinson, Marysville, wrote to USG. "I wrote to Secretary Delano a few days since (with whom I am well acquanted) saying I felt some interest in regard to the appointment of the Judge of the Dist Court for the Central Dist of Ohio in case such Dist should be formed—The more I think of it, the more I am persuaded that Judge Thomas C Jones of Delaware Ohio is the right man for that place . . ."—ALS, *ibid.* Related papers are *ibid.* Proposed legislation to create an additional U.S. judicial district in Ohio failed.

1871, FEB. 20. Frederick MacCrellish, San Francisco, to Frederick T. Dent. "I send by our friend Lieut Morey to deliver you a letter to President Grant. It is unsealed—read it an seal it up. Can the President receive such a letter—Can he (when travelling accept private hospitality) if so disposed receive hospitality from a private citizen who has *nothing to ask.* I tender the offer of my private residence for a few days to the President as a friend—as a return of his Courtesy (and yours) to me when at City Point in 1864 Dec 7th 8th & 9th and also as the chief magistrate of this great nation. I make the offer in all sincerity and if it can be accepted all right—if not the same."—ALS, ICarbS. See *San Francisco Chronicle,* Nov. 1, 1882.

1871, FEB. 21. Wayne MacVeagh, U.S. minister, Constantinople, to USG. "*Private* . . . The newspapers state that you are again badgered about putting some Pennsylvanian in your Cabinet in order to produce harmony in our state—If it is true let me beg of you to do nothing of the kind for the present—I have been more or less concerned in the political affairs in Pennsylvania for ten years; and have twice had a leading direction in her most important elections—I must therfore be very stupid not to have learned something about her politics—Now I am perfectly certain that any change in your Cabinet between this and the election will be a sign of weakness and a confession of weakness *always* in politics causes defection—Every member of your Cabinet is a good working member; and if as a whole it lacks political insight and political force it is 'too near the crossing of the stream to begin to swap horses—' This is peculiarly true of our state—Your offers to gentlemen in that state, of seats in your cabinet, have done great credit to your estimate of the value of high moral character in public affairs,—an estimate in which I heartily agree with you,—but I believe it is possible to find high moral character in combination with political experience and political ability—in our state as well as elsewhere—But this is not the wise time to do it—If you take any one of the hundred or two hundred men in Penna: who rather expect the place you will dishearten and dissatisfy all the rest; and as he will probably be a milk-and water man who has never had either prominence enough or force enough to make enemies will be utterly useless to you himself and will render a vigorous campaign in the state by others impossible—I know you care about the success of the party—even if you dont care a hang about your own re-election; and the success of the party dont depend on whether Brown or Jones has a seat in the Cabinet; but whether on the whole the popular intelligence of the country is satisfied with the honesty loyalty and success of the administration—Moreover we are not divided in Penna: as you are told—These stories are minted largely by men who wish to make profit out of them by putting some man in the Cabinet who will help them—A year,—or even six months ago a good strong active man from Penna: might have helped you, but not now—Any selection you are at all likely to make will do us great harm—"—ALS, USG 3.

1871, FEB. 22. Samuel F. Miller, U.S. Supreme Court, to USG. "As the term of Genl Clark as Marshal of the District of Iowa will soon expire, I beg leave to recommend the appointment of Peter Melendy to that place. Mr. Melendy served as Marshal for several years with general acceptance to the public, and especially so to me as presiding Judge of the Circuit Court. He was displaced by President Johnson for no cause other than political. He is in my opinion honest, capable and has the advantage of some experience. . . ."—ALS, DNA, RG 60, Records Relating to Appointments. Related papers are *ibid.* On March 7, USG nominated Peter Melendy as marshal, Iowa.

1871, FEB. 23. U.S. Representative William L. Stoughton of Mich. to USG. "We respectfully recommend the reappointment of James Henry Esq. as Marshall of the Western District of Mich We also have the honor to call your attention to the accompanying recommendations of the leading Republicans of the District"—ALS, DNA, RG 60, Records Relating to Appointments. U.S. Representative Thomas W. Ferry and U.S. Senator Zachariah

Chandler of Mich. favorably endorsed this letter.—ES, *ibid.* On Feb. 28, USG nominated James Henry as marshal, Western District, Mich.

1871, FEB. 24. USG endorsement. "Let the order named within be revoked, as recommended by the Secretary of the Interior."—Copy, DNA, RG 48, Lands and Railroads Div., Letters Sent. Written on a letter of Feb. 18 from Secretary of the Interior Columbus Delano to USG. "I have the honor to recommend that your order of the 10th ultimo, directing the removal of the land office at Fort Dodge, Iowa, to Des Moines, and its consolidation with the office at the latter place, be revoked. This recommendation is made at the instance of Senator Harlan, who is convinced that it is inexpedient at present to close the Fort Dodge office."—Copy, *ibid.* On the same day, Delano wrote to USG. "I have the honor to recommend that your order of 25th October last, removing the land office from Springfield to Bon Homme, Dakota Territory, be revoked."—Copy, *ibid.* On Feb. 24, USG favorably endorsed this letter.—Copy, *ibid.*

1871, FEB. 24. USG endorsement. "Let the rock described within be reserved for public purposes, as recommended by the Secretary of the Interior."—Copy, DNA, RG 48, Lands and Railroads Div., Letters Sent. Written on a letter of Feb. 23 from Secretary of the Interior Columbus Delano to USG. "I have the honor to recommend that a limestone rock, known as 'Grand Tower', rising to the height of about fifty feet above high water in the Mississippi river, in what would be, if surveyed, Sec. 20, T. 34 N., R. 14 E., 5. principal meridian, Missouri, be reserved for public purposes."—Copy, *ibid.*

1871, FEB. 25. USG proclamation discontinuing discriminatory duties on certain imports arriving on Portuguese ships after Portugal had discontinued comparable duties on goods arriving on U.S. ships.—DS, DNA, RG 130, Presidential Proclamations.

1871, FEB. 25. Brig. Gen. Oliver O. Howard, president, Howard University, to USG. "We have our first medical Commencement at our Church corner of 10th & G. Sts. on Wednesday evening next (March 1st) at 7½ o'clock. If you *could* be present it would gratify many of your true friends."—ALS (press), Howard Papers, MeB.

1871, FEB. 25. Henry D. Rowe and Charles Quinby, East Orange, N. J., to USG. "wee Caled at your place U. S. house Washington citty as, a matter of Duty Desiring an interview with you but after Wating from 12 o clock noon to 3 o clock p*m* giving our card to the clirk at the Doare in Due time and hoping but in vain for an interview and not being admetted to your presents and finding finding our time and means Short to Stay over night having arrived in Washington citty in the morning train night cars and obliged to return in the Same—I rote a fue Lines in a hurry and Gave it to the clirk at the Door with his promis to give it to you before we left but after a while he refused Saing you was very buisy with the (Secretarry of the interiors office) and Seamed as I thought rather arbitrary *however* you may have recieved the note it was rote in hast and without much form or worth as to the matter we wished to Lay before you—(as by Seeing you personally in matter) would have ben more Satisfactory we could Explain the Substance Matter to you and gain your attention to it—briefly—and press the procedings in the Matter we put on fille at the office of the interior on the 23d Day of february 1871—the Day we caled at your place . . . P—S—on the fille above Stated can be Seen a Copy of a *Grant Lease* from the crown of England to the trinity church of Newyork citty Covering much property and on the treaty of peace between England and the united States in 1783—became the territory of the united States and to the amount of over Some Sixty acres of ground bsids the three tracts of Annake Janse property which was included as pretended by the trinity church corporation though not Described as Such property in Said *Grant Lease* but claimed by the trinity church corporation and with the help of the Govenors Drove the heirs off of there property upon the pretence that the Said *Grant Lease* covered the Ground as also Known to them to be the property of (*Annake Janse and her heirs*) for which we the Standing committee of NewJersey have in their possesion Copys of the origial title of that portion of ground of *Annak Janse* and her *heirs* together with the certified copy of the will of Annake *Janse Dced* which also setforth and Discribes the Same it is well to be a protestant or *christian* but to be a protestant *Rober* is an other thing . . ."—LS, DNA, RG 48, Miscellaneous Div., Letters Received. On May 8, Quinby wrote to USG on the same subject.—ALS, *ibid.*, Lands and Railroads Div., Letters Received. Related papers are *ibid.* The heirs of Anneke Jans disputed with Trinity Church, New York City, and others, over property rights for decades.—*New York Times*, Dec. 29, 1870, Feb. 9, 1885.

1871, FEB. 27. Secretary of the Interior Columbus Delano to USG. "I have the honor to return, herewith, the following-named Enrolled Bills, viz: H. R. 343—'Joint Resolution for the relief of Lucy A. Smith, widow and administratrix of James Smith deceased'; and H. R. 2909—'An Act to enable J. H. Schnell, of California, to enter and pay for a section of public land in California, for his tea colony', and to state that I am aware of no just reasons why they should not receive your approval."—LS, OFH.

1871, FEB. 27. Secretary of State Hamilton Fish to USG. "Herewith I enclose to you two copies of the List of persons composing the Legations in the United States."—LS, OFH.

1871, FEB. 27. Maj. Gen. John M. Schofield, San Francisco, to USG. "I desire to ask your kind consideration of the case of the son of our greatly lamented friend, the late Chancellor Chauvenet. I need not attempt to refer in detail to the eminent services rendered by Mr. Chauvenet to the Government and to the country. Probably no man of our time has done more to promote the cause of high scientific education than he. His son, Hemple, who is a most worthy young man of honorable character and ambition, is about graduating at Washington University, and is very anxious to go to West Point to complete his scientific education. If in your power to give him an appointment at large I am sure it could not be bestowed upon one more worthy of it or who would appreciate it more highly. My intimate personal relations with the late Chancellor and consequent knowledge of his great worth cause me to feel an unusual interest in this case; and while I would not recommend an appointment which I did not believe fully justified upon its own merits, I should esteem the appointment of young Chauvenet a great personal favor to me."—ALS, DNA, RG 94, Correspondence, USMA. Related papers are *ibid.* Samuel Hemple Chauvenet did not attend USMA; for his father William, see *PUSG*, 1, 350–51.

1871, FEB. 27. George W. Haskell, Woodhull, N. Y., to USG. "in relation to the Bill on ~~B~~ Public Lands, Passed, Enabling Honorably Discharged Soldiers, Sailors, their Widows and Orphan Children to acquire Homsteads on the Public Lands of the United States with Amendments as reported by Mr Pomeroy from the Committee on Public Lands, I am Engaged to Write to you for an Honorably Discharged Soldier which claimes Public Land According to this Bill Passed which wishes if Possible to have you send or [c]ause to be sent a List [o]f Public Lands in the United States Stating which States ~~of~~ Contain Public Lands and Especially if there is any Public Land in East Tennessee, for Instance on the Cumberland Mountains, Namely Cumberland (Table Lands) ~~and if~~ (this Soldier and Myself wish to Emigrate to a warmer Climate as being more Agreeable to [o]ur Health as found by Experience. My Father was a Chaplin in the late war of a *Penna* Regiment was at ~~the~~ your Residence during the War was some acquainted with our Venerable Martyr~~s~~ and Family, and Coresponded with Him before his Death in relation to a Future world and a preperation in order to obtain it, as Father was at your Residence before the Death of Wm Lincoln and got some acquainted with him and Family. Father wrote to his Father after the Death of Willie in relation to the Future, on account of Wm Death, as his one Favorite Boy, to which we hope Both have gone to Meet the God of Nations, as well as Individuals from which he has received the Loving Smiles of God, and all True and Loyal People to God and their Goverment. as did our Venerable Father of his Country which put his trust in God and overcame ~~all~~ obstacles through Christ, Please Answer or cause to be Answered, this, soon as possible if ~~o~~ conveanient. Yours in Love with all Good and True Principals of Humanity"—ALS, DNA, RG 48, Lands and Railroads Div., Letters Received. William M. Haskell served as chaplain, 136th Pa.

1871, FEB. 27. Nag-ga-rash *et al.* to USG, Secretary of the Interior Columbus Delano, and Ely S. Parker, commissioner of Indian Affairs. "The petition of the undersigned Chiefs, head men, and other members of the Iowa tribe of Indians respectfully represents That being in open concil assembled we have deliberately considered & decided to petition our Great Father in Washington to authorize the survey and allotment in severalty of a sufficiency of our reservation to give to every head of a family, and to each of our young men and young women, a farm to be secured to them by patent; The *number* of acres to be allotted in each farm, we leave to the Hon. Secretary of the Interior We also request that a manual labor boarding School may be established for the education of our children"—DS (36 signatures—signed by mark), DNA, RG 75, Letters Received, Great Nemaha Agency. On March 1, Samuel M. Janney, superintendent of Indian Affairs, Omaha, wrote to Parker. "I returned last night from a journey to the Great Nemaha agency performed at the request of the Iowa tribe of Indians, who have recently become very desirous to have a portion of their reservation surveyed and allotted to them in severalty. I herewith transmit their petition requesting the allotment of a farm to every head of a family and to each of their young men & young women; the number of acres in each to be fixed by the Hon. Secretary of the Interior. Agent Lightfoot and I concur in thinking that eighty acres in each farm will be sufficient, and that a larger area than this would extend their settlement so widely as to increase the difficulty of educating their children. The manual labor boarding school which they ask for, will, I hope, be granted. There are, so far as I know, only four or five men among the Iowas who object to the allotment of land, and they rest their objection on the ground that they will be subjected to taxation. We told them they would not be taxed until they voluntarily became citizens of the united States. I ask for their petition an early and a favourable consideration."—ALS, *ibid.* On Dec. 8, Nag-ga-rash *et al.* petitioned USG and Congress. "Your Petitioners, Chiefs and head-Men of the Iowa Tribe of Indians, respectfully represent, That we are adopting the habits and Customs of Civilized life. That we are opening Farms, building Dwelling houses, raising Cattle, using Agricultural Implements, and educating our children in school houses, on our Reservation in the States of Nebraska and Kansas. That the annuity from our Trust Funds, is insufficient to enable us to progress in these improvements as rapidly as we desire. For our more rapid advancement in civilization, and for the objects above named, your Petitioners ask, that the proceeds recieved from the sale of our Trust lands, advertised by the Hon Sect'y of the Interior, and sold by him for Cash, on the First day of October, A. D. eighteen hundred and Seventy One, shall be paid to our Tribe through its proper Officers, instead of being permanently invested in Trust funds. . . ."—DS (12 signatures—11 by mark), *ibid.* See *HED*, 42-2-1, part 5, pp. 854, 872–75, 42-2-26; Martha Royce Blaine, *The Ioway Indians* (Norman, 1979), pp. 270–74.

1871, March 1. Ambrose E. Burnside, New York City, to USG. "Please allow me to introduce to you Genl Edward Jardine who served with me during the rebellion with great distinction—He was in New York during the riots of 1863 and rendered most important service to the authorities at that time—In his efforts to disperse the rioters he was fearfully wounded and mangled, from the effects of which he has not yet recovered and never can recover—You will remember I asked you for an appointment to West Point for his son,—You were not then able to grant his request, but kindly promised an appointment to Annapolis to one of his sons, which you subsequently gave—His eldest son is still anxious to obtain a military education and to join the service—I am personally acquainted with him, and am sure he will make his mark at the academy and in the army if he gets the appointment—Genl Jardine is not able to give him the education he desires, and I hope you may find it for the interests of the service to give him an appointment at large—The gallant services of Genl Jardine during the war, and his disabled condition certainly render him worthy of the consideration of the government, and I am sure you will be glad to see him and do all you can for him."—ALS, DNA, RG 94, Correspondence, USMA. James Jardine did not attend USMA; Augustus E. Jardine graduated from the U.S. Naval Academy in 1876.

On Jan. 28, 1873, Governor John F. Hartranft of Pa. wrote to USG. "I have the honor to commend to your favorable consideration for some eligible appointment in your gift, my old comrade and personal friend Genl J. Jardine of New York. The General is recognized as an earnest and active Republican, a zealous and untiring supporter of yourself, and withal an accomplished gentleman and soldier. I feel assured, any appointment conferred upon him will give general satisfaction, and be worthily bestowed."—LS, PHi. No appointment followed for Edward Jardine, already a weigher in the New York City Custom House.

1871, March 1. Governor John W. Geary of Pa. to USG. "If you have not completed the usual Committee appointed to attend the annual examination of the Naval Cadets at Annapolis, will you permit me to suggest the name of one of your particular friends *Revd G. D. Carrow D. D.* as a gentleman in every way fit for the appointment and eminently deserving the compliment. The party in the State owes much to the Doctors prudent counsels and vigorous pen, and he is a staunch supporter of your administration."—LS, OFH. On March 9, Orville E. Babcock wrote to Geary. "The President directs me to acknowledge the receipt of your letter of the 1st inst: and say that the list of Members of the Committee to visit Annapolis was completed before the receipt of your letter."—Copy, DLC-USG, II, 1. In a letter docketed March, 1869, Bishop Matthew Simpson had written to USG. "Will you permit me to ask your favorable consideration of the application of Rev G. D. Carrow, for the place of Minister to Mexico, or to some of the Spanish speaking countries. . . ."—ALS, DNA, RG 59, Letters of Application and Recommendation. A related paper is *ibid.*

On Feb. 11, 1871, John P. Newman, Washington, D. C., wrote to Secretary of the Navy George M. Robeson. "Be kind enough to convey my thanks to the President for the honor of appointing me on the Board of Visitors to the Naval Academy, to attend the Annual examination; & which appointment

I hereby accept."—Copy, OFH. Robeson received similar letters from James H. Wilson, New York City, George D. Perkins, Sioux City, Iowa, James L. Orr, Abbeville, S. C., and Thomas P. Saffold, Madison, Ga.—Copies (forwarded to USG), *ibid.* On April 17, Babcock wrote to Robeson. "The President directs me to say that, if any vacancy exists, he will be pleased to have you appoint John B. Henderson of Mo. as one of the Board of Visitors to the Naval Academy this year."—LS, DNA, RG 45, Letters Received from the President. No appointment followed. On March 13, 1869, U.S. Senator James Harlan of Iowa had written to USG. "I have been informed that the friends of B. F. Tefft. of Maine, intend to present his name for the position of Minister from the United States to some foreign government. I have known him for many years. He is a gentleman of great talents and acquirements,—has few equals as an author and in scholastic attainments; and is eminently practical in his modes of thought. In my opinion he would fill with great credit to himself and advantage to the government, any position abroad in the gift of the President, and *no appointment would give me greater satisfaction personally.*"—ALS, *ibid.*, RG 59, Letters of Application and Recommendation. Related papers are *ibid.* Benjamin F. Tefft was appointed to the 1871 board of visitors, U.S. Naval Academy. See *HED*, 42-2-1, part 3, pp. 76–84.

1871, March 1. Charles A. Spencer, Humboldt, Kan., to USG. "I saw an acct of the trouble among the cadetts at West. *Rt.* some of them were expelled from the school; I believe. thinking that there might be a vacancy now, I write to see what the chance would be for me to get a situation in the school. . . . Now Pres. Grant, I write to you just the same as though you were no more than any common man: for I guess you have not changed very mouch since you was in the front, in our last war. my Father was one of your soldiers, then, and he says you have a head and mind of your own, so if there is any chance for me to go to west Pt to school please write and let me know: and if not, I want to know it. if there is a chance let me know what I will have to do to get there, for I would really like to go."—ALS, DNA, RG 94, Unsuccessful Cadet Applications. See Endorsement, Jan. 13, 1871; letter to Frederick Dent Grant, Jan. 15, 1871.

1871, March 2. U.S. Senator Oliver P. Morton of Ind. to USG. "I am informed that Wm. D. Gallagher Esq will be an applicant for the position of appraiser at Louisville Ky. He is a gentleman of high character, is an ~~appli~~ excellent Republican and would I have no doubt discharge ably and faithfully the duties of the office. I cordially commend him to your favorable consideration"—ALS, DNA, RG 56, Appraiser of Customs Applications. U.S. Senator John Sherman of Ohio favorably endorsed this recommendation.—AES (undated), *ibid.* On March 9, USG nominated William D. Gallagher as pension agent, Louisville, in place of Samuel McKee.

On March 15, 1869, McKee, Washington, D. C., had written to USG. "I have the honor herewith to apply for the appointment of Minister Resident to Switzerland; and refer respectfully to the reccommendations accompanying this paper. I have for four years been the only Republican in Congress from my state Kentucky; and served my country in the army during the late Rebellion. The Republicans of Kentucky unanimously endorse me; and the papers contain the names of over 60 members of Congress, of the 40th & 41st Congress and a number of Senators, also letter from associate Justice Miller of the Supreme Court; and a letter from Hon Geo S Boutwell Secretary of the Treasury. I wish this mission over any other of its class, because, of the climate; and because of the further fact that I have a wife and two children one now 9 years old; who must go with me wherever I go. I most earnestly ask that my claims be considered and recognized, if not by this appointmt, to one equally as good"—ALS, *ibid.*, RG 59, Letters of Application and Recommendation. Related papers are *ibid.*

On Jan. 4, 1872, J. H. H. Woodward, Louisville, wrote to USG. "... Recently I have made affidavits before U. S. Commissioners W. A. Merriwether and James A. Beattie of this city, setting forth the fact that the Hon. Sam McKee while a Member of Congress and U. S. Pension Agent here, was continuously prosecuting claims as an Agent against the United States, thereby violating Sec. 2. of the Act of Feby 26, 1853, entitled an Act to prevent Frauds upon the Treasury of the United States.... Also that he violated the Internal Revenue Law in not paying the special tax for a Claim Agents License. He acknowledged his guilt, and the fact of receiving fees in cases specified by me, to W. A. Bullett Esq of this city, Asst Dist Atty of the U. S. Now, notwithstanding all this, Col. G. C. Wharton, the Dist Atty here, has refused to permit the Commissioners to issue the warrants for McKee's arrest. Now, Mr President, I would respectfully ask what kind of an administration of law is this? Here is a man walking the streets of Louisville, one of your most relentless enemies, who acknowledges himself a criminal, and yet when I myself, an unpretending citizen, go before the proper officers of the United States, make oath of true facts, in due form of law, against a criminal, no notice is taken.... With all the power I had, I opposed the confirmation of this man, as Pension Agent here, knowing him to be a bad man, but to little or no purpose at the time, and since then, you, yourself have found out his duplicity and unworthy character and removed him from Office, a thing for which, all good citizens must commend you...."—ALS, *ibid.*, RG 56, Letters Received from Congress.

1871, MARCH 3. To Senate. "I transmit to the Senate in answer to their resolution of February 1st 1871 a report from the Secretary of State with accompanying documents"—DS, DNA, RG 46, Presidential Messages. *SED*, 41-3-53. On the same day, Secretary of State Hamilton Fish had written to USG. "The Secretary of State to whom was referred the resolution of the Senate of the 1st ultimo, requesting the President, 'if consistent with the public interest, to communicate to the Senate all dispatches addressed by Hon. H. T. Blow, Minister of the United States to the Court of Brazil, referring to the following subjects: Trade between Brazil and the United

States; Cotton and its culture in Brazil; Material and financial condition of Brazil; The Paraguayan war; Ocean navigation; and also Mr. Blow's note addressed to Secretary of Foreign Affairs of the Brazilian Government on July 1, 1870, referring to the trade between Brazil and the United States, and the export duty on Coffee with translation of the replies of Baron de Cotegipe and the Viscount H. Viconte,' has the honor to lay before the President the papers called for by the said Resolution."—LS, DNA, RG 46, Presidential Messages. Related papers are *ibid.*

1871, March 3. To Senate. "I transmit to the Senate in answer to their resolution of the 2nd instant a report from the Secretary of State with accompaning documents"—DS, DNA, RG 46, Presidential Messages. *SED*, 41-3-52. On the same day, Secretary of State Hamilton Fish had written to USG. "The Secretary of State, to whom was referred the resolution of the Senate of the 2nd instant, requesting the President 'if not incompatible with the public interests to transmit to the Senate copies of any correspondence from the Legation of the United States at Constantinople relating to the restrictions on the passage of the straits of the Dardanelles and the Bosphorus by the ships of other nations' has the honor to lay before the President the correspondence called for by the resolution."—LS, DNA, RG 46, Presidential Messages. Related papers are *ibid.*

1871, March 3. Secretary of the Interior Columbus Delano to USG. "I have examined, with as much care and attention as my limited time and many pressing engagements would permit, enrolled Bill No. 1831, which originated in the House of Representatives. It is entitled 'An Act to confirm the title to the Rancho del Rio Grande, in New Mexico, to the heirs and legal representatives of the original grantees thereof.' The preamble recites that the Government of Spain, on the 4th of February, 1795, granted a certain tract of land, situate in what is now the Territory of New Mexico, and known as the Rancho del Rio Grande, to certain parties in common; that the title so granted was, April 20th, 1837, recognized by the legally constituted authorities of Mexico, and that, in the treaty between that power and the United States, the latter stipulated to guarantee the property held under the laws of former Governments. The enacting clause quit-claims to and confirms the title of the heirs and legal representatives of those parties to the tract of land, and bounds it as follows: On the south by the ridge of Bear Mountain. On the west by the Cañada or valley of Miranda and the road described in their original grant as leading to Pueblo Picorio. On the east by the ridge of the mountain of the River Don Fernando, and on the north by the boundaries of Don Manuel Montes Vigil, to hold the same to them and their heirs and assigns under and according to the terms of the original grant from the Government of Spain. The 2nd section makes it the duty of the Secretary of the Interior to direct the Surveyor-General of New Mexico to ascertain and fix, by actual survey, the boundaries of said tract of land, as above described, as soon as practicable, and then provides that, upon such survey being returned to the General Land Office, a patent shall be issued, in conformity to the provisions of the act, to the heirs and legal representatives of the parties aforesaid, with a proviso that nothing shall be construed to affect the rights of *bona fide* settlers upon the land under the laws of the United States. I am not able to state whether the recital of facts in the preamble is substantially accurate or not, but it will be perceived that the 1st section of the act absolutely confirms the title of the parties to the said tract of land. The Supreme Court has said that a confirmation by act of Congress makes a legal title without a patent. I regard it as the highest form of title known to our laws. The boundaries of the tract confirmed should be given so that its location may be fixed with unmistakable certainty. General boundaries by the natural features are given, but these do not afford a safe means of determining the exact limits and real extent of the tract. The loose and indefinite description of the lands furnishes a serious objection to your approval of the bill. Parties some time since claimed in a somewhat analagous case that a confirmed claim, the boundaries of which were given in general terms, covered an area of two million acres. The Department refused to authorize a survey, for which the parties applied, but the case furnishes a striking instance of the uncertainty of such general descriptions. It may well be contended that the 2nd section was designed to render the survey of the Surveyor-General, in this instance, conclusive as to the limits of the lands, and to require a patent to be issued upon it. If the supervisory action of the General Land Office and of this Department over the doings of the Surveyor-General is to be thus excluded, the objections to the legislation which accomplishes the result are insurmountable. Upon the whole, I cannot, consistently, with my views of duty, recommend you to approve the bill."—Copy, DNA, RG 48, Lands and Railroads Div., Letters Sent. USG did not sign the bill. See *CG*, 41–3, 1142, 1802; *HMD*, 39-2-16, 40-2-97.

1871, MARCH 3. Orville E. Babcock to John Wagner, Philadelphia. "The President desires me to enclose you his check for $118 00 the amount of your bill for cigars . . . P. S. Please acknowledge receipt"—Copy, DLC-USG, II, 1. On April 17 and on Jan. 11, June 18, and Nov. 13, 1872, Babcock wrote similar letters to Wagner.—Copies, *ibid.* On May 20, 1873, Babcock wrote to Wagner. "The President requests that you will send him 2000 Segars. Please let the assortment be the same as heretofore sent."—Copy, *ibid.*, II, 2. On May 26, Culver C. Sniffen wrote to Wagner. "Enclosed please find the President's check for $240. in payment of bill of cigars of 23d instant. Be kind enough to receipt the enclosed bill and return it."—Copy, *ibid.* On Sept. 27 and Oct. 2, Levi P. Luckey wrote to Wagner. "The President will be pleased to have you send him 2000. Cigars, of same qualities as you have been sending him, divided in the same proportion. Please add this bill with the one of Aug. 30, and he will remit the whole amount at the same time." "Enclosed please find draft on New York to your order for Three Hundred Dollars, the amount of the President's bill. Please acknowledge receipt . . ."—Copies, *ibid.* On Sept. 19 and 22, 1874, Sniffen wrote to Wagner. "The President directs me to request that you will send him one thousand cigars of the same quality you last sent" "The President directs me to forward the enclosed check to your order for $182. in payment of accompanying bill which please receipt and return. He requests me to say that had your bill of July 30 been received before it would have been paid earlier, but, this is the first time he has seen it."—Copies, *ibid.* On Dec. 31, Luckey wrote to Wagner on the same subject.—Copy, *ibid.* On Nov. 15, 1876, Sniffen wrote to Wagner. "The President directs me to request that you will send him one thousand cigars of the usual quality"—Copy, *ibid.*, II, 3. On Dec. 26, Sniffen noted: "Another order to above for 2000"—AN (initialed), *ibid.*

1871, MARCH 4. Franz Georges, Buffalo, to USG. "It is reported that Mr William Dorsheimer is applying for a Foreign Mission. Aside from Mr D's want of the proper qualifications for such place, the fact of his having in his adhesion to Andrew Johnson, just at the time when he made his assault on you, and while he was trying his best to ruin the Republican party, ought to be a bar to his success—Mr. D procured his present office by the aid of the Blairs father and sons, and signed the 'Philadelphia Call' so called, later, he joined the so called Revenue reformers, all in all, he is a poor Republican, Merely an Active successful Office seeker As regards influence with the Germans, he has none, nor ever had, If *you would please our nationality* send *Genl Franz Sigel* to *Berlin*"—ALS, DNA, RG 59, Letters of Application and Recommendation. On Jan. 31, Judge Charles Daniels, N. Y. Supreme Court, Buffalo, had written to USG. "Benjamin H. Austin, Jr, of this city is an applicant for the office of District Attorney for the Northern district of New York, Mr. Austin is well qualified as a lawyer to discharge the duties of that office, As a republican he has been uniform, consistent and zealous, ever since the organization of the present republican party. His integrity and fidelity are unexceptional, and I believe his appointment would prove to be satisfactory to the district, I must add however that I do not desire or intend by this note, to recall or qualify what I have already written in behalf of the appointment of Mr. Crowley, Should the appointment of the latter for any reason be deemed to be inexpedient, I believe that of Mr. Austin would meet the approbation of the district,"—ALS, *ibid.*, RG 60, Records Relating to Appointments. Related papers are *ibid.* On March 10, Thomas Murphy, collector of customs, New York City, wrote to USG. "The bearer of this, Mr Richard Crowley, is an old personal and political friend between whom and myself for several years have existed the most intimate relations. I know him thoroughly, and he possesses my entire and unbounded confidence. I know him to be true, honest, faithful and able;—a good lawyer, a good citizen, and a friend that don't require watching. If there is anything more that I can add or say on his behalf, please draw upon your imagination without limit."—ALS, *ibid.* Related papers are *ibid.* On March 8, Ambrose E. Burnside, Providence, R. I., had written to USG. "I had the pleasure several days ago of signing a recommendation for the appointment of Mr John A. Gardner of Providence to the office of Attorney Genl for R. I—Mr

Gardner is a most excellent, intelligent, and upright man, and a good lawyer—He is the choice of a large majority of our best citizens—I hope you will find it for the interest of the public service to appoint him, and I will esteem his appointment a personal favor—I hope to be in Washington about the 15th inst, when I will do myself the pleasure to call on you—"—ALS, *ibid.* Related papers are *ibid.* Also on March 8, U.S. Senator William Sprague and U.S. Representatives Benjamin T. Eames and James M. Pendleton of R. I. petitioned USG. "We the undersigned request the appointment of Stephen A. Cooke Jr. Esq. to the office of United States Attorney for the District of Rhode Island—"—DS, *ibid.* Related petitions are *ibid.* On March 11, Sprague, Eames, and Pendleton wrote to USG. "The undersigned respectfully request an interview before any nomination is made by you for the office of U. S. District Attorney for the Rhode Island District.—We will meet you at such time as may suit your convenience."—LS, *ibid.* On March 17, Horace Porter wrote to Attorney Gen. Amos T. Akerman. "The President directs me to say that he will be pleased to have you have prepared, nominations for Gardner to be U. S. Att'y. for Rhode Island; and for Crowley to be U. S. Att'y. for the West. Dist. N. Y. in place of Dorsheimer, and requests that they be sent to him before twelve o'clock today."—LS, *ibid.*, Letters Received. Richard Crowley's nomination was for the Northern District, N. Y.

1871, March 7. Harriet L. Fuller, Seville, Ill., to USG. "My husband Ichabod O Fuller was a loyal Soldier in the 72 Reg Ill,s Vol for three years lost his health by exposiere so he was unable to work in the winter although he did work endureing much suffering this winter he went into a coal bank to work becaus he was not so much exposed to the cold he was killed and I am left with Seven children the young one year old & I think I ought to have a pension from the ~~g~~Government to help me take care of my children"—ALS, DNA, RG 48, Miscellaneous Div., Letters Received.

1871, March 8. William A. Ricketts, deputy warden, Ala. Penitentiary, Wetumpka, to USG. "I hereby notify you of the escape of United States convict George Jones from Tates Mill S & N. R Rd on the 26th of February 1871. Said Jones was convicted of Mail robbery and sentenced to 15½ years in the Penitentiary of Alabama by the United States court in June 1868. Said Jones is a native of Alabama, he is 29 years old and is 5–6 inches high weighs 160# with Florid complexion light hair, blue eyes, and has an '*anchor*' tattooed on right arm and left foot off."—LS, DNA, RG 60, Letters from the President.

1871, March 10. Orville E. Babcock to H. de Mareil, *Messager Franco-Americain*, New York City. "The President received your letter and called the attention of his Cabinet to it (in Cabinet meeting) and expressed a hope that, a portion of the advertising would be given to your Journal."—Copy, DLC-USG, II, 1. De Mareil had written to USG. "Allow me respectfully to ask from you a recommendation to the heads of the various Departments of the Government to publish their advertisements in the 'Messager Franco Americain.' President Lincoln regarded it as very desirable that all these advertisements should be inserted in the 'Messager' for the purpose of giving the Franco-American portion of the population a share in the benefits of the purchases of Supplies and Stores. For this reason, he was so kind as to request that heads of the various Departments to authorize the 'Messager Franco American' to publish their advertisements, and I would solicit from Your Excellency a similar favor"—LS (undated), DNA, RG 45, Subject File, Div. XV; *ibid.*, RG 56, Miscellaneous Letters Received.

1871, MARCH 13. Russell R. Lowell, Jerome, Mo., to USG. "I am confident I can find arrest and return to the authorities of the State of Kansas Quantrall who led the party to Sack the city of Lawrence Kansas in 1863. What encouragements can you give me for payment of Expenses & Services incurred in doing this work. I will refer you to Hon S P Chase for refferance as to my Experance &C—I ask my own way to find and to return the man referred to, but all times would like your advice I want no Employment from the U S. only wish to do what I have referred to"—ALS, DNA, RG 60, Letters from the President. William C. Quantrill had died from wounds in Louisville on June 6, 1865.

1871, MARCH 14. Orvil L. Grant, Chicago, to USG. "Hon C B Farwell will present to you the case of Jas Geary who has been indited and sentenced to one years imprisenment in the State Penitentiary I know but little as to the extent of his guilt but strong sympathies are expressed in his behalf. The helpless condition of his family make his case an extreme one and hopes are entertained that he will receive Executive clemency Mrs Geary was confined last week and her health is so critical that it has been deemed imprudent to apprise her of the sentence of her husband. Hoping that you will give the matter a fair investigation . . ."—ALS, ICHi. On May 3, Horace Porter telegraphed to U.S. Representative Charles B. Farwell of Ill., Chicago. "Attorney General opposes and makes out a very bad case but decision will be made tomorrow. I shall advise you"—Copy, DLC-USG, II, 5. On May 4, Porter wrote to Farwell. "I supposed that upon our return from the west, the pardon would be all ready for the President's signature as directed before he left. The Attorney General on our return presented the enclosed report to the President stating facts of which he had no knowledge when he ordered the pardon and stated that he thought the interests of the of the Government would suffer if a pardon were granted. The report was made by an Officer of the Revenue Department in whom great confidence is reposed. Notwithstanding, the President feels that he has promised you the pardon; and, if upon reading the report you still think it ought to be granted the President will comply with your wishes. I regret exceedingly the delay, but I know you will fully appreciate the circumstances."—Copy, *ibid.*, II, 1. James Geary had been sentenced to one year of imprisonment and fined $1000 and costs for removing "tobacco from the manufactory without paying the special tax or making an entry in the proper book of such removal, as required by law."—Copy, DNA, RG 130, Pardon Records. On May 10, USG pardoned Geary, "excepting and conditioned upon payment of the said fine and costs."—Copy, *ibid.*; DS, Gallery of History, Las Vegas, Nev.

1871, March 14. Jacob B. Sagerty, Omaha, to USG. "I hope you will have leisuere to read my little request, if I am not asking too much, I am a young man twenty three years old and crippled so that I am not able to do very hard work. I took up a homestead in this state on the 12th day day of Dec 1870. . . . and I am not able to get the means necessary to live on it and improve it according to law. I am afraid it will be taken away from me. if I could hold it untill next Spring I think I would be able to do something with it. I hope you will try to fix it so I can hold it if it would not be Putting you to too much trouble. for I am worried a great deal about it. for I hoped to have a home when I took it, I worked for a man here one year and a half a Short time ago he broke up and I lost ~~all~~ all my wages but what little I had used for clothing & other little necessaries, if he had paid I would be allright, I am at work again so If I have good luck I would be ready next Spring I have no way to get anything but by own labor my parents died when I was young so I have got my living pretty hard I came from Ohio 1869 when I arrived in this place I had but 7 cents. I hope you will help me so I can hold my land it will be a sore thing for me indeed if I lose it perhaps you may think me an impostor and will take no notice of me. I could give good refference but you would not Know whether they were or not and another thing people would make fun of me for writing to the President of the United States. so I will say nothing aboutt it so if you cannot help me they will be none the wiser. hoping you will will be so kind as to assist me which I trust you will I will close my simple letter. I am a stranger to you will never have the opportunity perhaps to repay you for your trouble but I hope I can in some way favor you. I suppose you have thousands of such letters as this. ~~bidding~~ I bid you fare well and hoping you will pardon me for intrudiing on you I will close,"—ALS, DNA, RG 48, Lands and Railroads Div., Letters Received.

1871, March 15. To Attorney Gen. Amos T. Akerman. "The execution of Grady may be postponed at the request of his spiritual adviser until Saturday, or until Friday of next week, the present day fixed for the execution being Saint Patrick's day."—Copy, DLC-USG, II, 1. On March 14, Akerman had written to USG. "The petitions for a commutation in the case of James Grady, now under sentence of death in the District of Columbia for murder, which you have referred to me, according to Executive usage, have received a careful consideration. The principal facts in the case are the following: Mrs. Fanny Faulkner, a charity pensioner of Trinity Church, about seventy-four years of age, occupied a single apartment on Ohio-avenue, in Washington, and at the time of the commission of the offense was confined to her bed from an attack [o]f fever. The jury were satisfied from the evidence that while she was in this condition GRADY, who is a comparatively young and vigorous man, ravished her, and in the act did such violence to her person as caused her death within a few days, and accordingly they found him guilty of murder. After the verdict was rendered, he made a motion for a new trial, which, after argument, the Court overruled. He was then sentenced to suffer death on the 24th day of February last. You have reprieved him until the 17th day of March instant. I find no good reason for a belief, or even for a suspicion, that the law was improperly administered in the case, either by the Court or jury. I will now state the grounds upon which a commutation is asked in the written petitions, and in verbal communications, together with my opinion of their validity. It is alleged that, at the time of the perpetration of the offense, he was under the influence of liquor. This is no mitigation of the offense, either in law or reason. The codes of civilized communities generally, if not universally, hold a man responsible for crimes committed during voluntary drunkenness. A different rule would permit all persons who meditate crime to prepare themselves with a palliative by a real or simulated intoxication. In this instance the offender was not so stupefied by liquor that he could not understand and remember his licentious act, for he retired from Mrs. FAULKNER's room, when a witness entered, and then passing into a shop near by, boasted of having deflowered her. Second, it is urged in extenuation of the crime that he did not intend murder, but that he merely intended rape. It is the law of this District that a person who, in the perpetration of one felony commits another which was not within his design, is as guilty of the latter as if he had designed it. In the present instance it must be the judgment of all right-minded persons, that the homicide of this woman is not lessened in criminality by the circumstance that it was perpetrated in an effort to do an act which to worthy women is more terrible than murder. Third—It is alleged that GRADY has respectable parents, and they deserve commiseration; but I can not perceive any reason for favor to him on their account. This plea for mercy goes in its fair consequence to the extent of lightening the severity of the law upon all offenders who have worthy relatives. Criminals who have had the benefit of good domestic and social influences are more culpable than the neglected and the friendless. If men will not spare their relatives the mortification which must come from their crimes, I do not think that the Government should spare their relatives the mortification which comes from the punishment of their crimes. Fourth—It is alleged that he was not skillfully defended. I am informed that he had a zealous defense by respectable counsel, and I am satisfied that no counsel, however skillful, could have procured a different verdict, without misleading the jury. The law and the facts of the case authorized no other verdict. Fifth—It is alleged that the jurors who rendered the verdict recommend a commutation. This fact deserves a most respectful consideration. But the weight of such a recommendation must depend upon the reasons for it, and the jurors present no reasons, except some of those which I have above cansidered. It is not pretended that GRADY's character has been good. He has already been in the Penitentiary for horse-stealing. I am satisfied that the feeling which has moved many of the persons who have taken an interest for commutation in the case, is a dislike to the infliction of capital punishment. An objection to the law should be presented to the Legislature and not to the pardoning power. The Executive must assume the law to be right. Upon the whole, I find nothing in the case to justify any interference with the sentence which the law has pronounced. Though I pity this offender, I acknowledge a much stronger pity for his victim. She had but few safeguards except those which the law gives. He spurned these safeguards and dishonored and murdered her. The law cannot restore her to life, but it can proclaim that the severest penalties shall fall upon those who brutally destroy the old, the poor, the lonely and the sick."—*New York Times*, March 15, 1871.

1871, MARCH 15. Col. Robert Allen, asst. q. m., Washington, D. C., to USG. "In my personal interview with you a few days since I am apprehensive that I did not explain to you quite distinctly enough the reasons which led to the rejection of Mr W. D. Farrand by the Senate as U. S. Consul to Callao I beg now to be permitted to say, that Mr Farrand's confirmation was defeated by the persistent hostility of the previous Consul who was at the head of a *ring*, the nefarious schemes of which, were exposed by him; and whose overtures, to the new Consul, to make his office speculative, had been indignantly rejected,—thereby offending the Peruvian Officials who sympathised with Farrand's predecessor And, furthermore, Mr Farrand was commissioned to purchase two Monitors for the Peruvian Government and was involved in the course of the transaction in a controversy with the Firm of Swift & Co. of New York who exerted a powerful moneyed influence, which was directed in all its force against Farrands confirmation That Farrand has been shamefully treated, and the U. S. Government defrauded by the Firm of Swift & Co will appear very clearly, I think, in the enclosed printed statement Mr Farrand feels confident that his official conduct when understood by you, will meet your entire approbation, and he has no fear of an adverse judgement by the Senate I will not say, Mr President, how much I will be personally obliged if you can favor the application of Mr F. for the place he seeks"—ALS, DNA, RG 59, Letters of Application and Recommendation. On Dec. 6, 1869, USG had nominated William D. Farrand as consul, Callao, to replace James H. McColley, deceased; Farrand was not confirmed. On March 4, 1870, USG nominated David J. Williamson for this post.

1871, MARCH 15. E. S. Zevely, Washington, D. C., to USG. "This is respectfully to call your attention, in the nature of a petition, on behalf of the Ute Indians, NewMexico, well knowing your earnest desire to benefit that race. As appears from the last annual report of the present agent for these Indians, at the Abiquiu agency, ~~it appears~~ they are somewhat dissatisfied, (tho' considered friendly in general) on account of not receiving sufficient aid &c.

They also deny having made the treaty agreeing to go on the reservation in Colorado,—And now that this agency has been tendered to us, we earnestly hope that we may be authorized & instructed to give some satisfactory assurances to those Indians on our arrival, similar to the suggestions made by the agent in his report above alluded to. Otherwise, so far as we can understand, the field of usefulness there is not very promising at present."—ALS, DNA, RG 75, Letters Received, New Mexico Superintendency. On March 9, USG had nominated Zevely, a Lutheran, as agent for the Abiquiu Agency. See *HED*, 41-3-1, part 4, pp. 618–22, 42-2-1, part 5, pp. 820–25.

1871, MARCH 16. To King Amadeo I of Spain. "I have received the letter which Your Majesty was pleased to address to me on the 6th of January last, announcing your accession to the Throne of Spain. I offer to Your Majesty my sincere congratulations upon this auspicious event, with my best wishes that your reign may contribute to your own happiness and to the prosperity of that ancient Kingdom—I reciprocate, at the same time, the assurance of the sincere desire of Your Majesty to maintain those relations of amity and confidence which have heretofore subsisted between our respective countries—And so I pray God to have Your Majesty always in His safe and holy keeping—. . ."—Copy, DNA, RG 84, Spain, Instructions. Similar formal diplomatic letters prepared for USG may not appear in these volumes.

1871, MARCH 16. To Randolph Strickland, St. Johns, Mich. "There cannot be much delay in sending nomination to the Senate. Will wait until Monday."—Copy, DLC-USG, II, 5. Members of the 41st Congress had sent an undated petition to USG. "The undersigned respectfully request the appointment of Randolph Strickland of the State of Michigan one of the Board of Commissioners to receive, examine and consider the claims of loyal citizens of the States lately in rebellion . . ."—DS (90 signatures), DNA, RG 60, Applications and Recommendations. Strickland, who completed his term as U.S. representative on March 3, resumed a law practice in Mich.

1871, MARCH 17. To Senate. "I transmit to the Senate, in compliance with its resolution of the 14th instant, a report from the Secretary of State, making known that official notice has been received at the Department of State of the ratification, by the legislature of one, and only one, additional State—to wit, that of New Jersey—of the fifteenth amendment to the Constitution of the United States, since the 30th of March, 1870, the date of his certificate that three fourths of the whole number of States in the United States had ratified that amendment and that it had become valid to all intents and purposes as part of the Constitution of the United States."—DS, DNA, RG 46, Presidential Messages. *SED*, 42-1-2. On the same day, Secretary of State Hamilton Fish had written to USG transmitting this information.—LS, DNA, RG 46, Presidential Messages. On March 14, U.S. Senator Frederick T. Frelinghuysen of N. J. had proposed the resolution.—*CG*, 42–1, 91. See *PUSG*, 20, 130–33.

1871, MARCH 17. Clarence T. Smith, Philadelphia, to USG. "I have the honor to make application for an appointment as Physician and Surgeon to an Indian Agency or a position connected with the Indian Bureau where my profession would be of service. I have been among the Indians for the past three years in Montana and Dakota Territories and am acquainted with their various modes of life. I would respectfully state that in asking for the above appointment I am in no way seeking for gain any more than sufficient for the support of myself and family and will furnish the government if necessary ample reference and security; & if appointed will leave a growing practice which in a little while would pay me far better than any appointment of the kind in the Bureau; but having lived on the frontier for several years I am desirous of returning—I would respectfully refer you to Surg. A. B. Campbell U. S. A with regard to my services during the Small-Pox epidemic among the Blackfeet, Gros-Ventres Peigans & others—I am & have been an earnest supporter of the Administration,"—ALS, DNA, RG 75, Letters Received, Miscellaneous.

1871, MARCH 19. Richard Lamberson to USG. "in my humble way I have Concluded to write you afew lines Concerning oure Supreme Court that has benn sitting at nashville Reseantley they have Disregarded the Decison of the former Courts and have Ruind me by Reversing all of the first Deliverd opinons givein after the late Rebelion I was one of the Southern Symsaphisers but never went in the Rebelion and since the Rebelion I Brout suite for money I was swindled out of I will give you the Partickelerse in my humble way the first Case is this bfore the war I lond 400–00 dollarse in Gold to aman in Smith County and I moved to decalb in the fall of 59 Tucke Judgment on said debt and dureing the war in 62 said officcer raisd the Exicution and Collected the money with out my authrty and I Refusd to take it and told him the Plantive wase aunion man and I did not beleive he pad him Confederate and I would not take the Confed that it was only woth 10 on the doller in nashville and that would not have it and the officer said I had better take it if I did not I would bee sorry for it and I did not take it and shortley after words forist and his men about 4000 thousond strong well armd and Equiped and put up Printed advertisements Stating in them if we did not take this money we would bee put in Prisin and every thing we had Confiscatd and the Soaldurse Pointed them out to use and told use what they might Depend on and I did take the money under the Circumstances and after the ware I went down in Smith County and Comes up with the Plantiff of Said debt and told him he had treted me very bad he sed why so I told him he barid gold from me and paid it in Confedrate he sed he Paid in good money and Could prove it and I then suid the officer and Proved more than I have sed in this Case and gaind it with ease in Court below and it has binn in Supreme Court 4 yearse and they have maid a new Constitution and Elected Rebel Judges and that is the way they have treted me I would Rather aman had stold my money and have sued him in a Civil Case and lost it as to have lost this Suite in the Supreme Court at nashville they say I tuck it and that wase apayment and they Could have sed I let him get away therfore I Could not have Judgment Every word sed in this Case by me was Proven in Court before the plantiff in said Case and a young man he sent the money by to the officer by boath testifide in the Court before that he Paid him in State Banke money and it was only one per Cent Discount and the Confed was only worth 10 Cts in the doller and the officer Contended lancaster the plantiff Paid Confed Every word ritten was Proved in the Court before next Case was I Sold my land in Smith County in 59 and thear anote given due January the fist 62 and the purcher wanted to pay it in Confed and I would not take it the 1500–00 dollarse and I give him abond agreeing to the Bond to make title when said note was Paid off in good Curant money generl forist Come in the Cuntry with 4000 thusond men and Posted Said Printed Printed advertisement Stayting in that if anney Person refusd to take the money his Property would bee Confiscated and him put in Prisin and the Soaldierse Pointed out the advertisements and wond us of the Consiqencs and said Plantiff Came foward and Paid of Said note with Confed and went home and in afew dayse he Came againe and wanted his deede and the Soalderse was on had left and I told him he Could have his money Back but I ~~wol~~ would never make him adeede for the land and never did nor never will I Refusd the money Severl times before the army Come in the Cuntry I Suide Said fisher for the amount of Confed he paid me and got Judgment with ease Judg tilmon decided it was taken under deuress and it was not an Exicuted Contract thearfore I must have Judgment for the Confederate money paid to me under Deuress this nashville Supreme Court reverses the Judgment below and that is ahard thing I want you to let me know wether or not ther dicesion will Stand or not they are under disabilites and thearefore Cannot bee leagle officers I am down on all sutch men and partyse the Balance of my life you will Please rite me imeadiatley wether or not you thinke their Decisens will Stand wether or not you thinke tennessee will be reconstructed Please dont make this Publicke Anser imeadiatley"—ALS, DNA, RG 60, Letters from the President.

1871, March 21. Chief David King and eleven others, L'Anse, Mich., to USG. "We the undersigned Chippeway Indians of Lake Superior are informed by the white man that part of our Reservation has been sold without our sanction The Township which we hear is sold was selected by us previous to the writing of Treaty 1854, but when the Treaty was read to us we discovered that it was omited and on that account we refused to sign the Treaty But Mr Gilbert U. S. Commissioner assured us that it should be placed there and upon that condition we put our signatures to the Treaty and we knew that it was withdrawn from market and thus we felt assured that the land was secure to us If it be true that part of our Reservation is sold we ask you to take such measures for its redemption as your wisdom may indicate We know our kind Father that you will not do us any injustice nor allow the Government to cheat us out of our land we are confident in your faithfulness toward us and we look to you as our protector"—D, DNA,

RG 75, Letters Received, Mackinac Agency. On March 24, Peter Crebassa, L'Anse, wrote to USG. "Excuse me sir if I take the liberty to write you a few lines in r'gard of this reservation Township 51 Range 31 that was sold this winter Dear sir I shall explain you how this matter stands the treaty of 54 I was not there at Lapoint. but our ~~I~~Chiefs and Interpreter Rev'd Peter Marksman. Methodist Missionery told Me when the Commissioner Henry C. Gilbert call them to signe the treaty Peter Marksman read the treaty and thear was only one township for the Methodist Indians on the East side of the bay then the Chief ~~told~~ said one township is not enough for us for therre is another band of Indians to come in this reservation you must put another township. and we shall signe the treaty and the Commissionr said yes I will ad another township. and furthermore the said Commissionr said I will retain from sale in the land office so he done it. it retain from sale until this winter. some speculators take the advantage of there was only one township in the copy of the treaty. and in the treaty of 54 the mixed blood was to have 80 acres of land or Land scrips to select therre land were they please on the governement land but Dear sir we never got our scrips nor land and I have made application to our Agents. but they say you take your land in the reservation so I selected one section for my Family last summer and this section was sold this winter. and I make my application to you Dear sir We must have our land and I dont se no were where we can get our lands it is all bought as far has 20 or 30 miles from this place—it is only in the reservation where we can select our land if this township is returned to us for there is more land there the indians can huse. I have writteen to the Commissionr of Indian Affairs on the subject and send our claims the discribtion of our land. Dear sir I ask you only justice and I know you are only the man can do us this favor."—ALS, *ibid.* See *HED*, 42-2-1, part 5, pp. 924–27, 42-2-193.

On March 22, Joseph Me-daywis, chief, Dunningville, Mich., had written to USG. "Last Oct. 22d 1870 the Ind. Agt J W Long distributed the Patents or deeds to all the Otawa & Chipewa Indians who have made selections of Lands according to the stipulations of the Treaty made with them by the U. S Goverment at Detroit July 31st 1855 but I find there are several of the indians who are the head of Families and who had always lived in the States before the treaty came into opperation and we consider them are justly entitled to select lands under the Treaty aforesaid But these persons was unfortunately thrown out of their selections by some reason or cause unknown and was therefore unfortunately and unintentionaly overlooked and omitted though they are justly & Lawfully and equitably entitled to lands like the others because they being one of the parties connected with the treaty of July 31st 1855 I do therefore humbly entreat you to be graciously and Mercifully ~~to be gracious~~ pleased to consider the rights and title of these Indians and grant them the privilage to select lands and issue to them Pattents or deeds before all lands matters under the treaty are finaly brought to a close . . . In Concluseon I would say that you write to me at Dunningville P O Mich so I may know whether my request~~s~~ in behalf of these

Indians are granted—If any further evidence or testimony is required to proove the facts of these statements I and many of my fellow Chiefs can produce them"—ALS, DNA, RG 75, Letters Received, Mackinac Agency. On Aug. 4, Me-daywis *et al.* petitioned USG. "The undersigned Humble Petitioners having claims in the 'Treaty of July 31st 1855 for the Ottawas and Chippewas of Grand River' humbly petition the President that He will in mercy grant us the right and privilege to all our Children their proportion of Land on the Reservations in Mason, Oceana, and Muskegon Counties. As the Eighty Acres for Each Indian in the Treaty at the time of its Ratification is not sufficient for their future Homes induces us to humbly Petition You— . . . Signed in the presence of Henry Jackson Special Indian Interpreter"—D (12 signatures—signed by mark), *ibid.* On Dec. 20, 1872, Masis Shaw-be Koung and others, Bradley, Mich., wrote to USG. "We are of the Treaty of July 31st 1855, between the Ottawas and Chippewas of Grand River in the State of Michigan. We understand that all the Reservations in the Counties of Mason Oceana, and Muskegon are to come into market this present month. We humbly pray that you will be pleased in much mercy to order not to Have the Reservtions to come into Market. We have many valid reasons for this Petitioning. We read your Communication stating that you will do just and further prosperity of the Indians in your Protection. This made us Happy & much pleased & beleive that you will do as you say. We Have claims against the U. S. Government we therefore pray that you will be pleased to order a Delegation to visit you at Washington City to make final Settlement with this Great Government. Last Spring in the Month May we did request Our Agent for this Agency to present these things to you but we fear you did not Hear our words. Let us Hear from you soon. Write to Bradley P. O Alligan County Mich."—D (signed by mark), *ibid.* Charles K. Eddy and others in the lumber industry had petitioned USG to investigate corruption related to the sale of pine lands on a Chippewa reservation.—DS (printed—docketed May 25), *ibid.* See *HED*, 42-3-1, part 5, I, 586, 43-1-1, part 5, I, 543.

1871, March 22. To Senate. "In reply to the request contained in your Resolution of the 20th instant, I return herewith the resolution of the 17th instant, advising and consenting to the appointment of Thomas J Henderson to be Collector of Internal Revenue for the 5th District of Illinois. I have to request the return of a copy of the confirmation of Walter S. Brown, (on the same sheet,) for the guidance of the Treasury Department."—DS, DNA, RG 46, Nominations. The enclosure is *ibid.* On March 24, the Senate reaffirmed its confirmation of Thomas J. Henderson, a lawyer who had served as col., 112th Ill., as collector of Internal Revenue, 5th District, Ill.

1871, March 22. Peter Dougherty, Omena, Mich., to USG. "By request of the Indian of the Grand Traverse region, among whom I have been laboring as missionary over thirty years, I have copied the accompanying letter and enclose it to you. I would simply add they would be gratified to receive an answer from you. Any communication directed to Ah,go,sa Chief Omena P. O Lelenaw Co Michigan would reach them by the regular mail"—ALS, DNA, RG 75, Letters Received, Mackinac Agency. On the same day, Chief Ah,go,sa and nine others petitioned USG. "We the Indians residing on Grand Traverse Bay in the State of Michigan have met together to consult about our welfare. We write to you to inform you what our united earnest desire is. We wish you would give our young men* forty acres of land each as given in our treaty or to authorize them to take homesteads as white men are allowed to do. This is our earnest desire and we hope you will send an answer to this our communication By direction of the council we Chiefs & head men subscribe our names . . . *They mean those who have come of age since the last treaty was made."—Copy, *ibid.*

1871, March 22. Governor Edmund J. Davis of Tex. to USG. "I have the honor to transmit herewith, certified Copy of 'Joint Resolution instructing our Senators and requesting our Representatives in Congress to use their exertions to effect the removal of bands of Comanche and Kiowa Indians to a point at least one hundred and fifty miles from the civilized settlements or organized Counties in Texas'."—LS, DNA, RG 75, Letters Received, Kiowa Agency. See *HED*, 42-2-1, part 5, pp. 419, 918–20.

1871, March 24. To Senate. "In reply to the request contained in your Resolution of the 20th instant, I return herewith the resolution of the 17th instant advising and consenting to the appointment of Nicholas H. Owings of the Territory of Colorado, to be Register of the Land Office in Arkansas Valley Land District, in the Territory of Colorado. I have to request the return of a copy of the confirmation of Charles A. Cook (on the same sheet) for the guidance of the Department of the Interior."—DS, DNA, RG 46, Nominations. The enclosure is *ibid.* On March 31, USG withdrew the nomination of Nicholas H. Owings, who had served as capt., commissary of subsistence (1863–65). On Dec. 5, USG nominated Irving W. Stanton, formerly lt., 2nd Colorado Cav., as register, Arkansas Valley Land District, Colorado Territory. Stanton had been commissioned during the Senate recess.

1871, March 24. Carlos Butterfield, Washington, D. C., to USG. "At the present moment, when deep gloom hangs over the entire business community of these United States by reason of the fact that our foreign commerce and Shipping interests have sunk to an alarming and hitherto unparalleled point of depression, affecting injuriously every branch of trade, every field of productive industry, and consequently the financial resources of the nation, any measure which will open up an enlarged field for the enterprising commercial and industrial spirit of our people is surely worthy of our most serious consideration. . . . Partial relief, it is true, would be afforded to our shipping interests by reducing or abolishing the duty upon all materials that enter into the construction or equipment of vessels, but it is manifest that a mercantile marine cannot long exist unless it find profitable employment, and to supply it with profitable employment it must have commerce. Such a policy must be inaugurated as will open up the vast field of commercial enterprise stretching out before us on this Continent, and conduct to our ports the fruitful streams of a trade naturally ours, but now, unfortunately in the hands of others, in consequence of the neglect by former administrations, to create and establish the necessary policy. Some co-operative system of international measures between the independent States of America must be adopted that will secure to us the great advantages contended for as being within our reach that will enable us to compete successfully with our European rivals; build up our merchant marine, and give it profitable employment; enrich our business community and fill our national coffers. The magnitude and importance of the trade between the Spanish American States and other countries is evidenced by the fact, that according to reliable statistics, it amounts at the present time to more than $500.000.000. a year in gold, of which nearly $400.000,000. fall to the share of the maritime nations of Europe, and of this latter amount, the great bulk to England alone.... And there is no reason why, with a proper policy we should not almost monopolize the entire trade of Spanish America.... But apart from the mere pecuniary aspect of the subject, there are considerations connected with it that are worthy of the attention of the Statesman, the philanthropist and the lover of free institutions. Our sister States of Spanish America are related to us by ties stronger even ~~by~~ than those of consanguinity. Born, amid throes and convulsion, of the common parent of *freedom*, but under less happy auspices than ourselves, they deserve, and ought to receive, all such proper aid and encouragement at our hands as our more fortunate condition enables us to give. Watched over by us in their struggling infancy, recognized by us as legitimate heirs of independence, and, after their national existence had been established, saved by us from its attempted overthrow, they look to us for a continuation of our friendship, our sympathy, and our good offices. There can be no surer way to secure lasting peace to the States in question—domestic peace to each, and peace among themselves—than by the adoption of some beneficial policy within the power of the Administration. . . ."—Copy, OFH.

On June 19, 1869, Butterfield, New York City, had written to USG. "You will, I trust, excuse the liberty I take in thus addressing you at a time when you are seeking repose—but knowing that you are always willing to consider any question of great public good, & from our former acquaintance during the Mexican War, I venture to enclose you the accompanying documents asking for them the favor of your personal consideration. . . ."—ALS, DNA, RG 59, Letters of Application and Recommendation. Enclosures and related papers regarding trade policies and the appointment of Butterfield as special commissioner to the "Spanish American Republics" are *ibid.* Butterfield published books and pamphlets concerning U.S. and Mexican commerce. See *HRC*, 45-3-100.

1871, March 28. To Senate. "In answer to the Resolution of the Senate of the 16th instant, I transmit a Report from the Secretary of State and the papers which accompanied it."—DS, DNA, RG 46, Presidential Messages. *SED*, 42-1-7. On the same day, Secretary of State Hamilton Fish had written to USG. "The Secretary of State to whom was referred the Resolution of the Senate of the 16th instant, requesting the President, 'if compatible with the public interests, to transmit to the Senate, copies of the reports made to the Department of State by Samuel B. Ruggles, Delegate from the United States to the International Statistical Congress, at the Hague in the year 1869, with the documents accompanying said Reports,' has the honor to lay before the President the Reports mentioned in the subjoined list."—DS, DNA, RG 46, Presidential Messages. Related papers are *ibid.*

1871, March 30. To Senate transmitting a commercial treaty with Italy.—DS, DNA, RG 46, Presidential Messages. On April 15, the Senate ratified this treaty. On June 17, USG authorized Secretary of State Hamilton Fish to exchange ratifications of this treaty.—DS, DLC-Hamilton Fish.

1871, March 31. To Senate. "In answer to your Resolution of the 17th instant, requesting, 'if not incompatible with the public service, the report recently made of a board of officers of the Engineer Department on the condition of the Mississippi River near Vicksburg, Miss, with such remarks, suggestions, or recommendations as may be made by the Chief Engineer of the Army,' I herewith transmit a Report, dated 28th instant, with accompanying papers, received from the Secretary of War."—DS, DNA, RG 46, Presidential Messages. *SED*, 42-1-6. On March 28, Secretary of War William W. Belknap had written to USG supplying the information.—DS, DNA, RG 46, Presidential Messages.

1871, March 31. Elihu B. Washburne, Paris, to USG. "I take great pleasure in introducing to your acquaintance the Viscount de Lancastre, the new Minister of Portugal to the United States. The Viscount remained in Paris a long time during the siege and my relations with him have always been of the pleasantest and most agreeable character. You will find him a most accomplished gentleman and I feel assured that he will receive from you and the people of Washington a most cordial reception."—ALS (press), DLC-Elihu B. Washburne. On Oct. 18 and 20, Charles H. Lewis, U.S. minister, Lisbon, wrote to Secretary of State Hamilton Fish. "I was this day informed by the Minister for Foreign Affairs, that it is the intention of His Majesty the King of Portugal, to appoint Senhor João de Sousa Lobo, at present Secretary of the Portuguese Legation in London, Minister Plenipotentiary and Envoy Extraordinary to the Government of the United States, in the place of Viconde Lancestre. . . ." "In my Dispatch of the 18th Inst. announcing the appointment of Senhor Lobo, as Minister Plenipotenciary of the King of Portugal to the United States, I deemed it advisable to omit any mention of the reasons which had induced, first Senhor Coelho de Almeida, and more recently, the Viconde de Lancastre to resign the position, as these reasons were not referred to in the note addressed to me by the Secretary for Foreign Affairs. It is however generally understood here, that in both instances, the appointment was resigned on account of the insufficiency of the Salary allowed the Minister. Both the gentlemen previously appointed seem to have sought the *Honor* conferred by the appointment, but without any serious intention of going to Washington, as neither of them considered his private fortune sufficient to enable him to live there in the style he deemed becoming in his position. Senhor Lobo, the gentleman who has been lately appointed has announced his intention to set out for Washington in the course of the next month. . . ."—ALS, DNA, RG 59, Diplomatic Despatches, Portugal. On Jan. 12, 1872, Fish recorded in his diary that João de Souza Lobo was presented to USG.—DLC-Hamilton Fish.

[*1871, MARCH*]. Secretary of the Interior Columbus Delano endorsement. "Respectfully referred to the Prest"—AES (undated), OFH. Written on a letter of March 9, 1871, from U.S. Senator Matthew H. Carpenter of Wis. to Delano. "I have been confined to my bed for several days, and your letter of the 28th ult. has remained unopened until to-day. I have known Beadle for years. A more candid, sincere, energetic, & conscientious man never lived. He is a consistent Christian, a thorough & Radical Republican, and a gentleman worthy of your utmost confidence, in every way. It is because he would not pander to, and play into the hands of, a corrupt political ring, that they have turned upon him, determined to hunt him out of his office. You have one honest officer in Dakota, and I advise you to keep him."—ALS, *ibid.* On March 17, 1871, USG had nominated Lot S. Bayless to replace William H. H. Beadle as surveyor gen., Dakota Territory; on April 15, he withdrew this nomination.

[*1871, MARCH*]. William D. Cole, Grubville, Mo., to USG. "ihope you will excuse my boldness iwood most respectfully ask one Small favor of your excellency wood you please let me know whether the act has past congress allowing Soldiers a land warrent or not if it has please let me know and tel me how to proceed in obtaining mine Dear general ihope you will not forget me ihave Seen you often i was in your command at vicks burg i be longed to the 30th Mo' vol inft comdg by colonel farrar ihope you will Write to me as soon as your leasure will admit iremain your most umble servt and affectionate friend"—ALS (docketed March 4, 1871), DNA, RG 48, Lands and Railroads Div., Letters Received. See *PUSG*, 9, 209.

1871, APRIL 1. To Bradley Barlow. "I am in receipt of the two packages of Maple Sugar you were so good as to forward to me from Vermont. The Sugar is of a very fine quality and is a great luxury at this season of the year. Will you please accept my sincere thanks for the very kind remembrance."—Copy, DLC-USG, II, 1. Born in 1814 in Fairfield, Vt., Barlow was prominent in banking, railroads, and Vt. politics.

1871, April 1. Orville E. Babcock to Governor John M. Palmer of Ill. "The President directs me to inform of the receipt of your letter of the 29th inst. in relation to Lt. Geo: E Albee, and that under existing laws no appointments can be made to the Staff Corps. U. S. Statutes 3rd Sess. 40th Congress. page 318. Sec: 6."—Copy, DLC-USG, II, 1. On March 27, Palmer had written to USG. "Col W M Kilgour late of 75th Ills Infy. with whom you are no doubt acquainted has handed me the enclosed and asks me to recommend to your kind consideration his friend Lt Geo E Albee of the 24th U S Infy. Col Kilgour was after the close of the war appointed Capt in the regular Army and knew Lt Albee and formed a high opinion of him Esteeming Col Kilgour highly I would be personally obliged by anything done for his friend"—ALS, DNA, RG 94, ACP, 1318 1872. On the same day, William M. Kilgour, Springfield, Ill., wrote to USG. "I have the Honor to very Respectfuly ask that 1st Lieut—Geo E. Albee 24th Infantry be appointed to a position on the General Staff of the army, either In the, pay—Quartermaster—or Subsistance Department. I Have served with Lieut Albee and can state from personal observation, as well as from official Reports from His superior officers that He Is a very worthy officer, and justly merits such promotion"—ALS, *ibid.* Also on March 27, Erastus N. Bates, Ill. treasurer, wrote a similar letter to USG.—ALS, *ibid.*

1871, April 1. Governor Benjamin F. Potts of Montana Territory to USG. "It is due to you as well as to myself to frankly say to you, that my zeal to obtain the appointment of a good Lawyer as Chief Justice of this Territory has placed me, (without an Explanation) before you in the attitude of an insincere man—I hope my explanation sent Genl Giles A. Smith has satisfied you that I meant to do right as between the two applicants—and that my interference in the matter was dictated by an earnest desire to carry out your expressed wish, that Montana should be redeemed from the present Democratic misrule, and I could see no way by which so much could be done for the party as the appointment of a good Lawyer as Chief Justice of our Supreme Court. The former Chief Justice being a Democrat a popular Judge it behooved us to get a Republican his equal and if possible his Superior in order to strengthen our party and your Administration in this Territory I intended to do right and if I have not come up to your expectations, Will you please to indicate it and I will conform to your wishes in all matters wherein your wishes are known. I have greatly reduced the expendiatures of this Office and think I have the full confidence of the friends of your administration in this Territory."—Copy (press), Montana Historical Society, Helena, Mont. On March 14, USG had nominated Decius S. Wade as chief justice, Montana Territory, in place of Henry L. Warren. See John D. W. Guice, *The Rocky Mountain Bench: The Territorial Supreme Courts of Colorado, Montana, and Wyoming, 1861–1890* (New Haven, 1972), pp. 74–75.

1871, April 3. Secretary of the Navy George M. Robeson to USG. "The letter of Paymaster H. M. Denniston, submitted with yours of the 15th ult. is returned. Seamen, while serving as firemen and coal heavers are entitled to the thirty-three cents per day only for the days when they actually do duty as firemen or coal heavers; as, under the orders of the Department, a ship is not under steam except under particular circumstances. Thus seamen's pay, with proper allowances for the time when they do actual service as firemen will not exceed, in any instance, the regular monthly pay of firemen and coal heavers; and upon a proper carrying out of the orders of the Department, the question suggested by Mr. Denniston will not arise."—Copy, DNA, RG 45, Letters Sent to the President.

1871, April 3. Gilbert E. Parsons, Oswego, N. Y., to USG. "Confidential . . . This community is somewhat excited with reference to a change in the office of collector of customs at this port; and as a life long republican I make use of this medium to advise the appointing power of the true situation of the republican party here. There are Two wings to the party in this city and vicinity; one headed by Hon De Witt C. Littlejohn with the Commercial Advirtizer and times as an organ and the other now without any head with the Oswego Press newspaper as an organ. Dr Clark the present collector is identified with the latter and his retintion in office will be distateful to the former; Mr Root whose name has been sent to the Senate is identified with the former—the Littlejohn wing and is a fast personal and political friend of that gentleman and his appointment is very displeasing to the Press wing of the party. I do not think it easy to reconcile the two sections at present but believe that the appointment of Robert F. Child would be the best and most judicious action that can be made. Captain Child is a good true man and has held a subordinate position in the Custom house here since 1861 I therefore respectfully recommend his appointment."—ALS, DNA, RG 56, Collector of Customs Applications. On March 31, USG had nominated Elias Root as collector of customs, Oswego, in place of Charles C. P. Clark. On March 22, 1875, Mayor Benjamin Doolittle of Oswego and many others petitioned USG to reappoint Root.—DS, *ibid.* On Dec. 8, USG renominated Root.

1871, April 4. Orville E. Babcock to Sylvester Larned, Detroit. "Official duties prevent the President's attendance upon Friday at Senator Howard's funeral. Thanks for the invitation to your house"—Copy, DLC-USG, II, 5.

1871, April 5. USG proclamation authorizing Secretary of State Hamilton Fish to exchange ratifications of a consular convention with the Austro-Hungarian Empire.—DS, DLC-Hamilton Fish. See *PUSG*, 20, 442.

On Dec. 12, 1870, USG had written to the Senate. "I submit to the Senate for their consideration, with a view to ratification, a Convention relating to naturalization between the United States and the Austro-Hungarian Empire, signed at Vienna, on the 20th of September, 1870, which is accompanied by the papers mentioned in the subjoined list."—DS, DNA, RG 46, Presidential Messages, Foreign Relations, Austria-Hungary. The enclosure is *ibid.*

1871, April 5. USG endorsement. "Refered to the Sec. of the Treas. It looks to me as if the change herein asked should be made."—AES, DNA, RG 56, Collector of Customs Applications. Written on an undated petition from Alfred A. Farr and 93 others to USG. "The undersigned Ministers of the Methodist E— Church would, most respectfully request that our friend and brother *Hiram Dunn* be reappointed as Collector of Customs for the district of Champlain Mr. Dunn's unjust removal by Prest. Johnson demands we think his restoration. . . ."—Copy, *ibid.* In an undated note, John P. Newman wrote to USG. "Rev Mr Dunn, comes to me with the within letter from Bishop Simpson. Mr Dunn is an old friend & religiously & politically is a gentleman of great energy & intelligence. He desires an interview which I hope you can grant. He was deposed by Mr Johnson from the position of Collector of Customs, of Champlain District. N. Y. & now desires to be reappointed."—ANS, *ibid.* On May 12, John McGreggor, Altona, Clinton County, N. Y., and three others, "Republican Supervisors," petitioned USG. "The undersigned learning that conclusive proof of the importance and necessity of a change in collector of customs for this district has been forwarded to the Secretary of the Treasury we respectfully ask that H. Dunn Esq be appointed in place of Mr. Parmenter With the exception of a small 'ring' at Plattsburgh we are confident Mr. Dunn is nearly the unanimous choice of this county—Two of those opposed to Mr. Dunn's reappointment (Mr. Clark now assessor & Mr. Ransom Post-Master) were Mr. Dunn's deputies when he was collector and discharged by him as they would not consent to perform service while taking pay We earnestly entreat that the change be made immediately as the welfare of the party and interest of the department demand it"—DS, *ibid.* Ephraim Wells *et al.* petitioned USG. "Allow us to give the following facts in reference to the Champlain Collection District . . . The appointment of collector has always been conceded to this congressional district now represented by Hon. J. Rogers Democrat and we enter our protest to any change in this proper and established rule 5th Most conclusive proof in the shape of affidavits and otherwise is on file in the office of the Treasury that J. Parmenter has shown himself incompetant, inefficient, and negligent of his duties 6th Many prominent and influential Republicans of the county assert that the collector is not only derelict in official duties but runs his office in the interest of the democrat party and this caused the election of a Democrat Senetor two years ago—and last fall of a Dem. Congressman These papers are also on file 7th The proof we claim is abundant and also on file that H. Dunn should be reappointed to the place as collector from which Mr Johnson removed him more than four years ago not only as an act of justice to him but his appointment would save thousands of dollars to the revenue, and this congressional & Senatorial district to the Administration 8th We also learn Mr. Dunn's appointment is urged by Bishop Simpson. Dr. Newman and more than one hundred of the prominent clergy of the largest and truest denomination in the land and that those papers are on file . . ."—DS (undated—17 signatures), *ibid.*

George L. Clark, assessor of Internal Revenue, Plattsburg, N. Y., *et al.* petitioned USG. "The undersigned Republicans and members of the M. E. Church at Plattsburgh in the District of Champlain, having been informed that Mr. Hiram Dunn is endeavoring through the relation that he still holds in our church as a nominal Minister, and through the friendly influence of Ministers who stand deservedly high in our denomination, to procure the removal of Major Parmeter, from the position of Collector of Customs of the District of Champlain and his own appointment: We would most respectfully and earnestly: not only as Republicans, but in the interest of our church and the Cause of Religion where Mr. Dunn is known, enter our solemn protest against such appointment. Mr. Dunn has not been known throughout this County or District for the last ten years, as a religious man, but as an intriguing politician—and by desertion of the Republican cause and going over to the Johnson Democrats after his removal in 1866—and attending, conspicuously, the Democratic County, Congressional and State Conventions as a delegate—he showed in this such an entire lack of moral and political principle—that no intelligent Methodist or Republican, aside from those connected to him by marriage, has had any confidence whatever in him since—Major Parmeter the present Collector, and whose removal Mr. Dunn is endeavoring to procure, is to our personal knowledge, a true and reliable Republican and has always been since the formation of the party. He served as a Captain in the 118th Regt. of New York Volunteers and lost his right leg in the Battle of Coal Harbour while gallantly defending the cause of the country. He also had three sons in the service—one of whom died and lies buried at the 'Soldiers Home' in Washington. After all those sacrifices for us, and for our Children, and for the Country, we most earnestly remonstrate against Major Parmeters removal—and the appointment of such a man as, we regret to say, Mr. Dunn, whatever his position may once have been, has now become—"—DS (undated—8 signatures), *ibid.* A similar petition is *ibid.* On Dec. 6, 1870, USG had nominated Jacob Parmerter as collector of customs, Champlain, N. Y.; he continued in office.

1871, April 6. USG endorsement. "Respectfully refered to the Att'y. Gn. for his opinion."—AES, DNA, RG 60, Letters Received from the President. Written on a letter of April 3 from Amos Webster, Washington, D. C., to USG. "I have the honor to address you on the subject of my 'Commission' as Register of Wills for Washington County, District of Columbia, and to refer you to the following extracts, taken from the Constitution of Maryland, and subsequent Act of Congress, relating to the above Office, as follows: . . ."—LS, *ibid.* On April 15, Attorney Gen. Amos T. Akerman wrote to USG. "You have required my opinion upon the application of Mr A. Webster, Register of Wills for the District of Columbia, for an amendment of his commission. He quotes the following paragraph from the constitution of

Maryland:... This provision was in force in what is now the District of Columbia, at the time of the cession by Maryland. Mr. Webster conceives that it is in force still, and that his commission ought to run 'during good behavior' instead of 'during the pleasure of the President' If his office were created by the constitution of Maryland, and there had been no authorized legislation modifying the tenure, his claim would be well founded. But the Constitution of the United States gives to Congress the power of 'exclusive legislation in all cases whatsoever over such district (not exceeding ten miles square) as may, by cession of particular States and the acceptance of Congress, become the seat of the government of the United States.'... There being no other provision by law for the appointment of register of wills, the appointment is with the President, with the advice and consent of the Senate; and the tenure of the office is the President's pleasure, under the modification prescribed by the recent acts known as the Tenure of Office Acts. I am therefore of the opinion that the change which Mr Webster desires in his commission, is not authorized by law."—Copy, *ibid.*, Opinions. Webster had served at USG's hd. qrs. See *PUSG*, 15, 370–71.

1871, April 6. To Senate. "In reply to the request contained in your Resolution of the 30th ultimo I return herewith the Resolution of the 23d ultimo: 'That the Senate do not advise and consent to the appointment of Eli F. Jennings to be Assessor of Internal Revenue for the Third District of Alabama."—DS, DNA, RG 46, Nominations. On March 9, USG had nominated Eli F. Jennings to replace Luther Q. Morton as assessor of Internal Revenue, 3rd District, Ala. On April 19, the Senate reconsidered Jennings and tabled the vote on his approval. Jennings had been paymaster and capt., commissary of subsistence (1864–65); Morton continued in office.

1871, April 7. Orville E. Babcock to L. W. Lloyd, Red Banks, Miss. "The President directs me to convey to you his thanks for your kindness in sending him the spurs, which are a nice specimen of blacksmith work to be made with simple a hammer and file. He appreciates your kind intention and regrets that he cannot comply with your wish. He knows of no such place as you wish. He returns you certificate of citizenship with this letter and also the spurs, which have cost you ~~so~~ much labor and are so good an evidence of your handiwork, by Express."—Copy, DLC-USG, II, 1.

1871, April 8. William T. Bradshaw, Guyandotte, Cabell County, West Va., to USG and Congress. "Knowing Patriotism and good feeling towards all the Solderes who fought to Perpetuate our Government and Constitution and to Put down the Rebellioin I as one of the Soldires of the union Army make Bold to approach you Will See By the Army Polls on file Washington. that I Volenterd In 9th West Virginia Regiment Commanded at that time By Col Skinner and Company I Served tow years In the Regiment, and Was Discharged by Reason of Relistment as a Vetron in the 1st Va Vet Vol Ift. I do not make this Statement to Decieve as I Could not do it if felt disposed But to Show you my Present Condision. you will also see By the Pension Polls that I am a pensioner on the Bounty of the Government for my Suport, I am Disabled from Worke from a Gun Shot wound wi~~s~~tch I Recieved In the thy at the Battle of hall town Well to be Plain I can not walk about to do Worke more then one fourth of the time and I have a famley to Suport and my Pension is not Adequate therefore I know you all ~~fell~~ feel for the Sufferings of all the Soldiers that fought to uphold the Government of our fathers I have a Wife and three Children and I am not able to more then half feed and cloth them Look at the Picture and Carry it to your own fire side and a Small Pittance of all your Salaries Contributed for their Support Would not be felt or missed by you and now what ask is for you to keep me and famley from want by Contributing one or two days Pay of your Salaries in doing this you will have the Prayers and hart felt thanks one who was maimed for life In Contributing his part in Puting down the Rebellion . . . P S if you feel disposed help me Send ~~money~~ me a me Draft on the Banke at Iron ton Ohio"—ALS, DNA, RG 48, Miscellaneous Div., Letters Received.

1871, April 8. Thomas Murphy, collector of customs, Alonzo B. Cornell, surveyor of customs, and two others, New York City, to USG. "We understand that an effort is being made to have the son of Gen. John Hammond of this State appointed as one of the Cadets at large to West Point. Gen. Hammond is a leading citizen and Republican; served his country faithfully and well in the field during the late rebellion; is a member of the N. Y. State Republican State Committee; a warm friend always of the Administration; and we have positive proof of his warm friendship. We know of but few men in the State of N. Y. among the soldiers better disposed or more able to assist our friends"—LS, DNA, RG 94, Unsuccessful Cadet Applications. John Hammond, col., 5th N. Y. Cav., had been appointed bvt. brig. gen.

1871, April 10. USG endorsement. "Let the penalty of the bond named within be fixed at thirty thousand dollars, as recommended by the Secretary of the Interior."—Copy, DNA, RG 48, Lands and Railroads Div., Letters Sent. Written on a letter of April 8 from Walter H. Smith, act. secretary of the interior, to USG. "I have the honor to recommend that the penalty of the bond of the Receiver of Public Moneys in the land office at Walla Walla, Washington Territory, be fixed at thirty thousand dollars."—Copy, *ibid.* On March 17, USG had nominated Anderson Cox as receiver, Walla Walla.

1871, April 12. USG endorsement. "Refered to the Sec. of State. Before sending any other bearer of dispatches to Europe I want to see the Sec. of State in relation to sending Gn. Spinner."—AES, DNA, RG 59, Letters of Application and Recommendation. Written on a letter of the same day from Joseph B. Will, Washington, D. C., to Secretary of State Hamilton Fish. "I have the honor to apply for an appointment as Special Bearer of Despatches to one or more of our Legations abroad to take effect the 1st of June proximo."—ALS, *ibid.* Related papers are *ibid.* See *PUSG*, 19, 480.

1871, APRIL 14. USG endorsement. "The within resignation is accepted to take effect May 31, 1871."—E (initialed), DNA, RG 48, Appointment Div., Letters Received. Written on the resignation of Henry Van Aernam, commissioner of pensions, dated the same day.—ALS, *ibid.*

On March 19, 1869, Ignatius Donnelly, Washington, D. C., had written to USG. "I take pleasure in recommending Hon: Henry Van Aernam of New York for the position of Commissioner of Pensions. He is a physician by profession, and has therefore the kind of technical knowledge necessary in the place he seeks. He served during the war as Surgeon of the 154th N. Y. Vol: and Surgn in Chief of Brigade & Division, with great credit to himself and satisfaction to his superiors. He has since the war served four years in the House of Representatives of the U. S. and during all that time has served on the Com: on Invalid Pensions. He is every way qualified, by profession, legislative experience and personal character for the position of Commis. of Pensions. He is a kind hearted, just-minded, honorable gentleman and could not fail to perform the duties of the office to the satisfaction of the Executive."—ALS, *ibid.* Related papers are *ibid.*

On Nov. 2, 1870, C. Augustus Haviland, Chicago, wrote to USG. "I again ask your attention to Pension office matters in the hope that you will direct the attention of your new Sec'y to the manner in which soldiers are treated by Hon Henry Van Aernam. I believe Mr Cox was the cause of the retention of Mr Van A—. and that you can effectually *silence your enemies* by NOW causing the removal of one who is bringing disgrace upon the country."—ALS, *ibid.* On Feb. 17, 1871, Haviland wrote to USG enclosing clippings charging Van Aernam with incompetence.—ANS, *ibid.*

On March 8, the Medical Society of D. C. petitioned USG and Secretary of the Interior Columbus Delano. ". . . the large majority of the present Examining Surgeons of the Pension Bureau have served in the medical corps of the Volunteer forces during the late war: and whereas, none but regular physicians were admitted into that corps, or into the medical corps of the regular Army and Navy, and, therefore, none but regular physicians are provided with the medical experience required on Examining Boards: therefore—*Resolved*, that this Society deems the action of the Honourable Commissioner of Pensions, in excluding irregular practitioners from the Medical Examining Board under that Bureau, as made in the best interests of the public service: thereby leading to uniformity of action, increasing the efficiency of the Bureau, protecting the Government, and affording to the pensioner the benefit of the most skilled advice:—and it is earnestly hoped that the Government will not, in this instance, disregard the deliberate and expressed conviction of the whole legitimate medical profession of this country, by appointing to medical position or office a class of men whose practice is not based on experience and observation—the only true Ground-work of medical progress,—but upon arbitrary dicta, not verified after nearly a century of trial, and wholly opposed to the ordinary exposition of the natural laws of physical science:—. . ."—Copy, *ibid.*

On April 12, Tullio S. Verdi, Washington, D. C., wrote to USG. "I am deputed to forward the enclosed petitions to your Excellency. They beg for the removal of Dr. Van Aernum. Seventy two Medical organizations have been perfected in the U. S. for the purpose of securing the removal of that officer who has betrayed his official prerogatives by making of his office a means to proscribe six thousand professional men from holding office of trust under the U. S. Government. Fortyseven of said organizations are in the State of NewYork to which more than a thousand members belong. They have decided to make this a test question and will use their political privileges to see that justice be done. I know they are in earnest and as a republican and a friend of your administration I would beg that the cause of so much dissatisfaction be removed. We cannot afford many more splits in the republican party and particularly in the State of New York and I assure you that the non-removal of Dr. Van Armun will cost the republicans at least ten thousand votes in that State. Senator Conkling makes a great mistake in supporting Van Armun. From the moment this is known in Utica and Albany the Senator's action will meet with such a disapprobation from his people as will make him regret that he ever sided with that bigotted and unjust officer. Moreov[er] the homoeopathic physicians are under the delusion that Sen. Conkling is friendly to them, believing him a just man and one who has put the life of his children and wife, whenever needed, under the treatment of the very men who receive proscription at the hands of his friend Van Armun. Mr. President, for the sake of justice, for the welfare of your party, and for the respect that the Medical profession entertain for you I hope that you will remove Van. Arimun as speedily as possible, and ~~to~~thus to heal many a wound in our ranks before elections"—ALS, *ibid.*

On April 14, John M. Medows, Chicago, wrote to USG. "Would you like to know the truth in regard to one of your appointees? Of course you would. As one of the soverign people, as an old soldier who served under you for over two years, and received three wounds in battle with the Johnneys, and as a friend of your Administration (St Domingo and all) I claim your ear for a moment. Hon Dr. H Van Aerman is a humbug, a nuisance on general principles and a disgrace to the office of Pension ~~agent~~Commissioner. I have made inquiry of every person in this city engaged at all in business of prosecuting Pension claims, and of some ten or twelve persons who are endeavoring to prosecute their own claims, and there is just one voice in regard to him, and that is of condemnation. He has out of caprice and a desire to prove himself a greater man than all who have preceeded him invented and promulgated a vast mess of new rules and requirements making the getting of a Pension, and particularly a Mothers or Fathers Pension almost if not quite an impossibility. He refuses to reply to enquires as to what is wanted in pending cases though they may not have been heard from for years. He is a *nuisance*! There are more than two hundred cases from this city alone which have not been heard from for more than a year, though all the evidence called for had been sent to him, and repeated attempts made to get information both by the Agents and the parties themselves. . . ."—ALS, *ibid.*

On Feb. 4, John B. Rodgers, Washington, D. C., had written to USG. "The undersigned is informed there is likely to be a vacancy of Commissioner of pensions, in that event, Tennessee is not without her claims to your consideration during your administration, and your humble servant would be pleased to represent his state in that behalf, and is furthermore pleased that he has the unanimous approval and approbation of the Congressional delegation from Tennessee"—ALS, *ibid.* On Feb. 15, U.S. Senator Hiram R. Revels of Miss. wrote to USG. "At the wish of many white and colored citizens of the State of Mississippi, I take pleasure in placing before you the name of Mr T. P. Sears for the office of commissioner of pensions. The colored people of the south have a deep interest in the above officer and Mr Sears is evidently the man in whose hands they wish to place thier claims."—ALS, *ibid.* On March 17, Haviland wrote to USG. "There is one man whose name as Com of Pensions would satisfy the Country. That man is Your friend, Hon Wm Lawrence of Ohio. He has carefully considered many matters connected with the Pension office."—ALS, *ibid.* On April 7, O. Noble, president, Keystone National Bank, Erie, Pa., wrote to USG. "Majr A A Craig of our City is an applicant for the Office of Commissioner of Pentions—Permit me to State that Maj Craig was in the armey ~~of~~during the Rebelion & acquited himself with honor & fidelity as a Solgier & was honerably discharged at the close of the war—. . ."—ALS, *ibid.* Related papers are *ibid.* On April 14, USG nominated James H. Baker as commissioner of pensions.

1871, April 14. Thomas J. Hall *et al.*, Sackets Harbor, N. Y., to USG. "We, the undersigned Citizens, Electors, of the village of Sackets Harbor, and its vicinity have the honor thus to approach your Excellency with an appeal on behalf of 1st Lieut: Alonzo E. Miltimore, 1st U. S. Artillery, now stationed, and doing duty at the post of Madison Barracks as Acting Assistant Quartermaster and Acting Commissary of Subsistence, who we understand, has filed in the Adjutant Generals Office an application for an appointment as Captain and Quartermaster on the General Staff of the Army. . . . A number of us remember, with pleasure the time your Excellency filled the same position at Madison Barracks as that Lieut: Miltimore now occupies, and ask a favorable consideration of this appeal as a personal favor."—DS (22 signatures), DNA, RG 94, ACP, 4305 1871. On May 26, U.S. Senator Matthew H. Carpenter of Wis. endorsed this petition. "I cordially concur in the within I believe Miltimore is a good officer, and his father is a constituent and friend of mine"—AES, *ibid.* No appointment followed.

1871, April 14. William J. Smith, surveyor of customs, Memphis, Washington, D. C., to USG. "The bearer Major A. E. Alden is one of the leading & active Republicans of Middle Tennessee—entering the Army in sixty one he served with credit and distinction during the war for the suppression of the Rebelion. was appointed Commission of Registration by Gov Wm G. Brownlow and twice elected Mayor of Nashville by the Radical Republican party of that City—In all positions of honor & trust he has acted with unswerving fidelity & to the entire satisfaction of his party—Since the ascndency of the Rebels to the controle of the State Maj Alden like many other loyal men has ben completely ostrocized and unable to ingage in any business for a livelihood—His services are deserving of some recognition at the hands of the Administration. and I trust some appointment may be given him—"—Copy, DNA, RG 94, Applications for Positions in War Dept. Related papers are *ibid.* On May 12, Augustus E. Alden, Washington, D. C., wrote to Secretary of War William W. Belknap. "I have the honor to make application for the appointment of Post Trader at some one of the Posts on the Pacific Coast, either in Oregan. Nevada, or Arizona, . . ."—ALS, *ibid.*

1871, April 15. USG endorsement. "Respectfully refered to the Atty. Gn. for investigation."—AES, DNA, RG 60, Letters from the President. Written on a petition of April 8 from William Selden, Washington, D. C., to USG. "The petition of William Selden, late Marshal of the District of Columbia respectfully represents That he is an aged citizen of the District aforesaid having a just and equitable claim against the United States, amounting to the sum of $11220.02, for the maintenance, as Marshal aforesaid, of public prisoners confined in the jail of said District from the year 1857 to the year 1861, both inclusive. That the said claim, whereof the facts have always been admitted, has been heretofore rejected by certain officers of the government, acting as the claimant supposes, wholly beyond their jurisdiction and upon an erroneous construction of a certain statute of the United States. That the validity of said claim is entirely dependent upon the just interpretation of a certain enactment approved August 16. 1856 sec. 1. (11 Stat. 49.) and which has never received the consideration of the legal adviser of the government: The claimant supposing that his said claim is entirely sustainable with reference to said enactment, prays that the subject may be referred to the Honorable the Attorney General for his official opinion upon the merits of said claim under the just interpretation of the statute aforesaid."—DS, *ibid.* A related paper is *ibid.* On June 28, Attorney Gen. Amos T. Akerman wrote to USG transmitting a report on this matter from Benjamin H. Bristow, solicitor gen.—Copy, *ibid.*, Letters Sent to Executive Officers. On March 3, 1873, USG signed a bill awarding Selden his claim. See *CG*, 42–3, 1204–5, 2071, 2137; *SRC*, 42-3-418.

1871, April 17. Secretary of State Hamilton Fish to USG. "Judge Bingham desires the transfer of Mr Sheppard now Consul at Chin Kiang with a Salary of $3,000, to Tien Tsin, which is a fee consulate, with about $1000 to $1500—the object being the more healthful climate—The Speaker is very desirous of the appointment of Mr Edgecomb—to the Consulate at Capetown (vacated by recent resignation) Salary $1.000—I send nominations for both the above, for your approval. Also nomination of Capt. Lyon ~~of~~ at El Paso, which you authorised on Friday."—ALS (press), DLC-Hamilton Fish. For Willard W. Edgecomb, see *PUSG*, 20, 425.

On March 18, 1869, U.S. Representative John A. Bingham of Ohio had written to USG. "Eli T Sheppard a Soldier in the War for the Union desires to be appointed consul to Japan China or Africa, for his health. I sent letter by Secy Cox to the President. I want him appointed because he is a Soldier of the Union, a Scholar and gentleman."—ALS, DNA, RG 59, Letters of Application and Recommendation. On March 7, 1871, Bingham wrote to Fish concerning the transfer of Eli T. Sheppard, consul, from Chin Kiang to Tien Tsin.—ALS, *ibid.* Related papers are *ibid.* On April 17, USG nominated Sheppard as consul, Tien Tsin. On Aug. 9, Martin S. Kennedy, Cadiz, Ohio, wrote to USG. "It is understood here that E. T. Shepherd Consul to Chang Kiang China has resighned on account of ill health If that is so would you appoint me to fill his place. If I can satisfy you that I am worthy & can fill his place I can give all the security you ask can give reference to any in this county that know me My age is 40 years, am a Republican have always been. Have never had any office have never asked for one before Tis said that you never make a mistake in your appointments try me and I will do you good"—ALS, *ibid.* See *PUSG*, 20, 276, 284–85.

On April 8, Samuel A. Purviance, Pittsburgh, had written to Fish. "The friends of Capt Edwin Lyon are gratified to learn that his name will be presented to your department for a Consulship in Mexico where he is anxious to go to Regain his lost health. We have no more Competent or Meretorious young man in the 23d Congressional district of Penna as our Congressman Hon E McJunkin will inform you. His war Record is that of a most gallant soldier, as the wound which he bears in his breast (a ball having passed clear through him) will during life attest . . ."—ALS, DNA, RG 59, Letters of Application and Recommendation. On April 17, USG nominated Edwin Lyon as consul, Paso del Norte. On Nov. 27, George C. McClellan, Franklin, Pa., wrote to USG. "On account of having been a Shool and Class mate, I take the liberty of writing to you in behalf of my Nephew Capt Lyon who is in ill health in consequence of a gunshot wound in the lungs received during the Rebellion He is now Consul in New Mexico but he is poor, and the salary is not Sufficient to Support him and his family. The climate of N. M. agrees with him better than that of Pa. He wishes to get the appointment of Posttrader at a new Post which is about being established among the Apache Indians. He is a gentleman of good moral character, and if you were to give him the position I as well as all his numerous friends would feel under obligations to you—Please aswer this"—ALS, *ibid.*, RG 94, Applications for Positions in War Dept. McClellan, USMA 1843, named "McClelland" in military records and cashiered for drunkenness (1847), graduated last in USG's class.

1871, April 17. Orville E. Babcock endorsement. "*Respectfully referred to the Honorable Secretary of War.* who is requested to direct Gen. Hancock to give the surveying parties of the Northern Pacific R. R. Co. such protection as the strength of his force, and his other duties, will allow."—ES, DNA, RG 94, Letters Received, 1339 1871. Written on a letter of April 15 from Jay Cooke to Vice President Schuyler Colfax. "I am on my way back from New York, after a very pleasant meeting of the Directors of the Northern Pacific. I also spent an Evening with meeting nearly all the editors of the religious Press, including Henry Ward Beecher, Dr Prime, &c. very enthusiastic friends of the Northern Pacific. Gov. Smith, President of our road, desired me to write you and ask as a very great favor that you would see the President & get him to order placed at the disposal of the Company, under directions of Gen. Hancock, a sufficient body of troops, say 800 to 1000 in Dakota & Montana to protect our surveying parties. We desire to send at once clear through to the Rocky Mts., and want to put the road under contract so soon as these ~~con~~ surveys are completed. It is vastly important that the order should be given at once, and notice of it sent to us, so that we may arrange the whole expedition. If we are successful in selling our bonds rapidly it will not be much beyond the middle of Gen. Grant's second term before the locomotive reaches Puget Sound. I hope the President will not hesitate. We have not troubled the army until the very last moment, & now it is an absolute necessity that we should have their services."—L, *ibid.* On April 2 and 16, Maj. Gen. Winfield S. Hancock, St. Paul, had issued Special Orders Nos. 67 and 80, detailing small military escorts for Northern Pacific Railroad surveying parties.—*Ibid.*

On June 9, W. Milnor Roberts, chief engineer, Northern Pacific Railroad, New York City, wrote to Secretary of War William W. Belknap. "The Board of Directors of the Northern Pacific Railroad Compy. through their President, Hon. J. Gregory Smith, have instructed me to see you in person, with a view to obtain the requisite authority to secure adequate military escort to protect our engineering parties on surveys during the present season along the valley of the Yellowstone river. . . ."—ALS, *ibid.* On June 20, Roberts telegraphed to Belknap. "Our Board in Session Anxious to know shape escort likely to take,"—Telegram received, *ibid.* On June 21, Belknap wrote to Roberts. "I have received your telegram of yesterday in reference to an escort for the surveyors of your road, & answered briefly by telegraph, & have now the honor to state that in view of the reduction of the Army on the 1st of July it will be impossible to furnish a larger escort than that heretofore ordered by General Hancock, without withdrawing troops from stations where their presence is imperatively required."—Copy, *ibid.* On July 21, Hancock issued Special Orders No. 162, "directing the Commanding Officer of Fort Ellis, M. T., to proceed with all the available Cavalry at that post as an escort to Mr. *Milner Roberts,* Chief Engineer Northern Pacific Railroad Company, while engaged in making a reconnoissance down the Yellowstone River a distance of 250 miles, or so far as in the judgment of the Commanding Officer would be expedient and safe, . . ."—*Ibid.* Related papers are *ibid.* See John W. Bailey, *Pacifying the Plains: General Alfred Terry and the Decline of the Sioux, 1866–1890* (Westport, Conn., and London, 1979), pp. 80–83; Francis B. Robertson, "'We Are Going to Have a Big Sioux War': Colonel David S. Stanley's Yellowstone Expedition, 1872," *Montana*, 34, 4 (Autumn, 1984), 4–15.

On Oct. 5, U.S. Senator Alexander Ramsey of Minn., St. Paul, wrote to USG. "On yesterdy I took the liberty ~~of~~ to telegraph you on the subjet of the removal of the Military Hd. quarters of this Dept. from St Paul to some point on the Missouri river which rumor has it, is in contemplation. I do sincerly trust that no such purpose is entertained and in behalf of our people here who are your good friends ask that if there is such purpose at least it may be delayed until the ensuing spring. I respectfully submit, that if there were sufficnt reasons for the establishment of a Dept. Hd. qrs. at St Paul these reasons are stronger now. The Northen P. R. R. in one year will have reached the Missouri River, and Indian difficulties will be imminent right then from day to day as that road progresses. There is no line of Rail Road from Sioux City or from Omaha to a point on or near ~~to~~ the Missouri river where the Northen Pacific R. R. will be carried over that stream. From Sioux City to the probable crossing there will be six hundred miles without R. Road communication and with very uncertain river communiation During the construction of the Union Pacific R. R. there has been a Dept. Head Qrs. at the very door and that road could scarcely have been built without this ability (upon consultation with the officers of the road in a suden emergency) to concentrate troops promptly for its defence. Were Hd. qrs. at Omaha or Sioux City the commandig officer there would have to be communicated with by telegraph in a round about way or by mail, the latter consuming many days. As the construction of the N. P. R. Road progresses the troops will almost all that can be disposed of for such purpose be placed along this line for its protection as has been the case of the other line to the Pacific and it would seem to me Mr President, that at the commencmt of the line is the proper station from which to have a good look out over the whole work & from which to control all the troops. Before winter sets in with us, the Northen Pacific R. R. will be completed to the Red River & within two hundred & twenty five (225) miles of the Missouri river and within Eql distance of the international line on the north, where, even now, there is trouble brewing that may call for the intervention of Militry authority. It seems to me Mr President, not necessary that another Military Department should be united with this, and under present circumstances, the citizens of Minnesota would much regret to have Military Hd. qrs. removed from its prsnt location—such removal would be a serious loss to St Paul and to the state at large in its present commencemt of prosperity. It is almost certain that the Indian question will have to be settled on the line of the Northern Pacific R. Road and that the troops used in doing this will have to be moved over this road, and it would therefore seem that the center of Mility operations should be on the line of the road & where more appropriately than where they now are, at St Paul in Minnesota It does seem to me, Mr President, that the psent arrangemt of Departmnts west of the Mississippi river is a good one and hope you will not deem it a necessity to modify this one. At all events I repeat my request that no chage may be made if at all until the ensuing Spring"—ALS, *ibid.*, 4571 1871. On Oct. 11, Belknap endorsed this letter. "No order has been issued for change of Departments—The matter was awaiting the arrival of the President but no orders have as yet been given"—AE (initialed), *ibid.*

On June 2, Maj. Gen. John M. Schofield, San Francisco, had written to Horace Porter, Long Branch, N. J. "I understand the President proposes in a short time to discontinue the Military Divisions, and as a consequence to make several changes in Department Commanders. If you are at liberty to tell me what the probabilities are so far as I am concerned I would be very glad to know. As a matter of choice I would not prefer to command a Department on this coast after the Division is broken up. My old Department of the Missouri would Suit me perfectly, but my principal wish is not to go South, for the reason that repeated trials have shown that I cannot hope to enjoy good health in a Southern climate. Please do me the favor to give me such information as you properly can on this subject. With warm regards to the President and all who are with you at Long Branch . . ."—Copy, DLC-John M. Schofield. On June 16, Porter wrote to Schofield. "I received your letter in regard to the change in the Mil. Commands, and can say to you *confidentially* that changes will be made this fall, substantially as follows, Sheridan to retain his present Mil. Div, with his present Dep't Commanders, Dep't of East, McDowell at N. York, Dept of Centre Meade, at Phila, Dept of S. East, Terry Louisville, S. West, Halleck. N. Orleans, Columbia as at present, Arizo, Ord, California Schofield. There is nothing very definitely decided upon in regard to time of issuing order. I have no doubt the Sec. of War will be glad to gratify your wishes as far as he can, and I hope the final arrangement may be made satisfactory to you. I write in some haste as we leave town today for Long Branch."—ALS, *ibid.* See Schofield to Gen. William T. Sherman, July 2, concerning reorganization of military divs. and depts.—ALS, DLC-William T. Sherman.

On Oct. 31, Sherman wrote to Lt. Gen. Philip H. Sheridan, Chicago. "Yesterday I returned from Lancaster, Ohio, whither I had gone to attend the bedside and funeral of Mr Ewing, of which you have learned the particulars in the newspapers. By appointment the Secretary of War and I had a full conference with the President, at which it was finally concluded, that in as much as the Military Divisions of the Missouri, and Pacific had to be kept up, it would be better to let those of the Atlantic and South also remain in force. Nevertheless other changes were deemed necessary, the orders for which are now being arranged that materially affect your command. General Augur must go to Texas for reasons which I cannot now explain, and the President prefers to merge the Department of the Platte into that of the Missouri, instead of that of Dakota, because he would prefer to confide the management of the Mormons question to General Pope, supervised by you than to General Hancock, and the probabilities are that the latter can better superintend the arrangements necessary for the protection of the Northern Pacific Road from Saint Paul, than from Omaha. Of necessity

Omaha will for the time being cease to have the importance it has hitherto possessed as a Department Headquarters, and great pressure will be brought to bear on the President to restore it, but other changes which I will describe necessitate the formation of the Department of the Gulf, and it is not deemed wise to have too many Departments, as our General officers are limited in number, and by existing law cannot be increased. . . ."—Copy, DNA, RG 94, Letters Sent. See *HED*, 42-2-1, part 2, pp. 21, 27–29.

On Dec. 20, Sherman, Cadiz, Spain, wrote to Alfred M. Hoyt. ". . . at a Conference between the President, Sec of War and myself, I advised that the Dept of the Platte should be united with that of Dakota, to be commanded by Gen Hancock, whose HdQrs should be removed from St Paul to Omaha—General Grant said he was not willing to confide the Mormon question to General Hancock, because Hancock had shown political Aims, and he Gen Grant then ordered that the Dept of the Platte should be attached to the Dept of the Missouri. I told Gen Grant that the Poeple of Omaha and of Nebraska would make a fuss at the Change, and he then said that we should leave the Depot at Omaha which was all they ought to insist on. As soon as the order was published appeals came from Omaha, just as we expected and Senator Hitchcock came to me at the Astor House and I explained to him just how the case stood. Now I have no doubt the President has backed square down, and though he would not do so mean a thing as to throw off on me after I was away, he has allowed the inference to be drawn that it was my order he had reversed instead of his own, and now he probably thinks it is none of his business to correct this mistake of a Newspaper Correspondent—Yet I know there are men ~~already~~ in Washington who think it smart thus to treat an absent person, . . ."—ALS, DLC-William T. Sherman. On Dec. 21, Sherman wrote to U.S. Senator John Sherman of Ohio. ". . . The fling at me by the NewYork Herald abot breaking up the Departmt of the Platte was unjust, for it was the sole act of the President, after a full knowledge of the outcry it would cause. Grant has simply let down on this pressure, and now allows his understrappers to throw off on me—This is eminently mean—but he had done it more than once, merely saying he cannot prevent the misconstruction of newspaper Reporters. . . ."—ALS, *ibid.*

1871, APRIL 17. Orville E. Babcock to James H. Hackett, Brooklyn. "The President is in receipt of your letter of April 15th 1871. at the hand of the Hon: J. B. C. Davis' and in reply directs me to say, that should you conclude to come to Washington professionally he with your many friends will be pleased to welcome your reappearance on the Stage. The President wishes me to say that he expects to be absent from Washington some ten days immediately after the adjournment of Congress."—Copy, DLC-USG, II, 1. Hackett died on Dec. 28. See *New York Times*, Dec. 29, 1871.

On Jan. 12, 1865, Hackett, New York City, had written to John Hay, Washington, D. C. "Allow me—as I made two unsuccessful efforts to find you in your office the few days whilst I was in Washington last week—to thank you now for your particular favor;—in having submitted my note of 1st inst to the President's observation 'at his Excellency's earliest leisure & convenience' At the close of our interview last Sunday evening the President had the kindness to make a remark to me—I had just said—'It is very uncertain whether I shall ever again appear upon the Washington Stage; unless, perchance, at the desire of Lieutt Genl Grant; who, at Cairo in *Oct 1863*, expressed to me his great regret in never having had &,—for the reasons that I purposed to quit the Stage last winter at the East whilst he should be on duty in the West—never could expect—an opportunity to See my Falstaff for which he had long wished—' The President said—'Mr Hackett, I should myself like to see your Falstaff once more; and if Genl Grant may be in Washington at any time when it may also happen, to be convenient to you to come and act the character, I will try to arrange and let you know the time—' As I believe Mr Ford has the pleasure of your acquaintance, and his theater and corps seem likely to offer the best & readiest facilities for such an occasion, & of which yourself will soonest be aware, may I ask the favor, in such an event, of your first communicating with Mr Ford in reference thereto, &, if the previous arrangements of his theater admit of a negotiation with me for that particular evening, suggest his opening of one forthwith. Our kind-hearted President mentioned how constantly he was oppressed with the cares of State & incident to his chief magistracy, & how little time was allowed him for society or recreation—I could not but think that many who envy his high position, could they know the drudgery it imposes would conclude that the remarks of Shakespeare in regard to *Princes* will apply to *our* President—'Princes have but their titles for their glories; An outward honor for an inward toil; And for unfelt imaginations, they Often feel a world of restless cares. So that between their *titles* and *low* name, There's nothing differs but the *outward* fame.'"—ALS, RPB. Hackett's note of Jan. 1 to Hay is *ibid.* See *PUSG*, 15, 404; *Richard III*, act 1, scene 4.

1871, April 17. Richard W. Corwin, Narrowsburg, N. Y., to USG. "Desirous for an appointment to West Point as a Cadet and having neither moneyed or political influence to aid me in the usual way to obtain such a favor, I therefore, alone come to you. I have no claims for services rendered to my country but would willingly give her years of service in exchange for an education. Physically, I know I am fitted for the appointment, being in my nineteenth year, six feet one inch in highth and stout in proportion. My strength and perfect health I attribute, in a great measure to my entire abstinence from tobacco, wine, tea, coffee and all alcoholic compounds, none of which has ever passed my lifs. My family is of Hungarian descent and came to America about two hundred years ago, are stauch republicans and are of well known respectability, proof of which I can easily furnish. I am anxious to obtain a scientific education, my opportunities have been limited but I have made the most of them. In mathematics I have been partly through Trigonometry, and have devoted as much time as I could to Natural History, principally Ornithology and have made a handsome collection but am in the dark to classify or write about them for want of an education, and so I find myself cut off from every scientific pirsuit. Should my application impress you favorably and you would grant me an interview I would gladly come to Washington and abide by your decision as to the wisdom of making the appointment. I believe the appointments are to be made in June and if my application should be unfavorable, their is none to know my disappointment but you"—ALS, DNA, RG 94, Unsuccessful Cadet Applications. On the same day, Corwin wrote to Julia Dent Grant. "Pardon me, a boy of nineteen who resides in the wild woods of Sullivan County N. Y. who has no one to advise him, if in his great anxiety to have his letter safely placed in the hands of the President, has oversteped the bounds of etiquette in thus inclosing it under cover to you."—ALS, *ibid.* See Jerome C. Smiley *et al.*, *Semi-Centennial History of the State of Colorado* (Chicago, 1913), II, 235–37.

1871, April 19. Wilhelmina Bartholomew, Philadelphia, to USG. "Respectfully referred to Genl. U. S—Grant president of the United States asking that he will try and have the amount I have been swindled out of stopped against the swindler Franklin. B. Wonderly a pensioner of the United States, the Pension department have informed me that the matter is beyond their control, I believe the money can be justly stopped against him and therefore as a poor woman I appeal to you to Save myself the Expense of legal advice"—LS (signed by mark), DNA, RG 48, Miscellaneous Div., Letters Received. On March 22, Bartholomew, whose late husband, Charles, had been a private in Co. H, 31st Pa., had applied to Henry Van Aernam, commissioner of pensions, for action against Franklin B. Wonderly on losses totalling $218.—DS (signed by mark), *ibid.* On April 13, Van Aernam wrote to Bartholomew. ". . . I have respectfully to inform you that these transactions with Mr. Wonderly occurred at dates subsequent to your having received your money, and hence the matter is entirely beyond the control of this Office.—The papers are therefore respectfully returned.—"—LS, *ibid.*

1871, April 20. To J. W. Nicholson. "I have the honor to acknowledge the receipt of your letter of the 3d inst, informing me of my election as an honorary member of the U. S. Naval Lyceum at the Navy Yard N. Y. I wish you to accept for yourself and your associates, my sincere thanks for the compliment, which it affords me much pleasure to accept at your hands."—LS, U.S. Naval Academy Museum, Annapolis, Md.

1871, April 20. Secretary of the Interior Columbus Delano to USG. "I have examined 'An Act for the relief of the inhabitants of the town of Arcata, in Humboldt County, California', presented for your approval, and in regard thereto, have the honor to say that the records of this Department show that the tract of land mentioned in the act was, on the 6th November, 1869, awarded to F. T. Lansdale by my predecessor, Mr. Secretary Cox, in a case before the Department, to which the town of Arcata was a party, on appeal from the decision of the General Land Office, Mr. Lansdale has not yet, I am informed, completed his title to the tract, proceedings in the case being still pending in the General Land Office. While not questioning the right of Congress to dispose of public lands at its pleasure, I seriously doubt whether the act would have passed that body had the foregoing facts been known to it; and as I can perceive no valid objection to the interposition of delay in the matter, I would respectfully advise that the act be not approved."—LS, OFH. On Feb. 6, 1872, U.S. Senator Cornelius Cole of Calif. reintroduced this bill, remarking "that it passed both Houses during the last Congress, but failed to receive the signature of the President on account of some imaginary objection on the part of the Interior Department. I now have some papers, which I present with the bill, that I wish the committee to refer to that Department and see if they have any real objection."—*CG*, 42–2, 839. This bill never emerged from the Committee on Public Lands. See *ibid.*, 42–1, 194, 746–47.

1871, April 20. John M. Kelly, Brooklyn, to USG. ". . . I have engaged or rather beged of General Slocum our M C for Brooklyn to enable me to prepare & file a Bill to be laid before the English Commissnrs now at Washington to claim over 8 thousand Pounds Sterlg, and Eleven years Interest on same absolutely and equitably due to my wife deceased by her Fathers will Colonel Richard Seale who died at Rathangan Co Kildare, Ireland where my wife was Born He died about the year 1814 . . . I have been left without friend or help for the last 40 years to strugle as best I could to support my little family and has got some 9 hundred Dollars in Debt on their acct— . . ."—ALS, DNA, RG 59, Miscellaneous Letters. On July 10 and Dec. 18, Kelly wrote to USG on the same subject.—ALS, *ibid.* On July 29 and Dec. 3, 1872, Kelly wrote to USG. "From the opressive confused and degraded situation I have been entraped into I have troubled you within the last four years with some discordant random letters, . . ."—ALS, *ibid.*, Letters of Application and Recommendation. "Permit me most sincere and Respectfully to congratulate you on your instalation for a second term, . . . Patiently waiting your kind help"—ALS, *ibid.*, RG 60, Letters from the President. On March 16, 1873, Kelly again wrote to USG about recovering the inheritance.—ALS, *ibid.*, RG 59, Miscellaneous Letters.

1871, April 21. Orville E. Babcock to Governor William Claflin of Mass. "The President directs me to acknowledge the receipt of your letter of March 8th and to convey to you his thanks for the very cordial invitation extented to him to visit the city of Boston at the time of the anual meeting of the Society of the Army of Potomac. It will afford him great pleasure to be present upon that occasion."—Copy, DLC-USG, II, 1. On May 9, Babcock telegraphed to Theodore Lyman, Boston. "The President will not be able to visit Boston. He has telegraphed to Gov. Claflin. We all wish you a happy meeting."—Copy, *ibid.*, II, 5. See *Boston Transcript*, May 13, 1871.

1871, April 21. Philip O'Brien, Cassville, N. Y., to USG. "You have gained your chair by honor—and honor to Every one—Now the Subscriber Philip

O'Brien a soldier in the 81st Regiment Co "E" claims $10,000 for the Shooting of Rebel Gen Price—The Amount Advertised to be given—I am the Man who Shot said Gen Price at the first Battle of 'Fair Oaks' Saturday May 29. in the afternoon about 2. o'clock in the year 1862—I am a poor Man—and Earn my Bread by the Sweat of my Brow—I send this to you, hoping you will look after the matter and see that justice is done Me—I inclose you my Photograph picture so you can See the Man that done the Deed—I was 3 years and 10 Months in the war—and all the time in the *field*—I was wounded in the left Knee at the Battle of Cold Harbor June 2d 1863—I only get a Small pension of $2—per month—If I could get the said $10,000 it would help me much—My Dear General, for thus I address you, Do by me in this Matter as you Shall think is right and Just—And I shall be perfectly satisfied—Hoping to hear from you on the Subject— . . ."—ALS, DNA, RG 94, Letters Received, 1565 1871. On May 10, AG Edward D. Townsend endorsed this letter and related papers. ". . . It was not the usual policy of the Government to offer such rewards, and it is believed no such offer was ever made."—AES, *ibid.* The war dept. had found no record "of any rebel General *Price*, killed at 'Fair Oaks', Virginia."—E, *ibid.*

1871, April 24. Joseph Cooper, London, to USG. "At the request of the Anti Slavery Committee I take the liberty to enclose a Copy of a Minute adopted at its last meeting and earnestly solicit for it the favour of your obliging attention—Correspondence with the friends of freedom in Spain and Brazil has impressed the Committee [with the belief that the moral] influence of the United States in favour of the extinction of Slavery, would be of essential service at the present time and that its exertion would be highly appreciated by the philanthropists of both those Countries As to Cuba, the entire abolition of Slavery would probably quickly lead to a settlement of Affairs in that distracted Country—But the Spanish people are slow to move in any right direction—The last accounts which have reached us go to prove that neither party in Cuba is likely to get such decided advantage over the other as to bring about a permanent peace and that the War will Continue till the moral influence of your great Republic Coupled with the British Government shall intervene & put an end to it I feel that an apology is due from me for taking the liberty to address you, but knowing that the cause of justice and freedom every where, is dear to you, I trust you will kindly excuse it."—ALS, DNA, RG 59, Miscellaneous Letters. The resolution passed at a committee meeting of the British and Foreign Anti-Slavery Society is *ibid.*

1871, April 27. Orville E. Babcock to U.S. Representative William H. Lamport of N. Y., Canandaigua. "The President directs me to acknowledge the receipt of your letter relating to the removal of Mr. Anthony the present incumbent of the Post Office at Geneva and the appointment of Mr. Adams. He directs me to say that Mr. Anthony is a very fine Officer and his recommendations are very strong, that so long as there are no charges of misconduct in any way prefered against Mr. Anthony he does not think it best to make any change. The President directs me to say that should a charge be against Mr. Anthony requireing a change, you shall be notified before any change is made."—Copy, DLC-USG, II, 1. On April 12, 1869, USG had nominated Samuel N. Anthony as postmaster, Geneva, N. Y.

1871, April 28. John L. Evans, Bristol, England, to USG. "The important work you have lately had to carry through decided me not writing again on the subject of the Fiji Islands until you had a little time to consider how to receive and act upon in conjunction with your Representative Houses the annexing or granting a Protectorate Flag to that Group—I enclose for your information the Statistics for the past Year and I feel satisfied in reading them you will be pleased to notice the steady advancement in material prosperity—The number of American and British subjects at present in the Islands point to the necessity of a strong Government, and the sooner established the better for all concerned—Your Consul Dr Brower at Fiji and General Latham late Consul at Melbourne both have long since seen the desirableness of that Group being early governed by an Anglo Saxon Race—and as the place and people now seem prepared to receive and assist a good Government, the present seems a favourable opportunity of establishing one—I trust Sir you will give the matter a favourable consideration—"—ALS, DNA, RG 59, Miscellaneous Letters.

1871, April 28. Sigismund Kaufmann, New York City, to USG. "Permit me to introduce to your most favorable regard and esteem Mr. Benjamin Lehmaier; for many years a leading German citizen of this city and a prominent republican, Mr. Lehmaier, who is about going to Europe for some length of time, would, from his intimate knowledge, derived from a practical experience of the laws and customs of Germany and the United States, be admirably qualified to fill the position of American Consul for some German port. His appointment would gratify many of our German republicans and would be highly appreciated as a personal favor . . ."—LS, DNA, RG 59, Letters of Application and Recommendation. On the same day, Thomas Murphy, collector of customs, New York City, wrote to Secretary of State Hamilton Fish recommending Benjamin Lehmaier.—LS, *ibid.* On March 19, Simon Wolf, recorder of deeds, Washington, D. C., had written to Fish. "The enclosed papers were sent to me by General Pleasanton, for the purpose of joining in the request of Mr B. Lehmayer, I take great pleasure in doing so, as I know him to be competent and in every sense trustworthy. he was and is the Treasurer of the German Republican Asso, and has been very liberal at all times, and does not ask for this place on account of the salary. I hope that his request for one of the places asked for can be granted."—ALS, *ibid.* Enclosures and related papers are *ibid.* No appointment followed.

1871, April 29. USG endorsement. "Let the order named within be revoked, as recommended by the Secretary of the Interior."—Copy, DNA, RG

48, Lands and Railroads Div., Letters Sent. Written on a letter of April 27 from Secretary of the Interior Columbus Delano to USG. "I have the honor to recommend that your order of the 20th ultimo, directing the removal of the land office at Augusta, Kansas, to El Dorado, be revoked. Since the issue of the order, I have been satisfied that the change would not subserve the public interest, and the Kansas delegation have withdrawn their recommendation of it."—Copy, *ibid.*

1871, April 29. USG endorsement. "Let the islands named within be reserved for Light-House purposes, as recommended by the Secretary of the Interior."—Copy, DNA, RG 48, Lands and Railroads Div., Letters Sent. Written on a letter of April 27 from Secretary of the Interior Columbus Delano to USG. "I have the honor to recommend that Passage Island and Gull Island, to the Eastward of Isle Royale, Lake Superior, be reserved for Light-House purposes. This recommendation is made at the instance of the Secretary of the Treasury; and the Commissioner of the General Land Office informs me that there is no adverse claim to these lands."—Copy, *ibid.*

1871, April. Mary Beale Belfield, Richmond County, [*Va.*], to USG. "An aged widow thus appeals to your sympathies in her extremities. Having lived in affluence until the year 1863, when immediately after the death of my Husband I was visited by a raid of Federal Soldiers and reduced to poverty. My Husband was an an officer in the War of 1812 served as Major during the war, at time of his death was 77 or 8 and had been blind for years, I am now in my 78th year am extremely feeble and unable to render any aid towards my support My friend Doctr Douglass knew my circumstances before and since the war can tesify to the truth of this—I have never ~~have~~ received any pension under the last provison and your petioner will be most grateful to you for your all sufficent aid—in my extremity."—ALS, DNA, RG 48, Miscellaneous Div., Letters Received.

1871, April. Julian Neville, New Orleans, to USG. "Having been informed that some dissatisfaction exists as to the retention of Mr Dillingham in his present position of Naval Officer of this Port, and that his removal will probably take place at an early date, I respectfully submit my name as an applicant for such office and solicit your favorable consideration as to my appointment thereto. I can safely assure you that my appointment will afford general satisfaction as well as in no wise diminish the strength of your Administration, . . ."—ALS, DNA, RG 56, Naval Officer Applications. On May 20, James R. Beckwith, U.S. attorney, New Orleans, wrote to USG. "Mr Julian Neville of this City requests from me a statement of my knowledge of his antecedents as a union man and a republican. I take sincere pleasure in stating that I have long been acquainted with Mr Neville and knew him under circumstances well calculated to test the sincerity of his loyalty, the days when Louisiana first embarked in Secession, When to be loyal was to place one's life in jeopardy. Among the few men in Louisiana true to the

United States in those days. Mr Neville was conspicious, and as the price of his loyalty, became so unpopular as to lose almost entirely a most prosperous business, which for the same reason he has never been able to revive— . . ."—ALS, *ibid.* Related papers are *ibid.* On April 14, 1869, USG had nominated Neville as pension agent, New Orleans; on Dec. 2, 1873, USG nominated Neville as receiver, New Orleans.

On March 17, 1873, Pinckney B. S. Pinchback, Washington, D. C., wrote to USG. "Since we recommended Mr Marys appointment I have received a large number of telegrams from home thanking me for the part I have taken in this matter and as Mr Mary is the only appointment I have asked and knowing my people desire his appointment I most earnestly urge it, and hope my request in this respect will be granted"—ALS, ICHi. On March 10, U.S. Senator J. Rodman West of La., Pinchback, and others wrote to USG recommending Aristide Mary as naval officer, New Orleans.—LS, DNA, RG 56, Naval Officer Applications. On March 14, USG had nominated Charles Dillingham to continue as naval officer, New Orleans.

1871, April. C. A. Sleeper, Northport, Wis., to USG. "The enclosed communications not proving Satisfactory to a number of young men who served in the late rebelion and who are desirous to settle on a portion of the Land mentioned therein (and by whom I have been apointed to corispond with the differents departments on the subject) and also firmly believeing the policy of the present Administration, is to give to the poor man equal rights with the Capitalist Respectfaly submit the following to your consideration That the Menominee reservation in the State of Wisconsin contains ~~togather~~ many thousands of acres of valuable Land, togather considerable medium and in some cases unsaleable land That if the said sold at public auction alone, it excludes the poor man (who would prove ~~setler~~ an actual setler) from any chance of obtaining any Land upon which he may have determined to settle, and for this reason, Capitalists who wish to invest in these Lands atend the sale, and if a person not in the (ring) makes a bid one of the ring overbids him until the poor man is forced to retire The land goes to the highest bider who falls back and throws up his bid, a friend then deposits the apraised value at the Office and the Land falls into the hands of the (ring) or after one or two sales at enormous prices the poor man goes home and the (ring) buy at their own prices. this has been the case at sales of both State and Govt Land in this Country Neither is it uncommon for good Land to be apraised at a low figure while poor unsaleable land is put at a very high figure haveing call your atention to the above we Respectfaly ask First If the said Lands are not a part of the public domain how can the Govt dispose of and give to the purchaser a clear title to the Land in question Second Cannot a person wishing to settle on the above Lands make a claim under the Preemption laws and pay the apraised value at the Land Office at the the Land is advertised for sale Third Can a title be obtained of the Indians now in possesion with the cooperation of the Govt, by either private citizen or discharged Soldier If posible for you to pay your personal atention to this matter you will oblige a large number of fellow citizens"—ALS, DNA, RG 75, Letters Received, Green Bay Agency. On April 28, Henry R. Clum, act. commissioner of Indian Affairs, wrote to Sleeper informing him that "certain lands reserved for the Menomonee tribe . . . are not a portion of the public domain, and consequently are not subject to entry or settlement under the Homestead laws."—LS, *ibid.*

[*1871, April*]. U.S. Senator George G. Wright of Iowa *et al.* to USG. "We respectfully ask that Alexander Clark, a colored citizen of Muscatine, Iowa, be appointed to some prominent position within your gift. He is worthy and competent, is possessed of considerable oratorical ability and exerts a wide influence among the people of his race, whom he has been in the habit of addressing in several of the Western & Southern States. He was among the first, in a speech delivered at Memphis, Tennessee, to pronounce for Genl Grant for President, and is a working and ardent republican Resolutions are appended showing his indorsement at an emancipation celebration at Oskaloosa, Iowa, Jany. 3, 1871. Iowa having been among the first to admit colored citizens to the right of suffrage, there would be much fitness in favoring that State with an appointment for one of its colored citizens."—DS (8 signatures—dated on docket), DNA, RG 59, Letters of Application and Recommendation. On Dec. 20, 1872, Wright wrote to Secretary of State Hamilton Fish. "Judge Cotton of the House & myself called upon you on the 9th inst. in behalf of Alexr Clark of Muscatine, Iowa, an applicant for a consulship, and you offerred him an appointment to a Port in Hayti.—Upon advising him of your offer, he desires to know if the offer can remain open, for his determination, until Spring.—Not knowing how this may be, I beg to submit the enquiry for him—"—LS, *ibid.* Alexander Clark declined the appointment because of the low salary. See William J. Simmons, *Men of Mark: Eminent, Progressive and Rising* (1887; reprinted, New York, 1968), pp. 1097–1100.

1871, May 1. To Edward M. Gallaudet, president, National Deaf-Mute College, Washington, D. C. "I am in receipt of your letter of April 21st. I believe the Institute for the benefit of the deaf and dumb is doing and will do great good to those unfortunate persons throughout our Country. I regret that Congress did not appropriate the amount of money deemed necessary to place the Institute on a permanent basis."—Copy, DLC-USG, II, 1. Gallaudet used this letter to raise private funds for the college. An 1871 letter from Gallaudet to USG is listed in William Evarts Benjamin, Catalogue No. 27, Nov., 1889, p. 7. See Gallaudet, *History of the College for the Deaf 1857–1907* (Washington, 1983), pp. 110–11.

1871, May 1. Governor Rutherford B. Hayes of Ohio to USG. "I am well acquainted with the personal and official character of Mr Joseph W. Dwyer. I believe him to be a gentleman of unusual qualifications for public business. He is an energetic, perservering, capable and honest officer, and I take pleasure in recommending his retention in the service, and his assignment to this State."—LS (press), OFH. USG appointed Joseph W. Dwyer as supervisor of Internal Revenue, Northern Ohio.

1871, May 3. William Cogswell, Academy of Design, Chicago, to USG. "My Son, W. G. Cogswell, is soon to leave for Milan Italy, to reside there two or three years in the study of Music—In the absence of any other acquaintance to whom I can apply for a letter of Introduction to some one living there, I have thought best to ask you for a few lines to the american consul at that place or any other person that may best suit you—The object is that in case of necessity he may have someone to apply to who will know who he is, and where from—If I may be allowed to speak for my son inasmuch as you do not know him I will say he is *in all respcts* a gentleman—His age is 26—Mrs C— joins me in Respectful remembrance to yourself & family, your attention will be highly appreciated."—ALS, DNA, RG 59, Miscellaneous Letters. On July 21, 1868, Brig. Gen. Oliver O. Howard had written to Cogswell acknowledging "the reception of the engraving of General Grant and his family. I had great admiration for the original painting and wished when I first saw it that I might be able to duplicate it in some way. . . ."—LS (press), Howard Papers, MeB. See *PUSG*, 18, 216–17.

On Oct. 23, 1871, Homer Henderson, Columbus, Ohio, wrote to USG. "I have presented me, unsolicited, a paper signed by Gov. Hayes and each individual of this state government, recommending me to appointment as consul at Venice, Munich or other available consulship in Italy or South Germany The destruction of Chicago, and with it my studio, and what I may now term with modesty, a brilliant prospect, (my patrons being bankrupt) would make a residence abroad at this time, particularly desirable, should such a consulate be at disposal soon. If your Excellency should desire it I can procure in, addition, the names of Senator Sherman, Genl Warner, Hon. Jas. Wilson of Iowa, Senator Thurman, Genl Woods, Genl Logan, Mr J. Y. Scammon, or any prominent citizens of this place or Chicago. The only public consideration I could urge would be, that, by sending her artists to represent her abroad, the Govt would benefit American art, as in the case of Stillman &c. I write this in advance, to learn if my endorsed application will be acceptable; but if this give your Excellency either trouble or annoyance, I trust you will dismiss it without further thought and pardon the intrusion. . . . It may not be uninteresting to know that the portrait of your Excellency was detained in this city and thus happily escaped destruction. This I must look upon as very good fortune as all Healeys portraits of you were in the burnt district. Coggswells portrait of you was also destroyed *which may* be *considered as some compensation* for the *loss* of the *others*."—ALS, DNA, RG 59, Letters of Application and Recommendation. See *PUSG*, 19, 109–10. In 1885, Henderson painted "The Hero's Welcome," depicting USG's arrival in Heaven.—Copy (photograph), DLC-USG, VI, C.

1871, May 4. To John W. Forney, collector of customs, Philadelphia. "Your yesterdays letter received. Your request granted."—Copy, DLC-USG, II, 5.

1871, May 4. Jesse Root Grant, Covington, Ky., to USG. "I have known Dr Williams for ten or twelve years and feel safe in indorsing fully all Rev Dr Rilea has said for him Dr Rilea was our stationed Pastor here for two years, & knows Mr Williams well—"—AES, DNA, RG 59, Letters of Application and Recommendation. Written on a letter of May 2 from J. McKendree Reiley, Louisville, to USG recommending Amos F. Williams of Covington for a consulship.—ALS, *ibid.* On July 8, 1872, "J R Grant by Hannah Grant" wrote to "My. Honored Son." "Please have the kindness to look at the recommendations of Dr. A. F. Williams, of this place, for an appointment to a consulship—now in the hands of the Secretary of State—and by giving them favourable consideration you will much oblige . . ."—ALS, *ibid.* Related papers include a petition endorsed by USG's sister Mary Grant Cramer. No appointment followed.

Probably in late May, 1871, Jesse Grant, Elizabeth, N. J., wrote to Mrs. Isaac N. Morris. "Our Daughter Mary with her two children Came here yest on their way to Denmark, where her Husband is Resident Minister. My Wife & myself accompanied her, to see her safely on the steamer, on the 3rd of June—I expect to go to Washington, before the 3rd of June, & come back again before that tim[e] But I may not go untill after that time, & go direct home—I sent your first letter explaining you Nieces case & her letter to Mr Delano, requesting him to give her a clerkship but I do not expect it will be done for I see the Departments are discharging many of their Clerks both male & females Congress having withheld appropriations for that purpos When I get to Washington I will try to find out what can be done, & report progress Our Golding Wedding, would come off on the 24th of June Mr Corbin & Jennie say we must celebrate it here, or at Long branch But I expect we will go home before that time, and probaby not have it at all—Mrs Grant is a little too modest & unassuming to be willing to assume such notoriaty But I dont ~~entend~~ to be fooled out of that gratification . . ."—ALS, Morris Family Papers, IHi.

1871, May 5. To Nehemiah G. Ordway. "I had fully expected to be present at the ratification meeting this evening, but I have been detained until it is so late that I shall have to abandon the intention."—LS (facsimile), Superior Galleries, Nov. 6, 1993, no. 471. Born in N. H. in 1828, Ordway helped to organize the Republican Party in that state and served as sergeant at arms to the U.S. House of Representatives (1863–75). As local party chairman, Ordway directed the Republican victory in the first election for D. C. territorial government, April 20, 1871. See letter to Hannibal Hamlin, Feb. 21, 1871. On May 6, a local paper reported. "The complimentary serenade to Mr. N. G. Ordway, chairman of the republican executive committee, by republican voters of the District of Columbia, last evening, was the occasion of a very fine and imposing display. . . ."—*Washington Evening Star*, May 6, 1871.

1871, May 9. USG pardon. "Whereas, on the 16th day of May, 1870, one Robert Lindenfels was convicted in the Criminal Court of the District of

Columbia, of grand larceny and was sentenced to be imprisoned for one year; And whereas, in view of his youth, his frankness in confessing his crime, repentance, the probability of his reformation and the distress of his aged parents, Judge Humphreys and the Jury before whom he was tried, recommend his pardon, and U. S. Attorney Fisher, for these reasons and because of his great temptation, join in this recommendation; And whereas, the term for which he was sentenced has now almost expired: Now, therefore, be it known, that I . . . do hereby grant to the said Robert Lindenfels a full and unconditional pardon. . . ."—DS, NN.

1871, May 9. William E. Chandler, Washington, D. C., to USG. "With your permission I desire to withdraw the letter lately addressed by me to you relative to the issue of land patents to the Oregon and California Railroad Company"—ALS, OFH. On the same day, Orville E. Babcock wrote to Chandler returning the letter.—Copy, DLC-USG, II, 1. On May 13, Secretary of the Interior Columbus Delano wrote to USG. "I enclose herewith copy of Hon W. H. Smiths opinion affirming the right of the Oregon Central R. R. to assign to the Oregon & California R. R I also enclose cop~~ies~~y of my letter to the Atty Genl, and copy of his reply thereto, touching my decisions as Secretary of the Interior in regard to such assignment, and the recognition of its validity, by my immedeate predicessor I also enclose copy of my letter to W E Chandler Esqr, announcing to him my conclusions & giving reasons for the same All these papers are sent because Mr Chandler has appealed to you from my opinion, and I deemed it best to place the case within your reach, provided you desire to examine it"—ALS, OFH. On May 9, Attorney Gen. Amos T. Akerman had written to Delano. "In answer to your letter of the 8th instant, I have the honor to state that my recollection of what passed at the informal conferences between us, in regard to the case of the Oregon and California Railroad, entirely agrees with your own. . . . The letter of the counsel for certain parties in interest, Mr. Chandler, to the President, complaining of your refusal to require the opinion of the Attorney General in the case of the Oregon and California Railroad, seems to me to have been written under an erroneous conception of the relations between the Attorney General and the Heads of other Departments. I think that the Attorney General should be called on for an opinion only when the Head of the Department in which the question arises, sees a good reason for the call, and *not* whenever a litigant before a Department desires the opinion."—Copy, DNA, RG 60, Letters Sent to Executive Officers. See *SRC*, 41-1-3; *CG*, 41–2, 3209; John Tilson Ganoe, "The History of the Oregon and California Railroad," *Quarterly of the Oregon Historical Society*, XXV, 3 (Sept., 1924), 273–76.

1871, May 10. Orville E. Babcock to Mrs. R. H. Pennington, Wilmington, Del. "The President requests me to acknowledge the receipt of your two letters asking him to purchase a basket, or to find a purchaser. He requests you to enclose you five dollars and hopes it will fully recompense you for your work on the basket."—Copy, DLC-USG, II, 1.

1871, May 11. Mrs. M. C. Ames, Cincinnati, to USG. "Your worthy Father called to see me a few days ago, and in course of conversation he remarked that as I had done so much for our sick & wounded soldiers during the War my son should be sent to West Point. He then told me to write you myself and ask the favor, and that he would recommend him. The best recommendation I can give him is, he never disobeyed me in his life, he is just the right age and has a great talent for drawing and I think he could pass a very good examination He is a stepson of Dr. Ames, and that is one reason why I feel so anxious to provide for him myself. If you can do this Mr President you will confer a lasting obligation upon me and a favor I shall never forget or cease to fell grateful for, I can give the best of reference, for my son."—ALS, DNA, RG 94, Unsuccessful Cadet Applications. On Feb. 8, 1872, Ames again wrote to USG. "I have the honor of making application to your Excellency to appoint my son Oscar. Q. Ames. Cadet at West Point. His father served during the War. and he himself served as Orderly for more than a year He is a strong healthy boy and has quite a talant for drawing which I understand will be of advantage to him should he recieve the appointment. If you can make this appointment you will place under lasting obligations your friend"—ALS, *ibid.*

On Sept. 25, 1869, William Stoms, Cincinnati, had written to USG. "I would respectfully recommend to your favorable consideration the name of Dr. Fisher W. Ames, for the appointment as Consul to Callao, S. A. Dr. Ames—accompanied by his estimable lady, who was most assiduous in the performance of her self-imposed duties as nurse, cook and general attendant upon our sick and wounded soldiers during the War,—served with much credit as Asst. Surgeon and Surgeon in the U. S. Army during a period of five years, from 1861 to 1866. He is a highly accomplished, intelligent gentleman, well versed in the Spanish language, and would fill the position for which he applies with honor to himself and credit to the Government."—ALS, *ibid.*, RG 59, Letters of Application and Recommendation. See *PUSG*, 19, 542; letter to Samuel G. Howe, June 9, 1871.

1871, May 11. Ebenezier Y. Terrill, Sydney, to [USG]. "I writt these few lines to you hopeing that you will look into my case thatis if the law alows it if it does not of corse i cannot expect it i sailed from home in the year 1865 in the Ship James Arnold of New Bedford on a whaling Voyage during the first four months all went on well but after that i was most cruely illtreated until i ran away in New Zealand in 1867 after serving two years i was floged by the Captain and also by the Mate which i think is not lawfull and after two years of such life i ran away i applied fore redress to the Amerrican consul at the Bay of Island and got no satasfaction from him therefore i now apply to you as am in ill health and cannot follow my ocupation thereforre i want to get home once more to Wading River Long Island New York my name Ebenezier Yadiska Terrill My fathers name is William but whether he is liveing ore not i cannot tel not haveing herd from him since i left home i must inphorm you that i was in the second Connetticuc heavy artilary durring the war i will not weary you with any more i hope that i have not done any thing rong by these few lines if there is any thing to be done you can inphorm Mr. H. H. Hall U. S. Consul Sydney"—ALS, DNA, RG 59, Miscellaneous Letters. See *PUSG*, 20, 446–47.

On March 17, 1872, Patrick Hogan, Melbourne, wrote to USG. "... After living there as a citizen for nine years and serving three of them under your command in the army, I wish to to get back again to N. York, as I feel no peace since I left the flag of liberty, ..."—AL, DNA, RG 59, Miscellaneous Letters.

1871, MAY 12. To Postmaster Gen. John A. J. Creswell. "I shall be pleased to have you appoint Orrin B. Ingalls Post Master at Belvidere, Ills."—Copy, DLC-USG, II, 1. On May 15, USG nominated Orrin B. Ingalls as postmaster, Belvidere, Ill.; on May 23, the Senate rejected this nomination. On June 21 and 28, Orville E. Babcock wrote to Creswell transmitting USG's orders to appoint Ingalls, postmaster, Belvidere, and "Miss Laura Ingalls, Postmistress at Denmark, Oxford Co. Maine."—Copies, *ibid.* On Dec. 3, 1872, USG renominated Ingalls as postmaster, Belvidere; on Dec. 10, the Senate confirmed this nomination.

1871, MAY 12. Horace Porter to Secretary of War William W. Belknap. "The President directs me, for your information; to send you the following copy of a despatch sent this morning to Gen. Spooner U. S. Marshal Indianapolis Ind.—'Retain Harrison and Porter as lawyers in the Milligan case. By order of the President'—"—LS, DNA, RG 60, Letters from the President. Beginning on May 16, Benjamin Harrison and law partner Albert G. Porter defended Indiana officials in U.S. district court against a false arrest suit filed by Lambdin P. Milligan, subject of an 1866 U.S. Supreme Court decision. See G. R. Tredway, *Democratic Opposition to the Lincoln Administration in Indiana* (Indianapolis, 1973), pp. 257–61.

1871, MAY 12. U.S. Senator Oliver P. Morton of Ind. to USG. "I desire to recommend for the appointment of *Recorder of the General Land Office* in the Interior Department—*Frank M Heaton*—He is a faithful and competent man, a good Republican, and of excellent character. He has been a clerk in the Department for ten years, and desires a little promotion. He is from Indiana, and I cordially endorse him for the place."—LS, DNA, RG 48, Appointment Div., Letters Received. John P. Newman favorably endorsed this letter.—ES, *ibid.*

On May 13, H. Barber *et al.*, members of the finance committee, Assembly's Church, Washington, D. C., wrote to USG. "The undersigned, having learned that the office of Recorder of the General Land Office has become vacant, recommend the appointment of the Rev Charles B. Boynton to that position...."—DS (7 signatures), *ibid.* On May 18, USG nominated Charles B. Boynton as recorder, General Land Office.

1871, MAY 13. Clark E. Carr, editor, *Galesburg Republican*, Galesburg, Ill., to USG. "I have a *very especial* favor to ask of you and I hope that you will not think that I am asking too much as I am fully aware and entirely appreciate how much I am indebted to you My youngest brother George P. Carr who served with credit to himself during the war coming out as Captain now 29 years of age & now a Parish Judge in Louisana writes me that he has on file in the office of the Secretary of State, at Washington, the Strongest reccommendations from the Senators and representatives of Louisana for a consulship in Europe—He is a young man of good habits, and more than ordinary literary acquirements and has a fair knowledge of German and French He wishes a consulship or consular clerkship which will pay his expenses abroad and will fit him for the consular or diplomatic services—He is especially fitted by education for such a position and it would be *extremely gratifying* to me to have him appointed. The papers on file at the State Department show that he is heartily supported by the delegation in Congress from his State. I am doing all in my power to ~~merit~~ ~~the~~ return the obligations I am already under to you.... P S. Should the application be received with favor by you will you please to have me advised of the fact as my brother will be here in a few days."—ALS, DNA, RG 59, Letters of Application and Recommendation. Related papers are *ibid.* No appointment followed. On Aug. 21, 1865, Carr, Mendota, Ill., had written to U.S. Representative Elihu B. Washburne of Ill. "I wish that you would find out and write me immediately *certainly* whether my brother goes to Arkansas—I would like to know how Genl Grant thinks of him ..."—ALS, DLC-Elihu B. Washburne. On Nov. 25, 1867, U.S. Representatives Ebon C. Ingersoll and John A. Logan of Ill. had written USG recommending George P. Carr for a commission in the U.S. Army.—LS, DNA, RG 94, ACP, C1212 CB 1867. No appointment followed. On March 17, 1869, USG nominated Clark E. Carr as postmaster, Galesburg.

1871, MAY 17. USG endorsement. "Approved"—AES, DNA, RG 60, Records Relating to Appointments. Written on a letter of May 14 from Frederick A. Boswell to USG, resigning as D. C. justice of the peace. On March 29, 1869, Boswell had written to USG. "I most respectfully make application for re-appointment as a Justice of the peace for the County of Washington. District of Columbia. I was first appointed under President Lincoln, and Served by his appointment until Febuary last. when my commission expired. when I applied to President Johnson, and was refused on political grounds"—ALS, *ibid.* On April 1, USG nominated Boswell as D. C. justice of the peace.

1871, MAY 17. Orville E. Babcock to Hermann W. Hasslock, Nashville. "The President directs me to acknowledge the receipt of your letter of the 9th, and to inform you that his feelings towards you have always been and continue to be the kindest. He did wish to appoint you Post Master, but did not insist against the opinions and wishes and representations of those representing the district in Congress. He directs me to say that he still has the highest consideration and hopes to be able to give you some suitable appointment. The appointment of Gauger was not of my suggestion. I supposed it would afford you a good support."—Copy, DLC-USG, II, 1. On Sept. 1, 1869, Hasslock had written to USG. "The kind reception you gave me last spring, when I was in Washington encourages me to send you these lines. Since I had the honour to see you, I sold out my drugstore here in Nashville & was always under the firm conviction, that you would find me a situation either as U. S. Marshal here instead of E. S. Glasscock or abroad in any capacity you think me capable of considering that I am fully master of german english or french In the firm believe that I shall soon here from you . . ."—ALS, DNA, RG 60, Records Relating to Appointments.

On Oct. 3, 1871, Hasslock wrote to USG. "The leaders of the radical party here seem to think it necessary, that I should have some office, either the one mentioned or an other one of same QUALIFICATIONS & therefore some of the SIGNORS handed me the anext petition & prevailed on me to send it on. Hoping you will give a favourably decicion & excuse my intrusion . . ."—ALS, *ibid.*, RG 59, Letters of Application and Recommendation. A petition dated Sept. 30 recommending Hasslock for consul at Basle is *ibid.* On May 13, 1872, Babcock wrote to Hasslock. "The President desires me to acknowledge the receipt of your letter of the 16th ult:, and say that, there is no talk of suspending the Postmaster at Nashville. He also wishes me to say that your letter was mislaid or should have been answered sooner."—Copy, DLC-USG, II, 1. On April 11, 1873, Levi P. Luckey wrote to Hasslock. "The President directs me to acknowledge the receipt of your letter of the 6th inst, and say that a few days since he conversed with the Commissioner of Internal Revenue in regard to you, and that when the consolidation takes place, you will not find yourself forgotten."—Copy, *ibid.*, II, 2. On Jan. 19, 1874, USG nominated Hasslock as postmaster, Nashville.

1871, MAY 17. Orville E. Babcock to Alfred B. Mullett, supervising architect, Treasury Dept. "I informed the President, as you requested, that the Mr Burnham, spoken of in the public print as having a young child arrested, is now occupying a small building on the White House lot. The President will be pleased to know that he has been removed from the grounds."—Copy, DLC-USG, II, 1. A reporter described the incident in a local paper. "On last Monday night week, it will be remembered, policeman Doyle arrested a little boy, named Earnest Muretet, on the charge of stealing nine eggs from a man named Burnham, who lives in a shanty in the White Lot. The prisoner was a mere child, said to be but five and a half years old, and when the facts became known the public were much excited about the outrage, as they well might be. The child was taken out of bed where it was sleeping by Doyle, and was then kept at the station-house all night, on a table, from whence it was next morning taken to the Police Court, when Judge Snell promptly dismissed the case. . . . The President has very properly directed Mr. Mullett, Architect of the Treasury, to give notice to Burnham to remove his chattels from the White Lot. Serves him right. 3½ P.M.—Private Doyle has been severely reprimanded by the Police Board for conduct unbecoming an officer"—*Washington Evening Star*, May 18, 1871.

1871, MAY 19. James J. Reeves, Bridgeton, N. J., to USG. "You will pardon me for intruding a small matter upon your attention, but as it concerns a number of aged Pensioners I venture to do so. I have forwarded to the Commissioner of Pensions at Washington, no less than a dozen applications of soldiers of 1812 for Pensions—requesting in each case an acknowledgment of their receipt. *In no case have I received any answer of any kind* The aged pensioners—many of whom are near their graves—are anxious to know something about their claim—when they may be expected. I do not so much as hear whether the applications have been received at the Pension office & hence can give the aged Pensioners no satisfaction.—If our officials receive ample pay, as the Comm'r of Pensions & his assistants do, they should courteiusly & satisfactorally answer all letters written them ~~in~~ on matters of business. May I ask that this request ~~may~~ be considered"—ALS, DNA, RG 48, Miscellaneous Div., Letters Received.

1871, MAY 20. Edward Foster, Chattanooga, to "the united States of america." "your petitioner Edward Foster would Respectfully represent and show to the Honorable united States authorit~~ies~~y to who it may concern or to the supreme Power of the united states of america that he was Lawfully married to his wife according to the Laws of the united and of the state of virginia at abinton virginia in washington County by Liecens from the clerk of the county in said state & county, and the Rites of matrimony was also solemnized to ~~me~~ him by a Regular minister of the gospel, W. Leewood a Methodist minister of said county & state in the year of our Lord One thousand Eight hundred and sixty nine. in the month of July. and your petitioner further states that they have been Liveing together Evey since that time above specified as man and wife, and your petitioner further states that he is a Bright Mulato from the third generation, and your petitioner further states that he came to the state of Tennessee Live and to make that his home in the year of ~~our~~ ~~Eight~~ one thousand Eight hundred and sixty nine and there remain untill the year one thousand ~~one~~ eight hundred and seventy one, when as your petitioner was informed that there was an act passed by the Legislatuere of the state of Tennessee Reviving and old act of the Laws of the state prohibiting negroes & white peoples from marring or Living together as man and wife and your petitioner would further to your Hon that he was ~~on~~ in the month of March in year of one thousand Eight hundred and seventy one arrest for a white and having a colored woman for a wife and was then incosrated in prison and there keep untill the first day of May in the year (1871) and that that time the first of May (1871) when your petitioner was Ready for Trial ~~thy~~ and had all of his witnesses ready to prove that he was not a white man and was a Bright Mulato they refused to give your petitioner a Trial for fear he would come clear and thy would not get their cost of the proceeding and Entred an nollie and require your petitioner to scure scure the cost of the cause and turn turn him a Loose which amount of cost they refused to tell ~~me~~ your petitioner and they have now got ~~my~~ your petitioner house all that your petitioner haves and all he possess. in the word and then told him he ~~could go and thy would not both him any more~~ and his wife coudd not Live together in this said state and thy have been parted by said criminal court of Hamilton county your petitioner ferthr states that as now seeing all the trouble that any body could see by beig parted from Each other and they have seperated us from Living together and your petitioner appeal to your Hons for Justice and ~~we~~ your petitioner have been injure by said court at Least four hundred dollars by Looseing the house and Looseing the time as ~~I am pay~~ your petitioner is a mill Rite by tread and Lost two month word and your petitioner wife was also Loose time and was incosrated in prison at the same time. your Petitioner wages Regular for his work was $2 50 per day in which he had all that he could do, and your petitioner wife wages was a bout $15 00 per month. your petitioner state that he was born and Rised in Richmond virginia. and by being Jurney workman he came to chattanooga Tenn to do some work and then made the same his home and your petitioner wife was also, a virginia by birth and Rise if he is not intitl to his wife and under the provissions of the fourteenth & fifteenth amendment to the constutition of the united states of america & if he is not intitle to live with ~~w~~ his wife as the Laws of the state of Tennesese prohibits him from marring a white woman the Laws of the State prohibits the marring of colored people to white from the third generation in clusive and your petitioner is of the third generation, and your petitioner would show to your Hon that his mother was a Bright Mulato woman and his father a white man and now they or restraind of the Preveleges of Living together"—Affidavit, DNA, RG 60, Letters Received, Tenn.

On Aug. 24, 1872, T. F. Pegg, Rockwood, Tenn., wrote to USG. "I have been a citizen of Tennessee for the past five years. Three years ago I was married in the citty of Knoxville by a Minister of the Gospel to a Lady who is *mixed blooded* I suppose she is ⅙ or ⅛ Negro blood. Since we have been married Tennessee has adapted a new Constitution Containing a clause that for a white Person to marry a person with Negro blood in their veins Shall be indited before the Circuit Court and punished with a fine and imprisenment. I would respectfully ask you to write to me and if I am violating the Law let me know. I was of the impression that under the 15th amendment as my Wife is a citizen of the United States that she was legaly and Lawfuly my wife not withstanding Stat constitutions and Legislative acts prohibiting it I have been Indited and my trial will be at Circuit Court of December next. My means are limited and if there is any way to stop proceedings against me I would love to know it as it will involve me to push my case through all the courts to the Supreme Court of the United States, which I will be obliged to do a pay the penalty according to Tennessee Law which is $500.00 fine and imprisenment From this letter you can easily guess the political complexion of this part of the *foot stool* but here is one (and there are many more here) who will Support the Philadelphia nominees Hoping you will spare the time and do me the favor to write to me . . ."—ALS, *ibid.*, Letters from the President.

Also in 1872, Sanford Jacob, Metropolis, Ill., wrote to USG. "Your most humble appeals to Your excellencey for correction Your most humble has been arrested with my wife for marrieing her.—Your most humble presumed from reading the 13th and 14th a mendments that all a mericans citizens had a exclusive right to make a greements contracts from personal consents or legal. now Your excellencey if You please I will give you the cause of my arrest in the early part of 1871 for marri~~e~~ing a Wite Lady now Your honor I procured licences for marrieing this Lady and was legally married by a minister of the divine truth and had been married six months before being arrested and of ~~corse~~ course of that time six months after marriage she was labouring under impregnancey and laying there six months in that condition in jail during that time. Your honor ~~can~~ can well judge how things was when I was marching in the battles for this country I hoped to be able by the Laws of this great and free a merica for whitch I fought for the maintainance of I say Your excellencey I hoped to enjoy this pursuit of happiness whitch is the dearest pursuit of earth then to think after fighting for this country for near three years in the 68 Mo colored infantry for the maintancy of the a ~~m~~merican liberties now I am denied the right to enjoy them . . ."—ALS (docketed June 7), *ibid.*, Letters Received, Ill.

1871, May 20. Maria Hunter and Fanny Ricketts, Washington, D. C., to USG. "The Board of Lady Managers of the National Soldiers' & Sailors' Orphans' Home, most respectfully apply for the appointment to the United States Military Academy of George King, the son of non commissioned officer George King, who was killed at the battle of the Wilderness, in May, 1864, leaving four orphans who have been provided for in the Home since 1867. George King was adopted by Lincoln Post. GAR. last month, to prepare for admission to the Military Academy—in 1872."—LS, DNA, RG 94, Correspondence, USMA. King did not attend USMA.

On Feb. 17, 1870, John F. Guilfoyle, Baltimore, had written to Adolph E. Borie. "When the President and you visited the fair for the benefit of the Soldier's Orphans, at Baltimore, the President promised to give an appointment to West Point to one of the orphan boys. Being the oldest boy the ladies gave me the preference. I would be greatly obliged, If you would give me a little information in regard to the examination so that I can prepare for it Hoping you will pardon my presumption, . . ."—ALS, *ibid.* On May 24, 1871, U.S. Representative Benjamin F. Butler of Mass., Lowell, wrote to Secretary of War William W. Belknap. "I have endeavored to find among the soldiers' orphans some one who, I could be instructed, would pass examination as cadet at West Point. I have not succeeded. If the young gentleman named, John F Guilfoyle, is a soldier's orphan and would be acceptable, I should be very glad of his appointment, and in this I think I can speak for the Board of Managers of the National Asylum."—LS, *ibid.* Guilfoyle graduated from USMA in 1877. See *PUSG*, 20, 409.

1871, MAY 22. Secretary of State Hamilton Fish to USG. "The Iowa Senators are very anxious for the appointment of Mr Studer (recommended also by Genl Belknap,) to the Consulate—at Singapore—I think that Senator Harlan at least deserves great recognition, & shall be very glad if you think proper to sign the nomination"—ALS, DLC-Hamilton Fish. On the same day, USG endorsed this letter. "Approved."—AES, *ibid.* On May 23, USG nominated Adolphus G. Studer as consul, Singapore. See *PUSG*, 20, 410–11.

On May 31, U.S. Senator Phineas W. Hitchcock of Neb. wrote to USG. "I beg to recommend Hon. Thomas P. Kennard (late Secretary of the State of Nebraska) for appointment as Consul at Singapore—Mr. K— is an old resident of the State—always an active Republican—and a fair lawyer—I might add that Mr Taffe has written me recently in regard to procuring a foreign appointment for him (Mr K.) and he will if desired I have no doubt file a formal recommendation—I transmit herewith several communications which have reached me from other sources . . ."—LS, DNA, RG 59, Letters of Application and Recommendation. Related papers are *ibid.* Also on May 31, Fish wrote in his diary. "President gives the name of Thomas P. Kennard of Nebraska, for Consul at Ching Kiang—but being told of the importance of prudent & discreet men, at present for Chinese Consulates, & of the Judicial power they are called to exercise he reserves the question for inquiry, & whether he be a lawyer"—DLC-Hamilton Fish. On the same day, Horace Porter wrote to Hitchcock. "The President directs me to ask whether mr Kennard, whom you recommended for Consul, is a lawyer, as it requires a person with legal knowledge to fill the consulate mentioned."—Copy, DLC-USG, II, 1.

1871, MAY 24. U.S. Senator Simon Cameron of Pa. to USG. "Since I received Gen Porters' note, saying you could not go to Pennsylvania tomorrow, I have received a telegram from Mr Coleman asking me to bring you to his house on Friday or Saturday if you could not come tomorrow. I send this by Messenger and will keep the Car at Baltimore until your decision reaches me. I think we will conclude the session tonight."—LS, ICarbS.

On May 26, Horace Porter telegraphed to Commodore John L. Worden, superintendent, U.S. Naval Academy. "President thanks you for your invitation. He is compelled to go without his family tomorrow and return same evening."—Copy, DLC-USG, II, 5. On May 27, a Washington correspondent reported. "The President and Mrs. GRANT, with Miss NELLIE GRANT, Secretary ROBESON, Ex-Senator CATTELL, Marshal SHARPE, and several prominent officials, left here this morning for Annapolis, to attend the annual examination at the Naval Academy, and returned this evening."—*New York Times*, May 28, 1871.

1871, MAY 25. To Thomas H. Nelson, U.S. minister, Mexico City. "I take pleasure in introducing, and commending to your good offices, Dr Ord of

California, who purposes visiting Mexico"—Copy, DLC-USG, II, 1. On April 12, Brig. Gen. Edward O. C. Ord had written to Matías Romero concerning a visit by his brother Dr. James L. Ord.—*Archivo de Histórico de Matías Romero*, I, 521.

1871, MAY 26. Orville E. Babcock to Simon Wolf, D. C. recorder of deeds. "Please have the accompanying deed from Thompson *et al*—Trustees to Julia B. Grant, recorded, and send word by the bearer when it can be had. Enclosed find $5 with which the expenses are to be satisfied."—Copy, DLC-USG, II, 1. On the same day, a local paper reported. "Messrs. Fitch & Fox, real estate brokers, have sold to President U. S. Grant. lot of subdivision of square 285, improved by a three story brick residence, located on I street, between 12th and 13th streets, for $7,500 cash."—*Washington Evening Star*, May 26, 1871. Beginning on May 6, the *Evening Star* had advertised: "The BRICK RESIDENCE with mas[t]ic front, on I street, between 12th and 13th streets, north side, containing 12 rooms, with all the modern conveniences of bath room, water closet, gas and water, and known as the 'New York avenue Presbyterian Church Parsonage,' can be had, if purchased at once, at the low price of $8,000—a little more than the value of the lot, which is 25x142 feet, to a 30 foot alley. Application to be made to JAMES E. FITCH, of the Board of Trustees, office of Fitch & Fox, 515 7th street"—*Ibid.*, May 6, 1871.

On April 17, USG had nominated John W. Thompson, a local businessman and trustee of the New York Avenue Presbyterian Church, to the D. C. legislative council.

1871, MAY 26. James B. Eads, St. Louis, to USG. "When you were recently in St Louis you were so kind as to promise to grant a leave of absence to an officer of the Engineer Corps of the Navy for the purpose of permitting him to accept a position in the Bridge Company here, as an Inspector of the steel and iron work of the Superstructure of the Bridge. Mr Henry W. Fitch 1st Assistant Eng. U. S. N., is the gentleman of whom I spoke to you, and I hope you will kindly grant as long a leave of absence as is compatible with the regulations of the service, as his proposed duties will probably occupy a twelve month, and the experience that will be gained by him will I think prove of value to the Navy."—ALS, DNA, RG 45, ZB File. On April 12, USG had nominated Henry W. Fitch as Chief Engineer. Fitch was granted one year's leave from June 1.

1871, MAY 26. U.S. Senator John F. Lewis of Va. to USG. "Col. P. A. Davis, since the war a resident of Virginia, desires an official position at your hands. The first officer commissioned from his native state, Massachusetts, at the breaking out of the war, he served until May 1866, having attained the ranks of Major, and Brevet Colonel in the Adjt. General's Dept—the latter appointment having been made upon your personal recommendation. The County of Buckingham, throug his influence, at the election in Nov. last, was carried by the Republicans by more than 800 majority although there was a small majority of white registered voters. He has always sustained the reputation of a gallant officer, and a gentleman. The numerous friends he has made in my state, will be gratified if he can receive from you another recognition of his services in defense of his country, and the cause of the Union."—ALS, DNA, RG 59, Letters of Application and Recommendation. Additional papers are *ibid.* See *ibid.*, RG 94, ACP, D75 CB 1865; *PUSG*, 14, 453.

1871, May 29. USG endorsement. "Respectfully refered to the Sec. of War. I promised Gen. Howard to look into this case personally and to give it as favorable consideration as the facts would warrant."—AES, DNA, RG 94, ACP, 2794 1871. Written on a letter of the same date from Albert J. S. Molinard, Washington, D. C., to USG. ". . . as I have learned from Gen. Howard and Gen Dent, that you were kind enough to say that the papers, on their return to you by the Hon: Secretary of War, would b[e] acted upon by you immediately, (as they have been acted upon by the Secretary,) I beg to trespass on your valuable time long enough to ask you to consider my application which, I suppose has been returned to your Excellency for your decision, and to plead in extenuation of my troubling y[ou] about this, to me, important matter, my anxiety to have your Excellency's decision thereon, as I understood was promised, before your Excellency's departure from th[is] City."—ALS, *ibid.* On Oct. 30, 1870, Molinard had written to USG. ". . . All those who have been made acquainted with my case, as set forth in the enclosed paper, having been of the opinion that a great injustice had been done me, I trust that your Excellency may come to the same conclusion and restore me to the rank, active or retired,) which at the time of my being retired, was the reward of over twelve years continuous service, without leave of absence, in the swamps of Florida, the Western Indian country and the late war, where my being taken prisoner by the Guerrillas and their treatment of me, caused a sickness without which, I would never have appeared before any Retiring Board and would have won a name, had I not fallen by my guns—. . ."—ALS, *ibid.* Related papers are *ibid.* Molinard, USMA 1851, capt., 2nd Art., had been involuntarily retired as of Oct. 1, 1863.

1871, May 29. Horace Porter to Thomas A. Scott, Harrisburg, Pa. "No goods will be shipped to-day."—Copy, DLC-USG, II, 5. On the same day, Porter wrote to Maj. William Myers, asst. q. m., Washington, D. C. "Will you please have two (2) spring wagons at the Mansion at eleven o'clock tomorrow morning to haul the Presidents baggage to the Depot preparatory to leaving for Long Branch. And on Wednesday morning please have an ambulance at the Mansion at quarter past seven (7) to take the servants to the cars."—Copy, *ibid.*, II, 1.

1871, May 30. Governor Edmund J. Davis of Tex. to USG. "I have to recommend for your consideration in connection with the appointment at large of Cadets to West Point, the name of Master Andrew J. Houston, a son of the late Govr. Sam Houston of this State. Young Houston was tendered a nomination to West Point, by you, for this year (I beleive among the appointments at large) but could not be admitted on account of being a little under the age required. He is anxious to obtain a cadetship and would, I think, exert himself to prove a credit to the appointing power and the Institution. The services of his distinguished Father, in the cause of the Union, which to the last moment of his life he sustained, might perhaps warrant a departure from the rule which, I think, has generally been adopted by the President, of making these appointments at large from the sons of officers of the Army or Navy."—LS, DNA, RG 94, Correspondence, USMA. Andrew J. Houston entered USMA in 1871 but did not graduate.

1871, May 31. USG note. "During the absence or sickness at any time of the Hon *Geo S. Boutwell,* Secretary of the Treasury, the Hon *John F. Hartley,* while Assistant Secretary, is hereby authorized to perform the duties of Secretary until otherwise ordered."—DS, IHi.

Index

All letters written by USG of which the text was available for use in this volume are indexed under the names of the recipients. The dates of these letters are included in the index as an indication of the existence of text. Abbreviations used in the index are explained on pp. xiv–xix. Individual regts. are indexed under the names of the states in which they originated.